The Lyle
official
BOOKS
review

The Dollar conversions have been made at the rate of exchange
prevailing at the date of the sale.

SBN 0-86248-004-3
Copyright © Lyle Publications '80.
Glenmayne, Galashiels, Scotland.

ISBN 0-8256-9685-2
Order Number 450020
Quick Fox,
33 West 60th Street,
New York, N.Y. 10023.

Printed by Apollo Press, Worthing, Sussex, England.
Bound by R. J. Acford, Chichester, Sussex, England.

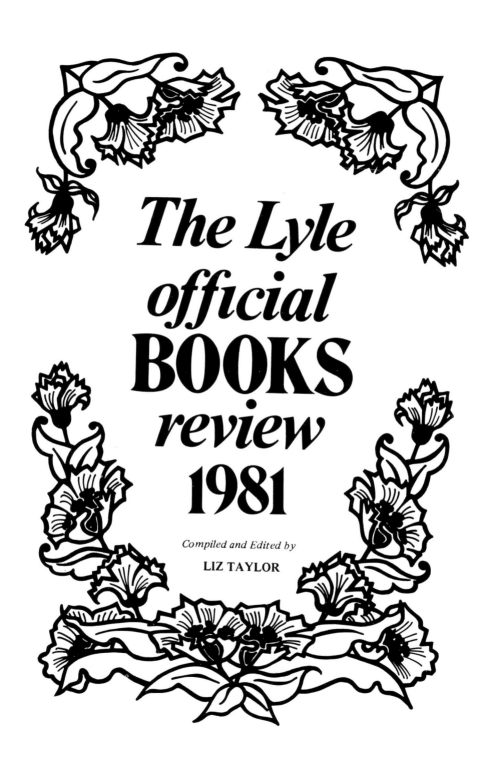

The Lyle
official
BOOKS
review
1981

Compiled and Edited by

LIZ TAYLOR

The publishers wish to express their sincere thanks
to the following for their kind help and assistance
in the production of this volume.

TONY CURTIS
JANICE MONCRIEFF
BRIAN HOLTON
NICOLA PARK
CARMEN MILIVOYEVICH
ELAINE HARLAND
MAY MUTCH
ROBERT SUTHERLAND
MARGARET ANDERSON

Introduction

A new enlarged and improved edition of our book about books.

Our subject is about books sold in auction, and we have covered the market by using as sources catalogues from major international book sales.

The list includes not only the very expensive and rare books but also those cheap 'little bargains' which collectors often find on the shelves of second-hand bookshops or even in local jumble sales. The date range runs from some of the earliest books ever printed to modern comics and books by living authors.

Book collecting is a passion which grows more popular every year and any one interested in the subject will find our book invaluable.

They will notice that we have taken the trouble to include fully detailed descriptions for every entry with particulars of the state of the book and its bindings, numbers and type of illustrations and any other relevant information such as date and place of printing or who owned the book in the past.

Where we give two different prices for the same book this is to show variations in price which can be caused by different auctions or disparate condition of the books themselves.

The Lyle Official Books Review is published every 1st November enabling Dealers and Collectors to begin each new year with an up-to-date knowledge of the current trends, together with the verified values of books of all descriptions.

Acknowledgements

Bennett Book Auctions (Tessa Bennett), 72 Radcliffe Terrace, Edinburgh.
Bonham's, Montpelier Galleries, Knightsbridge, London.
Christie, Manson & Woods International, Inc., 502 Park Avenue, New York.
Christie's, 8 King Street, St. James, London.
Christie's South Kensington, Old Brompton Road, London.
Lawrence, 19B Market Street, Crewkerne, Somerset.
Phillips, New Bond Street, London.
Sotheby's, Hodgson's Rooms, 115 Chancery Lane, London.
Sotheby's, 34 & 35 New Bond Street, London.
Sotheby's, 19 Castle Street, Edinburgh.
Sotheby's Belgravia, 19 Motcomb Street, London.
Sotheby's, Monaco, per Agent.
Spencer, Henry & Sons, 20 The Square, Retford, Yorkshire.
Swann's, New York, N.Y.
Taviner's, Prewett Street, Bristol.

BOOKS
review

The world of books has moved steadily forward through the year without any great excitement, but without any large setbacks. Books are making good prices and though there have been no spectacular leaps ahead, there has been a steady progress visible throughout the whole spectrum of book sales.

Some very interesting collections have come up for dispersal over the past twelve months which only goes to prove that anyone wanting to provide themselves with a valuable asset for the future should try to specialise.

For example a second section of the Findlay collection of conjuring books — built up over years for the love of a hobby by an amateur conjurer and hotel owner in the Isle of Wight — brought in buyers from all over the world to Sotheby's in London. Similarly a large collection of the works of Hans Christian Andersen which was held during March in Sotheby's Chancery Lane salerooms provided much justification for the lifelong dedication of collector Dr. Richard Klein who began collecting Andersen when he was a boy in Germany before the war. When he died in 1978 he had a collection of over six thousand items, not all of them books. They ranged from first edition copies in various languages to posters and gramophone records of Hans Christian Andersen — story songs by Bing Crosby and Danny Kaye. The whole sale brought in £36,262 and not surprisingly the top prices were recorded for rare books illustrated by top flight artists like Kay Neilsen, Heath Robinson, Edmund Dulac and Arthur Rackham .. a 'Fairy Tales' illustrated by Kay Neilsen and issued in 1924 sold for £740.

Amongst the other unusual collections to be dispersed during the period was a collection of books on the history of science and economics which was built up by Kenneth K. Knight, a Cambridge property developer. Christie's sold his collection in November and there were several very rare books among the lots, including 'Abstract of a Dissertation Read in the Royal Society of Edinburgh, 1785' in which James Hutton first expounded his theories on geology, on which much of the modern knowledge of the subject is based. This made over £3,000, although it had only cost Mr. Knight £22 a few years ago.

Yet another collection was one of

the main attractions at Bonham's — books on gynaecology and midwifery which had been collected by the late Alfred Hellman, M.D. Some of the books dated to the early days of printing and had very fine woodcut illustrations. Among the rarest examples were 1513 editions of the famous obstetrical textbook 'Der Swangern Frauwen und Hebammen Rosengarten' by Aucharius Roesslin, a physician from Wurms. Roesslin's famous illustrations of the position of a child in the womb make those books extremely significant for the development of obstetrics and gynaecology. Prices for Roesslin at the sale ranged from an astonishing £25,000 to £6,000.

Just to prove that collections do not have to be of very old books to be valuable, a New York auction of Bronte family manuscripts brought together connoisseurs across the Atlantic. The papers were sold on behalf of the Library Fund of the New York Grolier Club by Christie's in March. There were ten lots which made over £82,000 — a very handsome donation to the Fund from the Grolier Club member who gave the papers. The Bronte Society of Haworth bought one of the most expensive lots and therefore returned it to Britain — a set of thirty autograph letters from Charlotte Bronte to her friend Ellen Nussey covering the years 1835-1854, and documenting almost every part of Charlotte's life. The Bronte Society secured them for £40,723.

They also bought a letter from Branwell dated May 1831 which contained a poem in Charlotte's peculiar microscopic hand. The unhappy Branwell, who wrote under the pseu-

donym John Flower, was also represented in the sale by a forty thousand word manuscript, entitled 'Real Life in Verdopolis'. It went to a New York dealer for £4,072.

Yet another section of the fabulous Honeyman Collection of Scientific Books and Manuscripts came under the hammer at Sotheby's New Bond Street in May, taking the alphabetical progression up to M. Some very interesting prices were recorded at this sale, ranging from £17,000 for Stanislaw Lubieniecki's 'Theatrum Cometicum' of 1669, a first edition, with some very fine coloured engravings, to a mere £40 for a first edition copy of Petrus van Mussehenbroek's 'Introductio ad Philosophiam Naturalem' of 1762. More books from the Honeyman Collection are still to be sold and connoisseurs await the sale with interest.

Apart from the collections, there were of course many other interesting sales held over the past year. One of these was in Edinburgh, where Sotheby's held a two day auction in the Free Church College of surplus books from the College library. There were many rare books among the lots, including the first issue of the first book ever published in Glasgow, as well as the first books ever published in Kelso, Whitburn, Irvine, Annan and Kirkcudbright. Many of the lots were books of theological works, some very heavy going indeed, but most of these were bought as a roomful by a young American academic who also deals in theological literature.

But all subjects do not have to be as heavy as theology: there have been sales of books on the dance and sales of books and material on ballet and the theatre. Among the most interesting sales for many people are sales of autograph letters and manuscripts: it is not too sweeping to suggest that here Sotheby's hold a pre-eminent position, not only because of the scope and frequency of their sales in this area of the market but also because of the fascination of the catalogues they produce.

Some of these catalogues make fascinating reading in themselves. In a sale devoted to autograph letters and manuscripts from the Continent which contained a section on musicians and composers, they had such items as letters from Marcel Proust complaining about his ill health and admitting to feelings of guilt about his mother after her death in 1905. One fascinating letter from the Marquis de Sade shows him in an unexpected light when he asks nervously whether he would be safe if he travelled in a certain area of Provence which he had heard was affected by revolutionary fervour. It sold for £200. In the music section was a sheet of twenty different caricatures of Sir Thomas Beecham conducting, drawn in pen and ink by Frank Leah, which made £250.

Still in the realms of famous men, it was interesting to note the sale of one hundred and sixty-five lots of Napoleonica in Christie's sale of the library of North Mymms Park. A first edition of Flaubert's 'Salammbo' which he presented to Berlioz was also one of the highlights of a sale held by Sotheby's in Monte Carlo in November. Queen Victoria did not give rise to much enthusiasm when three copies of her 'Leaves from the Journal of Our Lives in the Highlands' came under the hammer

at Christie's and Edmiston's in Glasgow. Although they were privately printed copies, inscribed by the Queen to her personal physician Sir James Clark, one failed to find a buyer and the other two made £90 each. The Queen did better, however, at Christie's in South Kensington in March, when a copy of her 'Leaves from the Journal. . .' was sold for £400.

The main enthusiasm in the book world still remains concentrated on travel and natural history books, especially those with fine illustrations and in good condition. The sales results from all over the country and from abroad are full of interesting prices made by books in this category where the old favourites still hold sway, demanding brisk bidding whenever they appear for sale. A complete set of Captain Cook's travel books made £2,400 when the nine volumes came up for sale at Phillips, London in November, and an 1813 second edition of Captain J. G. Stedman's 'Narrative of a Five Years' Expedition against the Revolted Negroes of Surinam' with hand coloured maps and plates made £650. At Spencer's of Retford in January three volumes of Otto von Kotzbue's 'Voyage of Discovery into the South Seas and Baring Straits' 1821, made £550. It was however interesting that once pre-eminent travel books like David Roberts' 'Holy Land' were not commanding the high prices they have made at auction: when two copies came up at Sotheby's in Chancery Lane in January they sold at £3,400 and £4,800 — both below the estimates. On the other hand, at the same sale an above estimate price was recorded for 'Travels to Discover the Source of the Nile' by Sir James Bruce, which sold for £500. It might seem that

Roberts is one of the books that soared too high a few years ago and is now settling down to a more reasonable price.

Natural history books always seem to arouse great enthusiasm among buyers. At Phillips in May in London a Selby 'Illustrations of British Ornithology' dated 1819-34 sold for £7,000 and at Swann's in New York that great favourite John Gould's book on humming birds of 1849-61 made £15,178. A hitherto unknown ornithological book which turned up at a Taviner's book sale only showed that there are still some undiscovered treasures around. It was a volume of eighty-two fine hand coloured plates of birds dating from around 1835 and entitled 'Collection d'Oiseaux d'Europe'. It sold for £1,950. At the same sale a Country Life book of 1938 – 'Wild Chorus' by Peter Scott – sold for £150. Another Gould book – 'Birds of Europe' with an added monograph on the family of Toucans – sold for the high price of £14,000 at Sotheby's in January. The monograph, dated 1833-35, contained thirty-four lithographed plates by Gould and Lear and all but one of them were hand coloured. Another bird book at the sale which made more than had been expected was 'A Monograph on the Nectariniidae or the Family of the Sun-Birds' by G. E. Shelley which sold for £4,200.

Botanical books continue to maintain their good prices – Sotheby's sold three copies of Curtis' 'Flora Londiniensis' for prices ranging from £1,800 to £3,800 depending on their condition. A first octavo edition of 1824 of Redoute's 'Les Roses' with one hundred and sixty plates made £5,800, also at Sotheby's, and Gallesio's 'Pomona

Italiana' 1817-34 reached £4,800. The same price was recorded for six volumes of Elizabeth Blackwell's 'Herbarium Blackwellianum' 1750-73. A lovely 'Tulip Book' dating from around 1630 containing delightful watercolour drawings of specimen tulips for flower bulb buyers of the time made £6,956 when it was sold by Christie's at the Singer Museum, Laren, Holland in March.

Illustrated books are of course always the most popular with buyers and fortunately the mad craze for 'breaking' seems to have died down a little, leaving illustrated books prized and priced for themselves entire. One section of the illustrated market which however, like David Roberts, might seem to have flown a little too high recently is the children's book section, where top flight illustrators like Rackham, Dulac, Pogany and Kate Greenaway seem to have been resting at about the same level or slightly beneath it recently. Here condition is of premier importance because so many children's books have received heavy handling from young owners in their time and this can have a marked effect on the prices recorded.

Interesting prices recorded in the children's market over the year include £280 for Richard Doyle's 'In Fairy Land' and £60 for 'More Celtic Fairy Tales' compiled by Joseph Jacobs and illustrated by John Batten. One of the rising stars in the established firmament seems to be Eleanor Vere Boyle (E.V.B.) whose 1875 'Beauty and the Beast' made over £100 for the first time this year, Sir Arthur Quiller Couch's 'In Powder and Crinoline' with illustrations by Kay Neilsen made £210; a Hans Andersen's 'Stories' illustrated by

Edmund Dulac, admittedly a limited signed edition, sold for £190.

Another popular artist, Jessie Marion King illustrated 'Mummy's Bedtime Story Book by 'Marion'' which sold for £110. A low price was recorded for a first edition copy of 'Wind in the Willows' at only £80, but it was damaged. A. A. Milne's 'A Gallery of Children', however, soared to new heights when one of five hundred signed copies of 1925, with plates by Le Mair, sold for £110.

Less usual than the children's books were Russian books which appeared in a big way on the book market this year — Sotheby's had examples of the illustrative work of I. Yabilibin in their sale of children's books and drawings at the end of 1979, as well as a copy of Afarasiev's 'The Frog Princess' which made £105. Later in February 1980, there was a special sale of Russian books at Sotheby's in Chancery Lane where some very good prices were recorded in spite of the previous unpopularity of the subject. The most expensive item was 'A Game in Hell' by A. Kruchenykh and V. Khlebnikov, published in St. Petersburg in 1915, which was sold for £1,150. A Mayakovsky book 'Raucous Laughter' sold for £580 and a seven volume set of reference books on the treasures of Russian Art also published at St. Petersburg between 1901 and 1907 sold for £880.

A specialist area which has retained its prices and position unassailed is Private Press books: many very fine examples of these have cropped up for sale. They include a very rare Dante Gabriel Rossetti 'Sir Hugh and the Heron' which, though estimated at only £250-£320 at Sotheby's in February,

managed to sell for £2,100. It was Rossetti's first book and was printed in 1843 on Polidori's private press. English Illustrated and Private Press books which were sold at the end of 1979 on behalf of Trinity College, Oxford, made some very good prices, partly because they were in first class condition and partly because of their rarity. The private presses represented included the Ashendene Press — one of forty copies on Japanese vellum of their Virgil's 'Bucolica Georgica Aenis' made £1,200. Another Ashendene book — 'Don Quixote de la Mancha' with woodcut initials by Quick and Ford after Louise Powell sold for £700.

Nonesuch Press and Kelmscott Press were represented by Dante's 'Divine Comedy' (£145) and 'The Life and Death of Jason' with woodcuts after Burne Jones (£340). Other interesting items included a Cresset Press Milton — two volumes of 'Paradise Lost' and 'Paradise Regained' for £220; A Doves Press five-volume English Bible at £1,150 and a Fanfrolico 'A Hommage to Sappho' for £540. Of course there were many examples of the work of the Golden Cockerel Press, several with illustrations by artists like Eric Ravilious, Peter Barker-Mill and Eric Gill. One excellent example of the Golden Cockerel output was Evadne Lascaris' 'The Golden Bed of Kydno' with an extra set of plates signed by the artist Lettice Sandford, which sold for £250. Golden Cockerel Press also figured strongly in a sale held by Christie's in March where Eric Gill's illustrated 'Canterbury Tales' and his 'Troilus and Cressida' each sold for £1,400. Private press books are much sought after by collectors and are well worth looking out for, especially those with good illustrations.

Another specialist taste which repays its collectors is bindings. Over the year there have been some excellent examples of the work of the binder coming up for sale. In Sotheby's sale of Continental Illustrated Books at the end of last year there were some excellent bindings which demanded high prices. Rene Kieffer's binding on a 1906 copy of Pierre Louys' 'Les Aventures du Roi Pausole' put the price up to £420. Another interesting binding appeared on Magre's 'Les Soirs d'Opium' 1921, which had a brown morocco binding tooled in blind with the upper cover reproducing one of the twelve etched plates by Chimot. It sold for £340. A very high price of £2,400 was recorded for 'Prieres Ecclesiastiques' printed in Geneva in 1566 and covered with a Swiss embroidered binding of oval black fabric covered boards embroidered with silver thread in a floral motif.

Still in the realms of fine binding it has been noticeable over the year that there has been a steady rise in price of sets of books by standard authors providing they are uniformly and nicely bound. Books which might not have raised much interest a few years ago are now making very respectable prices. A uniformly bound green half levant set of the works of Oscar Wilde – twenty volumes in all – dating from 1892 to 1909 was sold at Christie's in South Kensington for £1,350 in the spring. Sir Walter Scott, who has often been a drag on the book market in the past, shared in this new trend to some extent at Taviner's in Bristol when £86 was paid for a forty-eight volume set of the Waverley novels with good full calf bindings.

Sir Walter Scott however came more into his own later on in the year when Sotheby's sold a complete set of his works in seventy-four volumes, all first editions, for £900. The Mellstock edition of the works of Thomas Hardy however outdid even that respectable price by making £1,300 – they were all signed by Hardy and had their original dust jackets.

Dickens too, who has often suffered from a too prolific output and too many editions, was redeemed at Phillips when an 1874 'Illustrated Library Edition' of his works, thirty volumes in tree calf gilt, made £500.

There has also been a rise in collector's interest in bookplates. Four portfolios of 18-20th century bookplates sold for £300 over an estimate of £30 to £40, at Christie's in December. Also a collection of 19th century bookplates mounted on 192 leaves made £440 at the same sale. Collectors would do well to watch out for good examples of bookplates when doing their browsing in the future.

Periodicals are another area of continually rising interest and consequently rising prices. At Bonham's in February one hundred and fifty volumes of the 'Illustrated London News' for the years 1842 to 1916 were estimated at around £120 and sold for £2,100.

Sotheby's later sold sixty-one volumes of the 'Illustrated London News' for 1843-81 for £1,100 and even more surprising volumes 1-69 of the 'Picture Post' (1938-55) for £1,000. 'The Studio' is always popular whenever it comes up for sale and Christie's in

South Kensington sold volumes 1-142 for the years 1893-1951 for £1,500. The book collectors' reference book, 'Book Auction Records' (volumes 1-71), sold for £700. 'Vanity Fair' always sells well too, and when thirteen volumes of colour plates from the magazine by artists like Spy and Ape came up at Bonham's in April they made £500. 'The London Magazine' 1732-81 in fairly poor condition made a surprising price of £900 when it came up for sale at Christie's — this price especially surprised the auctioneers who had estimated the lot of forty-nine volumes at around £80. All in all periodicals are on the way up if prices paid at auction are anything to go by. Though not a periodical, at least a piece of interesting ephemera, a Pirelli Calendar for 1973 sold for £40 to the Tate Gallery at Sotheby's, Chancery Lane in February. Another issue of the calendar which featured the nude photograph of Marilyn Monroe also sold for £35. Pamphlets, especially those relating to interesting events and times, are also making high prices at the moment. A collection of 17th century pamphlets covering the period 1684-92 and relating to politics and trade made £700 at Sotheby's in February.

Periodicals from a more recent time made surprising prices when Sotheby's sold a batch of I.P.C. back numbers late last year. Among the highlights of the sale were twenty-one volumes of 'Funny Folks' which made £400; 'Peg's Companion' 1921-32 £520; 'The Tatler' 1925-65 £540. A collection of ninety-three periodicals on wireless made £520.

Modern books always have their dedicated following. There were several items appearing over the year of great interest. The book that Winston Churchill later wished he had not written, 'Savrola' appeared in a first edition sale at Sotheby's in June and doubled its estimate to sell for £1,000. Churchill had inscribed it to Major General Ian Hamilton of Ladysmith and there is a story that when he was writing the inscription after dinner he complained to Hamilton about being so unthinking as to have such a difficult name to write 'especially for a fellow after dinner.'

A three part first edition of Tolkein's 'Lord of the Rings' sold for a the very high price of £2,300 at the same sale and a 1936 first edition of Sacheverell Sitwell's 'Conversation Pieces', with a dust jacket designed by Rex Whistler, sold for £350. D. H. Lawrence's 'Amores' — another first edition — sold for £310 and P. G. Wodehouse's first book, 'The Pothunters', sold for £400.

One of the biggest surprises in the first editions was Ian Fleming's 'Casino Royale', with dust jacket designed by the author, which sold for £420. Another high price was recorded for Katherine Mansfield's 'The Garden Party' with sixteen coloured lithographs by Marie Laurencin which made £150.

The old guidelines about buying books still hold good in every category — look for the condition first, then see if they have original dust jackets, see if they are illustrated, and check on the state of the plates. One of the charms of book collecting is the joy of the hunt and the thrill·of a good find. Persistence always reaps benefits in the end.

LIZ TAYLOR

A.A. OF THE WORLD
20 vols. only – coloured plates, illustrations, original cloth, dust jackets – New York 1959-67.
(Sotheby Humberts
Taunton) $45   £20

ABDRY, NICHOLAS
'An account of the breeding of worms in human bodies, with letter . . . on this subject from Nicholas Hartsoeker . . . and George Baglivi' – 1st Edn. in English, 5 plates, the last large folding, a little worming in upper margins at beginning, cont. panelled calf – H. Rhodes and A. Bell, 1701.
(Sotheby's
London) $215   £95

'ABEILLARD EN ELOIZE. HET LEEVEN EN DE LOTGEVALLEN'
1st Dutch Edn., half title, titles on endleaf, engraved frontis, a very few minor defects, original boards, joints just torn, uncut – Utrecht and Amsterdam, 1790.
(Sotheby's
London) $135   £60

ABRAHAM BEN REUVEN (Biblical Lexicographer)
Wormed throughout, written within typographical border, modern buckram, gilt. folio – Johan Ben Jacob Ashkenazi, Constantinople, 1742.
(Sotheby's, New Bond
Street) $115   £50

ABRAHAM, NICOLAS
'Le Gouvernement Necessaire a Chacun pour Vivre longuement en Sante' – woodcut device, tears, shaved, waterstaining, morocco, gilt, by Ludwig, g.e. – Paris, 1608.
(Sotheby's
Monaco) $1,000   £450

ACADEMY OF ARCHITECTURE AND ANNUAL ARCHITECTURE REVIEW
5 vols., cloth – 1893-97.
(Tessa Bennett,
Edinburgh) $16   £7

ACCOUNTS
Farm Mss. account book, 1842-43.
(Tessa Bennett,
Edinburgh) $45   £20

ACHENER, MAURICE – ZOLA, EMILE
'La Faute de L'Abbe Mouret' – woodcut frontispiece, 2 full page illustrations, 98 pictorial head and tail pieces and 49 picorial initials by Achener, frontispiece and initials in two colours, green half morocco, t.e.g., original wrappers bound in – G. et A. Mornay, Paris, 1922.
(Sotheby's,
Chancery Lane) $18   £8

ACKERMANN, RUDOLPH
'The Repository of Arts' – literature, fashions etc., vols. I-VIII only of 12, engraved titles and 284 plates including many hand coloured aquatint views of country seats and fashion plates, cont. half russia – 1823-26.
(Christie's,
St. James) $1,305   £580
'History of the Abbey Church of St. Peter's Westminster' – 2 vols., cont. aquatint plates, half morocco, gilt, bound without half titles, but with list of subscribers – 1812.
(Sotheby's, New Bond
Street) $190   £85
'The History of the Colleges of Winchester, Eton and Westminster' – First issue, 48 coloured aquatints, half calf repaired – 1816.
(Sotheby's, New Bond
Street) $1,800   £800

ACTON, HAROLD AND LEE YI-HSIEH, TRANSLATORS
'Glue and Lacquer, four cautionary tales from the Chinese' – 290 of 350 copies, frontispiece and full page illustrations by Eric Gill, original morocco backed cloth, t.e.g. – Golden Cockerel Press, 1941.
(Christie's S.
Kensington) $130   £58

ADAIR, J.
'A New and Exact Map of the Clyde' –
double page folio, mounted and framed,
some marginal defects – circa 1770.
(Tessa Bennett,
Edinburgh) $60   £26
'A Map of West Lothian' – double page
folio, mounted and framed – circa 1770.
(Tessa Bennett,
Edinburgh) $25   £10

ADAIR, JOHN
'The Description of the Sea Coast and
Islands of Scotland' – The Stirling
Maxwell copy, 6 engraved maps, three
double page, browning and soiling, 19th
century red toan backed cloth, rubbed.
Large folio – Edinburgh, 1703.
(Sotheby's, New Bond
Street) $720   £320

ADAM, R. and J.
'The Works in Architecture' – 3 vols., 102
plates only, soiling and some tears, unbound
folio – Paris, E. Thezard, 1901-02.
(Christie's S.
Kensington) $45   £20

ADAM, ROBERT
'Ruins of the Palace of the Emperor Dio-
cletian at Spalatro in Dalmatia' – 61
plates, spotting and soiling, half roan,
spine defective, covers detached, folio –
1764.
(Sotheby's, New Bond
Street) $1,125   £500

ADAMS, REV. JOHN
'Modern Voyages containing a variety of
Useful and Entertaining Facts Respecting
the Expeditions and Principal Discoveries
of Cavendish, Dampier, Anson etc.' – 2
vols., first edition, cont. sheep, slightly
worn, joints split – G. Kearsley, 1790.
(Sotheby's,
Chancery Lane) $11   £5

**ADAM'S ILLUSTRATED PANORAMA OF
HISTORY**
Folding coloured chart, mounted on linen,
slightly soiled, original half calf, rather worn,
folio – n.d.
(Sotheby Humberts
London) $30   £13

ADAN, EMILE – FLAUBERT, GUSTAVE
'Un Coeur Simple' – etched frontispiece,
vignette on title, 9 plates and 12 illustrations
by Champollion after Adan, blue morocco
gilt, inside borders gilt, marbled endpapers,
t.e.g., original wrappers bound in – No.
295 of 500 copies. – Librairie des Amateurs,
Paris, 1894.
(Sotheby's,
Chancery Lane) $9   £4

ADDISON, JOSEPH
'Remarks on several parts of Italy, etc. . . . .
1701, 1702, 1703' – 1st Edn., a few en-
graved illustrations of medals in the text,
half title, cont. sprinkled calf, rubbed –
1705.
(Sotheby's
London) $135   £60
'The Freeholder or Political Essays' – First
collected edition, bookplate of Josiah
Bullock of Faulkbourn, cont. sprinkled
calf, hinges cracked, gilt – 1716.
(Sotheby's, New Bond
Street) $250   £110

**ADDISON, JOSEPH AND STEELE, SIR
RICHARD**
'The Spectator' – 8 vols., 8 engraved
frontispieces spotted, cloth, original board,
worn, cracked – 1827.
(Sotheby's, New Bond
Street) $9   £4

ADDISON, T.
'Observations on the Disorders of Females
connected with Uterine Irritation' –
London, 1830.
(Bonham's) $945   £420

AELIANUS, CLAUDIUS
'Variae Historiae libri XIII (and other
works)' – 1st Edn., Greek letter, device on
title, repeated at end, some waterstaining,
18th century boards – Rome 1545.
(Sotheby's
London) $225   £100

AESCHYLUS
'Tragoediae VII' – Greek text, title with
woodcut device, slight browning and soiling,
17th century limp vellum, rubbed and
soiled – Antwerp, 1580.
(Sotheby's, New Bond
Street) $115   £50

AESOP

AESOP
'Fables – coloured illus. by E. J. Detmold, cloth gilt – n.d.
(Phillips
London) $100   £45
'The Fables . . . translated by Sir Roger L'Estrange' – number 55 of 350 copies, vignettes by C. M. Fiennes, original cloth backed boards, dust jacket soiled and frayed, unopened – Golden Cockerel Press, 1926.
(Christie's S.
Kensington) $115   £50

AGAPETUS
'Ad Justinianum Imp. Adhortationes' – The Dedication copy from Bishop Leonellus Chiericatus to Pope Innocent VIII, illuminated Mss. on vellum, 51 leaves, 16 lines written in a fine roman hand in black ink, initials in red, first leaf stained purple, illuminated renaissance border and initial. – early 19th century morocco, g.e. – Venice, October 1484.
(Christie's King
St.) $21,375   £9,500

AGRIPPA, CORNELIUS
'The Vanity of Arts and Sciences' – English portrait by Th. Burnford, cont. sprinkled calf – J. C. for Samuel Speed, 1676.
(Sotheby's
London) $405   £180

AIKIN, ARTHUR
'Journal of a Tour Through North Wales and Part of Shropshire' – 1st Edn., folding engraved plate, uncut, modern half calf, gilt – 1797.
(Sotheby's, New Bond
Street) $75   £32

AINSWORTH, W. HARRISON
'Sir John Chiverton, A Romance' – 1st Edn., half title, advertisement leaf at end, a very few spots, original boards, upper cover detached, spine slightly worn, uncut.
(Sotheby's
London) $80   £35

AITKEN, J.
'Principles of Midwifery or Puerperal Medicine' – Portrait and 15 plates, 3rd Edn. – n.d.
(Bonham's) $100   £45

Ad Justinianum Imp. Adhortationes by Agapetus. (Christie's)

ALASTAIR (V. VOIGHT) – WILDE, OSCAR
'Salome' – 9 plates by Alastair, original wrappers, uncut – G. Cres, Paris, 1922.
(Sotheby's,
   Chancery Lane) $100   £45

ALBANIS, BEAUMONT (JEAN FRANCOIS)
'Travels Through the Rhaetian Alps in the Year MDCCLXXXVI' – 1st Edn., 10 sepia aquatint plates, list of plates, a few leaves marginally dampstained, a little foxing, title soiled, disbound, folio – 1792.
(Sotheby's, New Bond
   Street) $790   £350

ALBANY, LOUISE, COUNTESS OF, WIFE OF YOUNG PRETENDER
Good series of 23 autograph letters, unsigned, in French – c. 75 pages large and small quarto, Florence, Livorno and Paris 1809 to 1820, to the Chevalier Francais Sobiraz in Carpentras.
(Sotheby's, New Bond
   Street) $790   £350

ALBERTUS MAGNUS
'Opus in Evangelium, Missus est Gabriel Angelus' – one large initial supplied in red and black, rubricated throughout, 111 leaves of 112, 18th century German half calf – Milan, 1488.
(Bonham's) $630   £280

'Ein Newer Albertus Magnus' – woodcut title printed in black and red, woodcuts throughout text. Modern vellum in cloth cover and case, cont. notes on fly leaf – Augsburg, 1579.
(Bonham's) $1,800   £800
'De Secretis Mulierum' – wrapper, most leaves stained, inner margin wormed – 1508.
(Bonham's) $100   £45

ALBIN, ELEAZAR
'A Natural History of Spiders and Other Curious Insects' – 53 hand coloured engraved plates, cont. mottled calf, worn, covers detached – 1736.
(Sotheby's
   Monaco) $5,625   £2,500

ALBINUS, BERNHARDUS SIEGFRIED
'Explicatio tabularum anatomicarum Bartholomaei Eustachii . . . auctor recognovit . . . denuo edidit' – half title, title in red and black with English vignette, 47 English plates acc. by one (in some cases two) outline plates, light waterstain on upper margins, new half calf, folio, Leiden, Joh. & Hermannus Verbeek, 1761.
(Sotheby's
   London) $855   £380
'Incones Ossium Foetus Humani' – 16 engraved plates in two states, cont. boards, worn – Leiden, 1737.
(Bonham's) $405   £180
'Plates of the human muscles carefully reduced from the original copy' – 17 tinted plates with explanatory text, 311 adverts at end, name: W. Farrar written on verso of all plates, original printed wrappers, rebacked (covering part of the printed matter on upper cover) – E. Cox and Son & T. Underwood, 1815.
(Sotheby's
   London) $125   £55

ALBUM
'ALBUM of approx. 80 engraved plates of NORTH EUROPE, CHINA, NATURAL HISTORY AND COSTUMES, ETC.' – a few crudely hand coloured, a few torn or imperfect, mostly slightly soiled, all mounted in half vellum album, worn – late 18th century.
(Sotheby's,
   Chancery Lane) $200   £90

ALBUM

ALBUM OF 70 AUTOGRAPH LETTERS
Includes a series of Messrs. Agnew from prominent artists like Millais, Tenniel, Frith etc., also Rowland Hill, Ruskin, Arthur Sullivan, Sir Walter Scott, Gladstone, Conan Doyle and Randolph Churchill. Portions of some letters signed by Dickens and Henry Kingsley – n.d.
(Lawrence of
Crewkerne) $495   £220

ALBUM
Album of 12 pencil sketches, a watercolour, hand coloured embossed picture of playing kitten etc. apparently kept by Jane Lane, Picardy Place, Edinburgh – circa 1837.
(Lawrence of
Crewkerne) $60   £25

ALBUM
Album with 29 accomplished drawings in pencil, wash and watercolour, average size 7in. x 10in., of Continental and English scenes – 1893-96.
(Lawrence of
Crewkerne) $225   £100

ALBUM DES TRAVESTISSEMENTS NOUVEAUX DE LA MAISON MOREAU
12 hand coloured lithographed plates, margins slightly soiled, original boards, rebacked, worn, g.e. – Paris, 1860.
(Christie's S.
Kensington) $60   £25

ALBUMASAR
'De Magnis Conjunctionibus: Annorum Revolutionibus: ac eorum Profectionibus: Octo Continens tractatus' – woodcut title, about 30 woodcut illustrations repeated to 270, woodblock initials, waterstaining, early 19th century half roan, rubbed, spine loose at head – M. Sessa, Venice, 1515.
(Christie's King
St.) $180   £80

ALCOTT, LOUISA M.
'Little Women' – part one of two, 2 vols., 1st Edns., wood engraved plates after May Alcott, original cloth gilt, spines soiled and somewhat frayed at head and foot – Robert Bros., Boston, 1869-68.
(Sotheby's, Hodgson's
Rooms) $70   £30

ALDINGTON, RICHARD
'Death of a Hero' – 1st Edn., original cloth, dust jacket designed by Paul Nash – 1929.
(Sotheby's,
Chancery Lane) $55   £24

ALECHINSKY, PIERRE
'Hayterophiles' – 11 etched plates, each signed and numbered by Alechinsky, 5 coloured, unsewn in original cloth portfolio with tie, folio – La Hune, Paris, 1968.
(Sotheby's,
Chancery Lane) $240   £106

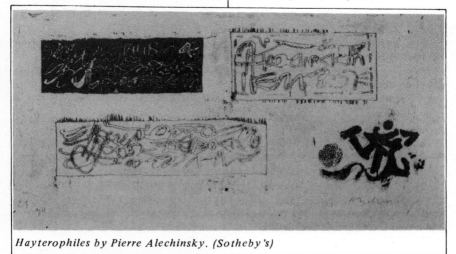

Hayterophiles by Pierre Alechinsky. (Sotheby's)

ALENCON, FRANCOIS DUC D'
Conspiratorial autograph letter signed, 1 page, folio, 28 December, 1580, to his uncle the duc de Montpensier, contemporary endorsement, slight foxing, strengthened at centre fold.
(Sotheby's, New Bond
  Street) $360 £160

ALEXANDER DE HALES
'Pars Quarta Summe Theologie' — title in woodcut architectural border, preceded by 'Tabula Questionum', woodcut initials, some in red with rubrication, old style calf — Anton Koburger, Lyon, 1516.
(Christie's King
  St.) $125 £55

ALEXANDER, L.
Hebrew Ritual and Doctrinal Explanation of the Whole Ceremonial Law of the Jewish Community — original cloth, worn — Printed by and for the Author, 1819.
(Sotheby's, New Bond
  St.) $80 £35

ALEXANDER, WILLIAM
'Picturesque Representations of the Dress and Manners of the Austrians' — 50 hand coloured plates, plate I and last leaf of text defective and mounted, some soiling, modern red half calf — 1813.
(Sotheby's
  London) $360 £160

ALEXIS OF PIEDMONT (pseud. i.e. Girolamo Ruscelli)
'The Secrets . . . Containing Many Excellent Remedies against divers diseases wounds, and other accidents, newly corrected and amended' — 5 parts in one vol., of which 2-4 are under separate title pages, black letter, woodcut device on the three sub titles, index at end, diced calf gilt, inner gilt border, red edges — William Stansby for Richard Meighen, 1615 — W. Stansby, 1614.
(Sotheby's
  London) $520 £230

ALEYN, CHARLES
'The Historie of . . . Henrie of that Name the Seventh, King of England . . . In a Poem' — 1st Edn., lacks portrait, former ownership inscription on verso of title, cont. sheep, worn, front cover detached, spine torn — 1638.
(Sotheby's
  London) $45 £20

ALI, MRS MEER HASSAN
'Observations on the Mussulmauns of India' — 2 vols., 1st Edn. List of subscribers, some spots, cont. green roan, rubbed — 1832.
(Sotheby's, New Bond
  Street) $70 £30

ALKEN, HENRY
'The Beauties and Defects in the Figure of The Horse' — leather backed pictorial boards, 54 figures in 18 plates, coloured —James Toovey, Piccadilly, 1881.
(Lawrence of
  Crewkerne) $25 £55

ALL ABOUT ANIMALS FOR OLD AND YOUNG
Photographic illus. of mainly zoo animals, decorated cloth gilt, oblong 4to — n.d. — circa 1900.
(Tessa Bennett,
  Edinburgh) $18 £8

ALLAN

ALLAN, JOHN H.
A Pictorial Tour in the Mediterranean' –
1st Edn., additional lithographed title, 40
tinted lithographed plates, half title, a
little spotting, original cloth, rebacked –
1843.
(Sotheby's, New Bond
    Street)   **$340**   **£150**

ALLEN, THOMAS
'A New and Complete History of the
County of York' – 3 vols., steel eng.
titles and plates on India paper, mostly
after N. Whittock, some spotting, cont.
calf, joints split – 1828-31.
(Christie's S.
    Kensington)   **$450**   **£200**

ALLESTREE, RICHARD
'The Gentleman's Calling' – 2nd Edn.,
engraved frontispiece, additional title page
and 2 plates, cont. calf – 1662.
(Sotheby's, New Bond
    Street)   **$40**   **£16**

ALLOM, T.
'A Series of Fifty Views of the Picturesque
Scenery and Lakes of Scotland' – eng.
additional title and 49 plates after T. Allom,
occasional spotting, cont. cloth, worn,
spine lacking – Edinburgh, n.d.
(Christie's S.
    Kensington)   **$65**   **£28**

ALLOM, THOMAS AND T. ROSE
'Westmorland, Cumberland, Durham and
Northumberland' – vol. I and II only of
3, engraved title and 139 views on 70
plates only, some leaves spotted and dampstained, original cloth, rubbed, lacks spine
– 1832.
(Sotheby's,
    Chancery Lane) **$225**   **£100**

**ALLOM, THOMAS AND THE REV.
ROBERT WALSH**
'Constantinople and the Scenery of the
Seven Churches of Asia Minor – 2 vols.,
folding map, 94 engraved plates, additional
eng. titles, frontis.s. and eng. titles slightly
spotted, the latter partly detached in vol.
I, cont. green blindstamped morocco, gilt,
spines slightly worn – n.d.
(Sotheby's
    London)   **$160**   **£70**

'Constantinople and the Scenery of the
Seven Churches of Asia Minor' – first and
second series, additional engraved vignette
titles, 94 engraved plates, 2 maps, 1 folding,
cont. half calf, gilt stamped, spine rubbed –
circa 1839.
(Sotheby's, New Bond
    Street)   **$180**   **£80**

ALMANAC FOR THE YEAR 1785
4 page engravings, with case, original
morocco gilt (this year not in Spielmann)
1¼ x 2¼in. – London, 1785.
(Phillips)   **$65**   **£28**

ALMANACH ROYALE FOR 1726
Cont. olive morocco gilt, arms of Bourbon
Conde on sides, g.e. – Paris, 1726.
(Phillips)   **$290**   **£130**

ALMANACK FOR 1780
'Old Poor Robin' – printed in red and
black, some marginal annotations, original
wrappers, soiled – 1779.
(Christie's S.
    Kensington)   **$7**   **£3**

ALPHERAKAY, SERGIUS
'The Geese of Europe and Asia' – large
quarter green morocco, spine gilt, t.e.g.,
coloured frontispiece and 24 coloured
plates by F. W. Frohawk, a very good
copy – Published in Russia, 1905.
(Lawrence of
    Crewkerne)   **$430**   **£190**

**AMEDEO OF SAVOY, LUIGI, DUKE OF
THE ABRUZZI**
'On the Polar Star in the Arctic Sea' – 2
vols., plates, maps, two in wallet at end of
vol. 2, original cloth, vol. 1 slightly affected by damp, inner hinge cracked – 1903.
(Christie's S.
    Kensington)   **$75**   **£32**

AMERICA
THEVET, A.
'Quatre Partie du Monde' – engraved map
of North and South America, including
Greenland, part of Asia, Antarctica, etc.,
embellished with groups of human figures,
animals, sailing ships, etc., worming, usually
restored with pen, margins shaved or cut –
Paris, 1575.
(Sotheby's, New Bond
    Street)   **$1,800**   **£800**

AMERICAN MERCURY, THE
Edited by H. L. Mencken, G. T. Nathan
and Charles Agnoff — 117 in all from No. 8
- 124 with some duplicates. Contributions
by James Stevens, Theodore Dreiser, Wm.
Faulkner and others — 1924-34.
(Sotheby's,
    Chancery Lane) $80   £35

AMERICAN PRIMER
'Being a Selection of Words the most easy of
pronounciation' — wood engraved vignette
on title, original printed wrappers — McCarty
and Davis, Philadelphia, circa 1820.
(Sotheby's,
    Chancery Lane) $55   £25

AMERICAN THEATRE
Large and interesting collection of programmes and press cuttings etc. of
American Theatres from circa 1819 to
1914 in 75 volumes including programmes
for Col. W. E. Sinn's Park Theatre,
Montauk and Mrs. F. B. Conway's
Brooklyn Theatre featuring all notable
actors and actresses of the period. Some
programmes printed on silk, some loose,
cont. half roan, worn. Folio.
(Sotheby's, New Bond
    Street) $1,915   £850

AMHURST, NICHOLAS
'Terrae Filius or the Secret History of
the University of Oxford' — 2 vols. in one,
2nd Edn., engraved frontispiece, cont.
calf, joints rubbed — 1726.
(Christie's S.
    Kensington) $65   £28

AMUNDSEN, ROALD
'The North West Passage' — 2 vols., 1st
English Edn., protrait, plates, illustrations
in text, 3 maps, 2 folding. Original cloth,
gilt — 1908.
(Sotheby's, New Bond
    Street) $160   £70
'The South Pole' — 2 vols., plates, folding
maps, original cloth, slightly rubbed, t.e.g.
— 1912.
(Sotheby's,
    Chancery Lane) $240   £105

ANAIS DAS BIBLIOTECAS E ARQUIVOS
Second series, vols. 1-10 bound in 5 vols.,
many folding tables and illustrations,
cloth 4to. —Lisbon, 1922-32.
(Christie's,
    St. James) $45   £20

'ANATOMICAL DIALOGUES OR A BREVIARY OF ANATOMY . . . CHIEFLY COMPILED FOR THE USE OF THE YOUNG GENTLEMEN IN THE NAVY AND ARMY'
4th Edn., 10 plates with explanatory text
at end, original boards worn, rebacked,
uncut — G.G. and J. Robinson, 1796.
(Sotheby's
    London) $80   £35

'THE ANCESTOR'
12 vols., plates, original boards — 1902-5.
(Phillips) $45   £20

ANDERSEN, HANS CHRISTIAN
'Digte' — 1st Edn., one leaf repaired, half
calf, contains Andersen's first fairy tale
'Dadningen' — Copenhagen, 1830.
(Sotheby's,
    Chancery Lane) $720   £320

'Out of the Heart, Spoken to the Little
Ones' translated by H. W. Dulcken — 1st
English Edn., wood engraved frontispiece
and 15 plates printed in colour, original
cloth, gilt — Routledge, 1867.
(Sotheby's,
    Chancery Lane) $75   £32
'Kjaerliched Paa Nicolai Taarn' — 1st Edn.,
calf backed boards, original upper cover
bound in — Copenhagen, 1829.
(Sotheby's,
    Chancery Lane) $75   £32
'Phantasier Og Skizzer' — 1st Edn., some
leaves browned, slightly spotted, modern
half roan — Copenhagen, 1831.
(Sotheby's,
    Chancery Lane) $290   £130
'Maurerpigen' — 1st Edn., presentation copy
inscribed by author to a fellow poet, cont.
half calf, slightly rubbed, slipcase — Bianco
Luno, 1840.
(Sotheby's,
    Chancery Lane) $765   £340

ANDERSEN

'The Improvisatore or Life in Italy' translated by Mary Howitt — 1st English Edn., original cloth backed boards, soiled, uncut — Richard Bentley, 1845.
(Sotheby's,
    Chancery Lane) $75   £32
'Winterabend-Geschichten' — 1st German Edn., spotted, original lithographed pictorial boards, soiled, slightly rubbed — M. Simion Leipzig, 1853.
(Sotheby's, Hodgson's
    Rooms) $45   £20
'The Will O' the Wisps are in Town and Other New Tales' — 1st English Edn., wood engraved frontispiece and 6 plates by M. E. Edwards and others, original cloth gilt, slightly marked — Alexander Strahan, 1867.
(Sotheby's,
    Chancery Lane) $80   £35

ANDERSON, G. W. (Editor)

'A New Authentic and Complete Collection of Voyages Round the World . . . containing Captain Cook's Voyages' — 86 plates, charts and maps. Some spotting, cont. half calf worn. Folio — n.d.
(Christie's S.
    Kensington)   £160   £70

ANDERSON, J.

'Historical and Genealogical Memoirs of the House of Hamilton' — engraved frontispiece and plate, original boards, uncut — Edinburgh, 1825.
(Tessa Bennett,
    Edinburgh) $27   £12

ANDERSON, J. C.

'Monuments and Antiquities of Croydon Church' — 11 lithographed plates, some coloured, spotting, original half calf, soiled and rubbed, g.e., ex library copy, folio — Croydon, 1855.
(Christie's S.
    Kensington) $45   £20

ANDERSSON, CHARLES JOHN

'Lake Ngami or Explorations and Discoveries During Four Years' Wanderings In the Wilds of South Western Africa' — 2nd Edn., 15 lithographed plates, 1 folding lithographed map, woodcut illustrations in text, spotting, original cloth gilt, rubbed, spine faded — 1856.
(Sotheby's, New Bond
    Street) $150 $65

ANDRAE, WALTER (Editor)

'Coloured Ceramics from Ashur' — plates, mostly coloured, illus. original cloth, folio — 1925.
(Christie's S.
    Kensington) $60   £25

ANDREWS, JOHN AND ANDREW DRURY

'A Map of the Country Sixty-Five Miles Round London' — 20 double page engraved maps, hand coloured in outline, slightly offset, 'Andrews' New Travelling Map of the South East Part of England' bound in, original half calf, worn, covers detached — 1776-78.
(Sotheby's,
    Chancery Lane) $655   £290

ANDREYEV, LEONID

'Abyss' — number 60 of 500 copies, frontispiece and illustrations by Ivan Lebedeff, original cloth backed boards — Golden Cockerel Press, 1929.
(Christie's S.
    Kensington) $40   £18

ANDRY, NICOLAS

'De La Generation de Vers Dans le Corps de L'Homme' — 3rd Edn., 2 vols., 23 plates with 7 folding, cont. mottled calf, spine gilt — Paris, 1741.
(Christie's, King
    St.) $100   £45

ANEL, DOMINIQUE

'L'Art de succer les plaies sans se servir de la bouche d'un homme avec un discours d'un specifique propre a prevenir certaines maladies Veneriennes' — 1st Edn., 3 folding plates, licence leaf at end, dampstained in outer margins just affecting printed line and numeral in plate 2, cont. calf — Amsterdam, Francois van der Plaats, 1707.
(Sotheby's
    London) $270   £120

ANGELONI, FRANCESCO

'La Historia Augusta da Giulio Cesare Infino a Constantino il Magno' — 1st Edn., numerous engravings in text, many full page, some soiling and browning, folio — Rome, 1641.
(Sotheby's, New Bond
    Street) $70   £30

ANGUS, W.
'The Seats of the Nobility and Gentry in Great Britain' – engraved title, 63 engraved plates, crimson morocco gilt – 1787.
(Phillips) $385   £170

ANOUILH, JEAN
'Ornifle ou le Courant D'Air' – original wrappers – La Table Ronde, Paris, 1955 .
(Sotheby's,
Chancery Lane) $25   £11

ANSTED, A.
'The Riviera' – 20 etched plates, some spotted, original cloth, gilt soiled, 8ct. folio – 1894.
(Sotheby Humberts
Taunton) $90   £40

ANTIQUARIAN AND ARCHAEOLOGICAL MISCELLANEA
From the Counties of Durham and Northumberland – 4 vols., plates, illustrations, original cloth – South Shields – n.d.
(Christie's S.
Kensington) $85   £38

ANTONIUS, FLORENTINUS
'Summa Confessionum' – 1st Edn., 143 leaves of 144, 27 lines, gothic letter, ornamental initial 'D' in red with decorative penwork in red and green, other initials in red, rubricated, cont. German blindstamped sheep over wooden boards, spine worn and repaired, rubbed – Cologne, 1468.
(Sotheby's, New Bond
Street) $6,300 £2,800
'De Censuris. De Sponsalibus et Matrimonio' – 1st Edn., 136 leaves, 40 lines, double column, gothic letter, initials supplied in red, 17th century vellum, slightly worn – Venice, 1474.
(Sotheby's, New Bond
Street) $1,305   £580
'Confessionale' – 123 leaves of 128, 23 lines, roman letter, some spotting and staining, 18th century stiff wrappers, worn and soiled – Florence, 1479/80.
(Sotheby's, New Bond
Street) $675   £300

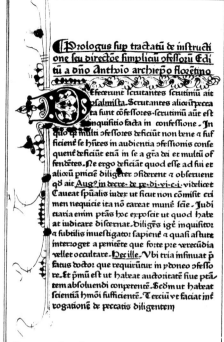

Summa Confessionum by Florentinus Antonius. (Sotheby's)

ANTONIUS, MARCUS AURELIUS
'His Meditations . . . translated by Meric Casaubon' – 1st Edn. of English trans., eng. portrait by Faithorne, 1 eng. plate, lacks first leaf, inner margin of portrait and title page repaired, touching text, tear in one blank margin and ink marginalia partly erased, causing small marginal hole, inner margins slightly dampstained, some pencilled marginalia, cont. panelled calf, rebacked, hinges split, slightly worn – 1634.
(Sotheby's
London) $90   £40

APIANUS, PETRUS
'Cosmographia, Per Gemman Phrysium Restituta' – 4 volvelles and many woodcut illustrations, some leaves stained, holed and repaired, some worming, 19th century paper boards, rubbed – A. Berckman, Antwerp, 1540.
(Christie's, King
St.) $1,125   £500

APIANUS

'Instrumentum Primi Mobilis . . . Accedunt iis Gebri Filii Affla Hispalensis'. Libri IX of astronomia, title in red and black with large woodcut, woodcut diagrams. Nuremberg 1534.

'Horoscopion' – title in red and black with large woodcut and woodcut illustrations in text – 1533.

'Folium Populi' – title and text in Latin and German, title in red and black, large woodcut and full page arms with large folding woodcut plate and 2 diagrams – 1533 – 3 works in one volume, all 1st Edns,, 18th century mottled sheep, gilt spine, folio.

(Sotheby's, New Bond
    Street) $3,375   £1,500

APOLLONIUS OF TYRE

'Historia Apollonii Regis Tyri' – number 15 of 300 copies, one of 75 with a set of the engraved plates, frontis, vignette on title and 4 illustrations by Mark Severin, original morocco gilt, edges damaged, spine dampstained, t.e.g., 4to. – 1956.

(Sotheby's,
    Chancery Lane) $170   £75

APPERLEY, CHARLES JAMES – 'NIMROD'

'Memoirs of the Life of the Late John Mitton, Esq.' – original green cloth gilt, lithograph title and three lithograph plates by Alken and Rawlins – reprint edition, n.d.

(Lawrence of
    Crewkerne) $25   £10

'The Life of a Sportsman' – hand coloured additional title and 37 plates by Henry Alken, original cloth, inner hinges split, portion of spine detached, stitching worn – Routledge, 1874.

(Christie's S.
    Kensington) $430   £190

APPERT, M.

'L'Art de Conserver . . . Animales et Vegetales' – signed limited edition, calf gilt – Paris, 1813.

(Phillips) $160   £70

'AQUATIC PARTY, THE'

7 wood engraved illustrations signed J. R. B. coloured by hand, one double page, original pictorial wrappers – Dean and Son, 1865.

(Sotheby's, Hodgson's
    Rooms) $45   £20

Folium Populi by Petrus Apianus. (Sotheby's)

Historia Apollonii Regis Tyri, illustrated by Mark Severin. (Sotheby's)

ARABIAN NIGHTS, THE
8 vols. including illustrations some in proof
state by Wood, Lalauze, Letchford, Harvey,
Marsillier, Westall and others from various
editions of the Arabian Nights — one vol.
full, the remainder half morocco, bookplates of Dyson Perrins, 4to.
(Christie's S.
Kensington) $360   £160

ARBUTHNOT, JOHN
'An Essay Concerning the Effects of Air on
Human Bodies' — 1st Edn., half title, worm-
ing, cont. calf, gilt, rubbed, bookplate of
the Royal College of Physicians — 1751.
(Sotheby's
Monaco) $720   £320
'An Essay Concerning the Effects of Air on
Human Bodies' — half title, no errata men-
tioned, cont. calf — J. & J. Tonson & S.
Draper, 1751.
(Sotheby's
London) $60   £25

**ARCHER, SIR GEOFFREY AND
GODMAN, EVA M.**
'The Birds of British Somaliland and the
Gulf of Aden' — vol. I and II only of 4,
plates, some coloured, folding maps,
original cloth, t.e.g. — 1937.
(Sotheby Humberts
Taunton) $110   £48

ARCHER, THOMAS
'Charles Dickens, Gossip about his Life,
Works and Characters' — plates on India
paper, illustrations, occasional spotting,
cont. half morocco, rubbed, folio, n.d.
(Christie's S.
Kensington) $70   £30

**ARCHIVES INTERNATIONAL DE LA
DANCE**
Introductory vol. 1932, 1933, Nos. 1-5,
1934; Nos. 1-6, 1935; together 19 vols.,
numerous illustrations in text, some
coloured, original printed wrappers —
Paris, 1932-36.
(Sotheby's, New Bond
Street) $85   £38

ARETAEUS CAPPADOX
'De acutorum ac diuturnorum morborum
causis & signi Lib. IV. De ... curatione Lib.
IV' — 1st Edn. in Greek, printers device on
title, old calf, spine gilt — Paris, Adr.
Turnebus, 1554.
(Sotheby's
London) $290   £130

ARETINO, PIETRO
'L'Aretin d'Augustin Carrache' — one of
575 copies, morocco, inner gilt dentelles,
t.e.g., slipcase — Paris, 1962.
(Sotheby's
Monaco) $945   £420

ARIOSTO, LUDOVICO
'Orlando Furioso' — 4 vols., engraved por-
trait, frontispiece and 46 other plates,
slight foxing, cont. calf, rebacked with
modern gilt spines — Baskerville,
Birmingham, 1773.
(Christie's S.
Kensington) $340   £150

ARISTOPHANES
'Comoedae undecim' — Greek text, Sessa's
cat-and-mouse device on title, a larger
version at end, lacks final blank, small tear
in 2HI, sheep backed boards, spine very
worn, with Heber copy, with stamp —
Venice, B. Zanettii for M. Sessa, 1538.
(Sotheby's
London) $160   £70
'Women in Parliament' — number 432 of
500 copies, plates and illustrations by
Norman Lindsay, original half morocco,
covers slightly nicked, t.e.g. — Fanfrolico
Press, 1957.
(Christie's S.
Kensington) $270   £120

ARISTOTELES, and others
'Problemata ad varias quaestiones &
philosophiam naturalem cognescendas ...
utilia' — italic letter, last three leaves
blank, cont. calf — Cologne, Officina
Birckmannica, 1601.
(Sotheby's
London) $80   £35

ARISTOTLE
'Aristotle's Complete Masterpiece;
Aristotle's Last Legacy' — a collection of
27 edns. of these are popular pieces,
many with frontis.s., ranging in date from
1707 to the end of the 19th century,
quarter vellum, calf, half calf, cloth —
1707-late 19th century.
(Sotheby's
London) $585   £250
'His Compleat and Experienc'd Midwife' —
woodcut frontispiece, old calf. Two
others included.
(Bonham's) $90   £40
'Compleat Masterpiece' — frontispiece
and illus. 22nd Edn., calf — 1741.
(Bonham's) $45   £20

ARISTOTLE

ARISTOTLE – CAROLUS, P.
'Generalis ad Libros Physicorum Introductio' – and BURNATUS, G. 'Primae Physicae in Partem Communem Synopsis' – mss. in ink of two courses of study, more than 1,000 pp. in Latin in neat regular hand, decorative dated titles, chapter headings and side notes, cont. calf, gilt floral centre, gilt spine, gilt and gauffred edges – Montauban, 1605.
(Christie's, King
St.) $495   £220

ARMENIAN
'Compendiose Notizie Sulla Congregazione de Monaci Armeni Mechitaristi di Venezia nell'Isola di S. Lazzaro' – two parts in one vol. Armenian and Italian text, 2 engraved plates, cont. roan backed, marbled boards – Tipografia di Suddetta Isola, Venice, 1819.
(Sotheby's, New Bond
Street) $160   £70

ARMENIAN PRAYER ROLL
Illuminated mss. on vellum, 4 membranes, written in black bolorgir script with headings and marginal letters in red, miniature of a saint, 90 x 60mm., some stains, edges browned, tear in text crudely repaired, wide colophon, written by scribe Kostandin at the monastery of Argelan – 933 (i.e. A.D.1484)
(Christie's, King
St.) $765   £340

ARMENIAN GOSPELS
Illuminated mss. on paper, 261 leaves, double column, 21 lines, written in black bolorgir script, with pagination and headings in red, five full page miniatures misbound, lacking St. Matthew, some leaves detached, torn, stained, stitching split, later calf, covers warped, spine wormed, jewelled metal cross in centre of upper cover, 243 x 162mm. – 16th century.
(Christie's, King
St.) $1,125   £500

ARMSTRONG, JOHN
'The Art of Preserving Health, a Poem' – 1st Edn., new half morocco – A. Millar, 1744.
(Sotheby's, New Bond
Street) $75   £32

ARMSTRONG, MARTIN
'The Puppet Show' – limited to 1,225 copies, original cloth backed boards, dust jacket – Golden Cockerel Press, 1922.
(Christie's S.
Kensington) $40   £18

ARNOLD, SIR THOMAS W.
'The Library of A. Chester Beatty, a catalogue of the Indian Miniatures' – 3 vols., 103 plates, 19 coloured, original buckram, folio – Oxford University Press, 1936.
(Sotheby's
Monaco) $5,400   £2,400

ARP, HANS
'On My Way' – 2 woodcuts by author, illustrations and reproductions, original wrappers – New York, 1948.
(Sotheby's,
Chancery Lane) $25   £10

ARP, JEAN, Sonia Delaunay, Alberto Magnelli and Sophie Taeuber-Arp
10 lithographs, title, 10 coloured lithographs wach combining designs of two or three of the four artists, unsewn, uncut, original folder and slipcase – Aux Nourritures Terrestres, Paris, 1950.
(Sotheby's,
Chancery Lane) $215   £95

ARROWSMITH, A.
'Map of South Italy and Adjacent Coasts' – eng. map, hand coloured in outline, on 8 folding sheets, each about 25 x 32in., mounted on cloth – 1807.
(Christie's S.
Kensington) $40   £18

ART, GOUT, BEAUTE
Nos. 16, 25, 30-33, 35, 38. 8 issues, numerous illustrations, by Colette, Dory, Vittroto, Scavone and others, Depicting clothing designed by Poiret, Worth, Molyneux, Patou and others, the majority coloured by hand or printed in colours, original pictorial wrappers, slightly soiled in slipcase – Paris, 1921-23.
(Sotheby's,
Chancery Lane) $430   £190

Art, Gout, Beaute, 1921-23.
(Sotheby's)

ART JOURNAL, THE
Plates, 6 vols., ranging between 1849 and 1898.
(Bonham's) $250 £110

ART JOURNAL, THE
15 vols., illus., various bindings – 1851-81.
(Phillips) $385 £170

'THE ART JOURNAL ILLUSTRATED CATALOGUE. THE INDUSTRY OF ALL NATIONS 1851'
Plates, illustrations, cont. half morocco, corners rubbed – 1851.
(Christie's S.
Kensington) $60 £25

ART OF KNOWING WOMEN, THE
Trans. Spring Macky, calf – 1730.
(Phillips) $215 £95

'ARTS DECORATIFS DE GRANDE BRETAGNE ET D'IRLANDE EXPOSITION'
Contributions by Walter Crane, Douglas Cockerell, Emery Walker and others, coloured and other plates, cloth gilt, boxed – Paris, 1914.
(Tessa Bennett,
Edinburgh) $95 £42
ASPIN, JEHOSHAPHAT
'The Naval and Military Exploits . . . in the Reign of George the Third' – 1st Edn., 34 hand coloured aquatint plates, slight browning and soiling, cont. red roan, worn – 1820.
(Sotheby's, New Bond
Street) $180 £80
ASTRUC
'A Treatise on all the Diseases Incident to Women' – old calf – 1743.
(Bonham's) $135 £60
ATKINS, J.
'The Navy Surgeon or A Practical System of Surgery' – 2nd Edn., binding poor – 1737.
(Tessa Bennett,
Edinburgh) $11 £5
ATKINSON, J.
'An Account of the State of Agriculture and Grazing in New South Wales' – folding coloured aquatint panorama of Port Jackson and part of the town of Sydney, large folding coloured map of New South Wales with vignettes and cartouche, 3 coloured aquatint plates and plate of gound plan of milking yard – 1st Edn. with half title, calf – Signet Arms – 1826.
(Bonham's) $2,590 £1,150
ATKINSON, THOMAS WITLAM
'Travels in the Regions of the Upper and Lower Amoor and the Russian Acquisitions on the Confines of India and China' – 1st American Edn., woodcut frontispiece and illustrations in text, folding map, slightly torn, original cloth, slightly worn – New York, 1860.
(Sotheby's New Bond
Street) $70 £30
'Oriental and Western Siberia' – 1st Edn., 20 coloured lithos, 1 folded map, 2 plates and 1 text leaf detached, very short tear in map, signature of Sarah Tyrconnel on title, original gilt cloth – 1858.
(Sotheby's
London) $160 £70

One of a collection of 39 mainly 17th century maps. (Lawrence of Crewkerne)

One of the 31 maps in the Rev. J. Hall Parlby's Atlas.(Lawrence of Crewkerne)

ATLAS
Collection of 39 maps mainly 17th century – folio 19th century half calf spine gilt, some scuffing, label missing. These maps by De Witt, the Allard family, the Danckers family, Schenk and others showing America, China, but chiefly Europe in particular the Netherlands and Germany. Collection formed in early 18th century, generally good condition. Approx. 20¾ x 25in. each.
(Lawrence of
    Crewkerne) $4,050   £1,800

ATLAS
Collection of 31 maps – mainly late 17th century, folio 19th century half calf, spine gilt, morocco label, some scuffing. Collection seems to have been formed at same time as English edition of Jansson's Atlas. Collection rebound in 19th century for Rev. John Hall Parlby of Manadon in Devon. Maps double paged, very good state, on guards throughout, uncoloured except for last. Almost all 20½in. x 24in.
(Lawrence of
    Crewkerne) $1,240   £550

ATTWELL, M. L. – BARRIE, J. M.
'Peter Pan' – mounted coloured plates by Attwell, original cloth, soiled, n.d.
(Christie's S.
    Kensington) $35   £15

ATWOOD, T.
'The History of the Island of Dominica' – half calf – 1791.
(Sotheby's
    Monaco) $1,915   £850

AUBREY, JOHN
Letters written to Eminent Personages in the 17th and 18th centuries to which are added Hearne's Journeys to Reading and Lives of Eminent Men – 2 parts in 3, half calf – 1813.
(Lawrence of
    Crewkerne) $80   £35

AUCTION HOUSE REVIEWS OF THE YEAR
9 vols., various, plates, illustrations, some coloured. Original cloth, dust jacket – 1960-78.
(Christie's S.
    Kensington) $85   £38

AUDEN, W. H.
'Spain' – 1st Edn., original wrappers, uncut – 1937.
(Sotheby's,
    Chancery Lane) $40   £18

AUDEN, W. H. AND ISHERWOOD, CHRISTOPHER
'Journey to a War' – 1st Edn., frontispiece, original cloth, holed – 1939.
(Sotheby's,
    Chancery Lane) $40   £18

AUDUBON, JOHN JAMES
'The Birds of America' – limited facsimile edition, 2 vols., additional facsimile titles and 40 facsimile coloured plates, original half linen, elephant folio – Ariel Press, 1972-73.
(Christie's
    St. James) $450   £200
'The original watercolour paintings . . . for the Birds of America . . . introduction by Marshall B. Davidson' – 2 vols., coloured plates, original cloth – 1966.
(Christie's S.
    Kensington) $95   £42

AUDUBON, JOHN JAMES AND BACHMAN, JOHN
'The Quadrupeds of North America' – 2nd Edn., 3 vols., 155 coloured lithographed plates, cont. maroon morocco, sides with gilt borders and central blind stamped medallions, spines gilt, g.e. – V. G. Audubon New York, 1854.
(Christie's
    St. James) $2,250   £1,000

AUGSBURG, GEORGES
'La Vie en Images de Serge Lifar' – number 250 of 500 copies of an edition limited to 535 copies. 61 line illustrations, original printed and decorative stiff wrappers, small tears, slightly soiled – Paris, 1937.
(Sotheby's, New Bond
    Street) $115   £50

AULDJO, JOHN
'Narrative of an Ascent to the Summit of Mont Blanc' – engraved plates on India paper, half calf, worn, 4to – 1828.
(Phillips) $585   £260

AULNOY, MARIE CATHERINE COUNTESS D'
'The Celebrated Tales of Mother Bunch' – etched frontispiece, a few leaves stained, original roan backed boards, worn – John Harris, 1830.
(Sotheby's
    Chancery Lane) $18   £8

AULT

AULT, NORMAN
Watercolour drawing of a turbaned figure
sailing a boat past an Oriental palace,
signed and dated 1913.
(Sotheby's,
    Chancery Lane) $135   £60

Twenty pen and ink drawings to illustrate
'The Shepherd of the Ocean' depicting
scenes from the times of Sir Francis Drake,
Charles I and the Middle Ages. One framed.
(Sotheby's,
    Chancery Lane) $260   £160

A series of 21 pen and ink drawings to illustrate 'The Seven Champions of Christen-
dom', comprising 12 drawings for the full
page illustrations, each signed, some dated
1913, and 9 smaller drawings for chapter
headings.
(Sotheby's,
    Chancery Lane) $200   £90

AULT, NORMAN AND LENA
Series of 12 watercolour drawings to illustrate 'Sammy and the Snarleywink' three
framed and glazed, three mounted and one
soiled. Drawings probably by Lena Ault
alone and the text by her husband.
(Sotheby's,
    Chancery Lane) $170   £75

**'AUNT LOUISA'S SHIPS, BIRDS AND
WONDER-TALES'**
comprising: The A.B.C. of Ships and
Boats; The Old Woman who lived in a
Shoe; Trial of the Sparrow who killed
Cock Robin; The Three Little Boggies,
4 separately issued works in one vol.,
printed in colour by Kronheim, original
cloth gilt — Warne, 1880.
(Sotheby's, Hodgson's
    Rooms) $85   £38

AUSTEN, JANE
'The Works' – 6 vols., portrait, five en-
graved frontispieces, dampstaining, cont.
mottled half calf, damaged by damp –
1904.
(Christie's S.
  Kensington) $80   £35
'Sandition' – fragment of a novel, second
impression, cont. cloth backed boards,
corners bumped – Oxford, 1925.
(Christie's S.
  Kensington) $7   £3

AUSTRALIA
2 share certificates for issue of land by
Western Australia Co. to Alexander C.
Ogilvy – 1840.
(Tessa Bennett,
  Edinburgh) $36   £16
8 maps, some coloured; 3 New Zealand,
all late 19th century.
(Phillips) $72   £32

AUSTRIAN INFANTRY
'Regulement Und Ordnung Des Gesammten Kaiserlich-Koniglichen Fuss-Volks' –
mss. in ink on paper in two volumes, 284
leaves, including 162 pictorial leaves,
illustrations in ink and wash and military
plans mostly in colour, 4 illustrated sub
titles, 2 armorial leaves, generally inscribed
on one side only. Cont. mottled calf, gilt,
Habsburg Imperial arms on upper covers,
royal arms on lower covers. Oblong folio
– Vienna, circa 1770.
(Christie's
  St. James) $8,550   £3,800

AVICULTURE, MAGAZINE THE
Various issues relating to foreign birds, in
4 vols., majority coloured lithographs –
1899-1914.
(Christie's S.
  Kensington) $160   £70

AVRIL, PAUL – FRANCE, HECTOR
'Sous le Burnous' – etched frontispiece,
vignette on title and 20 head and tail
pieces by Avril, green half morocco, t.e.g.,
No. 224 of 375 – Carrington, Paris, 1898.
(Sotheby's,
  Chancery Lane) $20   £9

AVRIL, PAUL – GAUTIER THEOPHILE
'Une Nuit de Cleopatre' – etched vignette
on title and 20 illustrations by Avril,
purple morocco gilt, gilt inside borders,
watered silk doublures and end leaves,
t.e.g., original wrappers bound in, 150 of
500 copies – Librairie des Amateurs,
Paris, 1894.
(Sotheby's,
  Chancery Lane) $160   £70

AVRIL, PAUL – UZANNE, OCTAVE
'L'Ombrelle, Le Gant, le Manchon' – 78
illustrations after Avril, original pictorial
wrappers, slightly soiled and worn, uncut,
pictorial silk folder, dampstained joints
split, ties defective – Quantin, Paris, 1883.
(Sotheby's
  Chancery Lane) $7   £3

AVRIL, PHILIPPE
'Voyage en Divers Etats d'Europe and
D'Asie entrepris pour decouvrir un nouveau
Chemin a la Chine' – 1st Edn., engraved
portrait, 3 plates, folding map, browning
and soiling, cont. calf, worn – Paris, 1692.
(Sotheby's, New Bond
  Street) $160   £70

Regulement und Ordnung Des Gesammten Kaiserlich-Koniglichen Fuss-Volks.
(Christie's)

AWDLEY, JOHN
'Alla Cantalena de Sancta Maria' — number
21 of 450 copies, illustrations by Lloyd
Haberly, original parchment — The Seven
Acres Press, 1926.
(Christie's S.
   Kensington)   **$56**   **£25**

AXE, PROF. J. WORTLER
'The Horse, Its Treatment in Health and
Disease' — 9 vols., plates, some coloured,
original decorated cloth — 1900.
(Christie's S.
   Kensington)   **$36**   **£16**

BABER, ZEHIR-ED-DIN MUHAMMED, EMPEROR OF HINDUSTAN
'Memoirs translated by John Leyden and
William Erskine' — 1st Edn., folding
engraved map, slight browning, cont.
polished calf, joints split, rubbed — 1826.
(Sotheby's, New Bond
   Street)   **$160**   **£70**

BABINGTON, WILLIAM, MARCET, ALEXANDER AND ALLEN, WM.
'A Syllabus of a course of chemical lec-
tures read at Guy's Hospital' — interleaved
copy, frontispiece of a chemical lecture
bench, half calf, gilt, hinges repaired —
William Phillips, 1816.
(Sotheby's, New Bond
   Street)   **$90**   **£40**

BACHAUMONT, F. DE
'Memoires Secrets, pour servir a l'histoire de
la Republique des Lettres en France' - 19
vols., cont. mottled calf, gilt spines, index
vol., not uniform, rubbed — Londres, 1781-
89; Bruxelles, 1866.
(Sotheby's
   Monaco)   **$1,910**   **£850**

BACK (CAPTAIN)
'Narrative of the Arctic Land Expedition
to the Mouth of the great Fish River . . .
Arctic Ocean, in the years 1833, 1834 and
1835' — folding map and 16 steel engraved
and litho plates, calf spine rubbed, 1st Edn.
— 1836.
(Tessa Bennett,
   Edinburgh)   **$315**   **£140**

BACKHOUSE, EDWARD, JUNIOR
'Original Etchings of Birds' — engraved title,
26 etched plates, including 20 of birds and
6 of animals, on India paper, 2 extra plates
loosely inserted, and a pen and ink sketch
on linen, tears, spotting, signed by Backhouse, C., on free end paper, cont. purple
morocco, gilt, upper cover and spine partly
detached, worn, g.e., sm folio — Ashburne,
1840.
(Sotheby's, New Bond
   Street)   **$855**   **£380**

BACKHOUSE, JAMES
'A Narrative of a Visit to the Australian
Colonies' — 1st Edn., 18 plates and maps, 4
folding, 5 torn, illustrations, spotted, origi-
nal cloth, rebacked, slightly rubbed — 1843.
(Sotheby's,
   Chancery Lane)   **$158**   **£70**

BACON, FRANCIS, VISCOUNT ST. ALBANS
'The Historie of the Reign of King Henry
the Seventh' — title within woodcut border, light staining, later morocco rubbed,
upper cover torn, folio — 1929.
(Christie's S.
   Kensington)   **$100**   **£45**
'Sylva Sylvarum' — additional engraved
title, lacking printed title, portrait, and
all after CI of the 'Articles of Enquiry',
slight browning and soiling, a few tears
and holes, book label after C. H. Wilkinson
on engraved title, cloth backed boards
rubbed and soiled — small folio, 1664.
(Sotheby's
   London)   **$34**   **£15**

'Of the Advancement and Proficiencie of Learning' – eng. title, portrait lacking, lower corners of Hhh-Jjj4 chewed, affecting a few letters, later half calf, rubbed, joints split, folio – Oxford, Leon, Lichfield, for Rob, Young & Ed. Forrest – 1640.
(Christie's S.
   Kensington) $56   £25
'The Essayes, First Complete Edition' – printed within line borders throughout, some browning and soiling, title and A4 slightly defective, title manuscript, lacking blank AI, some line borders shaved, early 19th century half calf, rubbed, spine defective, upper cover detached – 1625.
(Christie's S.
   Kensington) $630   £280
'The Essays' – 2 parts in one vol., continuous signatures, 4pp. advertisements at end, some browning, cont. mottled calf, slightly worn – 1696.
(Christie's S.
   Kensington) $135   £60
'Resuciatatio' – 2 parts in one vol., 3rd Edn., 2 engraved portraits, last leaf rubbed and holed, half calf, covers detached, folio – For William Lee, 1671.
(Christie's S.
   Kensington) $135   £60

BACON, ROGER
'The Cure of Old Age and Preservation of Youth' – translated by Richard Browne, 1st Edn. in English, 2 parts in one vol., advertisement leaf at end, calf, rebacked – Tho. Flsher and Edward Evets, 1683.
(Sotheby's, New Bond
   Street) $540   £240

BACON'S NEW MAP OF THE WAR IN VIRGINIA AND MARYLAND
Coloured map, 24 x 18½in., mss. note at lower right, framed and glazed – 1862.
(Christie's S.
   Kensington) $34   £15

BACONNIERE-SALVERTE, A. J. E.
'Eusebe Salverte'
'Des Sciences Occultes' – 2 vols., 1st Edn., romantic binding of half red calf, spines gilt, trifle worn – Paris, 1829.
(Sotheby's
   Monaco) $1,125   £500

BADEN-POWELL, LIEUT.-GEN. R. S. S.
'Scouting for Boys' – Parts 1, 2 and 4-6, 5 vols., illustrations, original pictorial wrappers, one slightly torn, covers of one loose – 1908.
(Sotheby's, Hodgson's
   Rooms) $50   £22

BADESLADE, T. AND TOMS, W. H.
'Chorographia Britanniae' – engraved double page title, 46 double page maps, tables, calf – 1742.
(Phillips) $765   £340

BAGLIVI, GIORGIO
'The Practice of Physick reduc'd to the ancient way of Observations . . . particularly of the Tarantula and the Nature of its poison' – 1st English Edn., some stains, name written on title page, new half calf – A. Bell etc., 1704.
(Sotheby's, New Bond
   Street) $520   £230

BAGULESCO, GEORGES
'Yamato Damashi. A Romance' – No. 15 of 130 copies, inscribed by the author 'A Madame et Mr. le General F. G. G. Piggott . . . Tokyo le 3 Avril 1938', folding coloured plate, one mounted colour illus., Japanese style decorated cloth, boxed – Kenkyusha Printing Co., n.d.
(Christie's S.
   Kensington) $90   £40

BAILEY'S MAGAZINE OF SPORTS AND PASTIMES
Vols. I-X and 67-69, First ten vols., half calf, morocco label. Other vols. in cloth – 1860-65 and 1897-98.
(Lawrence of
   Crewkerne) $18   £8

BAILLIE, MATTHEW
'A Series of Engravings accompanied with explanation which are intended to illustrate the morbid anatomy of some of the most important parts of the human body' – 2nd Edn., 73 plates by William Clift, explanatory text, half title, half roan gilt, uncut, arms of the Royal College of Physicians on upper cover – W. Bulmer and Co., 1812.
(Sotheby's, New Bond
   Street) $450   £200
'The Works to which is prefixed an account of his life' – 2 vols., portrait, calf gilt – Longham, 1825.
(Sotheby's, New Bond
   Street) $360   £160

BAINBRIDGE, G. C.
'The Fly Fisher's Guide' – 1st Edn., 8 hand coloured plates, some foxing, stitching loose, original boards, spine defective uncut, 8vo. – 1816.
(Sotheby's, New Bond
    Street)   **$290**   **£130**

BAINES, EDWARD
'The History of . . . Lancaster' – 2 vols., folding map, illustrations in text, library stamp on a few pages, original cloth, rather rubbed – 1868-70.
(Sotheby's,
    Chancery Lane)   **$45**   **£20**

BAKER, DAVID ERSKINE
'The Companion to the Play-House' – 2 vols., 1st Edn., dedicated to David Garrick, errata and ad. leaf at end of vol. I, title to vol. II very slightly browned and frayed, other leaves slightly spotted, some outer edges slightly soiled, modern half calf, labels, uncut – 1764.
(Sotheby's
    London)   **$225**   **£100**

BAKER, E. C. STUART
'The Indian Ducks and Their Allies' – additional title and 30 coloured plates after H. Gronvold, and others, some leaves slightly spotted, cont. half morocco, corners bumped – 1908.
(Christie's S.
    Kensington)   **$170**   **£75**

BAKER, SIR RICHARD
'A Chronicle of the Kings of England with a continuation to the year 1660 by E. Phillips' – additional engraved title with many engravings, mostly portraits, inlaid in larger sheets, cont. calf, rebacked with sheep, folio – 1730.
(Christie's S.
    Kensington)   **$115**   **£50**

BAKER, SIR SAMUEL WHITE
'The Albert N'Yanza' – 2 vols., 1st Edn., 2 partly coloured maps, 1 folded, 13 plates incl. 1 tinted litho, short tear in folded map, 1 section detached and 2 partly detached in vol. I, 1 partly detached in vol. II, signature of Sarah Tyrconnel on titles, original cloth, gilt, inner hinges slightly weak in vol. I – 1866.
(Sotheby's
    London)   **$80**   **£35**

'The Nile Tributaries of Abyssinia' – 2nd Edn., plates, maps, 1 folding, cont. half morocco – 1868.
'Rifle and Hound in Ceylon' – New Edn., plates, cont. calf, gilt, slightly rubbed – 1874.
'Wild Beasts and their Ways' – 2 vols., 1st Edn., plates, cont. half morocco, slightly rubbed – 1890.
'Eight Years in Ceylon' – New Edn., cont. calf, gilt – 1891.
(Sotheby's,
    Chancery Lane)   **$198**   **£88**
'Ismailia' – 2 vols., 1st Edn., engraved portrait, plates, 2 coloured maps, one folding and slightly torn, half titles lacking, half morocco, rubbed – 1874.
(Christie's S.
    Kensington)   **$146**   **£65**

BAKST, LEON, AND OTHERS
'The Russian Ballet in Western Europe 1909-1920' – with chapter on music by Eugene Goosens, 5 portraits, 66 reproductions of designs by Bakst, Picasso, Gontcharova, Matisse and others, most full page, 47 coloured, original buckram backed board, spine slightly soiled t.e.g. – 1921.
(Sotheby's,
    Chancery Lane)   **$295**   **£130**

BAKST, LEON – ARSENE, ALEXANDRE, AND COCTEAU, JEAN
'The Decorative Art of Leon Bakst' – portrait, 77 plates, 50 coloured, original half vellum, t.e.g., folio – Fine Art Society, 1913.
(Sotheby's,
    Chancery Lane)   **$585**   **£260**

BALBIRNIE, J.
'The Speculum applied to Organic Diseases of the Womb' – 1st Edn., presentation copy, cloth and another edition of the same – 1836.
(Bonham's)   **$160**   **£70**

BALDINUS, B. AND NEGRONUS, J.
'De Calceo Antiquo et de Caliga Veterum' – 2 parts in one, engraved additional title and plates, some folding, illustrations, cont. vellum – Amsterdam, 1667.
(Christie's S.
    Kensington)   **$56**   **£25**

BALDRY, A.
'Hubert Von Herkomer' – 2 frontispieces and plates, quarter vellum with wrapper, boxed, limited edition on large paper, handmade. 13 of 85 copies, folio – 1901.
(Tessa Bennett,
   Edinburgh)   **$22**   **£10**

BALDWIN, T.
'Airopaedia . . . the Narrative of a Balloon Excursion from Chester' – 4 plates, 2 coloured, title torn and mounted with slight loss, some soiling, calf, antique, 8vo – Chester, 1786.
(Sotheby's, New Bond
   Street)   **$2,790**   **£1,240**

BALFOUR, J.
'The Book of Arran' – frontispiece and plates, buckram, limited edition 55 copies – Glasgow, 1910.
(Tessa Bennett,
   Edinburgh)   **$85**   **£38**

BALL, CHARLES
'The History of the Indian Mutiny' – engraved additional titles and plates, double page map, hand coloured in outline, some spotting, cont. half morocco slightly rubbed – n.d.
(Christie's S.
   Kensington)   **$95**   **£42**

BALLANTYNE, R. M.
'The Kitten Pilgrims' – 1st Edn., coloured frontispiece, pictorial title and 10 plates and illustrations in text by the author, original cloth backed pictorial boards – 1882.
(Sotheby's, Hodgson's
   Rooms)   **$45**   **£20**
'Hudson's Bay' – 2nd Edn., wood engraved frontispiece and illustrations, cloth, 1848.
'The Wild Men of the West' – 1st Edn., 8 wood engraved plates, spotted, original cloth – 1863.
(Sotheby's,
   Chancery Lane)   **$34**   **£15**

BALLET
Edited by Richard Buckle – together 107 volumes, illustrations, original wrappers – 1939-52.
(Sotheby's, New Bond
   Street)   **$11**   **£5**

BALLET HOUSE
Programme for the 1914 season at Royal Theatre Drury Lane, illustrations, many coloured, by Leon Bakst, original wrappers, slightly soiled, 4to – 1914.
(Christie's S.
   Kensington)   **$80**   **£35**

BALZAC, HONORE DE
'Oeuvres' – 2 vols., presentation copy, illustrated, cloth, broken – Paris, 1831.
(Sotheby's, New Bond
   Street)   **$720**   **£320**
'Histoire de la Grandeur et de la Decadence de Cesar Birotteau' – 2 vols., 1st Edn., cloth, original wrappers, bound in – Paris, 1838.
(Sotheby's,
   Chancery Lane)   **$95**   **£42**
Autograph letter signed, 1 page, 16mo, no place, 30th August (1847) to M. Guerville at the Theatre Historique.
(Sotheby's, New Bond
   Street)   **$430**   **£190**

Autograph letter signed, 1 page octavo, postmarked, 26 July, 1837, to Mr. Schlesinger, entreating him to hurry the printer, a little browned, integral address leaf.
(Sotheby's, New Bond
   Street)   **$1,620**   **£720**

former lets go the arrow which, after piercing the lady, speeds on to the target where it remains sticking. The ribbon is still attached to the arrow that has passed through the lady and the end of it now hangs down in front of her. To prove that it is really true that the ribbon is through her body she moves it backwards and forwards through her body. Complete with all accessories. Price.................... See Price List

1299.   THE MYSTERIOUS ESCAPE.

A gigantic set of scales are seen standing in the centre of the stage. On one side of the scales a big cage is attached, instead of the ordinary weighing pan. A lady is asked to enter the cage and is weighed, the scales being made to exactly balance by the usual weights on the other side. The curtains of the cage are now closed, a pistol is fired, and, instantaneously, the scale carrying the weights falls and the cage end rises. On drawing the curtains, it is found that the cage is empty, but the lady is seen at the same moment, coming down the theatre through the audience on her way to the stage. To prove that the cage is absolutely hanging free it is swung round, so that all may see it. This is a first-class illusion, and the idea is brand new. Price on application.

BAMBERG, THEO.
'Amateur Catalog of Magic and Novelties' − original wrappers (copyrighted 1909). 'Illustrated Catalogue' − prices pasted over, last leaf slightly worn, folder, with original wrappers bound in, n.d., illustrations − New York, n.d.
(Sotheby's,
  Chancery Lane) $108   £48

BAMBOU, LE
Edited by Edouard Guillaume − 11 vols. of 12, lacking vol. 10, many illustrations by Andreas, Gambard, Mittis and others, slightly spotted, original wrappers, slightly soiled, some worn, upper cover of vol. I detached, uncut − E. Dentu, Paris, 1893.
(Sotheby's,
  Chancery Lane) $2.25   £1

BANKART, G. P.
'The Art of the Plasterer' − frontispiece, illustrations, original cloth, soiled, inner hinges worn − 1908.
(Christie's S.
  Kensington) $67   £30

BANKS, W.
'Views in North Wales' − engraved title and 32 plates by Banks, some detached, original cloth, g.e. − Chester and Bangor, n.d.
(Christie's S.
  Kensington) $72   £32

BANNET, IVOR
'The Amazons' − limited to 500 copies, this number 2 of 80 specially bound by Sangorski and Sutcliffe and signed by author and artist, frontispiece and full page illustrations by Clifford Webb, maps by Mina Greenhill, original morocco, t.e.g. − Golden Cockerel Press, 1948.
(Christie's S.
  Kensington) $315   £140

BAPTISTA, JOANNES
'Institutiones Christianae, seu Parvus Cathechismus Catholicorum' − device on title, 103 engravings in text by Petrus Canisius, Jesuit ownership inscription, cont. limp vellum − C. Plantin, Antwerp, 1589.
(Sotheby's, New Bond
  Street) $112   £50

BARBER, T.
'Picturesque Illustrations of the Isle of Wight' − title 40 plates, coloured engravings of Carisbrooke Castle loosely inserted, some spots, double page map, calf gilt, g.e. − 1834.
(Phillips) $85   £38

BARBERIIS, PHILIPPUS DE
'Opuscula' − 1st Edn., printed on vellum, 41 leaves of 70, 26 lines, roman letter, 4 hand coloured woodcut illustrations of Sibyls only − Rome, 1 December 1481.
(Sotheby's, New Bond
  Street) $1,125   £500
'Opuscula' − 1st Edn., printed on vellum, 41 leaves of 70, 4 hand coloured woodcut illustrations of Sibyls, disbound and loose. Joannes Philippus de Lignamine, Rome, 1 December 1481.
(Christie's S.
  Kensington) $900   £400

Opuscula by Philippus de Barberiis. (Christie's)

The Practice of the Most Successful Physitian Paul Barbette. (Sotheby's)

BARBETTE, PAUL
'The Practice of the Most Successful Physitian Paul Barbette' — 1st Edn. in English, engraved title by F. H. van House, printed title, a few dampstains, cont. calf worn — T. R. for Henry Brome, 1675. (Sotheby's, New Bond
    Street) $495   £220

BARBETTE, VANDER
Album containing photographs, cards and press clippings of Barbette collected by David Gray with biographical notes. Some items tipped in, original cloth, folio. (Sotheby's, New Bond
    Street) $90   £40

BARBIER, GEORGE — VERLAINE, PAUL
'Fetes Galantes' — 20 full page coloured illustrations, pictorial border to title, cover design by Barbier, original pictorial wrappers, backstrip and joints slightly worn, uncut, slipcase worn — H. Piazza, Paris, 1928. (Sotheby's,
    Chancery Lane) $520   £230

Le Bonheur du Jour pour 1920 ou Les Graces a la Mode, illustrated by
Barbier and Reidel. (Sotheby's)

BARBIER, GEORGE
'Le Bonheur du Jour pour 1920 ou Les
Graces a la Mode' – pictorial title, 3 illustrations in text, 16 plates and cover illustration by H. Reidel and Barbier, coloured
by hand, unsewn in original wrappers.
Oblong folio – Chez Meynial, Paris, 1920-
24.
(Sotheby's,
    Chancery Lane) $1,575   £700

**BARBIER, GEORGE – BOYLESVE,
RENE**
'Les Bains de Bade' – wood engraved pictorial title printed in two colours, 29
illustrations in text, all by Georges Aubert
after Barbier, marbled silk, t.e.g., original
wrappers bound in – G. Cres, Paris, 1921.
(Sotheby's,
    Chancery Lane) $360   £160

Celle qu'aima le Centaure.

**BARBIER, GEORGE – GRAMONT,
SANCHEDE**
'Anteros' – 5 illustrations by Barbier,
vellum, original wrappers, bound in, t.e.g.,
slipcase, no. 311 of 500 – La Belle Edition,
Paris, 1913.
(Sotheby's,
    Chancery Lane) $290   £130

BARBIER, GEORGE – GAUTIER, THEOPHILE
'Le Roman de la Momie' – coloured wood-cut illustration, title 31 illustrations, 2 ornamental letters and pictorial wrappers by Gasperini after Barbier, original wrappers uncut – A. and G. Mornay, Paris, 1929.
(Sotheby's,
    Chancery Lane) $510   £226

BARBIER, GEORGE – GUERIN, MAURICE DE
'Poemes en Prose, precedes d'une petite lettre sur les mythes par Paul Valery' – 28 wood engraved illustrations, 3 pictorial initials by Bouchet, printed in colours and gold, unsewn in original decorated wrappers, uncut, slipcase. Limited to 150 copies, this printed for Albert Bescombes – A. Blaizot, Paris, 1928.
(Sotheby's,
    Chancery Lane) $810   £360

BARBIER, GEORGE – REGNIER, HENRI DE
'Les Rencontres de Monsieur de Breot' – 34 illustrations, 10 pictorial initials and cover designs by Barbier, all coloured through stencils, brown half morocco, t.e.g., original wrappers bound in, by Trinckvel – A. and G. Mornay, Paris, 1930.
(Sotheby's,
    Chancery Lane) $250   £110

BARCLAY, JOHN
'Euphormio's Satyricon' – number 174 of 260 copies, plates by Derrick Harris, original cloth backed boards, folio – Golden Cockerel Press, 1854.
(Christie's S.
    Kensington) $95   £42
'Barclay his Argenis, or, the Loves of Poly-archus and Argenis. Faithfully translated . . by Kingsmill Long, Esquire' – 2nd Edn., engraved title, just shaved at head, portrait, full page engravings, hole in N8 affecting text, a few rust holes, occasional staining and soiling, one word defective, cont. calf, worn, upper joint split – 1636.
(Sotheby's
    London) $67   £30

BARCLAY, JOHN
'The Anatomy of the Bones of the Human Body represented in a series of engravings by Edward Mitchell, engraver' – New Edn. by R. Knox, 32 plates with explanatory text, original cloth, paper label rubbed, uncut – MacLachlan and Stewart, Edinburgh, 1829.
(Sotheby's, New Bond
    Street) $85   £38

BARHAM, R. H.
'Ingoldsby Legends' – 24 colour plates by A. Rackham, repair to text without loss, cloth, 4to – 1920.
(Phillips) $85   £38

BARING-GOULD, SABINE
'Iceland, Its Scenes and Sagas' – plates, some coloured, one folding map, torn and neatly repaired, cont. half morocco, worn, 4to., ex-library copy – 1863.
(Christie's S.
    Kensington) $95   £42

BARKER, GEORGE
'Alanna Autumnal' and 'Thirty Preliminary Poems' – 1st Edns., original cloth backed boards – Parton Press, 1933.
(Sotheby's,
    Chancery Lane) $135   £60

BARLES, LOUIS
'Les Nouvelles Decouvertes sur Les Organes des Femmes Servans a la Generation' – 1st Edn., errata leaf at end, engraved portrait, 6 plates, cont. calf worn – Esprit Vitalis, Lyon, 1674.
(Sotheby's, New Bond
    Street) $250   £110

BARLOW, FRANCIS
'Birds Curiously Engraved' – engraved
title and 7 plates by R. Gaywood – 17th
century.
(Phillips) $200   £90

BARNARD, GEORGE
'The Theory and Practice of Landscape
Painting in Water Colours' – seven thou-
sand plates printed in colour by Leighton
Brothers chromatic process, some spotting,
original cloth, stitching worn, g.e. – 1861.
(Christie's S.
    Kensington) $34   £15

**BARNES, ROBERT AND GREY,
SYDNEY**
'Story Land' – 32 coloured illustrations by
Robert Barnes, some full page, original
cloth backed pictorial boards – 1885.
(Sotheby's,
    Chancery Lane) $85   £38

BARNETT, P. NEVILLE
'Armorial Bookplates' – no. 226 of 300
copies signed by the author, mounted
frontis, illus. some mounted, one coloured,
original cloth – Sydney, privately printed,
1932.
(Christie's S.
    Kensington) $68   £30

BAROCCIO, ALFONSO
'Lectionum de Febribus, Liber Primus' –
all published, half morocco, folio – Ferrara
1616.
(Sotheby's
    Monaco) $1,575   £700

BARONIUS, CAESAR
'Annales Ecclesiastici Ex XII Tomis Editio
Altera' – folio, early suede, spine in compartments, slight rubbing and staining,
engraved title by Eberhard Keiser, initials,
head and tail pieces, no index, worming,
early bookseller's prices on inside of front
cover – Mainz, 1622.
(Lawrence of
    Crewkerne) $34   £15

BARR, MAURICE
'Visites au Jardin Zoologique d'Acclimata-
tion' – wood engraved plates and illustra-
tions in text, original cloth, stained –
Yours, 1867.
(Sotheby's, New Bond
    Street) $18   £8

BARRATT, T. J.
'The Annals of Hampstead' – 3 vols. limited
to 500 copies signed by author, portrait,
plates, some mounted and coloured, folding
maps, one loosely inserted in wallet at end
of vol. 2, illus., original cloth, extremities
rubbed, some tears, 4to – 1912.
(Christie's S.
    Kensington) $192   £85

BARRETT, A. W. (R. ANDOM)
'Sideslips or Misadventures on a Bicycle' –
illustrations by Arthur Frederic, original
cloth – 1898.
(Sotheby's,
    Chancery Lane) $27   £12

BARRIE, SIR JAMES
'Quality Street' – large pictorial parchment
gilt, t.e.g., 22 tissued and mounted plates
by Hugh Thomson, signed by artist, no. 58
of 1,000 copies – 1913.
(Lawrence of
    Crewkerne) $54   £24

BARRINGTON, DAINES
'Miscellanies' – 1st Edn., 2 eng. portraits,
one of the infant Mozart, 2 eng. maps, one
folding, 5 printed tables, 1 folding, a few
leaves and one plate detached, a few leaves
slightly spotted, cont. half calf, spine and
hinges split – 1781.
(Sotheby's
    London) $250   £110

BARROUGH, PHILIP
'The Method of Physick containing the
Causes, Signes and Cures of Inward Diseases
in Main Body from the Head to the Foote'
– 3rd Edn., corrected and amended,
roman letter, woodcut device on title,
cont. vellum, ties missing – Richard Field,
1601.
(Sotheby's, New Bond
    Street) $790   £350

BARROW, JOHN, JUNIOR
'Excursions in the North of Europe' – 1st
Edn., 8 woodcut illus., woodcut vignette on
title, 2 eng. folding maps, slightly spotted,
woodcuts in text, cont. half red morocco,
gilt, slightly rubbed – 1834.
(Sotheby's
    London) $85   £38

'Account of Travels into the Interior of Southern Africa' – large folding map, 1st Edn., half title, tree calf – 1801.
(Bonham's) $112 £50

BARROW, JOHN
'Dictionarium Polygraphicum or the Whole Body of Arts' – vol. I only, engraved frontispiece and folding plates, worming, cont. calf, worn – 1735.
(Christie's S. Kensington) $50 £22

BARROW, WILLIAM
'An Essay on Education' – 2 vols., 1st Edn., cont. half calf, gilt – 1802.
(Sotheby's, New Bond Street) $160 £70

BARROZZI, GIACOMO. da VIGNOLLA
'Architettura' – 31 eng. illus. only, modern calf, small folio – Rome, 1765.
(Christie's S. Kensington) $85 £38

BARTHELEMY, JEAN JACQUES
'Voyage de Jeune Anacharsis en Grece' – Atlas vol. only, half title, slightly damaged, 38 engraved maps, plans and views by Ambroise Tardieu, 2 folding, repaired, cont. calf backed boards, corners rubbed – Paris, 1824.
(Sotheby's, New Bond Street) $63 £28
'Maps, Plans, Views and Coins Illustrative of the Travels of Anacharsis the Younger in Greece' – 2nd Edn., 30 double page, maps and plates mounted on guards, one detached, cont. boards, worn, backstrip lacking – 1793.
(Christie's S. Kensington) $68 £30

BARTHOLINUS, THOMAS
'Historiarum Anatomicarum Rariorum Centuriae 1 et 11' – engraved title, 9 plates, 2 folding, woodcuts in text, short tear, cont. limp vellum – Martzan for P. Hauboldt, Copenhagen, 1654.
(Sotheby's, New Bond Street) $112 £50

BARTHOLOMAEUS DE CHAIMIS
'Interrogatorum seu Confessionale' – 173 leaves of 174, 27 lines, gothic letter, initials supplied in red and blue, rubricated throughout, 18th century vellum – Milan, 1478.
(Sotheby's, New Bond Street) $675 £300

BARTIN, F. TOWNEND
'The Retriever' – cloth, plates – n.d.
(Tessa Bennett, Edinburgh) $7 £3

BARTLETT, W. H.
'Walks About . . . Jerusalem' – vignette title, tinted litho front, 20 engraved views, morocco gilt – Virtue, n.d.
(Phillips) $100 £45
'Nile Boat' – engraved title, frontispiece, 33 plates including map, morocco gilt, g.e. – 1850.
(Phillips) $135 £60
'Forty Days in the Desert, on the Track of the Israelites; or a Journey from Cairo, from Wady Feiran to Mount Sinai and Petra' – 3rd Edn., additional engraved title, 26 engraved plates, 1 folding engraved map, woodcut illustrations in text, cont. green morocco by Proudfoot, gilt, rubbed and soiled, g.e. – 1849.
(Sotheby's, New Bond Street) $290 £130
'Pictures from Sicily' – engraved title, folding map and 23 plates, illustrations, original cloth, rubbed, faded, g.e. and a volume of 62 engraved plates – 1864.
(Sotheby's, Chancery Lane) $135 £60

BARTLETT, W. H. – BEATTIE, W.
'Switzerland' – 2 vols. in one, 2 eng. portraits, one detached, additional titles and 106 plates after Bartlett, occasional spotting, original cloth worn – Virtue and Co., n.d.
(Christie's S. Kensington) $565 £250

BARTLETT, W. H. and PROF. N. G. VAN KAMPEN
'The History and Topography of Holland and Belgium' – additional eng. title, folded eng. map, 61 eng. views, some slightly spotted, original cloth – n.d.
(Sotheby's London) $540 £240

BARTLEY, G.
'The Rhine from its Source to the Sea' – cloth gilt, wood engraved illustrations – 1888.
(Tessa Bennett, Edinburgh) $45 £20

BARTOLO

BARTOLO, PIETRO
'Le Antiche Lucerne Sepolcrali Figurate Raccolte Dalle Cave Sotterance e Grotti di Roma' — numerous engraved plates, cont. Italian red morocco, gilt, the Prince Lichtenstein copy, folio — Rome, 1691.
(Sotheby's
    Monaco)   **$3,600**   **£1,600**

BASAN, F.
'Recueil d'Estampes Gravees d'Apres les Tableaux du Cabinet de Monsignor le Duc de Choiseul' — engraved title, portrait, 6 leaves of engraved text and 128 fine engraved plates, the title 'avant l'adresse', a large copy in cont. calf, worn, repaired, bookplate of Alfred Pfeiffer — Paris, 1774.
(Sotheby Parke Bernet
    Monaco)   **$8,550**   **£3,800**

BASON, FRED.
'Fred Bason's Diary'; 'Fred Bason's Second Diary'; 'Fred Bason's Third Diary' — all 1st Edns., original cloth with wrappers and all inscribed and signed to Nicholas Bentley — 1950/52/55.
(Lawrence of
    Crewkerne)   **$56**   **£25**

BATE, GEORGE
'Pharmacopoeia Bateana or Bates' Dispensory translated by William Salmon' — 1st English Edn., engraved plate, some leaves slightly spotted, cont. calf, worn — 1694.
(Sotheby's, New Bond
    Street)   **$100**   **£45**

BATEMAN, THOMAS
'Delineations of Cutaneous Diseases Exhibiting the Principal Genera and Species Comprised in the Classification of the Late Dr. William' — 1st Edn., 76 coloured plates, a few thumbmarks, stained, half calf rubbed — Longman, 1817.
(Sotheby's, New Bond
    Street)   **$585**   **£260**

BATES, H.
'Naturalist on the River Amazon' — wood engravings, cloth gilt — 1876.
(Tessa Bennett,
    Edinburgh)   **$11**   **£5**

BATES, H. E.
'Flowers and Faces' — No. 111 of 325 copies signed by author, full page illustrations by John Nash, original morocco backed boards, t.e.g. — 1935.
(Christie's S.
    Kensington)   **$205**   **£90**
'The House with the Apricot' — No. 274 of 300 copies signed by author, illustrations by A. M. Parker, original morocco backed cloth, t.e.g. — 1933.
(Christie's S.
    Kensington)   **$135**   **£60**
'A German Idyll' — No. 109 of 307 copies signed by author, frontispiece and decorations by Lynton Lamb, original morocco backed cloth, t.e.g. — Golden Cockerel Press, 1932.
(Christie's S.
    Kensington)   **$125**   **£55**

'Flowers and Faces' — No. 315 of 325 copies, one of 25 not for sale, signed by author, wood engraved pictorial border to title page and 4 full page illustrations by John Nash, original morocco backed boards, t.e.g., 4to. — 1935.
(Sotheby's,
    Chancery Lane)   **$205**   **£90**

BATES, HENRY WATTEN
'The Naturalist on the River Amazon' –
2 vols., 1 folding map, repaired, plates,
margins shaved, modern calf backed
boards – 1863.
(Christie's S.
   Kensington)   **$56**   **£25**

BATESON, EDWARD AND OTHERS
'A History of Northumberland' – 15 vols.,
plates, some folding, illustrations, original
cloth, rather rubbed, t.e.g. – 1893-1940.
(Sotheby's,
   Chancery Lane)   **$405**   **£180**

BATTY, CAPTAIN ROBERT
'An Historical Sketch of the Campaign of
1815' – 6 folding plates, tables, original
boards – 1820.
(Phillips)   **$115**   **£50**

'French Scenery' – large paper copy,
engraved title and 65 plates, vignette view
at end, foxing, spotting, cont. calf backed
boards, spine worn, rubbed – 1882.
(Sotheby's, New Bond
   Street)   **$250**   **£110**
'Welsh Scenery' – large paper, half calf,
worn.
'Views of North Wales' – 2 vols., original
limp cloth – Chester and Bangor, 1859.
(Sotheby's, New Bond
   Street)   **$270**   **£120**

BATTY, ELIZABETH FRANCES
'Italian Scenery' – engraved title, 60
plates, engraved vignettes, cont. russia,
gilt, Signet arms on sides, covers detached,
spine missing, g.e. – 1820.
(Sotheby's, New Bond
   Street)   **$340**   **£150**

BAUCHART, E. Q.
'Les Femmes Bibliophiles de France' – 2
vols., No. 270 of 300 on papier de Hollande,
many plates and illustrations, wrappers –
Paris, 1886.
(Sotheby Parke Bernet
   Monaco)   **$4,500**   **£2,000**

BAUDELAIRE, C.
'Les Fleurs du Mal' – First publication, in
Revue des Deux Mondes, XXV annee, por-
trait added, boards, wrappers to original
part preserved – Paris, 1855.
(Sotheby Parke Bernet
   Monaco)   **$3,600**   **£1,600**

Another First Edition with the first state
of wrapper before the censorship ordered
by the courts soon after publication – Paris,
1857.
(Sotheby Parke Bernet
   Monaco)   **$42,750**   **£19,000**
'Les Epaves' – First Edn., no 2 of 10
copies on papier de Chine, frontispiece
by Rops, half morocco – Amsterdam,
1866.
(Sotheby Parke Bernet
   Monaco)   **$7,200**   **£3,200**
BAUDELAIRE, C. – CREPET, JACQUES
'Dessins de Baudelaire' – 16 reproductions,
unsewn in original wrappers, uncut –
Gallimard, Paris, 1927.
(Sotheby's,
   Chancery Lane)   **$45**   **£20**

Fine autograph letter signed, 1 page,
octavo, presumably Paris, 9 May, 1952, to
Maxime du Camp, integral address panel,
slight browning, with pencilled note signed
C. B. on third parge.
(Sotheby's, New Bond
   Street)   **$1,690**   **£750**

BAUDELOCQUE, J. L.
'Principes sur l'Art d'Accoucher par
Demandes et Reponses, en Faveur des
Sages Femmes . . . ' – First Edn., half
calf – Paris – with two others by the
same – 1775.
(Bonham's) $315   £140
'L'Art des Accouchements' – plates, First
Edn., old half calf, worn – Paris, 1781.
(Bonham's) $495   £220

BAUER, M. A. J.
'Histoire d'Aboulhassan Ali Ebn Becar Et
De Schemselnihar, D'Apres La Traduction
De Galland' – coloured illustrations by
Bauer, original wrappers, uncut – De Erven
F. Bohn, Harlem, 1929.
(Sotheby's,
    Chancery Lane) $35   £15

BAUM, FRANK L. (Editor)
'The Christmas Stocking Series – 6 vols.,
coloured illustrations, soiling, one vol.
lacking some leaves, original pictorial boards,
spines worn – 1905-11.
(Christie's S.
    Kensington) $70   £32

BAUWENS, M. AND OTHER
'Les Affiches Etrangeres Illustrees' – 62
coloured plates, including posters, by
Beardsley, Fabry, Heine, Rhead and others.
Numerous illustrations, some full page,
cont. half morocco, rubbed, t.e.g., original
wrappers bound in – Boudet, Paris, 1897.
(Sotheby's,
    Chancery Lane) $970   £430

BAYFIELD, ROBERT
'Enchiridion Medicum containing the causes,
signs and cures of all those diseases that do
chiefly affect the body of man' – First and
only? edn., engraved portrait by W.
Faithorne (inlaid), cont. calf, repaired – E.
Tyler for Joseph Cranford, 1655.
(Sotheby's, New Bond
    Street) $720   £320

BAYFIUS, LAZARUS
'De Re Navali' – First Edn., two parts in
one vol., many woodcuts, some full page,
cont. limp vellum – R. Stephanus, Paris,
1536.
(Christie's, King
    St.) $585   £260

*Enchiridion Medicum by Robert
Bayfield. (Sotheby's)*

BAYLE, PIERRE
'Dictionnaire Historique et Critique . . . revue,
corrigee et augmentee par l'auteur' – 4 vols.,
3rd Edn., engraved title vignettes, cont.
speckled calf, gilt spines, gilt dentilles, folio
– Bohm, Rotterdam, 1720.
(Sotheby's, New Bond
    Street) $225   £100

BAYLEY, F. W. N.
'Floral Poems with Pictures in the Flowers'
– six hand coloured plates, spotted, original cloth, soiled, g.e., large 4to. – n.d.
(Christie's S.
    Kensington) $80   £35

BAYLEY, JOHN
'The History and Antiquities of the Tower
of London' – 2 vols., 39 engraved plates,
some spotted, cont. half morocco, joints
split, worn – 1825.
(Sotheby's,
    Chancery Lane) $50   £22

BAYNARD, EDWARD
'Health, a poem showing how to procure,
preserve and restore it' – 4th Edn., lacks
half title, new boards – J. Robert, 1731.
(Sotheby's, New Bond
Street) $34   £15

**BAYROS, F. VON – BIERBAUM, OTTO
JULIUS**
'Das Schone Maedchen von Pao' – 7 plates
by Bayros, original cloth gilt, lettered in
Chinese on upper cover, designed by Paul
Renner, uncut. No. 486 to 600 – Munich,
1910.
(Sotheby's,
Chancery Lane) $180   £80

BEARDSLEY, AUBREY
'A Portfolio of Drawings Illustrating
'Salome' by Oscar Wilde' – 17 plates by
Beardsley, margins soiled, unbound as
issued, original portfolio, soiled, ties lack-
ing – folio – n.d.
(Christie's S.
Kensington) $146   £65

'La Morte d'Arthur' – introduction by Prof.
John Rhys and note on Beardsley by
Aylmer Vallance, from an edition limited to
1,600 copies, gilt decorated full blue cloth,
large – J. M. Dent and Sons Ltd., London,
1927.
(Sotheby's
Belgravia) $315   £140

'The Uncollected Works' – First edn.,
frontispiece portrait, many black and
white plates – 1925.
(Lawrence of
Crewkerne) $90   £40
'The Yellow Book' – illustrated quarterly,
vols. I-XIII, April 1894 to April 1897 com-
plete, decorations by Beardsley, Sickert,
Crane, Cameron and others; contributions
from Henry James, W. B. Yeats, Kenneth
Graham etc. – 1894-97.
(Lawrence of
Crewkerne) $315   £140

**BEARDSLEY, AUBREY – WILDE,
OSCAR**
'Salome' – pictorial title, contents lead
and 14 plates after Beardsley, black
morocco spine and fore edges, vellum plate
on covers, with maroon and gold onlays,
t.e.g., original wrappers bound in. By Benoil
– Paris, 1907.
(Sotheby's,
Chancery Lane) $350   £155

BEATRICE, PRINCESS
'A Birthday Book' – inscribed by Queen
Victoria, coloured lithographed frontis-
piece, detached and 14 plates, original
cloth, gilt, g.e. – 1881.
(Christie's S.
Kensington) $135   £60

BEATSON, LIEUT. COL. ALEXANDER
'A View of the Origin and Conduct of the
War with Tipoo Sultan' – portrait, frontis-
piece, folding plates and maps, some leaves
detached, cont. marbled calf, covers de-
tached – 1800.
(Christie's S.
Kensington) $50   £22

BEATTIE, WILLIAM
'The Danube' – engraved additional title,
two maps and 80 plates, occasional
staining, cont. half calf, rubbed – n.d.
(Christie's S.
Kensington) $470   £210
'The Bosphoros and the Danube' – part V
only, 23 engravings and one map,
cloth gilt, rubbed, g.e., 4to – 1842.
'Castles and Abbeys of England' – 2 vols.,
engravings, cloth gilt, g.e., 4to – circa
1840 – Goldsmith, O.
'The Earth and Animated Nature' – 6
vols., hand coloured plates, cloth gilt,
4to – circa 1880.
(Phillips) $135   £60

BEATTIE

'The Castles and Abbeys of England' – 2 vols., large paper copy, engraved portrait, plates, original cloth, gilt, slightly soiled – 1860.
(Sotheby's,
Chancery Lane) $56   £25
'Scotland . . . Illustrated' – 2 eng. titles, 118 plates and 1 folding map, text lacking, half morocco, by Bruyere, rubbed – 1838.
(Christie's S.
Kensington) $112   £50
'Switzerland' – 2 vols., 1st Edn., additional title pages with vignettes, 106 plates after Bartlett, folding map, engraved title and some plates spotted, cont. half morocco, gilt, hinges rubbed, t.e.g. – George Virtue, 1836.
(Sotheby's, New Bond
Street) $675   £300
'Waldenses' – illus. Bartlett and Brockedon, port., engraved title, 70 plates, no folding map, half calf, gilt, library mark on back, 4to – 1838.
(Phillips) $250   £110

BEATTIE, WILLIAM AND W. H. BARTLETT

'The Ports, Harbours, Watering Places, and Coast Scenery of Great Britain' – 6 original parts, 2 engraved titles and 123 plates only of 124, some slightly spotted and soiled, original roan backed boards, rubbed, part 6 worn and loose – 1842.
(Sotheby's,
Chancery Lane) $560   £250

BEAUCLERK, CAPTAIN LORD CHARLES

'Lithographic Views of Military Operations in Canada' – lithoed map and 6 hand coloured plates, slight spotting, original cloth backed card wrappers, backstrip and lower cover lacking, upper cover detached, folio – 1840.
(Christie's S.
Kensington) $1,912   £850

BEAUDIN, ANDRE – LIMBOUR, GEORGES

'Andre Beaudin' translated by Stuart Gilbert – 8 coloured lithographs and cover design by Beaudin, 157 reproductions, 12 in colour, original boards –Zwemmer, 1961.
(Sotheby's,
Chancery Lane) $11   £5

BEAUMARCHAIS, P. A. C. DE

'La Folle Journee ou le Mariage de Figaro' – 5 plates after St. Quentin, cont. mottled calf, gilt spine, trifle worn, the Comte de Suzannet copy – 1785.
(Sotheby Parke Bernet
Monaco) $12,375   £5,500

BEAUMONT, FRANCIS

'Sallmacis and Hermaphroditus' – No. 121 of 380 copies, coloured frontispiece and illustrations, all but two full page by John Buckland-Wright, original cloth, folio.
(Christie's S.
Kensington) $112   £50

BEAUMONT, FRANCIS AND FLETCHER, JOHN

'Cupid's Revenge' – 2nd Edn., 19th century half roan – 1630.
(Christie's S.
Kensington) $270   £120
'The Knight of the Burning Pestle' – 3rd Edn., margins thumbed, slight waterstains, red morocco by Sangorski – 1635?
(Christie's, King
St.) $250   £110

WIT WITH
OVT MONEY.

A COMEDIE,

As it hath beene Presented with good Applause at the private house in Drurie Lane, by her Majesties Servants.

Written by { Francis Beamount, and John Flecher. } Gent.

LONDON
Printed by Thomas Cotes, for Andrew Crooke, and William Cooke. 1639.

'Wit. Without Money, a Comedie' – 1st Edn., ink markings in margins, some edges untrimmed, brown calf by Roger de Coverley, gilt, g.e. – 1639.
(Christie's, King
St.) $810   £360

BECAT, PAUL EMILE – LOUYS, PIERRE
'Les Chansons Secretes de Bilitis' –
coloured etched frontispiece and 23 large
illustrations by Becat, facsimile of letter
from author, unsewn in original wrappers,
uncut, folder, slipcase – Marcel Lubineau,
Paris, 1938.
(Sotheby's,
    Chancery Lane) $180   £80

'Les Aventures du Roi Pausole' – 20
coloured etched illustrations by Becat, 6
full page, unsewn in original wrappers,
uncut, folder, slipcase – Le Vasseur, Paris,
1947.
(Sotheby's,
    Chancery Lane) $146   £65

BECKETT, GILBERT A
'The Comic History of Rome' – illustrations
and hand coloured plates by John Leech,
original cloth, spine faded, 4to – n.d.
(Christie's S.
    Kensington) $34   £15

BECKETT, SAMUEL
'En Attendant Godot' – 1st Edn., original
wrappers, slightly soiled, uncut – Paris,
1952.
(Sotheby's,
    Chancery Lane) $225   £100
'From an Abandoned Work' – 1st Edn.,
original wrappers – 1958.
(Sotheby's,
    Chancery Lane) $45   £20
'No's Knife' – 1st Edn., no. 31 of 100,
Series A copies, signed by author, original
parchment, gilt, g.e., slipcase – 1967.
(Sotheby's,
    Chancery Lane) $135   £60
'Poems in English' – 1st Edn., no. 83 of
100 copies, signed by author, original cloth,
uncut, unopened – 1961.
(Sotheby's,
    Chancery Lane) $146   £65

**BECKETT, SAMUEL AND ELUARD,
PAUL**
'Thorns of Thunder' – translated by
Beckett, 1st Edn., no. 117 of 575 copies,
frontispiece by Picasso, original cloth, dust
jacket design by Max Ernst – Europa Press,
1932.
(Sotheby's,
    Chancery Lane) $90   £40

BECKET, WILLIAM
'A Free and Impartial Enquiry into the
Antiquity and Efficacy of Touching for the
cure of the King's Evil. Letters to Dr.
Steigertahl and Sir Hans Sloane' – 2 parts
in one vol., quarter calf – J. Peele, 1722.
(Sotheby's, New Bond
    Street) $70   £30

BECKFORD, WILLIAM
'A Descriptive Account of the Island of
Jamaica' – 2 vols., 1st Edn., cont. calf,
gilt ornaments on spines – 1790.
(Sotheby's
    Monaco) $2,140   £950
'Vathek' – 1st Edn., slight browning,
early 20th century maroon levant morocco
by Riviere, gilt, upper cover detached, t.e.g.,
others uncut – 1786.
(Sotheby's, New Bond
    Street) $315   £140

BECKMANN, MAX – GLASER, CURT
'Max Beckmann' – 2 engravings and one
woodcut by Beckmann, each signed by
artist, reproductions, original half morocco,
t.e.g., dust jacket, slipcase – Munich, 1924.
(Sotheby's,
    Chancery Lane) $1,080   **£480**

BEDDOES, T.
'Observation on the nature and cure of
Calcus, Sea Scurvy, Consumption, Catarrh
and Fever, etc.' – 1st Edn., original boards,
uncut – 1793.
(Bonham's) $112   **£50**

BEDOYA, D. F. G. De
'Historia del Toreo' – illustrations, half
title, some leaves browned, cont. sheep,
rubbed – Madrid, 1850.
(Sotheby's,
    Chancery Lane) $160   **£70**

BEECHAM, SIR THOMAS
A sheet of 20 different caricatures of
Beecham conducting, signed by Beecham,
drawn in pen and ink by Frank Leah, 1899.
15 x 11in. framed and glazed, upper right
hand corner a little torn.
(Sotheby's New Bond
    Street) $560   **£250**

*Caricature of Sir Thomas Beecham
by Frank Leah. (Sotheby's)*

*Citoyen Collier by A. Beer and
N.F. Jacquemart. (Sotheby's)*

BEER, A. – JACQUEMART, NICOLAS FRANCOIS
'Citoyen Collier' Contes a Rire – etched frontispiece, offset, blue morocco gilt, leaf and flower border composed of coloured morocco inlays, inside borders gilt, t.e.g., by Rene Kieffer. No. 156 of 500 copies – Gay et Douce, Brussels, 1881.
(Sotheby's,
   Chancery Lane) $810   £360

BEERBOHM, SIR MAX
'Cartoons' – 15 coloured plates, cloth backed boards, folio – 1901.
(Phillips) $135   £60
'Fifty Caricatures' – 1st Edn., presentation copy, 48 mounted plates by Beerbohm, original cloth, spine faded and rubbed – 1913.
(Christie's S.
   Kensington) $45   £20
'Heroes and Heroines of Bittersweet' – nos. 428 of 900 copies, five mounted coloured plates by Beerbohm, margins browned, unbound as issued in original portfolios, soiled, corners bumped – folio, n.d.
(Christie's S.
   Kensington) $65   £28
'Zuleika Dobson' – 1st Edn., very slightly spotted, original cloth, rubbed – 1911.
(Sotheby's,
   Chancery Lane) $120   £52

BEETHOVEN, LUDWIG VAN
Autograph letter signed, 4 lines, re banking, a banker's draft transcription on verso and presentation inscription to Siegmund Ochs. Slim oblong – circa 1807.
(Sotheby's, New Bond
   Street) $5,625   £2,500

BEETON, ISABELLA
'Household Management' – 12 coloured plates, lacks front, half calf gilt – 1861.
(Phillips) $146   £65

BEEVERELL, JAMES
'Les Delices de la Grand Bretagne et de L'Irlande' – 8 vols., new edn., printed titles in red and black, double page engraved titles, plates and maps, half titles, cont. calf, worn – Leiden, 1727.
(Sotheby's, New Bond
   Street) $945   £420

BELCARI, F.
'Vita del Beato Giovanni Colombini' – 94 of 96 leaves lacing first two, stains and worming, cont. half calf over wooden boards, worn and wormed, folio – Florence, 1477.
(Sotheby's
   Monaco) $1,912   £850

BELCHER, JOHN AND MACARTNEY, M. E. (Editors)
'Later Renaissance Architecture in England' – 2 vols., plates, vol. 1 title detached, half morocco, corners slightly rubbed – Batsford, 1901.
(Christie's S.
   Kensington) $112   £50

BELIUS, MATTHIAS
'Notitia Hungariae Novae Historico Geographica' – 4 vols., all published, 1st edn., engraved portrait, frontispiece, folding map and folding plates, cont. calf, spine gilt, folio – Vienna, 1735-42.
(Sotheby's
   Monaco) $11,250   £5,000

Autograph letter by Ludwig van Beethoven, c. 1807. (Sotheby's)

BELL

BELL, CHARLES
'A System of Dissections' – 12 engraved plates, cloth, folio, 1st Edn. – Edinburgh, 1798.
(Tessa Bennett,
    Edinburgh) $50   £22
'The Hand, Its Mechanism and Vital Endowments as Evincing Design' – 1st Edn., woodcut illustrations, half title, original cloth, paper label, uncut – William Pickering, 1833.
(Sotheby's, New Bond
    Street) $340   £150

BELL, GERTRUDE
'The Arab War' – No. 339 of 500 copies, original morocco backed cloth, t.e.g. – 1940.
(Christie's S.
    Kensington) $270   £120

BELL, JAMES
'A New and Comprehensive Gazeteer of England and Wales' – 4 vols., 45 folding engraved maps, England and Wales, hand coloured, marginal browning, original cloth soiled, spines slightly torn, unopened – A Fullarton and Co., Glasgow, 1836.
(Christie's S.
    Kensington) $270   £120

BELL, JOHN
'Engravings of the Bones, Muscles and Joints' – 2nd Edn., 28 etched plates by author, half title, errata leaf, stains and thumbmarks, torn, old calf, rebacked – Longman, 1804.
(Sotheby's, New Bond
    Street) $360   £160
'Letters on Professional Character and Manners; on the education of a surgeon and the duties and qualifications of a physician addressed to James Gregory' – half title, paper discoloured, original boards, uncut, rebacked, advertisement leaf pasted inside – John Moir, Edinburgh, 1810.
(Sotheby's, New Bond
    Street) $225   £100
'Travels from St. Petersburg . . . to diverse parts of Asia' – 2 vols., Oswald ownership inscription, cont. calf, rubbed, joints and spines cracked – 1764.
(Christie's S.
    Kensington) $205   £90

BELL, M.
'Edward Burne Jones' – frontispiece and plates, cloth gilt, folio – 1893.
(Tessa Bennett,
    Edinburgh) $45   £20

BELL, THOMAS
'A History of the British Stalk-Eyed Crustacea' – illus., cont. half calf, corners scuffed – 1853.
(Christie's S.
    Kensington) $34   £15

BELLEGARDE, JEAN BAPTISTE MORVAN DE
'Reflections Upon Ridicule' – 1st edn., in English, rust hole in B8, cont. panelled calf, repaired – 1706.
(Sotheby's
    London) $112   £50

BELLI, SILVIO
'Libro del Misurar con la Vista' – 1st Edn., device on title, woodcut illustrations in text, some dampstaining, worming, modern boards – Per Domenico de'Nicolini, Venice, 1565.
(Sotheby's, New Bond
    Street) $290   £130

BELLORI, G. P.
'Ichnographia Veteris Romae' – engraved title, 27 plates, engraved head and tail pieces and initials, cont. mottled calf, gilt, rubbed, g.e., folio – Rome 1764.
(Sotheby's, New Bond
    Street) $270   £120

BELLOSTE, AUGUSTIN
'The Hospital Surgeon or A New Way to Cure Speedily all sorts of Wounds' – 1st Edn. of Vol. II, frontispiece in first vol., cont. calf – 1732.
(Sotheby's, New Bond
    Street) $90   £40

BELORDEAU, PIERRE
'Les Costumes Generales des Pays et Duche de Bretagne' – 2 parts in one vol., 1st Edn., titles printed with woodcut device, general title in red and black, some cont. ms. notes, some browning, cont. calf, worn – Chez Nicolas Buon, Paris, 1624.
(Sotheby's,
    Chancery Lane) $430   £190

BELZONI, G.
'Narrative of . . . Recent Discoveries . . . in Egypt and Nubia' — lithographed portrait, map lacking, cont. calf, joints split — 1820.
(Christie's S.
    Kensington)   **$70**   **£32**

BENEDICTUS, E.
'Nouvelles Variations' — 20 plates and cover design by Benedictus, coloured through stencils, loose in original cloth backed portfolio, rather worn, ties, folio — Albert Levy, Paris — n.d.
(Sotheby's,
    Chancery Lane)   **$305**   **£135**

BENEDICTUS, GULIELMUS
'Repetitio Capituli Raynutius, de Testamentis' — 1st Edn., title in red and black with woodcut device, 17th century mottled calf, gilt spine, somewhat worn, folio — A. Vincentius, Lyon, 1544.
(Sotheby's, New Bond
    Street)   **$135**   **£60**

BENEDICTUS
'Regula' — 1st Edn., 64 leaves of 68, 20 lines, gothic letter, 19th century boards — Bernardinus Benalius, Venice, 1489/90.
(Sotheby's, New Bond
    Street)   **$1,125**   **£500**

BENNETT, ARNOLD
'Journal 1929' — vellum, decorated boards, t.e.g., uncut, no. 48 of 75 copies on Saunders Handmade paper, signed by author with signed photograph of author in front — 1929.
(Lawrence of
    Crewkerne)   **$90**   **£40**

BENNETT, C.
'Famous Harness Horses' — vol. 2, plates, cloth, limited edition — 1932.
(Tessa Bennett,
    Edinburgh)   **$13**   **£6**

BENSON, STELLA
'Hope Against Hope and Other Stories' — large, buckram backed marbled boards, t.e.g. rest uncut, first edition, one of 650 copies signed by author and inscribed by her in pencil to Barbara, Mrs. Bentley — 1931.
(Lawrence of
    Crewkerne)   **$25**   **£10**

BENTHAM, JEREMY
'Plan of Parliamentary Reform' — 2nd Edn., errata notice at foot of contents page, a few leaves slightly spotted, cont. morocco backed boards, rubbed — 1818.
(Sotheby's
    London)   **$90**   **£40**

BENTINCK, C.
'Dornoch Cathedral and Parish' — plates and maps, quarter morocco — Inverness 1926.
(Tessa Bennett,
    Edinburgh)   **$45**   **£20**

BENTIVOGLIO, GUIDO
'Della Guerra di Fiandra' — 2 vols., cont. vellum — 1632 and 1636.
(Tessa Bennett,
    Edinburgh)   **$27**   **£12**
'Relationi' — woodcut portrait on title, slight flaw affecting text on 5 recto, cont. vellum boards, soiled, signature of Andrew Fletcher of Saltoun on title — Brussels, 1632.
(Sotheby's
    London)   **$56**   **£25**

BENTLEY, E. C.
'Those Days' — front cover a little soiled and faded, inscribed by author 'With love from Father' — n.d.
(Lawrence of
    Crewkerne)   **$27**   **£12**
'Biography for Beginners' — with 40 diagrams by G. K. Chesterton, large original pictorial boards, first edition — T. Werner Laurie — n.d.
(Lawrence of
    Crewkerne)   **$27**   **£12**
'The Original Publisher's Contract signed by Bentley and with autograph correction of a Christian name for 'Trent's Last Case', folio — 27 June, 1912.
(Lawrence of
    Crewkerne)   **$990**   **£440**
'Trent's Last Case' — original blue blind stamped cloth, first edition, coloured frontispiece illustration, dedicated to G. K. Chesterton, press photo of Bentley laid down inside cover, inscribed by author 'To My Wife' — Thomas Nelson, 1913.
(Lawrence of
    Crewkerne)   **$315**   **£140**

BENTLEY, NICOLAS
Collection of 25 works written and
illustrated by Nicolas Bentley from the
author's library, together with scrap albums
of press cuttings of book reviews and
articles etc. – n.d.
(Lawrence of
   Crewkerne)   **$385**   **£170**

BERESFORD, J. D.
'Signs and Wonders' – limited to 1,500
copies, original boards, soiled and rubbed
– Golden Cockerel Press, 1921.
(Christie's S.
   Kensington)   **$45**   **£20**

BERG, JOH. AUG.
'Sverige Framstaldt I Taflor' – 96 tinted
lithographed plates, one loose, text browned,
with a few tears, cont. morocco backed
boards, rubbed – Gothenburg, 1856.
(Sotheby's,
   Chancery Lane)   **$900**   **£400**

**BERKELEY, GEORGE, BISHOP OF
CLOYNE**
'Alciphron: or, The Minute Philosopher'
– 2 vols., 1st Edn., engraved vignettes on
titles, author's advertisement with errata
on verso, final blanks, slight offsetting, a
few leaves in vol. I slightly dampstained.
cont. sprinkled calf gilt, slightly worn –
1732.
(Sotheby's
   London)   **$180**   **£80**
'Siris; A Chain of Philosophical Reflections
and Inquiries, Concerning the Virtues of
Tar Water' – 1st Edn., mss. notes and
corrections in pencil, worming, cont. calf,
joints cracked – Dublin, 1744.
(Christie's, King
   St.)   **$360**   **£160**

BERKENHOUT, JOHN
'Symptomatology' – half title, advertise-
ment leaf at end, 8pp. cont. mss. 'Dr.
Cullen's arrangement of diseases' entered
after title, quarter calf – 1784.
(Sotheby's, New Bond
   Street)   **$90**   **£40**

BERKSHIRE SERIES, THE
Vol. 1-3, limited to 550 copies, original
cloth backed boards, vol. 1 slightly rubbed
and partly opened, vols. 2 and 3 unopened
and with dust jackets, spotted – Golden
Cockerel Press, 1926.
(Christie's S.
   Kensington)   **$63**   **£28**

**BERNARD, EMILE – RONSARD, PIERRE
DE**
'Les Amours' – 16 etched plates, woodcut
illustrations in text by Bernard, unsewn in
original wrappers, uncut, slipcase, worn –
Ambroise Vollard, Paris, 1915.
(Sotheby's,
   Chancery Lane)   **$45**   **£20**

BERNARDINO DE LAREDO
'Subida Del Monte Sion; Por La Via Contem-
plativa' – 1st Edn., title in red and black in
woodcut border. 31 woodcuts in text, 3
half page, and another with text in woodcut border, numerous woodcut initials, a
few historiated, 19th century sheep, very
scuffed – Juan Cromberger, Seville, 1
March, 1535.
(Sotheby's, New Bond
   Street)   **$1,465**   **£650**

BERNARDUS, SAINT
'Opuscula' — 345 leaves of 348, 40 lines in double column, gothic letter, staining, modern blind stamped sheep — Brescia, 1495.
(Sotheby's, New Bond
  Street) $585   £260

BERNIER, FRANCOIS
'The History of the Late Revolution of the Empire of the Great Mogul' — 4 vols. in one, I and II 2nd edn., vol. III and IV 1st Edn., (translated by Henry Oldenburg), engraved folding map, advertisements, vol. IV title and A1-E3 misbound but no loss of text, lacking blanks, bookplate of F. W. Cavendish-Bentinck, cont. panelled calf, neatly rebacked, corners restored — 1676-72.
(Sotheby's
  London) $225   £100

BERQUE, JEAN — LOUYS, PIERRE
'Trois Filles de Leur Mere' — 16 coloured plates by Berque, coloured by pochoir, unsewn in original wrappers, uncut, folder, slightly damaged, slipcase — Paris, circa 1947.
(Sotheby's,
  Chancery Lane) $112   £50

BERTHOD, FRANCOIS
'Emblemes Sacrez Tirez de l'Ecriture . . . augmentez d'Examples Tirez des Histoires de la Sainte Bible' — engraved title page, 34 engraved emblems, cont. calf, rubbed — Paris, 1699.
(Sotheby's, New Bond
  Street) $95   £42

BERTRAND DE MOLEVILLE, A. F.
'The Costume of the Hereditary States of the House of Austria' — 50 hand coloured aquatint plates, text in French and English, some leaves slightly soiled, cont. morocco, gilt, rubbed, upper cover detached, g.e. — 1804. (plates watermarked 1817).
(Sotheby's,
  Chancery Lane) $520   £230

BERTRAND — HENNIQUE, LEON
'Deux Patries' — 10 engraved illustrations by Leon Boisson after Bertrand, blue half morocco, t.e.g., original wrappers bound in,, no. 111 of 250 — Conquet, Paris, 1905.
(Sotheby's,
  Chancery Lane) $20   £9

BERTUCH, F. J.
'Bilderbuch, Pflanzen' — 2 vols., upwards of 190 hand coloured plates, half leather — circa 1840.
(Sotheby's
  Monaco) $12,825   £5,700

BERVE AND GRUBEN
'Greek Temples, Theatres and Shrines' — 212 plates, 36 coloured, 4to, cloth, in d.w. — 1963.
(Bonham's) $40   £18

BESANT, SIR WALTER
'Survey of London' — 10 vols., illus., cloth gilt, t.e.g. — 1902-12.
(Phillips) $292   £130

BESSARION, CARDINAL JOHANNES
'In Calumniatiorem Platonis' — 120 leaves, woodcut device of Aldus on title, slightly soiled and waterstained, cont. limp vellum, soiled, folio — Aldus, Venice, 1503.
(Christie's, King
  St.) $405   £180

BESTERMAN, THEODORE
'The Pilgrim Fathers' — no. 298 of 300 copies, frontispiece and illustrations by Geoffrey Wales, original morocco backed cloth, t.e.g. — 1939.
(Christie's S.
  Kensington) $75   £32

BETJEMAN, SIR JOHN
5 autograph letters, signed, an autograph card lettered calligraphically and signed, three typed letters signed, folio note with 2 autograph lines signed, and an ink sketch on card — in all some 90 lines. All to N. C. Bentley — 1952.
(Lawrence of
  Crewkerne) $315   £140
'Ghastly Good Taste' — original blue cloth backed pink boards, 1st Edn., inscribed by author on title, a good copy — 1933.
(Lawrence of
  Crewkerne) $100   £45
'Metro Land' — oblong cloth lithograph label, 16 coloured lithographs by Glynn Boyd Marte, no. 52 of 220, original red cloth box — Warren Press, 1977.
(Lawrence of
  Crewkerne) $70   £30

BETJEMAN

'Mount Zion or In Touch with the Infinte'
– decorative boards, paper label, 1st Edn.,
text within decorative borders, illus. by
Cronin Hastings, signed by author, slight
tears – James Press, 1933.
(Lawrence of
    Crewkerne) $270   £120
'On Oxford University Cheat' – 1st Edn.,
plates, illustrations, original cloth backed
boards, corners rubbed, t.e.g. – 1938.
(Christie's S.
    Kensington) $75   £32
'A Pictorial History of English Architecture'
– 1st Edn., no. 92 of 100 copies, signed by
author, illustrations, some coloured,
original buckram backed boards – 1972.
(Sotheby's,
    Chancery Lane) $60   £26

An amusing original ink sketch on a
quarto page 10 x 8in. of an elaborate
stone church titled 'Save Our Old Pre-
Saxon Church' and with a pencilled note
'Drawn by John Betjeman during a meeting
of the Committee of Management of the
Society of Authors' – 13 July, 1950.
(Lawrence of
    Crewkerne) $100   £45

BETJEMAN, SIR JOHN, 'EPSILON'
(pseud)
'Sir John Piers' – green paper wrappers,
1st Edn., inscribed by author, corrections
in Betjeman's hand – Mullingar, circa
1938.
(Lawrence of
    Crewkerne) $450   £200

BEVERIDGE, E.
'Coll and Tiree' – maps and plates, quarter
morocco – Edinburgh, 1903.
(Tessa Bennett,
    Edinburgh) $75   £32

BEWICK ALBUM
Approximately 180 wood engravings by
Thomas and John Bewick. Oblong folio,
red half morocco, engravings laid down –
n.d.
(Lawrence of
    Crewkerne) $430   £190

BEWICK GLEANINGS
'Being Impressions from the copperplates
and wood blocks engraved in the Bewick
workshop' – ed. J. Boyd, reproductions,
large paper edition signed by the editor,
4to. morocco, worn – Bonhams, 1866.
(Bonham's) $205   £90

BEWICK, JOHN
'Proverbs Exemplified' – black calf spine
gilt, morocco label, 50 woodcuts after
John Bewick – 1790.
(Lawrence of
    Crewkerne) $112   £50

BEWICK, JOHN AND BERQUIN, ARMAND
'The Looking Glass for the Mind or
Intellectual Mirror' – engraved frontis-
piece slightly spotted, 74 wood engraved
illustrations and tail pieces by John
Bewick, cont. tree calf, rebacked – J.
Cowder, 1794.
(Sotheby's,
    Chancery Lane) $100   £45

BEWICK, THOMAS

'A Collection of Newspaper Extracts —
taken from the Newspapers of the Day
and Designed to Afford some Amusement
to those who are Fond of the Every Day
Book' — 1st Edn., vignette title, engraved
frontispiece, engraved vignettes by Thomas
Bewick — Alnwick, 1839.
(Lawrence of
    Crewkerne) $11   £5
'The Fables of Aesop and Others' — half
calf, spine gilt, morocco label, some rubbing,
Imperial paper copy, vignette title, wood
engraved illustrations by Bewick, a good
copy — Newcastle, 1806.
(Lawrence of
    Crewkerne) $360   £160
'Fabliaux or Tales' Abridged from French
Mss. and translated into English verse —
with preface and notes, cont. mottled calf
gilt, morocco labels, engraved vignette
title and over 50 wood engraved illustrations by Bewick — 1796-1800.
(Lawrence of
    Crewkerne) $146   £65
'Figures of British Land Birds . . . (and) a
Few Foreign Birds' — vol. I (all published),
printed on rectos only, title with wood
engraved vignettes, slight browning, cont.
half calf, worn — Newcastle-upon-Tyne,
1800.
(Sotheby's
    London) $340   £150
'Four Broadsides' — printed and sold by
Emerson Charnley, Newcastle. Each with
15 cuts and borders — n.d.
(Lawrence of
    Crewkerne) $205   £90
'A General History of Quadrupeds' — 4th
Edn., title with wood engraved vignette,
wood engraved illustrations and vignettes
in text, slight browning, cont. half calf,
rubbed — Newcastle-upon-Tyne, 1800.
(Sotheby's
    London) $100   £45
'History of British Birds' — 2 vols., cont.
calf, gilt, morocco labels, 1st Edn. — 1797.
(Lawrence of
    Crewkerne) $340   £150
'The Figures of Bewicks Quadrupeds and
Vignettes' — special Impressions with
woodcuts on one side of the leaf only,
2nd Edn., with inserted autograph letter
from Miss Jane Bewick, 2 vols., 4to, half
morocco — Newcastle, 1824.
(Bonham's) $1,035   £460

'A General Directory of Quadrupeds' —
2nd Edn., woodcut vignettes by Bewick,
soiling, some pages missing, cont. tree
calf, worn, upper cover detached —
Newcastle-upon-Tyne, 1791.
(Christie's S.
    Kensington) $45   £20
'Youths Instructive and Entertaining
Story-Teller' — cuts by T. Bewick,
3rd Edn., modern calf (a few leaves
foxed) — Newcastle-upon-Tyne, 1778.
(Bonham's) $94   £42
'A Memoir of Thomas Bewick Written by
Himself' — embossed green cloth, spine
gilt, vignette title, engraved frontispiece,
vignettes and plates by Bewick, engraved
portrait loosely inserted — Newcastle,
1862.
(Lawrence of
    Crewkerne) $112   £50
'Percy, Thomas, Bishop of Dromore' A
Northumberland Ballad in Three Fits —
cloth backed boards, dedication, advertisement, wood engravings by Bewick —
Alnwick, 1806.
(Lawrence of
    Crewkerne) $56   £25

BEWICK, THOMAS AND JOHN

Goldsmith, Oliver and Parnell, Thomas —
'Poems' — diced cloth, spine gilt, wood
engraved vignettes on titles and 12 illus-
trations by the Bewicks, some browning —
1795.
(Lawrence of
    Crewkerne) $112   £50
'Robin Hood' — 2 vols., 1st Edn., half
titles, wood engraved illustrations and
vignettes by the Bewicks — 1795.
(Lawrence of
    Crewkerne) $45   £20
'Select Fables' — green morocco gilt by
Robertson, t.e.g., engraved frontispiece,
illustrated by Bewicks but altered by Nesbit.
A good copy — Newcastle, 1820.
(Lawrence of
    Crewkerne) $180   £80

BEWICK, THOMAS AND CLENNEL, L.

'Wood engravings for the Hive of Ancient
and Modern Literature' — original paper
wrappers, vignette title, wood engraved
illustrations by Bewick, versos blank —
1805.
(Lawrence of
    Crewkerne) $125   £55

BEYLE

BEYLE, HENRI 'STENDHAL'
'Vie de Henri Brulard' – 1st Edn., red half
morocco, original wrappers, bound in –
Paris, 1890.
(Sotheby's,
    Chancery Lane) $56   £25

BIANCONI, GIOVANNI LODOVICO
'Descrizione dei Circhi Particolarmente di
Quello di Caracalla' – engraved title vig-
nette, 20 engraved plates, 7 folding and 4
engraved vignettes in text, some spotting,
cont. wrappers, rebacked, uncut, folio –
Rome, 1789.
(Sotheby's, New Bond
    Street) $292   £130

BIBLE
'Biblia Germanica' – 2 parts, 583 leaves
only of 586, 109 hand coloured woodcut
illustrations in text, capitals, paragraph
marks etc., supplied in red and blue, slight
browning, soiling and worming, 18th century calf, worn, folio – Nuremberg, 1483.
(Sotheby's, New Bond
    Street) $19,125   £8,500

BIBLE – BOHEMIAN
1st Edn., of the Complete Bible in Czech –
578 leaves of 610, many leaves damaged
and repaired affecting text, blindstamped
antique calf, rubbed – Prague, August,
1488.
(Sotheby's, New Bond
    Street) $5,625   £2,500

BIBLE – ENGLISH
2 parts in one vol., titles within woodcut
border, book of psalms bound at end,
rubricated, cont. needlework binding,
worked with a central figure within stylized flowers, that on the front cover
possibly Hope with her anchor, joints
worn and repaired and front cover almost
detached – 1641-42.
(Sotheby's
    London) $205   £90

BIBLE – ENGLISH
'The Holy Bible' – pages ruled in red, cont.
Scottish binding of dark green morocco,
roll tooled border of alternating ornaments,
spine in alternate green and red compartments, central motto with arms, motto and
coronet of Hopetoun, Dutch coloured
floral gilt endpapers, covers rubbed and
scuffed – 1726.
(Christie's, King
    St.) $1,690   £750

BIBLE – IN FRENCH, OLD TESTAMENT
Title lacking some leaves torn with loss, woodcut illustrations, cont. calf, spine detached, folio – Lyons, Par Jean Pillehotte – 1585.
(Christie's S. Kensington) $90   £40

BIBLE– GERMAN
3 parts in one vol., translated by Martin Luther, 2 titles within woodcut border but lacks title to part 1, wormed, damaged and roughly repaired, slightly brown and spotted, cont. German blindstamped pigskin, slightly worn, folio – Egenolph, Frankfurt, 1599.
(Sotheby's, New Bond Street) $405   £180

BIBLE – HEBREW
'Biblia Hebraica Prout Opera Atque Studio Davidia Clodii . . . Recognita a John Henrico Majo . . . et ultimo Revisa a Johanne Leusdeno' – engraved frontispiece, preliminary matter in Latin, text in Hebrew, a few stains, cont. calf, gilt, crowned monogram of Karl XI of Sweden on sides, g.e. – Frankfurt on Main, 1712.
(Sotheby's, New Bond Street) $790   £350

BIBLE – HEBREW, – THORA, PENTATEUCH
Complete ms. roll on vellum written in brown ink, ashkenazi script, 45 lines, 325mm. wide, 39 sections stitched together, between 5 and 8 columns to each section, over plain wooden borders, early 19th century.
(Christie's, King St.) $1,465   £650

BIBLE – LATIN
'Biblia, ad vetustissima exemplaria castigata' – title with woodcut device, and within woodcut border, some dampstaining, a few leaves shaved, cont. calf, worn, spine defective at head and foot, metal clasps – Antwerp, Plantin, 1565.
(Sotheby's London) $80   £35

BIBLE, NEW TESTAMENT
Matthew (Torat Ha' Mashi'ach) Hebrew and Latin versions, Hebrew translation by Sebastian Munster with the Epistle of St. Paul to the Hebrews in Hebrew and Latin – 2 parts in one vol., 19th century calf, one cover detached – H. Petrus, Basle, 1557.
(Sotheby's, New Bond Street) $292   £130

BIBLIA LATINA
Part of Part 2 only, 122 leaves of 268, 48 lines, double column, gothic letter, some printing in red, large initials supplied in blue and red, water and dampstained throughout, extensive marginal repairs, 18th century reverse calf, worn, covers detached, early 16th century ownership inscriptions, folio – Paris, 1467/77.
(Sotheby's, New Bond Street) $2,925   £1,300

BIBLE
'The New Testament Translated Faithfully into English in the English College of Rhemes' – 1st Edn., of the Catholic version, marginal notes, antique style calf, joints rubbed – J. Fogny, Rheims, 1582.
(Christie's, King St.) $450   £200

BIBLIA – (ANTIGUO TESTAMENTO)
'Traducido del Hebreo al Castellano por Rabi Mose Arragel de Guadalfajara . . . por El Duque de Berwick y de Alba' – numerous coloured and other plates, 2 vols., folio; embossed calf – 1920-22.
(Bonham's) $70   £30

BIBLIA
'Das Ist Die Ganze Heilige Schrifft' – title in red and black, engraved frontispiece, portrait of Luther, 8 other portraits and 41 plates, many by Sandrart, modern morocco – Nuremberg, 1717.
(Christie's, King St.) $205   £90

BIE, JACQUES DE
'Les Vrais Portraits des Rois de France' –
title in red and black, engraved portraits
in text, 18th century sheep, cover detached,
folio – Paris, 1636.
(Sotheby's
    Monaco) $855   £380

BIEF, JONCTION SURREALISTE
Nos. 1-12 in one vol., a complete set,
illustrations, original cloth – La Terrain
Vague, Paris, 1958.
(Sotheby's,
    Chancery Lane) $50   £22

BIENVILLE, G. R.
'De La Nymphomanie' – modern cloth –
Amsterdam, 1771.
(Bonham's) $135   £60

BILIBIN, I. YA – AFANASIEV, A. N.
'Sestritsa Alenushka i Bratets Ivanushka' –
8 coloured illustrations, 3 full page, cover
designs by Bilibin, slightly spotted, original
pictorial wrappers, stained, worn – St.
Petersburg, 1903.
(Sotheby's,
    Chancery Lane) $215   £95

BILLARDON DE SAUVIGNY, L. E.
'Parnasse des Dames' – 5 vols., 5 engraved
titles by Ponce after Marillier, cont. French
red morocco, gilt, flat gilt spines, g.e., Duc
de Richelieu copy with his arms gilt on
cover, minor repairs – Paris, 1772-73.
(Sotheby Parke Bernet
    Monaco) $13,500   £6,000

BILLINGS, ROBERT W.
'The Architectural Antiquities of Durham'
– 15 original parts, 64 engraved plates,
some spotting, original wrappers, slightly
rubbed – 1844-45.
(Sotheby's,
    Chancery Lane) $95   £42

BILLS OF MORTALITY
London's Dreadful Visitation. A Collection
of bills of mortality for this present year,
beginning the 27th December 1664 and
ending the 19th of December following –
54 leaves and folding table, woodcut border in white on black ground with symbols
of death, half calf – E. Cotes, 1665.
(Sotheby's, New Bond
    Street) $495   £220

BINDING – BIBLE
English, authorized version, titles to Old
and New Testaments within woodcut
borders, Genealogies bound at beginning,
Metrical Psalms bound at the end. Fine
cont. English embroidered binding, richly
worked in coloured silks and silver thread
on plain satin ground, central device of
snake and beehive on both covers with a
dolphin like creature at foot, gilt and
gauffered edges – R. Parker and J. Bill,
1620.
(Sotheby's, New Bond
    Street) $1,125   £500

BINDOR, F.
'D. Y. Cameron, an Illustrated Catalogue
of his Etchings and Dry Points, 1887-
1932' – plates, limited edition 394/600
copies – Glasgow, 1932.
(Tessa Bennett,
    Edinburgh) $75   £32

BINYON, LAURENCE
'Brief Candles' – no. 89 of 100 copies,
signed by author and artist, illustrations by
Helen Binyon, original morocco, t.e.g. –
1938.
(Christie's S.
    Kensington) $75   £32

'The Followers of William Blake' – plates, some mounted and coloured, original cloth, t.e.g. – 1925.
(Christie's S.
    Kensington)   **$63**   **£28**
'Nizami, the Poem' described by Laurence Binyon – coloured plates, original cloth, some slightly nicked, folio – The Studio, n.d.
(Christie's S.
    Kensington)   **$34**   **£15**

BIRBECK, MORRIS
'Notes on a Journey in America' – folding coloured map, original boards – 1818.
(Phillips)   **$146**   **£65**

BISMARCK, COUNT VON
'Lectures on the Tactics of Cavalry . . . translated by N. Ludlow Beamish' – additional title and plates, some shaved, later half calf, rubbed. Another of the same in German, 1929 – 1827/29.
(Christie's S.
    Kensington)   **$80**   **£35**

BISSCHOP, JAN DE
'Signorum Veturum Icones' – 2 parts in one vol., engraved title, cut down and mounted, and 100 plates, a few stains, text (4 leaves) in Latin and Dutch, later half calf, rubbed, joints cracked , small folio, mid 17th century.
(Christie's S.
    Kensington)   **$190**   **£85**

BISSE, THOMAS
'The beauty of holiness in the Common-Prayer' – cont. red morocco, spine gilt in compartments, large made up lozenge on covers within dentelle border with infilled cornerpiece. – 1720.
(Sotheby's
    London)   **$125**   **£55**

BIZARRE, REVUE PERIODIQUE
Edited by Michel Laclos and others, first series, Nos. 1-2; second series Nos. 2, 3, 6-10, 15, 16, 26, 27, 34-35 and duplicates of No. 7 and 15: 17 issues in 16 parts. Illustrations and original wrappers – Paris, 1953-64.
(Sotheby's,
    Chancery Lane)   **$110**   **£48**

BLACK
'Black's General Atlas of the World' – coloured plate of flags (mounted) and 56 double page coloured maps, folio, cloth, morocco back – 1876.
(Bonham's)   **$90**   **£40**

BLACK, ADAM AND CHARLES
'General Atlas' – 54 maps, coloured in outline, some double page, a few loose, cont. half morocco, worn – Edinburgh, 1841.
(Sotheby's,
    Chancery Lane)   **$80**   **£35**

BLACKADDER, J.
'Berwickshire' – a large roll up linen backed map, hand coloured in outline, engraved by J. Ainslie – circa 1797.
(Tessa Bennett,
    Edinburgh)   **$135**   **£60**

BLACKER, J. F.
'The A B C of English Salt Glaze Stoneware from Dwight to Doulton' – plates illustrations, original cloth, dust jacket – 1922.
(Christie's S.
    Kensington)   **$50**   **£22**

BLACKIE & SON
'Atlas' – lacks title, coloured maps, half morocco – n.d. – and a collection of 19th century maps.
(Phillips)   **$90**   **£40**

BLACKMORE, EDWARD
'A Practical treatise on the Forms, Causes, Sanability and Treatment of Pulmonary Consumption' – errata leaf, original boards, uncut – Longman, 1832.
(Sotheby's, New Bond
    Street)   **$70**   **£30**

BLACKMORE, SIR RICHARD
'Discourses on the gout, a rheumatism and the King's Evil' – dampstained, cont. panelled calf, rubbed – J. Pemberton, 1726.
(Sotheby's, New Bond
    Street)   **$75**   **£32**
'Dissertations on a Dropsy, a Tympany, the Jaundice and the Stone and a Diabetes' – advertisement leaf at end, stained, panelled calf, rebacked – J. and J. Knapton, 1727.
(Sotheby's, New Bond
    Street)   **$430**   **£190**

BLACKSTONE, SIR WILLIAM
'Commentaries on the Laws of England' –
4 vols., 12th Edn., engraved portraits, cont.
calf, spines cracked, labels chipped – 1793-
95.
(Christie's S.
   Kensington)   **$112**   **£50**

BLAEU, G.
'Danubius' – hand coloured map – circa
1650.
(Phillips)   **$270**   **£120**
'Mansfeldia, Clivia' – 2 hand coloured
maps – circa 1650.
(Phillips)   **$250**   **£110**
'Dorsetshire' – hand coloured map, vig-
nette sailing ships, arms – circa 1650.
(Phillips)   **$315**   **£140**
'Norfolk' – hand coloured map – circa
1650.
(Phillips)   **$225**   **£100**
'Germania vulgo Deutchland' – hand
coloured map – circa 1650.
(Phillips)   **$340**   **£150**
'Trevirensis et Lusatia' – 2 hand coloured
maps – circa 1650.
(Phillips)   **$135**   **£60**
'Guiana' – hand coloured map, vignette
sailing ships – circa 1650.
(Phillips)   **$146**   **£65**
'Cyprus' – hand coloured map, cartouche
– circa 1650.
(Phillips)   **$405**   **£180**
'Hildesiensis and La Voigtlande' – 2 hand
coloured maps – circa 1650.
(Phillips)   **$190**   **£85**
'Nova Marchia et Brandenbourg' – 2 hand
coloured maps, cartouches – circa 1650.
(Phillips)   **$160**   **£70**
'Montgomery' – hand coloured map –
circa 1650.
(Phillips)   **$146**   **£65**
'Denbighshire' – hand coloured map –
circa 1650.
(Phillips)   **$100**   **£45**
'Novoforensis' – hand coloured map –
circa 1650.
(Phillips)   **$125**   **£55**
'Saxonia et Lusatia et Misnia' – 2 hand
coloured maps – circa 1650.
(Phillips)   **$135**   **£60**
'Silesia, Erpach' – 2 hand coloured maps
– circa 1650.
(Phillips)   **$146**   **£65**

'Wertheim and Meissen' – 2 hand coloured
maps – circa 1650.
(Phillips)   **$180**   **£80**
'Thuringia and Anhaltinus' – 2 hand
coloured maps – circa 1650.
(Phillips)   **$135**   **£60**
'Westphalia' – hand coloured map – circa
1650.
(Phillips)   **$190**   **£85**
'Pinnenberg' – hand coloured map, inset
town plan, cartouche – circa 1650.
(Phillips)   **$250**   **£110**

BLAEU, J.
'Gallovidia Vernacule Galloway' – double
page folio map, some pale hand colouring,
framed in plain oak – 17th century.
(Tessa Bennett,
   Edinburgh)   **$50**   **£22**

BLAEU, J. AND C.
'Westmoria comitatus' – eng. map, hand
coloured in outline, 12 x 15½in., slightly
stained, framed and glazed, 1695 or later.
(Christie's S.
   Kensington)   **$70**   **£30**

BLAEU, W. AND J.
'Le Theatre du Monde' – Part IV, Great
Britain, thick paper copy, architectural
engraved title, printed title label, 58
engraved maps, finely coloured by cont.
hand, historiated and other cartouches, 3
engravings in text hand coloured, plus a
duplicate of map of Devon similarly
coloured, loosely inserted, some maps and
text detached from guards, original vellum
gilt, roll borders, inner panel, cornerpiece,
g.e., soiled, folio – Amsterdam, 1646.
(Sotheby's, New Bond
   Street)   **$14,625** **£6,500**

BLAEU'S LIBRARY GLOBES
Unusually large pair of 17th century terrestrial and celestial globes on matching
wooden stands, coloured by hand and varnished, terrestrial globe embellished with
cartouches of sailing ships, monsters, compass roses etc., celestial globe with animals,
stars in magnitude etc., lettered in Latin,
worn and in places illegible, some surface
damage to both. Diameter of each 670mm.;
height 635mm. – Amsterdam, 1640-48.
(Sotheby's, New Bond
   Street)   **$11,250** **£5,000**

Kent, from Le Theatre du Monde by W. & J. Blaeu. (Sotheby's)

A pair of terrestrial and celestial globes by Blaeu, 1640-48. (Sotheby's)

BLAGDON

BLAGDON, F.
'An Historical Memento — Public Rejoicing — Centenary of the Accession of the Illustrious House of Brunswick' — 14 plates, 6 hand coloured aquatints, morocco, worn — 1814.
(Sotheby's, New Bond
   Street) $205   £90

BLAIR, R.
'The Grave, a Poem' — portrait, engraved title and 11 engravings, after William Blake, slight spotting, half morocco, rubbed, g.e., folio — 1813.
(Phillips) $270   £120

BLAKE, WILLIAM
Pencil Drawings — ed. Keynes, limited edition, cloth gilt, 4to — Nonesuch Press, 1856.
(Phillips) $65   £28
'America facsimiled at Edmonton by Wm. Muir'; 'Europe facsimiled by Wm. Muir'; 'The Song of Los facsimiled by Wm. Muir' — 3 works in one vol., each signed by Muir and limited to 50 copies, plates, those in second and third works hand coloured, cont. vellum, soiled, t.e.g., cont. wrappers bound in, folio — 1887-90.
(Christie's S.
   Kensington) $650   £290
'The First Book of Urizen facsimiled at Edmonton by Wm. Muir' — 2 works in one vol., cont. vellum, slightly soiled, t.e.g., original wrappers, bound in — n.d.
(Christie's S.
   Kensington) $495   £220
'Illustrations of the Book of Job' — folio paper covers, paper label, facsimile of 1826 edition. Engraved title and 21 tissued plates, only 1,000 copies — 1902.
(Lawrence of
   Crewkerne) $80   £35
'Songs of Experience' — black cloth gilt, partly uncut, printed in colours from a copy in the British Museum.
'Songs of Innocence' — black cloth gilt, partly uncut, printed in colours from a copy in the British Museum — Ernest Benn, 1926/7.
(Lawrence of
   Crewkerne) $70   £30

BLAND, J.
New Illustrated Catalogue of Extraordinary Novelties in Conjuring Tricks, Mechanical Automatons, Puzzles and Magical Apparatus' — wood engraved illustrations, printed slips with price alterations pasted in, original wrappers, somewhat worn, spine torn, g.e. — circa 1874.
(Sotheby's,
   Chancery Lane) $160   £70

BLANKAART, STEVEN
'Anatomia Reformata Sive Concinna Corporis Humani Dissectio, editio novissima' — engraved frontispiece by Penningen after Tideman, engraved portrait by Van Der Gucht after Plaatz, 84 engraved plates, cont. calf — Leiden, 1695.
(Sotheby's, New Bond
   Street) $405   £180

BLESSING
'The Blessing of the Ship, a Form of Prayer, formerly used by many of the sailors of Iona and the Isles' — hand coloured title and 14 leaves, original wrappers, small — printed and published by W. Muir, J. McCormick, 1887.
(Christie's S.
   Kensington) $160   £70

BLESSINGTON, COUNTESS OF, EDITOR
'Heath's Book of Beauty' – 3 vols., various,
engraved additional titles and plates, slight
spotting, cont. morocco by F. Westley,
slightly rubbed, g.e. – 1835-37.
(Christie's S.
Kensington) $70   £30

BLIGH, LT. WILLIAM
'The Log of H.M.S. Bounty 1787-1789'
– no. 161 of 500 copies, this one of 50
signed by Lord Mountbatten and specially
bound by Zaehnsdorf, plates, folding map,
original blue morocco, gilt inner dentelles,
contained in a cloth box, small folio –
Genesis Publications, 1975.
(Christie's S.
Kensington) $180   £80
'A Voyage to the South Seas' – 1st Edn.,
large paper, 6 engraved maps and plans of 7,
5 folding, lacks portrait, cont. half leather,
label, very worn – 1792.
(Sotheby's, New Bond
Street) $585   £260

BLOCH, MARCUS ELIESER
'Ichthyologie ou Histoire Naturelle
Generale et Particuliere des Poissons' – 2nd
Edn., 6 vols., titles with engraved vignettes,
half titles, 216 hand coloured engraved
plates, some heightened with silver, cont.
green half roan, uncut, slightly rubbed,
folio – Berlin, 1795.
(Christie's
St. James) $13,500   £6,000

BLOME, RICHARD
'Britannia, or A Geographical Description
of the Kingdoms of England, Scotland and
Ireland' – 47 engraved maps only, five
folding and reinforced, some soiled, some
lacking, 12 plates, title neatly laid down,
modern calf, folio – 1673.
(Christie's S.
Kensington) $3,375   £1,500
'The History of the Holy Bible' – plates,
maps by Blome, some folding, some leaves
torn, few detached, cont. calf, worn, covers
detached, folio – 1752.
(Christie's S.
Kensington) $290   £130

BLONDEL, J. A.
'The Power of the Mother's Imagination
over the Foetus examin'd' – 1st Edn.,
calf rebacked, some leaves foxed – 1729.
(Bonham's) $290   £130

BLONDEL, J. F.
'De La Distribution des Maisons de
Plaisance' – 2 vols., numerous engraved
plates, cont. calf, worn – Paris, 1737-38.
(Sotheby Parke Bernet
Monaco) $10,125   £4,500
'Architecture Francois' – 4 vols, 498
engraved plates, few plates slightly trimmed,
several torn without loss, cont. red morocco
gilt, g.e., slightly worn, folio – Paris, 1752-
56.
(Sotheby Parke Bernet
Monaco) $85,500   £38,000

Ichthyologie ou Histoire Naturelle ..... des Poissons, by M.E. Bloch. (Christie's)

BLORE

BLORE, EDWARD
'The Monumental Remains of Noble and
Eminent Persons, comprising the Sepul-
chral Antiquities of Great Britain' – 1st
Edn., large paper copy, 30 engraved plates,
19th century morocco gilt, rubbed, g.e. –
1826.
(Sotheby's, New Bond
    Street) $90   £40

BLUNDEN, EDMUND
'A Northamptonshire Poetess, Mary
Leapor' – First separate edition, limited
to 'a few copies', presentation copy
inscribed by author, slightly spotted,
original wrappers – Northampton, 1936.
(Sotheby's,
    Chancery Lane) $125   £55

'Undertones of War' – First Edn., presentation copy inscribed by author to John
Taylor, with autograph poem, original
cloth, uncut, dust jacket – 1928.
(Sotheby's,
    Chancery Lane) $745   £330

**BOATE, GERARD, THOMAS MOLYNEUX
AND OTHERS**
'Natural History of Ireland in Three Parts' –
11 engraved plates, 7 folding, 2 slightly torn,
some leaves soiled, cont. calf, worn, crudely
rebacked, upper hinge split, small 4to – Dublin,
1726.
(Sotheby's, New Bond
    Street) $215   £95

BOCCACCIO, GIOVANNI
'Il Decamerone' – 3 vols., engraved frontispiece by Demautort, cont. red morocco,
three gilt fillets enclosing the Artois arms,
gilt, inner gilt dentelles, spines gilt in three
compartments, green labels, g.e. – London
with Paris address of Delalain, 1789.
(Sotheby's, New Bond
    Street) $945   £420
'The Decameron . . . Translated by J. M.
Rigg' – 3 vols., including a portfolio of
additional plates by Louis Chalon, various
original bindings, slightly soiled, spines
torn and faded – 1906.
(Christie's S.
    Kensington) $50   £22
'Il Filocopo' – woodcut device on title,
shaved, waterstaining, 19th century calf –
J. Rapirio, Venice, 1551.
(Christie's, King
    St.) $112   £50
'Laberinto d'Amore con una epistola a
Messer Pino de Rossi' – rather spotted,
cont. black morocco, rebacked, g.e. –
Florence, 1525.
(Sotheby's, New Bond
    Street) $150   £65
'The Modell of Wit, Mirth, Eloquence
and Conversation' – part I only of
2nd and 3rd edns., 5 woodcuts in text,
lacking frontis, title badly stained, defective and mounted, large hole in A2 affecting text, a few leaves cropped or frayed,
tears in X8 and Aa5, M5-8 loose, some
staining and discolouration, cont. calf,
rebacked, worn – 1634.
(Sotheby's
    London) $18 $8

BOCCACCIO, J.
'Le Decameron' – 5 vols., 116 plates by
Aliamet and others after Gravelot, Boucher,
Cochin and Eisen, cont. blue morocco, sides
gilt with elaborate rococo plaque, flat gilt
spines, g.e. – Paris, 1757-61.
(Sotheby Parke Bernet
    Monaco) $126,000   £56,000

*Le Decameron by Boccaccio in a fine eighteenth century binding.
(Sotheby Parke Bernet, Monaco)*

BODIN, JEAN
'Les Six Livres de la Republique' – small
woodcut ornament on title with final
blank, slight browning and soiling, some
worming, 17th century calf, worn –
Geneva, 1577.
(Sotheby's, New Bond
 Street) $90 £40

[manuscript image]

BODONI, GIOVANNI BATTISTA,
Printer
Autograph letter signed, 1 page, folio,
Parma, 22 September 1771, to an unnamed
correspondent, integral blank.
(Sotheby's, New Bond
 Street) $405 £180

BOERHAAVE, HERMANN
'Elements of Chemistry Faithfully abridg'd
to which are added curious notes by a
Physician' – 17 plates with explanatory
text at end, panelled calf, rebacked, J.
Wilford, 1732.
(Sotheby's, New Bond
 Street) $430 £190
'A Method of Studying Physick containing
what a Physician ought to know in relation
to bodies, the laws of motion etc.' – trans-
lated into English by Mr. Samber, half title,
errata and advertisements, cont. panelled
calf – H. P. for C. Rivington, 1719.
(Sotheby's, New Bond
 Street) $540 £240

BOGAERT, ABRAHAM
'De Roomsche Monarchy' – 167 engraved
copper plate portraits, 6 engraved plates (2
folding), some tearing, browning and
soiling, cont. vellum – Utrecht, 1697.
(Sotheby's, New Bond
 Street) $270 £120

BOGHURST, WILLIAM
'Loimographia, an Account of the Great
Plague of London in the Year 1665' –
facsimile plate, original cloth – 1894.
(Sotheby's, New Bond
 Street) $70 £30

BOHNY

BOHNY, N.
'Neues Bilderbuch' — coloured illustrations, original cloth backed boards, partly disbound — n.d.
(Christie's, S.
  Kensington)   **$125**   **£55**

BOIARDO, MATTEO MARIA
'Orlando Innamorato' — different editions, two vols. in one, first title in woodcut, architectural border, second title in historiated border, with woodcut vignette, woodcut map, some worming and staining, 18th century mottled calf, gilt spine, covers wormed — De Sabbio, Venice, 1539-44.
(Christie's, King
  St.)   **$225**   **£100**

BOILEAU, ABBE NICOLAS
'De L'Abus des Nuditez de Gorge' — 2nd Edn., 18th century French red morocco, gilt, g.e., bookplate of Albert, Duc de Luynes — Paris, 1677.
(Sotheby Parke Bernet
  Monaco)   **$2,700**   **£1,200**

BOILEAU — DESPREAUX, NICOLAS
'Oeuvres Completes' — 3 vols., engraved portraits, blue morocco gilt — Paris, 1810.
(Sotheby's
  Monaco)   **$145**   **£650**

BOILEAU, JACQUES
'A Just and Sensible Reprehension of Naked Breasts and Shoulders . . . Translated by Edward Cooke' — later sheep, rebacked, spine and stitching split — Jonathan Edwin, 1678.
(Christie's S.
  Kensington)   **$250**   **£110**
'Historia Flagellantium de Recto et Perverso Flagrorum usu apud Christianos' — leaf before title blank, cont. calf, spine gilt, worn — J. Anisson, Paris, 1700.
(Sotheby's, New Bond
  Street)   **$90**   **£38**

BOILVIN, E. — RABELAIS, FRANCOIS
'Les Cinq Livres' — 5 vols. in one, 11 etched plates by Boilvin, brown morocco gilt, elaborate panels on cover and spine, inside borders gilt, morocco doublures, marbled endpapers, t.e.g. by Marius Michel. One of 15 copies on chine of an edition of 200 large copies — Jouaust, Paris, 1886.
(Sotheby's,
  Chancery Lane)   **$855**   **£380**

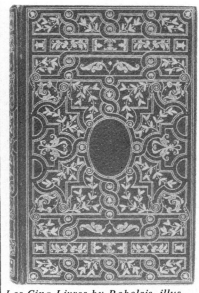

Les Cinq Livres by Rabelais, illustrated by E. Boilvin. (Sotheby's)

BOISSIER DE SAUVAGES, FRANCOIS
'Nosologie Methodique ou Distribution des Maladies en Classes' — 10 vols., one damaged, cont. mottled sheep, gilt spines — Lyon, 1772.
(Sotheby's
  Monaco)   **$1,915**   **£850**

BOIVIN, Mme. M. A. V.
'Memorial de L'Art des Accouchements' — portrait and woodcut plates, presentation copy, 2nd Edn., 2 vols. — Paris, 1817.
(Bonham's)   **$180**   **£80**
BOIVIN, Mme. M.A.V. — DUGES, A.
'Traite Pratique des Maladies de L'Uterus et des Annexes' — 41 coloured plates, 2nd Edn., oblong folio, modern boards — Bruxelles, 1834.
(Bonham's)   **$340**   **£150**

BOLDENYI, J.
'La Hongrie' and another on Hungary — plates, original decorative cloth, gilt — Paris, 1853.
(Sotheby Parke Bernet
  Monaco)   **$5,400**   **£2,400**

**BOLINGBROKE, HENRY ST. JOHN,
LORD VISCOUNT**
'Letters on the Study and Use of History'
— 2 vols., cont. calf, joints cracked — 1752.
(Christie's S.
　　Kensington)　　　　$50　　　£22

BOLIVAR, SIMON
Document signed discharging Don Jose
Olavarria with the rank of Colonel of
Cavalry, counter signed by Juan Salazar —
1 page, folio, printed heading 'Republica
Peruana', printed vignette at bottom, damp-
stained and a little foxed, filing holes, inte-
gral blank — 13 March, 1826.
(Sotheby's, New Bond
　　Street)　　　　$2,475　　　£1,100

BOLTON, ARTHUR T.
'The Architecture of Robert and James
Adam' — 2 vols., frontispieces, illustrations,
original cloth, soiled — 1922.
(Christie's S.
　　Kensington)　　　　$160　　　£70

BOLTON, JAMES
'History of Fungusses' — 4 vols., plates, W.
Strickland bookplate, calf gilt — 1788-91.
(Phillips)　　　　$720　　　£320

'Harmonia Ruralis' — Natural History of
British Song Birds — 40 coloured plates, half
calf rebacked — 1794.
(Bonham's)　　　　$675　　　£300

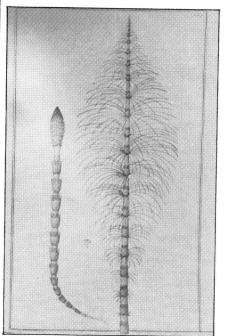

'New Figures of all the British Ferns . . .
copied from Nature' — autograph mss.,
title in red and black, 39 original watercolour drawings with coloured ruled borders and mss. captions on blank interleaves,
on Whatman paper, cont. green half
morocco, gilt, large folio — Stannary near
Halifax, 1795.
(Christie's
　　St. James)　　　　$5,625　　　£2,500

BONAPARTE, LUCIEN
'Choix de Gravures . . . d'apres Les Pein-
tures Originales' — plates, slight spotting,
cont. morocco — 1812.
(Christie's, S.
　　Kensington)　　　　$112　　　£50

THE LITTLE MERMAID.

AR, far away, out on the open sea, the water is as blue as the most beautiful corn-flowers, and as clear as the purest crystal; but it is very deep,—deeper than the longest cable can reach. Many a church-steeple would have to be piled one on the other before you could reach

BONAPARTE, PRINCE NAPOLEON, 1822-91

Son of Jerome Bonaparte, known as 'Plon Plon', good collection of about 85 autograph letters, signed, and letters signed 'Napoleon Bonaparte' etc., upwards of 100 pages, folio and octavo, Palais Royal, Avenue d'Antin, Genoa, Rome, Prangins and elsewhere, May 1843 to January 1891 to a variety of correspondents.
(Sotheby's, New Bond
   Street)   **$565**   **£250**

BOND, F. B. CANUM, DOM BEDE

'Roodscreens and Roodlofts' – 2 vols., plates, original cloth, faded and soiled – 1909.
(Christie's S.
   Kensington)   **$75**   **£32**

BONE, J.

'Edinburgh Revisited' – etched frontispiece, plates and illustrations by H. Fletcher, buckram gilt – 1911.
(Tessa Bennett,
   Edinburgh)   **$7**   **£3**

BONER, CHARLES

'Chamois Hunting in the Mountains of Bavaria' – New Edn., vignettes, lithographed frontis, 6 plates by Theodore Horschett, some spotting, cont. polished calf, corners and joints slightly rubbed – 1860.
(Christie's S.
   Kensington)   **$90**   **£40**

BONER, CHARLES – Translator

'A Danish Story Book' by Hans Christian Andersen, 1st English Edn., 4 lithographed plates coloured by hand, wood engraved illustrations, original red cloth, gilt, slightly worn – Grant and Griffith, 1847.
(Sotheby's,
   Chancery Lane)   **$112**   **£50**

BONETUS, THEOPHILUS

'A Guide to the Practical Physician' – half title, printed in double columns, 211 table in duplicate, paper discoloured, library stamps, cont. calf rubbed, folio – Thomas Flesher, 1684.
(Sotheby's, New Bond
   Street)   **$385**   **£170**

BONFILS, ROBERT – NERVAL, GERARD DE

'Sylvie' – coloured wood engraved illustrations and decorations by Bonfils, perforated and rubber stamped library marks, green half morocco, spine slightly soiled, t.e.g., original wrappers bound in, by Duval – Paris, 1919.
(Sotheby's,
   Chancery Lane)   **$14**   **£6**

BONFILS, ROBERT – REGNIER, HENRI DE
'Les Rencontres de M. de Breot' – 59 illustrations and decorations by Bonfils, coloured by hand, brown calf, each cover blindstamped with five landscape designs, original wrappers bound in, by Rene Kieffer – Kieffer, Paris, 1919.
(Sotheby's,
 Chancery Lane) $80 £35

BONNARD, C.
'Costumes Historiques' – 2 vols., 200 hand coloured plates, some heightened with gold, minor stains, half calf – Paris, 1845.
(Sotheby's, New Bond
 Street) $495 £220
'Costumes Historiques des XII-XV siecels' – 3 vols., 200 hand coloured plates by Paul Mercuri, half cloth, folio – Paris, 1860-61.
(Sotheby's
 Monaco) $4,950 £2,200

BONNARD, PIERRE
Charming filial letter signed, 3 pages, octavo, Paris no date, to his mother, very slightly browned.
(Sotheby's, New Bond
 Street) $450 £200

BOOK OF COMMON PRAYER
'Verve No. 17/18'. Couleur de Bonnard – 1 coloured lithograph after Bonnard, coloured and plain illustrations, original wrappers, cover design by artist – Paris, 1947.
(Sotheby's,
 Chancery Lane) $29 £13

BONNET, CHARLES
'Considerations sur les corps organises, ou l'on traite leur origine . . . developement . . . reproduction etc.' – 2 vols., 1st Edn., engraved vignette on title, half titles, cont. French calf, spines gilt – M. M. Rey, Amsterdam, 1762.
(Sotheby's, New Bond
 Street) $450 £200

BONNYCASTLE, JOHN
'An Introduction to Astronomy' – 2nd Edn., 20 engraved plates, 8 folding, advertisement leaf at end, occasional light spotting, cont. calf backed boards, extremities rubbed – 1787.
(Christie's S.
 Kensington) $75 £32

BOOK AUCTION RECORDS
Vol. 1 in two parts to 71; General Index, 6 vols. in 7; together 79 vols., all but two original cloth, some soiled or rubbed, a few minor hinges worn.
(Christie's S.
 Kensington) $1,575 £700

BOOK AUCTION RECORDS
Vol. 26, vols. 40-45 (duplicate 43), 47, 49, 50, 53, 61-68, 4th and 5th General Indexes, together 22 vols., cloth – 1929-1972.
(Phillips) $90 £40

BOOK OF COMMON PRAYER, THE
Plates, cont. morocco, rubbed, joints worn, head of spine chipped – 1713.
(Christie's S.
 Kensington) $112 £50

BOOK OF COMMON PRAYER, THE
Chromo lithographed plates, vignettes, ornaments and borders by Owen Jones, original morocco gilt, binding loose – 1845.
(Bonham's) $90 £38

BOOK OF HOURS

The illuminated Book of Hours made for Isabelle D'Este, 1474-1539. (Sotheby Parke Bernet, Monaco)

BOOK OF HOURS

Comprising the Hours of the Virgin (Use of Rome) preceded by a Calendar and Followed by the Offices of the Dead, the Penitential Psalms and Litany, the Fifteen Gradual Psalms and the Hours of the Cross, all in Latin — illuminated mss. on vellum, 240/11 text complete. Seven large illuminated initials in leafy designs in full colour and gold, five large historiated initials with full borders of floral designs, four full page miniatures with full borders enclosing further miniatures. A little rubbing, slight stains at ends, generally in good condition, late 19th century black morocco gilt inlaid with brown by Marius Michel, g.e. Written for Isabella D'Este 1474-1539, daughter of Ercole Este, Duke of Ferrara, Marchioness of Mantua. She was a patron of Raphael, Mantegna and Leonardo da Vinci — Florence 1490. (Sotheby Parke Bernet
　　Monaco)　　　$720,000　£320,000

72

(83)

The Blacksmith.   LXXI.   *Faber Ferrarius.*

The Blacksmith, 1.	*Faber ferrarius,* 1.
in his Smithy (or Forge) 2.	in *Ustrina* (Fabricâ) 2.
Bloweth the fire	inflat ignem
with a pair of Bellows, 3.	Folle, 3.
which he bloweth	quem adtollit
with his Feet, 4.	Pede, 4.
and so heateth the Iron:	atq; ita candefacit *Ferrum:*
And then he taketh it out	Deinde eximit
with the Tongs, 5.	Forcipe, 5.
layeth it upon the Anvil, 6.	imponit *Incudi,* 6.
and striketh it	& cudit
with an Hammer, 7.	Malleo, 7.
where the sparks, 8. fly off.	ubi *Stricturae.* 8. exiliunt.
And thus are hammer'd out,	Et sic excuduntur,
Nails, 9.	Clavi, 9.
Horse-shoes, 10.	Soleae, 10.
Cart-strakes, 11.	Canthi, 11.
Chains, 12.	Catenae, 12.
Plates, Locks and Keys,	Laminae, Serae cum *Clavibus,*
Hinges, &c.	Cardines, &c.
He quencheth hot Irons	Reitinguit candentia
in the Cool-trough.	Ferramenta in *Lacu.*

**BOOK OF TRADES, THE . . . or
LIBRARY OF THE USEFUL ARTS**
3 vols., part 1 and 2, 3rd Edn. 66 of 67
engraved plates, one loose, spotted and
discoloured, original roan backed boards,
worn — Tabart and Co., 1806/07.
(Sotheby's,
Chancery Lane) $250   £110

BOOTH, GENERAL WILLIAM
'In Darkest England' and 'The Way Out' —
folding colour plan, original cloth, spine
soiled — 1890.
(Christie's S.
Kensington) $5   £2

BOQUINUS, PETRUS
'Apodeixis Antichristianismi' — 1st Edn.,
18th century French citron morocco, gilt
spine, rubbed — E. Vignon, Geneva, 1583.
(Sotheby's, New Bond
Street) $35   £15

BORLASE, WILLIAM
'The Natural History of Cornwall' —
folding map, 25 engraved plates, diced calf
gilt, folio — Oxford, 1758.
(Phillips) $215   £95

BOSCHE, JAKOB
'De Arts Symbolica ad Erastum' — wood-
cut decorations, old boards, folio —
Augsburg, 1701.
(Sotheby's, New Bond
Street) $180   £80

BOSSCHERE, JEAN DE
'The Love Books of Ovid' translated by
J. Lewis May, no. 233 of 300 copies.
plates by Bosschere, some coloured,
original cloth — 1925.
(Christie's S.
Kensington) $50   £22

BOSSE, ABRAHAM
'La Pratique du Trait a Preuves de M.
Desargues' — 2 parts in one vol., 2 engraved
title pages, 1 frayed, engraved dedication,
114 engraved diagrams, soiled, damp
stained, old limp vellum, uncut — Paris 1643.
(Sotheby's, New Bond
Street) $70   £30

BOSSOLI, CARLO
'The Beautiful Scenery and Chief Places of
Interest Throughout the Crimea' — lithographed title, 52 lithographed plates, tinted
in several colours and finished by hand on
30 sheets, list of plates, marginal foxing,
original green cloth, contents loose, folio
— 1856.
(Sotheby's, New Bond
Street) $855   £380

BOSSUET, ABBE C.
'Traite Elementaire d'Hydrodynamique' —
2 vols., 18 folding plates, calf, spines
cracked — Paris, 1875.
(Phillips) $170   £75

BOSSUET, JACQUES BENIGNE
'Discours sur l'Histoire Universelle
jusqu'a l'Empire de Charlemagne' — a few
quires browned, green morocco gilt, by
Bradel l'Aine with his ticket, hinges and
edges a little rubbed, minor defect on
upper cover, g.e., pink silk doublures —
Didot l'Aine, Paris, 1784.
(Sotheby's, New Bond
Street) $360   £160

BOSTON

BOSTON, THE ALMANAC
14 volumes, various, original cloth –
Boston, 1846-75.
(Christie's S.
Kensington)   **$65**   **£28**

BOSWELL, HENRY
'Complete Historical Descriptions . . .
Views and Representations of England and
Wales' – bound in 2 vols., engraved frontis,
and about 215 plates and maps, title and a
few leaves of text creased or torn, cont. half
calf, worn covers detached, folio – Alex.
Hogg, n.d.
(Christie's S.
Kensington)   **$945**   **£420**

BOSWELL, JAMES
'Journals' – ed. F. A. Pottle, 3 vols.,
limited edition, illus. quarter vellum gilt –
1951-3.
(Phillips)   **$110**   **£48**
'The Journal of a Tour to the Hebrides' –
1st Edn., 13 line errata, tree calf, rebacked
- 1785.
(Phillips)   **$190**   **£85**
'The Life of Samuel Johnson' – 2 vols., 1st
Edn., first state, engraved portrait and 2
plates – 1791.
'The Principal Corrections and Additions to
the First Edition of Mr. Boswell's Life of
Dr. Johnson' – 1st Edn., cont. calf,
rebacked with original spines, rubbed –
1793.
(Sotheby's, New Bond
Street)   **$1,465**   **£650**
'A Letter to the People of Scotland' – 1st
London Edn., old russia, scuffed and worn –
1784.
(Christie's, King
St.)   **$170**   **£75**

BOTANIC GARDEN, THE
Edited by Benjamin Maud, vol. IV only, 2
engraved titles, 33 hand coloured plates,
cont. green half morocco, rubbed and worn
– 1831-32.
(Christie's
St. James)   **$450**   **£200**

BOTTEGHE OSCURE
Edited by Marguerite Caetani – nos. 7-20,
22, 24, 25 and 23 duplicates. 30 issues in
English, French, Italian, original wrappers,
some with dust jackets – Rome 1951-60.
(Sotheby's,
Chancery Lane)   **$130**   **£58**

BOTTONNI, ALBERTINO
'De Vita Conservanda' – woodcut device
on title, 18th century half vellum, cont.
signature of Cesare Rosetti – G. Bozza,
Padua, 1582.
(Sotheby's
Monaco)   **$1,350**   **£600**

BOUCHER, J. F. – FILS
'Premier Cahier d'Arabesques' – 48
engraved plates, half calf, gilt, bound with
copy of the Second Series of Boucher's
Meubles Divers with 59 of 60 plates, minor
stains, folio – Paris, circa 1780.
(Sotheby's, New Bond
Street)   **$270**   **£120**

BOUCHERY, OMER – DURAND-LEFEVRE, MARIE
'Les Cathedrales de Chartres a Beauvais –
18 etched illustrations by Bouchery, 7 full
page, 2 double page, unsewn in original
wrappers, uncut, folder slightly damaged,
slipcase – Henri Colas, Paris, 1950.
(Sotheby's,
Chancery Lane)   **$80**   **£35**

BOULESTIN, MARCEL
'The Conduct of the Kitchen' – one of 25
signed copies, with original signed,
engraved by J. E. Labourer, original binding – 1925.
(Phillips)   **$125**   **£55**

BOULTON, RICHARD
'Physico – Chyrurgical treatises of the
Gout, the King's Evil and the Lues
Venerea' – 4 parts in one vol., all under
separate title pages, cont. panelled calf –
W. Brand and J. Kent, 1714.
(Sotheby's, New Bond
Street)   **$205**   **£90**

BOULTON, WILLIAM B.
'The Amusements of Old London' – 2 vols.,
coloured plates, original cloth, gilt – 1902.
(Sotheby's,
Chancery Lane)   **$70**   **£30**

BOURDIN, FREDERIC – BEYLE, MARIE HENRI
'La Chartreuse de Parme' – 4 vols. in two,
etched frontispieces, vignettes on titles,
24 plates and 8 head and tail pieces, after
Bourdin, green half morocco, t.e.g.,
original wrappers, bound in by Asper –
Librairie des Amateurs, Paris, 1911.
(Sotheby's,
Chancery Lane)   **$30**   **£14**

BOURGEOIS, LOUISE
'Observations sur la Sterilitie' – vignette
on title printed in red and black, portrait,
2 vols., crushed blue morocco, gilt, g.e.
– Rouen, 1626.
(Bonham's) $385   £170

BOURNE, VINCENT
'Miscellaneous Poems, consisting of originals and translations' – woodcut illustrations, light spotting, bookplate of Sir
John Trollope, cont. polished calf, cracked
– 1772.
(Sotheby's, New Bond
    Street) $90   £38
'Poemata, Latine partim reddita, partim
scripta' – 1st Edn., cont. mottled calf,
upper joint cracked, gilt – 1734.
(Sotheby's, New Bond
    Street) $70   £30

BOUSSARD, J.
'Etudes sur l'Art Funeraire Moderne' – 1st
Edn., 200 plates, 16 plates of text, tipped
in at end, spotting, cloth, rubbed and
soiled, large folio – Paris, 1870.
(Sotheby's, New Bond
    Street) $270   £120

BOUTELL, C.
'Monumental Brasses of England' – illus.,
half morocco, gilt, folio – 1849.
(Phillips) $160   £70

BOUTET, HENRI
'Les Modes Feminines du XIX Siecle' –
Preface de Jules Claretie, 100 dry point
plates by Boutet, coloured by hand, red
morocco, wide gilt borders, upper cover
with monogram inlaid in green and cream
morocco, inside borders gilt, t.e.g., original
pictorial wrappers bound in, slipcase –
Societe Francaise d'Editions d'Art, Paris,
1902.
(Sotheby's,
    Chancery Lane) $970   £430

BOWDICH, T. EDWARD
'Mission from Cape Coast Castle to
Ashantee' – 1st Edn., 2 engraved maps,
one folding, 10 plates, including 7
engraved aquatints, 2 folding and 5pp.
engraved music, cont. calf – 1918.
(Christie's
    St. James) $630   £280

*Les Modes Feminines du XIX Siecle
by Henri Boutet. (Sotheby's)*

BOWEN, E.
Road Map, Tinmouth to Carlisle; Map of
Northumberland – hand coloured and
mounted – circa 1720.
(Tessa Bennett
    Edinburgh) $20   £9
'The World' – hand coloured mounted –
circa 1780.
(Phillips) $110   £48

BOWEN, ELIZABETH
'Seven Winters' – 1st Edn., no. 412 of 450
copies, original linen backed boards, uncut,
unopened – Cuala Press, Dublin, 1942.
(Sotheby's,
    Chancery Lane) $80   £35
BOWEN, ELIZABETH, AND OTHERS
'The Game of Consequences' – limited to
1,200 copies, frontispiece by Eric
Ravillious, occasional light spotting,
additional gathering, list of nine players
signed by them and artist, original cloth,
faded, dust jacket soiled and holed – 1932.
(Christie's S.
    Kensington) $50   £22

BOWEN, EMANUEL AND KITCHIN, THOMAS

'The Large English Atlas or A New Set of Maps of all the Counties of England and Wales' — 31 double page engraved maps only of 47, all hand coloured in outline with elaborate engraved cartouches, old half calf, very worn, large folio — J. and C. Bowles and R. Sayer, 1763.
(Christie's
   St. James) $2,475   £1,100

BOYD, JULIA

'Bewick Gleanings . . . remaining in the possession of her family until the death of the last Miss Bewick' — folio, half morocco rubbed, t.e.g., title in red and black, frontispiece portrait, 53 copperplate illustrations and woodcuts, signed by author — Newcastle 1886.
(Lawrence of
   Crewkerne) $55   £25

BOYDELL, JOHN AND JOSIAH

'An History of the River Thames' — 2 vols., large paper copy, 2 engraved folding maps, one uncoloured plate and 76 fine coloured aquatint views on thick paper, cont. diced calf, rebacked, preserving gilt spines, folio — 1794-96.
(Christie's
   St. James) $6,300   £2,800

BOYLE, JOHN, EARL OF ORRERY

'Remarks on the Life and Writings of Dr. Jonathan Swift' — portrait, marginal worming throughout, cont. speckled calf, joints rubbed, upper joint slightly split — 1752.
(Christie's S.
   Kensington) $55   £25

BOYLE, ROBERT

'Defensis Doctrinae de Elatere et Gravitate Aeris' — extracted from a larger work, one plate, spotted and stained, modern cloth backed boards — Geneva, Samuel de Tournes, 1680.
(Christie's S.
   Kensington) $34   £15
'Occasional Reflections upon Several Subjects' — 1st Edn., title in red and black, imprimatur leaf, pagination shaved, cont. calf, rebacked, upper cover detached — 1665.
(Christie's, King
   St.) $270   £120

BOYS, THOMAS SHOTTER

'Original Views of London' — 2 vols., facsimile reprint, coloured plates, original morocco backed cloth, slipcase — Guildford, 1954-55.
(Sotheby's,
   Chancery Lane) $95   £42

An History of the River Thames by John and Josiah Boydell. (Christie's)

BRABNER, J. H. F. (Editor)
'The Comprehensive Gazetteer of England
and Wales' – 6 vols., coloured maps and
plans, plates, original cloth, some covers
damaged by damp – n.d.
(Christie's S.
  Kensington) $30   £12

BRACKEN, H.
'The Midwife's Companion or A Treatise
on Midwifery' – 1st Edn., old calf, worn –
1737.
(Bonham's) $90   £40

BRACKENBURY, GEORGE
'The Campaign in the Crimea' – vol. 1 of
two, tinted lithographed title and 39
plates, spotting, original cloth, spine worn,
g.e. – 1855.
(Christie's S.
  Kensington) $60   £26

BRADFORD, REV. WILLIAM
'Sketches of the Country, character and
costume of Portugal and Spain' – 1st
Edn., engraved mounted frontispiece and
53 coloured aquatint plates, including the
13 supplementary coloured military plates,
modern red half morocco, folio – 1810.
(Christie's
  St. James) $720   £320

BRADLEY, RICHARD
'A Course of Lectures upon the Materia
Medica Ancient and Modern read at
Cambridge' – advertisements at end, cont.
panelled calf – Cha. Davis, 1730.
(Sotheby's, New Bond
  Street) $90   £40
'A Philosophical Account of the Works of
Nature . . . in the Animal, Mineral and
Vegetable parts of the creation' – 1st Edn.,
title in red and black, 29 hand coloured
engraved plates, one folding, cont. calf,
rubbed and worn – 1721.
(Christie's
  St. James) $135   £60

BRADLEY, THOMAS
'A Treatise on Worms and other Animals
which infest the Human Body' – 3 plates,
half title, original boards, rebacked, uncut
– T. Underwood and J. Souter, 1813.
(Sotheby's, New Bond
  Street) $90   £40

BRADSHAW, P. V.
'Art in Advertising' – plates, some
coloured, cloth gilt, 4to – n.d.
(Phillips) $80   £35

BRADSTREET, DUDLEY
'The Life and Uncommon Adventures of
Capt. Dudley Bradstreet' – 1st Edn., slight
browning and soiling, cont. calf, rebacked,
worn – Dublin, for the author, 1755.
(Sotheby's
  London) $125   £55

BRANDT, GERARD
'Het Leven en Bedryf van den Heere
Michiel de Ruiter' – 4th Edn., engraved
additional title and 7 plates – Amsterdam,
Rotterdam and Gravenhage, 1746.
(Christie's S.
  Kensington) $430   £190

BRANGWYN, FRANK
'Works' – No. 6 of the 70 copies, comprising the proof edition, signed by
the artist, 10 mounted coloured plates –
n.d.
(Christie's S.
  Kensington) $100   £45

**BRANGWYN, FRANK AND SCOTT,
MICHAEL**
'Tom Gringle's Log' – 2 vols., with plates
by Brangwyn, original cloth, slightly
rubbed – Philadelphia, n.d.
(Christie's S.
  Kensington) $20   £9

BRANTOME, PIERRE DE BOURDEILLE
'The Lives of Gallant Ladies' – 2 vols.,
signed by Robert Gibbings, loosely inserted,
plates by Gibbings, original parchment
backed boards – Golden Cockerel Press –
1924.
(Christie's S.
  Kensington) $145   £65

BRANTOME, PIERRE DE
'Memoires' – 10 vols., 18th century French
red morocco, covers gilt with arms of
Nicolas Segur, President au Parliament de
Bordeaux 1697-1755, spines gilt a la
grotesque, contents of different parts
lettered, g.e. – Jean de la Tourterelle,
Leiden, 1722.
(Sotheby Parke Bernet
  Monaco) $58,500   £26,000

BRAQUE

BRAQUE, GEORGES

'Catalogue de l'Oeuvre de Georges Braque, 1928-57' – 4 vols., numerous reproductions, some coloured, original cloth binders, coloured design by artist on upper covers, spine slightly soiled – Maeght, Paris, 1962-73.
(Sotheby's,
Chancery Lane) $80   £35
'Verve No. 31/32' Carnets Intimes de Georges Braque – numerous plain and coloured reproductions, original boards, cover design by artist – Paris, 1955.
(Sotheby's,
Chancery Lane) $45   £20

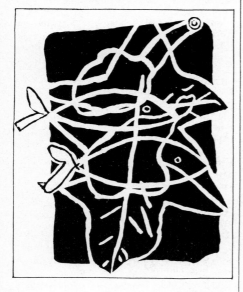

BRAQUE, GEORGES – CHAR, RENE

'Le Soleil des Eaux' – 4 etched plates, including coloured title by Georges Braque, unsewn in original wrappers, uncut, folder, slipcase – H. Matarasso, Paris, 1949.
(Sotheby's,
Chancery Lane) $740   £330

BRAQUE, GEORGES – GIEURRE, MAURICE

'G. Braque' – numerous plain and coloured reproductions, original cloth, coloured illustration on upper cover, slipcase – Editions Pierre Tisne, Paris, 1956.
(Sotheby's,
Chancery Lane) $18   £8

BRAQUE, GEORGES – PAULHAN, JEAN

'Les Paroles Transparentes' – 14 lithographs by Braque, 4 full page illustrations and 10 decorations on sub titles and upper cover, unsewn in original wrapper, uncut, folder, slipcase, folio – Bibliophiles de l'Union Francaise, Paris, 1955.
(Sotheby's,
Chancery Lane) $1,170   £520

BRAQUE, GEORGES – PONGE, FRANCIS AND MOURLOT, FERNAND

'Braque Lithographe' – lithographed frontispiece, title decoration, cover design by Braque, 153 reproductions, original wrappers, slipcase – Andre Sauret, Monte Carlo, 1963.
(Sotheby's,
Chancery Lane) $180   £80

BRAQUEMOND – ASSELINEAU, CHARLES

'Bibliographie Romantique' – 2nd Edn., etched frontispiece by Braquemond, original wrappers – P. Rouquette, Paris, 1872.
(Sotheby's,
Chancery Lane) $12   £5

BRASHER, REX
'Birds and Trees of North America' – 12
vols., no. 88 of an edition of 100, signed by
author on each title, 867 hand coloured
plates mounted on guards, contained in
half reversed pigskin loose leaf binders with
gilt lettering and bird design, oblong folio –
done in Chickadee Valley, near Kent,
Connecticut, 1929-32.
(Christie's
   St. James) $19,125   £8,500

BRASS HORNBOOK OF THE ALPHABET
Inscribed on reverse St. Pauls AD 1729 –
19th century.
(Lawrence of
   Crewkerne) $112   £50

BRASSINGTON, W. S.
'A History of Bookbinding' – plates, ori-
ginal cloth, 4to – 1894.
(Phillips) $270   £120

**BRAUN, GEORG AND HOGENBERG,
FRANZ**
'Contrafactur und Beschreibung von den
Vornembsten Stetten der Welt, Liber
Tertius' – vol. II only, text in German,
hand coloured engraved title, 51 hand
coloured engraved double page plates, detached and defective, 5 plates with tears,
cont. panelled calf, silver blocked cornerpieces and central arabesque, folio – G.
von Kempen, Cologne, 1582.
(Christie's
   St. James) $12,375   £5,500
'Civitatis Orbis Terrarium' – vol. II and
two only, of six in one vol., engraved
titles and 118 uncoloured plates, some
repaired or split, cont. German blindstamped pigskin over wooden boards,
metal clasps and cornerpieces, bevelled
edges, head of spine worn, folio –
Cologne and Antwerp, 1572-75.
(Sotheby's, New Bond
   Street) $21,375   £9,500

BRAY, MRS.
'Life of Thomas Stothard' – illustrations
extra illustrated by the insertion of c.
160 engravings etc., inlaid to size where
necessary and bound in, morocco, gilt,
n.d.
(Sotheby's, New Bond
   Street) $315   £140

BRAYLEY, E. W.
'A Topographical History of Surrey' – 5
vols., plates, cloth – 1850.
(Phillips) $125   £55

BREE, CHARLES ROBERT
'A History of the Birds of Europe' – 4
vols., 238 hand coloured engraved plates,
original red embossed cloth, gilt, spines
faded – 1863.
(Christie's
   St. James) $765   £340

BREHM, A. E.
'Merveilles de la nature' – 2 vols., plates
and illustrations, some foxing, red half
morocco, t.e.g. – Paris, 1880.
(Sotheby's
   Monaco) $855   £380

BRERELEY, JOHN
'The Protestants Apologie for the
Roman Church' – some headlines
cropped, title and last page soiled, cont.
calf, worn, upper cover loose – St. Omer,
English College Press, 1608.
(Sotheby's
   London) $68   £30

BRETON, ANDRE
'Le Surrealisme et la Peinture' – repro-
ductions, cloth – N.R.F., Paris, 1928.
(Sotheby's,
   Chancery Lane) $68   £30

BRETON DE LA MARTINIERE, J. B. J.
'China, Its Costume, Arts and Manu-
facturers' – 3 vols. of four only, 60
hand coloured plates, a few slightly smud-
ged, occasional slight soiling, later half
calf, head and foot of spines slightly
rubbed – 1818.
(Christie's S.
   Kensington) $225   £100
'Le Japon ou Moeurs, Usages et Costumes
des Habitans de cet Empire' – 4 vols., 51
engraved plates, 12 folded, half titles, some
torn, cont. mottled sheep backed boards,
spine gilt – Paris, 1818.
(Sotheby's, New Bond
   Street) $495   £220

BRETON, NICHOLAS
'The Twelve Moneths' – No. 450 of 500
copies, illustrations by Eric Ravillious,
original cloth, t.e.g., dust jacket – Golden
Cockerel Press, 1927.
(Christie's S.
   Kensington) $145   £65

BREYDENBACH, BERNARD VON
'Peregrinatio in Terram Sanctam' – 2nd
Latin Edn., 120 leaves, 52 lines, gothic
letter, woodcut frontispiece, large panoramas of Venice, partly mounted. Also
panoramas of Methone, Crete and Rhodes,
folding map of Palestine, 2 double page
views and illustrations in text, woodcut
oriental alphabets, late 18th century
boards, worn, folio – Peter Drach, Speier,
1490.
(Sotheby's, New Bond
    Street) $4,500   £2,000

BRIDGENS, R.
'Furniture with Candelabra and Interior
Decoration' – engraved title and 19 plates,
spotting, cont. cloth, affected by damp –
1838.
(Christie's S.
    Kensington) $80   £35

BRIGHAM, WILLIAM T.
'Ka Hana Kapa. The Making of Bark-cloth
in Hawaii' – 2 vols., including portfolio of
plates, some coloured, illustrations, original
wrappers and cloth, slightly torn –
Honolulu, 1911.
(Sotheby's,
    Chancery Lane) $475   £210

BRIGHT, RICHARD
'Reports of Medical Cases, selected with a
view of illustrating the Symptoms and Cure
of Diseases by a Reference to Morbid
Anatomy' – 16 fine coloured plates, half
title, library stamps on title, half morocco
– Richard Taylor for Longman, 1827.
(Sotheby's, New Bond
    Street) $900   £400

BRIGHTON, ROCK AND CO'S
'Pictorial Map of Brighton' – folding map
in original cloth with large engraved paper
label, 18¾ x 23½in. – 1851.
(Lawrence of
    Crewkerne) $34   £15

BRINDESI, J.
'Anciens Costumes Turcs de Constantinople'
– signed presentation copy, 22 hand coloured plates, some spotting and repairs,
cloth worn, folio – 1856.
(Phillips) $360   £160

BRISEUX, C. E.
'l'Art de Batir des Maisons de Campagne' –
2 vols., numerous engraved plates, cont.
calf, worn – Paris, 1743.
(Sotheby Parke Bernet
    Monaco) $45,000   £20,000

**BRISSAUD, PIERRE – BOYLESVE,
REME**
'Alcindor ou Suite a la Lecon d'Amour
dans un Parc' – vignette on title, 22
illustrations by Brissaud, coloured by
hand, small stain on one leaf, brown calf
blindstamped with floral centrepiece on
covers, inside borders gilt, marbled endpapers, original wrappers bound in, by
Rene Kieffer – Le Livre, Paris, 1920.
(Sotheby's,
    Chancery Lane) $135   £60

'BRITISH ISLES'
Hand coloured map – circa 1600.
(Phillips) $135   £60

**BRITISH MILITARY LIBRARY, THE
or JOURNAL**
2 vols., October 1798-September 1800, 13
coloured military costume plates, 35 maps
and plans, 13 folding leaves of music,
some maps slightly cropped, occasional
spotting, some tears, cont. red morocco,
gilt, worn, incomplete.
(Sotheby's, New Bond
    Street) $385   £170

BRITISH SPORTS AND SPORTSMEN
Plates and illus., limited edition, 11 vols.,
4to, morocco gilt, g.e., v.y. – n.d.
(Bonham's) $205 £90

BRITTEN, F. J.
'Old Clocks and Watches' – 2nd Edn., illus-
trations, original cloth, worn – 1904.
(Christie's S
  Kensington) $56 £25

BRITTEN, JAMES
'European Ferns' – coloured plates, half
calf, gilt, 4to – Cassell, n.d.
(Phillips) $108 £48

BRITTON, JOHN
'The Beauties of Wiltshire' – 3 vols.,
vignette titles, engraved plates, red morocco,
defective – 1801-25.
(Phillips) $135 £60
'Graphical and Literary Illustrations of
Fonthill Abbey' – large paper copy,
engraved title and 10 plates, 2 hand
coloured, subscribers' list, later half
morocco, rubbed – 1823.
(Sotheby's,
  Chancery Lane) $170 £75
'History and Description of Cassiobury
Park, Hertfordshire' – limited edition,
uncoloured copy, woodcut vignette on
title, 20 engraved plates, spotted, presentation inscription on title, cont. cloth
backed boards, large folio – Published by
author, 1837.
(Sotheby's, New Bond
  Street) $315 £140
**BRITTON, JOHN AND BRAYLEY,
EDWARD WEDLAKE**
'Devonshire and Cornwall Illustrated' –
2 parts in one vol., engraved titles printed
on India paper, torn, some loose, 1 coloured
and 69 steel engraved plates on India paper
with 138 views, slightly spotted and
soiled in places, dampstained, 19th century
half morocco, rubbed – 1829-31.
(Sotheby's, New Bond
  Street) $225 £100

BROCKEDON, WILLIAM
'Illustrations of the Passes of the Alps' –
2 vols., 108 engraved plates, 1 double page
map, some spotting, cont. half morocco,
rubbed – 1828-29.
(Sotheby's,
  Chancery Lane) $855 £380

'Road-Book from London to Naples' –
engraved title and 29 plates and maps. a
few small tears, rather soiled, original
cloth, rather worn, t.e.g. – 1835.
(Sotheby's,
  Chancery Lane) $85 £38

BRODIE, SIR BENJAMIN COLLINS
'Pathological and Surgical Observations
on Diseases of the Joints' – 1st Edn., 6
plates, 2 coloured, 4pp. advertisements,
original boards, rather worn, uncut –
Longman, 1818.
(Sotheby's, New Bond
  Street) $400 £180

BROMFIELD, WILLIAM
'Chirurgical Observations and Cases' – 2
vols., 18 folding plates, cont. calf – T.
Cadell, 1773.
(Sotheby's, New Bond
  Street) $205 £90

BRONTE, CHARLOTTE
'Poetry Past and Present' – inscription by
Charlotte Bronte dated 1849, with 4 line
quotation, green calf, gilt, g.e. – 1849.
(Phillips) $385 £170

BRONTE (SISTERS)
Novels – Thornton ed., 12 vols., portraits,
original cloth backs, slightly faded, 1898-
1901.
(Phillips) $112 £50

BROCK, A.
'Communion Tokens of Scotland' – plates,
wrappers bound in, half morocco, with
newspaper cuttings and pamphlets on
same subject – 1907.
(Tessa Bennett,
  Edinburgh) $45 £20

BROOKE, RALPHE
'A Catalogue and Succession of the Kings,
Princes . . . of this Realme' – title within
woodcut border, armorial woodcuts in
text, 4 leaves of errata at beginning, index
and errata leaf at end, outer edge of title
just browned, a few margins very slightly
dampstained, gilt bookplate of Lowther
Castle (Lonsdale), cont. calf, worn, folio
– William Jaggard, 1619.
(Sotheby's
  London) $67 £30

BROOKE

'A Discoverie of Certaine Errours Published in Print in the Much Commended Britannia, 1594 . . . to which are added the Learned Mr. Camden's Answer . . . and Mr. Brooke's Reply' – 2 parts in one vol., engraved portrait, browned, cont. calf, worn – 1724.
(Sotheby's, New Bond
    Street) $45   £20

BROOKE, RUPERT

'1914 and Other Poems' – 1st Edn., portrait, original cloth, uncut – 1915.
(Sotheby's,
    Chancery Lane) $108   £48
'The Old Vicarage, Grantchester' – inscribed by author's mother, woodcut by Noel Rooke, original wrappers, backstrip worn – 1916.
(Sotheby's,
    Chancery Lane) $108   £48

BROOKES, RICHARD M. D.

'The Art of Angling' – 4th Edn., engraved frontis by J. June, woodcuts of fish, ownership inscription on title, previous inscription deleted, causing slight perforation, frontis, just cropped, cont. sheep, slightly defective – For T. Lowndes, 1774.
(Sotheby's
    London) $225   £100

BROOKES, RICHARD

'The General Practice of Physic extracted chiefly from the Writings of the Most Celebrated Practical Physicians' – 2 vols., 1st Edn., cont. calf, rubbed – J. Newbery, 1751.
(Sotheby's, New Bond
    Street) $146   £65

BROUGHAM, HENRY

'An Enquiry into the Colonial Policy of the European Powers' – 2 vols., calf, rebacked – 1803.
(Phillips) $79   £35

BROWN, CORNELIUS

'The Annals of Newark upon Trent' – Woodbury type plates, verso of half title inscribed 'No. 48 Best Edition, Cornelius Brown', cont. dark green morocco, corners and joints rubbed, gilt inner dentelles, g.e. – London and Newark, 1879.
(Christie's S.
    Kensington) $68   £30

BROWN, HAROLD

'War With the Boers' – 5 vols., original pictorial cloth, a.e.g., titles in red and black, photographic illustrations – n.d.
(Lawrence of
    Crewkerne) $34   £15

BROWN, ISAAC BAKER

'On Some Diseases of Women Admitting of Surgical Treatment' – 9 plates, 8 coloured, woodcuts in text, advertisement leaves, original green cloth – Churchill, 1854.
(Sotheby's, New Bond
    Street) $68   £30

BROWN, J. H.

'Spectropia or Surprising Spectral Illusions Showing Ghosts Everywhere and of any Colour' – 16 lithographed plates coloured by hand, illustrations, original cloth backed pictorial boards, slightly soiled and rubbed – Griffith and Farran, 1866.
(Sotheby's,
    Chancery Lane) $100   £45

BROWN, JOHN AND CO., CLYDEBANK, SCOTLAND

Oblong folio album containing mounted photographs of their troopships, battleships, cruisers, steam yachts etc. and of the launching of the Lusitania – half morocco – circa 1900.
(Tessa Bennett,
    Edinburgh) $202   £90

BROWNE, JOHN

'Adenochoiradelogia: or, An Anatomick-Chirurgical Treatise of Glandules and Strumaes' – 3 parts in one vol., 1st Edn., engraved portrait, frontis, 2 licensing leaves before dedication, perforation in d7 barely affecting text, a few leaves slightly dampstained, bookplate of Hugh Cecil, Earl of Lonsdale, hinges weak, cont. sprinkled calf, spine gilt, just worn – 1684.
(Sotheby's
    London) $405   £180

BROWNE, JOSEPH

'Antidotaria or a Collection of Antidotes against the Plague and other Malignant Diseases' – half calf – J. Wilcox, 1721.
(Sotheby's, New Bond
    Street) $215   £95

'Institutions in Physick collected from the Writings of the most eminent Physicians' – 211 advertisements, cont. calf, spine gilt, Rolle bookplate – W. R. for Jonah Browne, 1714.
(Sotheby's, New Bond Street) $170 £75

BROWNE, RICHARD
'Medicina Musica or a Mechanical Essay on the Effects of Singing, Musick and Dancing on Human Bodies' – cont. calf – J. Cooke, 1729.
(Sotheby's, New Bond Street) $405 £180

BROWNE, SIR THOMAS
'Hydriotaphia, Urne Burial' – 1st Edn., engraved frontispiece, advert. leaf at end, water staining, 19th century roan backed boards, worn – 1658.
(Christie's, King St.) $180 £80
'A Letter to a Friend' – limited to 115 copies, original cloth backed boards – 1923.
(Christie's S. Kensington) $95 £42
'Pseudoxia Epidemica or Enquiries into very many received tenets and commonly presumed truths' – printed within double line border, cont. calf, second edition, folio – 1650.
(Sotheby's, New Bond Street) $205 £90
'The Works' – First collected edition, engraved portrait, 18th century half calf, very rubbed, folio – 1686.
(Sotheby's, New Bond Street) $68 £30

BROWNE, W. G.
'Nouveau Voyage dans La Haute et Basse Egypt en Syrie et dans le Dar-Four . . . 1792 jusqu'en 1798 . . . traduit par J. Castera' – 1st Edn., in French, folding engraved frontispiece, 3 engraved maps and plans, 2 folding, half titles, slight browning, modern calf, labels – Paris, 1800.
(Sotheby's, New Bond Street) $112 £50
'Travels in Africa, Egypt and Syria' – 1st Edn., 2 eng. plates, 2 folding maps, half title, title partly detached, cont. mottled calf, spine rubbed, hinges split – 1799.
(Sotheby's London) $125 £55

BROWNING, ROBERT
'Christmas Eve and Easter Day' – A Poem – 1st Edn., original cloth, extremities slightly rubbed – 1850.
(Christie's S. Kensington) $50 £22
'Pictor Ignotus, Fra Lippo Lippi, Andrea del Sarto' – no. 266 of 360 copies, original parchment backed boards – 1925.
(Christie's S. Kensington) $50 £22

BROWNLOW, JOHN
'The History and Design of the Foundling Hospital' – 1st Edn., engraved frontispiece portrait, 2 plates, original cloth – 1858.
(Sotheby's, New Bond Street) $27 £12

BRUCE, J. COLLINGWOOD
'The Roman Wall' – 3rd Edn., 45 plates, 2 folding maps, cont. half morocco, rubbed – 1867.
(Christie's S. Kensington) $68 £30

BRULLER, JEAN
'Releves Trimestriels' – Nos. 1-12 in one vol., 1 etched plate, 120 full page illustrations by Bruller, red cloth, slightly marked, original pictorial upper covers bound in – Paris, 1932-34.
(Sotheby's, Chancery Lane) $5 £2

BRUNELLESCHI, U.
'Contes du Temps Jadis' – 20 coloured plates, by Brunelleschi, original wrappers, soiled, spine chipped, uncut – l'Edition d'Art, Paris, 1912.
(Sotheby's, Chancery Lane) $56 £25

BRUNELLESCHI, U. – LAMARTINE, A. DE
'Graziella' – 27 illustrations, 4 full page, coloured through stencils, original wrappers, upper hinge loose – l'Editions d'Art, Paris, 1931.
(Sotheby's, Chancery Lane) $124 £55

BRUNELLESCHI, U. – MUSSET, ALFRED DE
'La Nuit Venitienne, Fantasio, les Caprices de Marianne' – 20 coloured plates and illustrations in text by Brunelleschi, book label on half title, original decorated wrappers, uncut – Paris, 1913.
(Sotheby's, Chancery Lane) $118 £52

BRUNELLESCHI

BRUNELLESCHI, U. – HERMANT, ABEL
'Phili' – 12 plates and numerous illustrations after Brunelleschi, coloured by hand,
slightly offset, unsewn in original wrappers,
uncut, morocco backed box, slipcase, no.
71 of 275 – edition de la Guirlande, 1921.
(Sotheby's,
   Chancery Lane)   **$700**   **£310**

**BRUNELLESCHI, U. – MUSSET,
ALFRED DE**
'La Nuit Venetienne' – 20 coloured plates
and pictorial head pieces in text by
Brunelleschi, blue morocco gilt, t.e.g.
original wrappers bound in – H. Piazza,
Paris, 1913.
(Sotheby's,
   Chancery Lane)   **$360**   **£160**

BRUNET, J.
'Manuel du Librairie' – 8 vols., anastatic
reprints, worn half leather – Paris, circa
1930.
(Sotheby Parke Bernet
   Monaco)   **$2,025**   **£900**

BRUSSEL, ROBERT
'Tamar Karsavina ou l'Heure Dansante au
Jardin du Roi' – limited to 500 copies on
Hollande, five brown and white illustra-
tions by Gir, original printed wrappers,
slightly torn and soiled, uncut – Paris.
circa 1910.
(Sotheby's, New Bond
   Street)   **$270**   **£120**

BRYAN
'Bryan's Dictionary of Painters and
Engravers' – edited by G. C. Williamson –
5 vols., cloth, buckram backs – 1925.
(Bonham's)   **$160**   **£70**

BRYANT, WILLIAM CULLEN (Editor)
'Picturesque America or the Land We Live
In' – 2 vols., large original morocco gilt,
engraved titles, 47 tissued steel engraved
plates – New York, 1872-74.
(Lawrence of
   Crewkerne)   **$200**   **£90**

BRYDEN, R.
'Etchings of Ayrshire Castles' – etched
titles and plates, quarter reversed calf,
limited edition 50 copies, signed by artist,
presentation copy, folio – 1889.
(Tessa Bennett,
   Edinburgh)   **$90**   **£40**

BUCHAN, JOHN
'The Watcher by the Threshold' – original
printed cloth, 1st Edn., – 1902.
(Tessa Bennett,
   Edinburgh)   **$22**   **£10**
'Scholar Gypsies' – etched title and
plates by D. Y. Cameron, original cloth
backed buckram – 1896.
(Christie's S.
   Kensington)   **$45**   **£20**

BUCHAN, P.
'Annals of Peterhead' – half morocco,
folding frontispiece and plates – Peterhead,
1819.
(Tessa Bennett,
   Edinburgh)   **$100**   **£44**

BUCHAN, WILLIAM
'Domestic Medicine or the Family Physician' – 1st Edn., name written on title page, cont. calf, rubbed – Balfour, Auld and Smellie, Edinburgh, 1769.
(Sotheby's, New Bond
   Street) $405   £180
'Advice to Mothers on the Subject of their own Health' – cont. tree calf – T. Cadell and W. Davies, 1803.
(Sotheby's, New Bond
   Street) $225   £100
'Some Friendly Cautions to the Heads of Families' – title laid down, some dampstains, cloth, uncut – John Rice, Dublin, 1791.
(Sotheby's, New Bond
   Street) $112   £50

BUCHANAN, ROBERT
'Comprehensive Atlas of Modern Geography' – 30 engraved hand coloured maps, original half leather – Edinburgh, 1829.
(Tessa Bennett,
   Edinburgh) $90   £40

BUCK, GEORGE
'The History of Richard the Third' – engraved portrait, cont. morocco, rubbed – 1646.
(Christie's S.
   Kensington) $68   £30

BUCKINGHAM, GEORGE VILLIERS, DUKE OF
'The Rehearsal, As it is now Acted at the Theatre Royal' – 3rd Edn., browned, wrappers, worn – Printed for Thomas Dring, 1675.
(Christie's S.
   Kensington) $100   £45

BUCKLAND, REV. WILLIAM
'Reliquiae Diluvianae' – 1st Edn., 27 eng. and lithoed plates and maps, 1 folding, 3 hand coloured, folding printed table, signature of Sarah Tyrconnel on title – 1823.
(Sotheby's
   London) $170   £75

BUDGEN, L. M.
'Acheta Domestica' – Episodes of Insect Life – 3 cols., hand coloured frontispiece and vignettes, occasional slight spotting, cont. half morocco, slightly rubbed – 1849-51.
(Christie's S.
   Kensington) $100   £45

BUFFET, BERNARD – MOURLOT, FERNAND
'Bernard Buffet, Oeuvre Grave' – 1952-56 – 11 coloured lithographs, including frontispiece and cover design, 66 reproductions, majority coloured, original wrappers – A. C. Mazo, Paris, 1967.
(Sotheby's,
   Chancery Lane) $56   £25

BUFFON, G. COMTE DE
'Oeuvres . . . annotees par M. Flourens' – 12 vols., hand coloured engraved plates, morocco backed boards, rubbed – Paris, circa 1850.
(Sotheby's
   Monaco) $2,925   £1,300
'A Natural History, General and Particular . . . translated . . by William Smellie' – 2 vols., hand coloured eng. plates, cont. half calf, soiled – 1866.
(Christie's S.
   Kensington) $110   £48

'Histoire Naturelle des Oiseaux' – 10 vols., 973 fine coloured plates of birds by Martinet without the 35 insect plates which are occasionally found, cont. French red morocco, gilt, g.e. – Paris, 1770-86.
(Sotheby Parke Bernet
   Monaco) $540,000 £240,000

BUILDERS' PRACTICAL DIRECTORY, THE
Coloured frontis, coloured plates, half morocco gilt, 4to — circa 1850.
(Phillips) $135   £60

BULLETIN de l'Effort Moderne' — Directeur Leonce Rosenberg — 25 vols. various, plates, some browning, original wrappers, slightly soiled — 1924-7.
(Christie's S.
Kensington) $720   £320

BULLMAN, E.
'The Medical Directory or Family Physician' — 2nd Edn., index and advertisement leaf at end, sprinkled calf — Canterbury, 1810.
(Sotheby's, New Bond
Street) $72   £32

BULLOCK, H. A.
'History of the Isle of Man' — 1st Edn., subscriptions list, engraved frontis, outer margin just cropped, engraved folding map, cont. half calf, very slightly rubbed — 1816.
(Sotheby's
London) $135   £60

BUMCHER, RICHARD
'Tretchikoff' — no. 1,143 of 1,500 copies signed by the artist, plates, some mounted and coloured, original binding, folio — Capetown, 1953.
(Christie's S.
Kensington) $56   £25

BUMPUS, JOHN
'A New Plan of London and its Environs' — engraved map with a little hand colouring, 16¼ x 30in., folding, mounted on cloth, slipcase — 1827.
(Christie's S.
Kensington) $63   £28

BUNBURY, HENRY WILLIAM 'GEOFFREY GAMBADO'
'An Academy for Grown Horsemen' — original boards rubbed and worn, frontispiece portrait roughly attached, 11 other plates by Dickinson after Bunbury — 1787.
(Lawrence of
Crewkerne) $68   £30

BUNWORTH, RICHARD
'A New Discovery of the French Disease' — 2nd Edn., corrected with large additions, cont. calf, rather worn — Henry Marsh, 1662.
(Sotheby's, New Bond
Street) $790   £350

BUNYAN, JOHN
'The Acceptable Sacrifice' — 4th Edn., browned and soiled, torn and holed, some loss of text, cont. sheep, worn — 1702.
(Sotheby's, New Bond
Street) $112   £50
'Der heilige Krieg . . . ubersetzet von J.L.M. C.' — title printed in red and black, additional eng. title, gothic letter, browned and soiled, cont. roan, worn — Hamburg, 1715.
(Sotheby's
London) $180   £80

BURBRIDGE, F. W. AND BAKER J. G.
'The Narcissus: its History and Culture' — 48 coloured lithographed plates, original cloth, faded — 1875.
(Christie's S.
Kensington) $450   £200

BURCKHARDT, JOHN LEWIS
'Travels in Nubia' — 1st Edn., eng. portrait, 3 eng. maps, 2 folding, half title, lacks advert leaf at end, maps very slightly spotted, signature of Sarah Tyrconnel on title — 1819.
(Sotheby's
London) $170   £75

BURGHLEY, W.
'A Collection of State Papers' — cont. calf, folio — W. Bowyer, London, 1740.
(Tessa Bennett,
Edinburgh) $23   £10

BURGUNDIA, ANTONIUS A.
'Mundi Lapis Lydius sive Vanitas per Veritate Falsi Accusata et Convicta' — 1st Edn., engraved title page by Theodore Ion van Merlen after A. van Diepenbeeck, 50 emblematic engravings in text, slightly spotted, some tears mostly repaired, 19th century boards, rubbed — Antwerp, 1639.
(Sotheby's, New Bond
Street) $450   £200

BURKE, E.
'An Account of European Settlements
in America' – 2 vols., 2 folding maps,
staining, calf gilt, worn, upper cover of
vol. 1 detached, 8vo – 1760.
(Phillips) $45 £20
'A Philosophical Enquiry into . . . the
Sublime and the Beautiful' – half title,
old calf, worn – 1757.
(Phillips) $385 £170

**BURKE, ROBERT O'HARA AND
WILLS, W. J.**
'The Burke and Wills Exploring Expedition;
an Account of the Crossing of Australia
with Biographical Sketches of Robert
O'Hara and William John Wills' –
Melbourne, 1861.
(Sotheby's, New Bond
Street) $495 £220

BURNES, ALEXANDER
'Travels into Bokhara' – 3 vols., 1st Edn., 5
eng. and 3 lithoed plates, one double page,
the former spotted, without the separately
published map as usual, lacks half titles and
last leaf in Vol. II – 1894.
(Sotheby's
London) $205 £90

BURNET, BISHOP GILBERT
'The History of the Reformation of the
Church of England' – 2 vols., 2nd Edn., 16
portraits, half titles, printed titles in red
and black, worming, 18th century panelled
calf, split, worn, folio – 1781-83.
(Sotheby's, New Bond
Street) $23 £10
'The Memoires of . . . James and William
Dukes of Hamilton and Castleherald' –
eng. portrait, later calf, rebacked, joints
cracked, folio – J. Grover for R. Royston,
1677.
(Christie's S.
Kensington) $68 £30

BURNET, THOMAS
'The Theory of the Earth' – the last two
books, separate title to last book and to
final 'Review', foxing, cont. calf, spine a
little chipped, g.e.g., bookplate of William
Norcliffe, folio – 1690.
(Christie's, King
St.) $112 £50

BURNS, J.
'Observations on Abortion' – modern
boards – 1806.
(Bonham's) $45 £20

BURNS, ROBERT
'Poems Chiefly in the Scottish Dialect' –
2nd, 1st Edinburgh Edn., faded portrait,
light browning and offsetting, early 19th
century half calf, worn – Edinburgh, 1787.
(Sotheby's, New Bond
Street) $315 £140
'Songs' – Selected by A. E. Coppard – no.
399 of 450 copies, illustrations by M. M.
Annesley, original cloth backed boards,
slightly rubbed – Golden Cockerel Press,
1925.
(Christie's S.
Kensington) $72 £32
'Tam O'Shanter A tale in verse' – illustra-
ted by George Cruikshank, coloured
plates and illustrations, decorated cloth,
4to – 1884.
(Tessa Bennett,
Edinburgh) $20 £9

**BURNS, ROBERT AND BLATHERWICK,
CHARLES**
'Twenty Five Sketches illustrating the
Songs of Burns' – 25 mounted water-
colour sketches by Blatherwick, weight
approximately 50lb.
(Tessa Bennett,
Edinburgh) $1,125 £500

BURTON, ISABEL
'Life of Captain Sir Richard Burton' –
2 vols., original cloth gilt – 1893.
(Phillips) $68 £30

BURTON, JOHN
'An Essay Towards A Complete New
System of Midwifery' – 18 engraved plates,
all but one folding, upper margins of a
few slightly shaved – 1751.
(Christie's S.
Kensington) $360 £160
'An Essay Towards A Complete New
System of Midwifery' – 1st Edn., 18 plates,
all except one folding – James Hodges,
1751.
(Sotheby's, New Bond
Street) $1,238 £550

BURTON, RICHARD F. (Translator)
'The Book of a Thousand Nights and a
Night' – 17 vols., including 7 vols.
'Supplemental Nights', no. 260 of 1,000
copies, plates, original cloth, some spines
slightly rubbed – Printed by the Burton
Club, n.d.
(Christie's S.
Kensington) $108 £48

BURTON

'Personal Narrative of a Pilgrimage to El-Medinah and Meccah' – 3 vols., 1st Edn., 14 plates, all but one lithographed – 1855-56.
(Christie's S.
  Kensington) $270   £120

BURTON, ROBERT
'The Anatomy of Melancholy' – 2 vols., limited edition, illustrated by E. McKnight Kauffer, original parchment backed boards, slightly marked, uncut, folio – Nonesuch Press, 1925.
(Sotheby's
  Monaco) $1,015   £450

BURTON, WILLIAM
'A General History of Porcelain' – 2 vols., plates, some coloured, cloth gilt – 1921.
(Phillips) $68   £30
'The Description of Leicestershire' – 2nd Edn., folding engraved map and 2 plates, subscribers' list, cont. half calf, slightly rubbed – Lynn, 1777.
(Sotheby's,
  Chancery Lane) $225   £100

BURY, LADY CHARLOTTE
'The Three Great Sanctuaries of Tuscany' – engraved title, 6 aqua plates, original cloth, 4to – 1833.
(Phillips) $95   £42

BURY, THOMAS TALBOT
'Coloured Views on the Liverpool and Manchester Railway' – 13 hand coloured plates – R. Ackerman, 1831.
(Christie's S.
  Kensington) $3,825   £1,700

BUSBEGUIUS, A. G.
'Travels into Turkey' – some spotting, cont. calf, spine bumped – 1744.
(Christie's S.
  Kensington) $112   £50

BUSHBY, MRS. (Translator)
'The Ice Maiden' by Hans Christian Andersen – 1st English Edn., wood engraved illustrations by Pearson after Zwecker, slightly rubbed, g.e. – Richard Bentley, 1863.
(Sotheby's,
  Chancery Lane) $45   £20

BUSSEMECHER, J.
'Europae Totius Orbis Terrarum Partis Praestantissimae ... Descriptio' – engraved architectural title, portrait on verso, 65 double page engraved map of 66, coloured by cont. hand, some maps torn or folded – Cologne, 1594-96.
(Sotheby's, New Bond
  Street) $9,450   £4,200

Europae Totius Orbis Partis Praestantissimae ..... Descriptio by J. Bussemecher. (Sotheby's)

BUSSIERE, GASTON — FLAUBERT, GUSTAVE
'La Legende de Saint Julien l'Hospitallier' — etched frontispiece, 5 plates and 16 illustrations, dark green half morocco, t.e.g., original wrappers bound in — Paris, 1912.
(Sotheby's,
Chancery Lane) $56   £25

BUTLER, A. G.
'British Birds' — 6 vols., illustrated by Frohawk, cloth gilt, g.e., 4to — 1896-99.
(Phillips) $64   £28
'Birds of Great Britain and Ireland, Order Passeres' — 2 vols., 115 coloured plates by F. W. Frohawk and H. Gronvold, occasional slight spotting — 1904-08.
(Christie's S.
Kensington) $248   £110
'Foreign Finches in Captivity' — 2nd Edn., 60 coloured plates by F. W. Frohawk — Hull and London, 1889.
(Christie's S.
Kensington) $180   £80

BUTLER, CHARLES
'The Feminin' Monarchi' or the Histori of Bee's' — 3rd Edn., 1st Edn. in Butler's phonetic spelling — Oxford, 1634.
(Sotheby's, New Bond
Street) $540   £240

BUTLER, JOSEPH
'The Analogy of Religion, Natural and Revealed' — 1st Edn., half title soiled, marginal waterstaining, cont. calf, rebacked, old spine preserved, rubbed — 1736.
(Sotheby's
London) $12   £5

BUTLER, S.
'Atlas of Ancient Georgraphy' — 21 maps, coloured in outline, half morocco gilt — 1829.
(Phillips) $85   £38

BUTLER, SAMUEL
'Records and Memorials' — 1st Edn., portrait, original wrappers, upper cover worn, lacking lower wrapper — Cambridge for Private Circulation, 1903.
(Sotheby's,
Chancery Lane) $5   £2

'Seven Sonnets and a Psalm of Montreal' — 1st Edn., original wrappers, detached and discoloured — Cambridge for Private Circulation, 1904.
(Sotheby's,
Chancery Lane) $112   £50

BUXTON, SIR THOMAS FOWELL
'An Enquiry Whether Crime and Misery are Produced or Prevented by our Present System of Prison Discipline' — 1st Edn., original boards and paper label, uncut, worn — 1818.
(Sotheby's, New Bond
Street) $270   £120

BUXTORF, JOHANNES THE ELDER
'Institutio Epistolaris Hebraica' — 2nd Edn., Hebrew and Latin, a model letter book including specimen letters from Maimonides, staining, original vellum — L. Konig, Basle, 1629.
(Sotheby's, New Bond
Street) $190   £85

BYNG, ADMIRAL JOHN
'The Trial of the Honourable Admiral John Byng at a Court Martial as Taken by Mr. Charles Fearne' — engraved plate mounted as frontispiece detached, cloth backed boards, folio — 1757.
(Christie's
St. James) $158   £70

BYROM, JOHN
'The Universal English Short-Hand' — 1st Edn., engraved plates, ownership inscription on title, cont. calf gilt, neatly rebacked, corners rubbed — Manchester, 1767.
(Sotheby's
London) $45   £20

BYRON, LORD GEORGE GORDON NOEL
'Manfred, a Dramatic Poem' — 1st Edn., 3rd issue, half title, dampstained, original drab wrappers, slightly worn — 1817.
(Sotheby's, New Bond
Street) $36   £16
'The Drawing Room Edition of Poetical Works' — 2 vols. in six, 2 engraved additional titles and 72 plates.
(Christie's S.
Kensington) $135   £60
'The Prisoner of Chillon' — chromolithographed text by W. R. Tymms after W. and G. Audsley — 1865.
(Christie's S.
Kensington) $40   £18

CABELL, J. B.
'Jurgen' — No. 477 of 500 copies, frontispiece and full page illustrations by John Buckland-Wright, original cloth — 1949.
(Christie's S.
Kensington) $158 £70

CABINET MAKER'S ASSISTANT, THE
Engraved additional title and plates, dampstains, cont. half calf, worn, folio — Blackie, 1853.
(Christie's S.
Kensington) $180 £80

CADPRYN-ROBERTS, J.
'British Sporting Prints' — 11 plates, folio — 1955.
(Phillips) $72 £32

CAESAR, CAIUS JULIUS
'De Bello Gallico Commentarii VII . . . cum scholis Franc. Hotomani . . . Ful. Ursini . . . Ald. Manutii' — 2 parts in one vol., woodcut device on title, 11 woodcuts, soiled and dampstained — Bartholomaeus Vicentius, Paris, 1574.
(Sotheby's, New Bond
Street) $180 £80
'Rerum ab se gestarum commentarii' — woodcuts including 2 maps, small wormhole in upper margin, upper hinge weak,— folio — Paris, Michael Vascosan, 1543.
(Sotheby's
London) $293 £130

CAETANI, MAGUERITE (Editor)
'Botteghe Oscure' — Nos. 1-23 in English, French and Italian, original wrappers, last six in dust jackets — Rome, 1949-59.
(Sotheby's,
Chancery Lane) $293 £130

CAHUN, CLAUDE
'Aveux Non Avenus' — 10 plates by Moore, original wrappers, spine slightly discoloured, unopened — Paris, 1930.
(Sotheby's,
Chancery Lane) $27 £12

CAHUSAC, LOUIS DE
'La Danse Ancienne et Moderne ou Traite Historique de la Danse' — 3 vols. in one, 1st Edn. Modern beige morocco by Fox of Los Angeles — Chez Jean Neaulme, the Hague, 1754.
(Sotheby's, New Bond
Street) $225 £100

CAILLER, PIERRE AND DAREL, HENRI
'Catalogue Illustre de l'Oeuvre grave et Lithographie de Maurice Barraud' — No. 67 of 1,065 copies — Geneva, 1944.
(Christie's S.
Kensington) $72 £32

CAIUS, JOHN
'The Works with a memoir of his life by John Venn' — edited by E. S. Roberts, portrait, plates, original buckram, t.e.g. — Cambridge, 1912.
(Sotheby's, New Bond
Street) $54 £24

CALBET, ANTOINE — LOUYS, PIERRE
20 coloured plates, headpieces and decorations on text by Calbet, slipcase, by G. Mercier — Albin Michel, Paris, 1923.
(Sotheby's,
Chancery Lane) $113 £50

CALBET, ANTOINE — NERCIAT, ANDREA DE
'Felicia ou mes Fredaines' — 17 coloured plates and 4 illustrations by Calbet, original wrappers, uncut, slipcase — Le Vasseur, Paris, 1933.
(Sotheby's,
Chancery Lane) $90 £40

CALDECOTT, RANDOLPH
'Graphic Pictures' — illustrated, original cloth gilt, worn, g.e., folio — 1891.
(Phillips) $86 £38
'Picture Books' — complete set, 16 vols., coloured illustrations, original wrappers, box — Routledge, n.d.
(Phillips) $158 £70

CALDER, ALEXANDER – AESOP
'Fables', Edited by Sir Roger l'Estrange,
50 illustrations by Calder – Paris, 1931.
(Sotheby's,
Chancery Lane) $90   £40

CALDERON, V. G.
'Lottery Ticket' – No. 341 of 400 copies,
frontispiece and full page illustrations by
Dorothea Braby, original cloth, soiled –
1946.
(Christie's S.
Kensington) $40   £18

CALEMARD, N.
'Abrege d'Astronomie' – half morocco,
slightly rubbed – London, 1801.
(Christie's. S.
Kensington) $40   £18

CALLAWAY, REV. HENRY
'The Religious System of the Amazulu . . .
in their own words' – 3 parts, stitched as
issued in original printed paper wrappers –
Natal, Capetown and London, 1868-70.
(Christie's
St. James) $326   £45

CALLIGRAPH MANUSCRIPT
'A Shew of Writing' written by Joseph
Hockaday of Hatherleigh in Devonshire,
June 4th, Anno Domini, 1731.
(Lawrence of
Crewkerne) $180   £80

CALLIS, ROBERT
'The Reading of Robert Callis upon the
Statute of Sewers' – 1st Edn., cont. notes
in ink on flyleaf – 1647.
(Christie's, King
St.) $101   £45

CALLOT, JACOMO
'Balli de Stessania' – engraved title and
23 engraved plates of the actors in the
'Commedia del Arte'. Title by Israel
Sylvestre after Callot – Paris, circa 1820.
(Sotheby's, New Bond
Street) $85   £38

CALVI, FRANCOIS DE
'Histoire Generale des Larrons Divisee en
Trois Livres' – separate titles for parts
2 and 3, slight foxing, cont. limp vellum,
soiled – Paris, 1639.
(Christie's, King
St.) $90   £40

CALVIN, JOHN
'The Institution of Christian Religion' –
translated by T. Norton, woodcut device
on title, worm hole, calf rebacked – A.
Hatfield, 1599.
(Phillips) $95   £42
'The Sermons' – translated out of French
into English by Arthur Golding – 1st
English Edn., woodcut initials, some
tearing, cont. calf, ties missing, worn – for
Lucas Harrison and George Byshop, 1577.
(Sotheby's, New Bond
Street) $146   £65

**CAMBRIDGE JOURNAL, THE
AND WEEKLY FLYING POST**
Nos. 44-110, lacking 72. Some browning,
staining and cropping, cont. half calf,
rubbed, folio – Cambridge, 1745/6.
(Sotheby's, New Bond
Street) $450   £200

CAMBRIDGE MODERN HISTORY, THE
Ed. Lord Acton, 14 vols., including atlas,
half calf worn – 1907-12.
(Phillips) $36   £16

CAMDEN, WILLIAM
'Britannia, New Translated into English' –
plates, 49 double page maps only, some
shaved or torn, lacking the map of Norfolk,
folio – Printed by F. Collins, for A. Salle
and A. J. Churchill, 1695.
(Christie's S.
Kensington) $1,530   £680
'Remaines Concerning Britaine' – some
water staining, 19th century half calf,
slightly worn – John Legatt for Simon
Waterson, 1614.
(Sotheby's, New Bond
Street) $50   £22

CAMERARIUS, JOACHIMUS
'Commentatio Explicationum omnium
Tragoediarum Sophoclis' – title page
browned, light staining at end, tear in fore
margins of N1-4, 18th century vellum
boards, label defective – Basel, J. Oporinus,
1556.
(Sotheby's
London) $68   £30

**CAMPAIGNS OF THE DUKE OF
WELLINGTON** – engraved portrait and
24 plates by Duplessi Bertaux after
Martinet, foxed, cont. red straight
grained morocco – Paris, 1817.
(Sotheby's, New Bond
Street) $180   £80

CAMPANELLA, THOMAS
'A Discourse Touching the Spanish
Monarchy' — 1st Edn. in English, some
browning and soiling — 1654.
(Sotheby's
 London) $72 £32

CAMPBELL, SIR ARCHIBALD
'Records of Argyll' — etched frontispiece
and plates, cloth gilt, limited edition no.
198 — 1885.
(Tessa Bennett,
 Edinburgh) $72 £32

CAMPBELL, COLEN
'Vitruvius Britannicus' — vol. 2 only,
engraved title and 65 plates, some tears
repaired, modern morocco, folio, 1717.
(Christie's S.
 Kensington) $180 £80

CAMPBELL, IRONS, J.
'Leith and Its Antiquities' — 2 vols., plates,
buckram gilt, printed for subscribers —
Edinburgh, n.d.
(Tessa Bennett,
 Edinburgh) $40 £18

CANADA RAILWAY NEWS CO.
'All Round Route and Panoramic View of
the St. Lawrence' — long folding panorama,
maps and illustrations and adverts, original
printed wrappers — 1881.
(Tessa Bennett,
 Edinburgh) $45 £20

CAMPE, J. H.
'Robinson der Jungere' — 3rd Edn., etched
frontispiece, cont. calf backed boards,
slightly worn — Wolfenbuttel, 1786.
(Sotheby's, Hodgson's
 Rooms) $55 £25

CANNON, R.
'Historical Records of the British Army' —
the First or Royal Regiment of Foot —
engraved title and 3 hand coloured plates —
circa 1836.
(Tessa Bennett,
 Edinburgh) $36 £16

CANTERBURY, DEAN OF
'The Riviera' — 12 coloured plates, illus.,
original cloth, rubbed, g.e. — 1870.
(Sotheby Humberts
 Taunton) $135 £60

CANTERBURY, DIOCESE OF
'Register — Mss. on Vellum' — Calendar
of saints' days, lists of churches and
tithes, one large initial with arms of
Cardinal Thomas Bouchier, 19th century
vellum — Canterbury, circa 1454-86.
(Christie's, King
 St.) $2,925 £1,300

CAPELLA, GALEAZZO
'l'Anthropologia' — 1st Edn., anchor device
on title, 18th century calf backed boards,
gilt spine, wormed — Aldus, Venice, 1533.
(Sotheby's, New Bond
 Street) $400 £180

CAPELLA, MARTIANUS MINNEUS FELIX
'De Nuptiis Philologiae et Mercurii' — 100
leaves, 42 lines and headline, roman letter,
woodcut device at end, worming, 18th century Italian half calf, very rubbed, 16th
century signature of Francesco Camerano
and his library stamp, folio — Modena,
1500.
(Sotheby's, New Bond
 Street) $1,240 £550

CAPPER, BENJAMIN PITTS
'A Topographical Dictionary of the United
Kingdom' — 46 hand coloured engraved
maps — 1808.
(Sotheby's
 London) $160 £70

CAPPER, JAMES
'Observations on the Passage to India' – 3rd
Edn., folding engraved plate and 3 maps,
cont. diced, spine rubbed – 1785.
(Christie's S.
   Kensington) $135   £60

CARBON, DAMIAN
'Libro Del Arte Delas Comadres O
Madrinas Y Del Regimento Delas Prenadas
Y Paridas Y Delos Ninos' – title printed
in red and black with fine woodcut
border, cont. limp vellum – 1541.
(Bonham's) $29,250   £13,000

CARERI, G.
'Giro del Mondo' – 6 vols., 3 frontispieces,
45 plates, Philippines, America, Persia, etc.,
calf – Napoli, 1699-1700.
(Phillips) $340   £150

CAREW, THOMAS
'A Rapture' – No. 370 of 375 copies, plates
by J. E. Laboureur, original cloth backed
boards, dust jacket soiled – 1927.
(Christie's S.
   Kensington) $50   £22

CAREY, HENRY
'Songs and Poems' – No. 26 of 300 copies,
signed by artist, illustrations by Robert
Gibbings, musical songs, original vellum,
bookplate of Kelly College – 1924.
(Christie's S.
   Kensington) $95   £42

CARION, JOHN
'The Three Bokes of Cronicles whyche
John Carion (A man singularly well sene
in the mathematicall sciences) Gathered –
added an appendix by John Funcke of
Nurenborough' – 1st Edn. in English,
19th century half calf – and another,
folio – 1550.
(Christie's, King
   St.) $225   £100

**CARLEGLE, EMILE CHARLES –
COLETTE, SIDONIE GABRIELLE**
'Nudite' – 1st Edn., 20 illustrations
by Carlegle, original wrappers, uncut,
unopened – Mappemonde, Paris, 1942.
(Sotheby's,
   Chancery Lane) $50   £22

CARNE, J.
'Syria, The Holy Land and Asia Minor' –
73 plates, 1st and 2nd series in one vol.,
morocco, g.e., rubbed – Virtue, n.d.
(Phillips) $95   £42

CARNELL, P. P.
'A Treatise on Family Wine Making' –
occasional slight spotting, original boards,
backstrip torn with loss – 1814.
(Christie's S.
   Kensington) $95   £42

**CARON, FRANCOIS AND SCHOUTEN,
JOOST**
'A True Description of the Mighty King-
doms of Japan and Siam' – no. 21 of 475
copies, plates and maps, original vellum
backed cloth, gilt – 1935.
(Sotheby's,
   Chancery Lane) $115   £50

CARON, JOHANNES
'Carmina Tumultuaria' – 1st Edn., 12
leaves, 37 and 22 lines, gothic letter,
woodcut device within border on title
page, 19th century half calf, worn –
Felix Baligault, Paris, 1496/97.
(Sotheby's, New Bond
   Street) $1,465   £650

CARR, JOHN
'The Stranger in Ireland' – 1st Edn., 16
sepia aquatints, 5 folding, 1 hand coloured
engraved plan, 2 plates partly detached,
original boards, uncut, spine worn, upper
cover detached – 1806.
(Sotheby's
   London) $360   £160

CARRUTHERS, R.
'The Highland Notebook' – cloth –
Edinburgh, 1843.
(Tessa Bennett,
Edinburgh) $28   £12

CARTARI, VINCENZO
'Le Imagini de i Dei de gli Antichi' – woodcut device on title, 87 engraved plates of
88, some in sepia, some shaved, holed,
foxed, cont. limp vellum, stained, spine
damaged – Venice, 1587.
(Christie's, King
St.) $145   £65

CARTE GENERAL DE LA MER ROUGE
11 sea charts, boards, folio – circa 1790.
(Phillips) $180   £80

CARTER, JOHN
'The Ancient Architecture of England' –
2 parts in one vol., 2 engraved titles,
engraved plates, half roan defective, folio
dated 1806.
(Phillips) $55   £25

CARTER, MATTHEW
'Honor Redivivus or An Analysis of Honor
and Armory' – 2nd Edn., engraved title
by R. Gatwood, frontis, armorial woodcuts
in text, lacks front free end paper, cont.
calf, both covers partly detached – For
Henry Herringman, 1660.
(Sotheby's
London) $45   £20

CARTWRIGHT, WILLIAM
'Comedies, Tragi Comedies with Other
Poems' – 1st Edn., engraved portrait by
Lombart, some staining, worming, old
mottled calf, gilt, worn, g.e., ownership
inscription of Mary Kemeys, 1670 on fly
leaf, 8vo – 1651.
(Sotheby's, New Bond
Street) $180   £80

CARUSO, ENRICO
The picture postcard collection formed by
Enrico Caruso and his mistress Ada
Giachetti comprising over 650 postcards,
contained in a box and 2 albums – circa
1899-1902.
(Sotheby's, New Bond
Street) $4,500   £2,000

CARY, J.
'Map of Surrey' – hand coloured double
page folio map and 18th century map of
Faringdon Ward, London.
(Tessa Bennett,
Edinburgh) $28   £12
'Middlesex' – hand coloured map – 1787.
(Tessa Bennett,
Edinburgh) $36   £16
'Actual Survey of the Country Round
London' – engraved title, explanation leaf,
51 hand coloured maps, one folding,
occasional browning, cont. speckled calf
– 1786.
(Christie's S.
Kensington) $400   £180
'Travellers Companion Pocket Atlas' –
42 maps coloured in outline on 22 sheets,
large folding map, half covers detached –
1791.
(Phillips) $85   £38

CARY, JOYCE
'The Horse's Mouth' – lithographed self
portrait, plates, original parchment backed
boards – 1957.
(Sotheby's,
Chancery Lane) $50   £22

CASANOVA, GIANCOMO
'Memoirs' – 12 vols., no. 244 of 1,000
copies, frontis, original parchment backed
boards, slightly rubbed, 4to. – n.d.
(Sotheby Humberts
Taunton) $14   £6

CASEMENT, ROGER
'Some Poems' – 1st Edn., portrait frontis-
piece, original wrappers, slipcase – Talbot
Press, Dublin, 1918.
(Sotheby's,
Chancery Lane) $45   £20

**CASSANDRE, A. M. – JOUVE, PIERRE
JEAN**
'Decor de Don Juan' – 20 plates by
Cassandre, 17 coloured, one double
page, unsewn in original wrappers, slip-
case – Kister, Geneva, 1957.
(Sotheby's,
Chancery Lane) $140   £62

CASSES, LOUIS FRANCOIS
'Voyage Pittoresque de la Syrie' – 2 vols.,
180 engraved plates, later half calf –
Paris, 1799.
(Christie's S.
Kensington) $3,265   £1,450

CASSON, SIR HUGH
Three autograph letters signed 'Hugh' or
initials incorporating three self caricatures
approx. 50 lines to N. C. Bentley – n.d.
(Lawrence of
   Crewkerne) $22   £10

CASTIGLIONE, B.
'Il Cortegiano' – device on title, cont.
French backless binding of brown calf
tooled to an entrelac design with black and
green strapwork – Venice, 1541.
(Sotheby Parke Bernet
   Monaco) $288,000 £128,000

CATANEO, GIROLAMO
'Dell' Arta del Misurare . . . libri due' –
woodcut diagrams, 2 folding, 1 double
page, table, shaved at foot, slight discolouration, stiff wrappers – Brescia, 1682.
(Sotheby's
   London) $115   £50

CATLIN, G.
'Adventures of the Ojibbeway and Ioway
Indians' – 2 vols. in one, illustrated, green
morocco, gilt and gauffered – 1852.
(Phillips) $115   £50
'Illustrations of the Manners and Customs
. . . the North American Indians' – 2 vols.,
illustrated, cloth gilt – 1857.
(Phillips) $125   £55

CATRA, CARLO AND PACCHIONI, G.
'Carla Caro Pittore' – 2nd Edn., presentation copy inscribed by Catra, plates,
some mounted and coloured, original
cloth, 4to – Milan, 1959.
(Christie's S.
   Kensington) $45   £20

CAUFEYNON, DR.
'Le Ceinture de Chastitie, son histoire, son
emploi autrefois et aujourd'hui'– several
photographs and plates, half crimson
morocco gilt – Paris, 1905.
(Sotheby's, New Bond
   Street) $100   £45

CAULFIELD, JAMES
'Portraits, Memoirs and Characters of
Remarkable Persons' – 3 vols., plates,
calf gilt – 1813.
(Phillips) $115   £50

CAUSE, D. H.
'De Koninglycke Hovenier' – 15 plates and
16 plans – Amsterdam, 1676.
(Phillips) $1,240   £550

CAVALCA, DOMENICO
'Pungi Lingua' – 3rd Edn., 117 leaves of
118, 31 lines, roman letter, wormed,
soiled, modern old style boards, cracked,
folio – Nicolaus Laurentii, Florence,
1476/77.
(Sotheby's, New Bond
   Street) $1,080   £480

CAVALIERI SAN BERTOLO, NICOLA
'Institutioni di Architettura Statica e
Idraulica' – 2 vols., 67 folding plates,
slight foxing – Mantua, 1831.
(Sotheby's, New Bond
   Street) $225   £100

CAVALLO, ADOLPHUS
'Tapestries' – 2 vols., plates, original
cloth, slipcase – Boston, n.d.
(Christie's S.
   Kensington) $55   £25

CAVE, WILLIAM
'Primitive Christianity' – 2 parts in one
vol., 1st Edn., additional engraved title
page by W. Sherwin, 18th century panelled
calf, gilt and blindstamped borders, spine
gilt – 1673.
(Sotheby's
   London) $18   £8

CAVENDISH, HENRY
'The Electrical Researches of . . . written
between 1771 and 1781. Edited by J.
Clark Maxwell' – 1st Edn., many illus.
and diagrams, original cloth, 8vo. –
Cambridge, 1879.
(Christie's
   St. James) $190   £85

CAWLEY, A. C. (Editor)
'Sir Gawain and the Green Knight' – no.
572 of 1,500 copies signed by the artist,
illustrations by Cyril Satorsky, original
cloth, slipcase, g.e. – The Limited
Editions Club, 1971.
(Christie's S.
   Kensington) $50   £22

CAXTON, WILLIAM
'A Leaf from Chaucer's Canterbury Tales
1478' – initial letter colour in red – F. & G.
1478.
(Phillips) $765   £340

CAYLUS, COMTE DE
'La Fee Paillardine ou la Princesse Ratee' —
one of 160 copies, coloured plates, dark
green morocco by H. Mangeat, tooled in
gilt, t.e.g., original wrappers bound in,
slipcase — Londres, 1931.
(Sotheby's
    Monaco) $1,015   £450

CELSUS, AULUS CORNELIUS
'De Medicina' — 93 leaves of 94, 45 lines
and headlines, roman letter, woodcut
device at end, waterstaining in margins,
worn, folio — Venice, 6 May, 1497.
(Sotheby's, New Bond
    Street) $540   £240
'De Re Medica Libri Octo' — roman letter,
woodcut initials and ornaments, vellum —
Venice, 1566.
(Sotheby's, New Bond
    Street) $145   £65

CELSUS, AURELIUS
'Of Medicine' — translated by James
Grieve — 1st Edn., in English, cont. calf,
worn — 1756.
(Christie's S.
    Kensington) $100   £45

CERIA — BIBESCO, MARTA LUCIA, PRINCESSE
'Catherine Paris' — 30 etched illustrations
by Ceria, original wrappers, spotted and
soiled, limited to 300 copies — Paris, 1928.
(Sotheby's,
    Chancery Lane) $5   £2

CERTAIN NECESSARY INSTRUCTIONS FOR THE CURE OF THE PLAGUE
22 leaves, black letter licence leaf before
title — John Bill and Christopher Barker,
1665.
(Sotheby's, New Bond
    Street) $400   £180

CERVANTES, SAAVEDRA, MIGUEL DE
'The Life and Exploits of Don Quixote' —
translated by C. Jarvis — 2 vols., engraved
plates, calf gilt, g.e. by Morrell, 4to, R.
Dodsley — 1742.
(Phillips) $250   £110

CESCINSKY, H. AND GRIBBLE, E. R.
'Early English Furniture and Woodwork'
— 2 vols., plates, morocco, gilt — 1922.
(Phillips) $200   £90

CESCINSKY, HERBERT
'English Furniture of the Eighteenth Century' — 3 vols., frontispieces, illustrations,
original half morocco worn, vol. 1 spine
lacking, vol. 1 and 3 partly disbound — n.d.
(Christie's S.
    Kensington) $72   £32

CESSNER, SALOMON
'Mort d'Abel' — engraved portrait and 5
plates after Monsiau, printed in colour,
cont. half calf, gilt — quarto — Paris, 1793.
(Sotheby's, New Bond
    Street) $630   £280

CEZANNE, PAUL
'Carnet Des Dessins' — 2 vols., facsimile
reproduction of a sketchbook, 160 pp.
accompanying text, original cloth folder,
slipcase, No. 50 of 1,050 copies — Quatre-
Chemins, Paris, 1951.
(Sotheby's,
    Chancery Lane) $80   £35
'Les Baigneuses', Texte de Jean Cassou —
facsimile reproductions of watercolours by
Cezanne, original wrappers, uncut, folder,
folio — Editart, Paris, 1947.
(Sotheby's,
    Chancery Lane) $55   £25

CHABERT, J. C.
'Galerie des Peintres ou Collection de
Portraits des Peintres les Plus Celebres de
Toutes les Ecoles' — 2 vols., 90 lithographs,
some foxing, worn, g.e., folio — Paris, 1822-
24.
(Sotheby's, New Bond
    Street) $225   £100

CHAFFERS, W.
'Marks and Monograms on European and
Oriental Pottery and Porcelain' — 14th
Edn., illustrations, original cloth, dust
jacket — 1946.
(Christie's S.
    Kensington) $35   £15

CHAGALL, MARC
'Bible' — 2 vols., 105 etched plates by
Chagall, unsewn in original wrappers,
uncut, folders, slipcase, folio — Teriade,
Paris, 1956.
(Sotheby's,
    Chancery Lane) $12,600   £5,600

'Verve' – vol. IX, no. 33/34, illustrations for the Bible by Marc Chagall, 18 coloured lithographs, 12 in black on versos and 105 reproductions, original pictorial boards – Paris, 1956.
(Sotheby's,
    Chancery Lane) $2,365   £1,050

CHAGALL, MARC – GENAUER, EMILY
'Chagall at the "Met"' – coloured and plain reproductions, original cloth, dust jacket, slipcase – New York, 1971.
(Sotheby's,
    Chancery Lane) $28   £12

CHAGALL, MARC – GOGOL, NIKOLAI V.
'Les Ames Mortes' – translated by Henri Mongault, 2 vols., 118 etchings by Chagall, unsewn in original wrappers, uncut, folders and slipcase, folio – Teriade, Paris, 1948.
(Sotheby's,
    Chancery Lane) $11,700   £5,200

CHAGALL, MARC – LA FONTAINE, JEAN DE
'Fables' – 2 vols., 102 etched plates by Chagall, unsewn in original wrappers, uncut, folders, large – Teriade, Paris, 1952.
(Sotheby's,
    Chancery Lane) $11,700   £5,200

CHAGALL, MARC – LASSAIGNE, JACQUES
'Dessins et Aquarelles pour Le Ballet' – one coloured lithograph by Chagall, original cloth, dust jacket, slipcase – Siecle, Paris, 1969.
(Sotheby's,
    Chancery Lane) $80   £35

CHAGALL, MARC – LEYMARIE, JEAN
'The Jerusalem Windows' – 2 coloured lithographs by Chagall, original cloth, dust jacket, slipcase – Andre Sauret, Monte Carlo, 1962.
(Sotheby's,
    Chancery Lane) $80   £36

CHAGALL, MARC – MOURLOT, FERNAND AND SORLIER, CHARLES
'The Lithographs of Chagall' – text in English, coloured lithographed frontispiece and dust jacket by Chagall, original cloth, dust jacket – Book and Art Shop, Boston, 1969.
(Sotheby's,
    Chancery Lane) $80   £35

CHAGALL, MARC – PAULHAN, JEAN
'De Mauvais Suites' – 10 coloured etched plates by Chagall, unsewn in original wrappers, decorated folder and slipcase, folio – Les Bibliophiles de l'Union Francaise, Paris, 1958.
(Sotheby's,
    Chancery Lane) $3,600   £1,600

CHAGALL, MARC – SORLIER, CHARLES
'The Ceramics and Sculptures of Chagall' – coloured lithographed frontispiece by Chagall, coloured and plain reproductions, original cloth, dust jacket – Andre Sauret, Monaco, 1972.
(Sotheby's,
    Chancery Lane) $45   £20

CHAIM BEN HACHAR BAER
'Mincha Ktana', Commentary on three Haftoror and Chapter 79 of the Psalms – The Widow and Sons of Jacob Proops, Amsterdam, 1789.
(Sotheby's, New Bond
    Street) $65   £28

CHAMBERLAINE, WILLIAM
'Tyrocinium Medicum or a Dissertation of the Duties of Youth Apprenticed to the Medical Profession' – 2nd Edn., 1 folding plate, title slightly dust soiled, cloth – For the author, 1819.
(Sotheby's, New Bond
    Street) $90   £40

CHAMBERS

CHAMBERS, E.
'Cyclopaedia: or, an Universal Dictionary of Arts and Sciences' – vol. 5 only, 150 engraved plates, folding specimens of printing types, spine gilt, slightly worn, folio – 1789.
(Sotheby's London) $180   £80

CHAMBERS, ROBERT
'Vestiges of the Natural History of Creation' – 1st Edn., presentation copy, inscribed on half title, by author, original cloth, uncut, rebacked, 8vo – 1844.
(Sotheby's, New Bond Street) $675   £300

CHAMBERS, SIR WILLIAM
'A Treatise on Civil Architecture' – 1st Edn., 50 plates, some discolouration, cont. calf worn, rebacked and repaired, folio – 1759.
(Sotheby's, New Bond Street) $250   £110

CHAMPION, F.
'Jungle in Sunshine and Shadow' – photographs, cloth – n.d.
(Tessa Bennett, Edinburgh) $15   £7

CHANCEL, ROGER
'Livre Noir' – 30 plates by Chancel, 25 coloured, dampstained, loose in original wrappers, uncut, half parchment folder, 2 corners frayed, spine detached, folio – Paris, 1945.
(Sotheby's, Chancery Lane) $20   £9

CHANDLER, R.
'Travels in Asia Minor and Greece or an Account of a Tour Made at the Expense of the Society of Dilettanti' – 2 vols., 3rd Edn., 8 engraved maps, charts and plans – 1817.
(Sotheby's, New Bond Street) $225   £100

CHANDLER, R. AND OTHERS
'Ionian Antiquities, published by order of the Society of Dilettanti' – 28 plates, some staining and spotting, covers and spine lacking, folio – 1769.
(Christie's S. Kensington) $90   £40

CHAPIUS, ALFRED AND JAUQUET, EUGENE
'The History of the Self Winding Watch' – coloured frontispiece, mounted facsimiles, illustrations, original cloth – 1956.
(Christie's S. Kensington) $40   £18

CHAPMAN, EDMUND
'An Essay on the Improvement of Midwifery Chiefly with Regard to the Operation' – 1st Edn., half title, cont. panelled calf – A. Blackwell, 1733.
(Sotheby's, New Bond Street) $720   £320

CHAPMAN, F. H.
'Architectura Navalis Mercatoria 1768' – 6 parts, plates, original wrappers – n.d.
(Phillips) $135   £60

CHAPMAN, JOHN AND ANDRE, PETER
'A Map of the County of Essex' – hand coloured double page engraved title, margins repaired, 23 pages mounted on guards, later half morocco, rubbed, folio – 1777.
(Christie's S. Kensington) $520   £230

CHARDIN, SIR JOHN
'Travels in Persia' – no. 684 of 975 copies, plates, original vellum backed cloth, gilt – 1927.
(Sotheby's, Chancery Lane) $50   £22
'Voyages . . . en Perse . . . Lieux de l'Orient' – 3 vols., frontispiece, 78 plates and maps, old calf rebacked – Amsterdam, 1711.
(Phillips) $630   £280

CHARLES VII, KING OF FRANCE
'Pragmatica Sanctio cum Glossis Egregii' – small repair to title, gilt – Paris, 1546.
(Sotheby Parke Bernet Monaco) $720   £320

CHARLETON, WALTER
'The Darkness of Atheism Dispelled by the Light of Nature' – engraved portrait, tiny holes, new half calf – J. F. for William Lee, 1652.
(Sotheby's, New Bond Street) $270   £120

CHARLEVOIX, PIERRE FRANCOIS XAVIER DE
'Histoire de l'Isle Espagnole ou de S. Domingue' – 2 vols., 1st Edn., 16 engraved maps, cont. French mottled calf, gilt spines – Paris, 1730-31.
(Sotheby Parke Bernet
    Monaco) $7,875   £3,500

CHARTER
Ms. on vellum – brown ink, 130 x 220mm. of William de Esseby granting an acre of land in Sutstoke to Adam de Brocgreve in return for annual rent of two silver pence, witnessed. With five others similar in buckram box – 13th century.
(Christie's, King
    St.) $360   £160

CHARTON, EDUARDO
'Viajeros Antiguos y Modernos' – 2 vols. in one, 21 plates, 15 hand coloured, half titles, cont. calf, slightly rubbed – Madrid, 1861.
(Sotheby's,
    Chancery Lane) $115   £50

CHASKUNI, ABRAHAM
'Zot Chukat Ha'atorah' Kabbalistic commentary on Luria's book Sepher Ha'kauvanot edited by Moshe Zacuto – title printed within architectural woodcut frame, repaired, modern cloth – Venice, 1659.
(Sotheby's, New Bond
    Street) $100   £45

CHASSEPOL, FRANCOIS DE
'The History of the Grand Visiers' – Englished by John Evelyn, Junior – engraved frontispiece, occasional foxing, some leaves detached; cont. sprinkled calf, rubbed – 1677.
(Christie's, King
    St.) $135   £60

CHASTEL, ROGER – ELUARD, PAUL
'Le Bestiare' – 88 etched illustrations and 42 initials by Chastel, unsewn in original pictorial wrappers, folder, slipcase, folio – Maeght, Paris, 1948.
(Sotheby's,
    Chancery Lane) $385   £170

CHATEAUVIEUX, MARQUE LULLIN DE, AND OTHERS
'La Suisse Illustree' – 2 vols., 87 engraved plates, 17 hand coloured, folding map hand coloured in outline, half titles – Paris, 1851.
(Sotheby's,
    Chancery Lane) $1,260   £560

CHATTERTON, THOMAS
'Poems supposed to have been written at Bristol by Thomas Rowley and Others in the Fifteenth Century . . . added a Preface . . . and a Glossary' – 1st Edn., engraved plate, cont. borders, uncut in buckram sleeve and slipcase – 1777.
(Sotheby's, New Bond
    Street) $315   £140

CHAUCER, GEOFFREY
'Troilus and Criseyde' – No. 180 of 225 copies, decorations and full page illustrations by Eric Gill, original morocco backed boards, corners rubbed, t.e.g. – Golden Cockerel Press, 1927.
(Christie's S.
    Kensington) $3,150   £1,400

CHAUMETON, F. P.
'Flore Medicale' – 8 vols., 424 hand coloured plates, occasional spotting, cont. marbled calf, corners rubbed – Paris, 1814-20-19.
(Christie's S.
    Kensington) $1,800   £800

CHAUNCY, SIR HENRY
'Historical Antiquities of Hertfordshire' – 1st Edn., engraved portrait, map and plates, later calf, worn – 1700.
(Sotheby's, New Bond
    Street) $315   £140

CHEESEMAN, T. F.
'Illustrations of the New Zealand Flora' – 2 vols., 251 plates, original cloth, interleaved copy – Wellington, 1914.
(Sotheby's, New Bond
    Street) $270   £120

CHESELDEN, WILLIAM
'The Anatomy of the Human Body' – 1st Edn., 23 plates some folding, advertisement leaf at end, cont. panelled calf – 1713.
(Sotheby's, New Bond
    Street) $675   £300

CHESELDEN

'A Treatise on the High Operation for the Stone' – 1st Edn., 17 plates, uncut – bookplate of Chichester Infirmary Library – John Osborn, 1733.
(Sotheby's, New Bond Street) $790 £350

CHESHIRE, JOHN
'A Treatise upon the Rheumatism as well as chronical' – advertisement leaf at end, name on title crossed out, cont. panelled calf – C. Rivington and S. Martin, 1735.
(Sotheby's, New Bond Street) $270 £120

CHESTERTON, GILBERT KEITH
Series of four original caricature pencil sketches entitled 'The Ruined Gamblers' each 5½ x 4½in., showing Nicolas Bentley, his wife and one of Mrs. Chesterton – n.d.
(Lawrence of Crewkerne) $360 £160

'The Wisdom of Father Brown' – original dark blue cloth spine faded, 1st Edn., coloured frontispiece by Seymour Lucas, ownership initials E.N.B.B. – 1914.
(Lawrence of Crewkerne) $45 £20

'Greybeards at Play, Literature and Art for Old Gentlemen' – 1st Edn., dedication to Edmund Clerihew Bentley with a 12 line original autograph poem in three stanzas – Brimley Johnson, 1900.
(Lawrence of Crewkerne) $945 £420

CHETHAM, JAMES
'The Angler's Vade Mecum' – 3rd Edn., double page plate, torn, cont. sheep, worn, upper cover loose, 8vo – 1700.
(Sotheby's, New Bond Street) $135 £60

CHETWYND, SIR GEORGE
'Racing Reminiscences' – 2 vols., 8vo half red morocco, spine gilt – 1891.
(Lawrence of Crewkerne) $18 £8

CHEYNE, GEORGE
'The English Malady or a Treatise of Nervous Diseases of all Kinds' – 1st Edn., 311 advertisements at end, name written on title page, cont. calf – G. Strahan and J. Leake, Bath, 1733.
(Sotheby's, New Bond Street) $450 £200

'An Essay of Health and Long Life' – 2nd Edn., cont. panelled calf – G. Strahan, 1725.
(Sotheby's, New Bond Street) $65 £28

The X-Ray Clock

CHICAGO MAGIC CATALOGUE
Catalogue nos. 6-10; 12 and 14-18, duplicates of nos. 12 and 18, two price lists and a few other loose leaves, in 13 vols., most with illustrations – Chicago, 1914-41.
(Sotheby's, Chancery Lane) $115 £50

CHILDS, GEORGE W.
'Specimens of Show Printing being Facsimiles in Miniature of Poster Cuts . . . Ledger Job Office' – many coloured, printed on one side of the leaf only – Philadelphia, n.d.
(Sotheby's, New Bond Street) $400 £180

CHILLIDA, EDOUARDO – GUILLEN, JORGE
'Mas Alla' – translated by Claude Esteban, calligraphic text, 17 wood engraved illustrations by Chillida, original wrappers, folio – Maeght, Paris, 1973.
(Sotheby's,
Chancery Lane) $475   £210

CHIMOT, EDOUARD – BAUDELAIRE, CHARLES
'Les Fleurs du Mal' – 24 coloured etched plates after Chimot, unsewn in original wrappers, uncut, unopened, folder, slipcase – Briffaut, Paris, 1941.
(Sotheby's,
Chancery Lane) $295   £130

CHIMOT, EDOUARD – LOUYS, PIERRE
'Les Poesies de Meleagre' – 15 coloured etched plates by Chimot, unsewn in original wrappers, uncut, partly unopened, folder, slipcase, damaged – Editions d'Art Devambex, Paris, 1926.
(Sotheby's,
Chancery Lane) $270   £120
'La Femme et le Plantin' – 16 coloured etched plates by Chimot, unsewn in original wrappers, uncut, morocco backed folder, slipcase. Limited to 211 copies – Editions d'Art Devambez, Paris, 1928.
(Sotheby's,
Chancery Lane) $270   £120
'Poemes Inedits 1887-1924' – 6 coloured etched plates by Chimot, unsewn in original wrappers, uncut, unopened, folder and slipcase. No. 73 of 109 copies – Pour l'Artiste et ses Amis, Paris, 1938.
(Sotheby's,
Chancery Lane) $385   £170

CHIMOT, EDOUARD – MAGRE, MAURICE
'Les Soirs d'Opium' – 12 coloured etched plates by Chimot, 21 wood engraved illustrations, slightly rubbed, uncut, original wrappers, bound in – Le Livre du Bibliophile, Paris, 1921.
(Sotheby's,
Chancery Lane) $765   £340

CHIPPENDALE, THOMAS
'Ornaments, and Interior Decorations in the Old French Style' – engraved title and 32 plates only, a little spotting or soiling, morocco backed boards, worn, folio – John Weale, n.d.
(Christie's S.
Kensington) $80   £35

CHODERLOS DE LACLOS, P. A. F.
'Les Liaisons Dangereuses' – 2 vols., engraved plates, light browning, early 20th century red morocco, gilt a little rubbed – Londres, 1796.
(Sotheby Parke Bernet
Monaco) $1,575   £700

CHODOWIECKI, D.
'A Collection of his engravings mostly for book illustrations' – 405 engravings some 10 or 12 to a page, in a cloth album, some before letters, a few 'eau fort', folio – circa 1760-1800.
(Sotheby Parke Bernet
Monaco) $36,000   £16,000

CHOISEUL, ETIENNE FRANCOIS DUC DE
'Recueil d'Estampes Gravees' – engraved plates, one lacking, spotting, later morocco – Paris, 1771.
(Christie's S.
Kensington) $495   £220

CHOMEL, NOEL
'Dictionnaire Oeconomique Contenant Divers Moyens d'augmenter son bien, et de conserver sa Sante' – 2 vols., a few wood-cut illustrations, cont. sprinkled calf, gilt spines, folio – Lyon, 1732.
(Sotheby Parke Bernet
Monaco) $3,600   £1,600

CHRONOLOGY OF THE CREATION OF THE WORLD TO THE YEAR 1828
Six hand coloured plates, soiling throughout, original wrappers, soiled and frayed – n.d.
(Christie's S.
Kensington) $14   £6

CHRISTIE, DAME AGATHA
'The Man in the Brown Suit' – 1st American Edn., presentation copy, inscribed by author, original cloth, slightly worn – New York, 1924.
(Sotheby's,
Chancery Lane) $270   £120

CHRONIK DER SACHSEN
Low German, 1st Edn., 210 leaves of 284, 43 lines, gothic letter, numerous woodcut illustrations and initials, folio – Peter Schoeffer, Mainz, 1492.
(Sotheby's, New Bond
Street) $3,375   £1,500

CHRYSOSTOMUS, JOANNES
'In Sanctum Jesu Christi Evangelium . . .' – 4 parts in two vols., slightly browned and spotted, initials in gilt on covers – Carola Guillard, Paris, 1543.
(Sotheby's, New Bond
Street) $1,800   £800

CHU-CHIA-CHEN
'The Chinese Theatre' – plates, one mounted and coloured, original morocco backed boards, worn – 1922.
(Christie's.
Kensington) $40   £18

CHURCHILL, CHARLES
'Poems' – 2 vols., 1st Edn., cont. calf, spines gilt, split, rubbed – 1763/5.
(Sotheby's, New Bond
Street) $180   £80

CHURCHILL, WINSTON S.
'My Early Life' – plates, maps, a few leaves detached, original cloth, worn – 1930.
(Christie's.
Kensington) $35   £15
'The Great War' – 26 issues, a complete set, illustrations and maps, original wrappers, slightly worn – George Newnes, 1933-34.
(Sotheby's,
Chancery Lane) $18   £8
'The River War' – 2 vols., 1st Edn., portraits, folding maps, some leaves soiled, original cloth, rubbed and soiled, inner hinges cracked – 1899.
(Christie's.
Kensington) $115   £50
'The Story of the Malakand Field Force' – 1st Edn., portrait frontispiece, maps, some folding, slightly spotted, tears, original cloth, worn and stained – 1898.
(Sotheby's,
Chancery Lane) $95   £42

CIBBER, COLLEY
'An Apology' – 2 vols., no. 279 of 450 copies, initials by Eric Gill, original cloth backed boards, soiled, unopened – Golden Cockerel Press, 1925.
(Christie's.
Kensington) $70   £30

CIBBER, THEOPHILUS
'The Lives of the Poets of Great Britain and Ireland to the time of Dean Swift' – 1st Edn., 5 vols., foxing, some defective, cont. calf – 1753.
(Christie's, King
St.) $145   £65

CICERO, MARCUS TULLIUS
'Cato Major or the Book of Old Age' –
Englished by William Austin, engraved and
printed titles, first and last leaves blank.
cont. sheep. Fine copy – William Leake,
1648.
(Sotheby's, New Bond
    Street) $720   £320
'Epistolae ad Familiares' – 225 leaves,
roman letter, woodcut on title, cont.
wooden boards, rebacked with calf, folio –
Octavianus Scottus, Venice, 1494.
(Christie's, King
    St.) $495   £220
'Opera Omnia' – engraved title, cont.
vellum, soiled – Amsterdam and Leiden,
1661.
(Christie's S.
    Kensington) $40   £18

CICERO, M. TULLIUS
'Paradoxa . . . ad M. Brutum, cum F. Sylvii
Ambiani Commentariis' – large device on
title, some staining, some lower margins
torn, cloth backed boards, 4to, sold with
another volume – J. Badius Ascensius,
Paris, 1532.
(Sotheby's, New Bond
    Street) $70   £30

CIPRIANI, G. B.
'Prints' – engraved portrait and 50 plates,
many tinted, modern half calf, gilt, folio
– Boydell, 1789.
(Sotheby's, New Bond
    Street) $900   £400

CIRELLI, FILIPPO AND VENTIMIGLIA, DOMENCIO
'Il Torneo di Caserta Nel Carnevale Dell'
Anno. 1846' – 1st Edn., 39 hand
coloured lithographed plates by G. Riccio,
cont. purple roan, folio – Naples, 1846.
(Sotheby's, New Bond
    Street) $900   £400

CLANVOWE, SIR THOMAS
'The Floure and the Leafe' – Edited by F.
S. Ellis, no. 300 of 310 copies, woodcut
initials, original holland backed boards,
uncut, 4to – 1896.
(Sotheby's,
    Chancery Lane) $260   £115

CLARENDON, EDWARD, EARL OF
'History of Rebellion and Civil Wars in
England' – 1st Edn., 3 vols., 3 portraits
and engraved titles, calf gilt, folio – 1702-4.
(Phillips) $215   £95
'The History of the Rebellion and Civil
Wars in England' – 7 vols., modern calf
backed boards – Oxford, 1849.
(Christie's S.
    Kensington) $50   £22

CLARE, M.
'The Motion of Fluids' – 9 plates, modern
calf gilt – 1737.
(Phillips) $90   £40

CLARK, CHARLES
'Engraved Alphabets' – twelve different
styles, original printed wrappers – circa
1850.
(Tessa Bennett,
    Edinburgh) $22   £10

CLARKE, SIR C. M.
'Observations on those Diseases of Females
which are Attended by Discharges' – 10
plates, some folding, 1st Edn., 2 vols., half
calf – 1814-21.
(Bonham's) $115   £50

CLARKE, H. G.
'Baxter Colour Prints' – plates, original
morocco backed cloth, soiled and slightly
rubbed, wrappers bound in at end –
1920-21.
(Christie's S.
    Kensington) $115   £50

CLARKE, HARRY, (Illustrator)
'Fairy Tales' by Hans Christian Andersen
– 40 plates, 16 coloured and illustrations
in text by Harry Clarke, original pictorial
cloth, soiled, t.e.g. – Harrap, 1916.
(Sotheby's,
    Chancery Lane) $295   £130

CLARKE, HARRY – POE, EDGAR ALLAN
'Tales of Mystery and Imagination' –
plates, some mounted and coloured, original cloth, dust jacket – New York, 1933.
(Christie's S.
    Kensington) $115   £50

CLARKE, J.
'Practical Essay on the Management of
Pregnancy and Labour' – 1st Edn., half
calf – 1793.
(Bonham's) $80   £35

CLARKE, STEPHEN
'Horticus Anglicus or the Modern English
Garden' – 2 vols., half calf, rubbed –
1822.
(Christie's S.
Kensington) $40   £18

**CLAUDE, GELEE AND EARLOM,
RICHARD**
'Liber Veritatis' – 3 vols., 3 engraved
frontispiece portraits, 300 sepia mezzo-
tint plates, folio.
(Christie's
St. James) $6,525   £2,900

CLAUDE, LORRAIN
'Liber Veritatis' – 1 vol., 100 plates, some
stained, disbound, folio – circa 1817.
(Phillips) $720   £320

CLAUDIANUS, CLAUDIUS
'Opera' edited by Thaddeus Ugoletus –
4th Edn., 128 leaves, 40 lines, roman
letter, woodcut initials, 19th century
blindstamped calf – Venice, 1500.
(Sotheby's, New Bond
Street) $400   £180

**CLAVE, ANTOINE – PUSHKIN,
ALEXANDER**
'La Dame de Pique' – translated by Prosper
Merimee, 10 lithographed plates by Claves,
unsewn in original wrappers, uncut, folder,
slipcase – Editions du Pre aux Clercs, 1946.
(Sotheby's,
Chancery Lane) $340   £150

CLAY, ENID
'The Constant Mistress' – no. 65 of 300
copies, signed by author and artist, full page
illustrations by Eric Gill, original cloth
backed boards, unopened – 1934.
(Christie's S.
Kensington) $200   £90

CLELAND, J.
'Annals of Glasgow' – 2 vols., half morocco
– Glasgow, 1816.
(Tessa Bennett,
Edinburgh) $12   £5

CLEMENS, S. L. 'MARK TWAIN'
'Tom Sawyer' – 1st Canadian Edn., origi-
nal cloth gilt, spine faded – Belford Bros.,
Toronto, 1876.
(Sotheby's,
Chancery Lane) $90   £40

CLEMENS, S. L. AND ELIOT, T. S.
'The Adventures of Huckleberry Finn' with
an Introduction by T. S. Eliot – presentation copy inscribed by T. S. Eliot, original cloth, dust jacket – The Crescent Press,
1950.
(Christie's S.
Kensington) $125   £55

**CLERICI, FABRIZIO – MARINO,
GIAMBATTISTA**
'Parigi 1615' – text in Italian and French,
lithographed vignette on title, 10 full page
illustrations, unsewn in original decorated
wrappers, cloth backed folder, slipcase –
Rome, 1952.
(Sotheby's,
Chancery Lane) $720   £320

CLIFTON, FRANCIS
'The State of Physick ancient and modern
briefly considered with a plan for the
improvement of it' – 2 folding tables,
cont. calf, rebacked – W. Bowyer for
John Nourse, 1732.
(Sotheby's, New Bond
Street) $95   £42

CLINTON-BAKER, H.
'Illustrations of 'New Conifers' – 4 vols.,
a complete set, plates, half morocco, 4to –
Hertford, 1909-35.
(Sotheby's, New Bond
Street) $630   £280

CLOUZOT, MARIANNE – OVIDIUS NASO, PUBLIUS
'Les Metamorphoses' – 24 etched plates by Marianne Clouzot, wood engraved initials and tail pieces, black half morocco, vellum covers, t.e.g., slipcase, folio, no. 132 of 300 – Editions Solac, Paris, 1947.
(Sotheby's,
Chancery Lane) $115   £50

CLUSIUS, CAROLUS
'Rariorum Plantarum Historia' – 2 parts and Appendix, many woodcuts, lacks title page and portrait, cloth, folio – Antwerp, 1601.
(Phillips) $1,395   £620

CLUVERIUS, P.
'Introductio in Universam Geographiam' – engraved title, 48 maps, 10 plates, calf gilt, 4to – 1711.
(Phillips) $650   £260

COBBETT, WILLIAM
'Porcupine's Works . . . exhibiting a faithful picture of the United States of America' – 12 vols., slight browning, cont. russia, gilt, arms of the Society of Writers to the Signet, Edinburgh on covers, split, rubbed – 1801.
(Sotheby's, New Bond
Street) $250   £110

COBDEN-SANDERSON, T. J.
'The Ideal Book or Book Beautiful' – limited to 310 copies of which this is 300, on paper, presentation copy, inscribed by author, original limp vellum, uncut, 4to – 1900.
(Sotheby's,
Chancery Lane) $370   £165

COCHIN AND BELLICARD
'Observations sur les Antiquities d'Herculaneum' – plates, some folding – Paris, 1757.
(Phillips) $90   £40

COCHRANE, THOMAS, 10th EARL OF DUNDONALD
'Servicios Navales que en Libertar al Chile y al Peru de la Dominacion Espanola Rindio el Conde de Dundonald' – blind-stamped blue cloth, mounted photographic frontispiece of Bernard O'Higgins, half title – James Ridgway, 1859.
(Lawrence of
Crewkerne) $115   £50

COCKBURN, MAJOR JAMES
'Swiss Scenery' – large paper copy, engraved vignette title, 60 plates, off-setting, spots, cont. calf backed boards, rubbed – 1820.
(Sotheby's, New Bond
Street) $1,015   £450

COCK ROBIN'S DEATH AND BURIAL
8 wood engraved illustrations, coloured by hand, slightly spotted, original pictorial wrappers, backstrip slightly torn – Routledge, Warne and Routledge, 1865.
(Sotheby's,
Chancery Lane) $28   £12

COCKBURN, WILLIAM
'The Symptoms, nature, cause and cure of a Gonorrhoea' – 1st Edn., 211 advertisement at end, large and thick paper, cont. calf gilt, spine rubbed, bookplate of Lord Bute – John Graves, 1713.
(Sotheby's, New Bond
Street) $215   £95

COCTEAU, JEAN
Autograph first draft of part of second act of 'La Machine Infernale', the scene between Anubis and the Sphinx, varying considerably from the first version with 14 pen and ink studies, 7 pages, quarto and an additional page of notes at the end in an exercise book – circa 1934.
(Sotheby's, New Bond
Street) $1,240   £550

COCTEAU

'Plain-Chant, Poeme' – 1st Edn., original
wrappers, faded, spine loose, partly
unopened, inscribed to Madame D.Erlanger
on half title dated June, 1923 – Paris, 1923.
(Sotheby's, New Bond
    Street) $118   £52
'Les Chevaliers de la Table Ronde Piece
en trois actes' – 1st Edn., frontispiece
after Cocteau, pages discoloured, original
wrappers, soiled, uncut. Autograph inscription on half title to 'Chere Catherine' with
a pen drawing of a woman's face – Paris,
1937.
(Sotheby's, New Bond
    Street) $135   £60
Pencil sketch showing 'Maalesh' signed, one
page, small folio.
(Sotheby's, New Bond
    Street) $295   £130

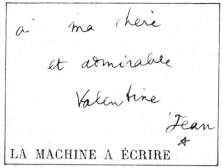

LA MACHINE A ÉCRIRE

'La Machine a Ecrire' – presentation copy,
inscribed by author to Valentine (Hugo),
original wrappers, fitted case – Paris, 1941.
(Sotheby's,
    Chancery Lane) $90   £40
'La Belle et La Bete' – presentation copy,
inscribed by author to Valentine (Hugo),
24 plates of stills from film, original
wrappers – Paris, 1946.
(Sotheby's,
    Chancery Lane) $85   £38

Autograph manuscript of an untitled poem
comprising four stanza of three and four
lines, illustrated with a charming sketch of
a woman in pen and ink, with autograph
corrections and revisions, one page, folio.
(Sotheby's, New Bond
    Street) $450   £200
'Les Chevaliers de la Table Ronde' –
presentation copy, inscribed by author to
Leclair, pen and ink sketch on title, frontispiece by author, cloth backed boards, original wrappers, bound in, fitted case –
Paris, 1937.
(Sotheby's,
    Chancery Lane) $250   £110

'25 Dessins d'un Dormeur' – 25 full page
illustrations, original wrappers, folder and
slipcase – Mermod, Lausanne, n.d.
(Sotheby's,
    Chancery Lane) $250   £110

COCTEAU, JEAN AND ARSENE, ALEXANDRE
'l'Art Decoratif de Leon Bakst' – 1st Edn., portrait, 77 plates, 50 coloured, browning on end papers, original half vellum, slightly worn, t.e.g., folio – Maurice de Brunoff, Paris, 1913.
(Sotheby's, New Bond
 Street) $585   £260

COHAUSEN, JOHANN HEINRICH
'Hermippus Redivivus or the Sage's Triumph over Old Age and the Grave' – 2nd Edn., cont. marbled boards, calf spine – J. Nourse, 1749.
(Sotheby's, New Bond
 Street) $45   £20

COHN, W.
'Chinese Paintings' – coloured and other plates, 2nd Edn. – 1950.
(Tessa Bennett,
 Edinburgh) $18   £8

COLAS, R.
'Bibliographie Generale de Costume et de la Mode' – 2 vols., cloth gilt – New York, 1969.
(Phillips) $90   £40

COLBATCH, SIR JOHN
'A Scheme for the Proper Methods to be taken should it please God to visit us with this Plague' – new boards – J. Darby, 1721.
(Sotheby's, New Bond
 Street) $160   £70

COLBEN, P.
'The Present State of the Cape of Good Hope' – frontispiece and 17 plates, cont. panelled calf – W. Innys, 1731.
(Bonham's) $430   £190

COLDEN, C.
'The History of the Five Indian Nations of Canada' – Thomas Pennant's copy with his bookplate, folding map, calf – 1755.
(Phillips) $190   £85

COL DE VILLARS, ELIE
'Receuil Alphabetique de Prognostics Dangereux et Mortels sur les differents maladies de l'homme' – 1st Edn., cont. calf – J. B. Coignard, fils, Paris, 1730.
(Sotheby's, New Bond
 Street) $55   £25

COLE, G. – ROPER, J.
'The British Atlas' – comprising a complete set of 57 county maps of England and Wales, with a general map of navigable rivers and canals and 21 plans of the cities and principal towns, worn, covers detached, 4to – 1810.
(Christie'S.
 Kensington) $655   £290

COLE, JACK
Collection of 21 scripts for films and shows including 6 duplicates for which Cole did the choreography, plastic or card folders – 1911-70.
(Sotheby's, New Bond
 Street) $70   £30

COLE, JOHN
'Historical Sketches of Scalby, Burniston and Cloughton' – 1st Edn., cont. silk covered boards, 8vo – Scarborough, 1829.
(Sotheby's, New Bond
 Street) $405   £180

COLERIDGE, SAMUEL TAYLOR
'La Chanson du Vieux Marin traduite par A. Barbier' – illustrated by Gustave Dore, numerous plates, original red cloth, gilt, spine torn, folio – Paris, 1877.
(Christie's
 St. James) $135   £60
'The Rime of the Ancient Mariner' – no. 51 of 110 copies signed by the illustrator, calligrapher and paper maker, mounted coloured plates by Errol le Cain, original half vellum, small folio, 1972.
(Christie's S.
 Kensington) $90   £40

COLETTE
'Cheri' – in 3 vols., illustrations by Vertes, wrappers, slipcovers – Editions de la Roseaeie, Paris, 1929.
(Sotheby Parke Bernet
 Monaco) $31,500   £14,000

COLIER, JOHN, 'TIM BOBBIN'
'The Miscellaneous Works – containing his view of the Lancashire Dialect' – 2 parts in one vol., 1st Edn., engraved portrait and 10 plates, slightly browned, 19th century cloth, worn – Manchester, 1775.
(Sotheby's, New Bond
 Street) $12   £5

LABOR EVANGELICA,
MINISTERIOS APOSTOLICOS
DE LOS OBREROS
DE LA COMPAÑIA DE IESVS,
FVNDACION, T PROGRESSOS
DE SV PROVINCIA
EN LAS ISLAS FILIPINAS.
HISTORIADOS
POR EL PADRE FRANCISCO COLIN,
PROVINCIAL DE LA MISMA COMPAÑIA,
CALIFICADOR DEL SANTO OFICIO,
Y SV COMISSARIO EN LA GOVERNACION
DE SAMBOANGA, Y SV DISTRITO.
PARTE PRIMERA
SACADA DE LOS MANVSCRIPTOS DEL PADRE
Pedro Chirino, el primero de la Compañia que paſò de los Reynos de
Eſpaña a eſtas Islas, por orden, y a coſta de la Catholica,
y Real Mageſtad.

CON PRIVILEGIO.

COLIN, FRANCISCO
'Labor Evangelica, Ministerios Apostolicos
de los Obreros de la Compania de Jesus,
Fundacion, y Progressos de su Provincia
en las Islas Filipinas' – 1st Edn., slightly
spotted, some leaves stained, cont. limp
vellum, slightly soiled, folio – Madrid,
1663.
(Sotheby's, New Bond
   Street)   **$1,620**   **£720**

**COLLECTION OF ONE HUNDRED
VIEWS IN GREAT BRITAIN**
99 of 100 engraved views, disbound, oblong
folio – J. Arnett, 1783.
(Phillips)   **$160**   **£70**

COLLIER, JEREMY
'Short View of the Immorality and Pro-
faneness of the English Stage' – 1st Edn.,
browned, cont. calf, rebacked – 1698.
(Sotheby's, New Bond
   Street)   **$145**   **£65**

COLLIN, RAPHAEL – LOUYS, PIERRE
'Les Chansons de Bilitis' – etched frontis-
piece, vignette on title, 6 plates and 25
illustrations by Chessa after Collin, black
morocco gilt – Librairie des Amateurs,
Paris, 1906.
(Sotheby's,
   Chancery Lane)   **$225**   **£100**

COLLINS, A.
'The Peerage of England' – vol. I, engraved
plates, calf – 1756.
(Tessa Bennett,
   Edinburgh)   **$14**   **£6**

COLLINS, DAVID
'An Account of the English Colony in New
South Wales' – 2nd Edn., engraved portrait frontispiece, 2 engraved maps, one
folding, 23 plates and 8 engraved illustrations in text, cloth backed boards, uncut –
1804.
(Christie's
   St. James)   **$630**   **£280**

COLLINS, S. H.
'The Emigrants Guide to . . . the United
States' – 4th Edn., folding map, original
cloth, soiled – Hull, Joseph Noble, n.d.
(Christie's S.
   Kensington)   **$72**   **£32**

COLLINS, WILLIAM
'The Poetical Works with Memoirs of the
Author by J. Langhorne' – 1st collected
Edn., advertisement leaf and blank at end,
with erratum, without half title as issued,
a few leaves very slightly spotted, later
half calf, spine gilt – 1765.
(Sotheby's
   London)   **$90**   **£40**

COLMAN, B. AND THORNTON, G.
'The Connoiseur' – 2 vols., original issues,
cont. half green morocco, gilt, folio –
1755-56.
(Sotheby's, New Bond
   Street)   **$675**   **$300**

COLNAGHI AND CO. (Publishers)
Dolby's Sketches in the Baltic, O'Reilly's
Sebastopol etc. – folio cloth, binding
defective, no title, 35 lithographed plates
and maps, some coloured, some foxing –
n.d.
(Lawrence of
   Crewkerne)   **$200**   **£90**

COLOMBE DE SEILLANS
'Imitation des Odes d'Anachreon en Vers
Francais . . . par Monsieur de S... et la Tra-
duction de Mademoiselle Lefevre' – 1st
Edn., Madame de Pompadour's copy with
her arms, gilt – Paris, 1754.
(Sotheby Parke Bernet
   Monaco)   **$3,600**   **£1,600**

COLONNA, F.
'Hyperotomachie ou Discours du Songe de Poliphile' – 2nd French Edn., title in woodcut border, 181 fine woodcuts in text, 19th century morocco binding, folio – J. Jerver, Paris, 1554.
(Sotheby Parke Bernet
   Monaco)   **$33,750**   **£15,000**

COLTON, WALTER
'Land and Sea in Bosphorus and Aegean' – 2 plates, original cloth, spine chipped – New York, 1851.
(Christie's S.
   Kensington)   **$28**   **£12**

COLUM, PADRAIC
'Creatures' – 1st Edn., no. 10 of 300 copies signed by author and artist, illustrations by Boris Artzybasheff, original cloth backed boards, slipcase worn – New York, 1927.
(Sotheby's,
   Chancery Lane)   **$55**   **£25**

COLUMBIA MAGIC TRICK MANUFACTURING COMPANY
Illustrated descriptive price list of magical apparatus and illusions – illustrations, slightly stained, original pictorial wrapper, discoloured – New York, circa 1890.
(Sotheby's,
   Chancery Lane)   **$225**   **£100**

COLUMBUS, CHRISTOPHER
'The Voyages' – no. 87 of 1,050 copies, plates and maps, original vellum backed cloth, gilt – 1930.
(Sotheby's,
   Chancery Lane)   **$45**   **£20**

COLUMNA, PETRUS GALATINUS
'Opus de Arcanis Catholice Veritatis . . . ' – 1st Edn., title and 12 plates within woodblock borders, numerous woodcut initials, calf backed boards, 18th century, folio – Ortona, 1518.
(Sotheby's, New Bond
   Street)   **$1,465**   **£650**

COLYNET, ANTHONY
'True History of the Ciuill Warres of France between the French King Henry the Fourth and the Leaguers' – engraved title, calf, upper cover detached – T. Orwin for Thos. Woodcock, 1591.
(Phillips)   **$180**   **£80**

COMBE, WILLIAM
'The First, Second, Third Tour of Doctor Syntax' – 3 vols., 11 3rd Edn., 111 1st Edn., coloured plates by Rowlandson, very browned and soiled, half calf, worn, broken – 1819-1821.
(Sotheby's, New Bond
   Street)   **$190**   **£85**
'The Tour of Doctor Syntax' – 3 vols., 78 plates after Rowlandson, original cloth – George Routledge, n.d.
(Christie's S.
   Kensington)   **$190**   **£85**
'Grand Master of Adventures of Qui Hi in Hindostan' – 26 hand coloured plates by T. Rowlandson, folding frontis, engraved title, calf gilt, g.e. – 1816.
(Phillips)   **$360**   **£160**

COMENIUS, J. A.
'Visible World of a Nomenclature and Pictures of All Chief Things that Are in the World', translated by Charles Hoole, 12th Edn., 155 woodcut illustrations and pictur alphabet – Printed for S. Leacroft, 1777.
(Sotheby's,
   Chancery Lane)   **$145**   **£65**

COMFORT, A.
Pen and ink drawings, Toll Houses and Other Drawings from Carlisle to Melrose, via Bonchester Bridge and Jedburgh' – cloth backed boards, oblong, n.d.
(Tessa Bennett,
   Edinburgh)   **$12**   **£5**

COMMELIN, CASPARUS
'Beschryvinge Van Amsterdam' – 2 vols., 1st Edn., engraved title and 51 of 52 plates and maps, vignettes in text, cont. blindstamped vellum, slightly rubbed, folio – Amsterdam, 1693.
(Sotheby's
Belgravia) $2,700   £1,200

COMMINES, P. DE
'Chroniques et Histoire . . . nouvellment reveue & corigee' – morocco, bound for Henri III's 'Confrerie des Penitents Blancs' with a skull, the royal arms, and motto gilt on spine, gilt medallion in centre of covers, g.e. – Jean Ruelle, Paris, 1560.
(Sotheby Parke Bernet
Monaco) $18,000   £8,000

COMMONPLACE BOOK
17th century, 33 leaves, ms. in ink neatly written in one hand, with a Poetical Miscellany, circa 1694-1716 of 9 poems, and accounts by Richard Bowater (the compiler), concerning shipments of cotton and sugar to and from Barbados, slight foxing, cont. calf, joints cracked and worn, folio.
(Christie's, King
St.) $250   £110

COMMONPLACE BOOK
17th century 'Juvenilities of some antiquity all save the two prefaces', mss, in ink neatly done in a single hand, fair copies of poems, 94 leaves plus one inserted leaf, cont. sheep badly worn, bookplate of Edward Mundy – 1674.
(Christie's, King
St.) $5,850   £2,600

'THE COMPLETE FARMER: or A GENERAL DICTIONARY OF HUSBANDRY . . . BY A SOCIETY OF GENTLEMEN'
4th Edn., 33 engraved plates, slight damp-staining, loose, original boards, worn, lacking spine, uncut – 1793.
(Sotheby's
London) $135   £60

CONOLLY, CYRIL
'The Unquiet Grave' – 1st Edn., no. 480 of 1,000 copies, frontispiece and 3 plates, original wrappers, slightly soiled – Horizon, 1944.
(Sotheby's,
Chancery Lane) $135   £60

CONRAD, JOSEPH
'One Day More' – 1st published Edn., no. 272 of 274 copies, original buckram backed boards, label on spine worn, soiled, uncut – Beaumont Press, 1923.
(Sotheby's,
Chancery Lane) $5   £2
'Youth, a Narrative' – 1st Edn., very slightly spotted, original cloth – 1902.
(Sotheby's,
Chancery Lane) $36   £16

CONSTANT, BENJAMIN
'Adolphe' – straight grain blue morocco gilt, g.e., by Vermorel – Paris, 1816.
(Sotheby Parke Bernet
Monaco) $10,125   £4,500

CONSTITUTIO CRIMINALIS THERESIANA
Engraved illustrations of tortures at the end, modern tan half pigskin, folio – Vienna, 1769.
(Sotheby's
    Monaco) $5,065   £2,250

CONTES DE MILLE ET UNE NUITS, ADAPTES PAR HADJI-MAZEM
Fifty coloured plates by Edmund Dulac, half mottled morocco, worn – Paris, 1907.
(Sotheby Parke Bernet
    Monaco) $1,350   £600

CONUNDRUMS, VICTORIAN
An amusing collection written in English and French on both sides of 20 cards fastened in concertina fashion with broad green ribbon and hand drawn and coloured enigmatic cover designs – circa 1860.
(Lawrence of
    Crewkerne) $90   £40

COOK, CAPTAIN JAMES
'First - Third Voyages' – 8 vols., engraved plates, plans and charts, many folding, first and second voyages, cont. sprinkled calf, third voyage half calf, gilt spines – 1785.
(Sotheby's
    Monaco) $31,500   £14,000
'The Voyages' – 2 vols., half calf, morocco labels, black and white illustrated maps, some folding – 1842.
(Lawrence of
    Crewkerne) $100   £45

COOK, CAPTAIN J. AND KING, J.
'A Voyage to the Pacific Ocean . . . for making Discoveries in the Northern Hemisphere' – 2nd Edn., 4 vols., including atlas, title and 1st page loose in vol. III, 93 plates, maps and charts, some folding, some spotting, half calf, lacks spines, 4to, and folio – 1785.
(Phillips) $2,205   £980

COOK, SIR T. A,
'Twenty Five Great Houses of France' – mounted frontispiece, illustrations, original half buckram, soiled, n.d.
(Christie's, S.
    Kensington) $55   £25

COOK, THEODORA ANDREA
'The Watercolour drawings of J. M. W. Turner' – no. 158 of 1,200 copies, portrait, coloured plates, original cloth, slightly rubbed, t.e.g. – 1900.
(Sotheby Humberts
    Taunton) $50   £22

COOKE, G.
'Topographical and Statistical Description of Suffolk' – plates and map.
'. . . of Norfolk' – plates and map – 2 vols. bound together, half calf – circa 1810.
(Tessa Bennett,
    Edinburgh) $40   £18

COOKE, G. A.
'Modern and Authentic System of Universal Geography' – 2 vols., frontis, plates, maps, preface sheet loose and torn, some spotting, cont. calf worn, spines cracked, 4to – circa 1807.
(Phillips) $85   £38

COOKE, JAMES
'Mellificium Chirurgiae or the Marrow of Chirurgery with the Anatomy of the Human Bodies' – revised by Thos. Gibson, errata and advertisement on last page, engraved portrait, 11 plates, some folding, worming – W. Marshall, 1693.
(Sotheby's, New Bond
    Street) $945   £420

COOKERY
Early 18th century English cookery book, mss. in ink in one hand, inscribed 'Mary Hardisty June ye 28, 1709' – 3 leaves missing, one detached and 7 loosely inserted, some torn, cont. limp vellum, badly worn.
(Christie's, King
    St.) $450   £200

COOKERY MANUSCRIPTS
'A Book of Incomperable Receipts for Phisick, Chirurgery, Preserving, Conserving and Candying and Cookery . . . 1711' – early 18th century cookery book, mss. on paper in three different hands, cont. inscriptions, more than 50 leaves. (And 2 early 19th century ms. cookery books.)
(Christie's
    St. James) $630   £280

COOPER

COOPER, SIR ASTLEY
'The Lectures on the Principles and Practice of Surgery' – 6 plates, 3 vols., binder's cloth – 1824-27.
(Bonham's) $225 £100

COOPER, ELIZABETH AND OLDYS, WILLIAM
'The Historical and Poetical Medley or Muses Library' – 3rd Edn., cont. calf, upper hinge broken – 1738.
(Christie's, King
 St.) $100 £45

COOPER, JAMES FENNIMORE
'The Prairie' – 3 vols., 1st English Edn., a few leaves spotted, cont. calf, gilt, rubbed, 8vo – 1827.
(Sotheby Humberts
 Taunton) $36 £16

COOPER, M.
'The History of South America' – engraved frontispiece and plates, slight soiling, morocco, extremities very slightly rubbed – 1789.
(Christie's S.
 Kensington) $45 £20

COOPER, THOMAS
'Thesaurus Linguae Romanae & Britannicae' – woodcut device on title page, lacks 3 leaves, cont. calf, worn, folio – 1588.
(Sotheby's, New Bond
 Street) $125 £55

COPPARD, A. E.
'Hips and Haws' – no. 398 of 500 copies, original cloth backed boards, dust jacket – Golden Cockerel Press, 1926.
(Christie's S.
 Kensington) $18 £8
'The Hundredth Story' – no. 315 of 1,000 copies, illustrations by Robert Gibbings, original morocco backed boards – 1931.
(Christie's, S.
 Kensington) $45 £20
'Pelagea and Other Poems' – no. 48 of 425 copies, illustrations by Robert Gibbings, original cloth backed boards, dust jacket, soiled – Golden Cockerel Press, 1926.
(Christie's S.
 Kensington) $65 £30

COPPER PLATE MAGAZINE, THE
Engraved title, 24 engraved views including Oxford, half calf gilt, oblong 4to – 1792.
(Phillips) $125 £55

COQUIOT, GUSTAVE
'Toulouse-Lautrec' – limited edition, plates, vellum backed boards, folio – Berlin, n.d.
(Phillips) $55 £25

CORDINER, C.
'Antiquities and Scenery of the North of Scotland' – vignette on title and 21 plates, cont. Irish tree calf gilt – Banff, 1780.
(Bonham's) $270 £120

CORDINER, JAMES
'A Description of Ceylon' – 2 vols., 1st Edn., 25 engraved and aquatint plates, a few folding, rather browned and soiled, cont. half calf, rubbed, 4to – 1807.
(Sotheby Humberts
 Taunton) $15 £7

CORELLI, MARIE
'The Devil's Motor' – mounted coloured plates, a few creased, original cloth, affected by damp – n.d.
(Christie's S.
 Kensington) $22 £10

CORNARO, LUIGI
'Sure and Certain Methods of Attaining a Long and Healthful Life' – Made English by W. Jones, 2nd Edn., a few leaves in the middle wormed, panelled calf, rebacked – Tho. Leigh and Dan Midwinter, 1704.
(Sotheby's, New Bond
 Street) $50 £22

CORNEILLE – FOUCHET, MAX POL.
'Femme de Nuit et d'Aube' – 7 large coloured lithographs and cover design by Corneille, each signed and dated by artist, unsewn in original cloth portfolio with ties, oblong folio – Georges Fall, Paris, 1966.
(Sotheby's,
 Chancery Lane) $135 £60

CORNEILLE, P.
'Le Cid' – engraved title, rubricated, cont. dark red morocco, gilt, minor repair, worn – Targa and Courbe, Paris, 1637.
(Sotheby Parke Bernet
 Monaco) $7,650 £3,400

CORNELIUS NEPOS
'Vitae Imperatorum' — 50 leaves, 29 lines
and headline, roman letter, wormed, waterstained, 17th century vellum, worn and
soiled, lacks ties — Venice, circa 1498.
(Sotheby's, New Bond
    Street)   **$200**   **£90**

CORONA
Edited by Martin Bodmer and Herbert
Steiner — vol. 1, nos. 1-6, vol. 2, nos. 1-2,
vol. 3, no. 4, 9 issues, contributions by
Lafcadio Hearn, Herman Hesse, Hugo von
Hofmannsthal, Thomas Mann, Rilke and
others, original wrappers — Bremer Press,
Munich, 1930-33.
(Sotheby's,
    Chancery Lane)   **$40**   **£18**

CORONELLI, VINCENZO
'Epitome Cosmografica' — 1st Edn., engraved title and 37 engraved double page and
folding plates, also round global maps,
cont. vellum — Venice, 1693.
(Christie's
    St. James)   **$1,080**   **£480**

CORONELLI, VINCENZO MARIA
'Isolario Descrittione Geografico-Histori-
ca sacro profana, antico moderno, di
tutte Isola . . . ' — 2 vols. in one, mss.
title in red and black, 2 dedication leaves,
numerous engraved portraits, maps,
plates and plans, later half vellum and
marbled boards, folio — 1696.
(Christie's
    St. James)   **$135,000**   **£6,000**

CORRARO, ANGELO
'Rome exactly describ'd, as to the present
state of it, under Pope Alexandre the
Seventh . . . translated into English' — 2
parts in one vol., portrait, imprimatur and
final blank, cont. sheep, rubbed — Escrick,
1664.
(Sotheby's
    London)   **$55**   **£25**

**'EL CORREO DE LA MODA, ALBUM DE
SENORITAS'** — 1 vol. only, 40 plates, 37
hand coloured, 3 folding, most shaved,
cont. morocco backed cloth, rubbed —
Madrid, 1865.
(Christie's S.
    Kensington)   **$180**   **£80**

CORY, CHARLES
'The Birds of Haiti and San Domingo' —
engraved map and 22 hand coloured lithographed plates, some foxing and spotting,
original cloth rubbed — Boston, 1885.
(Sotheby Parke Bernet
    Monaco)   **$9,000**   **£4,000**

**COSMETICS FOR MY LADY AND
GOOD FACE FOR MY LORD**
Collected recipes — no. 47 of 300 copies,
original cloth, slightly warped — 1934.
(Christie's S.
    Kensington)   **$75**   **£32**

COSTELLO, DUDLEY
'Piedmont and Italy' — 2 vols., vignette,
titles, engraved plates, gilt, g.e. —
1861.
(Phillips)   **$585**   **£260**

COSTUME
Album containing approximately 55 water-
colour drawings of costume from Greece,
Spain, France, Canary Island etc., some
with mss. captions, also pencil sketches of
Esquimaux, large quarto album, red
morocco gilt — 1820-30 approx.
(Lawrence of
    Crewkerne)   **$360**   **£160**

COSTUME

170 skilful watercolour drawings of costume, occupation, trade etc., over much of the world. 'Drawn by Avarilla Willoughby after she was 46 for her affectionate daughter Cecilia'. Most with mss captions — 1817-1831 approx.
(Lawrence of
Crewkerne) $1,035   £460

COSTUMES DES DIFFERENS DEPARTE-MENS DE l'EMPIRE FRANCAIS

Collection of 94 hand coloured engraved costume plates of France, Switzerland, Spain, Portugal etc., cont. red half calf, rubbed and worn — Chez Martinet, Paris, 1815.
(Christie's
St. James) $1,800   £800

COTERIE

Edited by Chapman Hall and others — nos. 1-7 in 6; The New Coterie, 2-4 and 6, contributions by Edmund Blunden, Roy Campbell, T. S. Eliot, Aldous Huxley, Edith Sitwell and others, illustrations, worming, original wrappers, some worn and some covers missing — 1919-27.
(Sotheby's,
Chancery Lane) $108   £48

COTTAGE BINDING
TRAPP, JOSEPH

'The Church of England Defended against the Calumnies and False Reasonings of the Church of Rome' — slight worming, cont. blue morocco tooled in gilt to a 'cottage' design, whole enclosed in a border of flowers, spine gilt with floral motifs, inner gilt dentelles, g.e., 8vo — 1727.
(Sotheby's, New Bond
Street) $720   £320

COTTON, CHARLES

'The Compleat Angler' — Part II — 1st Edn., thumbed, some pages shaved, old calf, rebacked with original spine — 1676.
(Christie's, King
St.) $270   £120

COTTON, NATHANIEL

'Visions in Verse for the Entertainment and Instruction of Younger Minds' — 11th Edn., engraved frontispiece, slightly soiled, 19th century blue straight grained morocco gilt, spine discoloured — Printed for J. Dodsley, 1787.
(Sotheby's,
Chancery Lane) $40   £18

COTTON, SIR ROBERT

'An Exact Abridgement of the Records of the Tower of London' — 1st Edn., edited by William Prynne, tears, holes, ink stain, cont. calf — 1657.
(Sotheby's, New Bond
Street) $78   £35

COUCH, JONATHAN

'A History of the Fishes of the British Islands' — 4 vols., 250 coloured plates of 252, original cloth, spines torn — 1862-65.
(Christie's S.
Kensington) $565   £250

COUNTRY GENTLEMAN'S VADE MECUM or HIS COMPANION FOR THE TOWN

18 letters from a Gentleman in London — 1st Edn., slightly browned, cont. panelled calf, joints split, signature and bookplate of Geoffrey Bosville of Gunthwaite, Yorks — 1699.
(Sotheby's, New Bond
Street) $450   £200

COURTELINE, G.

'Messieurs les Ronds-de-Cuir' — no. 67 of 590 copies, of which this is one of 60 on Papier Japon Imperial, 15 coloured plates by Sem, wrappers, uncut, worn — Paris, 1927.
(Sotheby Parke Bernet
Monaco) $3,600   £1,600

COURTIN, PIERRE — FAULKNER, WILLAIM

'Tandis que J'Agonise' — translated by M. E. Coindreau, engraved frontispiece and 24 illustrations by Courtin, unsewn in original wrappers, uncut, original box — Jean Boisseau, Paris, 1946.
(Sotheby's,
Chancery Lane) $225   £100

COURTNEY, LEWIS

'The Baxter Book' — plates, original cloth, rubbed — 1919.
(Christie's S.
Kensington) $33   £15

COVENTRY, FRANCIS

'The History of Pompey the Little or the Life and Adventures of a Lap Dog' — 1st Edn., engraved frontispiece by Boitard, slightly spotted, cont. calf, rubbed — M. Cooper, 1751.
(Sotheby's,
Chancery Lane) $70   £30

CREIGHTON

COWLEY, ABRAHAM
'The Mistress with Other Select Poems ...
edited by John Sparrow' – no. 961 of
1,050 copies, original cloth, unopened –
The Nonesuch Press, 1926.
(Christie's S.
Kensington) $18   £8
'The Works' – 8th Edn., engraved portrait
frontispiece, foxing, cont. panelled light
red morocco, gilt spine, g.e., rubbed –
1684.
(Christie's, King
St.) $340   £150

COX, DAVID
'A Treatise on Landscape Painting in
Watercolours' – limited to 250 copies,
this unnumbered, plates, some mounted
and coloured, original vellum, slightly
soiled, torn – The Studio, 1922.
(Christie's S.
Kensington) $75   £32

CRABBE, GEORGE
'Universal Technological Dictionary' – 2
vols., 60 engraved plates on 59 sheets, 1
folding, lacks first leaves, Tyrconnel bookplate, cont. calf, later vellum, corners and
spines, gilt, with the Tyrconnel crest and
coronet – 1823.
(Sotheby's
London) $100   £45
'Tales of the Hall' – 2 vols., half titles,
some spotting, original boards, corners
rubbed – 1819.
(Christie's S.
Kensington) $180   £80

CRAIG, EDWARD GORDON
'Dido and Aeneas' – a programme designed by Craig – illustrations by Craig,
addenda leaf loosely inserted, original
wrappers, torn – 1900.
(Christie's S.
Kensington) $40   £18

CRANACH, LUCAS
'Lucas Cranachs Stammbuch' – 8 plates,
hand coloured and heightened with gold,
3 leaves of facsimiles, some dampstains,
modern calf, large folio – Berlin, 1814.
(Sotheby's, New Bond
Street) $855   £380

CRANE, HART
'Collected Poems' and 'Letters' – 1st Edns.,
– New York, 1933 and 1953.
(Sotheby's,
Chancery Lane) $45   £20

CRANE, WALTER (Illustrator)
'Don Quixote of la Mancha' – retold by
Judge Parry, coloured plates and other
illustrations, cloth – 1900.
(Tessa Bennett,
Edinburgh) $45   £20
'A Flower Wedding' – coloured illus.,
original decorated boards.
'Line and Form' – illus. buckram gilt,
worn – 1905/1900.
(Phillips) $108   £48

CRANE, WALTER AND DELAND, M.
'The Old Garden and Other Verses' –
coloured decorations by Crane, original
cloth, soiled and rubbed, unopened –
1893.
(Christie's S.
Kensington) $27   £12

CRAVEN, RICHARD KEPPEL
'A Tour Through the Southern Provinces
of the Kingdom of Naples' – 1st Edn.,
engraved map and 13 engraved plates, half
calf, gilt – 1821.
(Christie's
St. James) $250   £110

CRAWFURD, JOHN
'Journal of an Embassy to the Court of Ava
1827 with an Appendix' – 2 parts in one
vol., 1st Edn., 10 plates including 5 aquatints, 3 hand coloured, 2 engraved maps, a
little spotting, marbled boards, rubbed –
1829.
(Sotheby's, New Bond
Street) $135   £60

CREIGHTON, CHARLES
'Illustrations of Unconscious Memory in
Disease including a Theory of Alternatives'
– 1st Edn., original cloth – 1886.
(Sotheby's, New Bond
Street) $100   £45

CREIGHTON, MANDELL
'Queen Elizabeth' – coloured frontispiece
plates, illustrations, cont. half morocco –
1896.
(Christie's S.
Kensington) $27   £12

115

CRELLIUS, J.
'De Uno Deo Patre' – 1st Edn., errata leaf
at end, minor browning, inscription partly ·
erased from title, 18th century French red
morocco, gilt spine, g.e., attractive copy –
S. Sternach, Rakow, 1631.
(Sotheby's, New Bond
    Street) $585   £260

CRESSET PRESS
SWIFT, JONATHAN
'Gulliver's Travels' – 2 vols., one of 195
copies, 2 engraved frontis. and 15 plates
by Rex Whistler, 12 hand coloured, cont.
half morocco over vellum boards in slipcase,
folio – 1930.
(Christie's
    St. James) $1,530   £680

CREVECOEUR, MICHEL GUILLAUME,
SAINT JEAN DE
'Voyage Dans la Haute Pensylvanie et dans
l'Etat de New York' – 3 vols., engraved
frontis, 4 maps, 6 plates, cont. calf backed
boards, rubbed, 8vo – Paris, 1801.
(Christie's
    St. James) $205   £90

CRIMEAN WAR
3 autograph letters signed C. A. W. to
Anthony Hudson of Norwich 1854-55, in
all 21½ pages, including 3 sketch plans and
a 30 line account of Balaclava written the
day after the action laying the blame
heavily on Captain Nolan.
(Lawrence of
    Crewkerne) $360   £160

CROCKER, A.
'The Elements of Land Surveying' – 1st
Edn., engraved title and 14 plates, illustra-
tions in text, slightly soiled, cont. calf,
rubbed – 1806.
(Sotheby's,
    Chancery Lane) $40   £18

CROCKETT, S. R.
'The Grey Man' – frontispiece and plates,
buckram gilt, large paper copy, limited to
250 copies, author signed – 1896.
(Tessa Bennett,
    Edinburgh) $36   £16
'The Stickit Minister' – frontispiece and
plates, buckram gilt, large paper copy,
limited to 350 copies, author signed –
1894.
(Tessa Bennett,
    Edinburgh) $40   £18

CROMWELL, OLIVER
Ls. 1 page with address leaf also signed
and sealed, somewhat dampstained, to Lord
Fairfax on army matters, Cockpit, May the
8th 1652, framed and glazed.
(Phillips) $250   £110

CROQUIS DE CHASSE
'Le Drag de Pau' – 13 tinted lithoed plates,
finished by hand, some spotting, original
cloth, soiled, with the Schwerdt bookplate
– n.d.
(Christie's S.
    Kensington) $450   £200

CROSBY, HARRY
'Red Skeletons' – no. 117 of 370 copies,
presentation copy, inscribed by author,
plates by 'Alastair' (H. H. Voight), original
wrappers, backstrip torn – Editions
Narcisse, Paris, 1927.
(Christie's S.
    Kensington) $295   £130

CROUCH, NATHANIEL
'Surprizing Miracles of Nature and Art' –
woodcuts in text (this edition not in Wing),
calf gilt – 1699.
(Phillips) $225   £100

CROWLEY, ALEISTER
'Diary of a Drug Fiend'; 'Magick in Theory
and Practice' – 1st Edns., original cloth and
original wrappers – 1922 and n.d.
(Sotheby's,
    Chancery Lane) $100   £45
'Works' – 3 vols. in one, 1st Edn., original
cloth, dampstained – 1905-07.
(Sotheby's,
    Chancery Lane) $100   £45

CRUCHLEY, G. F.
'County Atlas of England and Wales showing
all the Railways and all the Stations' – 45
of 46 country maps only, hand coloured in
outline, original cloth, disbound – 1875.
(Christie's S
    Kensington) $65   £28

CRUIKSHANK, GEORGE
'The Humorist . . . a Collection of Entertaining Tales etc.' – 4 vols., 1st Edn., 40
hand coloured aquatint plates, some
soiling, original boards, rebacked, blue
morocco bookform case, gilt, 12 mo. –
1819-20.
(Sotheby's, New Bond
    Street) $675   £300

'Scraps and Sketches' — 2 parts each including 6 hand engraved plates, original printed pink wrappers, adverts, small oblong folio — 1828 and 1829.
(Tessa Bennett, Edinburgh) $180   £80

CRUVERIUS, P.
'Italia Antiqua' — engraved title, portrait frontispiece, 14 folding engraved plates, 13 maps and a plan of Rome, vol. 2 title water stained, discolouring, cont. calf, worn, folio — Elzevir, Leiden, 1624.
(Sotheby's, New Bond Street) $180   £80

CUALA PRESS
A small collection of printed ephemera including 17 lists and announcements for books, prints etc. — 1905-43.
(Sotheby's, Chancery Lane) $225   £100

CUALA PRESS CHRISTMAS CARDS
127 in all with verses by Yeats, Russell, Colum and others, illustrations by Jack or Elizabeth Yeats, some signed by members of the Yeats family.
(Sotheby's, Chancery Lane) $1,920   £850

CUALA PRESS PRINTS
An almost complete collection of pictures, illustrated verses and decorated poems, 110 approximately, some hand coloured, various sizes.
(Sotheby's, Chancery Lane) $1,920   £850

CULLEN, WILLIAM (Editor)
'Synopsis Nosologiae Methodicae' — 1st Edn., cont. calf — Edinburgh, 1769.
(Sotheby's, New Bond Street) $790   £350

CULPEPER, NICHOLAS
'The Complete Herbal' — engraved frontispiece, soiled, hand coloured plates, cont. half calf, rubbed — 1848.
(Christie's S. Kensington) $115   £50
'A Directory for Midwives or a Guide for Women in their Conception, Bearing and Suckling of their Children' — cont. calf — 1655.
(Bonham's) $90   £40

'A Directory for Midwives; The English Physician' — 2 works in one vol., title of 1st work holed, cont. sheep, worn, spine lacking — 1777.
(Christie's S. Kensington) $85   £38
'Health for the Rich and Poor by Dyet without Physick' — cont. calf, rebacked, device of a brazier gilt on back cover — Peter Cole, 1656.
(Sotheby's Monaco) $675   £300
'Pharmacopiae Londonensis or the London Dispensatory' — worming, modern cloth, soiled — For Georg. Sawbridge, 1675.
(Christie's S. Kensington) $40   £18

CUMMINGS, E. E.
'1/20; Poems' — a selection made by the author, 1st Edn., original boards — Roger Roughton, 1936.
(Sotheby's, Chancery Lane) $115   £50

CUNARD, NANCY
'Parallax' — 1st Edn., original boards, cover design by Eugene McCown, rubbed and stained — Hogarth Press, 1925.
(Sotheby's, Chancery Lane) $110   £48

CUNNINGHAM, JOHN
'Poems, chiefly Pastoral' — 1st Edn., engraved frontis, slight browning, signature on title, modern brown quarter morocco — Newcastle, 1766.
(Sotheby's London) $70   £30

CURTEIS, THOMAS
'Essays on the Preservation and Recovery of Health wherein the Late Wines are Suspected' — last leaf blank, cont. panelled calf — Richard Wilkin and Henry Bonwick, 1704.
(Sotheby's, New Bond Street) $80   £35

CURTIS, JOHN HARRISON
'Observations on the Preservation of Health' — 1st Edn., engraved frontispiece of Mr. West and family, half calf — H. Renshaw, 1837.
(Sotheby's, New Bond Street) $110   £48

CURTIS

'A Treatise on the Physiology of Diseases of the Eye' – 2nd Edn., 2 coloured plates, half title, advertisements at end, title with a few thumbmarks, stains, boards, cloth spine, paper label worn – Longman, 1835. (Sotheby's, New Bond
Street) $170 £75

CURTIUS RUFUS, QUINTUS

'De Rebus Gestis Alexandri Magni' – marginal worming, cont. vellum, spine torn – Lyon, 1556. (Christie's S.
Kensington) $65 £28

CUSHING, J.

'The Exotic Gardener' – 2nd Edn., short marginal tear in one leaf, slightly affecting text, one or two leaves slightly spotted, cont. calf, worn – 1814. (Sotheby's
London) $40 £16

CUYER, EDWARD AND KHUFF, G. A.

'Le Corps Humain' – 1 vol. text, title in red and black, woodcut illustrations, 1 vol. with 27 coloured plates, two tinted, all with moveable flaps, half morocco rubbed – Bailliere, Paris, 1879. (Sotheby's, New Bond
Street) $22 £10

DALI, SALVADOR

'The Song of Songs of King Solomon' – 12 coloured etched plates by Dali, unsewn in original morocco backed cloth folder, slipcase, folio – Leon Amiel, Paris and New York, 1971. (Sotheby's,
Chancery Lane) $2,140 £950

DALI, SALVADOR – VALETTE, ROBERT D.

'Deux Fatrasies' – 3 etched plated and illustration on title by Dali, unsewn in original wrappers, uncut, half morocco, folder, slipcase – Cannes, 1963. (Sotheby's,
Chancery Lane) $450 £200

D'ALLEMAGNE, H. R.

'Du Khorassan au Pays des Backhtiaris' – 4 vols., no. 58 of an edition of 510, plates, illustrations, half vellum – Paris, 1911. (Sotheby Parke Bernet
Monaco) $9,000 £4,000

DAMPIER, WILLIAM

'Voyages and Discoveries' – no. 23 of 975 copies, folding maps, original vellum backed cloth, gilt – 1931. (Sotheby's,
Chancery Lane) $75 £34
'A New Voyage round the World' – no. 808 of 975 copies, plates and maps, original vellum backed cloth, gilt – 1927. (Sotheby's,
Chancery Lane) $90 £40

DANCE
Edited by Rudolf Orthwine and Lydia Joel –
12 vols., illustrations, buckram, original
wrappers, bound in New York.
DANCE MAGAZINE ANNUAL
Edited by Lydia Joel, 3 vols., illustrations,
original wrappers – New York – 1967-69.
(Sotheby's, New Bond
   Street)   **$85**   **£38**

DANCE INDEX
Edited by Lincoln Kirstein and others –
vol. I to VII, 80 vols., a complete set,
illustrations, black rexine, original wrappers,
bound in, dust jackets, slipcase – New York,
1942-48.
(Sotheby's, New Bond
   Street)   **$495**   **£220**

DANCE PERSPECTIVE
Edited by A. J. Pischl, Selma Jeanne Cohen
and others, together 65 vols., illustrations,
original pictorial wrappers, Index to Dance
Perspective and Current Bibliography for
Dance, three copies – New York, 1959-70.
(Sotheby's, New Bond
   Street)   **$270**   **£120**

DANCE SHEET MUSIC
Collection of 38 lithographed or engraved
sheet music and 16 covers, all depicting
dances, 3 in colour, some spotting and
soiling, some disbound and loose, all in
cloth binding, various sizes, various im-
prints – circa 1830-45.
(Sotheby's, New Bond
   Street)   **$495**   **£220**

DANCING TIMES
Edited by Philip J. S. Richardson, 25 vols.,
with South Africa Dancing Times, 45 vols. –
Johannesburg, 1935-70.
(Sotheby's, New Bond
   Street)   **$11**   **£5**

DANCKERTS, T.
'Asiae' – engraved map, hand coloured in
outline, 17½ x 11in., torn at fold, stained,
framed and glazed – n.d.
(Christie's S.
   Kensington)   **$80**   **£35**

DANIEL, W. B.
'Rural Sports' – 2 vols. in three, engraved
titles and plates, some browning and spott-
ing, cont. half calf, spines torn – n.d.
(Christie's S.
   Kensington)   **$95**   **£42**

DANIELE, FRANCESCO
'Le Forche Caudine' – engraved vignette
on title, folding plan, engravings in text,
calf backed boards, spine rubbed, folio –
Naples, 1812.
(Sotheby's, New Bond
   Street)   **$205**   **£90**

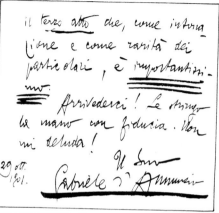

D'ANNUNZIO, GABRIELE
Autograph notes and letters relating to the
staging of his play 'Francesca di Rimini' in
1901, comprising 9 pages of notes, two
pages of rough sketches in pencil, 2 letters
of 1901, telegram and letter by D'Annunzio
to General de Rivera, 1897.
(Sotheby's, New Bond
   Street)   **$720**   **£320**

DANSDORF, CHRYSILLA VON
'Hearts Desire' – no. 69 of 70 copies,
engraved illustration on title and 7 plates
by John Buckland-Wright, an extra set of
engravings in wallet at end, original
morocco backed boards, spine darkened,
t.e.g. – Golden Cockerel Press, n.d.
(Christie's S.
   -Kensington)   **$695**   **£310**

DAPPER, OLFERT
'Umbstandliche Und Eigentliche Beschreibung von Africa' – 2 parts in one vol., 1st
Edn. in German, 56 engraved illustrations
in text, 29 engraved plates, 13 engraved
maps – Amsterdam, Jacob von Meurs,
1670-71.
(Sotheby's, New Bond
   Street)   **$1,690**   **£750**

DARAGNES, G. – BOURGES, ELEMIR
'Le Crepuscule des Dieux' – wood engraved
frontispiece by Daragnes, brown morocco,
slightly rubbed, inside borders gilt, patter-
ned endpapers, t.e.g. – Cres, Paris, 1919.
(Sotheby's,
Chancery Lane) $11   £5

DARBY, REV. CHARLES
'Bacchanalia or a Description of a Drunken
Club. A Poem' – 1st Edn., holed in one
leaf, stains, paper wrappers and folio –
1680.
(Christie's, King
St.) $135   £60

DARTON, WILLIAM AND SON
'The Western Hemisphere of the New
World and the Eastern Hemisphere of the
Old World' – 2 coloured maps, showing
Cook's voyages, varnished in cont. frames,
each 12 x 10in. – circa 1836.
(Lawrence of
Crewkerne) $63   £28

DARWIN, CHARLES
'On the origin of Species' – 5 thousand, 1
folding diagram, half title, 32 pages
publisher's catalogue at end, original cloth,
inner hinges slightly weak – 1860.
(Sotheby's
London) $170   £75
'The Variation of Animals and Plants
under Domestication' – 2 vols., 8vo, ori-
ginal green cloth, 1st Edn., illustrated –
1868.
(Lawrence of
Crewkerne) $180   £80
'On the Tendency of Species to Form
Varieties' – 1st Edn., lacks final blank,
buckram, 8vo, (Freeman 347) – 1858.
(Phillips) $855   £380

DARWIN, ERASMUS
'Zoonomia; or the Laws of Organic Life' –
4 vols., 3rd Edn., plates, some hand coloured,
cont. mottled calf, joints worn, one spine
label lacking – 1801.
(Christie's S.
Kensington) $56   £25

DARWIN, FRANCIS
'The Life and Letters of Charles Darwin' –
3 vols., portraits, original cloth, soiled and
rubbed – 1888.
(Christie's S.
Kensington) $65   £28

'DAS BUCH VOM KAISER' – A com-
memorative volume of the life of Franz
Josef I, with four frontispiece illustrations
by Koloman Moser, endplate and border
designs by Josef Hoffman, Max von Herzig,
Vienna. Richly gilt tooled tan leather
applied with gilt metal and enamel monogram
and crest, folio – Vienna, circa 1905.
(Sotheby's
Belgravia) $495   £220

DAUBIGNY, C. F. AND OTHERS
'Chants et Chansons Populaires de
France' – 3 vols., etched titles, 316
engraved illustrations or large pictorial
borders after Daubigny and others, most
with appropriate text, slightly spotted,
original pictorial boards, rather worn –
Delloye, Paris, 1843-44.
(Sotheby's,
Chancery Lane) $350   £155

DAUMAS, E.
'The Horses of the Sahara' – original cloth,
gilt, slightly rubbed, 8vo – 1863.
(Sotheby Humberts
Taunton) $45   £20

DAUMIER, H.
'Les Moeurs Conjugales' – 30 lithographs
from a series of 60, half cloth, original
wrappers – Paris, 1839-43.
(Sotheby Parke Bernet
Monaco) $24,740   £11,000

**DAUMIER, HONORE – ALHOY,
MAURICE AND LOUIS HAURT**
'Les Cent et Un Robert Macaire' – 2 vols.,
101 lithographs after Daumier, somewhat
spotted, cont. morocco backed boards,
gilt, slightly rubbed – Paris, 1839.
(Sotheby's,
   Chancery Lane) $585   £260

DAVENANT, SIR WILLIAM
'The Works' – 2 parts in one vol., 1st
collected edition, engraved portrait, reinforced at inner margin, cont. calf, rebacked,
slightly worn, folio – 1673.
(Sotheby's, New Bond
   Street) $190   £85

DAVENPORT, L. AND CO.
37 catalogues and lists in 24, including List
of Absolutely New Principles in Magic (circa 1899); All British Catalogue of New
Magical Novelties, 2 issues, n.d.; Illustrated
Catalogue of the Latest, English, American
and Continental Magical Novelties (circa
1910); Demon Series, 15 catalogues and
lists (circa 1930-1968), numerous illustrations, original wrappers or folders with
original wrappers, bound in – circa 1899-
1968.
(Sotheby's,
   Chancery Lane) $385   £170

DAVID, J. B.
'Anacreon Venge ou Lettres au Sujet de
la Nouvelle Traduction' – thick paper
copy, cont. French red morocco, gilt,
Madame de Pompadour's copy – Critico-
polis, Pierre l'Obervateur, Paris, 1755.
(Sotheby Parke Bernet
   Monaco) $36,000   £16,000

DAVIES, JOHN
'The Innkeeper and Butler's Guide, or A
Directory in the Making and Managing
of British Wines' – edges soiled, modern
half calf – Leeds, 1808.
(Christie's, King
   St.) $180   £80

DAVIES, RHYS
'Daisy Matthews' – no. 323 of 325 copies,
signed by author, illustrations by A. M.
Parker, original morocco backed cloth,
t.e.g. – 1932.
(Christie's S.
   Kensington) $70   £30

DAVIES, THOMAS
'Dramatic Miscellanies: consisting of
critical observations on several plays of
Shakespeare' – 3 vols., cont. sheep,
slightly soiled – 1784, Dublin.
(Sotheby's
   London) $160   £70

DAVILA, ENRICO CATERINO
'Histoire des Guerres Civiles de France' –
3 vols., large paper copy, titles printed
in red and black with engraved vignettes,
arms of the Society of Writers to the
Signet, Edinburgh, on covers, rubbed –
Amsterdam, 1757.
(Sotheby's, New Bond
   Street) $115   £50

DAVILA, H. C.
'A History of the Civil Wars of France' –
2nd English Edn., dampstains, rust holes,
cancelled stamp of the Bedford Library on
title page, 18th century panelled calf,
rebacked, worn – 1678.
(Sotheby's, New Bond
   Street) $35   £15

D'AVILIER, C. A.
'Cours d'Architecture' – additional engraved
title, numerous plates, letter to Duchess of
Sutherland dated 1833, loosely inserted,
cont. French mottled calf, label, spine gilt,
splits, rubbed, 4to – Paris, 1738.
(Sotheby's, New Bond
   Street) $385   £170

DAVILLIER, BARON C. H.
'Spain' – translated by J. Thomson, illus-
trated by G. Dore, cloth gilt – 1876.
(Phillips) $75   £32

DAVY, JOHN
'An Account of the Interior of Ceylon' —
14 aquatint plates, 2 hand coloured, lacks
maps, illus., slightly soiled, later half calf,
gilt spine, slightly rubbed, 4to.
(Sotheby Humberts
    Taunton) $1,915   £850

DAY, FRANCIS
'The Fishes of Great Britain and Ireland'
— 2 vols., plates, original cloth — 1880-84.
(Phillips) $250   £110

DE CANDIA AND SERVO BALORDO
A Very attractive collection of 161 pencil,
watercolour and gouache costume designs
for 'The Marriage of Figaro', and other
productions, with 14 hand coloured lithographs of costumes and 175 illustrations,
some signed — Italy, circa 1825.
(Sotheby's, New Bond
    Street) $11,700   £5,200

DE CHOU, GUILIELMO
'Veteran Romanorum Religio, Castramen-
tatio Disciplina Militaris' — 2 parts in one
vol., engraved title, folding plate and
illustrations in text, marginalia, some margins repaired, some leaves slightly soiled,
19th century half calf, rubbed —
Amsterdam, 1685.
(Sotheby Humberts
    Taunton) $67   £30

DE CHAIR, SOMERSET
'The First Crusade' — engravings by C.
Webb, half vellum gilt, 4to — Golden
Cockerel Press, 1945.
(Phillips) $112   £50

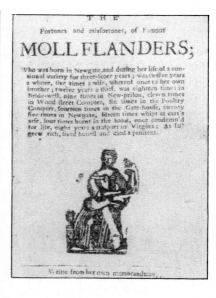

DEFOE, DANIEL
'The Fortunes and Misfortunes of Moll
Flanders . . . written from her own Mem-
orandums' — 8pp. type on last page much
larger than rest, crude woodcut on title,
disbound. A very rare or even unique
chapbook edition — Edinburgh, circa 1760.
(Sotheby's
    Edinburgh) $1,690   £750
'The Farther Adventures of Robinson
Crusoe, being the Second and Last Part of
His Life' — 1st Edn., first issue, stains,
cont. panelled calf, cracked — Printed for
W. Taylor, 1719.
(Sotheby's, New Bond
    Street) $225   £100
'A Letter to a Merry Young Gentleman,
entitled, Tho. Burnet, Esq.' — 1st Edn.,
2 page nos. cut into, slightly waterstained,
disbound — 1715.
(Sotheby's
    London) $125   £55

DEGAS, EDGAR
Curious autograph letter signed, 2 pages,
small octavo, envelope postmarked Paris,
26 May, 1884, to Mr. Bartholome,
envelope stamped and postmarked.
(Sotheby's, New Bond
    Street) $720   £320

DEGAS, EDGAR – HALEVY, LUDOVIC
'La Famille Cardinale' – portrait of author,
31 plates and head piece engraved by
Maurice Potin after monotypes by Degas to
illustrated this work, 6 plates in colour,
original wrappers, uncut, half morocco, fol-
der, slipcase, no. 162 of 350 copies –
August Blaizot, Paris, 1939.
(Sotheby's,
   Chancery Lane) $180   £80

DEGAS, EDGAR – LOUYS, PIERRE
'Mimes des Courtesanes de Lucien' – 22
engraved plates by Maurice Potin, 12
illustrations in text, all after Degas,
unsewn in original wrappers, uncut, no.
302 of 325 copies – A. Vollard, Paris,
1935.
(Sotheby's,
   Chancery Lane) $520   £230

DE LA MARE, WALTER
'Come Hither' – 2 vols., 1st Edn., no. 105
of 350 copies signed by author, illustrations
by Alec Buckels, original cloth backed
boards, t.e.g. – 1923.
(Sotheby's,
   Chancery Lane) $9   £4
Three Works, one 2nd Edn., two 1st Edns.,
all with pictorial wrappers and illustrations
in black and white by Barnett Freedman
and inscribed by him to Nick Bentley –
1935-40.
(Lawrence of
   Crewkerne) $50   £22

DE LA MARE, WALTER – 'Walter Ramal'
'Songs of Childhood' – 1st Edn., presentation copy, inscribed by author, frontispiece after Richard Doyle, original parchment backed cloth, gilt, t.e.g. – 1903.
(Sotheby's,
   Chancery Lane) $385   £170

'DE LA PLANTE A L'ORNEMENT'
A folio of 30 lithographic plates, art
nouveau, floral designs, printed list of con-
tents, title green cloth, folio – Gustav
Kolb and Ch. Gmelich, Goppingen, circa
1900.
(Sotheby's
   Belgravia) $520   £230

DE LISLE, G.
'l'Europe' – hand coloured map – 1708.
And four other including France.
(Phillips) $60   £25

DELKESKAMP, FREDERIC GUILLAUME
'Nouveau Panorama Du Rhine Depuis
Mayence Jusqu'a Cologne' – folding
engraved panorama, original roan backed
boards, rather worn – Frankfurt-am-Main,
1850.
(Sotheby's,
    Chancery Lane) $240   £105

DELLA BELLA, STEFANINO
'A Collection of Etchings' – 180 plates on
96 leaves, a few marginal tears, cont. half
morocco, worn, folio – 1818.
(Christie's S.
    Kensington) $1,980   £880

DE MOIVRE, A.
'The Doctrine of Chances' – 2nd Edn.,
engravings in text, errata leaf at end, old ms.
notes on two text pages and endleaves, title
partly detached, upper cover and front endleaves detached – 1738.
(Sotheby's
    London) $250   £110

DENHAM, MAJOR AND CLAPPERTON, CAPTAIN
'Narrative of Travels and Discoveries in
Northern and Central Africa' – 2 vols.,
plates and maps, linen backed boards –
1826.
(Phillips) $100   £45

DENIS, MAURICE – THOMPSON, FRANCIS
'Poemes' – translated by Elisabeth M.
Denis Graterolle, 67 coloured
lithographed illustrations by Maurice Denis,
13 full page, embossed morocco, uncut,
original wrappers bound in, folio –
Ambroise Vollard, Paris, 1942.
(Sotheby's,
    Chancery Lane) $450   £200

DENISON, JOHN
'A Three-fold Resolution, verie necessarie
to salutation' – 1st Edn., printed with line
borders, lacking first leaf and all after 2B12,
some dampstaining, cont. limp vellum,
rubbed and soiled – Richard Field for
Cuthbert Burbie, 1603.
(Sotheby's
    London) $70   £30

DENMAN, T.
'Collection of Engravings tending to Illus-
trate the Generation and Parturition of
Animals and of the Human Species' – 9
plates, 1st Edn., boards – 1787.
(Bonham's) $45   £20

DENNIS, JOHN
'Remarks upon Cato, A Tragedy' – 1st Edn.,
errata note at end of final leaf, slight dampstains, later half calf – for B. Lintott, 1713.
(Sotheby's
    London) $205   £90

DE NOLHAC, P.
'La Reine Marie Antoinette' – coloured
'Goupil' frontispiece, numerous illustra-
tions, a nice copy in half citron morocco,
gilt, by Pagnant – Paris, 1890.
(Sotheby Parke Bernet
    Monaco) $1,800   £800

DE QUINCEY, THOMAS
'Confessions of an English Opium Eater' –
1st Edn., cased in 18th century mottled
calf binding, rebacked, g.e. – 1822.
(Sotheby's, New Bond
    Street) $340   £150

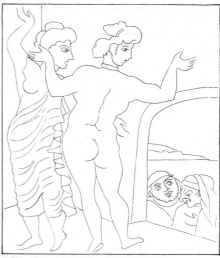

DERAIN, ANDRE – PETRONIUS, ARBITER
'Le Satyricon' – 69 engraved plates by
Derain, woodcut decorations, dark green
morocco, large folio – Au Depens
d'Amateur, Paris, 1951.
(Sotheby's,
    Chancery Lane) $2,590   £1,150

DERAIN, ANDRE – LA FONTAINE, JEAN DE
'Contes et Nouvelles en Vers' – 2 vols., 67 full page lithographs by Derain, brown morocco, t.e.g., slipcases by Rene and Michel Kieffer – Au Depens d'Un Amateur, Paris, 1950.
(Sotheby's,
   Chancery Lane) $855   £380

DERAIN, ANDRE – PETRONIUS, ARBITER
'Le Satyricon' – 33 engraved plates, 43 woodcut illustrations by Derain, unsewn in original wrappers, uncut, folder and slipcase, folio – Aux Depens d'Un Amateur, Paris, 1951.
(Sotheby's,
   Chancery Lane) $1,125   £500

DESAGUILIERS, JOHN THEOPHILUS
'A System of Experimental Philosophy' – advert leaf before title and 2 advert leaves at end, 10 engraved folding plates, cont. calf, rubbed, 4to – 1719.
(Christie's
   St. James) $400   £180

DESCARTES, RENE
'De Homine Figuris et Latinitate donatus a Florentio Schuyl' – 1st (authorised) Edn., device on title, 9 plates of 10, numerous ownership inscriptions, and ms. not on one plate, cont. sheep, slightly defective – Leiden, F. Moyardus and P. Leffen, 1662.
(Sotheby's
   London) $270   £120

DESGODETZ, ANTOINE
'Rome, in its Ancient Grandeur; with copious notes . . . under the superintendence of Mr. Charles Taylor' – bound in two vols., engraved plates, some spotting, cont. half morocco, rubbed, folio – 1848.
(Christie's S.
   Kensington) $115   £50
'Les Edifices Antiques de Rome' – engraved title and full page illustrations, cont. calf, rubbed, upper joint split, folio – Paris, 1682.
(Christie's S.
   Kensington) $1,300   £580

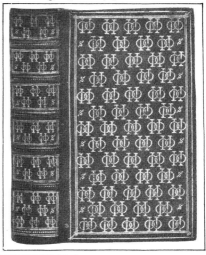

DES PORTES, P.
'Les Premieres Oeuvres . . . revues, corrigees & augmentees outre les precedent impressions' – device on title, 17th century French red morocco, gilt, sides and spine semeed with devices, typical of the Prince de Soubise collection – Robert le Mangier, Paris, 1583.
(Sotheby Parke Bernet
   Monaco) $29,250   £13,000

DETMOLD, E. J. – MAETERLINCK, M.
'The Life of the Bee' – 13 mounted
coloured plates by Detmold, original
parchment, soiled, upper joint slightly
torn – 1911.
(Christie's S.
   Kensington)   **$35**   **£15**

DEUCHAR, DAVID
'A Collection of Etchings after the Most
Eminent Masters of the Dutch and Flemish
Schools' – 3 vols., 3 engraved titles,
engraved dedication and 372 engravings on
303 plates, folio – Edinburgh, 1803.
(Sotheby's, New Bond
   Street)   **$1,915**   **£850**

DEVENTER, H.
'The Art of Midwifery Improv'd' – 5
folding plates, first English Edn., old
panelled calf – 1716.
(Bonham's)   **$540**   **£240**

DEWHURST, HENRY WILLIAM
'The Natural History of the Order of
Cetacea' – 1st Edn., 24 engraved and
lithoed plates, 7 page subscriber's list, 8
page adverts at end, original boards, uncut,
partly unopened – 1834.
(Sotheby's
   London)   **$295**   **£130**

DE WIT, F.
'Terra Sancta sive Promissionis, olim
Palestina' – hand coloured engraved map,
19 x 24in., slightly torn, framed and
glazed – n.d.
(Christie's S.
   Kensington)   **$430**   **£190**

DEZALLIER D'ARGENVILLE, A. J.
'l'Histoire Naturelle Eclaircie dans une
de ses Parties Principales' – engraved
frontispiece and 25 plates, cont. mottled
calf, slightly rubbed, spine chipped –
Paris, 1755.
(Sotheby's
   Monaco)   **$2,250**   **£1,000**

DIBDIN, T. F.
'The Bibliographical Decameron' – 3 vols.,
1st Edn., 37 plates, slight browning, cont.
polished calf, labels, spines gilt, rubbed –
1817.
(Sotheby's, New Bond
   Street)   **$225**   **£100**

DICKENS, CHARLES
'A Christmas Carol' – large parchment
decorated gilt, t.e.g., uncut, 12 tissued and
mounted plates by Arthur Rackham, 18
illustrations in black and white, no. 77 of
525 copies, signed by artist – 1915.
(Lawrence of
   Crewkerne)   **$225**   **£100**
'The Life and Adventures of Nicholas
Nickleby' – 1st Edn., first issue,
engraved portrait and plates, spotting and
staining, cont. half morocco, rubbed –
1839.
(Christie's S
   Kensington)   **$45**   **£20**
'Little Dorrit' – engraved plates by H. K.
Browne, half morocco rebacked – 1st Edn.
– 1857.
(Tessa Bennett,
   Edinburgh)   **$11**   **£5**
'The Works' with notes by Andrew Lang –
38 vols., Gadshill edition, plates, blue half
levant by A. & F. Denny Ltd., the spines
gilt in compartments – n.d.
(Christie's S.
   Kensington)   **$1,305**   **£580**

**'DICKINSONS' COMPREHENSIVE
PICTURES OF THE GREAT EXHIBITION
OF 1851'**
2 vols., 55 hand coloured proof lithographed plates by Nash, Haghe and Roberts,
one slightly torn, some leaves marginally
soiled, original morocco, worn, loose, g.e.
– 1854.
(Sotheby's,
   Chancery Lane)   **$3,040**   **£1,350**

DIDEROT, DENIS
'Le Neveu de Rameau' – one of 355 copies,
engraved plates by Naudin, red morocco by
Degoul, silk doublures, t.e.g., slipcase –
Paris, 1924.
(Sotheby's
   Monaco)   **$1,240**   **£550**

**DIDEROT, DENIS AND D'ALMEBERT,
JEAN**
'Encyclopaedie' – 33 anatomical plates,
24 chemical plates and 38 surgical plates
and a frontispiece to last section, all
accompanied by text, half calf, uncut,
folio – Paris, 1751.
(Sotheby's, New Bond
   Street)   **$720**   **£320**

DIERMERBROECK, ISBANDUS DE
'The Anatomy of Human Bodies' – trans-
lated by William Salmon, 2nd Edn. in
English, 16 engraved folding plates, folio –
W. Whitwood, 1694.
(Sotheby's, New Bond
    Street) $945   £420

DIGBY, SIR KENELM
'Of Bodies and of Mens Soul' – 4 parts in
one vol., separate title pages, rust hole,
polished calf gilt – S. G. and B. G. for John
Williams, 1669.
(Sotheby's, New Bond
    Street) $360   £160

DILETTANTI, SOCIETY OF
'Ionian Antiquities' – 2 vols., half calf,
covers detached, lacks 5 plates, folio –
1769.
(Phillips) $180   £80

DIODORUS SICULUS
'Bibliothecae Historicae Libri vi' and
'Cornelii Taciti Germania' – 2 parts in
one vol., 97 leaves of 102, 42 lines, roman
letter, 9 initials throughout the book,
finely painted in gold and colours, early
19th century roan backed boards, rubbed,
folio – Bologna, 1472.
(Sotheby's, New Bond
    Street) $1,575   £700

DION, CASSIUS 'NICAEUS'
'Rerum Romanarum a Pompeio Magno ad
Alexandrum Mamaeae Filium Epitome
Ioanne Xiphilino Authore, Guilielmo
Blanco Albiensi Interprete' – 2 parts in
one vol., 1st Edn., Latin and Greek text,
woodcut devices, initials and ornaments –
Robertus Stephanus, Paris, 1551.
(Sotheby's, New Bond
    Street) $250   £110

DIONIS, PIERRE
'L'Anatomie de l'Homme suivant La Circulation du Sang et les Nouvelles Decouvertes'
– 5th Edn., engraved frontispiece, portrait
after Boulogne, 24 engraved plates, cont.
calf – L. De Houry, Paris, 1716.
(Sotheby's, New Bond
    Street) $180   £80

DISCOURSE, A
'On Witchcraft on a Bill now depending in
Parliament to Repeal the Statute made in
the first year of the reign of King James I'
– quarter calf – J. Read, 1736.
(Sotheby's, New Bond
    Street) $225   £100

DISNEY, GERVASE
'Some Remarkable Passages in the Holy
Life and Death of Gervase Disney
Esq., to which are added Several Letters
and Poems' – 18th century calf, gilt spine,
cont. inscription on title – 1692.
(Christie's, King
    St.) $115   £50

DISRAELI, BENJAMIN
'Vindication of the English Constitution' –
1st Edn., copies of letters from the author's
father inserted, 2pp. of adverts, foxing,
later half calf, bookplate of Coningsby
Disraeli, 8vo – 1835.
(Christie's
    St. James) $315   £140

**D. M. T. (SUITE OF JEWELLERY
DESIGNS)**
Decorative title, printed leaf of dedication,
22 plates of jewellery designs by G. C.
after D. M. T., minor stains, old wrappers,
rebacked, card slipcase, two Russian
library labels, one with an elaborate inter-
laced cypher – Venice, 1751.
(Sotheby Parke Bernet
    Monaco) $72,000   £32,000

DOBELL

DOBELL, PETER
'Travels in Kamchatka and Siberia' – 2 vols., 1st Edn., 2 hand coloured aquatints, advert. leaf in vol. II, a few leaves very slightly spotted, loosely inserted A.L.s to Lady Tyrconnel, 1844, cont. half purple morocco, gilt – 1830.
(Sotheby's
   London) $250   £110

DODGSON, C. L. 'Lewis Carroll'
'Alice's Adventures Underground' – 1st Edn., facsimile of the author's manuscript and drawings, original cloth gilt, slightly soiled, spine faded, g.e. – 1886.
(Sotheby's,
   Chancery Lane) $155   £60

Rev. E. R. Dukes,

with the Author's sincere regard.

Man 27/79

EUCLID

AND HIS

MODERN RIVALS.

'Euclid and His Modern Rivals' – 1st Edn., presentation copy, inscribed by author, diagrams, original cloth, slightly rubbed – 1879.
(Sotheby's,
   Chancery Lane) $340   £150
'The Hunting of the Snark' – 1st Edn., frontispiece and 8 full page illustrations by Henry Holiday, very slightly spotted, original pictorial cloth, soiled, g.e. – 1876.
(Sotheby's,
   Chancery Lane) $160   £70

DODSLEY, R.
'The Oeconomy of Human Life' – large paper, text illustrations, cont. straight grain red morocco, g.e., inscription from J. Abdy to Julia Conyers 1807, folio – 1795.
(Sotheby Parke Bernet
   Monaco) $785   £350

DODWELL, EDWARD
'Views in Greece' – 30 coloured aquatint plates, mounted on card, printed slip in verso, lacks preface and some text, discoloured, disbound in original portfolio, roan backed boards, worn, lacking ties, folio – Rodwell and Martin, 1821.
(Sotheby's, New Bond
   Street) $12,375   £5,500

DOLCE, L.
'Dialogo della Institutione' – device on title and last page – Venice, 1547.
(Phillips) $160   £70

DOMINICUS, FERDINAND
'Bibliotheca Windhagiana ab Comite Joanne Joachimo ab, et in Windhag, Munzbach etc. Anno MDCLXXVIII Pro Usu Publico . . . fundata' – portrait, cont, half calf, rubbed, bookplate of E. von Friedlander – Vienna, 1733.
(Sotheby Parke Bernet
   Monaco) $2,250   £1,000

DONALDSON, T. L.
'Pompeii, illustrated with pictures and views' – 4 parts, 80 plates, 5 hand coloured, original printed wrappers, green leather spines, large folio – 1827.
(Sotheby's, New Bond
   Street) $385   £170

DONDE, ANTOINE
'Les Figures de la Vie, de la Mort, et des Miracles de Saint Francois de Paule . . . ' – 2 parts in one vol., 43 engraved plates, slight browning and soiling, cont. red morocco, gilt, worm, g.e., folio – Paris, 1671.
(Sotheby's, New Bond
   Street) $90   £40

DONERT, JOHN
'A New General Atlas of the World' – engraved title, and 46 maps, double page and mounted on guards, hand coloured in outline, two detached, a few additional maps loosely inserted, cont. morocco, covers detached, folio – 1842.
(Christie'S. S.
   Kensington) $90   £60

DONNE, JOHN
'A Declaration of the Paradoxe or Thesis that Self Homicide is not so naturally Sinne that it may never be Otherwise' — 1st Edn., first issue, lacks first blank, cont. calf, rubbed, corners repaired, new endpapers, small 4to — John Dawson, 1647.
(Sotheby's, New Bond
  Street) $450   £200

DONOVAN, EDWARD
'An Epitomie of the Natural History of the Insects of China' — 50 hand coloured engraved plates, cont. speckled calf, rubbed, joints cracked — 1798.
(Christie's S.
  Kensington) $4,275   £1,900
'An Epitomie of the Natural History of the Insects of India' — 58 hand coloured engraved plates, a few very slightly spotted, cont. calf, rubbed, joints cracked — 1800.
(Christie's S.
  Kensington) $4,275   £1,900
'The Natural History of British Insects' — 16 vols. in 8, 575 engraved plates, all but a few hand coloured, cont. calf, rubbed — 1802-1813.
(Christie's S.
  Kensington) $2,700   £1,200
'The Natural History of British Shells' — 5 vols. in two, 180 coloured plates, cont. red morocco, gilt, g.e., worn, 8vo — 1804.
(Sotheby's, New Bond
  Street) $1,015   £450

'The Natural History of British Birds' — 1st Edn., 10 vols., 244 hand coloured engraved plates, 4 half titles, original boards with printed paper labels on spines, uncut — 1794-1819.
(Christie's
  St. James) $4,950   £2,200

DORAT, CLAUDE
'Fables Nouvelles' — 2 vols. in one, engraved frontispieces, vignettes and culs de lampe by Delaunay, and others, modern tan morocco, gilt, g.e. — La Haye, 1773.
(Sotheby Parke Bernet
  Monaco) $3,600   £1,600

DORE, GUSTAVE — CERVANTES, S. M. DE
'Don Quixote' — engraved plates and illustrations after Dore, cont. half morocco, corners rubbed, hinges repaired — n.d.
(Christie's S.
  Kensington) $27   £12

DORE, GUSTAVE AND JERROLD, BLANCHARD
'London, a Pilgrimage' — folio, half morocco, gilt, rubbed, front cover loose, a.e.g. Engraved half title, frontispiece and 178 black and white illustrations after Dore, some full page and tissued, text within red border — 1872.
(Lawrence of
  Crewkerne) $115   £50

DOUGHTY, C. M.
'Travels, Arabia Deserta' — 2 vols., new edition, illustrations with folding map — 1923.
(Christie's S.
  Kensington) $90   £40

DOUGLAS, LORD ALFRED
'Collected Satires' — cloth, limited edition, 500 copies — Fortune Press, 1926.
(Tessa Bennett,
  Edinburgh) $20   £9

DOUGLAS, LADY JANE
'Letters . . . with several other Important pieces of Private Correspondence . . . together with an Introductory Preface, giving some Account of Lady Jane' — edited by James Boswell, half title, modern green morocco, gilt — For J. Wilkie, 1767.
(Sotheby's, New Bond
  Street) $340   £150

DOUGLAS, NORMAN
'Birds and Beasts of the Greek Anthology' — 1st Edn., no. 155 of 500 copies, signed by author, presentation copy, inscribed by author, frontispiece and two illustrations in text, original boards, uncut, dust jacket — Privately printed, 1927.
(Sotheby's,
  Chancery Lane) $120   £52

'Some Antiquarian Notes' – 1st Edn., half vellum – Naples, 1907.
(Sotheby's,
   Chancery Lane) $135   £60
'Some Limericks' – 1st Edn., limited to 110 copies, presentation copy, inscribed by author, original cloth, uncut – Privately printed, 1928.
(Sotheby's,
   Chancery Lane) $190   £85

DOVER, THOMAS

'The Ancient Physician's Legacy to his Country being what he has collected himself in forty-nine years practice' – 2nd Edn., many cont. mss. notes on fly leaves, very good readable hand, cont. panelled calf – 1732.
(Sotheby's, New Bond
   Street) $270   £120

DOW, ALEXANDER

'The History of Hindostan' – translated from the Persian, 3 vols., new edition, 7 engraved plates and 1 folding map, cont. diced russia by J. Young, Inverness – 1803.
(Christie's S.
   Kensington) $170   £75

DOYLE, SIR ARTHUR CONAN

'The Adventures of Sherlock Holmes' – 1st Edn., illustrations by Sidney Paget, original cloth, worn, recased, g.e. – 1892.
(Sotheby's,
   Chancery Lane) $100   £45
'The History of Spiritualism' – 2 vols., plates, original cloth, slightly rubbed – 1926.
(Christie's S.
   Kensington) $40   £18
'Hound of the Baskervilles' – 1st Edn., original red cloth gilt – 1902.
(Phillips) $170   £75
'The Memoirs of Sherlock Holmes' – 1st Edn., illus., slightly soiled, original cloth rubbed – 1894.
(Phillips) $180   £80

DOYLE, RICHARD

'Fairy Land. A Series of Pictures from the Elf World' – large folio, original green cloth gilt, 1st Edn., wood engraved title, frontispiece and 15 other plates with 36 illustrations in colour – 1870.
(Lawrence of
   Crewkerne) $340   £150

D'OYLY, SIR CHARLES

'Tom Raw, the Griffin . . . by a Civilian and an Officer' – 25 hand coloured plates, advertisements at end, foxed, soiled, original cloth, spine defective – 1828.
(Sotheby's, New Bond
   Street) $190   £85

DRAGE, WILLIAM

'A Physical Nosonomy - a small treatise of sicknesses and diseases from witchcraft and supernatural causes' – 2 works in one vol., tears, discoloured, new limp vellum – J. Dover for author, 1664.
(Sotheby's, New Bond
   Street) $855   £380

DRAKE, EDWARD CAVENDISH

'A New Universal Collection of Voyages and Travels' – 51 engraved plates and 7 maps, some browning, cont. calf, rubbed, inner hinges, cracked, folio – n.d.
(Christie's S.
   Kensington) $250   £110

DRAKE, SIR FRANCIS

'The World Encompassed' – no. 397 of 975 copies, plates and maps, original vellum backed cloth, gilt – 1926.
(Sotheby's,
   Chancery Lane) $60   £25

DRAKE, JAMES

'Anthropologia Nova or a New System of Anatomy' – 2nd Edn., two parts in one vol., 27 engraved plates, lacks the portrait and without the Appendix containing extra plates, cont. panelled calf – W. Innys, 1717.
(Sotheby's, New Bond
   Street) $55   £24

DRAYTON, MICHAEL

'The Bataile of Agincourt . . . the Miseries of Queene Margarite . . . Nimphidia (and other poems)' – 1st Edn., engraved portrait 'The Vision of Ben Jonson', some leaves slightly soiled, 18th century calf, rubbed, folio – 1627.
(Sotheby's, New Bond
   Street) $675   £300
'Poly Olbion or a Chorographicall Description of Tracts, Rivers, Mountaines, Forests and Other Parts of this Renowned Isle of Great Britaine' – 1st Edn., second issue, woodcut device on title, late 17th century panelled calf, gilt spine, folio – 1613.
(Christie's, King
   St.) $4,725   £2,100

Map of Cornwall from Michael Drayton's Poly Olbion. (Christie's)

DRESDEN GALLERY
'Recueil d'Estampes d'apres les plus
Celebres Tableaux de la Galerie Royale de
Dresden' – 2 vols., French and Italian text,
96 plates of 100, some double page, cont.
calf, very worn, large folio – Dresden,
1753-57.
(Sotheby's, New Bond
    Street) $2,140   £950

DRESSER, C.
'Studies in Design' – 60 coloured plates,
designs for wallpapers, friezes etc., half calf,
folio – circa 1890.
(Tessa Bennett,
    Edinburgh) $250   £110

DRESSER, H. E.
'A Manual of Palaearctic Birds' – 2 vols.,
plates, watercolour sketches, inserted limp
leather – 1902-3.
(Phillips) $315   £140

DRIBERG, J. H. (Translator)
'Initiations; translations from poems of the
Bidinga and Lango Tribes' – no. 5 of 325
copies, signed by translator, illustrations by
Robert Gibbings, original cloth, stained –
Golden Cockerel Press, 1932.
(Christie's S.
    Kensington) $55   £25

DRYDEN, JOHN
'Marriage a-la-Mode. A Comedy' – 1st Edn.,
lacks final blank, some leaves torn, last
leaf repaired, browned throughout, dark
blue half roan – 1673.
(Sotheby's
    London) $70   £30
'Songs and Poems' – limited to 500 copies,
this is no. 7 of 100 specially bound by
Sangorski and Sutcliffe and with extra set
of plates, decorations and coloured plates
by Lavinia Blythe, original morocco, t.e.g.,
slipcase, folio – 1957.
(Christie's S.
    Kensington) $430   £190

DUBE, PAUL
'The Poor Man's Physician and Surgeon
shewing the true method of curing all
sorts of distempers' – 1st English Edn.,
errata at end, some dampstains, old calf,
rebacked – 1704.
(Sotheby's, New Bond
    Street) $125   £55

DUBEUX, L.
'La Perse' – map and 86 engravings, slight
spotting, half calf, worn, spine cracked, 8vo
– Paris, 1841.
(Phillips) $75   £32

DU BOSC, J.
'L'Honneste Femme' – some browning and
staining, cont. limp vellum, slightly
stained and defective – Paris, 1639.
(Sotheby Parke Bernet
    Monaco) $675   £300

DUBOUCHET, H. – BEYLE, M. H.
'Stendhal'
'Le Rouge et Le Noir' – 3 vols., etched
frontispiece and 78 illustrations by
Dubouchet, mauve half morocco, t.e.g.,
original wrappers, bound in, by Rene
Kieffer, no. 267 of 500 copies – Conquet,
Paris, 1884.
(Sotheby's,
    Chancery Lane) $115   £52

DUBOURG, M.
'Views of . . . Rome and Its Vicinity' – 26
coloured plates, cloth gilt, rebacked, folio
– 1844.
(Phillips) $540   £240

DUBRAVIUS, JANUS
'A New Booke of Good Husbandry, very
Pleasant and of Great Profite for Gentlemen and Yomen' – 1st Edn., woodcut
arms on title, large woodcut and other
smaller initials, woodcut illustration, 19th
century calf, g.e., a little rubbed – 1599.
(Christie's, King
    St.) $2,250   £1,000

DUBUFFET, JEAN
'Elegies' – double page coloured lithograph
by Dubuffet, original wrappers, slightly
stained, uncut – Le Calligraphie, Paris,
1946.
(Sotheby's,
    Chancery Lane) $70   £30

DUCHARTRE, P. L.
'Legendes Croyances et Talismans des
Indiens de l'Amazone' – illus., limited
edition, morocco backed boards, 4to –
1923.
(Phillips) $80   £35

DUFF, E. GORDON
'Fifteenth Century English Books' – fac-
similes, original cloth backed boards,
soiled, rubbed – The Bibliographical
Society, 1917.
(Christie's S.
    Kensington) $65   £28

DUFY, RAOUL – ALLARD, ROGER
'Les Elegies Martiales' – 6 wood engraved
illustrations and 23 wood engraved head
and end pieces by Raoul Dufy, slightly
spotted, original wrappers, uncut – Paris,
1917.
(Sotheby's,
    Chancery Lane) $125   £55

DUGAZON, GUSTAVE
'Danses Nationales' – engraved title, music
and 6 hand coloured plates, heavy spotting,
cont. half morocco – n.d.
(Christie's S.
    Kensington) $115   £50

DUGDALE, WILLIAM
'Monasticon Anglicanum' – 3 vols. in one,
103 engraved plates, one torn, cont.
panelled calf, joints split, rubbed – 1718.
(Sotheby's,
    Chancery Lane) $190   £85

DUHRING, LOUIS ADOLPHUS
'Atlas of Skin Diseases' – 1st Edn., 36
coloured plates with explanatory text, half
morocco rubbed, upper cover loose –
Philadelphia, 1876.
(Sotheby's, New Bond
    Street) $190   £85

DULAC, EDMUND
'Rubaiyat of Omar Khayam' – 20
mounted colour plates by Dulac, slight
soiling, original cloth – n.d.
(Christie's S.
    Kensington) $65   £28

DULAC, EDMUND AND HOUSMAN, LAURENCE
'Stories from the Arabian Nights' – 20 mounted coloured plates by Dulac, original cloth, soiled – n.d.
(Christie's S. Kensington) $55   £25

DULAURE, J. A. J.
'Histoire de Paris et de ses Monuments' – coloured frontispiece, 51 engraved plates, illustrations, modern calf, gilt, g.e. – Paris, 1846.
(Sotheby's, Chancery Lane) $170   £75

DULCKEN, H. W. (Translator)
'What the Moon Saw' by Hans Christian Andersen – 1st English Edn., numerous wood engraved illustrations, upper hinge weak, original decorated cloth, slightly worn – Routledge, 1866.
(Sotheby's, Chancery Lane) $75   £32

DUMAS, A.
'Three Musketeers' – 2 vols., limited edition, illustrated by M. Leloir, half morocco gilt – 1892.
(Phillips) $85   £38

DU MAURIER, GERALD
'Trilby' – large paper, vellum backed buckram gilt, t.e.g., uncut, 12 illustrations by author, signed by author, no. 26 of 250 copies – 1895.
(Lawrence of Crewkerne) $22   £10

DUMONT, JEAN AND ROUSSET, JEAN
'Histoire Militaire du Prince Eugene de Savoye' – 3 vols., titles printed in red and black, engraved vignettes, maps and plans, cont. French mottled calf, spines worn, large folio – The Hague, 1729-47.
(Sotheby's, New Bond Street) $2,025   £900

DUNCAN, ISADORA
Album containing 76 photographs of Isadora Duncan and her friends, some showing her dancing, original decorative cloth edged with gold wire – circa 1922.
(Sotheby's, New Bond Street) $495   £220

DUNLOP, JOHN
'Mooltan, During and After the Seige' – lithographed additional title and 21 plates by A. Machure after Dunlop, spotting, cont. half morocco, worn, folio – 1849.
(Christie's S. Kensington) $200   £90

DUNN, S.
'The New World, Eastern and Western Hemispheres' – 2 partly coloured maps (matching) – 1781.
(Phillips) $80   £35

DUNSANY, E. P. LORD
'Time and the Gods' – limited edition, illus. by S. Sime, signed by artist and author, vellum backed boards, gilt – 1922.
(Phillips) $100   £45

DUNTON, JOHN
'Athenian Sport' or 'Two Thousand Paradoxes Merrily Argued with improvements from the Honourable Mr. Boyle, Lock, etc.' – 1st Edn., cont. panelled sheep, joints split – 1707.
(Sotheby's, New Bond Street) $70   £30

DURAND, J. N. L.
'Raccolta e Paralello delle Fabriche Classiche di tutti di tempi' – 4 vols., 226 engraved plates, a few slightly shaved or torn cleanly, titles and text in Italian and French, cont. morocco backed boards, rubbed, folio – Venice, 1834.
(Christie's S. Kensington) $430   £190

D'URFEY, THOMAS
'The Progress of Honesty or a View of
Court and City' — 1st Edn., cont. owner-
ship inscription, ms. annotations in margin,
cropped, stained and torn, disbound in
paper wrappers, folio — 1681.
(Christie's, King
St.) $110   £50

DURRELL, LAWRENCE
'The Black Book' — 1st Edn., original
wrappers, slightly worn, uncut — The
Obelisk Press, Paris, 1938.
(Sotheby's,
Chancery Lane) $270   £120
'The Alexandria Quartette' — First
collected edition, no. 426 of 500 copies,
signed by author, original buckram, t.e.g.,
slipcase — 1962.
(Sotheby's,
Chancery Lane) $190   £85

DURER, ALBRECHT
'Institutiones Geometricae' — Second issue
dated 1535 of second edition of Latin
translation by Camerarius, device on title,
numerous woodcut illustrations, several
full page, 19th century vellum boards,
joints splitting, folio — Christian Wechel,
Paris, 1535.
(Sotheby's, New Bond
Street) $1,800   £800

'Designs of the Prayer Book' — 46 litho-
graphed plates, a few spots and stains,
19th century half calf, rubbed, folio —
Ackermann's Lithographic Press, 1817.
(Sotheby's, New Bond
Street) $360   £160

DU TERTE, JEAN BAPTISTE DE
'Histoire Generale des Antilles Habitees
Par Les Francois' — 4 vols. in three,
engraved frontispiece and maps and plates,
many folding, some spotting, modern 18th
century style mottled calf, gilt spines —
Paris, 1667-71.
(Sotheby Parke Bernet
Monaco) $13,950   £6,200

DYKE, DANIEL
'The Mystery of Self Deceiuing or a Discourse and Discouerie of the Deceitful-
ness of Mans Heart' — 18th and 19th
century signatures on endpapers, light
stains, cont. calf, worn — 1628.
(Sotheby's, New Bond
Street) $100   £45

DYKES, W. R.
'Notes on the Tulip Species' — coloured
plates, original cloth, dust jacket —
1930.
(Christie's S.
Kensington) $240   £105

EARL, M.
'The Power of the Dog' — coloured plates,
half parchment — n.d.
(Tessa Bennett,
Edinburgh) $65   £28

**EARLY CRICKET, HINTON ST. GEORGE,
SOMERSET**
Rules for the Hinton St. George Cricket
Club, 13 July 1827, corrected for 1828,
written in ms. folio, with list of rules and
members with pencil annotations concern-
ing payment of subscriptions.
(Lawrence of
Crewkerne) $100   £45

'EASTERN LOVE'
Translated by Mathers — 12 vols., bound in
four, limited edition, engravings by Hester
Sainsbury, hand coloured, brown morocco
with black inlay, t.e.g., worming to margins
of last leaves vol. 1 — 1927.
(Phillips) $100   £45

EASTON, JAMES
'Human Longevity' — half title, original
boards, uncut, rebacked — James Easton,
London, Salisbury, 1799.
(Sotheby's, New Bond
Street) $100   £45

ECCLESIASTES or THE PREACHER
No. 90 of 250 copies, wood engraved
pictorial title and 12 illustrations by
Blair Hughes-Stanton, original vellum
backed cloth, t.e.g., 4to − 1934.
(Sotheby's,
    Chancery Lane) $405   £180

ECCLESIASTES or THE PREACHER
Crimson morocco sides with gilt lined
panels, overall floral design by T. J.
Cobden-Sanderson, dated 1889.
(Phillips) $360   £160

ECKEL, JOHN C.
'The First Editions of the Writings of
Charles Dickens and Their Values. A
Bibliography' − 8vo original cloth, t.e.g.,
portrait and 36 illustrations and facsimiles,
no. 218 of 750 copies − 1913.
(Lawrence of
    Crewkerne) $150   £65

**ECKERT, H. A. AND CHRISTIAN
WEISS**
'Les Armees d'Europe Representees en
Groupes Characteristiques' − 147 hand
coloured lithographed plates only, mostly
of German costumes, mostly mounted,
slightly soiled, cont. half morocco,
rubbed − Munich, 1838-43.
(Sotheby's,
    Chancery Lane) $4,725   £2,100

EDGEWORTH, MARIA
'Tales and Novels' − 18 vols., engraved
frontispieces and additional titles, cont.
half calf, spines gilt − 1832-3.
(Christie's S.
    Kensington) $180   £80

EDINBURGH AND PARIS
Two plans with outline hand colouring −
circa 1830.
(Tessa Bennett,
    Edinburgh) $22   £10

**EDINBURGH PRACTICE OF PHYSIC,
SURGERY AND MIDWIFERY**
21 engraved plates, 20 folding, 5 vols.,
cont. half calf − 1803.
(Bonham's) $100   £45

EDMONDS, CLEMENT
'Observations upon Caesar's Commentaries' − engraved title, 8 engraved double
page plates, woodcut portrait of Caesar,
19th century calf, folio − 1609.
(Christie's, King
    St.) $90   £40

EDMONDSTON, ARTHUR
'A View of the Ancient and Present State
of the Zetland Islands . . . and an account
of their Agriculture, Fisheries, Commerce'
− 2 vols., engraved map, half title, cont.
polished calf gilt, joints just torn −
Edinburgh, 1809.
(Sotheby's
    London) $110   £50

EDWARD, PRINCE OF WALES
7 A.Ls. signed E.P., St. James' palace
1924-26 and N.Y., to Harry and Mrs.
Brown, also 3 cards (2 of Christmas
Greetings from the Duke and Duchess of
Windsor).
(Phillips) $540   £240

EDWARDS

EDWARDS, BRYAN
'An Historical Survey of the French Colony
in St. Domingo' – 1st Edn., large folding
engraved map, cont. half russia – 1797.
(Sotheby's
Monaco) $1,980   £880

EDWARDS, GEORGE
'A Natural History of Uncommon Birds
and some other rare Animals, Quadrupeds,
Reptiles etc.' – 1st Edn., 4 vols., text in
English, hand coloured engraved frontis-
pieces, hand coloured engraved plates and
uncoloured portrait, 19th century calf,
rebacked, g.e. – 1743-51.
(Christie's
St. James) $6,075   £2,700

EDWARDS, JOHN
'A Demonstration of the existence and pro-
vidence of God' – cont. calf, rebacked – J.
D. for Jonathan Robinson and John Wyat,
1696.
(Sotheby's, New Bond
Street) $65   £30

EDWARDS, S. T. AND LINDLEY, JOHN
'Edwards's Botanical Register' – New
Series, vols. 1-10 complete, 688 coloured
plates, one detached, original cloth, spines
faded – 1838-47.
(Sotheby's, New Bond
Street) $3,825   £1,700

EDWARDS, SYDENHAM
'The Botanical Register, consisting of
coloured figures of exotic plants cultivated in British gardens' – vols. 1-15
only of 33, approx. 1,300 hand coloured
engraved plates after Edwards and others,
many folding, modern half parchment
boards – 1815-29.
(Sotheby's
London) $6,750   £3,000

EGAN, PIERCE
'Sporting Anecdotes' – 2 portraits, 4
coloured plates, half calf – 1825.
(Sotheby's, New Bond
Street) $250   £110

EGINHARTUS
'De Vita et Gestis Caroli Magni' – commen-
tary by Bessel, notes by Bolland and index
by Schmick – 19th century vellum boards
– Utrecht, 1711.
(Sotheby's, New Bond
Street) $110   £50

EISENBERG, BARON D'
'L'Art de Monter a Cheval' – engraved and
printed titles, 59 engraved plates by Picart,
18th century boards, very worn, oblong
folio – The Hague, 1733.
(Sotheby's, New Bond
Street) $2,475   £1,100

EISENMENGER, JOHANN ANDREA
'Entdecktes Judenthum' – 2 parts in one
vol., 2nd Edn., repaired, 19th century
brown half calf, very rare – Konigsberg,
1711.
(Sotheby's, New Bond
Street) $1,350   £600

ELIESER, LIEBERMANN SOFER
'Ma'ane Lashon', prayers for women, to
be recited – Old Yiddish, 4th Edn., 19th
century quarter calf, worn, rare –
Frankfurt am Oder, 1688.
(Sotheby's, New Bond
Street) $380   £170

ELIOT, T. S.
'Ash Wednesday' – 1st Edn., no. 545 of
600 copies, signed by author, original
cloth, gilt, t.e.g. – New York and London,
1930.
(Sotheby's,
Chancery Lane) $350   £155

'Old Possum's Book of Practical Cats' –
1st Edn., original cloth – 1939.
(Sotheby's,
    Chancery Lane) $40   £18
'Sweeney Agonistes' and 'The Rock' –
1st Edns., original boards – 1932 and 1934.
(Sotheby's,
    Chancery Lane) $55   £24

**ELLIS, GEORGE VINER AND FORD,
GEORGE HENRY**
'Illustrations of Dissections in a Series of
Original Coloured Plates . . . representing
the Dissection of the Human Body' – 29
original plates, 29 vols., 1st Edn. – 1863-67.
(Sotheby's, New Bond
    Street) $380   £170

ELLIS, HAVELOCK
'Kanga Creek' – limited to 1,375 copies,
original cloth backed boards, dust jacket
slightly torn – Golden Cockerel Press,
1922.
(Christie's S.
    Kensington) $45   £20

ELPHINSTONE, MOUNTSTUART
'An Account of the Kingdom of Caubul'
– 2 vols., new edition, 2 coloured frontispieces, 1 plate, 1 folding map, later half
calf, worn, ex-library copy – 1839.
(Christie's S.
    Kensington) $63   £28

EMPSON, WILLIAM
'Poems' – 1st Edn., original cloth, uncut –
1935.
(Sotheby's,
    Chancery Lane) $45   £20

ENCICLOPEDIA DELLO SPETTACOLO
Vol. I-IX Index, Supplement 1955-65 and
Supplement on Cinema, 12 vols. altogether,
1st Edn., numerous plates – Rome, 1954-
68.
(Sotheby's, New Bond
    Street) $540   £240

ENCOUNTER
Literature, Art, Politics, edited by Stephen
Spender, Irving Kristol and others – nos.
1-266 with some missing and index for
2-9, illustrations, original wrappers – Oct.
1953–November 1975.
(Sotheby's,
    Chancery Lane) $225   £100

**ENCYCLOPAEDIA BRITANNICA or A
DICTIONARY OF ARTS AND SCIENCES**
3 vols., 1st London Edn., 151 engraved
plates of 152, 4to – 1773.
(Sotheby's, New Bond
    Street) $1,575   £700

ENCYCLOPAEDIA BRITANNICA, THE
25 vols., 9th Edn., plates, illustrations,
cont. morocco, spines torn, some covers
detached, g.e. – Edinburgh, 1875.
(Christie's S.
    Kensington) $50   £22
ENCYCLOPAEDIA BRITANNICA, THE
32 vols. in 16, 11th Edn., original cloth,
slightly rubbed, spines faded – 1910-11.
(Christie's S.
    Kensington) $90   £40

ENCYCLOPEDIE METHODIQUE
'Marine' – 4 vols., with Atlas of plates,
171 of 175 engraved plates, 4to – Paris,
1783-87.
(Sotheby's, New Bond
    Street) $675   £300

ENGLISH MIDWIFE, THE
Containing directions to midwives, engraved
frontispiece, 7 folding plates, 23 woodcuts
in text, holed, stained, original sheep, worn
– Rowland Reynolds, 1682.
(Sotheby's, New Bond
    Street) $1,460   £650

ENGLISH PILOT, THE
'The Fourth Book Describing the West
India Navigation from Hudson's Bay to
the River Amazon' – 21 engraved maps
only of 22, engraved maps and woodcut
diagrams in text, defective, large folio –
1784.
(Sotheby's, New Bond
    Street) $3,600   £1,600

'THE ENGLISHWOMAN'S DOMESTIC MAGAZINE'
Vols. 1-6, 29 hand coloured plates, illustrations, original cloth, soiled, inner hinges cracked – n.d.
(Christie's S.
Kensington) $150   £65

ENGRAMELLE, MARIE DOMINIQUE JOSEPH
'La Tonotechnie ou l'Art de Noter les Cylindres et tout ce qui est Susceptible de Notage dans les Instumens de Concerts Mechaniques' – 1st Edn., half title, engraved frontispiece, 4 folding tables, 4 folding plates, cont. calf backed boards – Paris, 1775.
(Christie's, King
St.) $1,575   £700

ENGRAVINGS
A collection of 30 17th century Dutch and French engravings including some by Van Avent, de la Bella, Danex and Le Potre, water stained, torn and repaired, 17th century calf rebacked, oblong – circa 1650.
(Christie's, King
St.) $490   £220

'EPIGRAMMI LATINI TRADOTTI IN VERSI ITALIANI'
cont. mottled calf, gilt, spine chipped at head – Parma, Bodoni, 1798.
(Sotheby's
London) $90   £40

EPSTEIN, JACOB
'Epstein 1956' introduction by Laurie Lee – photographic illustrations, folio, original cloth, no. 86 of 200 copies, signed by Epstein and Lee – n.d.
(Lawrence of
Crewkerne) $27   £12

ERASMUS, D.
'Apophthegmatum Opus' – woodcut device on title, later panelled calf, 8vo – Robertus Stephanus, Paris, 1547.
(Sotheby's, New Bond
Street) $160   £70
'Adagiorum Chiliades Quator' – title within a woodcut border of the classical authors, a few other pages within woodcut border, cont. blindstamped calf, rebacked, folio – Froben, Basle, 1517.
(Sotheby's
Monaco) $6,300   £2,800

ERNST, MAX
'Une Semaine de Bonte ou Les Sept Elements Capitaux' – 5 parts, 182 illustrations, collaged wood engravings, original wrapper, card slipcase – Jean Bucher, Paris, 1934.
(Sotheby's,
Chancery Lane) $1,460   £650

EROTICA
A large collection, many illlustrated, various bindings, various sizes, 19th and 20th centuries.
(Sotheby's
  Monaco) $15,750   £7,000

ESNAULT-PELTERIE, ROBERT
'L'exploration par Fusees de la Tres Haute Atmosphere et la Possibilite des Voyages Interplanetaires' – 1st Edn., original paper wrappers, repaired, in buckram folder, 8vo – Paris, 1928.
(Christie's
  St. James) $225   £100

ESPERANCE – OVIDIUS NASO (Publius)
'L'art d'Aimer' – 14 coloured lithographed plates by Esperance, unsewn in original wrappers, uncut, unopened, folder, slipcase – Les Propylees, Paris, 1940.
(Sotheby's,
  Chancery Lane) $15   £7

ESTATE MAPS
2 large folio atlases with hand coloured maps on vellum of Kilcash Estate, Tipperary, property of Earl of Ormonde, some damaged, calf defective, folio, Surveyed R. Corfield – 1809.
(Phillips) $190   £85

ETAT ACTUEL DE LA MUSIQUE DU ROI ET DES TROIS SPECTACLES DE PARIS
Engraved title, frontispiece and 4 engraved plates, cont. red morocco gilt, g.e. – Paris, 1770.
(Christie's, King
  St.) $585   £260

ETHIOPIC SERVICE BOOK
Ms. on vellum, 141 leaves, double column written in small, clear script in red and black ink, occasional musical notation, list of contents at foot, calf backed wooden boards in leather carrying case with straps in buckram box – early 19th century.
(Christie's, King
  St.) $360   £160

'EUCLID ELEMENTS; The Whole Fifteen Books, translated and edited by Isaac Barrow'
Device on title, diagrams in text, upper margins wormed, cont. calf, slightly worn and stained – R. Daniel for William Nealand, 1660.
(Sotheby's
  London) $45   £20

EUCLIDES
'Elementa' With notes by Campanus Noviensis – 137 leaves of 138, 52 lines, woodcut borders, numerous woodcut diagrams, modern calf backed boards, folio – Vicenza, June 1491.
(Christie's, King
  St.) $1,910   £850

EUSEBIUS CAESARIENSIS
'Evangelica Praeparatio', translated by Georgius Trapezuntius, edited by Hieronymus Bononius – 106 leaves of 108, 47 lines and head line, roman letter, modern older style vellum, 17th century deleted Franciscan ownership inscription, folio – Treviso, 1480.
(Sotheby's, New Bond
  Street) $585   £260

EUTROPIUS
'Breviarum Historiae Romanae' – Editio Princips, 96 leaves of 104, 32 lines, roman letter, early 20th century half morocco, folio – Rome, 1471.
(Sotheby's, New Bond
  Street) $450   £200

EVANS, MARIAN 'GEORGE ELIOT'
'Daniel Deronda' – 8 parts in 4 vols., 1st Edn., first issue, half titles, cont. green half morocco gilt – 1876.
(Sotheby's, New Bond
  Street) $180   £80

EVELYN, JOHN
'Silva or a Discourse of Forest Trees' – portrait, 32 plates only, one folding table, some leaves torn, soiling, modern calf, large 4to – York, 1776.
(Christie's S.
  Kensington) $65   £28
'Memoirs . . . Edited . . . by William Bray' – 5 vols., plates, some folding, cont. half morocco – 1827.
(Christie's S.
  Kensington) $50   £22

EVELYN, J.
'Sculptura' – portrait and plates, calf – 1755.
(Bonham's) $146   £65

EVERARD, H.
'History of the Royal and Ancient Golf Club St. Andrews 1754-1900' – cloth, gilt – 1907.
(Tessa Bennett,
  Edinburgh) $124   £55

EVERGREEN REVIEW

Edited by Barry Rosset and Donald Allen, nos. 1-30 contributors include Samuel Beckett, Allen Ginsberg, Michael Hamburger, Henry Miller, Jean Paul Sartre etc., illustrations, original wrappers – New York, 1957-63.

(Sotheby's, Chancery Lane) $90   £40

EVERITT, GRAHAM

'English caricaturists and Graphic Humourists of the 19th century' – plates, occasional spotting, original cloth, rebacked in red calf, t.e.g. – 1886.

(Christie's S. Kensington) $67   £30

EXCELIMANNS, BARON KARLO

'Eventful Life of Napoleon Bonaparte' – 4 vols., 21 coloured plates, calf gilt – 1828.

(Phillips) $70   £30

'EXCURSIONS IN THE COUNTY OF ESSEX'

2 vols., folding map and town plan, plates, calf gilt – 1818-1819.

(Phillips) $170   £75

'EXCURSIONS IN THE COUNTY OF SURREY'

1 folding map, 1 engraved frontis, 44 engraved and folding plans of 50, modern half calf – 1821.

(Phillips) $70   £30

'EXCURSIONS IN THE COUNTY OF SUFFOLK'

2 vols., engraved additional titles, joints cracked – 1818-19.

(Christie's S. Kensington) $115   £50

EXHORTATIO DE CELEBRATIONE MISSAE

10 leaves, 32 lines, gothic letter, 2 large ornate woodcut initials, lightly spotted, modern boards – Heinrich Knoblochtzer, Strasburg, 1428.

(Sotheby's, New Bond Street) $315   £140

EXPLANATION OF THE WORKS OF THE TUNNEL UNDER THE THAMES FROM ROTHERHITHE TO WAPPING

9 engraved plates, some folding, original wrappers – 1836.

(Christie's S. Kensington) $80   £35

EXPOSITIO HYMNORUM SECUNDUM USUM SARUM

Part I only, 68 leaves, mixed lines, black letter, large woodcut on title page and another on verso of title, device on last page, blue morocco by Riviere – Richard Pynson, 1497.

(Sotheby's, New Bond Street) $2,475   £1,100

EYRE, E. J.

'Journals of Expeditions of Discovery into Central Australia' – 2 vols., 22 plates, maps lacking, worn ex-library copy – 1845.

(Christie's S. Kensington) $170   £75

EYTON, THOMAS CAMPBELL

'A Monograph on the Anatidae or Duck Tribe' – original cloth, damp marked, 22 plates of 24 including 6 hand coloured lithographed plates by Edward Lear – 1838.

(Lawrence of Crewkerne) $200   £90

FABER STAPULENSIS, JACOBUS
'Introductiones Logicales' – 30 leaves, 37-39 lines, gothic letter, woodcut device on title page, woodcut initials, worming, water stains, modern half calf – Guillaume Balsarin, Lyons, circa 1498-99.
(Sotheby's, New Bond
    Street) $1,460   £650

FABRE
'Fabre's Book of Insects' – coloured plates by E. Detmold, boxed – 1936.
(Tessa Bennett,
    Edinburgh) $80   £36

FABRETTI, RAFFAELE
'De Aquis et Aqueductibus Veteris Romae Dissertationes Tres' – 1st Edn., 3 folding maps, engravings in text, cont. French calf, gilt, arms of Jean-Jacques Charron, Marquis de Menars (1643-1718) – J. B. Bussotti, Rome, 1680.
(Sotheby's, New Bond
    Street) $430   £190

FADEN, W.
'England and Wales and Scotland' – folding coloured linen map, 1801, and a map of Scotland in a leather case.
(Tessa Bennett,
    Edinburgh) $11   £5

FAENZI, VALERIO
'De Montium Origine . . . Dialogus' – 1st Edn., woodcut device on title, modern calf, gilt – Venice, 1561.
(Sotheby's, New Bond
    Street) $945   £420

FARHRENHEIT, DANIEL GABRIEL
'Experimenta Circa Gradum Caloris Liquorum Nonnullorum Ebullientum Instituta . . . ' – altogether 5 papers extracted from Philosophical Transactions of the Royal Society, vol. 33, bound in one volume, modern half calf. Complete set of Fahrenheit's published writings – 1724.
(Sotheby's, New Bond
    Street) $430   £190

FAIRBURN, J.
'London and Westminster' – hand coloured map, 1801.
(Phillips) $80   £35

FAIRCHILD, THOMAS
'The City Gardener' – 2 plates, one folding, title in red and black, last leaf blank, new half calf – T. Woodward and J. Peele, 1722.
(Sotheby's, New Bond
    Street) $160   £70

FAIRLEY, JOHN
'The London Art of Cookery' – 10th Edn., portrait, illus., cont. sheep, rebacked, worn – 1801.
(Christie's S.
    Kensington) $50   £22

FALCONER

FALCONER, WILLIAM
'A Dissertation on the Influence of the
Passions Upon Disorders of the Body' –
2nd Edn., portrait, cont. calf – C. Dilly,
1791.
(Sotheby's, New Bond
   Street) $160   £70

FALE, THOMAS
'Horologiographia, the Art of Dialling,
teaching an easie and perfect way to make
all kinds of Dials upon any plain plat
howsoever placed' – black letter, woodcuts
by Jacocus Hondius, soiling and staining,
cont. limp vellum.
(Sotheby's, New Bond
   Street) $630   £280

FAMILY COMPANION, THE
'For Health or Plain, Easy and Certain
Rules . . . which will infallibly keep
families free from diseases' – cont.
panelled calf – F. Fayram, 1729.
(Sotheby's, New Bond
   Street) $110   £50

**FAMILY OF SCARLETT OF JAMAICA
AND GIGHA, CO. ARGYLL**
500-600 letters and documents, including
approximately 60 letters and documents
from Jamaica, some 17th century inden-
tures signed by George IV and Queen
Victoria, pedigree researches, ship and
consignment notices, original poems,
school exercises etc – 18th and 19th
centuries.
(Lawrence of
   Crewkerne) $900   £400

FARADAY, MICHAEL
'Chemical Manipulation, being Instructions
to Students in Chemistry' – bound in 3
vols., 1st Edn., woodcut diagrams in text,
cont. half russia, covers detached, spines
missing, uncut, half red morocco cases.
Faraday's own copies – W. Phillips, 1827.
(Sotheby's, New Bond
   Street) $4,050   £1,800
'Course of Six Lectures on the Chemical
History of a Candle; to which is added a
Lecture on Platinum . . . edited by William
Crookes' – 1st Edn., illustrations in text,
publisher's catalogue at end, original cloth,
spine rubbed, half red morocco case –
Griffin, Bohn and Company, 1861.
(Sotheby's, New Bond
   Street) $90   £40

FARADAY, WINIFRED (Translator)
'The Wisdom of the Cymry, translated
from the Welsh Triads' – no. 58 of 60
copies, woodcut title by Avril Mackenzie
Grieve, morocco, t.e.g. – 1939.
(Christie's S.
   Kensington) $85   £38

FARQUHAR, GEORGE
'The Beaux Stratagem – Introduction by
Bonamy Dobree' – no. 335 of 537 copies,
signed by Dobree, plates by J. E. Laboureur,
original cloth backed boards, t.e.g. –
Douglas Clevedon, Bristol, 1929.
(Christie's S.
   Kensington) $22   £10

FARRERE, CLAUDE
'Le Peur de Mr. de Fierce' – limited to 450
copies, coloured plates by Arnoux, red
morocco, gilt, by Lagrand, rough gilt edges,
original wrappers, bound in – Paris, 1922.
(Sotheby's
   Monaco) $1,235   £550

FARRIER, THE POCKET
. . .' or approved receipts that cure accidents that may happen to a horse' – 34pp.
interleaved with many mss. additions, 16
mp. – W. Williams, Shrewsbury, 1790-
1800.
(Sotheby's, New Bond
   Street) $180   £80

FASHION
A volume containing 48 hand coloured
plates, some soiling, cont. half calf, spine
lacking – mid 19th century.
(Christie's S.
   Kensington) $200   £90

FAUJAS DE SAINT FOND, B.
'Descriptions des Experiences de la
Machine Aerostatique de M. M. de
Montgolfier' – 2 vols., 1st Edn., 14 plates,
uncut, half red morocco case – Cachet,
Paris, 1783-84.
(Sotheby's, New Bond
    Street) $1,080   £480

FAULKNER, THOMAS
'An Historical and Topographical Account
of Fulham' – 1st Edn., large paper copy,
with 106 portraits, plans and view, woodcuts in text, cont. russia, gilt, rebacked,
g.e., 4to – 1813.
(Sotheby's, New Bond
    Street) $405   £180

**FEARNSIDE, W. G. AND THOMAS,
HARRAL** (Editors)
'The History of London' – 2 parts in one
vol., engraved additional titles and plates,
some slight spotting, cont. half calf,
rubbed – n.d.
(Christie's S.
    Kensington) $160   £70

FEATHERSTONHAUGH, G. W.
'A Canoe Voyage up to the Minnay Sotor'
– 2 vols., two lithographed frontispieces,
two folding maps, illustrations, some
spotting, original cloth, soiled, recased –
1847.
(Christie's S.
    Kensington) $170   £75

FELICE, M. DE
'Encyclopedie, ou Dictionnaire Universal
Raisonne des Connoissances Humaines . . .
Planches' – 6 vols. only, 154 plates, 7 fold-
ing, 3 slightly torn, including 84 on
Natural History and 52 on Horology, some
soiling, cont. calf, worn – 1777.
(Christie's S.
    Kensington) $180   £80

FELICIANO, FRANCESCO
'Libro Di Arithmetica & Geometria Specu-
lativa & Practicale' – 1st Edn., title with
woodcut border, woodcut diagrams, some
repairs, slight staining, modern vellum
backed boards, ownership inscriptions –
Bindoni and Pasini, 1527.
(Sotheby's, New Bond
    Street) $585   £260

FELLOWES, E. H. AND PINE, EDWARD
(Editors)
'The Tenbury Letters' – no. 246 of 300
copies, facsimile letters, original cloth, t.e.g.,
unopened – 1942.
(Christie's S.
    Kensington) $15   £7

FELTHAM, JOHN
'A Tour through the Island of Mann, in
1797 and 1798' – 1st Edn., wood engraved
vignette on title, engraved folding map and
table, 3 engraved plates, illustrations in text,
cont. calf, label, slightly rubbed – Bath,
1798.
(Sotheby's
    London) $110   £50

FENN, LADY ELEANOR
'The Rational Dame or Hints Towards
Supplying Prattle for Children' – engraved
frontispiece with 9 plates and 89 illustra-
tions, original roan backed boards, worn –
John Marshall, 1806.
(Sotheby's,
    Chancery Lane) $95   £42

FER

FER, NICOLAS DE
'Les Beautes de la France' — engraved title and 67 engraved plates, views and maps, cont. calf, oblong folio — Paris, 1724.
(Tessa Bennett,
    Edinburgh) $450   £200

FERGUSON, JAMES
'An Introduction to Electricity' — 3rd Edn., 3 folding plates, title browned, cont. sheep, worn — For W. Strahan and T. Cadell, 1778.
(Sotheby's, New Bond
    Street) $110   £48
'Lectures on Select Subjects in Mechanics, Hydrostatics, Hydraulics, Pneumatics and Optics. With the Use of Globes, the Art of Dialling' — 2 vols., plates separately, 6th Edn., 36 folding engraved plates, text slightly foxed, cont. calf and half calf, rubbed — For W. Strahan, J. Rivington, 1784.
(Sotheby's, New Bond
    Street) $150   £65

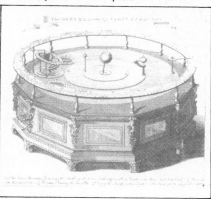

'Astronomy Explained Upon Sir Isaac Newton's Principles and Made Easy to those who have not studied Mathematics' — 1st Edn., 14 folding plates, cont. calf, gilt, splits in joints, bookplate of John Plumptre, the Kenney copy — For the Author, 1756.
(Sotheby's, New Bond
    Street) $630   £280

FERGUSSON, ADAM
'An Essay on the History of Civil Society' — cont. calf, 5th Edn. — London, 1782.
(Tessa Bennett,
    Edinburgh) $50   £22

FERMAT, PIERRE DE
'Varia Opera Mathematica' — 1st Edn., edited by Samuel de Fermat, 5 engraved plates, diagrams in text, some leaves browned or stained, 18th century vellum boards, half red morocco case, book label of J. Manzoni — J. Pech, Toulouse, 1679.
(Sotheby's, New Bond
    Street) $4,500   £2,000

FERNEL, JEAN
'Cosmotheoria, Libros Duos Complexa' — 1st Edn., second issue with reprinted title page, woodcut diagrams and initials, dark olive morocco, folio — Paris, 1528.
(Sotheby's, New Bond
    Street) $1,910   £850

FERRARI, F.
'Costume Eccelsiastici Civile e Militari della Corte di Roma' — vignette on title and 60 coloured plates, half calf, worn — 1823.
(Bonham's) $160   £70

FERRARI, GIOVANNI BATTISTA
'Hesperides Sive de Malorum Aureorum Cultura et Usu Libri Quatuor' — 1st Edn., engraved frontispiece, 100 engraved plates of plants and citrus fruits, or allegorical scenes by Cornelis Bloemaerts and others — Rome, 1646.
(Sotheby's, New Bond
    Street) $2,025   £900

FERRARIUS, OCTAVIANUS
'De Re Vestiaria' – 2 vols., engraved
additional titles, 17 plates and full page
illustrations, vol. 2 affected by damp, its
title wormed, cont. mottled calf, vol. 2
rebacked, bookplate of the Earl of Oxford
– Padua, 1654.
(Christie's S.
Kensington)　　　$135　　　£60

FERRIAR, JOHN M. D.
'An Essay Towards A Theory Of Appari-
tions' – ownership inscription cut from
upper margin of title page, cont. half
calf, just rubbed – 1813.
(Sotheby's
London)　　　$100　　　£45

FERRIS, SAMUEL
'A General View of the establishment
of Physic in England as a science . . . by
the incorporation of the College of
Physicians, London' – half title, cont. calf,
sides decorated with gilt and blind, spine
gilt, g.e., presentation copy – C. Whitting-
ham, 1795.
(Sotheby's, New Bond
Street)　　　$180　　　£80

**FESCH, CARDINAL, JOSEPH, uncle of
Napoleon I**
Autograph letter signed and three letters
signed, 4 pages, quarto, Rome and Paris,
February 1805 and July 1837, to various
correspondents, together with a statement
of Fesch's bank account and also a docu-
ment signed by the Arch Chancellor
Cambaceres granting Fesch a share of the
Rhine navigation fees – 1811.
(Sotheby's, New Bond
Street)　　　$360　　　£160

FEUILLEE, LOUIS
'Journal des Observations Physiques,
Mathematiques et Botaniques, faites par
l'order du Roy sur Les Cotes Orientales
de l'Amerique Meridionale et dans les
Indes Occidentales, depuis l'Annee 1707
jusques en 1712' – vol. I and II of 3 in
one vol., 73 plates and plans, engravings
in text – Pierre Giffart, Paris, 1714.
(Sotheby's, New Bond
Street)　　　$125　　　£55

FIAMELLI, GIOVANNI FRANCESCO
'La Riga Matematica' – 1st Edn., water-
stained, corroded, worm holes, disbound,
stitching broken, ownership inscription
on title of monastery at Chiavari near
Genoa – circa 1605.
(Sotheby's, New Bond
Street)　　　$70　　　£30

FICHTE, JOHANN GOTTLIEB
'Der Geschlossne Handelsstaat. Ein
Philosophischer Entwurf als Anhang zur
Rechtslehre und Probe Einer Kunstig zu
Lieferden Politik' – 1st Edn., title slightly
foxed, wrappers, uncut – Tubingen, 1880.
(Sotheby's, New Bond
Street)　　　$675　　　£300

FICINO, MARSILIO
'De Le Tre Vite . . . prolungare la Vita' –
device on title, vellum – M. Tremazzino,
Venice, 1548.
(Sotheby's
Monaco)　　　$1,575　　　£700
'Sopra lo Amore o ver' Convito di
Platone' – device on title and last page,
some marginal water staining, half vellum –
Florence, Neri Dortelata, 1544.
(Sotheby's
London)　　　$200　　　£90

FIEFFE, EUGENE
'Napoleon et La Grande Imperiale' –
vignette title, frontis, 20 coloured plates,
quarter morocco gilt, g.e. – 1859.
(Phillips)　　　$225　　　£100

FIELDING, HENRY
'Amelia' – 1st Edn., 4 vols., slight foxing
and gathering, cont. calf, gilt spines,
green and red morocco labels, rubbed,
small 8vo – 1752.
(Christie's
St. James)　　　$360　　　£160

FIELDING, T. H.
'Cumberland, Westmorland and Lancashire'
— large paper, 44 hand coloured aquatints,
cont. half morocco, partly uncut, folio —
1822.
(Sotheby's, New Bond
    Street) $495   £220

FIENUS OR FEYENS, JOANNES
'A new and useful Treatise of Wind Offend-
ing Man's Body' — translated by William
Rowland, panelled calf, rebacked, uncut —
Benjamin Billingsley, 1676.
(Sotheby's, New Bond
    Street) $425   £190

FIGARO ILLUSTRE — BRUSSEL,
ROBERT
'Le Ballet' — coloured frontispiece, 2
coloured plates, numerous illustrations
in text, modern half cloth — Paris, 1911.
(Sotheby's, New Bond
    Street) $60   £26

FIGATELLI, GIUSEPPE MARIA
'Retta Linea Gnomonica' — 2nd Edn.,
device on title, 7 folding plates, woodcut
diagrams in text, errata leaf at end, boards,
spine worn — Modena, 1675.
(Sotheby's, New Bond
    Street) $225   £100

FINART AND OTHERS
'Armees Etrangeres' — 30 hand coloured
lithographed plates by Finart, Lehnert,
Le Pan, Madou and Roland, lithographed
by Delonois, Frey and others, half cloth,
oblong 4to — Paris, circa 1840.
(Sotheby's, New Bond
    Street) $900   £400

FINE ART
A collection of miscellaneous books on the
fine arts, mostly 20th century and including many exhibition catalogues.
(Sotheby's
    Monaco) $6,300   £2,800

FINE, ORONCE
'Protomathesis' — first collected edn., title
in woodcut architectural border, woodcut
illustrations and initials, cont. limp vellum,
folio — Paris, 1532.
(Sotheby's, New Bond
    Street) $8,325   £3,700

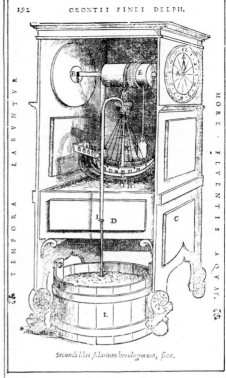

Secundi Libri solarium horologiorum, figura.

'De Solaribus Horologis et Quadrantibus.
Libri Quatuor' — first separate edn., edited
by Jean Fine, illustrations and diagrams,
19th century red morocco, joints rubbed —
G. Cavellat, Paris, 1560.
(Sotheby's, New Bond
    Street) $630   £280

FINDEN, W. AND E.
'Landscapes of Interesting Localities Men-
tioned in the Holy Scriptures' — 2 vols., 93
engraved plates after Turner and others, 2
folding maps, one torn, slight spotting
original morocco, gilt, slightly rubbed, g.e.
— mid 19th century.
(Sotheby's, New Bond
    Street) $290   £130

FINN, F.
'Indian Sporting Birds' — coloured plates,
cloth gilt — 1915.
(Phillips) $110   £50

FIRBANK, RONALD
'Extravaganzas' and another — 1st Edn.,
original cloth — New York, 1935.
(Sotheby's,
   Chancery Lane) $45   £20
'Prancing Nigger' — 1st Edn., coloured
frontispiece by R. E. Locher, original
cloth — New York, 1924.
(Sotheby's,
   Chancery Lane) $63   £28
'The Flower Beneath the Foot' — 1st Edn.,
portrait by Augustus John, vignette on
title by Wyndham Lewis and decoration on
endpaper by C. R. W. Nevinson, original
cloth, slightly worn — 1923.
(Sotheby's,
   Chancery Lane) $55   £25

FIRMICUS MATERNUS, JULIUS
'De Nativitatibus' — 1st Edn., edited by
Antonius Laurus, 119 leaves of 120, 45
lines and head line, roman letter, woodcut
diagrams and initials, title soiled, 19th
century calf — Simon Bevilaqua, Venice, 1497
1497.
(Sotheby's, New Bond
   Street) $3,825   £1,700

'De Nativitatibus' with other tracts — 376
leaves including 2 blanks, 38 lines and head
lines, roman and greek letter, woodcuts of
signs of the zodiac, 18th century red
morocco, gilt, g.e., folio — Aldus, Venice,
1499.
(Sotheby's, New Bond
   Street) $12,375   £5,500

FIRST RAILROAD IN GERMANY, THE
Between Nuremberg and Furth — 6 lithographed sections and front coloured by
hand, lacking 2 parts of bellows, original
slipcase, worn — G. W. Faber and Nurnt,
circa 1835.
(Sotheby's,
   Chancery Lane) $925   £410

FIRST WORLD WAR PROPAGANDA
12 coloured plates by Raphael Kirchner
and others, cont. half morocco — Paris,
Librairie de l'Estampe, circa 1914-15.
(Christie's S.
   Kensington) $55   £25

**'FISHER'S COUNTY ATLAS OF
ENGLAND AND WALES'**
48 maps, hand coloured in outline, one
folding and 2 double paged, some
slightly shaved, cont. half calf, spine
and corners rubbed — 1842-5.
(Christie's S.
   Kensington) $430   £190

FISHMONGERS' COMPANY
Ms. charter in Latin of an assignment
between Robert Little, fishmonger, to
Andrew Pikeman and Thomas Lyncoln,
fishmongers and citizens of London.
Cont. endorsements, two red wax seals
pendent on vellum strips in velvet lined
buckram box — 116 x 278mm. — London,
3 April, 1382.
(Christie's, King
   St.) $430   £190

FITZGERALD, R.
'Salt Water Sweetened, or A True Account
of the great advantages of this new Inven-
tion both by sea and by land . . . likewise
a Letter of the Honourable Robert Boyle
to a Friend upon the same subject' —
1st Edn., modern wrappers, rare — For
Will Cademan, 1683.
(Sotheby's, New Bond
   Street) $500   £220

FITZHERBERT, SIR ANTHONY
'La Graunde Abbregement de le Ley' — 3
parts in one vol., 2nd Edn., dampstained,
brittle and frayed, wormed, cont. London
calf over wooden boards, very rubbed,
lacks clasp, new endpapers, folio — John
Rastell, 1517.
(Sotheby's, New Bond
   Street) $1,915   £850

FITZHERBERT, JOHN
'Here Beginneth a Ryght Fruteful Mater:
& Hathe to Name the Boke of Surveyinge
and Improvementes' — 3rd Edn., black
letter, title within woodcut border, woodcut initials, 19th century half russia, cloth
case — Robert Redman, circa 1535.
(Sotheby's, New Bond
   Street) $2,025   £900

FLAMSTEED, JOHN

'Atlas Coelestis' – engraved portrait by
Vertue after Gibson, vignette on title,
27 double page engraved star maps, 19th
century dark blue half morocco, worn,
half red morocco case, folio – 1753.
(Sotheby's, New Bond
    Street)   **$5,850**   **£2,600**
'Historiae Coelestis Britannicae' – 3 vols.,
1st Edn., engraved portrait by Vertue after
Gibson, plates, some browning, cont. calf,
joints split, one cover detached, half red
morocco cases – H. Meere, 1725.
(Sotheby's, New Bond
    Street)   **$4,275**   **£1,900**

FLAUBERT, GUSTAVE

'Salammbo' – 1st Edn., one of 25 copies on
paper de Hollande, cont. red morocco, gilt
by Lortic, original wrappers, preserved,
Duchesse de Camastra copy with her arms
and bookplates, presentation copy from
author to Berlioz – Paris, 1863.
(Sotheby Parke Bernet
    Monaco)   **$108,000**   **£48,000**

'Salambo' – translated by E. Powys
Mathers, no. 337 of 500 copies, wood
engraved frontis, and 16 pictorial head and
tail pieces by Robert Gibbings, original
buckram backed boards – 1931.
(Sotheby's,
    Chancery Lane)   **$125**   **£55**
'Salambo', translated by E. Powys Mathers,
no. 224 of 500 copies, cloth backed
boards, corners rubbed, t.e.g. – Golden
Cockerel Press, 1931.
(Christie's S.
    Kensington)   **$158**   **£70**

FLAXMAN, JOHN

'Lectures on Sculpture' – 1st Edn., lithoed
portrait and 51 lithoed plates, 1 plate
detached, bookplate of Walter Cecil
Carpenter, original cloth, head of spine
worn, lower hinge split – 1829.
(Sotheby's
    London)   **$90**   **£40**

FLEMING, SIR ALEXANDER

'Penicillin its practical application' – 1st
Edn., illustrations, original cloth, slightly
soiled – 1946.
(Sotheby Humberts
    Taunton)   **$215**   **£95**

FLEMING, IAN

'Casino Royale' – 1st Edn., original cloth,
dust jacket, designed by author – 1953.
(Sotheby's,
    Chancery Lane)   **$945**   **£420**

FLETCHER, JOHN

'Rule a Wife and Have a Wife' – 1st Edn.,
ms. alterations, some worming, red half
morocco by Sangorski – Oxford, 1640.
(Christie's, King
    St.)   **$405**   **£180**
'The Tragedy of Rollo Duke of Normandy'
– 2nd Edn., lower margin cropped affecting text, red morocco by Sangorski, g.e. –
Oxford, 1640.
(Christie's, King
    St.)   **$340**   **£150**

FLETCHER, PHINEAS

'The Purple Island, or the Isle of Man . . .
to which is added Christ's Victory and
Triumph . . . by Giles Fletcher' – 2 parts
in one vol., new edition, lacking blanks
between parts, a few margins slightly
soiled, or with perforations, bookplate of
Edward Dalton, original boards, spine
slightly torn – 1783.
(Sotheby's
    London)   **$22**   **£10**

FLINT, SIR WILLIAM RUSSELL

'Drawings' – folio, original cloth backed
boards, t.e.g., dust wrapper, 134 plates,
no. 35 of 500 copies, signed by artist, a
good copy in original slipcase – 1950.
(Lawrence of
    Crewkerne)   **$125**   **£55**

'Minxes Admonished or Beauty Reproved' – limited to 550 copies this no. 59 of 150 specially bound by Sangorski and Sutcliffe and signed by Flint, original morocco, t.e.g., folio – 1955.
(Christie's S.
  Kensington) $250   £110

FLINTON, GEORGE
'Manual of Godly Prayers and Litanies Newly Annexed, Taken out of Many Famous Authors' – handsome restoration binding of citron morocco – Antwerp, 1671.
(Sotheby's, New Bond
  Street) $1,806   £800

FLORIAN, C. (Translator)
'Chronica Frankfurter' – 3 vols. in one, plates, vellum worn, folio – 1706.
(Phillips) $270   £120

FLOWER, ROBIN (Translator)
'Love's Bitter Sweet, translations from the Irish Poets of the Sixteenth and Seventeenth Centuries' – 1st Edn., limited to 500 copies, original linen backed boards, uncut, unopened – Cuala Press, Dublin, 1925.
(Sotheby's,
  Chancery Lane) $33   £15

FLOYER, SIR JOHN
'A Comment on Forty Two Histories described by Hippocrates in the first and third book epidemics' – Library stamp on last page, cont. marbled boards, rebacked – J. Isted, 1726.
(Sotheby's, New Bond
  Street) $190   £85

FLUDD, ROBERT
'Philosophia Moysaica. In Qua Sapientia Creationis & Creaturarum Sacra Vereque Christiana . . . Explicatur' – 2 parts in one vol., 1st Edn., engraving on title, engravings and woodcuts in text, cont. calf, folio – Petrus Rammazenius, Gouda, 1638.
(Sotheby's, New Bond
  Street) $450   £200

'FLUIDO ELETTRICO II APPLICATO A SPIEGARE I FENOMENI DELLA NATURA'
1st Edn., woodcut ornament on title, full page woodcut, Italian poem on electricity – Bellelli, Ancona, 1772.
(Sotheby's, New Bond
  Street) $85   £38

FOGGO, D.
'Tyro's Atlas' – 31 hand coloured maps, engraved title, small – Edinburgh, n.d.
(Tessa Bennett,
  Edinburgh) $125   £55

PRATICHE
DE FIORETTI MERCHANTILI,
vtilissime a ciascheduna persona, di mandare a memoria le breue Inuetioni fabrichate sopra il Valutar de pesi, & misure, & altre in struttioni neccessarie da sapere.
Et anchora a quadrare Muraglie, Tasselli, & Coperti & Tuade, Fieno, & Legne: Con la decchiaratione, & Exempli loro come legendo intenderai.

FONDULI, OLIVIERO
'Practiche de Fioretti Merchantili, Utilissime a Ciascheduna Persona, di Mandare a Memoria le breve Inventioni Fabrichate Sopra il Valutar de Pesi & Misure & Altre Instruttioni Neccessarie da Sapere' – 1st Edn., woodcut portrait on title, vellum, the Kenney copy – Pelegrino Bonardo, Bologna, 1560.
(Sotheby's, New Bond
  Street) $1,125   £500

FONTANA, DOMENICO
'Della Transportatione dell' Obelisco Vaticano et delle Fabriche di nostro Signore Papa Sisto V . . . Libro Primo' – 1st Edn., engraved title, frontispiece with portrait of author, 38 plates, cont. Italian vellum, gilt, hand painted arms of Pope Sixtus V, from the library of the Marquess of Bute, folio – Domenico Basa, Rome, 1590.
(Sotheby's, New Bond
  Street) $13,500   £6,000

FONTANO, CARLO
'Templum Vaticanum et Ipsius Origo' –
1st Edn., Latin and Italian titles, and text,
79 engraved plates by Alessandro Specchi,
9 folding, one double page, slight browning and staining, 19th century vellum
scuffed, rubbed library stamp of Tullabeg
College, folio – Rome, 1694.
(Sotheby's, New Bond
    Street) $1,690   £750

FONTENELLE, BERNARD LE BOVIER DE
'Entretiens sur la Pluralite des Mondes' –
cont. calf, worn, from the Earl of Pem-
broke's library – Pierre Mortier,
Amsterdam, 1686.
(Sotheby's, New Bond
    Street) $160   £70

FOOT, JESSE
'The Life of John Hunter' – cont. tree
calf – T. Becket, 1794.
(Sotheby's, New Bond
    Street) $315   £140

FORAIN, J. L.
'Publications de la Vie Parisienne, Nous,
Vous, Eux' – no. 62 of 75 copies on paper
de Chine, signed by artist, half morocco,
original wrappers preserved – Paris, 1893.
(Sotheby Parke Bernet
    Monaco) $790   £350

FORBES, JAMES
'Oriental Memoirs' – 1st Edn., 4 vols.,
engraved portrait and 94 engraved plates,
29 coloured aquatint and lithographed
plates, cont. green ribbed cloth, a little
rubbed and worn – 1813.
(Christie's
    St. James) $1,125   £500

FORCADEL, PIERRE
'Arithmetique entiere et abregee' – 1st Edn.,
large device on title, some water staining,
title soiled, cont. limp vellum, defective
ownership inscription of Raymond Dufont
– Charles Perier, Paris, 1565.
(Sotheby's, New Bond
    Street) $150   £65

FORDYCE, W.
'A History of Coal, Coke, Coal Fields . . .
Iron, its Ores, and Processes of Manufacture'
– double page map and 33 plates, 1 folding,
2 tables, some leaves slightly spotted, cont.
half calf, slightly rubbed – 1860.
(Sotheby's,
    Chancery Lane) $540   £240

FORDYCE, SIR WILLIAM
'A New Inquiry into the Causes, Symptoms
and Cure of Putrid and Inflammatory
Fevers . . .' – 1st Edn., library stamps on
title page, cont. marbled boards, new calf
spine – T. Cadell, 1773.
(Sotheby's, New Bond
    Street) $315   £140

FORESTER, THOMAS
'Rambles in the Islands of Corsica and
Sardinia' – 9 lithographed plates, some
coloured, illustrations, original cloth,
slightly worn – 1858.
(Sotheby's,
    Chancery Lane) $180   £80

FORREST, R. S.
Collection of 72 prints, dry points and
etchings by R. S. Forrest, mainly views of
Edinburgh and other parts of Scotland.
(Tessa Bennett,
    Edinburgh) $85   £38

FORSTER, E. M.
'The Story of the Siren' – 1st Edn.,
unopened, original wrappers – Hogarth,
1920.
(Phillips) $135   £60

FORSTER, JOHANN REINHOLD
'History of the Voyages and Discoveries
Made in the North' – translated from
German, 3 engraved maps, 2 folding,
modern half calf – 1786.
(Christie's
    St. James) $340   £150

FORSTER, THOMAS
'Researches about Atmospheric Phenomena'
– 2nd Edn., 6 plates by F. C. Lewis after
the author, printed in colour – For Baldwin,
Cradock and Joy etc., 1815.
(Sotheby's, New Bond
    Street) $50   £22

FORSYTH, ROBERT
'The Beauties of Scotland' – 5 vols., cont.
half calf gilt, boards scuffed, vignette titles,
folding coloured map, 108 engraved plates,
tables, plates clean – Edinburgh, 1805-8.
(Lawrence of
    Crewkerne) $90   £40

FOSSE, CHARLES L.
'Idees d'un Militaire pour la Disposition des Troupes confiees aux jeunes officiers dans la Defense et l'Attaque des petits postes' – 1st Edn., 11 engraved colour plates by Louis Bonnet after the author's designs, from Carlton House library with bookplate and arms of George IV as Prince of Wales – Paris, 1783.
(Sotheby's, New Bond
   Street) $405   £180

FOSTER, J. J.
'Miniature Painters, British and Foreign' – plates, author's edition, 2 vols., bindings soiled – 1903.
(Bonham's) $100   £45

FOTHEGILL, GEORGE A.
'Notes from the Diary of a Doctor, Sketch Artist and Sportsman' – coloured frontis, title and plates, illustrations, original cloth, slightly soiled, folio – York, 1901.
(Christie's S.
   Kensington) $45   £20

FOUCAULT, LEON
'Sur Les Vitesses Relatives de la Lumiere dans l'air et dans l'eau' – 1st Edn., presentation copy, folding plate, slight foxing, green morocco backed boards, original printed wrappers, bound in – Bachelier, Paris, 1853.
(Sotheby's, New Bond
   Street) $290   £130

FOUJITA – LOTI, PIERRE
'La Troisieme Jeunesse de Madame Prune' – 11 coloured etched plates and 6 illustrations by Foujita, half morocco, t.e.g., original wrappers, bound in, by Flammarion – Editions d'Art Devambez, Paris, 1926.
(Sotheby's,
   Chancery Lane) $470   £210

FOURCROY, ANTOINE-FRANCOIS DE
'Synoptic Tables of Chemistry intended to serve as a summary of the lectures delivered on that science in the public schools of Paris', translated from the original French by William Nicholson – 12 double page tables, original boards, repaired, uncut, half blue morocco case, large folio – 1801.
(Sotheby's, New Bond
   Street) $1,800   £800

FOURIER, JOSEPH
'Theorie Analytique de la Chaleur' – 1st Edn., 2 plates, half title, slight foxing, half blue morocco, gilt, g.e. – Firmin Didot, Paris, 1822.
(Sotheby's, New Bond
   Street) $675   £300

FOURNIER, ALAIN
'Le Grand Meaulnes' – 1st Edn., no. 202 of the special copies, purple morocco, lilac morocco and tapestry doublures, slipcase by J. van West, original wrapper preserved, inscription from author to Remy de Goncourt – Paris, 1913.
(Sotheby Parke Bernet
   Monaco) $10,125 £4,500

FOX-DAVIES, A. C.
'Armorial Families' – 2 vols., 7th Edn., original cloth, slightly rubbed – 1929-30.
(Christie's S.
   Kensington) $80   £35

HIERONYMI FRACASTORII.

FRACASTORO, GIROLAMO
'Homocentrica eiusdem de Causis Criticorum dierum per ea quae in Nobis Sunt' – woodcut portrait of the author, diagrams in text, soiling, modern red half morocco, title inscribed 'Ad Baptiste Zucculii usum' – Venice, 1538.
(Sotheby's, New Bond
   Street) $585   £260

FRAENKEL

FRAENKEL, MICHAEL
'Bastard Death' – 1st Edn., no. 225 of
400 copies, presentation copy, inscribed
by Henry Miller, original wrappers, uncut –
Paris and New York, 1936.
(Sotheby's,
    Chancery Lane)   **$135**   **£60**

FRANCE
Carriages - 18 pages of notes and drawings
of different carriages including attractive
sketches or diagrams in pen and ink and
coloured washes, notes in French, folio –
early 19th century.
(Sotheby's, New Bond
    Street)   **$1,240**   **£550**

FRANCE, ANATOLE
'Oeuvres Completes' – 22 vols., plates and
illustrations, each volume with a 'tirage
a part' of the illustration on chine,
wrappers, uncut – Paris, 1925-30.
(Sotheby Parke Bernet
    Monaco)   **$3,375**   **£1,500**

L'ANNEAU D'AMÉTHYSTE

'Histoire Contemporaine. L'Anneau
d'Ametheyste' – 1st Edn., no. 22 of 40
copies on Japon, green morocco gilt by
de Samblanx, inscription by author on
half title – Paris, 1899.
(Sotheby Parke Bernet
    Monaco)   **$8,550**   **£3,800**

FRANCHETTI, GAETANO
'Storia del Duomo di Milano' – 30 engraved
plates, tinted lithographed title and 39
plates, spotting, original cloth, spine worn,
g.e. – Milan, 1821.
(Christie's S.
    Kensington)   **$80**   **£35**

FRANCIS, G. W.
'Dictionary of Practical Receipts' – cloth,
gilt – 1853.
(Phillips)   **$35**   **£15**

FRANCIS I, HOLY ROMAN EMPEROR
Document signed 'Franciscus' acknow-
ledging the services of the 'Coen'
brothers, suppliers to the Imperial Court
and army, 10 pages on vellum – Vienna,
23 May, 1746.
(Sotheby's, New Bond
    Street)   **$90**   **£40**

Series of ten autograph letters signed
'francois' written in idiosycratic and semi-
phonetic French, 29 pages, quarto,
December 1738-1765.
(Sotheby's, New Bond
    Street)   **$1,350**   **£600**

FRANKLAND, SIR EDWARD
'Experimental Researches in Pure, Applied and Physical Chemistry' – First collected Edn., presentation copy, inscribed from author, 2 plates, 4 graphs, woodcuts in text – John van Voorst, 1877.
(Sotheby's, New Bond
    Street) $290   £130

EXPERIMENTS

A N D

OBSERVATIONS

O N

ELECTRICITY,

M A D E   A T

Philadelphia in *America*,

B Y

Mr. BENJAMIN FRANKLIN,

A N D

Communicated in feveral Letters to Mr. P. COLLINSON, of *London*, F. R. S.

L O N D O N :

Printed and fold by E. CAVE, at *St. John's Gate*. 1751.
(Price 2s. 6d.)

FRANKLIN, BENJAMIN
'Experiments and Observations in Electricity made at Philadelphia in America . . . communicated in several letters to Mr. P. Collinson of London F.R.S.' – 3 parts in one vol., 1st Edn. of parts I and III, 2nd Edn., of part II. Folding plate, woodcuts, red morocco case – E. Cave, 1751-54.
(Sotheby's, New Bond
    Street) $10,125   £4,500

FRANKLIN, J. BENJAMIN
'A Cheap Trip to the Great Salt Lake City' – unopened, margins browned, original wrappers, soiled and torn, disbound – Ipswich, n.d.
(Christie's S.
    Kensington) $22   £10

FRANKLIN, SIR JOHN
'Narrative of a Journey to the Shores of the Polar Sea – 1819-22' – 1st Edn., 31 engraved plates, 10 hand coloured, 4 folding engraved charts, worn, upper cover detached – 1823.
(Sotheby's, New Bond
    Street) $245   £110

FRASER, ROBERT W.
'Parish Kirks and Manses in Scotland' – 25 tinted lithographed plates, original morocco backed cloth, rubbed.
(Sotheby's,
    Chancery Lane) $80   £35

FRAUNHOFER, JOSEPH VON
'Bestimmung des Brechungs-und Farben-zerstreuungs-Vermogens Verschiedener Glasarten in: Denkschriften der Koniglichen Academie der Wissenschaften zu Munchen' – vol. V, 3 plates, 2 folding, wrappers, uncut – Munich, 1817.
(Sotheby's, New Bond
    Street) $790   £350

FRAZER, SIR J. G.
'The Golden Bough' – 3rd Edn., 12 vols., with bibliography and index, cloth – 1920.
(Phillips) $100   £45

FREART, ROLAND
'A Parallel of the Antient Architecture with the Modern Made English . . . by John Evelyn' – First English Edn., engraved and printed titles, numerous full page engravings, modern calf backed boards, folio – 1664.
(Sotheby's, New Bond
    Street) $65   £28

FREAS, F. K.
'The Art of Science Fiction' Introduction by Isaac Asimov – no. 556 of 1,000 copies, signed by author, illustrations, original morocco slipcase – Norfolk, Va. 1977.
(Christie's S.
    Kensington) $45   £20

FREEDMAN, BARNETT
'Set of Proofs for his Illustrations for the Six Volume Edition of 'War and Peace' – 41 coloured lithographs and 39 other illustrations in black and white, autograph inscription – 1938.
(Lawrence of
    Crewkerne) $260   £115

FREEMAN, STEPHEN
'The Ladies' Friend and Family Physical
Library' – 5th Edn., folding plate, original
boards, uncut, spine torn – For the author,
1787.
(Sotheby's, New Bond
Street) $115   £50

FRENCH, JOHN
'The Art of Distillation . . . to which is
added . . . Sublimation and Calcination . . .
as also, the London Distiller' – 4th Edn.,
woodcuts of apparatus in text, some
staining, cont. sheep, rebacked, bookplate
of Earl Fitzwilliam – E. Cotes for T.
Williams, 1667.
(Sotheby's, New Bond
Street) $225   £100

FRENCH TRELLICE
17 engraved plates, the last after designs by
Andre le Notre, half calf, leather label with
title on front cover – Chez Daumont, Paris,
1760-80.
(Sotheby Parke Bernet
Monaco) $9,000   £4,000

FRESNEL, AUGUSTIN JEAN
'Memoire sur la Diffraction de la Lumiere
(Extrait des Annales de Chimie et de
Physique)' – 1st Edn., drop title, folding
plate, original wrappers, defective, cloth
case – Paris, 1815.
(Sotheby's, New Bond
Street) $385   £170

FRESNOY, CHARLES ALPHONSE DU
'L'Art de Peinture' – in Latin with prose
translation by Roger de Piles, 1st Edn.,
waterstaining, later English reversed calf,
ownership inscription of Jean Racine
above woodcut ornament on title – Paris,
1668.
(Christie's, King
St.) $900   £400

FREUD, SIGMUND
'Die Traumdeutung' – 1st Edn., cont.
half roan, spine faded, ownership inscrip-
tion on title of Dr. T. H. Bertschinger –
Franz Deuticke, Leipzig and Vienna, 1900.
(Sotheby's, New Bond
Street) $6,075   £2,700

FREUDENBERG, S. AND DUNKER, B. A.
'Marguerite de Valois, Queen of Navarre,
Les Nouvelles' – 3 vols., 73 etched plates
after Freudenberg, head and tail pieces
after Dunker – Nouvelle Societe Typo-
graphique, Basle, 1780-81.
(Sotheby's,
Chancery Lane) $290   £130

FREY, JOHANN
'Ein New Visier Buchlein, Welches Innhelt
wie man durch den Quadraten auff eines
yeden Lands Eych, ein Rutten zu Beray-
tten und damit yetlichs unbekants Fass
Visieren, und solches innhalt erkennen
soll' – 1st Edn., woodcut on title, diagrams
and initials, modern limp vellum. Rare
early work on gauging – Nuremberg, 1531.
(Sotheby's, New Bond
Street) $1,915   £850

FRIEDLANDER, WALTER (Editor)
'The Drawings of Nicolas Poussin' – 4
vols., including one vol. of mounted
plates, unbound as issued in original
portfolio, original cloth, slight soiling –
1963.
(Christie's S.
Kensington) $335   £150

FRIKELL, W.
'The Magician's Own Book', edited by W.
H. Cremer – 1st Edn., wood engraved
frontispiece, slight spotting, original cloth,
spine slightly soiled – 1871.
(Sotheby's,
Chancery Lane)　　$40　　£18

FRISCH, JODOCUS LEOPOLD
'Die Welt im Feuer, oder das Wahre Verge-
hen und Ende der Welt, durch den letzten
Sund-Brand' – 2nd Edn., title printed in
red and black, 12 hand coloured engraved
plates, some browning, cont. half calf,
worn – Sorau, Gottlob Hebold, 1747.
(Sotheby's, New Bond
Street)　　$495　　£220

FRISI, PAOLO
'Operum' – 3 vols., first collected Edn.,
engraved medallion portrait to vol. I,
14 folding plates, cont. half vellum,
soiled, from the Signet Library with arms
gilt on sides – Milan, 1782-85.
(Sotheby's, New Bond
Street)　　$315　　£140

FROBISHER, MARTIN
'The Three Voyages' – edited by V.
Stefansson, 2 vols., no. 58 of 475 copies,
plates and maps, original vellum backed
cloth, gilt – 1938.
(Sotheby's,
Chancery Lane)　　$150　　£65

FROISSART, SIR JOHN
'Chronicles . . . translated . . . by Thomas
Johnes' – 12 vols. only, 3rd Edn., 53
aquatint plates, one folding map, cont.
russia, joints worn – 1808.
(Christie's S.
Kensington)　　$50　　£22

FROMENTIN, E.
'Dominique' – large paper, half morocco –
Paris, 1863.
(Sotheby Parke Bernet
Monaco)　　$4,500　　£2,000

FROST, ROBERT
'North of Boston' – 1st Edn., second state
very slightly spotted, original green cloth,
spine gilt – David Nutt, 1914.
(Sotheby's,
Chancery Lane)　　$40　　£18

FROUDE, J. A.
'History of England' – 12 vols., cont. half
calf – n.d.
(Christie's S.
Kensington)　　$100　　£45

FRYER, JOHN
'A New Account of East India and Persia'
– 1st Edn., engraved portrait, 8 plates and
maps, 3 folding, some worming, soiling
and discolouration, 19th century half calf,
rubbed, folio – 1698.
(Sotheby's, New Bond
Street)　　$430　　£190

FUCHS, EDOUARD
'Die Frau in Der Karikatur' – plates, some
coloured, some double page and mounted
on guards, one folding, original pictorial
cloth, slightly soiled, 4to – Munich, n.d.
(Christie's S.
Kensington)　　$75　　£32

FUCHS, LEONHARD
'De Historia Stirpium Commentarii
Insignes' – 1st Edn., woodcut portrait of
the author, 512 full page woodcuts of
plants by V. R. Speckle, cont. German
blindstamped pigskin over wooden boards,
half red morocco case, folio – Basle, 1542.
(Sotheby's, New Bond
Street)　　$12,375　　£5,500
'Herbal in Dutch' – woodcut illustrations,
title and some leaves lacking, others
detached or torn, cont. calf, folio – n.d.
(Christie's S.
Kensington)　　$450　　£200

FULLARTON, ARCHIBALD AND CO.
'The Parliamentary Gazetteer' – 12 parts,
39 maps, all double page or folding, some
torn, others stained, boards, worn – circa
1840.
(Christie's S.
Kensington)　　$190　　£85

FULLER, FRANCIS
'Medicina Gymnastica or a Treatise Con-
cerning the Power of Exercise with Respect
to the Animal Oeconomy and the Great
Necessity of it in the Cure of Several Dis-
tempers' – 2nd Edn., licence leaf before
title, cont. panelled calf, upper hinge torn
– R. Knaplock, 1705.
(Sotheby's, New Bond
Street)　　$65　　£28

FULLER

FULLER, LOIE
'Rules and Regulations to Dancers and a few Suggestions to Dancers' — autograph manuscripts in English, in ink, in cloth folder and morocco and cloth box — n.d.
(Sotheby's, New Bond
    Street)   **$270**   **£120**

FULLER, THOMAS
'The History of the Worthies of England' — 1st Edn., engraved frontispiece portrait, early 19th century diced russia gilt, rebacked, folio — 1662.
(Christie's, King
    St.)   **$250**   **£110**

FULLER, WILLIAM
'A Collection of 12 Items in 8 Volumes by or about, or connected with the imposter, William Fuller, particularly in relation to the birth of the Prince of Wales, the son of James II', slight browning and soiling, a few leaves cropped, calf or half calf, rubbed, one vol. disbound — 1688-1718.
(Sotheby's
    London)   **$180**   **£80**

FULTON, ROBERT
'A Treatise on the Improvement of Canal Navigation' — 1st Edn., 17 engraved plates, some foxing and soiling, cont. calf very worn, spine repaired, 4to — I. and J. Taylor, 1796.
(Sotheby's, New Bond
    Street)   **$810**   **£360**

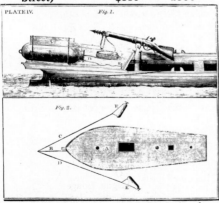

'Torpedo War and Submarine Explosions' — 1st Edn., 5 wood engraved plates, brown half roan worn, original marbled wrappers, bound in, half blue morocco case — William Elliot, New York, 1810.
(Sotheby's, New Bond
    Street)   **$2,140**   **£950**

FUMEE, MARTIN
'A History of the Troubles of Hungarie' — device on title, cont. sprinkled sheep, gilt spine, ownership inscription on title page, folio — 1600.
(Sotheby's
    Monaco)   **$790**   **£350**

FUNDAMENTUM AETERNAE FELICITATIS
32 leaves, 30 lines and head line, gothic letter, woodcuts of Virgin and Child and St. Anne. Initials in red throughout, a few stains, red morocco by Sangorski and Sutcliffe — 1497-98.
(Sotheby's, New Bond
    Street)   **$1,125**   **£500**

'FUNNY FOLKS'
21 volumes — 1875-94.
(Sotheby's,
    Chancery Lane)   **$900**   **£400**

FURNISS, HARRY
'Confessions of a Caricaturist' — 2 vols., illustrations, cloth gilt, t.e.g., 1901; 'Harry Furniss at Home' — illus. cloth gilt, t.e.g., 1904.
(Phillips)   **$70**   **£30**
'Parliamentary Views' — limited edition, plates, original binding, worn, oblong 4to — Bradbury and Agnew, n.d.
(Phillips)   **$35**   **£15**

FURTENBACH, JOSEPH
'Architectura Universalis. Das Ist; Von Kriegs; Statt-Und Wasser Gebawen' — 1st Edn., title printed in red and black, engraved frontispiece, portrait of author, 60 plates of military fortification and buildings, 1635. Bound in same volume with 'Buchsenmeistery-Schul, Darinnen Die New Angehende Buchsenmeister und Feurwercker' — folding engraved frontispiece and engraved portrait of Berthold Schwartz, inventor of gunpowder, 1643.
(Sotheby's, New Bond
    Street)   **$8,100**   **£3,600**

GAGE, T.

'A New Survey of the West Indies of the English American His Travail by Sea and Land' — 4 full page maps, 2nd Edn., folio, cont. calf, one map slightly defective — E. Cotes and John Sweeting, 1655.
(Bonham's) $450   £200

GALE, T.

'Electricity or Ethereal Fire Considered .. Comprehending both the Theory and Practice of Medical Electricity' — 1st Edn., browned, cont. sheep, worn, flyleaf inscribed 'Jesse Everett's property, April 11th, 1816' — Troy, 1802.
(Sotheby's, New Bond
  Street) $270   £120

GALEN

'Opera' — 5 vols., 1st Edn. in Greek, edited by Torresani and Opizo, anchor device on titles and at end of each volume, small tears, slightly soiled, g.e., folio — Venice, 1525.
(Sotheby's, New Bond
  Street) $24,750   £11,000

GALERIE THEATRALE OU COLLECTION DES PORTRAITS EN PIED DES PRINCIPAUX ACTEURS DES TROIS PREMIERS THEATRES DE LA CAPITALE

vols. 1 and 2 only of three, 1st Edn., 96 coloured plates of 144 of actors and dancers. Later half morocco, gilt spines with red morocco labels, slightly rubbed, marbled edges, folio — Chez Bance Aine, Paris, 1812-20.
(Sotheby's, New Bond
  Street) $900   £400

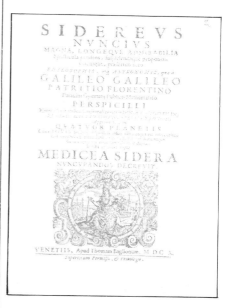

GALILEI, GALILEO

'Siderius Nuncius Magna, Longeque admirabilia Spectacula Pandens' — 1st Edn., device on title, 5 engravings of surface of the moon, woodcut diagrams, modern vellum boards, half green morocco case, first description of the scientific use of the telescope — T. Baglioni, Venice, 1610.
(Sotheby's, New Bond
  Street) $27,000   £12,000

GALILEO

'Le Operazioni del Compasso Geometrico, et Militare' – 1st Edn., woodcut diagrams, some spotting, cont. limp vellum, lacking ties – Padua, 1606.
(Sotheby's, New Bond
   Street) $15,750   £7,000
'Il Saggiatore' – 1st Edn., engraved title, portrait, engravings in text, browned and stained, cont. vellum boards, panelled in gilt, g.e., half red morocco case – circa 1623.
(Sotheby's, New Bond
   Street) $855   £380
'Istoria e Dimostrazioni Intorno alle Macchie Solari' – 1st Edn., engraved portrait of author, 38 full page engravings of sunspots, 5 plates of Jovian satellites, woodcut diagrams, 18th century mottled calf, half red morocco case – Giacomo Mascardi, Rome, 1613.
(Sotheby's, New Bond
   Street) $2,700   £1,200

'Discorsi e Dimostrazioni Matematiche, intorno a due nuove scienze attenenti alla Mecanica & i Movimenti Locali' – 1st Edn., device on title, woodcut illustrations and diagrams, errata leaf, some waterstaining, cont. limp vellum, worn, half red morocco case, ownership entries. The foundation of modern mechanics – Appresso gli Elsevirii, Leiden, 1638.
(Sotheby's, New Bond
   Street) $3,375   £1,500

GALLERY OF MODERN BRITISH ARTISTS, THE
steel engraved additional title and plates after Turner, Roberts, Prout and others, some spotting, original cloth, g.e. – n.d.
(Christie's S.
   Kensington) $100   £45

GALLETLEY, A.
'Ancient Towers and Doorways . . . relating to Celtic and Norman Ecclesiology in Scotland' – plates and text illustrations, gilt, folio, limited edition, no. 72 of 300 copies – 1896.
(Tessa Bennett,
   Edinburgh) $45   £20

GALSWORTHY, JOHN
'The Plays' – no. 890 of 1,275 copies signed by author, original cloth, t.e.g., 8vo – 1929.
(Sotheby Humberts
   Taunton) $100   £45

'Dialogo . . . sopra i due Massimi Sistemi del Mondo Tolemaico e Copernicano' – 1st Edn., fine engraved frontispiece by Stefano della Bella, woodcut diagrams, cont. limp vellum, spine slightly torn, half red morocco case – G. B. Landini, Florence, 1632.
(Sotheby's, New Bond
   Street) $5,850   £2,600

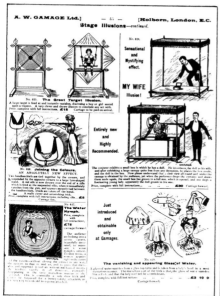

GAMAGES

21 catalogues in three volumes, illustrations, the earliest catalogue defective, cloth backed boards or cloth, 2 spines worn, original wrappers of all but the earliest bound in, some worn – circa 1909-59.
(Sotheby's,
    Chancery Lane) $380   £170

GARCIA DE LA LENA, CECILIO

'Disertacion en Recomendacion y Defensa del Famoso vino Malagueno Pero Ximen y Modo de Formario' – large paper copy, engraved frontispiece, folding diagram, cont. vellum, loose edges worn – Malaga, 1792.
(Sotheby's, New Bond
    Street) $180   £80

GARDINER, CAPTAIN A. F.

'Narrative of a Journey to Zoolu Country' – 24 plates of 26, some spotting, 2 folding maps, half calf gilt – 1836.
(Phillips) $65   £28

GARNETT, T.

'Observations on a Tour Through the Highlands' – 2 vols., map, tinted plates, calf, worn – 1800.
(Sotheby's, New Bond
    Street) $165   £75

GARNIER, JULES – LE ROUX, HUGUES

'Les Jeux du Cirque et la Vie Foraine' – 211 wood engraved illustrations by Garnier, all but one coloured by hand, light brown calf, covers blindstamped with large floral bouquet, inside borders gilt, marbled endpapers, t.e.g., original wrappers, bound in, by Rene Kieffer – Plon, Paris, 1899.
(Sotheby's,
    Chancery Lane) $200   £90

GARRAN, A.

'Picturesque Atlas of Australasia' – 3 vols., illus., half morocco gilt, folio – 1886.
(Phillips) $160   £70

GARTH, SIR SAMUEL

'Ovid's Metamorphoses in Fifteen Books translated by the Most Eminent Hands' – additional engraved title, engraved frontispiece and 15 engraved plates, waterstained, cont. calf, worn, folio – 1717.
(Christie's, King
    St.) $100   £45

GASCOYNE, DAVID

'Man's Life is this Meat' – 1st Edn., original boards – The Parton Press, 1936.
(Sotheby's,
    Chancery Lane) $170   £75

GASS, PATRICK

'Journal of the Voyages and Travels of Lewis and Clarke from the Mouth of the River Missouri through the Interior Parts of North America to the Pacific Ocean' – 1st London Edn., original paper boards, spine worn – 1808.
(Sotheby's, New Bond
    Street) $540   £240

GAUTIER, HENRY (Engineer)
'L'Art de Laver ou Nouvelle Maniere de
Peindre sur le Papier' – 1st Edn., 1 engraved
plate with final blank, browned and soiled,
tears and holes, slightly affecting text, cont.
calf worn, spine defective – Chez Thomas
Amaulry, Lyons, 1687.
(Sotheby's, New Bond
    Street) $205   £90

GAUTIER, T.
'Constantinople' – 2 vols., plates, original
cloth, dust jackets – 1854.
(Christie's S.
    Kensington) $45   £20

GAVARNI, PAUL AND OTHERS
'Le Museum d'Histoire Naturelle' – 41
engraved plates, some double page, 15 of
flowers and birds coloured by hand,
woodcut engravings in text by Gavarni,
slightly spotted, original pictorial cloth,
gilt, slightly rubbed, g.e., bookplate of
J. R. Abbey – L. Curmer, Paris, 1854.
(Sotheby's,
    Chancery Lane) $190   £85

**GAVARNI, PAUL – BALZAC, HONORE
DE, AND OTHERS**
'La Peau de Chargin' – First illustrated
Edn., engraved vignette on title, illustra-
tions in text after Baron, Gavarni and
others, cont. half morocco gilt, spine
slightly faded – Paris, 1838.
(Sotheby's,
    Chancery Lane) $175   £78

5° d'un cercle de badauds amassés autour d'un Paillasse;

**GAVARNI, PAUL – BALZAC, HONORE
DE; SAND, GEORGE AND OTHERS**
'Le Diable a Paris' – 4 vols., in two,
numerous wood engraved illustrations
after Gavarni, Grandville, Bertall and
others, cont. morocco backed boards, gilt,
by Costey – Paris, 1868.
(Sotheby's,
    Chancery Lane) $160   £70

**GAVARNI, PAUL – DUMAS,
ALEXANDRE**
'La Dame Aux Camellias' – 20 wood
engraved plates after Gavarni, blue morocco,
wide gilt borders gilt, red watered silk
doublures, g.e., original pictorial cloth
bound in, slipcase, by Parnant, plus two
alternative wrappers – Librairie Moderne,
Paris, 1858.
(Sotheby's,
    Chancery Lane) $540   £240

**GAVARNI, PAUL – SAND, GEORGES
AND OTHERS**
'Le Diable a Paris' – 2 vols., 208 wood
engraved illustrations after Gavarni, vignettes after Bertall and others, some leaves
slightly soiled, cont. half calf, somewhat
worn – Paris, 1845-46.
(Sotheby's,
    Chancery Lane) $100   £45

GAY, JOHN
'Fables' – engraved frontispieces, title and
67 illustrations, cont. calf, rebacked –
Darton and Harvey for Rivington and
others, 1793.
(Sotheby's,
    Chancery Lane) $110   £48

GEIKIE, W.
'Etchings Illustrative of the Scottish Character and Scenery' — plates, cloth —
Edinburgh and Glasgow, n.d.
(Tessa Bennett,
Edinburgh) $30   £14

GENTLEMAN'S MAGAZINE FOR 1731-1845 with Index vols. for 1-20 and 1-56,
calf, some gilt spines, worn, many joints
cracked and defective — 1731-1845.
(Christie's
St. James) $2,700   £1,200

GEOGRAPHIA ANTIQUA
'Being a Complete set of Maps of Ancient
Geography' — 32 of 33 double page
copper plates, maps, leather backed boards
— 1803.
(Tessa Bennett,
Edinburgh) $54   £24

GEOGRAPHICAL ANTIQUA
Maps of Ancient Geography engraved from
Cellarius, 33 double page maps mounted
on guards, some staining and worming, cont.
half calf, worn — 1825.
(Christie's S.
Kensington) $85   £38

GERARD, JOHN
'The Herball or Generall Historie of Plantes'
— 3rd Edn., engraved title page by Payne,
botanical woodcuts in text, woodcut
initials and ornaments, 19th century red
straight grained morocco by Riviere, gilt
fillets, blindstamped border, spine gilt, inner
gilt fillets, folio — Adam Islip, Ioice Norton
and Richard Whitakers, 1636.
(Sotheby's, New Bond
Street) $2,025   £900
'The Herball or Generall Historie of Plantes
... enlarged ... by Thomas Johnson' —
engraved title, slightly stained, woodcut
illustrations, 18th century panelled calf,
covers detached, folio — 1633.
(Christie's S.
Kensington) $1,910   £850

GERARD, THOMAS
'A Survey of Dorsetshire' — folding map,
6 engraved plates of arms, bookplate Duke
of Bedford, calf, upper cover detached,
small folio — 1732.
(Phillips) $205   £90

'GERM, THE'
Facsimile of the 1850 Edn., 5 portraits,
original wrappers, carton — 1901.
(Phillips) $36   £16

GERMAN COOKERY BOOK
Manuscript on paper, 350 pages, ms. index
at end, calf — 1764.
(Sotheby's
Monaco) $1,575   £700

GERNING, BARON JOHANN ISAAC VON
'A Picturesque Tour along the Rhine ...
engravings from the drawings of M. Schutz
... translated from the German by John
Black' — 24 coloured aquatint plates some
watermarked 1818, folding engraved map,
some spotting and offsetting, red morocco
gilt, damaged, rubbed, 4to — R. Ackermann
1820.
(Sotheby's, New Bond
Street) $2,700   £1,200

GERNSHEIM, HELMUT
'Julia Margaret Cameron' — plates, original
cloth, dust jacket — 1948.
(Christie's S.
Kensington) $100   £45

GHOSE, SUDHIN N.
'Folk Tales and Fairy Stories from India' —
limited to 500 copies, this no. 65 of 100
specially bound by E. W. Hiscox, plates
by S. E. Carlile, original morocco, t.e.g.,
slipcase — 1961.
(Christie's S.
Kensington) $160   £70

GIAMBULLARI, PIER FRANCESCO
'Origine della Lingua Fiorentina' — some
waterstaining, modern limp vellum —
Florence, L. Torrentino, 1549.
(Sotheby's
London) $125   £55

GIBBINGS, ROBERT
'The 7th Man' — no. 88 of 500 copies,
illustrations by author, original cloth
backed boards, g.e. — 1930.
(Christie's S.
Kensington) $85   £38

GIBBON, EDWARD
'Critical Observations on the Sixth Book of
the Aeneid' — 1st Edn., half title, modern
wrappers — 1770.
(Sotheby's, New Bond
Street) $450   £200

GIBBON
'Decline and Fall of the Roman Empire' –
8 vols., portrait, one map, cont. half
morocco – 1828.
(Christie's S.
   Kensington) $75   £32

GIBRALTAR, SIEGE OF
'Remarkable Occurrences During the Siege
of Gibraltar' – mss. in ink, title page, map
in ink and watercolour, day by day account
of the siege from 20 January to 11 June,
1727. Neatly written on 49 pages, 19th
century half roan, rubbed.
(Christie's, King
   St.) $205   £90

GIBSON, FRANK
'Charles Condor, His Life and Work' –
plates, some coloured, slight spotting, ori-
ginal buckram, soiled, t.e.g. – 1914.
(Christie's S.
   Kensington) $225   £100

GIBSON, J.
'History of Glasgow' – half calf – Glasgow,
1777.
(Tessa Bennett,
   Edinburgh) $11   £5

GIBSON, W.
'The Farrier's Dispensatory' – some leaves
stained, cont. panelled calf, split – 1721.
(Christie's S.
   Kensington) $45   £20

GIDE, A.
'L'Immoraliste' – 1st Edn., green morocco
by Louis Pinard, wrappers preserved,
presentation copy, inscribed by Gide to
Marcia Bley – Paris, 1902.
(Sotheby Parke Bernet
   Monaco) $14,625   £6,500
'Le Traite du Narcisse' – 1st Edn., limited
to 12 copies of which this is no. 4 of 5 on
chine, half blue morocco by Loisellier,
original wrappers preserved – Paris, 1891.
(Sotheby Parke Bernet
   Monaco) $38,250   £17,000

GILBERT, WILLIAM
'The Magic Mirror, a Round of Tales for
Young and Old' – 1st Edn., wood engraved
illustrations after W. S. Gilbert, some
leaves spotted, original cloth, gilt, g.e. –
1866.
(Sotheby's,
   Chancery Lane) $65   £28

GILBERT, WILLIAM
'De Magnete' – 1st Edn., woodcut device
on title with woodcut arms on verso, folding woodcut diagram, woodcut illustrations
and diagrams, cont. limp vellum, folio –
1600.
(Christie's, King
   St.) $2,925   £1,300

GILBERT, WILLIAM SWENCK
'Iolanthe and Other Operas' – original cloth
gilt, t.e.g., 32 tissued colour plates by Wm.
Russell Flint – 1910.
(Lawrence of
   Crewkerne) $80   £35

GILL, ERIC
'Art and Prudence' – no. 411 of 500 copies,
plates by author, original cloth – Golden
Cockerel Press, 1928.
(Christie's S.
   Kensington) $235   £105
'Art and Love' – engravings, one of 35
copies with an extra set of engravings in
pocket at end, signed, vellum gilt –
Bristol, 1927.
(Bonham's) $560   £250
'The Lord's Song' – no. 124 of 500 copies,
full page illustrations by author, original
cloth, unopened, first Golden Cockerel
book to make use of Gill's Perpetua
Roman and Felicity Italic types – Golden
Cockerel Press, 1934.
(Christie's S.
   Kensington) $160   £70

GILPIN, W.
'Observations on Several Parts of England'
– 2 vols., 30 plates, half morocco gilt –
1808.
(Phillips) $85   £38

GIOVIO, PAOLO
'Historiarum sui Temporis' – 2 vols. in one,
old inscriptions and scribbles on title and
last few leaves, 18th century panelled calf,
worn, folio – M. Vascosan, Paris, 1558-60.
(Sotheby's, New Bond
    Street) $200   £90

GIRARDIN, R. DE
'Promenard ou Itineraire des Jardins
d'Ermononville' – large paper, 2 leaves
of engraved music, 25 sepia plates by or
after Merigot, cont. French red morocco,
gilt – Paris, 1788.
(Sotheby Parke Bernet
    Monaco) $16,875   £7,500
'Promenades ou Itineraire deJardins de
Chantilly' – large paper, a folding plan,
20 plates mostly by or after Merigot,
cont. French green morocco, gilt, gilt
edges – Paris, 1791.
(Sotheby Parke Bernet
    Monaco) $15,750   £7,000

GLASGOW
'Illustrated Catalogue for the Exhibition of
Portraits' – photographs, cloth – T. Annan,
Glasgow, 1868.
(Tessa Bennett,
    Edinburgh) $18   £8
GLASGOW
Post Office Directory for 1842-43 –
Glasgow, 1842.
(Tessa Bennett,
    Edinburgh) $9   £4

GLASSE, MRS. H.
'The Compleat Confectioner' – 1st Edn.,
soiled internal scribblings and worm holes,
cont. calf, worn – London, Mrs. Ashburner's
China Shop, 1760.
(Sotheby's, New Bond
    Street) $360   £160

GLASSPOOLE, MICHAEL
'Mr. Glasspoole and the Chinese Pirates' –
no. 66 of 315 copies, frontispiece and
illustrations by Robert Gibbings, original
cloth, slightly soiled, unopened – Golden
Cockerel Press, 1935.
(Christie's S.
    Kensington) $65   £28

GLEADALL, ELIZA EVE
'The Beauties of Flora with Botanic and
Poetic Illustrations' – vol. II of two, hand
coloured and engraved title, 21 hand finished coloured lithographed plates, original
embossed cloth gilt, g.e. – 1836.
(Christie's
    St. James) $855   £380

GLENNIE, REV. J. D.
'Views on the Continent' – lithographed
title, 25 lithographed plates, cont. roan
backed cloth, worn, folio – 1841.
(Christie's
    St. James) $945   £420

GOBAT, REV. SAMUEL
'Journal of a Three Year's Residence in
Abyssinia' – 1st Edn., engraved folded
map, slightly spotted, lacks first leaf, cont.
half calf by E. Paul, Southampton – 1834.
(Sotheby's
    London) $190   £85

GOBINEAU, COMTE DE
'Nouvelles Asiatiques' – no. 16 of 20 copies
on Japon Imperial of an edition of 570,
plates in two states by Maurice de Becque,
tan morocco, gilt by Vermorel, ornamental
spine, g.e., original pictorial wrappers preserved – Paris, 1926.
(Sotheby's
    Monaco) $3,600   £1,600

**GOBLE, WARWICK – VAN MILLIUGERI,
A.**
'Constantinople' – coloured plates by
Goble, original cloth, spine soiled, t.e.g. –
1906.
(Christie's S.
    Kensington) $40   £18

GODDARD, R. H.
'A Method of Reaching Extreme Altitudes'
– 1st Edn., 10 plates, wrappers, 8vo –
Washington, 1919.
(Sotheby's, New Bond
    Street) $900   £400

GODWIN, WILLIAM
'Enquiry Concerning Political Justice and
Its Influence on Morals and Happiness' –
2 vols., 2nd Edn., half titles, cont. calf,
gilt spines, rubbed – 1796.
(Sotheby's, New Bond
    Street) $335   £150

GOETHE, JOHANN WOLFGANG VON
'Faust' – large decorated parchment gilt,
bevelled boards, t.e.g., rather soiled, 31
full page tissued coloured plates by Willy
Pogany, no. 247 of 250 copies, signed by
artist – 1908.
(Lawrence of
   Crewkerne)   **$75**   **£35**

GOGARTY, OLIVER ST. JOHN
'Elbow Room' – 1st Edn., limited to 450
copies, signed by author on fly leaf,
original linen backed boards, uncut, unopened – Cuala Press, Dublin, 1939.
(Sotheby's,
   Chancery Lane)   **$75**   **£35**

*To Ernest Boyd
(...... ......)*

WILD APPLES: BY
~~OLIVER GOGARTY~~

Oliver St. J. Gogarty

THE CUALA PRESS
DUBLIN, IRELAND
MCMXXVIII

'Wild Apples' – 1st Edn., limited to 50
copies, presentation copy, inscribed by
author on title, original linen backed
boards, uncut with bookplate of the
author – Cuala Press, Dublin, 1928.
(Sotheby's,
   Chancery Lane)   **$425**   **£190**

GOLD, CAPTAIN CHARLES
'Oriental Drawings sketched between the
years 1791 and 1798' – 49 hand coloured
aquatint plates, music notation in text,
some modern mss. notes, later black half
morocco, inner hinges strengthened in
maroon morocco protective jacket – 1806.
(Sotheby's, New Bond
   Street)   **$1,235**   **£550**

GOLDSMITH, O. AND PARNELL, T.
'Poems' – 1st Edn., woodcuts by Bewick,
half green morocco, rubbed, some margins
stained – W. Bulmer, 1795.
(Bonham's)   **$100**   **£45**

GOLDSMITH, OLIVER
'The Beauties of English Poesy' – 2 vols.,
1st Edn., cont. marbled calf, gilt, hinges
cracked – William Griffin, 1767.
(Sotheby's, New Bond
   Street)   **$200**   **£90**

GONCOURT, EDMOND DE
'La Fille Elisa' – 1st Edn., calf backed
boards, slightly rubbed – Paris, 1877.
(Sotheby's,
   Chancery Lane)   **$24**   **£11**
'Catalogue Raisonne de l'Oeuvre d'Antoine
Watteau' – half calf, wrappers, presenta-
tion copy, with inscription by author to
Mme Vigneres, some damage to spine –
Paris, 1875.
Sotheby Parke Bernet
   Monaco)   **$675**   **£300**

**GONTCHAROVA, NATALIA – KESSEL,
J.**
'Le The de Captaine Sogoub' – 6 etched
plates by Gontcharova, morocco backed
boards, original wrappers bound in, uncut –
Au Sans Pareil, Paris, 1926.
(Sotheby's,
   Chancery Lane)   **$215**   **£95**

GOODRICH, S. G.
'The Book of Trades, Arts and Professions
by Peter Parley' – 1st Edn., 16 wood
engraved plates and a few illustrations in
text, slightly spotted, original cloth, gilt,
soiled – Darton and Co., 1855.
(Sotheby's,
   Chancery Lane)   **$75**   **£32**

**GORGUET, AUGUSTE FRANCOIS –
FRANCE, ANATOLE**
'Le Lys Rouge' – pictorial half title,
heightened with gold, 18 coloured plates,
wood engraved frontispiece and 35 tinted
illustrations by Gorguet, deep red morocco
gilt, floral sprays on upper cover, woven
silk doublures and endleaves, g.e., original
wrappers bound in, slipcase by Rene
Kieffer – Romagnol, Paris, 1903.
(Sotheby's,
    Chancery Lane)   **$470**   **£210**

GOSSE, PHILIP HENRY
'The Birds of Jamaica' – 2 vols., 52 hand
coloured lithographed plates, cont. cloth,
not uniform – Van Voorst, 1847-49.
(Christie's
    St. James)   **$7,875**   **£3,500**

GOTCH, J. ALFRED
'The Old Halls and Manor Houses of
Northamptonshire' – folding map, plates,
illustrations, original cloth, soiled – 1936.
(Christie's S.
    Kensington)   **$55**   **£25**

GOTHEIN, MARIE LOUISE
'A History of Garden Art' – 2 vols., plates,
illustrations, original cloth – 1928.
(Christie's S.
    Kensington)   **$145**   **£65**

GOULD, R. F.
'The History of Freemasonry' – 3 vols.,
plates, a few coloured, original morocco,
worn, g.e. – 1886-87.
(Christie's S.
    Kensington)   **$65**   **£28**

GOURLAY, G.
'Anstruther or Illustrations of Scottish
Country Life' – cloth gilt – Anstruther
and Cupar, Fife, 1888.
(Tessa Bennett,
    Edinburgh)   **$50**   **£22**

GOWER, W. R.
'Atlas of the Pathological Anatomy of the
Eyeball' – plates, original cloth gilt, folio
– 1875.
(Phillips)   **$125**   **£55**

GRAAF, R. DE
'De Mulierum Organis Generatione Inservientibus' – engraved title, portrait and
plates, 1st Edn., old calf, first account of
the 'Graafian follicle'.
(Bonham's)   **$155**   **£70**

GRAHAM, D.
'An Impartial History of the Rise, Progress
and Extinction of the Late Rebellion in
Britain, 1745 and 1746' – woodcut frontis-
piece, half calf, 8th Edn., – J. and M.
Robertson, Glasgow, 1808.
(Tessa Bennett,
    Edinburgh)   **$50**   **£22**

GRAHAM, R. B. CUNNINGHAME
'The District of Menteith' – illustrated by
Sir D. Y. Cameron, limited edition, signed
by author and artist, quarter calf gilt,
folio – 1930.
(Phillips)   **$70**   **£32**

GRAHAM, W.
'The One Pound Note . Banking in Scotland
and Its Adaptability to England' – cloth –
1886.
'The One Pound Note – in Great Britain' –
cloth – 1911 – 1886-1911.
(Tessa Bennett,
    Edinburgh)   **$45**   **£20**

GRAHAME, KENNETH
'Wind in the Willows' – illustrated by
Arthur Rackham, limited edition, half green
morocco, gilt, t.e.g. – 1951.
(Phillips)   **$540**   **£240**

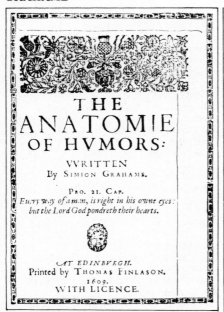

GRAHAME, SIMION
'The Anatomie of Humors' – 1st Edn.,
printed within woodcut borders through-
out, copy in early 19th century red
morocco, g.e., with bookplate of Thos.
Jolley, the fruit merchant – Finlason,
Edinburgh, 1609.
(Sotheby's
Edinburgh) $6,300   £2,800

GRAMMONT, LE SIEUR DE
'Heartsease and Honesty' – limited to 300
copies, this no. 16 of 25 on hand made
paper and specially bound, signed by translator Helen Simpson and Tirzah Ravilious,
designer of woodcut borders, original parchment, t.e.g., unopened – Golden Cockerel
Press, 1935.
(Christie's S.
Kensington) $125   £55

GRANDVILLE, J. J.
'Cent Proverbs' – wood engraved frontispiece, 49 plates and illustrations in text
after Grandville, spotted, original pictorial
cloth, gilt rebacked, preserving spine,
rubbed, g.e. – Paris, 1845.
(Sotheby's,
Chancery Lane) $55   £25

'Petites Miseres de la Vie Humaine' –
wood engraved frontispiece, title 47 plates,
illustrations in text after Grandville, upper
margins slightly stained, slightly spotted,
original pictorial cloth gilt, rubbed, spine
repaired, g.e. – H. Fournier, Paris, 1846.
(Sotheby's,
Chancery Lane) $150   £65
'Vie Privee et Publique des Animaux' –
illustrations, occasional foxing, calf backed
boards – Paris, 1867.
(Sotheby's
Monaco) $2,250   £1,000

**GRANDVILLE, J. J. – BALZAC,
HONORE DE**
'Scenes de la Vie Privee et Publique des
Animaux' – 2 vols., wood engraved frontis-
piece, 199 plates, numerous illustrations
after Grandville, preliminaries and end-
leaves slightly spotted, cont. vellum
backed boards, slightly marked – J.
Hertzel, Paris, 1842.
(Sotheby's,
Chancery Lane) $180   £80

**GRANDVILLE, J. J. – BERANGER, P. J.
DE – RAFFET, D. A. M.**
'Oeuvres Completes' – 3 vols., 120 wood
engraved plates after Grandville and Raffet,
portrait, slightly spotted, cont. morocco
gilt, slightly rubbed, spines slightly faded,
g.e., by Simier – H. Fournier Aine, Paris,
1837.
(Sotheby's,
Chancery Lane) $110   £50

GRANDVILLE, J. J. – DELORD, TAXILE AND OTHERS
'Les Fleurs Animees' – 2 vols., 2 engraved pictorial titles and 52 plates after Grandville, all but two coloured by hand, original morocco backed cloth, lower cover of first stained, slightly rubbed – Garnier, Paris, 1867.
(Sotheby's,
    Chancery Lane) $335   £150

GRANDVILLE, J. J. – FLORIAN, J. P. C. DE
'Fables' edited by P. J. Stahl – wood engraved title, 5 sub titles, 79 plates after Grandville, slightly spotted, cont. morocco backed cloth gilt, slightly rubbed, g.e. – Garnier Freres, Paris, n.d.
(Sotheby's,
    Chancery Lane) $70   £32

GRANDVILLE, J. J. – LA FONTAINE, JEAN DE
'Fables' – 2 vols., 2 wood engraved titles, half title, 240 plates, 12 pictorial sub titles, vignettes in text after Grandville, slightly spotted and torn, cont. morocco gilt, slightly rubbed, g.e. – H. Fournier Aine, Paris, 1839.
(Sotheby's,
    Chancery Lane) $110   £48

GRANT, J.
'Old and New Edinburgh' – 4 vols. in two, numerous wood engraved plates and illustrations, half calf – n.d.
(Tessa Bennett,
    Edinburgh) $70   £30

GRANVILLE, A. B.
'St. Petersburgh, A Journal of Travels to and From that Capital' – 2 vols., 1st Edn., 37 plates and maps, 2 folding, illustrations, half title in vol. 1 some leaves slightly spotted, cont. cloth, soiled – 1828.
(Sotheby's,
    Chancery Lane) $180   £80

GRAPHIC, THE
29 vols., illustrated, original cloth, folio – 1900-15.
(Phillips) $495   £220

GRATTAN, WILLIAM
'Adventures of the Connaught Rangers' – 1808-1814 – two copies, 2nd series, uniform half calf spines, gilt morocco labels by Morrell, a good set – 1847 and 1853.
(Lawrence of
    Crewkerne) $180   £80

REFLECTIONS
On the
WEEKLY
Bills of Mortality
For the Cities of
LONDON and WESTMINSTER,
and the Places adjacent :

But more especially, so far as it relates to
THE
PLAGUE,
AND OTHER
MOST MORTAL DISEASES
that we English-men are most subject to,
And should be most careful against,
in this our Age.

LONDON:
Printed for *Samuel Speed*, at the Rainbow in
Fleet-street. 1 6 6 5.

GRAUNT, JOHN
'Reflections on the Weekly Bills of Mortality for the Cities of London and Westminster so far as it relates to the Plague and
other Mortal Diseases' – 46 pp., new cloth,
4to – Samuel Speed, 1665.
(Sotheby's, New Bond
Street) $785 £350

GRAVES, ROBERT
'Love Respelt' – 1st Edn., no. 64 of 250
copies, signed by author, illustrations by
Aemilia Laracuen, original buckram backed
boards, dust jacket – 1965.
(Sotheby's,
Chancery Lane) $100 £45
'Man Does, Woman Is' – 1st Edn., no. 72
of 175 copies signed by author, original
cloth – 1964.
(Sotheby's,
Chancery Lane) $85 £38

GRAVES, ROBERT AND OTHERS
'Poems for Shakespeare' – edited by
Christopher Hampton and Graham Fawcett,
2 vols., no. 32 of 100 copies, signed by the
then living poets, portraits, original calf
backed cloth, gilt, g.e., slipcases – The
Globe Playhouse Trust Publications, 1972-
73.
(Sotheby's,
Chancery Lane) $155 £68

GRAVESANDE, W. J. S. VAN'S
'Physica Elementa Mathematica' – 2 vols.
in one, vol. 1 2nd Edn., 71 folding engraved
plates only, cont. calf, rubbed – Leiden,
1725-21.
(Christie's S.
Kensington) $135 £60

GRAY, GEORGE ROBERT
'A Fasciculus of the Birds of China' – 12
hand coloured lithographed plates, original
plates, original cloth backed boards with
paper label, corners worn, folio – 1871.
(Sotheby's, New Bond
Street) $585 £260

'The Genera of Birds' – 3 vols., over 183
coloured lithographed plates and numerous
uncoloured lithographed plates, some
double page, cont. red half morocco, gilt,
g.e., folio – 1844-49.
(Christie's
St. James) $16,875 £7,500

GRAY, JOHN EDWARD
'Illustrations of Indian Zoology' – 2 vols.
in one, lithographed portrait, 202 coloured
plates, finished by hand, and 14 additional
lithographed plates, modern red half
morocco, original printed wrappers to part
one, folio – 1830-34.
(Christie's
St. James) $4,500 £2,000

GRAY, THOMAS
'Elegy Written in a Country Churchyard'
foreword by Christopher Sandford – no.
291 of 750 copies, frontispiece and full
page illustrations by Gwenda Morgan,
original cloth backed boards – Golden
Cockerel Press, 1949.
(Christie's S.
   Kensington) $70   £32

GREEN, THOMAS
'The Universal Herbal' – 2 vols., engraved
titles, frontispiece, plates, old sheep, covers
loose, 4to – 1823.
(Phillips) $225   £100

GREEN, VALENTINE
'The History and Antiquities of Worcester'
– 2 vols., engraved titles, portrait, folding
plan and 22 plates, later half calf, covers
detached – 1796.
(Christie's S.
   Kensington) $125   £55

GREENAWAY, KATE
'Alphabet' – coloured frontispiece and
illustrations, original pictorial boards,
backstrip torn and with loss – George
Routledge and Sons, n.d.
(Christie's S.
   Kensington) $35   £15
'A Day in a Child's Life' – Music by
Myles B. Foster – coloured illustrations
and decorations by Kate Greenaway,
original cloth backed pictorial boards,
soiled and slightly rubbed – Routledge,
1881.
(Sotheby's,
   Chancery Lane) $72   £32
'The Language of Flowers' – coloured
illustrations by Kate Greenaway, slightly
spotted, original imitation morocco, gilt –
Routledge, 1884.
(Sotheby's,
   Chancery Lane) $80   £35

GREENAWAY, KATE AND WEATHERLY,
GEORGE
'The Little Folks Painting Book' – 107
wood engraved illustrations after Kate
Greenaway, frontispiece coloured by a
former owner, some leaves spotted,
original wrappers, slightly soiled – Cassell,
1879.
(Sotheby's,
   Chancery Lane) $40   £18

'Dame Wiggins of Lea and Her Seven
Wonderful Cats' – edited by John Ruskin –
large paper copy, illustrations, original
cloth, gilt – George Allen, 1885.
(Sotheby's,
   Chancery Lane) $110   £50

GREENE, GRAHAM
'Stamboul Train' – 1st Edn., slightly
spotted, original cloth – 1932.
(Sotheby's,
   Chancery Lane) $45   £20

GREENVILLE, COLLINS
'Shetland' – double page folio, hand
coloured map – circa 1654.
(Tessa Bennett,
   Edinburgh) $35   £16

GREENWOOD, JAMES
'The London Vocabulary, English and Latin
put into a New Method, proper to Acquaint
the Learner with Things as well as Pure
Latin Words' – 11th Edn., 26 woodcut
illustrations, decorations, half calf – C.
Hitch, 1749.
(Sotheby's,
   Chancery Lane) $180   £80

GREGORY

GREGORY, LADY
'The Kiltartan Poetry Book: Prose Translations from the Irish' − 1st Edn., limited to 400 copies, original linen backed boards, uncut, unopened − Cuala Press, Dundrum, 1920.
(Sotheby's,
  Chancery Lane) $80   £35

GREIG, T. WATSON
'Ladies' Dress Shoes of the Nineteenth Century' − frontispiece and 21 coloured plates, original cloth backed printed boards, folio − David Douglas, Edinburgh, 1900.
(Tessa Bennett,
  Edinburgh) $190   £85

GREW, NEHEMJAH
'Musaeum Regalis Societatis, or A Catalogue and Description of the Natural and Artifical Rarities belonging to the Royal Society and Preserved at Gresham Colledge, Whereunto is Subjoyned the Comparative Anatomy of Stomachs and Guts' − folio, calf rebacked, rubbed, 28 of 30 engraved plates and diagrams in text − For the author, 1681.
(Christie's, King
  St.) $55   £25

GRIGSON, GEOFFREY
'Samuel Palmer, the Visionary Years' − plates, original cloth, dust jacket, slightly torn − 1947.
(Christie's S.
  Kensington) $40   £18

GRIMMS OTHER TALES
Translated by Ruth Michaelis-Jena and Arthur Ratcliff, limited to 500 copies, this no. 41 of 75 signed by artist, and specially bound, frontispiece and full page illustrations by Gwenda Morgan, original morocco, t.e.g., unopened − Golden Cockerel Press, 1956.
(Christie's S.
  Kensington) $145   £65

GRINDEL, EUGENE
'Jacques Villon ou l'Art Glorieux' − no. 13 of 1,800 copies, presentation copy inscribed to Sir Gerald Kelly by the author, with an etching by Villon signed and numbered 13 of 50 − Paris, Louis Carre, 1948.
(Christie's S.
  Kensington) $605   £270

GROSS, CHAIM
'The Gates of Prayer 1845-1960' − artist's pre-publication proof, 6 aqualithos by Gross, loose as issued, original wraps, folio − 1960.
(Phillips) $90   £40

GROSZ, GEORGE
'Gedichte und Gesange' − pictorial title, 4 full page illustrations, tail piece and cover design by Grosz, sewn, loose as issued, original wrappers, uncut, folder and slipcase − Josef Portman, Litomysl, 1932.
(Sotheby's,
  Chancery Lane) $1,125   £500

GSELL FELS, DR.
'Switzerland, Its Scenery and People' − wood engraved plates and text illustrations, cloth gilt, folio − 1881.
(Tessa Bennett,
  Edinburgh) $505   £225

GUADAGNI, CARLO ALFONSO
'Specimen Experimentorum Naturalium Quae Singulus Annis in Illustri Pisana Academia' − 1st Edn., 8 engraved folding plates − Pisa, 1764.
(Christie's, King
  St.) $110   £50

GUARINI, GIOVANNI BATTISTA
'Il Pastor Fido, the faithful shepherd with
an addition of divers other poems . . . by
Richard Fanshawe' – engraved title by
Cross, cont. calf, gilt spine, rubbed and
chipped – 1648.
(Sotheby's, New Bond
   Street) $145   £65

GUARMANI, CARLO
'North Najd. A Journey from Jerusalem to
Anaiza in Quasim' – limited to 475 copies,
this unnumbered, illustrations, folding map
in wallet at end, original cloth, unopened,
4to – 1938.
(Christie's S.
   Kensington) $95   £42

GUATTANI, G. A.
'Memorie Enciclopediche Romane Sulle
Belle Arti' – plates, 4 vols., vellum – 1806.
(Bonham's) $65   £30

GUERIN, M.
'Description de l'Academie Royale des
Arts de Peinture et de Sculpture' – 1st Edn.,
7 folding plans, cont. calf, rubbed, book-
plate of William Constable, F.R.S. –
Paris, 1715.
(Sotheby's, New Bond
   Street) $100   £45

**GUERIN-MENEVILLE, FELIX
EDOUARD (Editor)**
'Dictionaire Pittoresque d'Histoire
Naturelle et des Phenomenes de la Nature'
– 9 vols. in 10, 719 engraved plates only,
no. 460 lacking, all but a few hand
coloured, some bound out of numerical
sequence, one upside down, a little
browning or spotting, early leaves of vol. 9
detached, cont. morocco backed boards,
rubbed – Paris, circa 1883.
(Christie's S.
   Kensington) $1,690   £750

GUEVARA, ANTONIO
'Mount Calvarie' the second part. Trans-
lated out of Spanish to English – 1st Edn.,
title very soiled, some water staining –
Adam Islip for Edward White, 1597.
(Sotheby's, New Bond
   Street) $90   £40

GUIDOTT, THOMAS
'De Thermis Britannicis, Accesserunt
Observationes Hydrostaticae, Chronomati-
cae et Miscellanea' – 2 parts in one vol.,
1st Edn., engraved title plate, 6 of 8 plates,
2 folding, spotted, modern calf backed
boards – 1691.
(Sotheby's, New Bond
   Street) $40   £18

**GUIGNEBAULT, PAUL – HUYSMANS,
J. K.**
'En Rade' – 19 coloured etched plates
and wood engraved decorations in text by
Guignebault, dark green morocco gilt, t.e.g.,
original wrappers bound in, slipcase by
Rene Kieffer, no. 24 of 250 copies –
Blaizot and Kieffer, Paris, 1911.
(Sotheby's,
   Chancery Lane) $900   £400

GUILLEMEAU, JACQUES
'De l'Heureux Accouchement des Femmes'
– 1st French Edn., engraved title and
woodcuts, vellum, slight browning,
inscription on verso of title – Paris, 1609.
(Bonham's) $3,600   £1,600

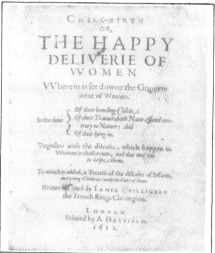

'Childbirth or the Happy Delivery of
Women . . . a treatise of the diseases of
Infants and Young Children with the Cure
of them, translated from the French' –
woodcuts of foetus, instruments etc., 1st
English Edn., vellum, g.e., in cloth cover
and morocco slipcase – A. Hatfield, 1612.
(Bonham's) $2,025   £900

GUILLEMEAU

'Childbirth or the Happy Delivery of Women . . . with a Treatise on the Nursing of Children' – numerous woodcuts, 2nd English Edn., old calf, rebacked, bookplate of James, Earl of Derby – London, 1635.
(Bonham's)　　　$1,462　£650

GUILLERMUS, EPISCOPUS PARISIENSIS

'Rhetorica Divina' – 152 leaves, 32 lines and chapter headings, gothic letter, Jean Petit's device on title page, rubricated throughout, small hole in text – Paris, 1500.
Sold with Bonaventura's 'Breviloquium' and other tracts, edited by Johannes Gerson – parts one and three only, full page woodcut device, small woodcut and a few grotesque initials, mostly rubricated, 19th century citron morocco, gilt, g.e., rather rubbed – Rouen 1502.
(Sotheby's, New Bond
　Street)　　　$855　£380

GUILLUM, JOHN

'A Display of Heraldrie' – 2nd Edn., illustrations many neatly hand coloured at a later date, slight soiling, cont. calf, rebacked, old spine laid down, joints worn, small folio – Printed by Richard Badger for Ralph Mob, 1632.
(Christie's S.
　Kensington)　　　$135　£60

GUIZOT, F.

'L'Histoire de France' – 5 vols., illus., cloth gilt, g.e., 4to – 1873-76.
(Phillips)　　　$18　£8

GWILYM, DAFYDD AP

'Selected Poems translated by Nigel Heseltine, preface by Frank O'Connor' – 1st Edn., no. 78 of 280 copies, original linen backed boards, uncut, unopened – Cuala Press, Dublin, 1944.
(Sotheby's,
　Chancery Lane)　　　$33　£15

HABERSHON, WILLIAM G.

'Records of Old London, Vanished and Vanishing' – folio, half brown morocco, t.e.g., spine with gilt emblems and raised bands, coloured lithographs and 36 mounted and hinged fine colour plates by Waldo Sargeant – Virtue and Co., n.d.
(Lawrence of
　Crewkerne)　　　$108　£48

HAFIZ, SHEMSEDDIN MOHAMMED

'The Poems . . . done into English verse . . . by John Payne' – 3 vols., this copy numbered 142, original parchment, soiled, t.e.g., printed for the Villon Society by private subscription – 1891.
(Christie's S.
　Kensington)　　　$90　£40

HAGEN, G. VON ADEL AUSS M.

'Comitiologia Ratisbonensis de Anno 1654. Das Ist; Was bey Selbigem Reichstage zu Regenspurg . . sich erzeidt hat . . . item; Unpassionierte Gedancken Wider Dess Hippoliti de Lapide . . . De Ratione Status Genanntem Buch' – folding plate, wrappers, lacking upper cover – Frankfurt, 1657.
(Sotheby's, New Bond
　Street)　　　$50　£22

HAGER, JOSEPH

'A Dissertation on the Newly Discovered Babylonian Inscriptions' – 1st Edn., one of 230 copies, 5 engraved plates, slight browning, half calf, worn – 1801.
(Sotheby's, New Bond
　Street)　　　$72　£32

HAGGARD, SIR H. RIDER
'King Solomon's Mines' – 1st Edn., torn, advertisements, original cloth, stained, rather worn – 1885.
(Sotheby's,
    Chancery Lane)   **$27**   **£12**
'Jess' – 1st Edn., original cloth, spine worn, faded – 1887.
(Sotheby's,
    Chancery Lane)   **$30**   **£14**
'Allan Quatermain' – 1st Edn., 20 wood engraved plates and illustrations in text after C. H. M. Kerr, original cloth, gilt – 1887.
(Sotheby's,
    Chancery Lane)   **$45**   **£20**
'Cetywayo and His Neighbours' – 1st Edn., spotting, original cloth, slightly rubbed – 1882.
(Sotheby's,
    Chancery Lane)   **$200**   **£90**
'Cleopatra' – 1st English edn., illustrations, original cloth – 1889.
(Sotheby's,
    Chancery Lane)   **$9**   **£4**

HAHNEMANN, S. AND DEVRIENT, CHAS CHARLES H. (translator)
'The Homeopathic Medical Doctrine, or Organon of the Healing Art' – 1st English Edn., 6 leaf bookseller's catalogue bound in before title, original boards, lower hinge cracked, head of spine and printed paper label slightly worn – Dublin, 1833.
(Sotheby's
    London)   **$165**   **£75**

HAHNEMANN, SAMUEL
'Organon der Heilkunst' – portrait, recent boards – Dresden and Leipzig, 1829.
(Sotheby's
    Monaco)   **$1,575**   **£700**

HAKEWILL, JAMES
'A Picturesque Tour of Italy' – engraved title, 63 plates, slight foxing and offsetting, cont. green morocco, gilt, Signet arms on sides, rubbed, g.e. – 1820.
(Sotheby's, New Bond
    Street)   **$315**   **£140**

HAKLUYT SOCIETY
'Missions to the Niger' – edited by E. W. Bovill – 4 vols. – 1964-66.
(Bonham's)   **$65**   **£30**

HALE, SIR MATTHEW
'The Primitive Origination of Mankind, considered and examined according to the Light of Nature' – 1st Edn., portrait, tail page and portrait foxed, small hole in 2K4, cont. calf, worn, rebacked – 1677.
(Sotheby's
    London)   **$65**   **£30**

HALL, LIEUT. FRANCIS
'Travels in Canada and the United States' – 1st Edn., folding map, half calf, worn – 1818.
(Phillips)   **$155**   **£70**

HALL, JOSEPH
'A Recollection of Such Treatises as Have Been Heretofore Severally Published' – 2 parts in one vol., engraved title, late 17th century calf, slightly worn, folio – 1621.
(Sotheby's, New Bond
    Street)   **$30**   **£14**

HALL, M.
'Commentaries on some of the More Important Diseases of Females' – 8 coloured plates, 1st Edn., boards, uncut, with two others – 1827.
(Bonham's)   **$180**   **£80**

HALL, S. C.
'The Baronial Halls, and ancient picturesque Edifices of England' – 2 vols., 71 tinted lithos, 1 plate and a few text leaves detached in vol. 1, cont. half green roan, a little rubbed, folio – 1858.
(Sotheby's
    London)   **$155**   **£70**

HALL, T.
'The Queen's Royal Cookery' – 2nd Edn., woodcut frontis, some browning, blank portions of 4 leaves torn away at foot, slight worming of two or three leaves slightly affecting text, sprinkled calf, gilt, by Bayntun – 1713.
(Sotheby's
    London)   **$540**   **£240**

HAMERTON, P. G.
'Etchings and Etchers' – 1st Edn., 35 plates after Palmer, Haden, Rembrandt and others, some spotting, original morocco backed cloth, rubbed, g.e., large 8vo.
(Christie's S.
    Kensington)   **$855**   **£380**

HAMILTON

HAMILTON, A.
'A Treatise of Midwifery' – old calf –
Edinburgh, 1781.
(Bonham's)   **$155**   **£70**
'A Treatise on the Management of Female
Complaints and of Children in Early
Infancy' – 1st Edn., old calf – Edinburgh,
1792.
(Bonham's)   **$200**   **£90**

HAMILTON, ALEXANDER
'A New Account of the East Indies' – 2
vols., no. 55 of 975 copies, plates and maps,
original vellum backed cloth, gilt – 1930.
(Sotheby's,
   Chancery Lane)   **$65**   **£28**

HAMILTON, GUSTAVUS
'The Elements of Gymnastics for Boys and
of Callisthenics for Young Ladies' –
engraved folding 42 plates, 2 folding,
spotted, cont. morocco, lacking part of
spine – Printed for A. K. Newman, 1840.
(Sotheby's,
   Chancery Lane)   **$215**   **£95**

HAMILTON, JAMES
'Observations on Purgative Medicines' –
2nd Edn., cont. tree calf, joints cracked –
Edinburgh, 1806.
(Christie's S.
   Kensington)   **$65**   **£28**

**HAMILTON, VEREKER M. AND
FASSON, STEWART M.**
'Scenes in Ceylon' – plates, errata slip,
cont. morocco backed cloth, rubbed,
oblong folio – n.d.
(Sotheby Humberts
   Taunton)   **$90**   **£40**

HAMILTON, SIR WILLIAM
'Collection of Engravings from Ancient
Vases' – vol. 1, text and 60 plates, quarter
leather, uncut, folio – 1st Edn., author's
presentation copy – 1791.
(Tessa Bennett,
   Edinburgh)   **$108**   **£48**

HANDIQUER DE BLANCOURT
'L'Art de la Verrerie' – 2 vols., 8 engraved
folding plates, cont. speckled calf – Paris,
1718.
(Tessa Bennett,
   Edinburgh)   **$270**   **£120**

HANLEY, JAMES
'Drift' – 1st Edn., limited to 500 copies,
presentation copy, signed by author,
original cloth, dust jacket – 1930.
(Sotheby's,
   Chancery Lane)   **$115**   **£52**
'The German Prisoner' – 1st Edn., no.
99 of 500 copies, presentation copy,
inscribed by author, frontispiece by Wm.
Roberts, original cloth gilt – Privately
printed, 1930.
(Sotheby's,
   Chancery Lane)   **$45**   **£20**

HANNA, S.
'Notes of a Visit to Some Parts of Haiti'
– engraved title and plates – 1836.
(Tessa Bennett,
   Edinburgh)   **$55**   **£24**

HARD, A. O.
'Swedish Costumes' – 10 hand coloured
lithographed plates, 1 torn, some leaves
spotted, some loose, original boards,
slightly worn – Stockholm, 1858.
(Sotheby's,
   Chancery Lane)   **$235**   **£105**

HARDING, JAMES DUFFIELD
'Sketches at Home and Abroad' – folio,
half morocco rubbed, spine defective,
lithographic title and dedication to
Louis Philippe, fixed and loose, 50
tissued tinted lithographed plates, foxing
– n.d.
(Lawrence of
   Crewkerne)   **$1,845**   **£820**
'Seventy Five Views of Italy and France'
– 75 mounted India paper plates,
spotting, cont. half morocco, worn, front
inner hinge split, g.e., folio – 1834.
(Christie's S.
   Kensington)   **$380**   **£170**

HARDMEYER, J.
'The Lake of Lucerne' – plates, illustrations
in text, original wrappers, slightly soiled,
loose – Zurich, n.d.
'Relief-Panorama of the Rhine' – folding
coloured panorama, in two sections,
original wrappers, slightly soiled –
Cologne, n.d.
(Sotheby's,
   Chancery Lane)   **$90**   **£40**

HARDY
'Hardy's Anglers' Guide Coronation
Number' – stiff wrappers, coloured and
other illustrations – 1937.
(Tessa Bennett,
Edinburgh) $15   £7

HARDY, FRANCIS
'Memoirs of the Political and Private Life
of James Caulfield, Earl of Charlemont'
– 1st Edn., large paper copy, engraved
portrait, browning, cont. sprinkled calf,
label, spine gilt, rubbed – 1810.
(Sotheby's, New Bond
Street) $55   £25

HARDY, THOMAS
'Jude the Obscure' – 1st Edn., map, fron-
tispiece, soiling, original cloth, extremi-
ties rubbed, inner hinge cracked, t.e.g. –
1896.
(Christie's S.
Kensington) $35   £15
'Works: The Wessex Novels' – 18 vols.,
maps, original cloth, spines of eight
faded, rubbed – 1902-15.
(Sotheby's,
Chancery Lane) $125   £55

HARE, AUGUSTUS J. C.
'Walks in Rome' – 2 vols. – 1871.
'Days near Rome' – 2 vols. – 1875.
'Cities of Northern and Central Italy' – 3
vols. – 1876.
'South-Eastern France' – 1890.
'South-Western France' – unopened –
1890.
'North-Western France' – 1895 – folding
maps, the second work signed by the
author, original cloth, gilt, a few rubbed
and soiled, and 10 later editions.
(Sotheby's,
Chancery Lane) $180   £80

HARLEIAN MISCELLANY, THE
8 vols., cont. calf, rebacked, some covers
detached, rubbed – 1744-46.
(Christie's S.
Kensington) $65   £30

HARLOW, V. T.
'Raleigh's Last Voyage' – no. 35 of 775
copies, plates and maps, original vellum
backed cloth, gilt – 1932.
(Sotheby's,
Chancery Lane) $60   £26

HARMSWORTH, DESMOND
'Desmond's Poems' – 1st Edn., limited to
75 copies, presentation copy, inscribed by
author, original cloth backed boards,
damaged, unopened – Cuala Press, 1930.
(Sotheby's,
Chancery Lane) $70   £32

**HARRAL, THOMAS AND IRELAND,
SAMUEL**
'Picturesque Views of the Severn' – 2 vols.,
52 lithographed plates, half titles, cont.
cloth, slightly worn – 1824.
(Sotheby's, New Bond
Street) $200   £90

HARRIOT (OR HARIOT), THOMAS
'Artis Analyticae Praxis' – folio, early
calf, title repaired, clean copy – 1631.
(Lawrence of
Crewkerne) $1,575   £700

HARRIOTT'S TABLES
'For the Preservation and Improvement of
Landed Estates and the Promoting and
Increasing the Growth of Timber Upon
Them' – original marbled paper stiff
wrappers, details of crops etc. on eleven
farms from 1789 to 1795, small oblong
folio – circa 1795.
(Tessa Bennett,
Edinburgh) $55   £24

HARRIS, MOSES
'The Aurelian: or Natural History of
English Insects; namely Moths and Butterflies' – engraved frontis, title vignette and
45 hand coloured plates, one unnumbered,
no. 1 cut down and mounted, titles and
90 pages of text in English and French,
cont. diced calf, rubbed, joints cracked,
folio – 1766 (but later).
(Christie's S.
    Kensington)   **$4,500**   **£2,000**

HARRIS, WILLIAM CORNWALLIS
'The Wild Sports of Southern Africa' –
1st Edn., 7 plates including 3 tinted
lithos, folding map, half title, original
cloth, gilt, spine grayed – 1839.
(Sotheby's
    London)   **$100**   **£45**

HARRISON, J. E.
'Greek Vase Painting' – illustrated, cloth
gilt, folio – 1927.
(Phillips)   **$65**   **£30**

HARRISON, P.
'Elfin Song' – A book of verse and pictures, coloured plates and other illustrations, cloth gilt – n.d.
(Tessa Bennett,
    Edinburgh)   **$30**   **£14**

HARRISON, WALTER
'A New and Universal History Description
and Survey of London and Westminster' –
plates, maps, some folding, others misbound, some leaves detached, cont.
reversed calf, worn, covers detached, folio –
1775.
(Christie's S.
    Kensington)   **$560**   **£250**

HARROD, W.
'The History of Market Harborough' –
plates, some folding and torn, original
cloth backed boards, worn – Market
Harborough, 1808.
(Christie's S.
    Kensington)   **$50**   **£22**

HART, CAPTAIN LOCKYER WILLIS
'Character and Costumes of Afghannistan'
– lithographed map, 24 of 26 plates,
spotting, tears, original morocco backed
cloth, lettered in gilt, disbound, folio –
1843.
(Christie's S.
    Kensington)   **$380**   **£170**

HARTE, WALTER
'Essays on Husbandry' – 1st Edn., 5
engraved plates, woodcuts in text, errata
leaf, last leaf blank, cont. sprinkled sheep,
gilt fillets, one or two small holes at base
of spine – 1764.
(Sotheby's
    London)   **$155**   **£70**

HARTLEY, J. AND OTHERS
'History of the Westminster Election . . .
by the lovers of Truth and Justice' – 15
plates of 16 after Rowlandson, foxing,
19th century half morocco, rubbed – 1784.
(Sotheby's, New Bond
    Street)   **$65**   **£30**

HARVEY, JOHN
'The Life of Robert Bruce, King of Scots' –
a poem, light spotting, cont. calf, rubbed,
joints and spine cracked – Edinburgh,
John Catnach, 1729.
(Christie's S.
    Kensington)   **$135**   **£60**

HARVEY, W.
'Anatomical Exercitations Concerning the
Generation of Living Creatures to which
are added Particular Discourses of Births
and Conceptions etc.' – portrait by
Faithorne, 1st English Edn., old calf, rebacked, lower margins slightly water
stained – 1653.
(Bonham's)   **$1,690**   **£750**

HARVEY, W.
'Phycologia Britannica' – 4 vols., 1st Edn.,
360 chromolithographed plates, 6 double
page, half titles, spine adhesive perished,
many leaves detached, signature of Sarah
Tyrconnel on titles, bookplate of Walter
Cecil Carpenter, original cloth, spines
faded – 1846-51.
(Sotheby's
    London)   **$245**   **£110**

HARVEY, W. W.
'Sketches of Hayti' – 1st Edn., folding
lithographed frontispiece, modern half
morocco, gilt spine, uncut – 1827.
(Sotheby's
    Monaco)   **$1,685**   **£750**

HASSALL, ARTHUR
'Christ Church, Oxford' – one of 50
copies, signed coloured plates, buckram
gilt, t.e.g., 4to.
(Phillips)   **$95**   **£42**

HASSALL, W. O.
'The Holkham Bible Picture Book' — 2nd
Edn., plates, original half morocco, folio
— The Dropmore Press, 1954.
(Christie's S.
  Kensington) $65   £30

HASSELL, J.
'Tour of the Grand Junction' — 24
coloured aquatint plates, cont. red
morocco gilt, g.e., slightly worn — 1819.
(Bonham's) $720   £320

HASSELQUIST, FREDERICK
'Voyages and Travels in the Levant . . .
1749-52 . . . Containing Observations in
Natural History, Physick, Agriculture and
Commerce' — 1st Edn., in English, half
title, slight browning, cont. sprinkled calf,
labels, splits in joints, rubbed — 1766.
(Sotheby's, New Bond
  Street) $270   £120

HASTED, C. E.
'History of Kent' — edited by H. M. Drake,
part 1, The Hundred of Blackheath, all
published, plates, preliminaries spotted,
modern half calf — 1886.
(Sotheby's,
  Chancery Lane) $90   £40

HATTON, THOMAS AND CLEAVER,
ARTHUR
'A Bibliography of the Periodical Works
of Charles Dickens. Bibliographical,
Analytical and Statistical' — 4to green
buckram, gilt, large paper edition, 31
illustrations and facsimiles, fine copy —
1933.
(Lawrence of
  Crewkerne) $180   £80

HAUKSBEE, FRANCIS
'Physico Mechanical Experiments on
Various Subjects' — 1st Edn., 8 engraved
plates with 7 folding, cont. gilt panelled
red gilt morocco, joints and corners a
little rubbed, g.e., small 4to — 1709.
(Christie's
  St. James) $1,080   £480

HAVARD, HENRY
'Dictionnaire de l'Ameublement et de la
Decoration' — 4 vols., plates, some
coloured, half morocco, t.e.g., others
uncut — Paris, circa 1890.
(Sotheby's
  Monaco) $4,725   £2,100

'Histoire et Philosophie des Styles' — 2
vols., limited edition, photogravure plates,
some coloured, original cloth — Paris,
1899-1900.
(Sotheby's
  Monaco) $2,925   £1,300

HAWKER, COLONEL PETER
'Instructions to Young Sportsmen in all
that Relates to Guns and Shooting' —
half red morocco, 3rd Edn., revised and
enlarged, 10 plates, 4 coloured and
frontispiece repaired — 1824.
(Lawrence of
  Crewkerne) $90   £40
'Diary' — 2 vols., portrait, plates, half
calf gilt — 1893.
(Phillips) $22   £10

HAWKESWORTH, JOHN
'The Adventurer' — 2 vols., Nos. 1-140,
original issues, cont. half green morocco,
gilt, folio — 1753-54.
(Sotheby's, New Bond
  Street) $945   £420

HAWKINS, SIR RICHARD
'The Observations' — no. 10 of 475 copies,
original vellum backed cloth, gilt — 1933.
(Sotheby's,
  Chancery Lane) $55   £24

HAWTHORNE, NATHANIEL
'A Wonder Book for Boys' — 1st English
Edn., 8 wood engraved plates slightly
spotted, original blue cloth gilt, spine
soiled, g.e. — Henry G. Bohn, 1852.
(Sotheby's,
  Chancery Lane) $65   £28

HAY, R. AND SYNGE, P. M.
'Dictionary of Garden Plants' — signed
limited edition, illus. green morocco gilt
decorated with overlays of leaves in three
colours, g.e., by Zaehnsdorf, Arcadia
Press, 1970, fleece lined box.
(Phillips) $135   £60

HAYDEN, A.
'Spode and His Successors' — 24 colour
plates and 64 illustrations in black and
white, cloth gilt — 1925.
(Bonham's) $55   £25

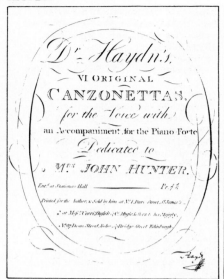

HAYDN, JOSEPH
Dr. Haydn's VI Original Canzonettas for the Voice with an Accompaniment for the Piano-Forte — 1st Edn., engraved throughout and signed at foot of title page by Haydn, slight soiling and spotting, altogether 23 works in one volume. Dedicated to Mrs. John Hunter who anonymously wrote the words.
(Sotheby's, New Bond
Street) $1,800   £800

HAYNES, JOHN
'Great Britain's Glory of an Account of the Great Numbers of Poor Employ'd in the Woollen and Silk Manufactories' — inscriptions and scribblings in ink on endpapers, severely stained, foxing, cont. panelled calf, worn, joints split — 1715.
(Christie's King
St.) $90   £40

HAZLITT, WILLIAM
'Lectures on the English Poets' — 1st Edn., half title with advertisement on verso, errata leaf at beginning, without advertisement leaves at end, cont. diced russia gilt, spine restored preserving original, one label lacking, the other torn — 1818.
(Sotheby's
London) $55   £25

HEAPHY, THOMAS
'The Likeness of Christ; Being and Inquiry into the Verisimilitude of the Received Likeness of our Blessed Lord' — edited by Wyke Bayliss — 12 plates in gold and colours, illustrations in text, slight spotting, frontispiece detached, original red morocco, gilt, rubbed and soiled, folio — 1880.
(Sotheby's, New Bond
Street) $11   £5

HEBREW MANUSCRIPT
Esther Scroll, illuminated ms. on vellum in sepia ink, Sephardic script, 12 columns, each 33 lines, separated by 13 large figures of the Esther history surrounded by border of floral devices, Turkish or Persian, the text late 18th century, illumination possibly early 19th century, in 19th century ivory case, chipped.
(Christie's, King
St.) $7,875   £3,500

HECTOR, W.
'Selections from the Judicial Records of Renfrewshire' — facsimile documents, cloth — Paisley, 1876.
(Tessa Bennett,
Edinburgh) $20   £9

HEGINBOTHAM, HENRY
'Stockport Ancient and Modern' — 2 vols., plates, illustrations, cont. half morocco, rubbed — 1877-92.
(Sotheby's,
Chancery Lane) $90   £40

HEINE, HEINRICH
'Nuits Florentins' — no. 10 of 15 copies, and edition of 266 containing a suite of illustrations in colour with duplicates in black illustrated by Grigory Gluckmann, morocco, gilt by Chavellier, t.e.g., large — Paris, 1925.
(Sotheby's
Monaco) $2,250   £1,000

HELIODORUS, BISHOP OF TRICCA
'L'Histoire Aethiopique . . . contenant dix livres, translated by J. Amyot, Bishop of Auxerre' — woodcut device on title and final leaf, woodcut head pieces and initials, preliminary and final leaf very slightly browned, a very few other spots, one margin just torn, bookplate of Sir Thomas Gerard Bart, later mottled calf, label, slightly defective, upper hinge weak, folio — Paris pour Vincent Sertenas, 1559.
(Sotheby's
London) $340   £150

HELMONT, JAN BAPTISTA VAN
'Ortus Medicinae Progressus Medicinae
Novus in Morborum Ultionem ad Vitam
Langam . . . editio quarta' — 2 parts in one
vol., edited by Franciscus Mercurius van
Helmont, engraved title with portraits,
some worming and dampstaining, gnawed
by mice, cont. calf, rubbed, folio — J. B.
Devenet, Lyons, 1655.
(Sotheby's, New Bond
   Street) $270   £120

HELPS, A.
'The Spanish Conquest in America' — 4
vols., maps and illustrations, calf gilt —
1855-61.
(Tessa Bennett,
   Edinburgh) $63   £28

HELVETIUS, JOHANNES
'Selenographia; Sive Luna Descriptio' — 1st
Edn., title in red and black, additional
engraved title, 107 engraved diagrams and
maps, 3 double page folding maps, 26
engraved illustrations and one engraved
volvelle (detached), lacks portrait, waterstaining in upper margin, cont. sprinkled
calf, gilt spine, worn, joints cracked, upper
cover partly detached, spine chipped —
Danzig, 1647.
(Christie's, King
   St.) $6,750   £3,000

HELVOT, PERE
'Histoire Abrege et Costumes Colores des
Ordres Monastiques' — 2 vols., coloured
plates, original boards — Paris, 1837.
(Sotheby's, New Bond
   Street) $290   £130

HEMM, J. P.
'Portraits of the Royal Family in Penman-
ship' — 8 plates, one slightly torn, soiled,
prospectus and list of subscribers in
original wrappers, slightly soiled — n.d.,
but subscribers' list 1831.
(Christie's S.
   Kensington) $290   £130

HENDERSON, E.
'Biblical Researches and Travels in Russia'
— 6 plates, 3 maps, 4to, calf gilt — 1826.
(Phillips) $65   £30

HENFREY, ARTHUR AND OTHERS
'The Garden Companion . . . January to
October, 1852' — 20 hand coloured
lithographed plates, cont. half morocco,
extremities slightly rubbed — 1852.
(Christie's S.
   Kensington) $180   £80

HENRY VIII, KING OF ENGLAND
'Miscellaneous Writings' — no. 352 of 365
copies, decorations by Robert Gibbings,
original parchment backed boards, soiled,
corners rubbed, unopened — 1924.
(Christie's S.
   Kensington) $80   £35

HENRY, DAVID (Editor)
'An Historical Account of all the Voyages
Round the World' — 4 vols., plates, folding
maps, a few slightly torn, staining, cont.
half calf, worn — 1774.
(Christie's S.
   Kensington) $65   £28

HENRY, G. M.
'Coloured plates of the Birds of Ceylon' —
parts 1-3 only of four, 48 coloured plates,
some leaves loose, original wrappers, slightly
torn, one spine repaired — Colombo, 1927-
30.
(Sotheby Humberts
   Taunton) $200   £90

HENTZY, R.
'Promenade Pittoresque dans l'Eveche de
Bale' — 2 vols., 44 hand coloured plates,
cont. calf, joints and spines cracked —
The Hague, 1808-09.
(Christie's S.
   Kensington) $2,925 £1,300

HEQUET, P.
'De l'Indecence aux Hommes d'Accoucher
les Femmes et de l'Obligation aux Femmes'
— 1st Edn., 1708.
(Bonham's) $180   £80

HERBELOT, BARTHELEMY D'
'Bibliotheque Orientale, ou Dictionaire
Universel contenant generalement tout ce
qui regarde la connoissance des Peuples
de l'Orient' — 1st Edn., title printed in
red and black, some discolouration, tears,
cont. calf, joints split, very worn — Paris,
1697.
(Sotheby's
   London) $155   £70

**HERBERT, EDWARD, LORD OF
CHERBURY**
'The Autobiography' — no. 106 of 300
copies, illustrations, original buckram,
folio — Gregynog Press, 1928.
(Christie's S.
   Kensington) $200   £90

HERCHENHEIM

HERCHENHEIM, F.
'Panorama of the Rhine' – 11½in. x 7ft.
with appendix, some repairs, original
boards – n.d.
(Phillips) $90   £40

HERIOT, GEORGE
'Travels Through the Canadas' – 1st Edn.,
tinted aquatint frontispiece and 25 tinted
aquatint plates, 1 line engraved plate, 1
hand engraved double page map, cont.
russia, rebacked in brown morocco, triple
gilt fillets, marbled edges, gilt – 1807.
(Sotheby's, New Bond
        Street) $2,025   £900

HERISSON, E.
'Nouvel Abrege de Geographie Universelle,
Ancienne et Moderne, Physique et
Historique' – 2 vols., including atlas, 51
double page maps, 2 folding, coloured in
outline, text foxed, modern Spanish calf
– Paris, 1816.
(Sotheby's, New Bond
        Street) $290   £130

HERMANN, P.
'Paradisus Bavus, Innumeris Exoticis
Curiosis Herbis and Rarioribus Plantis'
– 1st Edn., title page, engraved frontispiece and 109 of 111 engraved plates after
drawings by author, some foxing, a few
plates lightly stained in red, some initial
leaves, modern cloth – Elzivir, Leiden,
1698.
(Sotheby's, New Bond
        Street) $630   £280

HERMANNIDES (RUTGERUS)
'Britannia Magna – Geographico-historico
descriptio' – additional engraved title,
large engraved folding map, 31 double
page town plans, cont. vellum –
Amsterdam, 1661.
(Christie's, King
        St.) $720   £320

HERON BOOKS
A Collection of 70 volumes only, plates,
original rexine, gilt, various dates.
(Sotheby Humberts
        Taunton) $18   £8

HERRERA, ALONSO DE
'Agricultura General . . . de la Labranza del
Campo' – cont. vellum, lacks ties, gilt –
Don Antonio de Sancha, Madrid, 1777.
(Sotheby's, New Bond
        Street) $72   £32

HERRICK, ROBERT
'Poetical Works' – 4 vols., boards, t.e.g.,
rest uncut, coloured frontispiece and other
illustrations by Albert Rutherston, out of
series of 750 – Cresset Press, 1928.
(Lawrence of
        Crewkerne) $75   £35

HERTZ, HEINRICH
'Untersuchungen ueber die Ausbreitung
der elektrischen Kraft' – 1st Edn., 40
diagrams in text, cont. half roan, spine
slightly worn, 8vo – Leipzig, 1892.
(Sotheby's, New Bond
        Street) $450   £200

HERVE, FRANCIS
'A Residence in Greece and Turkey with
Notes of the Journey Through Bulgaria,
Servia, Hungary and the Balkans' – 2 vols.,
1st Edn., 12 tinted lithographed plates,
slight browning, original cloth, rubbed and
soiled – 1837.
(Sotheby's, New Bond
        Street) $180   £80

HERVEY, LORD JOHN
Memoirs of the Reign of George I from his
Accession to the Death of Queen Caroline
. . . edited by Rt. Hon. John Wilson Coker'
– 2 vols., grained calf gilt by Morrell,
morocco labels, inner dentelles, frontis
portraits, fine copies – 1848.
(Lawrence of
        Crewkerne) $55   £25

HEYLYN, PETER
'The History of St. George of Cappadocia
. . . and the Institution of the Most Noble
Order of St. George' – 1st Edn., additional
engraved title, cont. limp vellum – 1631.
(Christie's, King
        St.) $90   £40

HEYWOOD, THOMAS
'The Life of Merlin' – 1st Edn., engraved
frontispiece, some browning, a few small
holes, early 19th century polished calf,
spine gilt, rubbed – 1641.
(Sotheby's, New Bond
        Street) $135   £60

HIAM, FRANK

'Catalogues for 1881, circa 1888 and circa 1895 (2 copies, one lacking portrait), 4 vols. in 3 illustrations, somewhat soiled and spotted, original wrappers or folder with original wrappers bound in, worn, covers of the first loose − circa 1881-95.
(Sotheby's,
    Chancery Lane) $360   £160

HIBBERD, SHIRLEY

'New and Rare Beautiful-Leaved Plants' − 54 coloured plates, original cloth, spine faded, stitching shaken − 1870.
(Christie's S.
    Kensington) $65   £28

HIERONYMO DA FERRARA

'Epistola de Contemptu Mundi' − edited by Charles Fairfax Murray, limited to 156 copies of which this is 150, printed in red and black, woodcut illustrations by W. H. Hooper after the editor, ornamental border and initial, original holland backed boards, uncut, 8vo − 1894.
(Sotheby's,
    Chancery Lane) ' $405   £180

Mr. Frank Hiam's Latest Price List.

THE MYSTERIOUS STEW PAN.

Two rings are borrowed and placed in the pan with 2 eggs, some spirits of wine poured over them ; this is set on fire, lid placed on, and upon the lid being taken off, two live doves, with the rings attached to them, are taken from the pan, and the rings returned to the owners ; the pan and cover can be examined.—Price 10/6.

THE FAIRY FLOWER POT.—(A WONDERFUL NOVELTY).

A pretty flower-pot is filled with mould and some seed ; a paper cover having been examined is placed on ; a borrowed watch is now fired at the pot, and upon the cover being taken off, the pot is seen full of flowers ; they are lifted out of the pot with the watch hanging to the root, and the watch is handed back to the owner.—Price £1 and £1 4 0

THE MECHANICAL CHANGING RED AND WHITE ROSE.
(VERY EFFECTIVE.)

A red rose is shown to the company, but a white rose being preferred, the performer charms it into a white one before the eyes of the company.—Price 6/6.

Frank Hiam's Catalogues, 1881-95.
(Sotheby's)

Epistola de Contemptu Mundi by Hieronymo da Ferrara, illustrated by
C.F. Murray. (Sotheby's)

HIGGINS

HIGGINS, F. R.
'Arable Holdings, Poems' – 1st Edn., no.
23 of 300 copies, signed by author in
title, original linen backed boards, uncut –
Cuala Press, Dublin, 1934.
(Sotheby's,
   Chancery Lane) $90   £40

**HILARY, SAINT, BISHOP OF
POITIERS**
'Lucubrationes olim per dies, Erasmum . . .
emendatae' – woodcut device on title,
woodcut initials, dampstains, worming,
soiled, 19th century paper boards,
rubbed, folio – Carolae Guillard, Paris,
1544.
(Sotheby's, New Bond
   Street) $110   £50

HILDBURGH, W. L.
'Medieval Spanish Enamels' – original
cloth, dust jacket – 1936.
(Christie's S.
   Kensington) $85   £38

HILL, JOHN
'Eden, or a Compleat Body of Gardening'
– uncoloured engraved frontispiece and 60
plates, lower corner of one page torn away,
cont. calf, rubbed, lower joint split, folio –
1757.
(Christie's S.
   Kensington) $785   £350

HILLS, ROBERT
'Etchings of Cattle and Sheep' – title
lacking, 77 plates, most with two or more
etchings, some spotting, cont. calf, rubbed,
rebacked, folio – 1806-09.
(Christie's S.
   Kensington) $515   £230

HIND, HENRY YOULE
'Narrative of the Canadian Red River
Exploring Expedition of 1857 and of the
Assiniboine and Saskatchewan Exploring
Expedition of 1858' – 2 vols., 1st Edn.,
20 tinted wood engraved plates including
2 frontispieces, wood engravings in text,
8 hand coloured maps, plans and profiles,
cont. green half calf, rubbed – 1860.
(Sotheby's, New Bond
   Street) $1,125   £500

HINDLEY, CHARLES
'The Life and Times of James Catnach,
Ballad Monger' – 230 illustrations, includ-
ing 42 after Bewick, some coloured, 12
pages of advertisements at end, some
leaves soiled, original cloth, rather worn –
Catnach Press, 1878.
(Sotheby's,
   Chancery Lane) $80   £35

HIPKINS, A. J.
'Musical Instruments' – limited edition,
50 coloured plates, 2 loose, some spots,
half morocco, 4to – 1888.
(Phillips) $215   £95

HIPPOCRATES
'Oeuvres' – 4 vols., limited edition,
coloured plates, half morocco, t.e.g.,
others uncut, original wrappers bound in –
Paris, 1932-34.
(Sotheby's
   Monaco) $1,575   £700

HIPPOPOTAMI AND QUACK MEDICINE
Charming printed broadside illustrating 'Le
Grande e Maravigliose Virtu Del Dente Del
Hippopotami . . .', decorated with a wood-
cut of the hippopotamus, trimmed to
the border, a few slight fox marks, minor
tears in margin – For Cesare Scaccioppa,
Rome, 1625.
(Sotheby's, New Bond
   Street) $425   £190

**HISTOIRE DE LA VIE ET PASSION DE
NOSTRE SAUUEUR IESUS CHRIST**
2 parts in one vol., engraved throughout,
printed on rectos only, title within hand
coloured ornamental borders, 122 hand
coloured three-quarter page illustrations,
lacking a few leaves, browned and soiled,
cont. calf, worn – Paris, 1693.
(Sotheby's
   London) $360   £160

'HISTOIRE DES RECHERCHES SUR LA QUADRATURE DU CERCLE'
8 folding plates, one torn, one detached, staining, cont. calf, worn – Paris, 1754.
(Christie's S.
   Kensington) $65   £28

HISTORY OF BIRDS
Etched title and 29 full page illustrations, original boards with etched labels on covers, slightly worn – 1803.
(Sotheby's,
   Chancery Lane) $190   £85

HISTORY OF PRINCE LEE BOO, THE ... SON OF ABBA THULLE
Engraved frontispiece and 2 plates coloured by hand, original printed wrappers, soiled, rebacked – Printed for Thomas Hughes, 1830.
(Sotheby's,
   Chancery Lane) $18   £8

HITLER, ADOLF
'Mein Kampf' – quarter morocco, slipcase, presentation copy by a Burgermeister (1939), and an album of cigarette cards laid within text, Adolf Hitler Bilder aus dem leben des Fuhrers, coloured frontis, cloth backed boards, 4to – Munchen, 1935.
(Tessa Bennett,
   Edinburgh) $40   £18

HOBBES, THOMAS
'Leviathan' – 1st Edn., with 'head' ornament on title and three heads on centre of ornament on A4 recto, engraved additional title, 18th century calf, rubbed, head of spine chipped, folio – Andrew Crooke, 1651.
(Christie's S.
   Kensington) $1,395   £620
'Philosophicall Rudiments Concerning Government and Society' – 1st Edn. in English, engraved plate and two engraved illustrations, 19th century calf, worn – 1651.
(Christie's, King
   St.) $110   £50

HOBHOUSE, J. C.
'A Journey Through Albania to Constantinople' – 2 vols., 2nd Edn., 23 plates and maps, 17 coloured, some double page or folding, double page sheet of engraved music, dampstained, spotted, cont. cloth backed boards, soiled and slightly worn, joints split – For James Cawthorn, 1813.
(Sotheby's, New Bond
   Street) $335   £150

HOBSON, ROBERT LOCKHART
'The George Eumorfopoulos Collection Catalogue of the Chinese, Corean and Persian Pottery and Porcelain' – 6 vols., limited to 750 copies, plates, some coloured, original cloth, uncut – 1925-28.
(Sotheby's
   Monaco) $24,750   £11,000
'Chinese Ceramics in Private Collections' – no. 371 of 625, mounted coloured plates, illus., original cloth, soiled, 4to – 1931.
(Christie's S.
   Kensington) $170   £75

HODGSON, JOHN
'A History of Northumberland' – 3 parts in 7 vols., plates, illustrations, some leaves slightly spotted or dampstained, cont. calf, gilt, slightly rubbed – Newcastle-upon-Tyne, 1858-20.
(Sotheby's,
   Chancery Lane) $920   £410

HODGSON, MRS. WILLOUGHBY
'Old English China' – coloured and plain plates, uncut, cloth, 8vo – 1913.
(Christie's
   St. James) $55   £25

HOFFMANN

HOFFMANN, DR. HEINRICH
'The English Struwwelpeter or Pretty
Stories and Funny Pictures' – 29th Edn.,
wood engraved illustrations coloured by
hand, original printed boards, covers
loose soiled – Rutten and Loenig,
Frankfurt, 1875.
(Sotheby's,
   Chancery Lane) $33   £15

HOFSTEDE DE GROOT, CORNELIS
'A Catalogue Raisonne of . . . Dutch
Painters of the Seventeenth Century' –
5 vols. only, original cloth, extremities
bumped – 1908-13.
(Christie's S.
   Kensington) $55   £25

HOGARTH, WILLIAM
26 original parts, engraved plates, spotting,
original wrappers, some torn with a little
loss – 1833.
(Christie's S.
   Kensington) $55   £25

HOGENBERG, NICOLAUS
'Series of 23 engraved plates, including
3 portraits, depicting the history of the
revolt of the Netherlands against Spanish
rule from 1566 to 1570' – 20 plates
with captions in German verse, 19th
century boards, oblong – n.d.
(Christie's, King
   St.) $540   £240

HOGG, T.
'A Practical Treatise of the Carnation' –
6 hand coloured plates, original cloth –
1839.
(Tessa Bennett,
   Edinburgh) $75   £34

HOGG, THOMAS JEFFERSON
'The Athenians', correspondence between
Hogg and his Friends, edited by Walter
Sidney Scott, limited to 350 copies, this
no. 10 of 50 copies signed by editor,
collotype facsimiles and specially bound,
original morocco, t.e.g., slipcase –
Golden Cockerel Press, 1943.
(Christie's S.
   Kensington) $85   £38

HOLBEIN, HANS
'Les Images de la Morte' – woodcut device
on title, and 49 of 53 woodcuts by
Holbein, title slightly stained and frayed,
small hole and tears, later ownership
signature on title and some ms. notes in
text, slightly loose, cont. panelled calf,
later stamp of Royal Austrian Eagles on
both covers, worn, corners and head of
spine torn – Lyons, a l'escu de Cologne,
par Jehann Frellon, 1547.
(Sotheby's
   London) $675   £300
'The Dance of Death' – engraved additional title, laid down, portrait and 46
plates, spotting, cont. tree calf, joints
cracked, spine rubbed – 1811.
(Christie's S.
   Kensington) $65   £30

HOLCOT, ROBERT
'In Librum Sapientiae Regis Salomonis
Praelectiones. CCXIII' – woodcut initials,
late 17th century inscriptions on title,
cont. calf, rubbed, folio – Basle, 1586.
(Christie's, King
   St.) $180   £80

HOLE, W.
'Hibernia' – early hand coloured map of
Ireland, framed black hogarth – 17th
century.
(Tessa Bennett,
   Edinburgh) $75   £34

HOLINSHED, RAPHAEL
'The First and Second Volumes of the
Chronicles' – 2 vols. in one, badly frayed,
some waterstaining and foxing, minor
worming, cont. calf, rubbed, spine
chipped – Basle, 1586.
(Christie's, King
   St.) $180   £80

HOLLAND, SAMUEL
'The Provinces of New York, New Jersey
with Part of Pensilvania and the Province
of Quebec' – drawn by Major Holland,
hand coloured, reverse plain, title cartouche with view, inset plans of City of
New York, Amboy and mouth of Hudson
River, two sheets joined in middle,
slight tears, unframed – 57 x 35in.
(Lawrence of
   Crewkerne) $225   £100

HOLLANDE, LA
'Costumes et Paysages' — 10 mounted
photographs, including one on title of
fishing villages of Volendam and Marken
and their inhabitants, coloured by hand,
loose in original cloth portfolio — J. M.
Schalekamp, Amsterdam, circa 1900.
(Sotheby's, New Bond
    Street)   **$65**   **£28**

HOLLEY, G.
'The Falls of Niagara' — wood engraved
plates and illustrations, tree calf gilt —
1883.
(Tessa Bennett,
    Edinburgh)   **$35**   **£16**

HOLME, C. (Editor)
'The Art of the Book' — cloth — Studio,
1914.
(Tessa Bennett,
    Edinburgh)   **$65**   **£30**

**HOLY BIBLE, LATIN INCLUDING
APOCRYPHA**
6 parts in one vol., woodcut device on
titles, page 29 torn, calf gilt, small 4to —
H. Middleton (S.T.C. 2056) — 1580-79.
English psalms in metre bound in at end.
(Phillips)   **$65**   **£30**

HOMANN, J. B.
'Atlas Silesiae' — 20 hand coloured double
page maps, boards, large folio — Nuremberg,
1750.
(Phillips)   **$2,250**   **£1,000**
'Atlas Novus' — 3 vols., pictorial engraved
title and 367 engraved plates, including two
world maps, 314 maps some folding, 40
engraved plans of European cities, some
coloured by cont. hand, some margins
shaved, tears in some maps, some repairs,
18th century half calf, morocco labels, a
little worn, folio — Nuremberg, n.d.
(Sotheby's, New Bond
    Street)   **$85,500**   **£38,000**

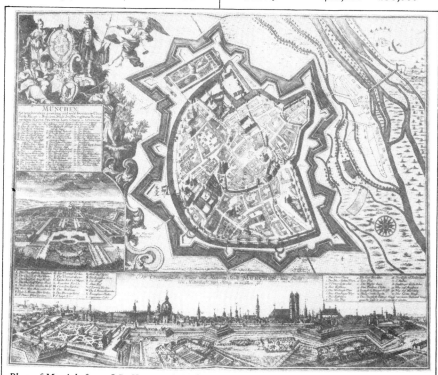

Plan of Munich from J.B. Homann's 'Atlas Novus'. (Sotheby's)

HOME

HOME, ROBERT
'Select View in Mysore, the Country of
Tippoo Sultan' – 1st Edn., large paper,
29 hand coloured engraved plates, 4
folding plans, 1 coloured, some discolouration and soiling, brown morocco,
gilt, worn, g.e. – 1794.
(Sotheby's, New Bond
    Street) $495   £220

HOMER
'Iliad and Odyssey' – engravings by John
Flaxman, etc (3) oblong folio, half
morocco, worn – 1805.
(Bonham's) $22   £10

HOOK, T. E.
Thomas Dibdin, Thomas More and others.
A collection of 18 plays, mainly early 19th
century, bound in 2 vols., one with frontis
after Stothard, some with advertisement
leaves, slightly spotted, cont. half calf,
defective – 1789-1820.
(Sotheby's
    London) $90   £40

HOOKE, ROBERT
'Micrographia or some Physiological
Descriptions of Minute Bodies made by
Magnifying Glasses with Observations and
Enquiries thereupon' – 1st Edn., title
printed in red and black, engraved with
arms of the Royal Society, 38 plates, 13
folding, 4 double page, cont. calf, worn,
joints repaired, bookplate of William
Constable, F.R.S., folio – Jo. Martyn and
Ja. Allestry, 1665.
(Sotheby's, New Bond
    Street) $5,400   £2,400

HOOKER, J. D.
'Cryptogamic Botany of the Antarctic
Voyage of H.M. Discovery Ships' – 66
plates, cloth – 1845.
(Phillips) $115   £52

HOOKER, R.
'Of The Laws of Ecclesiastical Politie' – 6
parts in one vol., engraved title, frontis.,
boards worn, folio – 1676.
(Phillips) $65   £30

**HOOKER, WILLIAM AND SALISBURY,
R. A.**
'The Paridisus Londinensis: containing
plants cultivated in the vicinity of the
Metropolis' – 2 vols., titles stating vol. I
and vol. II part 1 respectively, 119 hand
coloured plates, a few folding, occasional
spotting, cont. half calf, rubbed, joints
cracked – 1806-07.
(Christie's S.
    Kensington) $3,035   £1,350

HOOPER, R.
'The Morbid Anatomy of the Human
Uterus' – 21 coloured lithographed plates
all with stamp of the Med. and Chir. Soc.
of Aberdeen, half calf – 1832.
(Bonham's) $425   £190

HOPE, W. H. ST. JOHN
'Windsor Castle, an Architectural History'
– 3 vols., including portfolio of plans,
no. 406 of 1,050 copies, plates, illustrations,
original parchment, soiled, t.e.g., folio –
1913.
(Christie's S.
    Kensington) $80   £35

HOPKINS, JOHN
'Amasia or the Works of the Muses' – 3 vols.
in one, engraved frontispiece, waterstained,
torn and repaired, cont. calf, stained,
rebacked – 1700.
(Christie's, King
    St.) $135   £60

HOPPUS'S PRACTICAL MEASURER
Folding frontispiece, torn, staining, cont.
morocco, rubbed – Manchester, 1847.
(Christie's S.
    Kensington) $35   £15

HOPTON, ARTHUR
'Baculum Geodaeticum, sive Viaticum, or
Geodeticall Staffe' – 1st Edn., mostly
black letter, title within woodcut border,
3 folding tables and woodcut plan, diagrams in text, 19th century diced russia,
gilt, by R. Storr, Grantham, with his
ticket. Joints partly repaired, g.e., half
red morocco case, signature of James
Collyns at foot of title and of William Love
on original flyleaf – Nicholas Okes for
Simon Waterson, 1610.
(Sotheby's, New Bond
    Street) $1,125   £500

HORAE BMV
In Latin and French, preceded by a Calendar in French followed by Penitential Psalms, Office of the Cross and the Holy Ghost, Office of the Dead, Prayers and Hymns to the Virgin and Saints, 15 Joys and Pleas to the Lord, short Mass of the Holy Ghost and Virgin, illuminated ms. on vellum, 199 leaves, 12 large miniatures in floral, moulded or fleur de lys frames, calendar with occupations, figures and zodiac in grisaille, 19th century calf gilt, spine broken and upper cover detached — Paris, last quarter of 14th century.
(Christie's, King
   St.) $24,750   £11,000

HORAE BMV (USE OF ROME)
'Ces Presentes Heures a l'Usaige de Romme' — on vellum, 77 leaves of 96, set in fine woodcut border, woodcut device of Pigouchet incorporating Adam and Eve on title, woodcut of anatomical man, 13 full page woodcuts, initials illuminated in gold on red and blue backgrounds, rubbed, stained, 19th century morocco rubbed — Pigouchet, Paris, 14th April, 1497.
(Christie's, King
   St.) $1,460   £650

HORATIUS FLACCUS, QUINTUS
'Opera cum Quibusdam Annotationibus' — 219 leaves of 220, 74 lines of commentary round text and head line, roman and gothic letter, numerous woodcut illustrations, woodcut device at end, late 16th century vellum, soiled and worn, folio, first illustrated edition and first edition printed in Germany — Johann Gruninger, Strasbourg, 1498.
(Sotheby's, New Bond
   Street) $1,125   £500

HORE, J. P.
'The History of Newmarket . . . to the end of the Seventeenth Century' — 3 vols., frontispiece, original cloth — Newmarket and London, 1885-86.
(Christie's S.
   Kensington) $55   £25

HORNE, HENRY
'Essays Concerning Iron and Steel, the first containing Observations on American Sand Iron; the second, Observations, founded on Experiments, on Common Iron Ore' — 1st Edn., cont. sheep, worn, rebacked, the Kenney copy for T. Cadell, 1773.
(Sotheby's, New Bond
   Street) $900   £400

HORNE, THOMAS HARTWELL
'Landscape Illustrations of the Bible' —
engraved by W. and E. Finden — 2 vols.,
steel engraved additional titles and 94
plates, occasional spotting, cont. half
morocco, inner hinges split, cover detached,
g.e. — John Murray, 1836.
(Christie's S.
Kensington) $110   £50

HORSMAN, GILBERT
'Precedents in Conveyancing, Settled and
Approved' — 3 vols., 1st Edn., vol. II
wormed, cont. calf, joints split, worn, one
label missing, folio — 1744.
(Sotheby's, New Bond
Street) $13   £6

HOSKINS, G. A.
'Travels in Ethiopia' — frontis., folding
map, plates — 1835.
(Phillips) $425   £190

HOUGHTON, CLAUDE
'The Beast' — no. 9 of 250 copies, signed
by author and artist, plates by Alfred E.
Kerr, original cloth, t.e.g. — Quota Press,
Belfast, 1936.
(Christie's S.
Kensington) $40   £18

HOUGHTON, WILLIAM
'British Freshwater Fishes' — 41 coloured
plates, one detached, cont. morocco
backed cloth — William Mackenzie, n.d.
(Christie's S.
Kensington) $630   £280

HOUSE OF COMMONS
'Bengal, Fort St. George and Bombay
Papers' — folding maps and plates,
folio boards, uncut — 1804.
(Bonham's) $50   £22

HOUSMAN, JOHN
'A Descriptive Tour, and Guide to . . .
Cumberland, Westmorland, Lancashire,
and a part of the West Riding of Yorkshire'
— 2nd Edn., additional plates, 4 engraved
maps and town plans, 5 engraved plates,
errata and advertisement leaf at end,
plates numbered in pencil, a few leaves
slightly browned, 2 upper margins strengthened, upper hinge weak, cont. calf
gilt, worn, rebacked, joints rubbed —
Carlisle, 1802.
(Sotheby's
London) $45   £20

HOUSMAN, LAWRENCE
'The Field of Clover' — 8vo original green
pictorial cloth, uncut, 1st Edn., inscribed
by author, decorated and illustrated by
Clemence Housman — 1907.
(Lawrence of
Crewkerne) $11   £5

HOWARD, BRIAN
'God Save the King' — 1st Edn., limited to
150 copies, presentation copy, inscribed to
Nancy Cunard, slightly spotted, original
roan backed decorated boards, cover design
by John Banting, rubbed — Hours Press,
Paris, 1931.
(Sotheby's,
Chancery Lane) $405   £180

HOWARD, JOHN
'The State of the Prisons in England and
Wales' — with Appendix, 1st Edn., 2 parts
in one, 21 plates, some repaired, mounted,
lacking title to part 1, half morocco gilt,
4to — 1777-84.
(Phillips) $315   £140

HOWIE, D.
'History of the Lanark Rifle Volunteers' —
cloth — 1887.
(Tessa Bennett,
Edinburgh) $31   £14

HOWITT, SAMUEL
'The British Sportsman' — engraved title
and 71 plates, spotting, cont. marbled
calf, rebacked, rubbed — 1800.
(Christie's S.
Kensington) $1,800   £800

HOWITT, W.
'Ruined Abbeys and Castles of Great
Britain' — photographic illustrations,
cloth gilt — 1864.
'Ruined Castles of North Wales' — photo-
graphic illustrations, cloth gilt — 1864.
(Phillips) $125   £55

HOWLANDS, J.
'The Carpenter and Joiner's Assistant' —
engraved plates, half morocco — n.d.
(Tessa Bennett,
Edinburgh) $36   £16

HOWLET, ROBERT
'The School of Recreation' — original
calf, spine worn, corners repaired, 1st Edn.,
final advertisements, lacks engraved frontispiece, some staining — 1684.
(Lawrence of
Crewkerne) $110   £50

HOZIER, H. M.
'The Franco Prussian War' – 2 vols. in 6,
one additional engraved title, 53 plates,
3 plans, 13 double page maps, 3 hand
coloured, 1 folding map, slightly torn,
spotting, original cloth, soiled, g.e., 4to –
n.d.
(Christie's S.
  Kensington) $450   £200

HUDSON, W. H.
'Letters to R. H. Cunninghame Graham' –
no. 32 of 250 copies, two portraits by Sir
William Rothenstein, original morocco
backed cloth, t.e.g. – Golden Cockerel
Press, 1941.
(Christie's S.
  Kensington) $100   £45

HUEBERIN, MARIE ANNE
'Koch Buch' – mss. on paper, c 100 pages,
cont. half calf, worn and repaired – 1783.
(Sotheby's
  Monaco) $1,690   £750

HUGHES, G.
'The Natural History of Barbados' – large
paper, map, plates, mostly coloured, calf,
repaired, folio – 1750.
(Sotheby's, New Bond
  Street) $1,235   £550

HUGHES, JOHN
'A Complete History of England with the
Lives of all the Kings and Queens' – 3 vols.,
1st Edn., engraved frontispiece and 29
engraved plates, cont. sprinkled panelled
calf, covers detached, folio – 1706.
(Sotheby's, New Bond
  Street) $110   £50

HUGHES, RICHARD
'Gipsy Night and Other Poems' – limited to
750 copies, portrait by Pamela Bianco, a
few spots, original cloth backed boards,
dust jacket soiled – Golden Cockerel Press,
1922.
(Christie's S.
  Kensington) $45   £20

HUGHES, THOMAS SMART
'Travels in Sicily, Greece and Albania' – 2
vols., 1st Edn., 14 engraved plates and
plans, 1 folding engraved map, slight browning, 19th century half calf, rubbed – 1820.
(Sotheby's, New Bond
  Street) $675   £300

HUGNET, GEORGES
'La Belle en Dormant' – original wrappers,
1st Edn., lacking part of upper cover, 2
coloured embossed scraps on upper cover,
slightly stained, uncut, limited to 510
copies of which this is 341, presentation
copy inscribed by author to Princesse C.
de Rohan – Editions des Cahiers Libres,
Paris, 1933.
(Sotheby's,
  Chancery Lane) $65   £30

HUGO, JEAN
A.L.S. 1¾ pages, 21st May, no year, addres-
sed to Chere Amie and with watercolour
sketch at head of letter, framed and glazed.
(Sotheby's, New Bond
  Street) $50   £22

HUGO, R. P. LUDOVICUS
'Vita Sancti Norberti' – woodcut ornaments, slightly browned, cont. inscription,
cont. vellum boards, hinges weak, slight
wear on foot of spine, folio – Prague, 1732.
(Sotheby's, New Bond
  Street) $11   £5

HUGO, VICTOR
'L'Art d'Etre Grand-Pere' – 1st Edn., half
green morocco by Maylander, original wrap-
pers, presentation inscribed by author –
Paris, 1877.
(Sotheby's
  Monaco) $1,350   £600

HUGUES

HUGUES, D'HANCARVILLE, P. F.
'Monumens du Culte Secret des Dames
Romaines' – 1st Edn., additional engraved
title, 50 engraved plates, cont. mottled
calf, gilt, slightly rubbed – Nancy, 1784.
(Sotheby's
Monaco) $3,150   £1,400

HULME, F. EDWARD
'Familiar Wild Flowers' – 1st, 2nd, 3rd, 4th
and 5th series, 5 vols., green calf gilt,
morocco labels, tissued colour plates,
black and white illustrations in text – n.d.
(Lawrence of
Crewkerne) $45   £20

HULME, N.
'A Treatise on the Puerperal Fever' – plate,
1st Edn., new boards, calf back – 1772.
(Bonham's) $90   £40

HULSIUS, LEVINUS
'Erster Tractat Der Mechanischen Instru-
menten' – 4 parts, 2nd German Edn. of
parts 1-3, 1st German Edn. of part 4,
engraving on each title page and engraved
arms on dedication. Plates and folding
table, engravings and woodcuts in text,
some browning, cont. vellum boards,
soiled, label of the Biblioteka Julinska –
Frankfurst, 1632-33.
(Sotheby's, New Bond
Street) $1,690   £750

HULTON, P. AND QUINN, D. B.
'The American Drawings of John White,
1577-90' – 2 vols., plates, some coloured,
cloth – British Museum, 1964.
(Sotheby's
Monaco) $3,150   £1,400

HUMBOLDT, ALEXANDER VON BARON
'Kosmos. Entwurf Einer Physischen
Weltbeschreibung' – 5 vols. in 6, and atlas,
1st Edn., 42 plates, 39 coloured, cont.
brown half morocco, rubbed, bookplate of
Herbert McLean Evans, Atlas roan backed
boards, worn, folio – Stuttgart and
Tubingen, 1845-62.
(Sotheby's, New Bond
Street) $790   £350

HUME, DAVID
'History of England' – 6 vols., uniform calf,
some spines worn, tables missing – 1759-
62.
(Phillips) $45   £20

ABSTRACT

O F

A BOOK lately PUBLISHED;

E N T I T U L E D,

A

TREATISE

O F

Human Nature, &c.

W H E R E I N

The CHIEF ARGUMENT of that
BOOK is farther ILLUSTRATED and
EXPLAINED.

L O N D O N:
Printed for C. BORBET, at *Addison's Head,*
over-against St. *Dunstan's Church,* in *Fleet-
street.* 1740.
[Price fix Pence.]

'An Abstract of a Book Lately Published
Entitled a Treatise of Human Nature' –
light spotting, bound with six other works,
cont. speckled calf, upper cover detached,
spine cracked – 1740.
(Christie's S.
Kensington) $10,575   £4,700

HUME, FRANCES (Translator)
'The Story of the Circle of Chalk' – no. 4
of 1,000 copies, coloured plates by John
Buckland-Wright, original cloth – The
Rodale Press, n.d.
(Christie's S.
Kensington) $45   £20

HUMPHREYS, H. NOEL
'The Miracles of Our Lord' – 16 chromolithographed leaves by Humphreys,
original embossed papier mache binding,
spine torn, disbound, g.e. – 1848.
(Christie's S.
Kensington) $65   £28
'Genera and Species of British Butterflies'
– 33 hand coloured plates, including
title page, original cloth, neatly rebacked
using original spine – 1860.
(Sotheby's
London) $200   £90
'The Coinage of the British Empire' – 24
plates, 12 chromolithographed, margin of
one torn, original armorial papier mache
boards, one corner chipped, disbound –
David Bogue, 1855.
(Christie's S.
Kensington) $40   £18

HUNSLEY, W.
'Camel Howitzer Battery Planned, Raised
and Commanded by Captain I. H. Frith'
– lithographed title and six plates,
soiling marbled wrappers, backstrip
lacking and detached covers – St. Thomas'
Mount, 1837.
(Christie's S.
Kensington) $70   £32

HUNT, JOHN LEIGH
'The Feast of the Poets, with Notes, and
other Pieces in Verse' – 1st Edn., half
title, advertisement leaf at end, ms. correction in text on verso of final leaf, a very
few spots, lower hinge weak, original
boards, rebacked in cloth, slightly soiled –
For James Cawthorn, 1814.
(Sotheby's
London) $45   £20

HUNTER, CAPTAIN JOHN
'An Historical Journal of the Transactions
at Port Jackson and Norfolk Island' –
engraved title, portrait, soiled, 15 plates
and maps, some folding, some spotting and
stains, later half calf, worn, cover detached,
ex library copy, 4to – 1793.
(Christie's S.
Kensington) $675   £300

HURLOCK, JOSEPH
'A Practical Treatise upon Dentition' – 1st
Edn., some spotting, title page clumsily
tipped in, cont. calf, rebacked with cloth,
worn – 1742.
(Sotheby's
Monaco) $10,125   £4,500

HUTCHINGS, J. M.
'In the Heart of the Sierras the Yo Semite
Valley' – illus., cloth gilt – 1886.
(Phillips) $80   £35

HUTCHINS, JOHN
'History and Antiquities of the County of
Dorset' – 4 vols., 3rd Edn., titles in red and
black, 126 views and plans, 5 double page
or folding, numerous pedigrees, some on
double page plates, engravings and illustrations in text, cont. half calf, joints and
corners worn, folio – 1861-70.
(Sotheby's, New Bond
Street) $540   £240

HUTCHINSON, FRANCIS
'An Historical Essay Concerning Witchcraft'
– 1st Edn., cont. calf, worn – 1718.
(Sotheby's,
Chancery Lane) $200   £90

HUTTON, CHARLES
'A Treatise on Mensuration both in Theory
and Practice' – 1st Edn., 1 plate, woodcut
diagrams in text by Thomas Bewick, errata
leaf at end, cont. calf backed boards,
joints split, worn – T. Saint for author,
Newcastle on Tyne, 1770.
(Sotheby's, New Bond
Street) $135   £60

HUTTON, JAMES
'Theory of the Earth with Proofs and
Illustrations' – 2 vols., 1st Edn., 6 folding
plates, half titles, cont. mottled calf, covers
worn, rebacked – Edinburgh for Cadell,
Junior, 1795.
(Sotheby's, New Bond
Street) $1,235   £550

HUXLEY, ALDOUS
'Brave New World' – 1st Edn., original
cloth, dust jacket, worn – 1932.
(Sotheby's,
Chancery Lane) $110   £50

HUXLEY, THOMAS HENRY
'Evidence as to Man's Place in Nature' –
1st Edn., frontispiece, wood engraved
illustrations in text, half title, 8 pages of
publisher's advertisements at end, original
green cloth, half green morocco case,
signature of W. Houghton, 1863 on half
title – Williams and Norgate, 1863.
(Sotheby's, New Bond
    Street) $110   £50

HUYGENS, CHRISTIAAN
'The Celestial Worlds Discover'd or Con-
jectures Concerning the Inhabitants,
Plants and Productions of the Worlds in
the Planets' – 1st Edn. in English, 5
folding plates, 19th century marginal
annotations, cont. calf, upper cover
detached, lower joint split, bookplate
of Daniel Cresswell, Trinity College,
Cambridge – For Timothy Childe, 1698.
(Sotheby's, New Bond
    Street) $585   £260

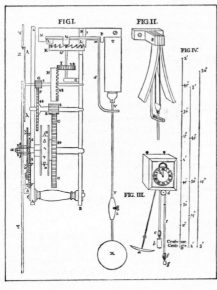

'Horologium Oscillatorium Sive de Motu
Pendulorum ad Horologia Aptato Demon-
strationes Geometricae' – 1st Edn.,
woodcut diagrams, one full page, some
browning, cont. calf, gilt spine, half red
morocco case, folio – Paris, 1673.
(Sotheby's, New Bond
    Street) $4,275   £1,900

HUYSMANS, J. K.
'A Rebours' – no. 6 of 10 copies on
papier imperial du Japon, containing 3
suites of plates and 3 original drawings of
an edition of 200 copies, illustrated by
Coussens, red morocco by Maylander,
silk doublures, original wrappers bound
in, slipcase – Paris, 1927.
(Sotheby's
    Monaco) $6,750   £3,000

HYGINUS, CAIUS JULIUS
'Poeticon Astronomicon' – edited by
Jacobus Sentinus and J. L. Santritter – 2nd
Edn., 57 leaves of 58, 31 lines, gothic letter,
47 allegorical woodcuts of principal con-
stellations, planets and signs of the zodiac,
19th century calf, slightly rubbed, half red
morocco case. Gilbert Redgrave's copy with
his bookplate and a note by him dated
1891 – Erhard Ratdolt, Venice, 1482.
(Sotheby's, New Bond
    Street) $7,875   £3,500

HYMEN
'An Acute Description of the Ceremonies
Used in Marriage' – old calf – 1760.
(Bonham's) $90   £40

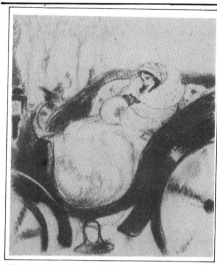

ICART, LOUIS — DUMAS, ALEXANDRE
'La Dame au Camellias' — 25 coloured
etched plates by Icart, slightly spotted —
original wrappers, uncut — Guillot, Paris,
1938.
(Sotheby's,
Chancery Lane)　$150　　£65

ILLUMINATED MS GOSPELS
Four gospels in Armenian, with Life of
Christ, Eusebian Letter, and Concordance,
256 leaves in Bolorgir script by the scribe
Karapet of Berkri. Marginal devices,
headpieces and capitals illuminated in
rich colours and gold, with sixteen miniatures, 18th century tooled calf, good
condition generally — S. E. Turkey, 15th
century.
(Sotheby's, New Bond
Street)　　$22,500　£10,000

ILLUMINATED MS QUR'AN
328 leaves of fine Naskhi script by the
scribe Ibn Abi Al-Qasim Abdul Jawad Al-
Nayrizi, with interlinear Persian translation in red, illuminated devices in margins,
Sura headings in gold on illuminated panels,

slight discolouration, in cont. lacquer
binding, morocco spine — Qajar, late 19th
century.
(Sotheby's, New Bond
Street)　　$6,750　　£3,000

ILLUSTRATED LONDON NEWS, THE
A quantity of unbound copies dated
between January 1875 and August 1868.
(Christie's S.
Kensington)　　$170　　£75
ILLUSTRATED LONDON NEWS, The
Illustrated, 150 volumes of years 1842-
1916.
(Bonham's)　　$4,950　£2,200

IMPORTATION CERTIFICATES
19 certificates authorising Andrew Russell
as authorised importer of various pro-
ducts including wine and coffee from
Rotterdam, written in Dutch — 1686 and
1695.
(Tessa Bennett,
Edinburgh)　　$180　　£80

INDENTURE
Ms. indenture in Latin, London, 15 August,
1370 between John de Tame, barber of
London, and John Churchman of the
Master Grocers' Co. and Richard Grace
relating to repayment to Tame of £100,
on vellum, 104 x 257mm., with red wax
seal pendant, buckram box, velvet lined.
(Christie's, King
St.)　　$290　　£130

INNES, HAMMOND
'The Conquistadors' — no. 151 of 265
copies signed by author, coloured plates,
illustrations, original tan morocco, gilt
inner dentelles — 1970.
(Christie's S.
Kensington)　　$90　　£40

INRAY, COMTE DE
'Bibliographie des Ouvrages relatifs a
l'Amour' — 4 vols. in three, 4th Edn.,
binder's cloth — Paris, 1894-1900.
(Sotheby's
Monaco)　　$2,475　£1,100

INTERIOR OF THE CRYSTAL PALACE

INTERIOR OF THE MAGNIFICENT NEW CRYSTAL PALACE AT SYDENHAM
3 lithographed sections and front, coloured by hand, title in German, French and English, the whole forming its own box, three sides missing, one loose – Germany, circa 1855.
(Sotheby's,
    Chancery Lane) $235   £105

INTERNATIONAL LIBRARY OF FAMOUS LITERATURE
20 vols. illustrated, half calf, spines bleached – 1899.
(Phillips) $70   £32

IONIDES, ALEXANDER C.
'Ion: a Grandfather's Tale' – 1st Edn., no. 173 of 200 copies, original linen backed boards, spin soiled, uncut – Cuala Press, Dublin, 1927.
(Sotheby's,
    Chancery Lane) $90   £40

IRELAND, SAMUEL
'Graphic Illustration of Hogarth' – 2 vols., 100 plates only, mezzotint, spotting, vol. 2 title repaired, later half calf, worn – 1794-9.
(Christie's S.
    Kensington) $90   £40
'A Picturesque Tour Through Holland, Brabant' – 2 vols., aquatint plates, half calf gilt – 1790.
(Phillips) $380   £170
'Picturesque Views of the Inns of Court' – 21 hand coloured views, diced calf, gilt – 1800.
(Phillips) $360   £160

'Picturesque views on The Upper, or Warwickshire Avon' – 1st Edn., 31 plates, engraved map, cont. half calf, rubbed, large 8vo – 1795.
(Sotheby's, New Bond
    Street) $270   £120
'Picturesque Views on the River Thames' – 52 sepia plates, 2 vols., boards, uncut – 1791.
(Bonham's) $495   £220

ISHERWOOD, CHRISTOPHER
'Sally Bowles'; 'Lions and Shadows'; 'Goodbye to Berlin' – 1st Editions, original cloth – Hogarth Press, 1937/38/39.
(Sotheby's,
    Chancery Lane) $145   £65
'The Condor and the Cows' – 1st Edn., cloth – 1949.
(Tessa Bennett,
    Edinburgh) $22   £10

ISIDORUS, HISPALENSIS
'Etymologiae, editio princeps' – 262 leaves of 264, 38 lines roman letter, rubricated, woodcut diagrams and map, worming, repaired, stained, 18th century French mottled calf, folio – Gunther Zainer, Augsburg, 1472.
(Sotheby's, New Bond
    Street) $4,275   £1,900

ITALY
Album of photographs of large views of Italy and others – half morocco, oblong folio – circa 1869.
(Tessa Bennett,
    Edinburgh) $315   £140

J

JABIR IBN HAIYAN
'Alchemiae Gebri Arabis . . . Libri cum Reliquis' – title within woodcut border, woodcuts in text, device at end, some browning and marginal stains, modern blue half morocco case, ownership inscription on title of Ferdinand Ruger, 1553 and another signature 'Nopitsch' – Joannes Petreius, Berne, 1545.
(Sotheby's, New Bond
    Street) $4,275   £1,900

JACKSON, SIR CHARLES
'English Goldsmiths and Their Marks' – frontis, original cloth – 1949.
(Christie's S.
    Kensington) $55   £25

JACKSON, MRS. E. NEVILL
'Silhouette Notes and Dictionary' – plates, 10 mounted and coloured, original cloth, dust jacket, 4to – 1938.
(Christie's S.
    Kensington) $22   £10

JACKSON, RICHARD
'The Interest of Great Britain Considered with Regard to her Colonies' – 1st Edn., modern paper wrappers, 8vo – 1760.
(Christie's.
    St. James) $90   £40

JACOBS, J. B.
'Ecole Pratiques des Accouchements' – 21 engraved plates, old half calf, with pasted on imprint of Bruxelles – 1785.
(Bonham's) $335   £150

JACOBS, JOSEPH (Editor)
'More English Fairy Tales' – no. 24 of 160 copies on Japanese vellum signed by the publisher, plates in 2 states by John Batten, original boards, t.e.g. – David Nutt, 1894.
(Christie's S.
    Kensington) $145   £65

JACOBUS DE VORAGINE
'Legenda Aurea' – in Dutch translation, part 2 only of two, double column, black letter, woodcut on title page and 82 illustrations in text, 19th century half calf, rebacked, worn, folio – Christian Snellaert, Delft, 1489.
(Sotheby's, New Bond
    Street) $4,500   £2,000

JAMES I (KING)
'The Peace Maker or Great Brittaines Blessing . . . ' – woodcut Royal arms and ornaments, cont. calf, rebacked, rubbed, small 4to – Printed by John Beale, 1620.
(Sotheby's, New Bond
    Street) $190   £85

JAMES I, KING OF ENGLAND
'The Works of the Most High and Mighty Prince James' – 1st Edn., engraved title, portrait frontispiece, woodcut arms, bound for Charles Prince of Wales, brown morocco, gilt panelled sides with double fillet borders etc., spine tooled with undulant design, rebacked, folio – 1616.
(Christie's, King
    St.) $19,125   £8,500

JAMES THE FIRST OF SCOTLAND
'Political Remains' – folding engraved frontispiece, later cloth rebacked – Edinburgh, 1783.
(Tessa Bennett,
    Edinburgh) $11   £5

JAMES, HENRY
'The Aspern Papers' – 2 vols. – 1888; 'Essays in London' – 1793; 'The Private Life' – 1893; 'The Spoils of Poynton' – 1897; 'The Awkward Age' – 1899 – 1st Edns., the second unopened, original cloth, spines rubbed and faded.
(Christie's S.
    Kensington) $225   £100

JAMES, JOHN
'The Theory and Practice of Gardening' – 32 engraved plates, 28 double page and mounted on guards, four folding, dedication leaf detached, cont. panelled calf, joints cracked – 1712.
(Christie's S.
    Kensington) $585   £260

JAMES, OWEN
'The Grammar of Ornament' – coloured additional title and plates, original cloth, rubbed cracked, t.e.g. – 1910.
(Christie's S.
    Kensington) $145   £65

JAMES, PHILIP
'Children's Books of Yesterday' – 1st Edn., illustrations, some coloured, original cloth – Studio, 1933.
(Sotheby's,
    Chancery Lane) $65   £30

JANE, CECIL (Translator)
'A Spanish Voyage to Vancouver and the North-West Coast of America' – no. 33 of 525 copies, plates and maps, original vellum backed cloth, gilt – 1930.
(Sotheby's,
    Chancery Lane) $135   £60

JANE, F. T.
'Fighting Ships' – 1904, 1909, 1914, 1916, 1918, 1926, 1935, 1937-56, 1959, 1960, together 25 vols. in 19, illus., all but one in original cloth – 1904-60.
(Phillips) $2,475   £1,100
'All the World's Aircraft' – plates, cloth, worn – 1942.
(Phillips) $27   £12

JANSON, J.
'America Septentrio' – hand coloured map, vignette sailing ships – circa 1650.
(Phillips) $315   £140
'Devon' – hand coloured double page folio map, mounted and framed – 17th century.
(Tessa Bennett,
    Edinburgh) $155   £70
'Holy Island and Farne Island' – 2 maps on one sheet, partly coloured – circa 1650.
(Phillips) $65   £28
'Nortfolcia; vernaculae Norfolke' – engraved map, a little hand colouring, 15 x 19½in. – Amsterdam, 1646.
(Christie's S.
    Kensington) $85   £38

JAPAN
An album containing a series of hand tinted photographs, street sellers, views, etc., half morocco, oblong folio − circa 1870-80.
(Tessa Bennett,
Edinburgh) $11   £5

JARDINE, SIR WILLIAM
'The Naturalist's Library' − 6 vols. only, 6 engraved portraits and titles with vignettes, 164 engraved plates, all but 10 hand coloured, original cloth, partly unopened − Edinburgh, 1833-40.
(Sotheby's
London) $290   £130

JEFFREY, THOMAS
20 maps including title from 'The County of York Surveyed' − upper margins all badly dampstained, folio − 1771.
(Phillips) $100   £45

JENKINS, JAMES
'The Martial Achievements of Great Britain and Her Allies . . . from 1799 to 1815' − 54 hand coloured aquatint plates, including 2 titles with vignettes, slight browning and soiling, early 19th century red half roan, worn, uncut, large folio − early 19th century.
(Sotheby's, New Bond
Street) $900   £400
'Naval Achievements of Great Britain from 1793-1817' − engraved title, 2 hand coloured aquatint plates of Nelson and St. Vincent, 55 hand coloured aquatint plates and one uncoloured plan, cont. diced russia, rebacked − 1817.
(Christie's
St. James) $5,175   £2,300

JENNER, EDWARD
'An Inquiry into the Causes and Effect of the Variolae Vaccinae' − 3rd Edn., ownership inscription excised, some spotting, original boards, rebacked, soiled, 4to − 1801.
(Christie's S.
Kensington) $335   £150

JESSE, EDWARD
'Anecdotes of Dogs' − plates, original cloth, t.e.g., soiled − 1846.
(Christie's S.
Kensington) $145   £65

JESSEL, FREDERIC
'A Bibliography of works in English on Playing Cards and Gaming' − 1st Edn., original buckram, uncut − 1905.
(Sotheby's,
Chancery Lane) $105   £48

JESUS CHRIST, THE SAYINGS OF
Arr by J. S. Mackail, lime green morocco elaborately tooled overall, floral design with shamrocks and tulips, title panel in centre, figure of dove above −
Doves Bindery, 1894.
(Phillips) $765   £340

JEWELLERS, GOLD AND SILVER-SMITHS' PATTERN BOOK
197 plates only, browning cloth, soiled, 4to − A. Fischer, n.d.
(Christie's S.
Kensington) $200   £90

JOANNES, GIOGOVIENSIS
'Computus Chirometralis' − 1st Edn., gothic letter, full page woodcut on title, cont, annotations, modern black morocco by the French binders, Garden City, N.Y. − Cracow, 1507.
(Sotheby's, New Bond
Street) $3,150   £1,400

JOHN BULL

'JOHN BULL'
Vols. I-IX, cont. issues 2-472, general title and index to each vol., signature of Sarah Tyrconnel on some titles, cont. half calf, worn, a few covers detached, folio — 1820-29.
(Sotheby's
  London) $315   £140

JOHN, W. D.
'Nantgarw Porcelain' — plates, some coloured, original morocco, worn — Newport, 1948.
(Christie's S.
  Kensington) $65   £28

JOHNSON, ABRAHAM
'Lucina sine Concubitu . . . a letter to the Royal Society' — no. 112 of 500 copies, plates by Hester Sainsbury, original parchment backed boards, t.e.g. — Golden Cockerel Press, 1930.
(Christie's S.
  Kensington) $27   £12

JOHNSON, FRANCIS
'A Dictionary, Persian, Arabic and English' — some leaves stained, cont. calf, rubbed, 4to — 1852.
(Sotheby Humberts
  Taunton) $135   £60

JOHNSON, SAMUEL
'A Dictionary of the English Language' — 2 vols., 1st Edn., slight browning and soiling, a few short tears, the first six leaves of vol. 2 defective with some loss of text, repaired, 19th century half roan, large folio, 1755.
(Sotheby's
  London) $900   £400
'A Journey to the Western Islands of Scotland' — 1st Edn., 6 line errata leaf, cont. half calf, worn — 1775.
(Christie's S.
  Kensington) $85   £38
'The Lives of the most eminent English Poets' — 4 vols., 2nd first London Edn., portrait, some browning, marginal water-staining at end of vol. III, cont. calf, spines slightly worn, new labels — 1781.
(Sotheby's
  London) $110   £50

JOHNSON, REV. W. M. AND EXLEY, THOMAS
'The Imperial Encyclopaedia' — 5 vols. including one volume of plates and maps, some folding, occasional spotting, cont. diced calf, some spines torn with loss, spine of vol. 1 lacking — n.d.
(Christie's S.
  Kensington) $55   £25

JOHNSTON, A. K.
'The National Atlas' — 41 double page maps, coloured in outline, original half morocco, soiled, stitching weak, g.e., folio — Cowan and Co., Edinburgh, n.d.
(Christie's S.
  Kensington) $80   £35

JOLY, G.
'Memoires' — 2 vols., edited by J. F. Bernard, cont. French red morocco, gilt, arms of Louis Antoine de Pardaillan, duc d'Antun 1665-1736, a fine copy — De Leers, Rotterdam, 1718.
(Sotheby Parke Bernet
  Monaco) $15,750   £7,000

JONES, DAVID
'In Parenthesis' — 1st Edn., frontispiece and 2 plates, original cloth — 1937.
(Sotheby's,
  Chancery Lane) $70   £32

JONES, GWYN
'The Green Island' — no. 341 of 500 copies, frontispiece and illustrations by John Petts, original cloth, t.e.g. — Golden Cockerel Press, 1946.
(Christie's S.
  Kensington) $50   £22

'Sir Gawain and the Green Knight' —
limited to 360 copies, this no. 13 of 60
signed by translator (Gwyn Jones),
coloured plates by Dorothea Braby, original morocco, specially bound, t.e.g.,
slipcase, folio — Golden Cockerel Press,
1952.
(Christie's S.
   Kensington) $200   £90

JONES, GWYN AND THOMAS
(Translators)
'Mabinogion' — no. 536 of 550 copies,
frontispiece and full page illustrations by
Dorothea Braby, original half morocco,
t.e.g., folio — Golden Cockerel Press, 1948.
(Christie's S.
   Kensington) $630   £280

JONES, HENRY
'The Bird Paintings (edited by) Bruce
Campbell' — one of 500 copies, 24
coloured plates, green half rexine, slipcase,
oblong folio, 1976.
(Sotheby's
   London) $290   £130

JONES, OWEN AND LOCKHART, J. G.
(Translator)
'Ancient Spanish Ballads' — 4 chromolithographed titles and woodcut borders
by Jones, tinted plates, illustrations,
spotting, cont. vellum, gilt with black and
red morocco inlays, slightly soiled, gilt and
gauffered edges — 1842.
(Christie's S.
   Kensington) $160   £70

JONES, T.
'History of Brecknock' — 4 vols., maps,
plans, half morocco gilt — 1909-30.
(Phillips) $145   £65

JONSON, BEN
'A Croppe of Kisses, lyrics chosen by John
Wallis' — limited to 250 copies, this no.
12 of 50 specially bound by Sangorski and
Sutcliffe, original morocco, t.e.g., folio —
Golden Cockerel Press, 1937.
(Christie's S.
   Kensington) $225   £100
'Works' — engraved portrait, torn and laid
down with a loss of lower corner margin,
cont. panelled calf, rebacked, old spine
laid down, folio — Thomas Hodgkin for
Herringman (and others), 1692.
(Christie's S.
   Kensington) $290   £130

IACOBVS . I . REX . SCOTORVM .

IACOBVS I. An. Chrif. 1424.
CORPORE non ingens, invictus robore mentis,
Omnigena auxit regna beata bonis.

I

JONSTON, J.
'Inscriptiones Historicae Regum Scotorum'
— 1st Edn., 11 engraved plates, 10 portraits
and royal coat of arms, repaired, good but
washed copy in 19th century blue morocco,
gilt, g.e., slightly worn, bookplate of Wm.
Barr Knox — Amsterdam, Claesson for A.
Hart, Edinburgh, 1602.
(Sotheby's
   Edinburgh) $360   £160

'Historiae Naturalis de Quadrupedibus' —
engraved title and 80 engraved plates;
'Historiae Naturalis de Insectis' —
engraved title and 28 plus 12 plates;
'Historiae Naturalis de Exanguibus
Aquaticis' — 20 plates;
'Historiae Naturalis de Piscibus' — engraved
title and 44 of 47 plates,
'Historiae Naturalis de Avibus' — engraved
title and 62 plates — 5 vols. in one, cont.
blindstamped vellum, folio — J. J. F.
Schipper, Amsterdam, 1657.
(Christie's, King
   St.) $720   £320
'Theatrum Universale Omnium Animalium
Quadrupedum' — title in red and black
with engraved vignette, additional engraved
title, 80 engraved plates by M. Merian, a
few stained, cont. calf, gilt, spine, folio —
Heilbronn, 1755.
(Christie's, King
   St.) $495   £220

JOSEPH BEN MOSHE

JOSEPH BEN MOSHE OF KREMENETZ
'Beur Al Sepher Mitzvot Gadol' — commentary on the Code of Moses of Coucy —
1st Edn., some water staining, cont. half
calf, worn — Juan di Gara, Venice, 1605.
(Sotheby's, New Bond
    Street) $335   £150

JOSEPH JUSHPA HANN NEURLINGEN
'Joseph Ometz' — A book of customs —
rare 1st Edn., some portions in Old
Yiddish, repaired, browned, 19th century
vellum backed, marbled boards, worn —
J. Kellnar, Frankfurt am Main, 1723.
(Sotheby's, New Bond
    Street) $495   £220

JOSEPHINE
Autograph letter signed to Barras, 1 page,
quarto, no place, 1795-6, asking him as a
favour to grant to one Citizen Maulhion
the position he is seeking.
(Sotheby's, New Bond
    Street) $675   £300

JOSEPHUS, FLAVIUS
'The Genuine and Complete Works of'
edited by Maynard, engraved plates and
maps, old calf, folio — J. Cooke, circa
1790.
(Phillips) $110   £50

JOURDAIN, MARGARET AND ROSE, F.
'English Furniture, the Georgian Period' —
coloured frontispiece, plates, original
cloth, spine slightly faded, dust jacket —
Batsford, 1953.
(Christie's S.
    Kensington) $55   £25

'JOURNAL, A'
Later the 'Illustrated Journal of
Australasia' — vol. I, II and IV only,
illus. original cloth, slightly rubbed —
Melbourne, 1856-58.
(Sotheby's,
    Chancery Lane) $315   £140

'JOURNAL DES DEMOISELLES'
1 vol. only, 16 hand coloured and 2
folding uncoloured plates, cont. morocco
backed cloth, slightly soiled — Paris, 1881.
(Christie's S.
    Kensington) $70   £32
Coloured costume plates and transfer
pattern sheets, 2 vols. — 1851-53.
(Bonham's) $315   £140

JOURNAL OF MODERN LITERATURE
Edited by Maurice Beebe — vols. 1-3,
excepting vol. 2, no. 5, vol. 4, 5, 6, 23
issues in all, illustrations, original wrappers
— Philadelphia, 1970-77.
(Sotheby's,
    Chancery Lane) $33   £15

JOUVE, PIERRE-JEAN
18 works by the author and two others,
all 1st editions, all inscribed to Anthony
Bertram by author, original wrappers,
some slightly soiled.
(Sotheby's,
    Chancery Lane) $58   £26

JOYCE, JAMES
'Exiles' — 1st American Edn., dampstained, original cloth backed boards,
stained and worn — New York, 1918.
(Sotheby's,
    Chancery Lane) $22   £10
'Finnegans Wake' — 1st Edn., original
cloth, spine discoloured, uncut — 1939.
(Sotheby's,
    Chancery Lane) $135   £60
'Ulysses' — 1st Edn., no. 460 of 1,000
copies, slightly spotted, few leaves stained,
two leaves with slight holes, original
wrappers, torn and soiled, detached, lacking spine, stitching weak, uncut — Paris,
1922.
(Sotheby's,
    Chancery Lane) $560   £250

'A Portrait of the Artist as a Young Man'
— 1st English Edn., original cloth — The
Egoist Ltd., 1916.
(Sotheby's,
    Chancery Lane) $180   £80

**JUBINAL, ACHILLE AND SENSI,
GASPARD**
'La Armeria Real ou Collection des Principales Pieces de la Galerie d'Armes Anciennes
de Madrid' — 2 parts in one vol., 2 engraved
titles, wood engraved initials, head pieces
and 20 illustrations, 81 lithographic plates
by Gaspard Sensi, spotted, cont. morocco
backed boards, folio — Paris, circa 1840.
(Sotheby's, New Bond
    Street) $158   £70

JUDD'S MAGICAL AND CONJURING

THE VENTRILOQUIAL CHAMPIONS
COPYRIGHT

JUDD, A. M.
'The Professional Wizard's Guide to the
Selection and Purchase of Magical and
Conjuring Tricks' — wood engraved
illustrations, folder worn, original wrap-
pers bound in — New York, circa 1890.
(Sotheby's,
    Chancery Lane) $605   £270

5 Brownlow-st. Drury-lane, London, W   19

E V E N I N G   P A R T I E S
Attended by Professor JUDD.
With a selection of beautful Conjuring Tricks
and startling Illusions; many of Robert Houdin's
and Stodare's stage Tricks being performed in
the Drawing-room.
    Terms for Illusions   ...   £1   1   0
    Illusions and Ventriloquism   1   11   6
        Travelling Expenses extra.

JUDD, PROFESSOR W. J.
'Illustrated Descriptive Catalogue With
Prices Of Conjuring Tricks, Magical
Apparatus etc.' — 25 wood engraved
illustrations, cloth backed boards, original
pictorial wrappers bound in, crease marked
— Rutley and Co., circa 1870.
(Sotheby's,
    Chancery Lane) $605   £270

**JUDICIUM CUM TRACTATIBUS
PLANETARIIS**
20 leaves, 32 lines, gothic letter, full page
woodcut representing the earth and planets
surrounded by the elements, slight staining
and browning, 18th century sheep, worn,
rebacked, very rare — Philippus de
Mantegatiis, Milan, 1496.
(Sotheby's, New Bond
    Street) $7,875   £3,500

**JUNGNICKEL, LUDWIG HEINRICH —
FLEISCHER, VICTOR**
'Tierfabeln des Klassischen Altertums' —
24 coloured lithographed plates and illustrations in text by Jungnickel, half morocco,
t.e.g., limited to 185 copies of which this is
23, signed by artist.
(Sotheby's,
    Chancery Lane) $30   £13

JUSTICE, JEAN
'Dictionary of Marks and Monograms of
Delft Pottery' — illustrations, original
cloth, dust jacket — 1930.
(Christie's S.
    Kensington) $100   £45

JUSTINIANUS, D.
'Sacratissimi Principi Institutionum' —
engraved additional title, folding tables,
some torn, cont. vellum rubbed —
Amsterdam, 1687.
(Christie's S.
    Kensington) $33   £15

JUVENALIS, DECIMUS JUNIUS
'Mores Hominum, The Manners of Men,
described in Sixteen Satyrs' — engraved
portrait, frontispiece and 15 plates only,
one leaf of text bound upside down, cont.
mottled calf, rubbed, joints torn at head
and foot, folio — R. Hodgkinson, 1660.
(Christie's S.
    Kensington) $200   £90

'Mores Hominum. The Manners of Men,
described in Sixteen Satyrs . . . translated
by Sir Robert Stapylton' — large brown
copy, additional engraved title, 16 engraved
plates by Hollar, slight browning, a little
worming, not affecting text, bookplate of
Sir William Nigel Gresley, early 19th century calf, slightly worn, large folio — 1660.
(Sotheby's
    London) $338   £150

JUVENILE
'A Visit to the Theatre' by the author of
'Juliet' — 32 hand coloured etched plates,
quarter morocco, 3rd Edn. — 1820.
(Tessa Bennett,
    Edinburgh) $75   £34

'The Book of Games or, A History of
Juvenile Sports' — 23 of 24 coloured
plates (copper), quarter morocco, outer
corner 2 11 defective — London, 1810.
(Tessa Bennett,
    Edinburgh) $40   £18

JUVENILE LIBRARY
'A Picture of the Seasons with Anecdotes
and Remarks on Every Month of the Year'
— wood engraved frontispiece, vignette on
title, 4 full page illustrations, very slightly
spotted, original roan backed boards,
soiled and rubbed — Printed for S. and A.
Davis, 1818.
(Sotheby's,
    Chancery Lane) $55   £25

**JUX FEXIRBUCH, ODER DER
ZAUBERER**
Lithographed throughout including frontispiece and 80 plates coloured by hand,
some pencilling, original wrapping repaired,
worn, an early flick book — Prague, circa
1840.
(Sotheby's,
    Chancery Lane) $235   £105

KACID-MIOSIC, ANDRIJA
'Ragzor Ugodni Naroda Slowinskoga',
edited by W. J. Dunder — 2 vols., text printed with gilt borders, Tsar Nicolas I's copy
with Tsarkoe Selo library stamp, cont.
Viennese calf, elaboratly gilt with red, green
and black, silk liners, g.e. slight wear but
an imposing binding — Vienna, 1836.
(Sotheby's, New Bond
 Street) $675 £300

KAMA SUTRA OF VATSAYANA
Vellum gilt, reprint — 1883.
(Phillips) $55 £25

KANDINSKY, VASSILY
'The Art of Spiritual Harmony' — title
stamped, 'presentation copy', 9 plates,
occasional spotting, original cloth backed
boards, rubbed — 1914.
(Christie's S.
 Kensington) $65 £28

KANE, RICHARD
'Campaign of King William and Queen
Anne from 1689 to 1712 . . . with the Most
Essential Exercise of Cavalry' — calf gilt
rubbed, rebacked, morocco label, 1st Edn.,
a folding map of Europe by Hermann Moll,
5 engraved plates — 1745.
(Lawrence of
 Crewkerne) $45 £20

KANNEMAN, JOHANNES
'Passio Jesu Christi Necnon Alius Tractatus
De Christi Passione Una Cum Legenda S.
Catherinae' — 3rd Edn., 88 leaves, 33 lines,
first tract double column, gothic letter, one
initial in blue, others in red, some rubrica-
tion, woodcut on title page, worming,
browning, early 19th century boards, worn
— Peter Wagner, Nuremberg, 1491.
(Sotheby's, New Bond
 Street) $1,350 £600

KANTER'S MAGIC SHOP
4 catalogues, comprising one unnumbered
(copyright 1939), no. 8 (2 copies) and no. 9,
illustrations, original wrappers or folders
with original wrappers bound in, very
slightly worn, and one other, an imperfect
duplicate — Philadelphia, 1939-50.
(Sotheby's,
 Chancery Lane) $65 £30

KAPPIEL, A. W. AND KIRBY, W. E.
'British and European Butterflies and
Moths' — 30 coloured plates, illustrations,
some soiling, original cloth, g.e., — n.d.
(Christie's S.
 Kensington) $65 £30

**KARO, JOSEPH AND ELIJAH GAON
OF WILNO**
'Tur Yore De'ah' Rabbinic code — printed
on blue paper throughout, title in red and
black, cont. calf backed boards, worn,
folio — Yecheskel Ben Moshe and Simcha
Simmel, Grodno, 1806.
(Sotheby's, New Bond
 Street) $1,170 £520

KAUFFER, E. McKNIGHT
'The Art of the Poster' — numerous
coloured and plain plates, illustrations,
cloth backed boards, edges rubbed, folio —
1924.
(Christie's
 St. James) $145 £65

KAVANAGH, PATRICK
'The Great Hunger' — 1st Edn., no. 15 of
250 copies, original linen backed boards,
uncut, unopened — Cuala Press, Dublin,
1942.
(Sotheby's,
 Chancery Lane) $105 £48

KAY, STEPHEN
'Travels and Researches in Caffraria' — 5
engraved plates and folding map, some
leaves slightly spotted and soiled, modern
half calf — 1833.
(Sotheby's,
 Chancery Lane) $105 £48

KEAN, EDMUND
Autograph signed Coutts and Comp.
cancelled cheque made out to Mr. Drago
for £13.12s. dated 25th August, 1825,
framed and glazed with Theatre Royal,
Drury Lane Theatre Bill with Kean as
Penruddock in 'The Wheel of Fortune'
mounted, framed and glazed, 3rd June,
1822.
(Sotheby's, New Bond
   Street) $65   £28

**KEATE, GEORGE AND WILSON,
CAPTAIN H.**
'An Account of the Pelew Islands' – 1st
Edn., engraved portrait frontispiece, 15
plates, folding map, some plates slightly
foxed, modern half calf, gilt – 1788.
(Sotheby's, New Bond
   Street) $215   £95

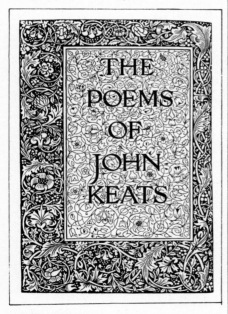

KEATS, JOHN
'Poems' edited by F. S. Ellis – limited to
307 copies, this is no. 300, printed in red
and black, ornamental woodcut border,
title and initials, original limp vellum, silk
ties, uncut, slipcase, 8vo – 1894.
(Sotheby's,
   Chancery Lane) $650   £290

KEITH, G. SKENE
'General View of the Agriculture of
Aberdeenshire' – folding hand coloured
map, 4 engraved plates and 2 folding plans,
original cloth backed boards – Aberdeen,
1811.
(Tessa Bennett,
   Edinburgh) $125   £55

KELLY, CHRISTOPHER
'An Authentic History . . . forming a Complete Universal History' – 2 vols., new edn.,
maps, some dampstains, cont. calf, rubbed
– n.d.
(Christie's S.
   Kensington) $90   £40

KELLY, R. TALBOT
'Egypt Painted and Described' – no. 316 of
500 copies, signed by author, coloured
plates, one leaf detached, original cloth,
soiled, t.e.g., 4to – 1902.
(Christie's S.
   Kensington) $70   £32

KEMBLE, J. P.
'Fugitive Pieces' – 1st Edn., half morocco,
slightly rubbed, unopened – York, W.
Blanchard, 1780.
(Sotheby's
   London) $290   £130

KENNEDY, E. S. (editor)
'Peaks, Passes and Glaciers' – second series,
vol. 2, folding maps, original cloth – 1862.
(Christie's S.
   Kensington) $45   £20

KENNEDY, WILLIAM
'The Continental Annual, and Romantic
Cabinet, for 1832' – engraved frontispiece.
additional title, both detached, and 11
plates on India paper – n.d.
(Christie's S.
   Kensington) $55   £25

KENNETT, BISHOP WHITE
'Parochial Antiquities Attempted in the
History of Ambrosden, Burcester etc.' –
1st Edn., engraved vignette title, 8 plates
only of 9, 7 folding, cont. panelled calf,
spine repaired, rubbed – Oxford, printed
at the Theater, 1695.
(Sotheby's,
   Chancery Lane) $80   £35

KETURA (MARRIAGE CERTIFICATE)
Certificate of marriage between Samuel
Kanoni and Esther Seror, illuminated mss.
on paper, signed and witnessed, written
with an ornamented border, worn in
folds, spotted, framed – Oran, 1864.
(Sotheby's, New Bond
   Street)   **$1,125**   **£500**

Otto Keyens
kurtzer Entwurff
von
Neu-Niederland
Vnd

G U A J A N A

Einander entgegen gesetzt/
Vmb den Vnterscheid zwischen warmen und
kalten Landen herauß zu bringen/
Und zu weisen

Welche von beyden am füglichsten zu bewohnen/
am behendesten an zu bauen und den besten Nutzen
geben mögen.

Denen Patronen/ so da Colonien an zu legen
gesonnen / als auch denen Personen und Familien/ die
ihr Vaterland zu vergessen sich bey dergleichen Bevölckerung
nach fremden Küsten und Reichen gebrauchen
lassen wollen.

Auß dem Holländischen ins Hochteutsche
versetzt
durch
T. R. C. S. C, S,

Leipzig
Im Ritzschischen Buchladen.
M. DC. LXXII.

KEYE, OTTO
'Kurtzer Entwurf Von Neu Niederland und
Guajana' – 1st Edn. in German, library
stamps of the Salzburg Museum Library,
later boards, 4to – Leipzig, 1672.
(Sotheby's, New Bond
   Street)   **$1,080**   **£480**

KEYNES, SIR GEOFFREY
'Bibliotheca Bibliographici; A Catalogue
of the Library' – limited to 500 copies,
plates, original cloth – The Trianon Press,
1964.
(Christie's S.
   Kensington)   **$108**   **£48**

KEYS, JOHN
'The Antient Bee-Master's Farewell or,
Full and Plain Directions for the Manage-
ment of Bees' – two engraved plates, one
torn and badly repaired, later half calf,
slightly rubbed – 1796.
(Christie's S.
   Kensington)   **$180**   **£80**

KHLEBNIKOV, VELEMIR
'Zangezi' – one of 2,000 copies, original
printed wrappers, rather torn – Moscow,
1922.
(Sotheby's, New Bond
   Street)   **$650**   **£290**

KIDDER, EDWARD
'Receipts of Pastry and Cookery' –
engraved portrait, title and text, slight
soiling, a few leaves shaved, affecting some
letters, cont. calf, worn – circa 1740.
(Christie's S.
   Kensington)   **$360**   **£160**

KILBURNE, RICHARD
'A Topographie of Kent' – engraved por-
trait, lacks map, cropped, stained, vellum
rebacked and worn – 1659.
(Sotheby's, New Bond
   Street)   **$31**   **£14**

**KILLWITZ, KATHE – HAUPTMANN,
GERHART**
'Die Weber' – vignette on title, 6 plates
and tailpiece by Killwitz, scarlet calf
gilt, t.e.g., original pictorial wrappers
bound in, No. 104 of 230 copies –
Erich Steinbal, Frankfurt, 1917.
(Sotheby's,
   Chancery Lane)   **$348**   **£155**

KILNER, DOROTHY
'The First Principles of Religion and Existence of the Deity' – 2 parts in one vol., 1st Edn., engraved frontispiece, original sheep backed boards, soiled, lacking spine, covers loose – John Marshall, 1787.
(Sotheby's,
Chancery Lane) $95   £42

KIMBELL, JOHN
'An Account of the Legacies, Gifts, Rents, Fees appertaining to the Church and Poor of the Parish and Church of St. Alphege, Greenwich' – engraved title, plates, folding map, cont. cloth, rebacked – 1816.
(Sotheby's,
Chancery Lane) $27   £12

KING, DANIEL
'The Vale-Royal of England' or the County Palatine of Chester Illustrated . . . also an Excellent Discourse of the Isle of Man' – engraved additional title, 16 plates, 1 folding, double page, town plan and 2 maps and illus., cont. calf, rubbed and rebacked, folio – 1656.
(Christie's S.
Kensington) $360   £160

KING, EDWARD
'Munimenta Antiqua; or Observations on Ancient Castles' – 4 vols. in two, First Edition, 167 engraved or aquatint plates, or folding, later half morocco, rubbed – 1799-1806.
(Sotheby's,
Chancery Lane) $495   £220

KING JAMES VII
'Alphabetical Abridgement of the First Parliament of King James the VII – 1685 and 1686' – cont. calf, notes bound in – Edinburgh, 1698.
(Tessa Bennett,
Edinburgh) $7   £3

KING, JESSIE M. AND MORRIS, WILLIAM
'The Defence of Guinevere and Other Poems' – decorative title, plates and vignettes by King, original cloth, affected by damp, t.e.g. – 1904.
(Christie's S.
Kensington) $95   £42

KINGLAKE, ALEXANDER WILLIAM
'The Invasion of the Crimea' – 9 vols., uniform half calf, spines gilt, t.e.g., illustrated folding plans etc., a good set – 1888-1892.
(Lawrence of
Crewkerne) $100   £45

KINGSLEY, CHARLES
'The Water Babies' – limited Edn., signed by the artist Warwick Goble, coloured illus., original vellum gilt (lacks one tie) – 1909.
(Phillips) $290   £130

KINSEY, W. M.
'Portugal Illustrated' – 1st Edn., additional engraved title, 30 engraved plates, 4 plates of music and 9 hand coloured aquatint costume plates, 1 folding engraved map, browning lacks half title, cont. blue russia, rebacked, rubbed, 8vo. – 1828.
(Sotheby's, New Bond
Street) $245   £110

KIPLING, RUDYARD
Collection of periodicals and cuttings containing contributions by Rudyard Kipling. The Youth's Companion, Boston, 1898 – 'The Burning of the Sahara Sands': The World's Sunday Magazine New York, 1898 – 'Kipling describes a Floating City of Twelve Thousand Souls': Pearsons Magazine 1897 – 'The Tomb of His Ancestors': series of eight 'Letters to the Family' from the Morning Post, 1908. Over thirty others, mostly poems printed in English and American newspapers before 1910, in folder.
(Sotheby's,
    Chancery Lane) $155   £70
'Plain Tales from the Hills' – vol. 1 only of the Sussex edition of Kipling's works, no. 311 of 525 copies signed by the author, original brown morocco gilt, slight mark on upper cover, uncut, unopened – 1937.
(Sotheby's,
    Chancery Lane) $108   £45
'Poems, 1886-1929' – 3 vols., no. 339 of 525 copies signed by the author, engraved frontispiece by Francis Dodd, signed by the artist, original morocco spines and parts of two covers faded, slightly rubbed, t.e.g. – 1929.
(Sotheby's,
    Chancery Lane) $180   £80

KIRBY, JOHN
'The Suffolk Traveller' – 1st Edn., cont. calf, rebacked, rubbed – Ipswich, 1735.
(Sotheby's,
    Chancery Lane) $170   £75

KIRBY, JOSHUA
'Dr. Brook Taylor's Method of Perspective Made Easy' – 2 vols. in one, 2nd Edn., engraved frontispiece and 51 plates, vol. 1 lacks title, cont. rough calf, upper cover loose – Ipswich, 1755.
(Sotheby's,
    Chancery Lane) $215   £95

KIRBY, W. F.
'European Butterflies and Moths' – 1 vol. in two, 62 plates all but one coloured, occasional spotting, cont. half morocco – 1898.
(Christie's S.
    Kensington) $225   £100

KIRKBY, JOHN
'The Doctrine of Ultimators' – 1st Edn., original boards, stained vellum spine, inner hinges broken, uncut, bookplate of Baron Camoys, Stonor Park – 1748.
(Sotheby's
    London) $45   £20

KIRKLAND, T.
'A Treatise on Child Bed Fevers' – half calf – 1774.
(Bonham's) $155   £70

KITCHIN, T.
'A New Map . . . North and South and West Indies' – 2 folding sheets, coloured in outline – R. Sayer, 1786.
(Phillips) $80   £35

KLASS, ALFONS, SOLATANZER VOM K. K. HOFOPERNTHEATER WIEN
'Album von Grosen Tanz, Schaal und Ensemble Gruppen, Aufzugen und Ensemble Tanzen' – 2 vols., autograph drawings in pencil and watercolour – Vienna, 1850.
(Sotheby's, New Bond
    Street) $1,462   £650

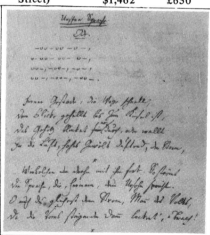

KLOPSTOCK, FRIEDRICH GOTTLOB
Early autograph version of his ode 'Die Deutsche Sprache' comprising 7 quatrians, 3 pages, quarto, note of authentification on verso of second leaf in hand of Dr. Botha – Before 1783.
(Sotheby's, New Bond
    Street) $8,100   £3,600

KLOPSTOCK

Early autograph version of his ode 'Der Kranz' comprising 24 lines, 2 pages, slight browning at edges — before 1782.
(Sotheby's, New Bond
    Street) $6,750   £3,000

KNAPP, J. L.

'Gramina Britannica' — 1st Edn., 119 hand coloured engraved plates, some plate nos. neatly corrected by hand, piece torn from one blank text margin, Tyrconnel bookplate, cont. calf, lacks backstrip, covers detached — 1804.
(Sotheby's
    London) $315   £140

KNELLER, SIR GODFREY

'The Kit Kat Club done from the original paintings of Sir Godfrey Kneller by Mr. Faber' — mezzotint title, 47 mezzotint portraits, one torn, some spotting, late 18th century russia, hinges and corners worn, Signet library copy, folio — 1735.
(Sotheby's, New Bond
    Street) $1,000   £450

KNIGHT, CHARLES

'Pictorial Museum of Animated Nature; and the Companion for the Zoological Gardens' — 2 vols., 4,000 wood engravings. With another copy of volume 11 in later edition with coloured frontispieces, folio — 1856-58 and circa 1875.
(Sotheby's, New Bond
    Street) $11   £5

KNIGHT, RICHARD PAYNE

'A Discourse on the Worship of Priapus' — 40 plates, original half morocco, rubbed, t.e.g. — 1865.
(Christie's S.
    Kensington) $85   £38

KNIGHT, T. A.

'Pomona Herefordiensis' — 1811.
(Bonham's) $1,575   £700

KNOWLER, WILLIAM (Editor)

'The Earl of Stratforde's Letters and Dispatches' — 2 vols. in one, frontispiece, torn, cont. calf, covers detached — 1739.
(Christie's S.
    Kensington) $50   £22

KNOX, R.

'Historical Relation of Ceylon' — 14 plates, 1 map, tear in map and page 90 repaired, no. portrait, W. Strickland bookplate, calf gilt, folio — 1681.
(Phillips) $360   £160

KOEHOORN, BARON MINNO DE

'The New Method of Fortification . . . translated . . . by Tho. Savery' — 14 plates, 12 folding, torn, title detached, cont. panelled calf, rebacked. Printed for Daniel Midwinter — London, 1705.
(Christie's S.
    Kensington) $125   £55

KOMENSKY, JOHN AMOS

'The Labyrinth of the Wind and the Paradise of the Heart' — no. 277 of 370 copies, frontispiece and illustrations by Dorothea Braby, original cloth, t.e.g. — Golden Cockerel Press, 1950.
(Christie's S.
    Kensington) $95   £42

KONODY, P. G. — SIR MARION CONWAY AND LIONEL CUST

'The King's Pictures' — 3 vols., plates, mostly mounted, a few coloured, some detached, original wrappers, slightly torn and soiled — vol. 2 boxed — n.d.
(Christie's S.
    Kensington) $45   £20

KORAN, THE

Commonly called the Alcoran of Mohammed, translated into English immediately from the original Arabic by George Sale, 1st Edn. of this translation, engraved folding map, slight browning, cont. calf rebacked — 1735.
(Christie's, King
    Street) $170   £70

KORAN

'The Koran, commonly called the Alcoran of Mohammed . . . to which is prefixed a preliminary discourse by George Sale' — title in red and black, folding map and 3 folding plates only of 4, cont. calf, rebacked, head of spine nicked, corners repaired — 1734.
(Sotheby's
    London) $101   £45

KORAN, ALCORAN OF MAHOMET
First English Edn., translated by Du Ryer,
cont. calf, 1649.
(Phillips) $270   £120

KRAUS, JOHANN ULRICH
'Heilige Augen-Und Gemuths-Lust
vorstellend alle Sonn-Fest-und
Feyrtagliche Nicht nur Evangelien Sondern
auch Epistelen und Lectionen, jene
Historisch Diese auch Emblemmatisch, und
mit Curieusen Einfassungen in vielen
Kupffer-Stucken' — 113 engraved plates of
119, some browning and soiling, early 19th
century calf, gilt, rubbed, folio — Augsburg,
1706.
(Sotheby's, New Bond
    Street) $360   £160

KRUCHENYKH, A.
'Yazyk Lenina' (The Language of Lenin) —
one of 5,000 copies, illustrations by G.
Klutsis, original printed wrappers by V.
Kulagina-Klutsis, slightly frayed — Moscow,
1925.
(Sotheby's, New Bond
    Street) $790   £350

**KRUCHENYKA, A. AND KHLEBNIKOV,
V.**
'Igra V Adu' (A Game in Hell) — 2nd Edn.,
lithographed throughout on thin paper,
illustrations by K. Melevich and O.
Rosanova, original wrappers, slightly
soiled and frayed — Svet, St. Petersburg,
1915.
(Sotheby's, New Bond
    Street) $2,590   £1,150

KRUSINSKI, JUDE, Jesuit
'The History of the Revolution of Persia
. . . Done into English . . . Father Du
Cerceau' — lacks map, title and some
leaves frayed by damp at lower outer
edge, old boards, worn at foot of spine,
uncut, library stamp of Tullabeg College
on title — Dublin, 1729.
(Sotheby's
    London) $22   £10

L

LABORDE, A.
'Descriptions des Nouveaux Jardins de la France' — text in English, French and German, fine engraved plates, few with overslips, boards, worn, folio — 1808.
(Sotheby's, New Bond
    Street) $2,925   £1,300

LABORDE, LEON DE
'Voyage de l'Arabie Petree' — engraved title with vignette, 65 plates, and maps, mostly on India paper, a few double page or folding, somewhat foxed, cont. green half morocco gilt, covers very worn, large folio — Paris, 1830.
(Sotheby's, New Bond
    Street) $675   £300

LACLOS, PIERRE A. F. CLOSDERLOS DE
'Les Liaisons Dangereuses' — translated into English by Ernest Dowson, 2 vols., no. 712 of 1,020 copies, plates by 'Alastair' (H. H. Voight), original wrappers, spotted, backstrips creased, unopened — The Black Sun Press, Paris, 1929-30.
(Christie's S.
    Kensington) $170   £75

LA COLOMBIERE, M. DE
'Les Hommes Illustres et grands Capitaines Francois qui sont Peints dans la Galerie du Palais Royal' — engraved plate of Arms at end and 25 portraits by Heince and Bignon in borders of engraved arms and scenes relating to the subject, leaves browned, ink stains, old calf backed marbled boards, worn and broken, folio — Paris, 1690.
(Christie's, King
    St.) $110   £50

LACOMBE, JEAN DE
'A Compendium of the East being an Account of Voyages to the Grand Indies' — no. 219 of 300 copies, plates, original cloth, folio — Golden Cockerel Press, 1937.
(Christie's S.
    Kensington) $225   £100

LA CONDAMINE, C. M. DE
'Relation Abregee d'un Voyage Fait Dans l'Interieur de l'Amerique Meridionale . . . Nouvelle Edition' — engraved folding frontispiece, 1 engraved folding map, cont. mottled calf, spine gilt, marbled edges — Maestricht, 1778.
(Sotheby's, New Bond
    Street) $290   £130

LA CONQUE, ANTHOLOGIE DES PLUS JEUNES POETES
Nos. 1-11, all published, original wrappers, uncut, half morocco slipcase. Edited by Pierre Louys with poems by him, Verlaine, Mallarme and Swinburne — 1891-92.
(Sotheby Parke Bernet
    Monaco) $8,550   £3,800

LACOSTE, EUGENE
Very attractive collection of 84 watercolour costume designs, 54 for 'Ballet de Sylvia' on India paper some heightened in gold, some with autograph captions, some creasing, all stamped Vente 1909 Eugene Lacoste. Mounted and tipped into a cloth album.
(Sotheby's, New Bond
    Street) $3,600   £1,600

**LACTANTIUS, LUCIUS COELIUS ·
FIRMIANUS**
'Opera' — 208 leaves of 228, 37 lines,
roman and a little greek letter, some
spotting and staining, modern calf backed
boards by McLeish, folio — Johannes de
Colonia and Johannes Manthen, Venice,
1478.
(Sotheby's, New Bond
Street) $495   £220

LACUNA, ANDREAS
'Epitome Galeni' — woodcut devices on
title and last pages, waterstaining, cont.
blindstamped calf over wooden boards,
rebacked, spine preserved, lacks clasps,
folio — Basle, 1551.
(Sotheby's, New Bond
Street) $540   £240

LACY, CHARLES DE L.
'The History of the Spur' — plates, cloth
gilt, 4to — n.d.
(Phillips) $65   £30

LADIES CABINET, THE
Coloured costume plates in 6 vols., cloth —
1844-1846.
(Bonham's) $450   £200

**LADIES' LIBRARY, THE or ENCYCLO—
PAEDIA OF FEMALE KNOWLEDGE IN
EVERY BRANCH OF DOMESTIC
ECONOMY**
2 vols., engraved portraits and 4 plates,
cont. calf, worn — 1790.
(Christie's S.
Kensington) $180   £80

LAET, J. DE
'L'Histoire du Nouveau Monde ou Descrip-
tion des Indes Occidentales' — 1st French
Edn., title printed in red and black, 14
double page engraved maps, illustrations
in text, all coloured by hand, some worm-
ing, restored and rebacked, folio —
Leiden, 1640.
(Sotheby's, New Bond
Street) $4,950   £2,200

**LAFAYETTE, MARSHAL AND
MARQUIS DE**
A.L.s. Paris, 6 Nov. 1830. Ip with endorse-
ment by the Marquis of West Meath,
expressing admiration for the Irish.
(Phillips) $145   £65

LA FONTAINE, J.
'Fables Choisis' — 4 vols., large paper frontispiece and 275 plates after Oudry, cont.
red morocco gilt by Douceur, gilt on sides,
joints repaired, slipcases, folio — Paris,
1755-59.
(Sotheby Parke Bernet
Monaco) $248,625   £110,500

'Contes et Nouvelles' — 2 vols., 2 portraits
and 80 plates after Eisen and others, cont.
red morocco, gilt, exceptionally fine copy
of the Fermiers Generaux Edition —
Amsterdam, Paris, 1762.
(Sotheby Parke Bernet
Monaco) $139,500   £62,000

211

LA FONTAINE

'The Fables . . . translated . . . by Walter
Thornbury' – plates and illus. after
Gustave Dore, cont. half calf, extremities
worn – n.d.
(Christie's S.
    Kensington) $33   £15

'Les Amours de Psyche et de Cupidon' –
large paper, the portrait in two states, 8
plates in three states, each eau forte and
avant la lettre, cont. red morocco gilt, g.e.,
by Bozerain jeune, signed at foot of spine,
bookplate of C. Bardi – Paris, 1795.
(Sotheby Parke Bernet
    Monaco) $36,000   £16,000

LA MORT ET LE MOURANT, Fable CXLIII.

'Fables Choisis' – 4 vols., 1st Edn. of the
Oudry plates, engraved portrait, frontispiece and plates by Oudry, cont. red
morocco, gilt, rebacked, slightly marked,
folio – Paris, 1755-59.
(Sotheby Parke Bernet
    Monaco) $67,500   £30,000

LA FOSSE, J. C. DE

'Premier Livre de Trophees' – 30 fine
engraved plates, including titles, by Le
Canu, Tardieu and Fessard, manuscript
title inserted at the beginning, 19th
century half calf, rubbed, folio – Paris,
circa 1770.
(Sotheby's, New Bond
    Street) $2,025   £900

LALAUZE, A. – OHNET, GEORGES

'Serge Pannine' – 10 etched plates by
Lalauze, a few leaves slightly spotted,
green half morocco, marbled end papers,
t.e.g., original wrappers bound in, by Rene
Kieffer – Ollendorff, Paris, 1890.
(Sotheby's,
    Chancery Lane) $27   £12

RELATION
DE CE QVI S'EST PASSE'
DE PLVS REMARQVABLE
AVX MISSIONS DES PERES
De la Compagnie de IESVS
EN LA
NOVVELLE FRANCE,
és années 1662. & 1663.
Enuoyée au R. P. André Caſtillon, Pro-
uincial de la Prouince de France.

A PARIS,
Chez SEBASTIEN CRAMOISY, Et SEBAST.
MABRE-CRAMOISY, Imprimeurs ordinaires
du Roy & de la Reine, ruë S. Iacques,
aux Cicognes.

M. DC., LXIV.
AVEC PRIVILEGE DV ROY

LALEMANT, JEROME

'Relation de ce qui s'est Passe de plus
Remarquable aux Missions des Peres de la
Compagnie de Jesus en la Nouvelle France
es annees 1662 et 1663' – woodcut device
on title page, half title, light browning,
cont. sheep, rubbed, small 8vo – 1664.
(Sotheby's, New Bond
    Street) $1,690   £750

LAMB, CHARLES

Letters – 2 vols., plates, half green morocco
gilt, t.e.g. – 1892.
(Phillips) $33   £15

212

'Specimens of English Dramatic Poets' —
1st Edn., half title, marginal tear in R8 and
small hole in S7 just affecting text, a few
other leaves with slight tears or perforations,
all but one marginal, a few leaves slightly
spotted, cont. russia, sides gilt with broad
ornate roll borders, floral tool in compartments of spine — 1808.
(Sotheby's
   London) $65   £30

LAMBARD, WILLIAM
'Eirenarcha or of the Offices of the Justices
of Peace' — letterpress title within woodcut border, woodcut arms on verso, device
on penultimate leaf, light soiled, cont.
presentation copy with 'Duties of Con-
stables' — 2 works in one vol., mostly
black letter, early sheep, joints slightly
cracked, rubbed, 8vo — 1582/83.
(Sotheby's, New Bond
   Street) $1,800   £800
'A Perambulation of Kent' — 2nd Edn.,
black letter, title in typographical border,
folding woodcut map, full page, woodcut
map, 19th century inscriptions, maps
shaved, calf, worn, covers detached, small
4to — 1596.
(Sotheby's, New Bond
   Street) $315   £140

LA MOTTE FOUQUET, H. A.
'Ondine . . . illustre par Arthur Rackham'
— limited edition, mounted coloured
plates, original parchment boards, gilt,
slightly rubbed, t.e.g. — Paris, 1912.
(Sotheby Parke Bernet
   Monaco) $3,375   £1,500

LA MOTTE, G. M. DE
'Traite Complet des Accouchements
Naturels' — 1st Edn., old French calf, gilt
back — Paris, 1772.
(Bonham's) $540   £240

LANCASTER, COUNTY PALATINE
Hand coloured showing the Hundreds
showing key, compass rose and large
vignette of Belvoir Castle, approx. 25½ x
31½in. — Greenwood and Co., Feb. 1830.
(Lawrence of
   Crewkerne) $11   £5

LANDOR, A. HENRY SAVAGE
'In the Forbidden Land' — 2 vols., plates,
some coloured, 1 folding map, slightly
torn, illustrations, original cloth, soiled,
worn — 1898.
(Christie's S.
   Kensington) $70   £32

'LANDSCAPE ANNUAL, THE for 1830-
39; and a duplicate of 1837'
Together 11 vols., engraved titles and 236
plates only of 243, some leaves spotted, a
few loose, a vol. with library stamps, original morocco, rubbed, 3 spines worn, 1
cover detached, g.e. — 1830-39.
(Sotheby's,
   Chancery Lane) $495   £220

LANDSCAPE ANNUALS
A Collection of 130 steel engraved plates —
Italian, French and Spanish with other
views — circa 1828-30.
(Tessa Bennett,
   Edinburgh) $75   £35

LANDSEER, SIR EDWIN
'Selections from the Work of Sir Edwin
Landseer' — 1 vol. only, 25 coloured
mounts, occasional slight browning,
original portfolio, soiled, folio — n.d.
(Christie's S.
   Kensington) $65   £28
'The Works' — 2 vols., steel engraved
plates, illustrations, red morocco gilt,
slightly rubbed, folio — J. S. Virtue and
Co. — n.d.
(Christie's S.
   Kensington) $135   £60

LANDSEER, THOMAS
'Monkeyana' — 6 parts each comprising 4
fine etchings on India paper plus title,
original engraved wrappers, 2 advert leaves
— 1827.
(Tessa Bennett,
   Edinburgh) $180   £80

LANDSEER, THOMAS AND BARROW, JOHN HENRY
'Characteristic Sketches of Animals' —
additional engraved title and 32 engraved
plates, engraved text vignettes, frontis
and engraved title spotted, Tyrconnel
bookplate, cont. half green calf, short
cracks in hinges, rubbed, folio — 1832.
(Sotheby's
   London) $200   £90

LANDT, REV. G.
'A Description of the Faroe Islands' – one folding map, two plates, some spotting, cont. calf, rebacked, covers detached – 1810.
(Christie's S.
   Kensington)   **$135**   **£60**

LANG, ANDREW
'Ballads and Lyrics of Old France' – 1st Edn., 500 copies printed, slightly spotted, original cloth gilt, somewhat stained, uncut – 1872.
(Sotheby's,
   Chancery Lane)   **$27**   **£12**
'Books and Bookmen' and 'The Library' – cloth – 1892 and 1881.
(Tessa Bennett,
   Edinburgh)   **$30**   **£14**

'The Yellow Fairy Book' – 1st Edn., no. 107 of 140, large paper copy, numerous illustrations by H. J. Ford, original boards, worn and soiled – 1894.
(Sotheby's,
   Chancery Lane)   **$125**   **£55**

LANGHAM, W.
'The Garden of Health' – 2nd Edn., cont. calf rubbed, the Burton Constable copy – 1653.
(Sotheby Parke Bernet
   Monaco)   **$2,700**   **£1, 200**

LANGLEY, BATTY
'The City and Country Builder's and Workman's Treasury of Design' – 200 engraved plates, some spotted, title repaired in fold, cont. sheep, rebacked, slightly worn – 1770.
(Sotheby's, New Bond
   Street)   **$245**   **£110**

L'ARBALETE
Revue de Litterature, nos. 2, 5, 6 and 8-13, nine issues, some limited editions, contributions by Hemingway, Kafka, Lorca, Henry Miller and others, original wrappers, uncut, Marc Barbezat, Lyon, 1941-48.
(Sotheby's,
   Chancery Lane)   **$155**   **£70**

LARIONOV, MIKHAIL
Charcoal caricature of Diaghilev and Prokofiev, mounted, framed and glazed, exhibited at Edinburgh Festival in 1954.
(Sotheby's, New Bond
   Street)   **$1,800**   **£800**

LARKHALL, DICK
'London by Night or Gentlemen's Complete Guide to all the Fun, Frolic and Amusement of which this little village abounds' — folding coloured frontispiece by Cruikshank, original cloth, 16 mo. — 1841.
(Sotheby's, New Bond
  Street) $405   £180

'L'ART DE BIEN TRAITER . . . PAR L.S.R.'
some dampstaining, cont. morocco, joints slightly split, head of spine chipped — Lyon, Chez Claude Bachelu, 1693.
(Christie's S.
  Kensington) $180   £80

LATHAM, JOHN
'A General History of Birds' — 10 vols., one of a few copies on large paper with plates on Papier Velin, engraved plates, coloured and finished by hand, cont. green half morocco, gilt spines, g.e. — Winchester, 1821-24.
(Sotheby Parke Bernet
  Monaco) $76,500   £34,000

LATHBURY, JOHN
'Liber Moralium Super Threnis Ieremiae' — 292 leaves, 40 lines and headline, double column, gothic letter, fine woodcut border of birds, flowers and foliage, in a fine cont. Oxford binding blindstamped calf over wooden boards in a very fine state of preservation, vellum endpapers, some lower edges uncut, folio — Theodoricus Rood, Oxford, 31 July, 1482.
(Sotheby's, New Bond
  Street) $56,250   £25,000

LATIN BIBLE
Double column with the prologue of Jerome, the first defective, also index initials supplied in red, rubricated stamped calf, paste downs from early plainsong ms. folio, w.a.f. (probably Basel, J. Amerbach 1B 37927).
(Phillips) $170   £75

LATROBE, C. I.
'Journal of a Visit to South Africa' — 1st Edn., 16 plates including 12 hand coloured aquatints, lacking the folding map, disbound, some leaves detached — 1818.
(Sotheby's, New Bond
  Street) $270   £120

LAUGHLIN, JAMES (Editor)
'New Directions in Prose and Poetry' — vols. 1 and 2, contributions by Cummings, Henry Miller, Pound, Gertrude Stein and others, original wrappers on boards — Norfolk, Conn., 1936-37.
(Sotheby's,
  Chancery Lane) $45   £20

ÉLÉGIE FRATERNELLE
par
André SALMON

LAURENCIN, MARIE
'Eventail' — with poems by Andre Breton, Max Jacob and others, 10 etched plates by Laurencin, original wrappers, soiled, backstrip worn — Paris, 1922.
(Sotheby's,
  Chancery Lane) $740   £330

LAURENT, HENRI
'Le Musee Royal' — 2 vols., 161 engraved plates, one heavily browned, some spotting, cont. half morocco, rubbed, g.e., folio — Paris, 1816-18.
(Christie's S.
  Kensington) $1,170   £520

LAURENT

LAURENT, PETER EDMUND
'Recollections of a Classical Tour Through Greece, Turkey and Italy' – 2 vols., 2nd Edn., 4 hand coloured aquatint plates, half titles, cont. calf, worn – 1822.
(Sotheby's, New Bond
    Street) $190   £85

LAVATER, CASPAR
'L'Art de Connaitre les Hommes par la Physionomie' – 10 vols., engraved portrait and numerous engraved plates, occasional foxing, late 19th century morocco backed boards, some worn – Paris, 1806-09.
(Sotheby Parke Bernet
    Monaco) $5,625   £2,500

LAWRENCE, ADA AND G. STUART GELDER
'Early Life of D. H. Lawrence' – 1st Edn., limited to 749 copies, this copy unnumbered, illustrations, original parchment, unopened, dust jacket – G. Orioli, Florence, 1931 (1932).
(Sotheby's,
    Chancery Lane) $55   £25

LAWRENCE, D. H.
'David' – 1st Edn., limited to 500 copies, slightly spotted, original cloth – 1926.
(Sotheby's,
    Chancery Lane) $27   £12
'Lady Chatterley's Lover' – 1st Edn., no. 859 of 1,000 copies, signed by the author, somewhat spotted, original boards, soiled, upper joint split, lacking foot of spine, uncut – Privately Printed, Florence, 1928.
(Sotheby's,
    Chancery Lane) $170   £75
'Look! We have come through' – 1st Edn., original cloth, soiled, faded, spine torn – 1917.
(Christie's S.
    Kensington) $14   £6

LAWRENCE, RICHARD
'Elgin Marbles from the Parthenon at Athens' – 1st Edn., 50 etched plates, list of subscribers, slight browning, cont. green morocco, gilt, rubbed, g.e., oblong folio – 1818.
(Sotheby's, New Bond
    Street) $290   £130

LAWRENCE, T. E.
'More Letters to Bruce Rogers' – limited to 300 copies, original cloth, slightly marked, dust jacket – Privately Printed, 1936.
(Sotheby's,
    Chancery Lane) $495   £220
'Secret Despatches from Arabia' – No. 969 of 1,000 copies, portrait, original morocco backed cloth, soiled – Golden Cockerel Press, 1939.
(Christie's S.
    Kensington) $245   £110
'Seven Pillars of Wisdom' – 1st published Edn., no. 2 of 750 copies, portraits, plates, folding maps and facsimiles, original pigskin backed buckram gilt, slightly rubbed and soiled, t.e.g. – 1935.
(Sotheby's,
    Chancery Lane) $110   £50

LAYARD, A. H.
'The Monuments of Nineveh' – first series only, 101 plates, a few coloured, some spotting, marginal fraying and soiling, unbound as issued in original portfolio, worn, folio – 1849.
(Christie's S.
    Kensington) $380   £170
'Nineveh and Its Remains' – 2 vols., 6th Edn., plates and maps, some folding, illustrations in text, slight spotting, cont. polished calf, labels, spines gilt, slightly rubbed – 1854.
(Sotheby's, New Bond
    Street) $40   £18

LEAR, EDWARD
'Journal of a Landscape Painter in Corsica' – wood engraved illustrations and 40 plates, 1 map, occasional spotting, original cloth, spine torn, inner hinges worn – 1870.
(Christie's S.
    Kensington) $145   £65
'Illustrated Excursions in Italy' – vol. 2 only, 25 lithographed plates, one map, original cloth, disbound – 1846.
(Christie's S.
    Kensington) $380   £170

LE BEAU GARCON OU LE FAVORI DE FORTUNE
2 parts in one vol., 1st Edn., cont. half calf, repaired, worn, Marie Antoinette's copy with her arms on side – London and Paris, 1784.
(Sotheby Parke Bernet
    Monaco) $10,800   £4,800

LEBEGUE, LEON – LECLERC, MARC
'La Passion de Notre Frere le Poilu' –
coloured frontispiece, in form of tryptych
and illustrations by Lebegue, blue
morocco backed cloth, original pictorial
wrappers bound in – Paris, 1918.
(Sotheby's,
   Chancery Lane) $20   £9

LEBEGUE, LEON – STRAPAROLA,
G. F.
'Les Facetieuses Nuits' – 50 plates by
Lebegue, coloured by hand, pictorial
initials, red half morocco, t.e.g., original
wrappers bound in – Carrington, Paris,
1908.
(Sotheby's,
   Chancery Lane) $40   £18

LE BLANT, JULIEN – MAISTRE,
XAVIER DE
'Les Prisonniers du Caucase' – etched
vignette on title, 8 illustrations by Muller
after Le Blant, dark brown morocco gilt,
inlaid border of red, light green and dark
green, inside borders gilt, silk doublures,
t.e.g., original wrappers bound in, slipcase
–Librairie des Amateurs, Paris, 1897.
(Sotheby's,
   Chancery Lane) $67   £30

LEBRUN, N.
'Petite Bibliotheque pour les Enfants' – 3
vols., original wrappers – Dresden, 1827.
(Phillips) $65   £30

LE BRUYN, CORNELIUS
'Travels into Muscovy, Persia and Part of
the East Indies' – 2 vols., 1st English Edn.,
engraved frontispiece, portrait, 3 engraved
double page maps, 262 engravings on 139
plates, cont. calf, rubbed, folio – 1737.
(Sotheby's, New Bond
   Street) $585   £260

LECKY, W. E. H.
'History of England' – 8 vols., half
morocco gilt – 1878.
(Phillips) $70   £32

LECOMTE, H.
'Costumes Civils et Militaires de la
Monarchie Francaise' – 2 vols., 380 hand
coloured plates, half morocco, gilt, folio –
Paris, 1820.
(Sotheby's, New Bond
   Street) $855   £380

LECTIONARY FOR THE USE OF ST.
GERMAIN D'AUXERROIS in Paris in
Latin
Mss. on paper, written in black ink in fine
sloping italic script, decorative head
pieces, tail pieces, initials etc. throughout,
red morocco, richly gilt, in fine condition,
g.e. – Paris, 1760.
(Sotheby Parke Bernet
   Monaco) $67,500   £30,000

LEE, HARRY
List of books, two copies, one with U.S.
prices, 11 volumes in five, some with
illustrations, original wrappers or folders
with original wrappers bound in – circa
1925-40.
(Sotheby's,
   Chancery Lane) $65   £30

LEE, NATHANIEL
'The Rival Queens or the Death of
Alexander the Great' – 1st Edn., cropping,
modern half cloth – 1677.
(Sotheby's, New Bond
   Street) $22   £10

LEFEBURE, F.
'Livre Nouveau de Toutes Sortes D'Orfev-
ries' – 11 of 12 engraved plates, each with
a view (St. Denis, Pont de Rouen etc.)
Mounted in a vellum album, on flyleaf
a charcoal sketch of a woman by Helleu,
signed – Paris, 1700?
(Sotheby Parke Bernet
   Monaco) $18,000   £8,000

LE GALLIENE, R.
'The Romance of Perfume' – decorated
boards and drawings by George Barbier
– New. York and Paris, 1928.
(Tessa Bennett,
Edinburgh) $22   £10

LEGER, FERNAND– RIMBAUD, A.
'Les Illuminations' – Preface de Henry
Miller, 15 full page lithographs by Leger,
6 coloured through stencils, red and black
morocco, covers centrally divided and
decorated in green and scarlet morocco,
t.e.g., original wrappers bound in, slipcase by Rene Kieffer, Grosclaude,
Lausanne, 1949.
(Sotheby's,
Chancery Lane) $1,395   £620

**LEICHHARDT, FRIEDRICH WILHELM
LUDWIG**
'Journal of an Overland Expedition in
Australia from Moreton Bay to Port
Essington' – 7 engraved plates, 7
engravings in text, publisher's advertise-
ments at beginning and end, original green
ribbed cloth, rebacked – 1847.
(Christie's
St. James) $270   £120

LEIGH, CHARLES
'The Natural History of Lancashire,
Cheshire and the Peak in Derbyshire' –
engraved portrait, laid down, 24 plates,
1 double page map, hand coloured in
outline, cont. calf rubbed and rebacked,
folio – Oxford, 1700.
(Christie's S.
Kensington) $155   £70

LEIGH, DOROTHY
'The Mother's Blessing or the Godly
Counsell of a Gentlewoman' – some tears
and browning, spots and stains, slightly
rubbed, 12 mo – Robert Allot, 1634.
(Sotheby's, New Bond
Street) $110   £50

LEIGH, PERCIVAL
'Manners and Customs of Ye Englishe
Drawn . . . by . . . Doyle' – 2 vols. in one,
plates by R. Doyle, slight soiling, inner
margin of title torn, cont. half calf, worn,
front inner hinge split – n.d.
(Christie's S.
Kensington) $35   £15

LEIGHTON, J.
'Strath Clutha or the Beauties of the
Clyde' – engraved plates, half calf – J.
Swan, Glasgow, n.d.
(Tessa Bennett,
Edinburgh) $50   £22

LELEND, C. G.
'Gypsy Sorcery and Fortune Telling' –
illustrations, some spotting, original
cloth, worn – 1891.
(Christie's S.
Kensington) $40   £18

**LE LIVRE DE MILLE NUITS ET UNE
NUIT**, Translated Dr. J. C. Madrus
16 vols., no. 23 of 25 copies on vellum,
slightly soiled, original wrappers, front
covers decorated by Georges Barbier,
dated 1928 – Editions de la Revue
Blanche, Paris, 1899-1904.
(Sotheby Parke Bernet
Monaco) $65,250   £29,000

**LELOIR, LOUIS – MOLIERE, JEAN
BAPTISTE**
'Theatre Complet' – 8 vols., etched por-
trait, 30 plates by Flameng after Leloir,
mauve morocco, inside borders gilt,
marbled endpapers, t.e.g. original wrap-
pers bound in, by R. Thevenet –
Librairie des Bibliophiles, Paris, 1876.
(Sotheby's,
Chancery Lane) $360   £160

LEMAIRE, MADELEINE – HALEVY, LUDOVIC
'L'Abbe Constantin' – 18 coloured plates and 18 head and end pieces by Madeleine Lemaire, blue morocco, red morocco doublures, flowered silk endleaves, g.e., original wrappers bound in, morocco backed slipcase, by B. Lebaron – Calmann Levy, Paris, 1888.
(Sotheby's,
   Chancery Lane) $18   £8

LEMBERGER, ERNST
'Portrait Miniatures of Five Centuries' – coloured plates, original vellum gilt – n.d.
(Phillips) $65   £28

LEMERY, LOUIS
'A Treatise of all sorts of Food . . . translated by D. Hay' – title in red and black, worming, cont. sprinkled sheep, rubbed, 8vo – 1745.
(Sotheby's, New Bond
   Street) $170   £75

LE MUET, PIERRE
'Maniere de bien bastir pour toutes sortes de personnes' – 2 parts in one vol., 2nd Edn., device on printed title, plates, mostly double page, numerous full page engravings, washed copy, some minor repairs, recent panelled calf, gilt, folio – Paris, 1647.
(Sotheby's, New Bond
   Street) $425   £190

LENAU, NICOLAUS, pseudonym of Nicolaus Niembusch, 1802-50.
Autograph verses entitled 'Sucht, Sucht' comprising 26 lines written on both sides of an octavo sheet and signed at end.
(Sotheby's, New Bond
   Street) $2,700   £1,200

LEO, JOHANNES, AFRICANUS
'Historiale Description de l'Afrique' – 2 vols in one, titles with woodcut borders, 2 double page engraved folding maps, slightly soiled, woodcut illustrations in text, modern calf, spine gilt with red morocco label, folio – Par Jean Temporal, Lyons, 1556.
(Christie's
   St. James) $720   £320

LEONARDO, DOMENICO
'Le Delizie Della Villa Castellazzo' in verso – 24 double engraved plates, cont. vellum, trifle worn, vellum – Milan, 1743.
(Sotheby Parke Bernet
   Monaco) $68,625   £30,500

LEONARDO DA VINCI
'Traite de la Peinture' – 31 plates, late 18th century cont. dark blue morocco, gilt, gilt edged, de Bure's copy with his collations and inscription – Paris, 1716.
(Sotheby Parke Bernet
   Monaco) $14,625   £6,500

LE PAUTRE, P.
'Livre de Tables qui sont dans les Apartemens du Roy sur Lesquelles sont Posee les Bijoux du Cabinet des Medailles' – 6 double engraved plates, 19th century red morocco gilt by Hardy – Chez Daigremont, Paris, circa 1700.
(Sotheby Parke Bernet
   Monaco) $8,550   £3,800

LERMONTOV, MIKHAIL YURIEVITCH
'A Song about Tsar Vasilyevitch' – no. 732 of 750 copies, decorations, format and binding designed by Paul Nash, original morocco, dampstained – The Aquila Press, 1929.
(Christie's S.
   Kensington) $50   £22

LEROQUAIS, ABBE V.
'Le Breviaire de Philippe le Bon' – 2 vols., no. 413 of an edition of 900 on papier velin fort, 20 fine colour plates and 102 black and white plates, large paper loose in card portfolio, a bit worn – Brussels, 1929.
(Sotheby Parke Bernet
   Monaco) $900   £400

LEROUX, AUGUSTE – FLAUBERT, GUSTAVE
'Un Coeur Simple' – etched frontispiece, 4 plates and 17 illustrations, blue half morocco, slightly rubbed, t.e.g., original wrappers bound in, Paris, 1913.
(Sotheby's,
   Chancery Lane) $54   £24

LEROY, W. D.
Six catalogues in five vols., 47 plates, original wrappers or folders with original wrappers bound in, somewhat worn, and one other – Boston, circa 1896-1910.
(Sotheby's,
   Chancery Lane) $235   £105

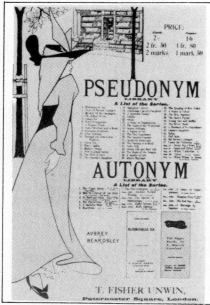

**'LES AFFICHES ETRANGERES
ILLUSTRES'**
A large bound volume containing 62 litho-
graphic plates by various European,
American and Japanese artists, includes
Beardsley, Private Livemont, Will Bradley
etc., together with half tone illustrations –
G. Boudet, Paris, 1897.
(Sotheby's
   Belgravia)   **$1,395**   **£620**

LES ARTS
Numbers 1-180 in 28 vols., plates, illustra-
tions, cont. cloth, slightly soiled – 1902
-19.
(Christie's S.
   Kensington)   **$70**   **£32**

LESLIE, CHARLES
'Philalethes', A view of the Times, their
Principles and Practices – vol. II-IV of 4
in one vol., original issues, 148 of 150 nos.,
2 titles, 3 with prefaces and indexes, lacks
1st title and last 2 nos., occasional light
browning, a few small dampstains in upper
blank margins, cont. panelled calf, Signet
Arms, gilt on sides, slightly worn, folio –
11th October 1707-26 March 1709.
(Sotheby's
   London)   **$135**   **£60**

**LETTRES CABALISTIQUES . . . Entre
deux Cabalistes divers Esprits elementaires
et le Seigneur Astaroth'** – 7 vols., New Edn.,
cont. calf, joints worn – The Hague, 1754.
(Christie's S.
   Kensington)   **$85**   **£38**

LEUSDEN, JOHANNES (Editor)
'Liber Psalmorum' Hebrew and Latin –
woodcut ornamentation on title, old
ownership inscription, 19th century calf
backed boards, worn – Balthasar Lobee,
Utrecht, 1688.
(Sotheby's, New Bond
   Street)   **$125**   **£55**

LE VACHER DE CHARNOIS
'Costumes et Annales des Grands Theatres
de Paris' – 48 issues in two volumes, large
paper, 46 engraved plates, many hand
coloured, 10 engraved leaves of music,
cont. mottled calf, spines gilt with red and
green morocco labels – Paris, 1786.
(Christie's
   St. James)   **$855**   **£380**

LEVASSEUR, VICTOR
'Atlas National Illustre des 86 Departe-
ments et des Possessions de la France' –
title, statistical table and 98 maps, hand
coloured in outline and with ornamental
surrounds and vignettes, tears and a little
soiling, original morocco backed boards,
worn, partly disbound, folio, Paris, 1856.
(Christie's S.
   Kensington)   **$405**   **£180**

LEVINSON, ANDRE
'Serge Lifar, destin d'un Canseur' – no. 21
of 80 copies on velin d'arches of edition
limited to 1,930 copies, frontispiece after
Picasso, 60 plates, signed inscription by
Lifar, dated Paris, 1935, original printed
wrappers, unopened – Paris, 1934.
(Sotheby's, New Bond
   Street)   **$75**   **£35**

LEWIN, WILLIAM
'The Birds of Great Britain' – 2nd Edn.,
8 vols. in 2, large paper copy, titles and
text in English and French, frontispiece
and 336 hand coloured engraved plates,
full levant morocco, spines gilt in six
compartments with raised bands, g.e.
(Christie's
   St. James)   **$9,000**   **£4,000**

LEWIS, CHARLES G. (Engraver)
'Landscapes British and Foreign' – 30
engraved plates, dust soiled, original
cloth gilt, g.e., worn, oblong folio – Art
Union of London, 1874.
(Sotheby's, New Bond
  Street) $495   £220

LEWIS, G. GRIFFIN
'The Practical Book of Oriental Rugs' –
plates, some coloured, original cloth,
slightly soiled, t.e.g. – Philadelphia, 1921.
(Christie's S.
  Kensington) $65   £30

LEWIS, S.
'The Topographical Dictionary of Scotland'
– hand coloured map of Scotland in sections, cloth – London, 1846.
(Tessa Bennett,
  Edinburgh) $60   £26
'Lewis Atlas Comprising the Counties of
Ireland' – engraved title, contents leaf, 33
maps, hand coloured in outlines, one fold-
ing and slightly repaired, a few lightly
soiled, original cloth, faded, spine torn,
free endpapers lacking – 1840.
(Christie's S.
  Kensington) $85   £38
'A Topographical Dictionary' – 44 hand
coloured maps only, of 45, 12 folding,
some torn spotting, cont. cloth, covers
detached, spine lacking – circa 1840.
(Christie's S.
  Kensington) $110   £50

LEWIS, W.
'The Roaring Queen' – one of 30 copies
with original etching by Michael Ayrton
signed by Mrs. Lewis, Walter Allen and
Michael Ayrton, buckram, in slipcase –
1973.
(Bonham's) $65   £30
'The Art of Being Ruled'; 'Time and
Western Man'; 'The Childermass' – 1st
Edn., original cloth, spines faded –
1926/27/28.
(Sotheby's,
  Chancery Lane) $110   £48
'The Enemy – A Review of Art and
Literature' – Edited by Wundham Lewis,
no. 2, two copies, illustrated and cover
design by editor, rather worn, covers
detached – 1927.
(Sotheby's,
  Chancery Lane) $65   £28

LHUYD, EDWARD
'Archaeologica Britannica . . . an account
of the languages, histories and customs of
the original inhabitants of Great Britain' –
vol. I, 1st Edn., engraved Sheldonian
device on title page, cont. panelled calf,
gilt, folio – 1707.
(Sotheby's, New Bond
  Street) $155   £70

LHUYD, HUMPHREY
'Commentarioli Britannicae Descriptionis
Fragmentum' – woodcut device on title,
a few ms. notes in text, some leaves slightly
spotted, lacking final blanks, later vellum,
label, slightly soiled – Cologne, 1572.
(Sotheby's
  London) $200   £90

LIBRETTI
An Attractive Collection of 60 Opera and
Ballet Libretti performed at the Teatro
della Pergalo, Florence between 1815 and
1834, vignettes and arms on title pages,
named cast lists, uniformly bound in cont.
red straight grained morocco for Ferdinand
III and Leopold II, Dukes of Tuscany, with
their gilt arms on covers – Florence, 1815-
34.
(Sotheby's, New Bond
  Street) $1,460   £650

LIBRETTI
Important and very interesting collection
of approximately 670 libretti of operas
and ballets collected by Jeanne Charles,
the dancer. Many first editions, some with
woodcut and lithographed ornaments,
vignettes, headpieces and initials. Many
with original and cont. wrappers, some
in cont. cloth backed boards, some spotted
and stained and some incomplete – 1614-
1896.
(Sotheby's, New Bond
  Street) $12,500   £5,550

LIEBNIZ, GOTTFRIED WILHELM VON
Autograph letter signed, in German, 2
pages, quarto, Berlin, February, 1703,
to an unnamed Count, thanking him for
his letter. Slight staining, splitting at
centre fold.
(Sotheby's, New Bond
  Street) $2,925   £1,300

LIFAR, SERGE

'Pensees sur la Danse' – no. 446 of 450
copies of an edition limited to 755 copies,
signed by publisher, 7 lithographed
plates after Aristide Maillol, original stiff
printed wrappers, uncut, folio – Paris,
1946.
(Sotheby's, New Bond
    Street)   **$125**   **£55**

'LIFE AND ADVENTURES OF THREE FINGERED JACK, THE TERROR OF JAMAICA'

Etched folding frontispiece, coloured by
hand, original wrappers, slightly spotted,
backstrip torn, uncut – Orlando Hodgson,
1830.
(Sotheby's,
    Chancery Lane)   **$65**   **£28**

LIFE AND LETTERS

Edited by Desmond MacCarthy and
others – No.s 1-64 with some missing and
73 duplicates, 128 issues, contributions
by Max Beerbohm, Robert Graves, Thos.
Hardy, Aldous Huxley, Virginia Woolf and
others – 1928-35.
(Sotheby's,
    Chancery Lane)   **$70**   **£32**

LIGHT, HENRY

'Travels in Egypt, Nubia, Holy Land, Mount
Libanon and Cyprus ... 1814' – 1st Edn.,
19 engraved plates, 1 folding engraved map,
woodcut vignettes in text, slight browning
and soiling, cont. half calf, worn – 1818.
(Sotheby's, New Bond
    Street)   **$290**   **£130**
'Sicilian Scenery' – large paper copy,
English and French text, 62 plates on
India paper, in two states, first state of
one plate missing, slight spotting and
soiling, brown half roan, very worn, folio
– 1823.
(Sotheby's, New Bond
    Street)   **$225**   **£100**

LIGHTFOOT, JOHANNES

'Horae Hebraicae et Talmudicae in
Quattuor Evangelistas' – title printed in
black and red, engraved frontispiece,
original parchment – Leipzig, 1683.
(Sotheby's, New Bond
    Street)   **$100**   **£45**

LILIAS, ZACHARIAS

'Orbis Breviarium' – 1st Edn., 130 leaves,
26 lines, roman letter, full page red painted geographical diagrams, woodcut device
on last page, 19th century stained vellum
– Florence, 1493.
(Sotheby's, New Bond
    Street)   **$2,025**   **£900**

L'IMAGE

Nos. 1-12 bound in one volume, one wood
engraving by Lucien Pessarro, wood
engraved illustrations after Mucha, Vallaton,
de Feurem Schwabe and others, morocco
backed boards, original wrappers bound in
at end, t.g.e. – Paris, 1896-97.
(Sotheby's,
    Chancery Lane)   **$720**   **£320**

LIMBORCH, P.
'History of the Inquisition' – 2 vols. in
one, plates, half calf gilt, 4to – 1731.
(Phillips) $125   £55

LINDLEY, JOHN
'The Ornamental Flower Garden and
Shrubbery' – 4 vols., 288 coloured plates,
a few folding, occasional spotting, cont.
morocco backed cloth – 1853.
(Christie's S.
   Kensington) $1,685   £750

LINDLEY, JOHN AND EDWARDS, S. T.
'Botanical Register: or Ornamental Flower
Garden and Shrubbery' – one vol. only,
69 hand coloured plates, 3 folding, 1
detached, cont. cloth backed boards,
soiled – 1839.
(Christie's S.
   Kensington) $360   £160

LINDSAY, W. S.
'History of Merchant Shipping and Ancient
Commerce' – 4 vols., plates and maps,
some spotting, unopened, original cloth
rubbed, 8vo. – 1874-76.
(Phillips) $180   £80

LINK, WILLIAM
'The Hudson by Daylight' – original pictorial boards, 16 plates and other illus.
adverts., large folding coloured map of
River from New York Bay to head of tide
water, extending to approx. 7ft.6in. –
1878.
(Lawrence of
   Crewkerne) $65   £30

LINNAEUS, SIR CHARLES
'A Genuine and Universal System of
Natural History' – 7 vols., engraved por-
trait and numerous hand coloured engraved
plates, cont. tree calf, two covers detached
– 1802-06.
(Christie's
   St. James) $1,350   £600

LINSCHOTEN, JAN HUYGEN VAN
'Histoire de la Navigation de Jean Hugues
de Linschot Hollandois; Aux Indes
Orientales' – 3 parts in one vol., 3rd
enlarged edition, engraved titles, portrait,
30 of 36 double and folding engraved
plates, torn, repaired, worming, cont.
vellum, slightly soiled, folio – Evert
Cloppenburgh, Amsterdam, 1638.
(Sotheby's, New Bond
   Street) $245   £110

LISZT, F.
'F. Chopin' – 1st Edn., morocco, worn,
presentation note from the author to
Delacroix mounted at front and a note to
this provenance inserted – Paris, 1852.
(Sotheby Parke Bernet
   Monaco) $20,250   £9,000

LITTLE, A.
'Anthology of Modern Irish Verse' –
selected by Lennox Robinson, 1st Edn.,
limited to 300 copies, original linen
backed boards, spine slightly soiled, uncut,
unopened – Cuala Press, Dublin, 1928.
(Sotheby's,
   Chancery Lane) $50   £22

LIVINGSTONE, D.
'Missionary Travels and Researches in South
Africa' – maps and plates, folding map in
pocket at end, 1st Edn., second issue, cloth,
inner joints worn – 1857.
(Bonham's) $55   £25

LIVY
'T. Livius Patavinus Historicus' – R.
Ascham's copy, with his signature, some
notes by him, stained and thumbed,
sprinkled calf covers, folio – J. Schoffer,
Mainz, 1518.
(Christie's, King
   St.) $5,175   £2,300

LIZARS, D.
'Edinburgh Geographical Atlas' – in original parts, lacking some, 53 hand coloured maps, folio – circa 1840.
(Phillips) $145   £65

LIZARS GUIDE TO THE EDINBURGH₁ AND NORTHERN RAILWAY
Text and folding map with vignettes, ₁tes, cloth cover, gilt, folio – circa 1850.
(Tessa Bennett,
  Edinburgh) $100   £44

LIZARS, W. H.
'New Edinburgh School Atlas' – 35 hand coloured maps, some soiling, a few marginal tears, original cloth, rebacked – Edinburgh, n.d.
(Christie's S.
  Kensington) $65   £28

LIZARS, W. H. AND BROWNE, JAMES
'Picturesque Views of Edinburgh' – engraved title and 51 plates, some leaves slightly spotted and soiled, later half morocco, slightly rubbed – Edinburgh, 1825.
(Sotheby's,
  Chancery Lane) $145   £65

L.J.A.
'Le Livre d'Or des Familles ou la Terre Sante Illustree' – 58 tinted lithographed plates, one folding map – Brussels, 1849.
(Christie's S.
  Kensington) $145   £65

LOBEL-RICHE – BAUDU, RENE
'Agora' – 23 etched illustrations by Lobel-Riche, 8 full page, unsewn in original wrappers, folder, slipcase – Le Compte des Auteurs, Paris, 1925.
(Sotheby's,
  Chancery Lane) $40   £18

LOBO, JERONYMO
'Voyage Historique d'Abissinie . . . Traduite du Portugais . . . Par M. Le Grand' – title printed in red and black, engraved frontispiece, 2 folding maps, some browning, cont. vellum boards, soiled – Paris and The Hague, 1728.
(Sotheby's, New Bond
  Street) $215   £95

LOCKE, JOHN
'Some Familiar Letters between Mr. Locke and Several of his Friends' – slight browning, modern half calf – 1708.
(Sotheby's, New Bond
  Street) $135   £60

LOCKHART, R. H. BRUCE
'Jan Masaryk' – a personal memoir, no. 32 of 100 copies signed by the author, specially bound, one plate, original blue niger morocco, dust jacket – The Dropmore Press, 1951.
(Christie's S.
  Kensington) $45   £20

LOCOMOTIVE GAME OF RAILROAD ADVENTURES
Aquatint sheet remounted on linen and coloured by hand, spiral track with 48 illustrations around a large illustration of Britannia, very slightly soiled, original cloth gilt folder, soiled – Edward Wallis, 1840.
(Sotheby's,
  Chancery Lane) $260   £115

LODGE, EDMUND
'Portraits of Illustrious Personages of Great Britain . . . with Biographical and Historical Memoires' – vols. I-III of four, 1st Edn., 180 engraved portraits, slight spotting, modern red calf morocco, gilt, g.e., folio – 1821-28.
(Sotheby's, New Bond
  Street) $90   £40

LOGAN, JAMES
'Scottish Gael' – 2 vols., 2 coloured frontispieces, plates, some coloured, quarter calf gilt – 1831.
(Phillips) $65   £28

LOGGAN, DAVID
'Oxonia Illustrata' — 1st Edn., engraved throughout, 40 double page engraved plates, some tears, cont. English red morocco gilt, roll tooled sides, early 19th century Carew bookplate and later morocco book label of Vernon Watney, folio — Oxford, 1675.
(Christie's, King
St.) $2,025   £900

'LONDON INTERIORS'
2 parts in one vol., engraved additional title and plates, cont. half calf, slightly rubbed, n.d.
(Christie's S.
Kensington) $55   £25

LONDON MAGAZINE, THE
Edited by John Lehmann and Alan Ross — vols. 1-8, new series vols. 1-11 with some missing, indexes and 296 duplicates, together 502 issues, contributions by T. S. Eliot, Louis MacNeice, William Plomer, Philip Larkin, Ted Hughes and others, illustrations, original wrappers — 1954-1971.
(Sotheby's,
Chancery Lane) $200   £90

LONGUS
'Les Amours Pastorales de Daphnis et de Chloe' — printed on vellum, 29 specially coloured gouache plates, cont. French red morocco, silk liners, by Bradel with his ticket, folio, Prince Galitzin copy — Paris, 1787.
(Sotheby Parke Bernet
Monaco) $247,500   £110,000

LORY, GABRIEL
'Voyage Pittoresque de Geneve a Milan par le Simplon' — 2nd Edn., 30 hand coloured aquatint plates of 35, half title, stained and holed, cont. straight grained half morocco, worn and loose, spine detached — Basle, 1819.
(Sotheby's, New Bond
Street) $6,750   £3,000

LOUDON, MRS. JANE
'British Wild Flowers' — 60 coloured plates, slight tears, some leaves spotted, original cloth gilt, slightly faded, upper hinge weak, uncut — 1847.
(Sotheby's, New Bond
Street) $785   £350

LOUDON, J. C. (Editor)
'An Encyclopaedia of Plants' — illustrations, original boards, soiled and rubbed — 1836.
(Christie's S.
Kensington) $40   £18

LOUNGER, THE
A periodical paper edited by Henry Mackenzie — nos. 1-101 bound in one vol., spotted, cont. half backed boards, rubbed, folio — Edinburgh, 1785-87.
(Sotheby's, New Bond
Street) $335   £150

LOUTHERBOURG, P. J. DE
'The Romantic and Picturesque Scenery of England and Wales' — coloured title, 18 coloured aquatint plates, cont. half red morocco, folio — 1805.
(Sotheby's, New Bond
Street) $1,235   £550

LOUYS, PIERRE
'Aphrodite' — 3 vols. in two, 2 engraved frontispieces, 14 engraved or dry point illustrations, half morocco, t.e.g., by Gauche — Davidoff, Tiflis, 1928.
(Sotheby's,
Chancery Lane) $85   £38
'Oeuvres Choisis' — 10 coloured plates, unsewn in original wrappers, uncut, folder, slipcase — Paris, 1950.
(Sotheby's,
Chancery Lane) $45   £20
'Poesies Erotiques' — 72 illustrations printed in bistre, unsewn in original wrappers, uncut, unopened, slipcase damaged — Rome, 1937.
(Sotheby's,
Chancery Lane) $78   £35

LOUYS

'Les Chansons de Bilitis' – no. 6 of 25 copies only, numerous fine illustrations by George Barbier, cont. cream morocco, chemise and slipcase, binding in Jansenist style by G. Crette with two coloured originals mounted inside covers in gilt and platinum borders, g.e., – Pierre Bouchet, Paris, 1929.
(Sotheby Parke Bernet
    Monaco) $607,500 £270,000

LOW, FRANCES H.
'Queen Victoria's Dolls' – coloured illustrations by Allan Wright. Original cloth, slightly rubbed – 1894.
(Christie's S.
    Kensington) $50   £22

LOW, Lt. C. R.
'Her Majesty's Navy' – 3 vols., illus., half morocco gilt – n.d.
(Phillips) $245   £110

LOWE, E. J.
'Beautiful Leaved Plants' – 60 coloured plates, occasional light spotting, original cloth, spine clipped at foot – 1864.
(Christie's S.
    Kensington) $75   £35

'Ferns: British and Exotic' – 8 vols., new edition, coloured plates, occasional spotting in a few vols., original cloth, soiled, some inner hinges cracked, ex library copy – 1872.
(Chrsitie's S.
    Kensington) $135   £60
'Our Native Ferns' – 2 vols., coloured plates, cloth gilt – 1874-1869.
(Phillips) $85   £38

LOWNDES, WILLIAM
'A Report containing an Essay for the Amendment of the Silver Coins' – 1st Edn., some foxing, 18th century calf, rubbed, joints worn – 1695.
(Christie's, King
    St.) $225   £100

LUCAS, MRS. E. (Translator)
'Fairy Tales' by Hans Christian Andersen – coloured frontispiece, decorated title and 90 illustrations by Charles Robinson, Thos. Heath Robinson and William Heath Robinson, 38 full page, original pictorial cloth designed by Charles Robinson, slightly worn, t.e.g. – Dent, 1899.
(Sotheby's,
    Chancery Lane) $125   £55

LUCAS, F. E.
'Gilgamesh, King of Erech' – no. 176 of
500 copies, full page illustrations by
Dorothea Braby, original cloth, t.e.g. –
Golden Cockerel Press, 1948.
(Christie's S.
   Kensington) $27   £12

LUCAS, F. L. (Editor)
'The Golden Cockerel Greek Anthology' –
limited to 206 copies, this no. 7 of 80 with
20 illustrations and bound by Zaehnsdorf,
frontispiece and full page illustrations by
Lettice Sandford, original half morocco,
slipcase, t.e.g., folio – Golden Cockerel
Press, 1937.
(Christie's S.
   Kensington) $315   £140

LUCANUS, M. A.
'Pharsalia. Translated into English Verse by
Nicholas Rowe' – 1st Edn., of this trans-
lation, engraved vignette on title, engraved
initials, lacks frontis, cont. calf, joints split
– Printed for Jacob Tonson, 1718 (1719).
(Sotheby's
   London) $33   £15

LUCOCK, B.
'Jamaica; Enslaved and Free' – cloth –
1846.
(Phillips) $36   £16

LUCRETIUS CARUS, TITUS
'Breve Spositione di Tutta l'Opera di
Lucretio' – wormed throughout, cont.
parchment, upper cover split – Pietro
Paganini, Venice, 1589.
(Christie's S.
   Kensington) $45   £20

LUDLOW, CAPTAIN WILLIAM
'Bengal troops on the line of march – a
panoramic sketch by an officer of that
army' – lithographed strip of text in
three columns, coloured lithographed
title, finished and coloured by hand, and
19 coloured lithographed strips all cut
and mounted in an album, oblong folio –
circa 1840.
(Sotheby's, New Bond
   Street) $900   £400

LUGAR, ROBERT
'Villa Architecture – a collection of
buildings executed in England, Scotland
etc.' – 42 engraved plates and plans
including many coloured aquatints, modern
half calf, folio – 1828.
(Sotheby's, New Bond
   Street) $1,125   £500

LUKE, SAINT
'The Birth of Christ from the Gospel according to Saint Luke' – no. 117 of 370 copies,
frontispiece and full page illustrations by
Noel Rooke, original morocco backed
boards, t.e.g. – Golden Cockerel Press,
1925.
(Christie's S.
   Kensington) $70   £32

LUMSDEN, ANDREW
'Remarks on the Antiquities of Rome and
its Environs' – 1st Edn., engraved portrait,
12 plates and plans, 48 fine original watercolour drawings by Martorana of Rome,
some foxing and offsetting, cont. dark
blue straight grain morocco gilt, rubbed,
g.e. – W. Bulmer sold by G. Nicol, 1797.
(Sotheby's, New Bond
   Street) $2,925   £1,300

LUNARDI, VINCENT
'An Account of the First Aerial Voyage in
England' – author's signature on title, 2nd
Edn., 2 folding diagrammatic plates,
stitched as issued, 8vo – 1784.
(Christie's
   St. James) $200   £90

LUPI, ANTONIUS MARIA
'Dissertatio et Animadversiones ad Nuper
Inventum Severae Martyris Epitaphium' –
15 engraved plates, 7 folding, 5 engravings
and numerous illustrations in text, slightly
dampstained, cont. limp vellum, slightly
worn, folio – Palermo, 1734.
(Sotheby's, New Bond
   Street) $100   £45

**LURCAT, JEAN – SUPERVIELLE,
JULES**
'La Fable du Monde' – 34 coloured lithographs and cover designs by Lurcat, 5
double page, 4 on sub titles, remainder in
text, 3 of which are double page, unsewn
in original wrappers, uncut, vellum backed
boards, folder, slipcase, slightly rubbed,
folio. – Andre et Pierre Gonin, Lausanne,
1956.
(Sotheby's,
   Chancery Lane) $340   £150

LUSHINGTON, HENRIETTA
'Hacco the Dwarf or The Tower on the
Mountain' – 1st Edn., 4 wood engraved
plates after G. J. Pinwell, original cloth
gilt, recased, spine soiled, g.e. – Griffith
and Farran, 1865.
(Sotheby's,
Chancery Lane) $25 £12

LUSSICH, A. D.
'Celebrated Shipwrecks' – half calf –
Monte Video, 1894.
(Phillips) $245 £110

LUTHER, MARTIN
'A Commentary on St. Paul's Epistle to
the Galatians' – folio, cont. calf, rubbed,
morocco label, advertisements – M. Lewis,
1774.
(Lawrence of
Crewkerne) $18 £8

LUYKEN, JAN
'Icones Biblicae Veteris and N. Testament'
– engraved double page title and 56 double
page plates of 61, worming in lower blank
margin, bound with 8 plates by Van der
Gucht after James Thornhill and engraved
dedication and tapestry design by Picart,
18th century calf, spine and hinges worn,
folio – P. Mortier, Amsterdam, 1708.
(Christie's, King
St.) $380 £170

LYALL, ALFRED
'Rambles in Madeira and Portugal, in the
Early Part of 1826' – 1st Edn., engraved
folding map, lacking first leaf, a few
leaves slightly spotted, upper hinge weak,
cont. half calf, slightly worn, upper joint
just torn – 1827.
(Sotheby's
London) $65 £30

LYDEKKER, RICHARD
'The Royal Natural History' – 6 vols., 70
of 72 coloured lithoed plates only, 2
slightly torn, one detached, illustrations,
original cloth, slightly rubbed – 1893-96.
(Christie's S.
Kensington) $55 £25
'Wild Oxen, Sheep and Goats' – no. 115
of 500 copies, signed by publisher, 28
hand coloured plates by J. Smith, illus.
original cloth, soiled, 4to – Rowland
Ward, 1898.
(Christie's S.
Kensington) $855 £380

LYDGATE, JOHN (Translator)
'The Auncient Historie and Onely Trewe
and Syncere Cronicle of the Wars Betwixte
the Grecians and the Troyans' –
woodcut historiated title, woodcut initials,
antique style morocco by Mounteny in
morocco case, g.e., folio – T. Marshe, 1555.
(Christie's, King
St.) $3,600 £1,600

LYDIS, MARIETTE
'Lettres de La Religieuse Portugaise' – 8
lithographed illustrations, 7 full page by
Lydis, unsewn in original wrappers, uncut,
unopened – Hazan, Paris, 1947.
(Sotheby's,
Chancery Lane) $40 £18

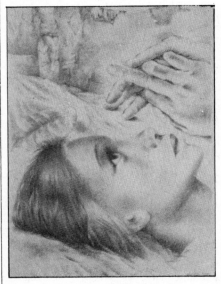

'Lettres de La Religieuse Portugaise' – 8
lithographed illustrations by Lydis, 7 full
page, unsewn in original wrappers, uncut,
folder, slipcase, folio – Fernand Hazan,
Paris, 1947.
(Sotheby's,
Chancery Lane) $190 £85

**LYDIS, MARIETTE – BAUDELAIRE,
CHARLES**
'Petits Poemes en Prose' – 22 etched
plates by Lydis, unsewn in original wrap-
pers, uncut, unopened, cloth box – Aux
Presses de la Cite, Paris, 1948.
(Sotheby's,
Chancery Lane) $260 £115

LYDIS, MARIETTE — MONTHERLANT, HENRI DE
'Les Jeunes Filles' — 12 coloured lithographed plates by Lydis, unsewn in original wrappers, unopened, morocco backed box, slipcase — G. Govone, Paris, 1938.
(Sotheby's,
  Chancery Lane) $470   £210

LYDIS, MARIETTE — VERLAINE, PAUL
'Parallelement' — 15 dry point plates by Lydis, unsewn in original wrappers, uncut, folder, slipcase — Guillot, Paris, 1949.
(Sotheby's,
  Chancery Lane) $135   £60

LYLY, JOHN
'Sixe Court Comedies' — first collected edn., second state of title, lower marginal worming, cont. vellum binding with blindstamped royal arms and a couplet in cont. hand, 12 mo. — 1632.
(Sotheby's, New Bond
  St.) $245   £110

LYNA, F.
'Le Mortifiement de Vaine de Rene d'Anjou Plaisance de Rene d'Anjou' — no. 513 of an edition 830 on papier velin fort, 10 coloure plates, 32 black and white plates, wrappers, unopened, in cardboard folio — Paris, 1926.
(Sotheby Parke Bernet
  Monaco) $225   £100

LYNDEWODE, WILLIAM
'Constitutiones Prouinciales, Editio Princeps' — 348 leaves of 350, gothic type, double column, 46 and 60 lines, rubricated throughout, calligraphic initial in red and blue, many ms. notes and alterations in cont. hand, some damage, cont. calf over wooden boards, severely wormed and defective, folio — Theodoric Rood, Oxford, 1483.
(Christie's, King
  St.) $42,750   £19,000

LYON, CAPTAIN C.
'Narrative of Travels in Northern Africa' — folding hand coloured map and 17 hand coloured plates, cont. calf gilt, 1st Edn. — 1821.
(Tessa Bennett,
  Edinburgh) $290   £130

LYSON, REV. DANIEL
'The Environs of London' — gilt and blind-stamped calf, with 83 vignettes, maps and plates as called for, many extra plates, a number folding, some foxing — 1796-1800.
(Lawrence of
  Crewkerne) $225   £100

LYSON, REV. DANIEL AND LYSONS, SAMUEL
'Magna Britannia — volume the fourth including Cumberland' — 1st Edn., 42 engraved plates, including 1 county map, offset, spotting, cont. calf by J. Clarke, gilt border, spine gilt, morocco labels, gilt dentelles — 1816.
(Sotheby's, New Bond
  Street) $100   £45
'Magna Britannia' — 6 vols., engraved plates and maps, some coloured, others folding, cont. half calf, slightly rubbed — 1806-22.
(Sotheby's,
  Chancery Lane) $720   £320

LYTTLETON, GEORGE COURTNEY
'The History of England' — 3 vols., engraved frontispieces and plates, some soiling, folding maps, first few leaves of vol. I creased, frontispiece and title of vol. II detached, cont. tree calf, extremeties rubbed, upper cover of vol. II detached, joints cracked, folio — 1805.
(Christie's S.
  Kensington) $27   £12

M

M . . . .
'L'Art de Rendre les Femmes Fidelles' –
2 parts in one volume, cont. quarter calf
by de Raci of Versaillies, worn, Marie
Antoinette's copy with her arms gilt on
sides, later in Stuart de Rothesay collection
– Geneva and Paris, 1779.
(Sotheby Parke Bernet
　　Monaco)　　　$18,450　　£8,200

M. W.
'The Queen's Closet Opened' – 3 parts in
one vol., 4th Edn., 7 leaf bookseller's
catalogue at end, one leaf of cont. mss.
recipes tipped in, cont. sheep, worn,
spine split, soiled – 1658.
(Sotheby's
　　London)　　　$250　　　£110

McADAM, JOHN LOUDON
'Remarks on the Present System of Road
Making' – 1st Edn., modern half pigskin,
8vo – Bristol, 1816.
(Sotheby's, New Bond
　　Street)　　　$585　　　£260

MACAULAY, KENNETH
'The History of St. Kilda' – 1st Edn., folding engraved map, half title, slight dampstaining, 19th century half calf, rubbed
– 1764.
(Sotheby's, New Bond
　　Street)　　　$245　　　£110

McBEY, J.
'Etchings and Dry Points from 1902 to
1924' – catalogue by Martin Hardie,
quarter reversed leather, signed etched
frontispiece and other plates, limited edition
452/525 copies – Colnaghi, 1925.
(Tessa Bennett,
　　Edinburgh)　　　$170　　　£75

McCOY, F.
'Natural History of Victoria' – 2 vols.,
200 plates, mostly coloured cloth, 8vo –
Melbourne, 1885-90.
(Sotheby's, New Bond
　　Street)　　　$495　　　£220

EMBL. XVI.
Aliud idem.

Vn'altro il medefimo.

MACCIO, PAULO
'Emblemata' – engraved title, dedicatory
engraving of the Virgin, 81 engraved
emblematic sepia plates, uncut, soiled,
some offsetting, modern morocco –
Bologna, 1628.
(Christie's, King
　　St.)　　　$1,000　　　£450

MACCULLOCH, JOHN
'A Description of the Western Islands of
Scotland' – 3 vols., 1st Edn., 43 engraved
plates and maps, 3 folding, 10 hand
coloured, half titles, signature of Sarah Tyrconnel on titles,
Tyrconnel bookplate, cont. calf and half
calf, Tyrconnel crest on text vol., worn –
1819.
(Sotheby's
　　London)　　　$245　　　£110
'Remarks on the Art of Making Wine' – 2nd
Edn., corners shaved, cont. diced calf,
modern spine label – 1817.
(Christie's S.
　　Kensington)　　　$85　　　£38

MACDONAGH, DONAGH
'Veterans and Other Poems' – 1st Edn., no.
163 of 270 copies, original linen backed
boards, uncut, unopened – Cuala Press,
Dublin, 1941.
(Sotheby's,
    Chancery Lane) $21   £10

MACDONAGH, THOMAS AND OTHERS
'Poems of the Irish Revolutionary Brother-
hood' – 1st Edn., original boards, spine
worn, uncut – Boston, 1916.
(Sotheby's,
    Chancery Lane) $22   £10

MACDONALD, GEORGE
'Annals of a Quiet Neighbourhood' – 3
vols., 1st Edn., original cloth, spines soiled,
uncut – 1867.
(Sotheby's,
    Chancery Lane) $215   £95
'Phantastes' – 33 illustrations by Arthur
Hughes, original cloth, slightly rubbed,
t.e.g. – 1905.
(Sotheby's,
    Chancery Lane) $33   £15

'At The Back of the North Wind' – wood
engraved illustrations by Arthur Hughes,
original pictorial cloth gilt, joints slightly
rubbed – 1882.
(Sotheby's,
    Chancery Lane) $80   £35

'Dealings with the Fairies' – 1st Edn.,
engraved frontispiece and 11 plates after
Arthur Hughes, slightly spotted, original
cloth gilt, lower joint slightly worn, g.e.
– 1867.
(Sotheby's,
    Chancery Lane) $380   £170

MACDONALD, CAPTAIN R. J.
'The History of The Dress of the Royal
Regiment of Artillery' – coloured plates,
illustrations, occasional slight spotting,
original cloth backed boards, soiled,
rubbed, large 4to – 1899.
(Christie's S.
    Kensington) $72   £32

MACFARLANE, CHARLES
'Constantinople in 1828' – 2 vols., 2nd
Edn., two hand coloured engraved frontispieces, two double page plates, mounted
on guards, one folding, cont. half calf,
slightly rubbed – 1829.
(Christie's S.
    Kensington) $200   £90

MACGILL, W.
'Old Ross-shire and Scotland' – 2 vols.,
plates, cloth – Inverness, 1909 and 1911.
(Tessa Bennett,
    Edinburgh) $60   £26

McKAY, A.
'History of Kilmarnock' – cloth –
Kilmarnock, 1909.
(Tessa Bennett,
    Edinburgh) $13   £6

MACKENNA

MACKENNA, F. SEVERNE
'Chelsea Porcelain, the Gold Anchor Wares'
– yellow cloth, gilt, 64 plates, signed by
author – Leigh on Sea, 1952.
(Lawrence of
    Crewkerne) $65   £30

MACKENZIE, C.
'Institutions of the Law of Scotland' –
calf, 4th Edn., – J. Watson, Edinburgh,
1706.
(Tessa Bennett,
    Edinburgh) $20   £9

MACKENZIE, GEORGE
'Mac's Mysteries' – catalogue nos. 204 and
2 others unnumbered, presentation copies,
inscribed by the manufacturer to J. B.
Findlay, each being the first catalogue off
the press and 4 others, original wrappers or
folders with original wrappers bound in –
circa 1940-45.
(Sotheby's,
    Chancery Lane) $80   £35

MACKENZIE, SIR GEORGE STEUART
'Travels in the Island of Iceland' – 2nd
Edn., 14 engraved plates, one folding,
including 8 hand coloured aquatints, and
one plate of engraved music, 3 engraved
maps, 1 fading and partly coloured, 4
folding printed tables, half title, one plate
and a few leaves spotted, worn, lacks
upper cover, lower detached – 1812.
(Sotheby's
    London) $380   £170

MACKENZIE, HENRY
'Julia de Roubigne' – 2 vols., some leaves
detached, margins browned, cont. calf –
1777.
(Christie's S.
    Kensington) $72   £32
'The Man of Feeling' – 2nd Edn., cont. calf,
joints worn – 1771.
(Christie's S.
    Kensington) $65   £30

MACKY, JOHN
'Memoirs of the Secret Service of John
Macky Esq., during the Reigns of King
William, Queen Anne and King George I' –
half calf, spine gilt, morocco label, 1st Edn.,
title inscribed De la Bibliotheque de la
Chevalier D'Eon – 1753.
(Lawrence of
    Crewkerne) $45   £20

MACLAREN, ARCHIBALD
'The Fairy Family, a Series of Ballads and
Metrical Tales Illustrating the Fairy
Mythology of Europe' – 1st Edn., engraved
frontispiece, title after Burne-Jones, origi-
nal cloth, spine discoloured – 1857.
(Sotheby's,
    Chancery Lane) $235   £105

MACLEAN, SIR JOHN (Editor)
'The Berkeley Manuscripts' – First series,
3 vols., some spotting, original cloth
backed boards, worn, one cover detached –
Gloucester, printed by John Fellowes for
the subscribers – 1883-85.
(Christie's S.
    Kensington) $33   £15

McNAIR, ROBERT FRENCH
'The Colours of the Grenadier Guards' –
coloured plates, one slightly worn, some
leaves detached, original cloth backed
boards, worn – 1869.
(Christie's S.
    Kensington) $40   £18

MACNEICE, LOUIS
'Blind Fireworks' – 1st Edn., original
cloth – 1929.
(Sotheby's,
    Chancery Lane) $80   £35

MACQUOID, PERCY
'History of English Furniture' – 4 vols.,
plates, some loose, cloth gilt, some
pages in Age of Mahogany stuck together,
4to – 1904-08.
(Phillips) $170   £75

MACROBIUS, AMBROSIUS AURELIUS THEODOSIUS
'In Somnium Scipionis' Libri II 'Eiusdem
Saturnaliorum' Libri VII – 8 woodcuts,
woodcut initials, slightly dampstained,
spotted and soiled – Joannis Soter,
Cologne, 1527.
(Sotheby's, New Bond
     Street) $135   £60

MADOX, THOMAS
'Baronia Anglica; an history of Land
Honors and baronies and on Tenure in
Capite, verified by records' – folio,
calf rebacked, 1st Edn., vignette title,
illus., index – 1736.
(Lawrence of
     Crewkerne) $110   £50

MAETERLINCK, M.
'Hours of Gladness' – translated by da
Mattos, illustrated by Detmold, cloth gilt
– 1912.
(Phillips) $110   £50
Autograph draft of 'L'Ombre des Ailes'
with autograph deletions and corrections,
many passages entirely scored through,
173 numbered pages, dated 10 May, 1936
to August, 1936, octavo.
(Sotheby's, New Bond
     Street) $2,250   £1,000

MAGALOTTI, COUNT L.
'Travels of Cosmo, the Third, Grand Duke
of Tuscany, through England during the
Reign of King Charles the Second' –
engraved portrait frontis, 38 sepia aquatints, half title, cloth covered with paper,
a little rubbed – 1821.
(Sotheby's, New Bond
     Street) $495   £220

MAGRIEL, PAUL
'A Bibliography of Dancing' – 3 vols.
including the two supplements, 1st Edn.,
frontispiece, plates, original cloth and
printed wrappers – New York, 1936-39.
(Sotheby's, New Bond
     Street) $180   £80

MAHRATTA WAR
Mss. journal of a British Naval officer
captured by the French and handed over
to the Indian forces of Hyder Ali – 65 pp.
of quarto journal, modern half calf,
approx. 18,000 words – 1781-82.
(Lawrence of
     Crewkerne) $225   £100

MAILLOL, ARISTIDE
'Daphnis and Chloe' – translated
by George Thornley, 51 woodcut illustrations and 4 initials by Maillol, original
vellum, uncut, slipcase – A. Zwemmer,
1937.
(Sotheby's,
     Chancery Lane) $945   £420

MAILLOL, ARISTIDE – LONGUS
'Daphnis and Chloe' – 48 woodcut
illustrations and 4 initials by Maillol,
unsewn in original wrappers, uncut,
folder, slipcase – Philippe Gonin, Paris,
1937.
(Sotheby's,
     Chancery Lane) $1,035   £460

MAILLOL

MAILLOL, ARISTIDE – OVID
'L'Art d'Aimer' – 12 lithographed plates, 11 woodcut illustrations, 4 initials by Maillol, slightly spotted, unsewn in original wrappers, folder and slipcase, folio – Philippe Gonin, Lausanne, 1935.
(Sotheby's,
    Chancery Lane) $1,530   £680

MAILLOL, ARISTIDE – RONSARD, PIERRE DE
'Livret de Folastries' – 43 etched illustrations by Maillol, including two on covers, unsewn in original wrappers, slipcase, folder, folder with signed pictorial bookplate by V. Fleissig – Editions Ambrose Vollard, Paris, 1939.
(Sotheby's,
    Chancery Lane) $630   £280

MAILLOL, ARISTIDE – VIRGIL
'Les Georgiques' – translated by l'Abbe Jacques Delille, 2 vols., text in Latin and French, 104 woodcut illustrations and 18 initials by Maillol, unsewn in original wrappers, uncut, folder, slipcase – Philippe Gonin, Paris, 1937-50.
(Sotheby's,
    Chancery Lane) $1,350   £600

'The Eclogues' – in original Latin with English prose translation by J. H. Mason, 43 woodcut illustrations, 3 initials, pressmark by Maillol, original cloth backed boards, slipcase – Cranach Press, Weimar, 1927.
(Sotheby's,
    Chancery Lane) $1,215   £540

MAISTRE, X.
'Voyage Autour de ma Chambre' – no. 13 of 20 copies on yellow paper of a total edition of 35, a nice copy in cont. red morocco, sides gilt with a roll of fruiting vine, gilt spine, g.e. – A. A. Renouard, Paris, 1814.
(Sotheby Parke Bernet
    Monaco) $9,000   £4,000

MAITLAND CLUB, THE
An almost complete set of the publications of the Maitland Club, 74 publications in 96 columes, lacking only the first volume of Terry's No. 19 (Criminal Trials) from the regular series of publications, numerous plates, mostly original boards, uncut, some vols. repaired or worn but a sound set – Glasgow and Edinburgh, 1928-59.
(Sotheby's
    Edinburgh) $1,710   £760

MAJORCA
DUCHETTI, CLAUDIO
'Majorca Insula' – engraved map, with
attractive pictures of buildings, hills, etc.,
verso blank – Rome, 1570.
(Sotheby's, New Bond
   Street) $405   £180

MALKIN, BENJAMIN HEATH
'The Scenery, Antiquities and Biography
of South Wales' – 1st Edn., 12 tinted
plates by Laporte, folding engraved map,
half title, 19th century green half morocco,
joints worn, t.e.g., 4to – 1804.
(Sotheby's, New Bond
   Street) $155   £70

MALLARME, S.
'L'Apres-Midi d'Un Faune' – 1st Edn., no.
151 of 195 copies, frontispiece and 3
vignettes, by Edouard Manet, wrappers in
card slipcase, quatrain by Mallarme on
first leaf and a P.C. by him inserted –
Paris, 1876.
(Sotheby Parke Bernet
   Monaco) $65,250   £29,000

MALORY, SIR THOMAS
'Birth, Life and Acts of King Arthur' –
2 vols., illustrated by Aubrey Beardsley,
cloth gilt – 1893.
(Phillips) $180   £80

MALTHUS, REV. T. R.
'Principles of Politicial Economy considered with a view to their Practical
Application' – 1st Edn., slightly spotted,
small hole in margin of X7, another margin
just torn, one leaf with slight stain, cont.
half calf, spine gilt, joints very slightly
worn – 1820.
(Sotheby's
   London) $85   £38

MANDEVILLE, BERNARD
'The Fable of the Bees' – 2 vols. – 1723-24.
'A Letter to Dion' – 1st Edn. – 1732.
Three volumes in two, cont. calf, joints
cracked and covers scuffed, covers of both
waterstained.
(Christie's, King
   St.) $245   £110

MANET, EDOUARD
Early autograph document asking the president of the Academy of Florence for permission to work on the frescoes in the
Church of the Annunziatia for ten days,
one page, no place but Florence, October
1857, slightly browned, integral blank.
(Sotheby's, New Bond
   Street) $540   £240

**MANET, EDOUARD – MALLARME,
STEPHANE**
'L'Apres Midi d'un Faune' – 1st Edn., wood
wood engraved frontispiece, head and
endpiece and ex libris after Manet, original
wrappers, worn and soiled, black and white
silk ties, folio – A. Derenne, Paris, 1876.
(Sotheby's,
   Chancery Lane) $2,360   £1,050

MANIN, LEONARDO CONTE
'Memorie Storico-critiche Intorno la Vita,
translazione e invenzioni di S. Marco
Evangelista, Principale Protettore di
Venezia' – 2nd Edn., 6 plates, 4 double
page, cont. boards, uncut, folio – Venice,
1835.
(Sotheby's, New Bond
   Street) $35   £16

MANN, THOMAS
'Der Tod in Venedig, Novelle' – presen-
tation copy, inscribed by author, original
cloth, spine slightly faded – Berlin, 1930.
(Sotheby's,
   Chancery Lane) $80   £35

Signed photograph inscribed to Mr. Wm.
W. Seward stamped as proof in two places
but without affecting the face, 25 x 20cm.
(Sotheby's, New Bond
   Street) $270   £120

MANNING, FREDERICK
'Her Privates We. By Private 19022' – 1st
Edn., original pictorial cloth – 1930.
(Sotheby's,
   Chancery Lane) $85   £38

MANNING, REV. OWEN AND BRAY,
WILLIAM
'The History and Antiquities of the
County of Surrey' – 3 vols., folio, half
morocco buckram boards, spines gilt, 1st
Edn., 20 engraved plates, 4 plans, 3 folding
tables, catalogues of books on Surrey,
appendix, spotting – 1804-1814.
(Lawrence of
   Crewkerne) $180   £80
MANSFIELD, JARED
'Essays, Mathematical and Physical: contain-
ing New Theories and Illustrations' – 1st
Edn., 13 folding plates, errata leaf, very
foxed, cont. calf, rebacked, 8vo – Wm. M.
Morse, New Haven, 1800.
(Sotheby's, New Bond
   Street) $70   £30
MANSFIELD, KATHERINE
'The Garden Party' – no. 1,183 of 1,200
copies, 16 coloured lithographed illustra-
tions, 10 full page by Marie Laurencin,
original cloth, dust jacket – Officina
Bodoni for the Verona Press, 1939.
(Sotheby's,
   Chancery Lane) $335   £150

MANUSCRIPT
A Manuscript notebook in various hands,
containing instructions for the performing
of dances, receipts for money owed and
received, songs, the symptoms of various
animal ailments and their cures . . . – some
browning, some leaves detached, cont.
calf, worn – late 17th or early 18th
century.
(Christie's S.
   Kensington) $65   £30

MANUSCRIPT
Double page vellum leaf from a service
book, 4 line stave; Cluverius: map of
Africa, partly coloured, 1681 – both
framed and glazed.
(Phillips) $65   £28

MANUSCRIPT
Vespers for the feast of Trinity, 6 folios
with two illuminated initials, one rubbed,
4 line stave; De Lisle double page map of
Near East extending from Libya to the
Indus, partly coloured, some damage in
fold, contained in large folio, 18th century
red morocco binding richly gilt.
(Phillips) $95   £42

MANWOOD, JOHN
'A Treatise and Discourse on the Lawes of
the Forrest' – 1st Edn., light waterstaining,
cont. calf, spine worn – Thomas Wright
and Bonham Norton, 1598.
(Sotheby's, New Bond
   Street) $495   £220

MARCET, MRS. JANE
'Conversations on Botany' – 2nd Edn.,
20 coloured plates, 1 double page, cont.
calf, spine defective, lacks label – 1818.
(Sotheby's, New Bond
   Street) $95   £42
'Conversations on Chemistry' – 2 vols.,
15 plates, calf gilt – 1817.
(Phillips) $100   £45

MARCHAND, PROSPER
'Histoire de l'Origine et des Progres de
l'Imprimerie' – 2 parts in one volume, 1st
Edn., title printed in red and black with
engraved vignette, engraved frontispiece,
slightly dampstained, cont. calf, spine gilt,
slightly worn – The Hague, 1740.
(Sotheby's, New Bond
   Street) $125   £55

MARCUS, JACOB ERNST
'Het Studie-Prentwerk' – 1st Edn., additional engraved title in Dutch and 93 of 105 engraved plates, printed title in French and 6 page biography in French and Dutch, cont. calf backed boards, rebacked, folio – Amsterdam, circa 1850.
(Sotheby's, New Bond
    Street) $855   £380

MARDRUS, J. C. (Translator)
'Le Livre de Mille Nuits et Une Nuit' – 8 vols., coloured plates after Persian miniatures, text within ornamental borders, original morocco backed boards, rubbed, t.e.g., 4to – Paris, n.d.
(Christie's S.
    Kensington) $125   £55

MARGUERITE DE NAVARRE
'Marguerites Suite de Marguerites' – 2 vols., device on titles and last leaves, text illustrations, rubricated, French olive morocco, Madame de Pompadour's copy, with her arms gilt in centre of covers, g.e. – De Tournes, Lyons, 1547.
(Sotheby Parke Bernet
    Monaco) $123,750   £55,000

'Le Nouvelles (Heptameron Francaise)' – 3 vols., 76 plates by Gutenberg and others after Freudenberg, a fine and large copy, bound for Gustavus III King of Sweden in cont. French red morocco, front covers gilt with Swedish royal arms, spines flat gilt with flowers, stars and the Swedish crown, g.e. – Berne, 1780-81.
(Sotheby Parke Bernet
    Monaco) $67,500   £30,000

MARGUERITE DE VALOIS, QUEEN OF NAVARRE
'L'Heptameron' – title within woodcut border, ornamental initials, slight browning, late 18th century russia, rubbed covers detached – Paris, 1560.
(Sotheby's, New Bond
    Street) $450   £200

MARIE ANTOINETTE, QUEEN OF FRANCE
Document authorising payment to six Swiss guards, 1 page, 2 October, 1785 with Louis XVI, King of France, three line autograph subscription to a memorandum on Payments de 1774/75, 1 page, 3 October 1774. Bound with four allegorical engravings of Marie Antoinette and Louis XVI, 19th century blue morocco, richly gilt, arms of Louis XVI in centre of each cover.
(Sotheby Parke Bernet
    Monaco) $15,750   £7,000

MARIE LOUISE, EMPRESS,
Second wife of Napoleon I
Autograph letter signed 'Louise', 4 pages, small octavo, Presburg, 27 August, 1830, to her son William describing her journey from Schonbrunn to Hungary, splitting at centre fold.
(Sotheby's, New Bond
    Street) $405   £180

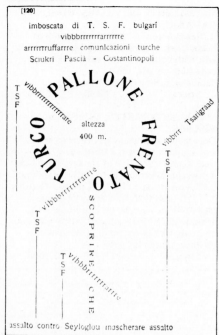

[120]

imboscata di T. S. F. bulgari vibbbrrrrrrarrrrre arrrrrruffarrre comunicazioni turche Sciukri Pascià - Costantinopoli

PALLONE FRENATO TURCO SCOPRIRE CHE

vibbrrrrrrrrrrrare

Tsarigraad

altezza 400 m.

T S F — vibbbrrrr

T S F

T S F — vibbbrrrrrrrrarrre

T S F

assalto contro Seyloglou mascherare assalto

MARINETTE, F. T.
'Zang Tumb Tumb, Adrianopoli Ottobre 1912, Parole in Liberta' – 18th thousand, presentation copy, inscribed by author, portrait, folding sheet, original wrappers with typographical design, slightly worn, uncut – Edizioni Furutiste de Poesie, Milan, 1914.
(Sotheby's,
Chancery Lane) $145   £65

MARINETTE, F. T. AND OTHERS
'I Manifesti del Futurismo' – prima series, 7th thousand original wrappers, uncut – Edizioni di Lacerba, Florence, 1914.
(Sotheby's,
Chancery Lane) $90   £40

MARKHAM, GERVASE
'The English Housewife containing the inward and outward virtues as her skill in Physick, Surgery, Cookery, Extraction of Oyls etc., now and eighth time amended' – some soiling, cont. calf, rebacked – W. Wilson for George Sawbridge, 1664.
(Sotheby's, New Bond
Street) $290   £130

'The Inrichment of the Weald of Kent' – 4th Edn., slight browning, modern calf backed boards, slightly rubbed – 1649.
(Sotheby's
London) $65   £30

MARLIANI, BARTHOLOMEA
'Urbis Romae Topographia' – woodcut device on title and at end, 5 plates and numerous woodcut illustrations in text – Rome, September, 1544.
(Christie's, King
St.) $1,238   £550

MARMONTEL, J. F.
'Didon' – 1st Edn., gilt wrappers, elaborate green morocco binding, gilt arms of Louis XVI on covers – Paris, 1783.
(Sotheby Parke Bernet
Monaco) $15,750   £7,000
'The Shepherdess of the Alps' – 2nd Edn., wood engraved frontispiece, signed E. W. coloured by hand, slightly soiled, marbled wrappers – W. Mason, 1820.
(Sotheby's,
Chancery Lane) $22   £10

MARRYAT, JOSEPH
'A History of Pottery and Porcelain' – 2nd Edn., coloured plates, frontispiece with portions of guard leaf adhering, illustrations, cont. morocco – 1857.
(Christie's S.
Kensington) $45   £20

MARSHALL, WILLIAM
'On Planting and Rural Ornament' – 2 vols., 3rd Edn., some spotting, cont. half calf, rubbed, split joints – 1803.
(Christie's S.
Kensington) $65   £28

MARTIALIS, MARCUS VALERIUS
'Ex Museo Petri Scriverii, Vita per Petrus Crinitus' – engraved title, boards rubbed – Janssonius, Amsterdam, 1630.
(Sotheby's, New Bond
Street) $22   £10

MARTIN, BENJAMIN
'The Natural History of England' – vol. 1 only, engraved maps and plates, most folding, occasional slight spotting, cont. calf, soiled, spine gilt, joints cracked – 1759.
(Christie's S.
Kensington) $360   £160

MARTIN, CHARLES – VALOTAIRE, MARCEL
'Les Artistes du Livre 2; Charles Martin' –
portrait by Dignemont, 16 plates and 16
illustrations, some coloured, unsewn in
original wrappers, uncut, folder, spine
faded – Henry Babou, Paris, 1928.
(Sotheby's,
    Chancery Lane)   **$110**   **£50**

MARTIN, DR. LOUIS
'L'Eschole de Salerne En Vers Burlesque
et Poema Macaronium de Bello Hugenotico'
– engraved title page, slightly spotted and
soiled, cont. limp vellum, lower cover
slightly damaged – J. Henault, Paris, 1653.
(Sotheby's, New Bond
    Street)   **$72**   **£32**

MARTIN, R. MONTGOMERY
'History of the British Colonies' – 5 vols.,
1st Edn., 26 engraved maps, 9 folding, all
but one coloured in outline, advert leaf in
vol. II, half titles, original cloth, partly
unopened, slightly worn – 1834-5.
(Sotheby's
    London)   **$290**   **£130**
'The History, Antiquities, Topography and
Statistics of Eastern India' – 3 vols., plates
and plans, map, hand coloured in outline,
later half calf, rubbed – 1838.
(Christie's S.
    Kensington)   **$125**   **£55**

'The Indian Empire' – 3 vols. in two,
additional titles, plates and maps, spotting,
cont. half morocco, rubbed – n.d.
(Christie's S.
    Kensington)   **$33**   **£15**

MARTIN, THEODORE
'The Life of His Royal Highness, The
Prince Consort' – 5 vols., portrait, plates,
slight worming to title, spotting, cont. red
calf, extremeties slightly rubbed – 1879.
(Christie's S.
    Kensington)   **$40**   **£18**

MARTINEAU, A. AND STEIN, H.
'Nouvel Atlas Illustre de la France et les
colonies' – 120 of 121 coloured maps, 5
double page, 2 folding, torn, original
morocco backed cloth, worn, folio –
Paris, 1902.
(Christie's S.
    Kensington)   **$33**   **£15**

MARTINEAU, HARRIET
'Eastern Life' – 3 vols., cont. half morocco,
spines gilt, extremeties rubbed – 1848.
(Christie's S.
    Kensington)   **$65**   **£28**

MARTY, A. E. – DAUDET, ALPHONSE
'Lettres de Mon Moulin' – coloured vignette
on title, illustrations, decorations and
initials by Marty, original pictorial wrappers,
uncut, slipcase, slightly discoloured – H.
Piazza, Paris, 1940.
(Sotheby's,
    Chancery Lane)   **$40**   **£18**

MARTYN, THOMAS
'Thirty Eight Plates with Explanations . . .
Linnaeus System' – coloured plates, modern
half calf – 1788.
(Phillips)   **$145**   **£65**

MARWICK, J.
'Early Glasgow' – plates, buckram –
Glasgow, 1911.
(Tessa Bennett,
    Edinburgh)   **$11**   **£5**

MASEFIELD, JOHN
'King Cole' – no. 160 of 780 copies
signed by author, illustrations by Judith
Masefield, original parchment backed
boards, slightly soiled, t.e.g. – 1921.
(Christie's S.
    Kensington)   **$33**   **£15**

MASEFIELD

'Poetry' – no. 30 of 275 copies signed by author, original cloth, soiled, t.e.g. – n.d. (Christie's S.
Kensington) $15 £7
'Some Memories of W. B. Yeats' – 1st Edn., no. 83 of 370 copies, frontispiece, original linen backed boards, uncut, unopened – Cuala Press, Dublin, 1940.
(Sotheby's,
Chancery Lane) $70 £32

MASON, MRS. CHARLOTTE

'The Lady's Assistant for Regulating and Supplying her Table' – 3rd Edn., ads on verso of final leaf, some worming, mainly marginal, but no real loss of text, a few ms. notes, cont. sprinkled calf, slightly worn – 1777.
(Sotheby's
London) $135 £60

MASON, G. H.

'The Costume of China' – 59 of 60 hand coloured plates, text in English and French, last page of text loose, half calf worn, covers detached, folio – 1800.
(Phillips) $225 £100

MASON, J.

'Ice World Adventures in the Arctic Regions' – pictorial cloth, folding map – circa 1880.
(Tessa Bennett,
Edinburgh) $9 £4

MASON, J. AND BELLEW

'Plan of North Leith and Plan of the Regality of the Canongate' – hand coloured – 1813.
(Tessa Bennett,
Edinburgh) $22 £10

MASSACHUSETTS, ANCIENT AND HONOURABLE ARTILLERY COMPANY

Souvenir portrait album of members, original red cloth gilt, 425 photographic plates and three other plates – Best Printing Co., Boston, Mass, 1903.
(Lawrence of
Crewkerne) $50 £22

MASSE, H.

'Pewter Plate' – cloth – 1904.
(Tessa Bennett,
Edinburgh) $25 £12

MASSINGER, PHILIP

'A New Way to Pay Old Debts' – 1st Edn., woodcut device on title, margins cropped, holes, occasional staining, dark blue morocco, gilt by Zaehnsdorf, g.e., small 4to – 1633.
(Sotheby's, New Bond
Street) $190 £85

MASSON, ANDRE – MAUROIS, ANDRE

'Les Erophages' – 16 coloured etched plates, 2 etched cover designs by Masson, unsewn in original wrappers, uncut, decorated folder, slipcase worn, folio – Les Editions le Passarelle, Paris, 1960.
(Sotheby's,
Chancery Lane) $380 £170

MASSON, ANDRE – PAULHAM, JEAN

'Les Hain-Teny' – 19 coloured etchings by Masson, comprising vignette on title, 17 plates and cover design, unsewn in original wrappers, decorated folder and slipcase, uncut, folio – Les Bibliophiles de l'Union Francaise, Paris, 1956.
(Sotheby's,
Chancery Lane) $920 £410

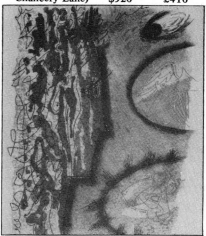

MASSON, ANDRE – SARTRE, JEAN PAUL

'Vingt Deuz Dessins sur le Theme du Desir' – 8 coloured lithographs by Masson, comprising 2 double page plates, 2 full page plates, 2 initials and cover design, 22 reproductions, unsewn in original wrappers, uncut, cloth box, folio – Fernand Mourlot, Paris, 1961.
(Sotheby's,
Chancery Lane) $315 £140

MASSON, L. F. R.
'Les Bourgeois de la Compagnie du Nord
Ouest' – 2 vols., title to first vol. inscribed
by author, modern morocco backed
boards, 8vo – Quebec, 1889-90.
(Sotheby Humberts
    Taunton) $215   £95

'MASTER MUSICIANS' SERIES
Published by Dent, 10 volumes, cloth,
gilt – 1900-1906.
(Tessa Bennett,
    Edinburgh) $6   £3

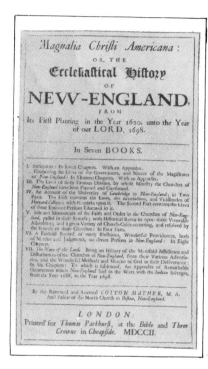

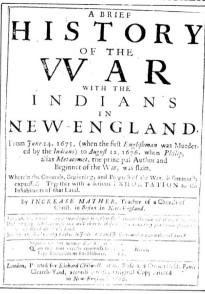

MATHER, INCREASE
'A Brief History of the War with the
Indians in New England' – 1st English
Edn., half title, head margins shaved, blue
morocco by Riviere, g.e., a trifle marked,
small 4to – 1676.
(Sotheby's, New Bond
    Street) $2,925   £1,300

MATHERS, E. POWYS (Translator)
'A Circle of the Seasons, a translation of
the Ritu-Samhara of Kalidasa' – no. 339 of
500 copies, plates by Robert Gibbings,
original cloth, t.e.g. – Golden Cockerel
Press, 1929.
(Christie's S.
    Kensington) $90   £40

'Love Night' – no. 91 of 200 copies, illustrations by John Buckland Wright, some
full page, original parchment backed cloth,
t.e.g. – Golden Cockerel Press, 1936.
(Christie's S.
    Kensington) $145   £65

'Maxima and the Considerations of Cham-
fort' – 2 vols., no. 91 of 550 copies,
original boards, dust jackets spotted and
torn, vol. 1 unopened – Golden Cockerel
Press, 1926.
(Christie's S.
    Kensington) $55   £25

MATHER, COTTON
'Magnalia Christi Americana or the
Ecclesiastical History of New England' – 7
parts in vol. 1, 1st Edn., folding engraved
map with medallion watermark with lion,
advertisment at end, cont. panelled calf,
slightly worn, folio – 1702.
(Sotheby's, New Bond
    Street) $2,475   £1,100

MATHERS

'Eastern Art of Love' – coloured plates, 12 vols., cloth gilt, morocco backs, somewhat worn – J. Rodker, 1927-30.
(Bonham's) $55   £25
'Procreant Hymn' – no. 60 of 200 copies, plates by Eric Gill, original cloth, t.e.g. – Golden Cockerel Press, 1926.
(Christie's S.
   Kensington) $335   £150

MATISSE, HENRI – D'ORLEANS, CHARLES

'Poemes' – lithographed throughout in colour with 54 illustrations and decorated pages by Matisse, title and 45 pages of text in his hand within decorated borders, unsewn in original wrappers, lithographed cover designs, uncut, slipcase, folio – Teriade, Paris, 1950.
(Sotheby's,
   Chancery Lane) $400   £380
'Poemes' – lithographed throughout in colour with 43 illustrations and decorated pages by Matisse, title and 45 pages of text in his hand within decorative border, unsewn in original wrappers, lithographed cover design, uncut, slipcase, folio – Teriade, Paris, 1950.
(Sotheby's,
   Chancery Lane) $900   £400

MATISSE, HENRI – RONSARD, PIERRE DE

'Florilege des Amours' – 127 lithographed illustrations by Matisse, printed in bistre, including 2 on covers, 23 full page, slightly offset, unsewn in original wrappers, uncut, velvet backed folder, decorated slipcase – Albert Skira, Paris, 1948.
(Sotheby's,
   Chancery Lane) $2,925   £1,300

MATTA, SEBASTIAN

'Come Detta Dentro Vo Significando' – 22 etched illustrations by author, 4 small illustrations in black, remainder in colour, three double page, each printed in two plates, and 10 are full page, unsewn as issued in original wrappers, slipcase, folio – Editions Meyer, Lausanne, 1962.
(Sotheby's,
   Chancery Lane) $810   £360

MATTHIOLUS, PETRUS ANDREAS

'Commentarii in Sex Libros Dioscoridis' – 2 parts in one vol., numerous woodcut illustrations in text, browned, a little worming, 18th century calf backed marbled boards, worn, folio – Frankfort a-M, 1598.
(Sotheby's, New Bond
   Street) $1,000   £450

MATURIN, CHARLES ROBERT
'Melmoth the Wanderer' with a memoir and
bibliography of works, 3 vols., portrait,
original cloth, slightly worn, uncut, 1892.
(Sotheby's,
    Chancery Lane) $30   £14

MAUCHLINE BINDING
Cabinet Album 'Land of Scott' — 5 vignette
views on front cover, glazed folding views —
n.d.
(Tessa Bennett,
    Edinburgh) $18   £8
Photograph Album, morocco backed
wooden boards, engraved vignette of
Aberfeldy on front cover, small — circa
1900.
(Tessa Bennett,
    Edinburgh) $27   £12

**MAUDIN, BERNARD — GERALDY,
PAUL**
'La Guerre, Madame' — cover design, title
vignette and 27 illustrations by Maudin,
15 full page, 2 double page, dark blue half
morocco, original wrappers bound in —
Paris, 1916.
(Sotheby's,
    Chancery Lane) $9   £4

MAUGHAM, W. SOMERSET
'Cakes and Ale' — no. 648 of 1,000 copies,
signed by author and Graham Sutherland,
original lithographed portrait and illustrations by·Sutherland, facsimiles and original
mushroom and blue calf, t.e.g., slipcase —
1954.
(Sotheby's,
    Chancery Lane) $160   £70
'The Vagrant Mood' — 1st Edn., no. 449 of
500 copies, signed by author, original calf,
t.e.g., unopened, slipcase — 1952.
(Sotheby's,
    Chancery Lane) $110   £48

MAUND, B.
'The Gardener's Edition of the Botanic
Garden' — 12 original parts only, 12
hand coloured plates, original wrappers,
some lacking, most torn. Together with
45 hand coloured botanical plates by E. D.
Smith bound with related text — 1845-46.
(Christie's S.
    Kensington) $270   £120

MAUPASSANT, G. DE
'Contes du Jour et de la Nuit' — 1st Edn.,
illustrated by P. Cousturier, half brown
morocco, gilt, by Lortic, wrapper preserved,
Duchess de Camastra copy — Paris, 1885.
(Sotheby Parke Bernet
    Monaco) $8,550   £3,800
'Des Vers' — 1st Edn., half green morocco,
gilt, by Lemardeley, wrappers preserved,
the Duchess of Camastra copy — Paris, 1880.
(Sotheby Parke Bernet
    Monaco) $1,125   £500

'Contes Choisis' — no. 10 of 25 copies on
Japon, illustrations by G. Jeannoit and
others, portrait, half brown morocco, the
Duchesse de Camastra copy, and an ALs
by the author — Paris, 1886.
(Sotheby Parke Bernet
    Monaco) $3,600   £1,600

MAURY, M. F.
'Physical Geography of the Sea' — 8 folding
plates, original cloth gilt — 1855.
(Phillips) $45   £20

MAWE, J.
'Travels in the Interior of Brazil' — map and
8 plates, one coloured, 4to, cont. calf, title
badly foxed -- 1812.
(Bonham's) $425   £190

MAWE

'Travels in the Interior of Brazil, particularly in the Gold and Diamond Districts of that Country' – 1st Edn., 8 plates, one coloured map, 19th century dark blue half calf, some wear – 1812.
(Sotheby's, New Bond
 Street) $720   £320

MAXWELL, SIR H.

'The Story of the Tweed – title and 20 plates, buckram gilt, folio, limited edition 174/375 copies – 1905.
(Tessa Bennett ,
 Edinburgh) $80   £36

MAYER, LUIGI

'Views in Egypt, Palestine and Other Parts of the Ottoman Empire' – 3 vols. in one, 96 coloured aquatint plates, text and plates watermarked 1801, cont. russia, gilt, rebacked, corners worn, folio – 1804.
(Sotheby's, New Bond
 Street) $2,475   £1,100

MAYHEW, AUGUSTUS

'Paved with Gold' – 1st Edn., engraved additional title, 24 plates only of 25, by H. K. Browne, original cloth, soiled, front inner hinge split – 1858.
(Christie's S.
 Kensington) $15   £7

MAYHEW, HENRY

'The Rhine; Upper Rhine' – together 2 vols., engraved vignette titles and 38 plates by Birket Foster, a few loose and a little soiled, original gilt stamped cloth, soiled – 1856-58.
(Sotheby's,
 Chancery Lane) $790   £350
'The World's Show 1851' – 1st Edn., original cloth, engraved title by Dalziel, 9 folding etched plates by George Cruikshank – 1851.
(Lawrence of
 Crewkerne) $13   £6

MAYNWARING, EVERARD

'Historia et Mysterium Luis Venerae' – 1st Edn., title printed in red and black, browned, 18th century vellum boards, slightly rubbed and soiled – Frankfurt and Hamburg, 1675.
(Sotheby's, New Bond
 Street) $180   £80

MAYORAS, M. H.

'English Needlework Carpets' – some plates coloured, original cloth, dust jacket – Leigh on Sea, 1963.
(Christie's S.
 Kensington) $33   £15

MAZZELIA, SCIPIONE

'Descrittione del Regno di Napoli' – 1st Edn., title with large woodcut device, numerous woodcut coats of arms in text, ms. headings, dampstains, worming, slightly defective, 17th century calf, very worn – Naples, 1586.
(Sotheby's, New Bond
 Street) $110   £50

Hec figura signat-quomodo filius prodig⁹ cũ patre ac suis amicis cenat-que historia mistice cene oñi est repsentatiua ╬ vt sequit ╬

MEDER, JOHANNES

'Quadragesimale Novum de Filio Prodigo' – 1st Edn., 224 leaves of 232, mostly double column, gothic letter, 18 woodcut illustrations, cont. blindstamped pigskin backed boards, small wormholes, cont. signature – Michael Furter, Basle, 1495.
(Sotheby's, New Bond
 Street) $3,825   £1,700

MEDIAEVAL MANUSCRIPTS
50 original leaves from Western Europe,
XII to XVI century, no. 39 of an edition
of 40 sets, descriptive text, in original
buckram box, large folio – circa 1960.
(Christie's, King
   St.) $5,850   £2,600

MEDICI, CARLO DI GABRIELE
Autograph letter, signed, one page, folio,
Florence, August, 1532, to Agostino del
Nero, integral address leaf, part of the
address in the same hand written on ori-
ginal paper tag secured by wafer seal bear-
ing Medici arms, in fine condition.
(Sotheby's, New Bond
   Street) $100   £45

MEDWIN, THOMAS
'Journal of the Conversations of Lord
Byron' – 1st Edn., slight browning, lacking
half title, half roan, rubbed – 1824.
(Sotheby's, New Bond
   Street) $85   £38

MEEK, CHARLES
'The Will to Function' – no. 99 of 300
copies, original cloth, t.e.g. – Golden
Cockerel Press, 1929.
(Christie's S.
   Kensington) $9   £4

MELDOLA, DAVID (Editor)
'Hanhagat Ve'limud Hatalmidim Ve'darchei
Yesod Ha'limud and Darchei Ha'gemara' –
2 parts in one volume, 2nd Edn., cont. calf,
gilt, rubbed – J. Jansson, Amsterdam, 1754.
(Sotheby's, New Bond
   Street) $170   £75

MELFORD, CHARLOTTE
'The Twin Sisters or Two Girls of Nineteen'
– 1st Edn., etched frontispiece coloured by
hand, original printed wrappers, spotted –
Dean and Munday, 1824.
(Sotheby's,
   Chancery Lane) $40   £18

MELOMBRA, G.
'Pratica Universale - di Misurare' – 2
engraved titles, engravings throughout, 2
parts in one vol., vellum, repaired –
Fiorenza, 1630.
(Bonham's) $155   £70

MELUN, MARQUISE DE
'Memoire' – drophead title, cloth, cont. ms.
endorsement at end, the Goncourt copy
with a note by Edmond on flyleaf –
Montalant, Paris, 1750.
(Sotheby Parke Bernet
   Monaco) $225   £100

MELVILLE, L.
'The Fair Land of Gowrie' – plates and
map, cloth – Coupar, Angus, 1939.
(Tessa Bennett,
   Edinburgh) $20   £9

MENDES PINTO, FERDINANDO
'Historia Oriental de las Peregrinaciones' –
1st Spanish Edn., engraved arms on title,
worming, foxing and waterstaining,
running titles shaved, 19th century half
calf, folio – Madrid, 1620.
(Christie's, King
   St.) $495   £220
'The Voyages and Adventures of'. Done
in English by H. C. Gent. 1st English Edn.,
title in red and black, cont. calf, folio –
1653.
(Christie's, King
   St.) $765   £340

MENPES, DOROTHY AND MORTIMER
'Venice' – large white cloth decorated
gilt, t.e.g. bevelled edges, uncut, 100
coloured and tissued plates by Mortimer
Menpes, no. 107 of 500 copies signed
by the artist, a fine copy – A. and C.
Black, 1904.
(Lawrence of
   Crewkerne) $40   £18

MERCIER, LOUIS SEBASTIEN
'New Pictures of Paris' – 2 vols., original
boards spines defective, one cover
detached, uncut – 1800.
(Lawrence of
   Crewkerne) $22   £10

MERCURIALIS

MERCURIALIS, HIERONYMUS
'De Arte Gymnastica Libri Sex' — engraved
title vignette, additional engraved title, 6
folding engraved plates, many full page
woodcuts, cont. calf rebacked —
Amsterdam, 1672.
(Christie's, King
St.)　　　　$202　　£90

MEREDITH, GEORGE
'Jump to Glory Jane' — limited to 1,000
copies, plates and illustrations by Lawrence
Housman, original pictorial boards, slightly
soiled — 1892.
(Christie's S.
Kensington)　　$63　　£28
'Modern Love' — 1st Edn., original cloth,
slightly rubbed — 1862.
(Christie's S.
Kensington)　　$34　　£15

MERIMEE, PROSPER
'Colomba' — red morocco, gilt, slipcase,
by Rene Aussourd, original beige wrappers repaired, bound in — Paris, 1841.
(Sotheby Parke Bernet
Monaco)　　$2,250　　£1,000
'Lettres a la Comtesse de Montijo, mere
de l'Imperatrice Eugenie' — 2 vols., no.
259 of 500 copies on papier velin, plates,
some coloured, rubricated, wrappers,
unopened, bit worn — Paris, 1930.
(Sotheby Parke Bernet
Monaco)　　$225　　£100

MERY, F.
'Les Joyaux, Fantasie . . . Mineralogie
des Dames par le Cte Foelix' — coloured or
tinted plates by Gavarni within paper cut
borders, original violet morocco, gilt, g.e.
— G. de Gonet, Paris, 1850.
(Sotheby Parke Bernet
Monaco)　　$2,700　　£1,200

MESURES
Edited by Henry Church, Bernard Groet-
huysen, Henri Michaux and others,
vol. 1, no. 6, vol. 6, no. 2; vol. 5 lacking
no. 1 and 4, 20 issues, vol. 1 and vol. 2
limited to 1,800 copies, original wrappers
— Paris, 1935-40.
(Sotheby's,
Chancery Lane)　　$130　　£58

METCALF, J. AND CARMICHAEL, J. W.
'Eight Views of Fountains Abbey with a
Historical Description by T. Sopwith' —
8 engraved plates in india paper, marginal
spotting and some fraying, original wrap-
pers, soiled and torn, folio — Ripon and
Newcastle, 1832.
(Christie's S.
Kensington)　　$45　　£20

METEYARD, ELIZA
'The Life of Josiah Wedgwood' — 2 vols.,
portrait, illus., original cloth, soiled,
joints cracked — 1865-66.
(Christie's S.
Kensington)　　$75　　£35

METHODIUS
'Revelationes Divinae a Sanctis Angelis
Factae' — 48 leaves of 68, 36 lines, gothic
letter, numerous woodcuts, worming,
browning, spotting, 19th century boards
slightly worn — Michael Furter, Basle,
1500.
(Sotheby's, New Bond
Street)　　$1,000　　£450

METZ, C. M.
'Imitations of Ancient and Modern Draw-
ings' — tinted and sepia title and 71 plates,
cont. half calf, joints split, folio — 1789.
(Christie's S.
Kensington)　　$145　　£65

MEURSIUS, JOHANNIS
'Elegantiae Latini Sermonis seu Aloisa
Sigea Toletana de Arcanis Amoris et
Veneris' — engraved title and frontispiece,
18th century mottled calf, gilt spine, g.e. —
Elsevier, Leyden, 1774.
(Christie's, King
St.) $65   £30

MEYER, FRANZ
'Marc Chagall, Life and Work' — translated
by R. Allen, buckram, over 1,250 illustrations including mounted colour plate,
mint copy — New York, n.d.
(Lawrence of
Crewkerne) $90   £40

MEYRICK, S. AND SMITH, C.
'The Costume of the Original Inhabitants
of the British Islands' — frontispiece and
24 plates, all hand coloured aquatints,
calf, rebacked, folio — 1815.
(Sotheby's, New Bond
Street) $450   £200

MICHAEL SCOTUS
'Mensa Philosophica' — 50 leaves, 39 lines
and headline, gothic letter, woodcut title,
a few initials, rather stained, blue morocco
by Sangorski and Sutcliffe — Heidelberg,
1489.
(Sotheby's, New Bond
Street) $1,170   £520

MICHELENA, A. — HUGO, VICTOR
'Hernani' — etched portrait frontispiece
after Deveria, 5 plates and 10 illustrations
by L. Boisson after Mechelena, red half
morocco, t.e.g., original wrappers, bound
in by Strodbants — Conquet, Paris, 1890.
(Sotheby's,
Chancery Lane) $25   £11

MIDDLETON, CONYERS
'The History of the Life of Marcus Tullius
Cicero' — 2 vols., 1st Edn., engraved
medallion portrait, headpiece and initial in
each volume, cont. calf, rebacked, some-
what rubbed, bookplate of Charles,
Viscount Bruce of Ampthill — 1741.
(Sotheby's
London) $45   £20

MIDDLETON, J.
'Grecian Remains in Italy' — coloured
aquatints, cont. morocco, worn, folio —
1812.
(Sotheby's, New Bond
Street) $1,350   £600

MIDHURST, SUSSEX
Interesting group of documents concerned
with Midhurst, Didling Dumpford,
Woolbeding etc., folio — 1791.
(Lawrence of
Crewkerne) $360   £160

MIEGE, GUY
'The New State of England' — 3 parts in
one volume, 1st Edn., additional engraved
title, general title signed 'Will. Fleming',
slight browning, cont. mottled calf, rubbed
— 1691.
(Sotheby's
London) $80   £35

MILES, H. D.
'British Field Sports' — plates, some
coloured, cont. half morocco, soiled — n.d.
(Christie's S.
Kensington) $495   £220

MILES, W. J.
'Modern Practical Farriery' — 5 vols., plates,
some coloured, original cloth backed boards,
inner hinges cracked, 4to — n.d.
(Christie's S.
Kensington) $40   £18

MILFORD, JOHN
'Observations . . . Tour Through the
Pyrenees, Switzerland . . .' — 2 vols.,
boards — 1818.
(Phillips) $135   £60

MILITARY LETTERS
2 small folio indexed books containing an
interesting collection of letters concerning
6th Dragoon Guards from War Office and
Horse Guards — 1851 and 1852.
(Tessa Bennett,
Edinburgh) $170   £75

MILL, JOHN STUART
'Elements of Political Economy' — 1st
Edn., calf — 1821.
(Phillips) $360   £160
'Principles of Political Economy' — 2 vols.,
1st Edn., advert at end of vol. I, titles lightly
spotted, a few annotations in pencil, half
calf, gilt, arms of Christ Church, Oxford on
upper covers, extremities rubbed, g.e. —
1848.
(Christie's S.
Kensington) $520   £230

MILLAIS

MILLAIS, J. G.
'Breath from the Veldt' – illus., original
cloth, folio – 1895.
(Phillips) $110   £50
'British Deer and Their Horns' – coloured
frontispiece and 185 text and full page
illustrations, cloth, binding defective,
most leaves loose – 1897.
(Bonham's) $45   £20

MILLAIS, J. G. AND OTHERS
'The Gun at Home and Abroad' – 2
vols., folio, morocco gilt, some staining,
t.e.g., rest uncut, colour and black and
white plates, some dampstaining – 1913.
(Laerence of
    Crewkerne) $180   £80

MILLER, EDWARD
'The History and Antiquities of
Doncaster' – 10 engraved plates and
folding map slightly torn, illus., rather
soiled, original boards, lacks spine, worn,
loose – Doncaster, n.d.
(Sotheby Humberts
    Taunton) $90   £40

MILLER, HENRY
'Black Spring' – 1st Edn., original pictorial
wrappers, slightly worn, uncut – Obelisk
Press, Paris, 1936.
(Sotheby's,
    Chancery Lane) $470   £210
'Tropic of Capricorn' – 1st Edn., errata
slip tipped in on title, original pictorial
wrappers, slightly worn, uncut –
Obelisk Press, Paris, 1939.
(Sotheby's,
    Chancery Lane) $200   £90

MILLER, PHILLIP
'Figures of the Most Beautiful, Useful and
Uncommon Plants' – 306 engraved plates,
coloured by hand, 2 folding, old calf,
broken, 10 pages slightly defective – 1771.
(Bonham's) $2,700   £1,200
'Gardener's Dictionary' – frontispiece and
4 plates loose, half calf worn, folio, 1759.
(Phillips) $145   £65

MILLER, THOMAS (Editor)
'Turner and Girtin's Picturesque Views of
English, Scotch and Welsh Scenery' –
engraved portrait and 30 plates, original
cloth, gilt, spine rubbed, g.e. – 1873.
(Christie's S.
    Kensington) $110   £48

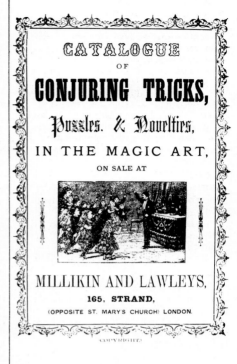

CATALOGUE

OF

CONJURING TRICKS,

Puzzles, & Novelties,

IN THE MAGIC ART,

ON SALE AT

MILLIKIN AND LAWLEYS,

165, STRAND,

(OPPOSITE ST. MARYS CHURCH) LONDON.

(COPYRIGHT)

MILLIKIN AND LAWLEY
Three catalogues, original wrappers, cloth
backstrip, folio – circa 1895.
(Sotheby's,
    Chancery Lane) $360   £160

MILLO, ANTONIO
'Isolario et Portolano di me Antonion
Millo' – showing more than 90 Mediterranean islands, autograph mss. on paper,
97 leaves, in two parts, cont. limp vellum,
soiled, wanting ties – Venice, late 16th
century.
(Sotheby's, New Bond
    Street) $16,875   £7,500

MILNE, A. A.
'When we were Very Young' – no. 43 of
100 copies on hand made paper, signed
by Milne and Ernest H. Shepherd, cloth
backed boards in dust jacket, uncut, small
4to – 1924.
(Christie's
    St. James) $1,575   £700

'Winnie the Pooh' – one of 300 copies signed by Christopher Milne, illus. by Ernest H. Shepherd, red morocco, gilt, g.e., by Zaehnsdorf, cloth slipcase, 8vo – 1976. (Christie's

    St. James) $180   £80

'The House at Pooh Corner' – presentation copy, one of 300 copies on hand made paper, signed by Milne and Ernest H. Shepherd, illus. by Shepherd, cloth backed boards in dust jacket, uncut and unopened, small 4to – 1928. (Christie's

    St. James) $675   £300

MILTON, JOHN
'Works', plates, 2 vols., calf gilt, worn – 1741-42.
(Phillips) $55   £25

I WHO E'RE WHILE
THE HAPPY GARDEN SUNG,
BY ONE MANS DISOBEDIENCE
    LOST, NOW SING
RECOVER'D PARADISE
    TO ALL MANKIND,
BY ONE MANS FIRM OBEDIENCE
    FULLY TRI'D
THROUGH ALL TEMPTATION,
    AND THE TEMPTER FOIL'D
IN ALL HIS WILES,
    DEFEATED AND REPULST,
AND EDEN RAIS'D
    IN THE WAST WILDERNESS.
¶ Thou Spirit who ledst this glorious Eremite
Into the Desert, his Victorious Field
Against the Spiritual Foe, and broughtst him thence
By proof the undoubted Son of God, inspire,
As thou art wont, my prompted Song else mute,
And bear through highth or depth of natures bounds
With prosperous wing full summ'd to tell of deeds
Above Heroic, though in secret done,
And unrecorded left through many an Age,
Worthy t' have not remain'd so long unsung,
¶ Now had the great Proclaimer with a Voice
More awful than the sound of Trumpet, cri'd
Repentance, and Heavens Kingdom nigh at hand
To all Baptiz'd: to his great Baptism flock'd
  12

'Paradise Lost, Paradise Regained'... to which are added Samson Agonistes and Poems both English and Latin' – 2 vols., limited to 315 copies of which this is one of 25 on vellum, original limp vellum, uncut, slipcase, 4to – 1902-05. (Sotheby's,

    Chancery Lane) $1,755   £780

MINIATURE BOOK
'Plaisir et Gaiete' – illus., last leaf cleanly torn, cont. morocco, gilt, 1 x 0.7in. – Paris, Marcilly, 1837. (Christie's S.

    Kensington) $95   £42

MINIATURE BOOK
'The New Testament' – cont. morocco, contained in metal case, 0.7 x 0.6in. – Glasgow, David Bryce and Son, 1895. (Christie's S.

    Kensington) $65   £28

MINIATURE BOOK – GASC. F. E. A.
The smallest French and English Dictionary in the World – original cloth, slightly soiled, in original hinged metal case, 1 x ¾in. – Glasgow, n.d. (Christie's S.

    Kensington) $100   £45

MINIATURE BOOK
'Les Quatre Elemens, l'Eau' – two coloured plates, slight soiling, original decorated boards, slightly soiled, 3¼ x 2in. – n.d. (Christie's S.

    Kensington) $90   £40

MINIATURE BOOK OF HOURS
All in Latin, illuminated mss. on vellum, text complete, 12 historiated initials in burnished gold and full colour, half page miniature with full border. Elaborate Portuguese late 16th century metal binding of ornate silver gilt filigree design of scrolls, springs, etc – North West Italy, probably Milan, 1455-70. (Sotheby Parke Bernet

    Monaco) $146,250   £65,000

MINIATURES

MINIATURES PERSANES EXPOSEES AU MUSEE DES ARTS DECORATIFS JUIN – OCTOBRE 1912
2 vols., no. 7 of an edition limited to 150, 195 plates, 21 in colour, unbound as issued in board portfolio, worn, folio – Paris, 1913.
(Sotheby Parke Bernet
   Monaco)   **$9,000**   **£4,000**

MINORCA
DUCHETTI, CLAUDIO
'De Minorca Insula' – engraved map, attractive pictures of buildings, hills, etc., a few early mss. additions of names, verso blank – Rome, 1570.
(Sotheby's, New Bond
   Street)   **$470**   **£210**

MIRABEAU, H. G. R. COMTE DE
'The Secret History of the Court of Berlin' – 2 vols., 1st English Edn., half titles, cont. calf, joints cracked, gilt – 1789.
(Sotheby's, New Bond
   Street)   **$85**   **£38**

MIRK, JOHN
'Liber Festivalis' – 2 parts in one volume with continuous signatures, 33 lines, double column, black letter, historiated initial, holed, torn, shaved, browned and stained, late 16th century limp vellum, 2 of 4 ties still remaining, worn – Johan Notary, circa 1506.
(Sotheby's, New Bond
   Street)   **$540**   **£240**

MIRO, JOAN – BROSSA, JOAN AND OTHERS
'Obra Inedita Recent' – 11 coloured lithographs by Miro, 4 double page including cover design, remainder full page, unsewn in original wrappers, uncut, cloth folder, slipcase – Barcelona, 1964.
(Sotheby's,
   Chancery Lane)   **$1,460**   **£650**

MIRO, JOAN – ERNST, MAX AND TANGUY, YVES
'L'Antitete' – 3 vols., 23 etched plates by Ernst, Tanguy and Miro, 8 irregularly shaped plates by Miro, limp vellum folders and slipcase, stained – Bordas, Paris, 1949.
(Sotheby's,
   Chancery Lane)   **$11,250**   **£5,000**

'MISSALE AD USUM INSIGNIS ECCLESIAE SARISBURIENSIS'
Woodcut illus., and initials, musical scores, printed in red and black Gothic letter, 2 full page illus., late 17th century mottled calf, rubbed, joints split, folio – Paris, apud Guillelmum Merlin, 1555.
(Christie's S.
   Kensington)   **$8,550**   **£3,800**

'MISSALE ROMANUM'
Title slight rubbed, inner margin torn with a little loss, last leaf pasted down, cont. calf, gilt, worn — Apud Ionnem Moretum, 1605.
(Christie's S.
Kensington)　　$65　　£28

MISSALS
Five volumes of missals with engraved plates, a few tears, one in red morocco gilt and the others in worn calf, 2 spines missing and some covers detached — Paris, Venice and Milan, 17th and 18th century.
(Sotheby's, New Bond
Street)　　$170　　£75

MITFORD, MARY RUSSELL (Editor)
'Findens' Tableau of the Affections' — engraved additional title, original morocco gilt, rubbed, hinges cracked — 1838.
(Christie's S.
Kensington)　　$45　　£20

'The Tableaux. A Series of Graphic Scenes' — plates, some spotting, one leaf detached, original cloth, soiled, folio — J. Hogarth, n.d.
(Christie's S.
Kensington)　　$45　　£20

MODERN TRAVELLER, THE
'Africa' — 3 vols., folding map, plates, half calf gilt — 1829.
(Phillips)　　$45　　£20

'MODERN TRAVELLER, THE, GREECE'
2 vols. only, folding engraved map and 7 plates, a few leaves slightly spotted, cont. half calf — 1826.
(Sotheby's,
Chancery Lane)　　$18　　£8

MOGG, EDWARD
'Paterson's Roads' — half calf, spine gilt, morocco label, 18th Edn., frontispiece general map, 10 plates on 7 folding sheets, additional map of banks of the Wye and course of Chepstow steam packets etc — 1826.
(Lawrence of
Crewkerne)　　$33　　£15

MOLIERE, J. B. P. DE
'Oeuvres' — 6 vols., portrait, plates and vignettes after Boucher and others, cont. French red morocco, gilt, arms in centre of covers, g.e. — Paris, 1734.
(Sotheby Parke Bernet
Monaco)　　$56,250　　£25,000

Complete Works of Moliere, illustrated by Boucher et al.
(Sotheby Parke Bernet, Monaco)

MOLIERE

'Oeuvres' – 6 vols., portrait and 33 plates after Moreau, a fine set in cont. French red morocco, spines gilt a la grotesque, g.e., small bookplate of a crowned eagle – Paris, 1773.
(Sotheby Parke Bernet
   Monaco) $94,500   £42,000

ΜΥΣΚΟΤΟΜΙΑ:
OR, THE
ANATOMICAL
Adminiftration
Of all the
MUSCLES
Of an Humane
BODY,
As they arife in Diffeƈion.

As alfo an Analitical T A B L E, reducing each Mufcle to his Ufe and Part.

Colleƈed for Private ufe,

By WILLIAM MOLINS
Mr. in Chyrurgery:

And Publifhed for the general good of all Praƈitioners in the faid Art.

London, Printed by John Field for Edward Husband, Printer to the Honorable Houfe of Commons, and are to be fold at his Shop at the golden Dragon in Fleetftreet near the Middle

MOLINS, WILLIAM
'Anatomical Administration of all the Muscles of the Humane Body as they arise in Dissection' – 1st Edn., border of printer's ornaments to title page, blank, cont. sheep, worn, spine defective at top and bottom, small 8vo – John Field for Edward Husband, 1648.
(Sotheby's, New Bond
   Street) $855   £380

MOLL, HERMAN
'The North part of Great Britain called Scotland' – a folding linen backed coloured map, buckram folder, a reprint of the 1714 edition – 1896.
(Tessa Bennett,
   Edinburgh) $50   £22
'The North West part of Turkey in Europe' – hand coloured map, lightly mounted – 1726.
(Tessa Bennett,
   Edinburgh) $11   £5

MOLLIEN, GASPARD THEODORE
'Travels in the Interior of Africa to the Sources of the Senegal and Gambia' – edited by T. E. Bewdich, first English Edn., engraved portrait, engraved folding map, 6 aquatint plates, vocabulary and advertisements at end, soiled, offset in places, 19th century half calf, joints and corners rubbed – 1820.
(Sotheby's, New Bond
   Street) $180   £80

MONARDES, NICOLAS
'Joyful newes out of the new found world' – woodcut illustrations, title and Ee1 (last leaf of text) lacking, some leaves detached, staining, stitched – 1577.
(Christie's S.
   Kensington) $160   £70
'La Historia Medicinal de las cosas que se traen de Nuestras Indias Occidentales que Sirven en Medicina' – several woodcuts in text, woodcut devices on one sub title, wormed – Alonson Escrivano, Seville, 1574.
(Sotheby's, New Bond
   Street) $1,015   £450

MONATLICHE UNTERREDUNGEN
'Eineger Guten Freunde von Allerhand Buchern und Andern Annehmlichen Geschlichten – separate title to each of 12 parts, 11 engraved frontispieces, one leaf torn and skilfully repaired, cont. vellum – Jan – Dec. 1698.
(Christie's, King
   St.) $70   £30

MONCRIF, F. A. P. DE
'Moncrif's Cats' – limited to 400 copies, no. 98 of 100 specially bound by Hiscox, plates, original morocco, t.e.g., slipcase – Golden Cockerel Press, 1961.
(Christie's S.
   Kensington) $190   £85

MONGEZ
'Tableaux, Statues . . . de la Galerie de
Florence et du Palais Pitti' − 4 vols. in
2, illus., half morocco gilt, folio − 1789-
1807.
(Phillips) $170   £75

MONKHOUSE, W. COSMO
'The Turner Gallery' − 3 vols., engraved
additional title and plates, some leaves
detached, cont. cloth, affected by damp −
n.d.
(Christie's S
   Kensington) $585   £260
'The Works of Sir Edwin Landseer' −
plates, illustrations, cont. morocco, gilt,
rubbed, g.e., folio − n.d.
(Christie's S.
   Kensington) $145   £65

MONROE, MARILYN
An Album of photographs, some coloured,
press clippings, telegrams, rehearsal sche-
dules and letters, with biographical notes
by David Gray. Mostly mounted or tipped
in, some loose, original rexine, square folio
− America, circa 1953-60.
(Sotheby's, New Bond
   Street) $1,350   £600

MONROE, MARILYN AND COLE, JACK
Black and white negative and 2 photographs
of Monroe and Cole dancing stamped
'Hollywood Accessories Co. 6413
Willoughby Ave.' − 1960.
(Sotheby's, New Bond
   Street) $425   £190

MONTAIGNE, MICHEL DE
'Essays Made English by Charles Cotton' −
3rd Edn., 3 vols., frontis, in 1 and 2, cont.
calf, 8vo − 1700.
(Christie's
   St. James) $65   £30

'Les Essais' − 3 vols., slight browning, cont.
sprinkled calf, labels, spines gilt, rubbed −
Paris, 1725.
(Sotheby's, New Bond
   Street) $250   £110

**MONTALBANO, MARCHESE MARCO
ANTONIO DE LA FRATTA**
'Pratica Minerale' − 1st Edn., woodcut
device on title, additional engraved title,
21 full page engraved plates, 7 engraved
illustrations, all in sepia, some waterstaining, modern half calf − Bologna, 1678.
(Christie's, King
   St.) $520   £230

MONTANUS, ARNOLDUS
'Atlas Chinensis, being a Second Part of
a Remarkable Passage in Two Embassies
from the East India Company of the
United Provinces . . . English'd . . . by
John Ogilby' − 1st Edn. in English, title
printed in red and black, additional
engraved title, 38 engraved plates, 1
double page engraved map, modern mottled half calf, labels, spine gilt, slightly
rubbed, large folio − 1671.
(Sotheby's, New Bond
   Street) $560   £250

MONTERGUEIL, G.
'Henri IV' − coloured illustrations and
mounted plates by H. Vogel, original cloth,
spine faded and torn, g.e., folio − Paris,
1907.
(Christie's S.
   Kensington) $50   £22

MONTESQUIEU, C. S. DE
'Le Temple de Gnide' − engraved through-
out, illustrations after Eisen, cont. red
morocco, gilt, gilt edges, in modern
morocco box. Dedicated to George III −
Paris, 1772.
(Sotheby Parke Bernet
   Monaco) $40,500   £18,000

MONTESQUIOU, COUNT ROBERT DE
'La Divine Comtesse' Preface by Gabriele
d'Annunzio − 26 plates, 2 coloured, one
illustration, green half morocco, t.e.g.,
original wrappers bound in − Goupil et
Cie, Paris, 1913.
(Sotheby's,
   Chancery Lane) $22   £10

MOORCOCK, MICHAEL
'Elric of Melibone' – illustrations and
coloured frontispiece by Bob Gould, ori-
ginal morocco – Hartford, Conn., 1977.
(Christie's S.
Kensington) $45   £20

**MOORE, GEORGE AND LOPEZ,
BERNARD**
'Martin Luther' – 1st Edn., original cloth,
worn, Lord Esher's copy, box – 1879.
(Sotheby's,
Chancery Lane) $340   £150

MOORE, HENRY
'Heads, Figures and Ideas' – edited G.
Grigson, coloured illus., original boards,
folio – 1958.
(Phillips) $110   £50

**MOORE, HENRY – GOETHE, JOHAN
WOLFGANG VON**
'Promethee' translated by Andre Gide –
16 coloured lithographs by Henry Moore,
unsewn in original wrappers, box, folio –
Henri Jonquieres, Paris, 1950.
(Sotheby's,
Chancery Lane) $765   £340

MOORE, JAMES
'A Narrative of the Campaign of the British
Army in Spain' – 2nd Edn., engraved
portrait, 2 folding maps, browning, cont.
russia, joints split, rubbed – 1809.
(Sotheby's, New Bond
Street) $65   £28

MOORE, THOMAS
'The Ferns of Great Britain and Ireland' –
nature printed by Henry Bradbury, 51
plates, some spotting and stains, some mar-
ginal repairs, original cloth, rubbed, spine
torn, inner joints worn, g.e., folio – 1855.
(Christie's S.
Kensington) $315   £140
'Nature Printed British Ferns' – 2 vols., oct-
avo edn., engraved additional titles, 121
coloured plates, some spotting, cont. half
morocco, rubbed – Printed titles n.d.,
engravings 1859.
(Christie's S.
Kensington) $180   £80
'Works' – 9 vols., spotted, cont. straight
grained morocco, one cover detached –
Paris, 1823-24.
(Christie's S.
Kensington) $40   £18

MOORE, REV. THOMAS
'The History of Devonshire from the
Earliest Period to the Present' – 3 vols., 3
engraved titled, 2 folding engraved maps,
92 steel engraved plates mostly by William
Deeble, 17 illustrations in text, cont. straight
grained morocco, rubbed – 1829-36.
(Sotheby's, New Bond
Street) $22   £10

**MOORE, THOMAS AND STEVENSON,
SIR JOHN**
'Irish Melodies' – engraved title and 2
plates, some leaves torn, spine chipped,
cont. half morocco, folio – n.d.
(Christie's S.
Kensington) $22   £10

MOORE, TOM
'Lyrics and Satires' – Selected by Sean
O'Faolain – 1st Edn., no. 82 of 130 copies,
5 illustrations by Hilda Roberts, original
cloth backed decorated boards, uncut –
Cuala Press, Dublin, 1929.
(Sotheby's,
Chancery Lane) $95   £42

MORAES, RUBENS BORBA DE
'Bibliographia Brasiliana' – 2 vols., plates,
illustrations, original cloth – Amsterdam
and Rio de Janeiro, n.d.
(Christie's S.
Kensington) $40   £18

MORAND, PAUL
Fine collection of 176 AL's, a few with sketches, 34 typed Ls. and 15 autographed postcards, 220 pages, folio – 1914-18 and 1925.
(Sotheby's, New Bond
    Street) $1,170   £520

MORANT, PHILIP
'The History and Antiquities of Colchester' – engraved frontis. laid down with marginal loss, 7 plates, 1 folding, 1 map, repaired, soiled, cont. calf, rebacked – 1748.
(Christie's S.
    Kensington) $55   £25

MORDEN, ROBERT
'Dorsetshire' – hand coloured map, 14½ x 16½in., framed and glazed – 1695 or later.
(Christie's S.
    Kensington) $75   £35
'Geography Rectified' – 2nd Edn., title and some leaves lacking, 76 engraved maps, one torn, small hole in another, some soiling and marginal fraying, later calf, worn – 1688, Wing M2620.
(Christie's S.
    Kensington) $1,125   £500
'Norfolk' – hand coloured map double page – 17th century.
(Tessa Bennett,
    Edinburgh) $45   £20
'North Wales' – hand coloured engraved map, 14½ x 16½in., margins torn, framed and glazed – 1695 or later.
(Christie's S.
    Kensington) $35   £15
'Playing Card Maps – Essex – 7 of Hearts; Yorkshire – King of Clubs – circa 1676.
(Phillips) $180   £80

MORE, HENRY
'Enchiridion Metaphysicum' – 1st Edn., title in red and black, engravings in text, some marginal worming, soiling, cont. panelled calf, rebacked, the Kenney copy, small 4to – Ed. Flescher for W. Morden, 1671.
(Sotheby's, New Bond
    Street) $100   £45

MORE, SIR THOMAS
'Utopia' – no. 249 of 500 copies, decorations by Eric Gill, original cloth, t.e.g. – Golden Cockerel Press, 1929.
(Christie's S.
    Kensington) $110   £50

MOREAU, ADRIEN – HUGO, VICTOR
'Guy Blas' – etched portrait, 5 plates and 10 illustrations by Champolin after Moreau, brown half morocco, t.e.g., original wrappers bound in, by Canape, no. 268 of 500 – Conquet, Paris, 1889.
(Sotheby's,
    Chancery Lane) $22   £10

MOREAU DE SAINT MERY, M. L. E.
'De La Danse' – very slight spotting, cont. boards – Bodoni, Parma, 1801.
(Sotheby's, New Bond
    Street) $55   £25

MORERI, LOUIS
'Le Grand Dictionnaire Historique' – 3 vols., titles printed in red and black, slight browning and soiling, cont. calf, folio – Alyons/Amsterdam, 1674-1716.
(Sotheby's, New Bond
    Street) $200   £90

MORIER, SIR JAMES
'Journey Through Persia, Armenia and Asia Minor to Constantinople' – 29 maps and plates, half calf, gilt, 4to – 1812.
(Phillips) $225   £100

MORIN, LOUIS – NODIER, CHARLES
'Le Dernier Chapitre de Mon Roman' – coloured illustrations by Morin, mauve half morocco slightly rubbed, t.e.g., original pictorial front wrapper bound in – Paris, 1895.
(Sotheby's,
    Chancery Lane) $50   £22

MORLAND, GEORGE AND BLAGDON, FRANCIS
'Authentic Memoirs of the Late George Morland' – 20 hand coloured or colour printed plates, one engraved facsimile, early 20th century blue morocco by Morrell, gilt rubbed, large folio – 1824 or later.
(Sotheby's, New Bond
    Street) $5,000   £2,200

MORRIS, B. R.
'British Game Birds and Wild Fowl' – 60 fine coloured plates, 4to, half calf worn – 1855.
(Bonham's) $1,125   £500

MORRIS

MORRIS, F. O.
'A History of British Birds' – 8 vols., 358
hand coloured plates, some leaves detached,
a few vol. partly disbound, original cloth,
rubbed – n.d.
(Christie's S.
    Kensington)   **$675**   **£300**
'A History of British Butterflies' – plates,
71 hand coloured, slight spotting and
original cloth – 1853.
(Christie's S.
    Kensington)   **$125**   **£55**

MORRIS, WILLIAM
Autograph letter signed 2½ pp. 20 lines
to Mr. Clark from Kelmscott House,
Hammersmith, No. 25 n.y.
(Lawrence of
    Crewkerne)   **$22**   **£10**

'A Dream of John Ball and a King's
Lesson' – limited to 311 copies, printed
in red and black, woodcut frontis, after
Sir Edward Burne Jones, ornamental
borders, initials, original limp vellum,
silk ties, uncut, 8vo – 1892.
(Sotheby's,
    Chancery Lane)   **$405**   **£180**

" The Glittering Plain" &
the first book printed by
William Morris bound
by me at Hampstead 1892
T. J. Cobden-Sanderson.

'The Story of the Glittering Plain' –
limited to 206 copies, this is 200, ornamental woodcut border, initials, limp
vellum, straps with silver gilt clasps, uncut,
by T. J. Cobden-Sanderson with his autograph note – 1891.
(Sotheby's,
    Chancery Lane)   **$5,625**   **£2,500**

MORTICELLARIUM AUREUM
210 leaves of 222, 35 lines and headline,
gothic letter, woodcut on title page,
woodcut initials, coloured green throughout, rubricated, 19th century half roan,
worn, cont. ownership inscription –
Gerard Leeu, Antwerp, 1488.
(Sotheby's, New Bond
    Street)   **$1,235**   **£550**

MORTON, H. V.
A collection of works in 18 volumes, 17
1st Edns., 14 inscribed by author, plates,
illustrations, 14 in cont. calf, slightly
faded, four in modern half morocco, all
with gilt ornaments on spines, t.e.g. – 1925-
43.
(Sotheby Humberts
    Taunton)   **$60**   **£26**

MOSCHINI, GIANNANTONIO
'Nuova Guida per Venezia' – engraved title
and 21 plates, 4 folding, cont. boards,
slightly rubbed – Venice, 1834.
(Sotheby's,
    Chancery Lane) $110   £50

MOSES, HARRIS
'The Aurelian, a Natural History of British
Moths and Butterflies' – 45 fine hand
coloured plates and title, original half
morocco, folio, inner hinges broken – 1840.
(Tessa Bennett,
    Edinburgh) $2,700   £1,200

MOSS, FLETCHER
'Pilgrimages to Old Homes' – 7 vols.,
plates, original cloth gilt rubbed – 1901-
1920.
(Phillips) $110   £48

MOTRAYE, AUBREY DE LA
'Travels Through Europe, Asia and into∘
Part of Africa' – 3 vols., 1st Edn., 58
engraved plates, many folding, 5 folding
engraved maps, list of subscribers, cont.
calf, worn, folio – 1723-32.
(Sotheby's, New Bond
    Street) $1,125   £500

MOTTEVILLE, F. L. DE
'Memoires pour servir a l'Histoirie d'Anne
d'Autriche' – 6 vols., a fine set in cont.
French red morocco, flat gilt spine, g.e.,
bookplate of C. M. de Talleyrand-Perigard
– 1754-1838 – F. Chaguion, Amsterdam,
1750.
(Sotheby Parke Bernet
    Monaco) $31,500   £14,000

MOTTLEY, JOHN
'A Survey of the Cities of London and
Westminster, Borough of Southwark and
Parts Adjacent . . . by Robert Seymour' –
vol. 1 only of 2, a few engraved plates,
some browning and soiling, cont. calf,
worn, folio – 1734.
(Sotheby's, New Bond
    Street) $45   £20

MOTTRAM, R. H.
'Strawberry Time and the Banquet' – no.
167 of 250 copies, signed by author,
illustrations by Gertrude Hermes, original
morocco backed cloth, t.e.g. – Golden
Cockerel Press, 1934.
(Christie's S.
    Kensington) $50   £22

MOULE, THOMAS
'Bibliotheca Heraldia Magnae Britanniae.
An Analytical Catalogue of Books on
Genealogy, Heraldry . . .' – large paper
copy, frontispiece, cont. morocco slightly
rubbed, spine repaired, g.e. – 1822.
(Christie's S.
    Kensington) $55   £25
'The English Countries Delineated' – 2
vols., 2 engraved titles, 4 plates and 59
maps, mostly hand coloured, a few
folding, cont. half calf, slightly rubbed –
1837.
(Sotheby's,
    Chancery Lane) $1,350   £600

MOUNTFORT, WILLIAM
'The Fall of Mortimer: an Historical Play,
(adapted by John Wilkes)' – 2nd Edn. –
1763.
(Sotheby's
    London) $45   £20

MOXON, JOSEPH
'Mechanick Exercises or the Doctrine of
Handyworks Began Jan. 1, 1677 and
intended to be Monthly continued' –
2 vols., engraved portrait and 17 plates
in vol. I and 33 plates in vol. II, torn
and crudely repaired, some plates
shaved, modern leather, small 4to – For
Joseph Moxon, 1677-80 and 1683.
(Sotheby's, New Bond
    Street) $2,475   £1,100

MOZART, WOLFGANG AMADEUS
Autograph sketch leaf comprising a
draft for a vocal composition – 2 pages,
20 filled staves, 88 bars, written in 3
differing colours of ink, text in German,
changes of key in French, a few alterations
and deletions – 1778-79.
(Sotheby's, New Bond
    Street) $27,000   £12,000

MUCHA

MUCHA, ALPHONSE AND VEROLA, PAUL
'Rama Poeme Dramatique' – no. 265 of 400 copies, five coloured plates by Mucha, original wrappers – Paris, 1898.
(Christie's S.
Kensington) $335   £150

MUIR, PERCY
'English Children's Books' – 1st Edn., coloured plates, original cloth, dust jacket – 1954.
(Sotheby's,
Chancery Lane) $50   £22

MULLENS, W. H. AND SWANN
'A Geographical Bibliography of British Ornithology' – 6 parts, original wrappers – 1919-20.
(Phillips) $55   £25

MULLER, ADOLF AND KARL
'Thiere der Heimath' – coloured lithograph plates, illustrations, original cloth, spotted – Kassel, 1897.
(Christie's S.
Kensington) $50   £22

MUN, T.
'Englands Treasure by Forraign Trade, or The Ballance of our Forraign Trade is the Rule of our Treasure' – 1st Edn., with licence leaf before title and catalogue of books, 4pp., cont. calf – Wing 3037, Kress 1243. – 1664.
(Bonham's) $4,275   £1,900

MUNDAY, ANTHONY
'A Briefe Chronicle of the Successe of the Times from the Creation of the World to this Instant' – 1st Edn., cont. calf with gilt crest in centre of both covers, rubbed and rebacked, Edward Mundy bookplate – 1611.
(Christie's, King
St.) $150   £65

MUNNINGS, SIR ALFRED
'Autobiography' – vol. 2 and 3 only, vol. 2 inscribed on half title by the author, title slightly torn, plates, original cloth, dust jacket – 1951-52.
(Christie's S.
Kensington) $105   £48

MUNSTER, SEBASTIAN
'Terra Sancta' – hand coloured woodcut map, latin text on verso, 10 x 13½in., slightly soiled – mid 16th century.
(Christie's S.
Kensington) $190   £85
'The World After Ptolemy' – uncoloured map, wide margins – circa 1559.
(Phillips) $1,235   £550

MURPHY, W. S.
'The Textile Industry' – coloured and other illustrations, and model of Openshed loom in separate envelope, 8 vols., original cloth gilt – Gresham Publishing Co., 1910-11.
(Bonham's) $65   £30

MURRAY, AMELIA
'Letters from the United States, Cuba and Canada' – 2 vols., 1st Edn., folding engraved map, half titles, original cloth, slightly worn – 1856.
(Sotheby's, New Bond
Street) $65   £30

MURRAY, HUGH
'Historical Account of Discoveries and Travels in Africa' – 2 vols., cont. diced calf morocco labels, 7 maps, 3 folding, foxing, appendix – Edinburgh, 1818.
(Lawrence of
Crewkerne) $65   £28

MURRAY, J.
'Bathymetrical Survey of the Scottish Fresh Water Lochs' – vol. 1, half morocco – 1910.
(Tessa Bennett,
Edinburgh) $20   £9

MUSGRAVE, WILLIAM
'De Arthritide Symptomatica Dissertatio' – 1st Edn., old calf using boards from another binding, worn – Exeter, 1703.
(Christie's, King
St.) $65   £30

MY
We Konstantin Bal'mont, Vyacheslav Ivanov, Ryurik Ivnev, Aleksandr Kusikov, Lev Nikulin, Boris Pasternak, Semen Rubanovich, Ivan Rukavishnikov, Sergei Tretyakov, Vel. Khlebnikov, Vadim Shershenvich – original wrappers, rather frayed – Moscow, 1920.
(Sotheby's, New Bond
Street) $450   £200

N

NADASDY, COUNT FERENCZ III
'Mausoleum Potentissimorum ac
Gloriosissimorum Regni Apostolici
Regum & Primorum Militantis Ungariae
Ducum' — numerous engraved plates,
some browning, half calf, folio —
Nuremberg, 1664.
(Sotheby Parke Bernet
   Monaco) $2,475   £1,100

NANSEN, FRIDTJOF
'The First Corssing of Greenland . . .
translated from the Norwegian by Hubert
Majendie Gepp' — 2 vols., 1st Edn., portraits, plates, illustrations in text, coloured
folding maps, Nansen's autograph in vol. 1
— original pictorial cloth, worn and
discoloured — 1890.
(Sotheby's, New Bond
   Street) $160   £70
'Farthest North' — 2 vols., plates, some
coloured, 4 folding coloured maps, one
slightly torn, illus., slight soiling, original
cloth, affected by damp — 1897.
(Christie's S.
   Kensington) $15   £7

NAPIER, JOHN
'The Construction of Logarithms . . . and
a catalogue of Napier's Works' by William
Rae Macdonald — original cloth, soiled
— Edinburgh, 1889.
(Christie's S.
   Kensington) $27   £12

'NAPOLEON I, Emperor of the French,
Funerailles de l'Empereur Napoleon' —
lithographed title and 22 plates, 14 hand
coloured, slightly spotted and soiled, a
few marginal tears, cont. half roan, rubbed
— Paris, n.d.
(Sotheby's,
   Chancery Lane) $560   £250

NAPOLEON I
Bonaparte as Army Commander in Chief
Army in Italy, 1½ pp. folio with engraved
heading about supplies and payment.
(Phillips) $425   £190

'Zaire' — Italian and French text, cont.
French morocco gilt, flower and leaf corner
ornaments, g.e., side covers with triple
tulips, Doves Bindery design of T. J.
Cobden-Sanderson dated 1889, Lady
d'Abernon bookplate — 1889.
(Phillips) $495   £220

NARBOROUGH, SIR JOHN
'An Account of Several Voyages and
Discoveries . . . South Seas' — title in red
and black, 2 folding maps, loose table,
19 plates, old calf, lower cover detached —
1694.
(Phillips) $605   £270

NASH, OGDEN
Autograph letter signed, 1 p. folio, 20 lines
to Nicolas Bentley from New Hampshire,
August 1970, concerning their coming
collaboration in Nash's 'Bad Riddance' —
1970.
(Lawrence of
   Crewkerne) $90   £40

NASH, PAUL AND OTHERS
'Sermons by Artists ' — no. 129 of 300
copies, frontispiece by Elizabeth Corsellis,
original morocco backed boards, t.e.g. —
Golden Cockerel Press, 1934.
(Christie's S.
   Kensington) $155   £70

**NATIONAL SOCIETY FOR PROMOTING
THE EDUCATION OF THE POOR . . .**
Monthly Journal — 8 vols., cont. cloth,
periodical 1850; 1853-57; 1859-60.
(Sotheby's, New Bond
   Street) $180   £80

NATTES, JOHN CLAUDE
'Scotia Depicta or the Antiquities, Castles,
Public Buildings, Noblemen and Gentle-
men's Seats . . . of Scotland' — 48 etched
plates by James Fittler, old cloth backed
boards, uncut, worn, oblong folio — 1804.
(Sotheby's, New Bond
   Street) $190   £85

NATURAL HISTORY CARDS

MONKEY

The nimble Monkey with great Eafe
Can Imitate what e'er he Sees
But what's the worft when underftood
He Mimics bad, and Shuns the good

APPLICATION

That Child, who is on mifchief bent
Will never give his Friends Content

NATURAL HISTORY CARDS
12 cards each with an engraved illustration
of an animal coloured by hand and a
rhyme below — W. Tringham, circa 1780.
(Sotheby's,
    Chancery Lane) $215   £95

NATURAL HISTORY PRINTS
A collection of approximately 230 hand
coloured plates of butterflies, insects,
crabs, shell fish and other sea creatures,
some slightly soiled, torn, disbound, 8vo
— n.d.
(Sotheby Humberts
    Taunton) $135   £60

NAVIGATION AND MATHEMATICS
Mss. in ink in Latin, neatly written by one
scribe and incorporating numerous
examples, problems and diagrams dated
1663, 48 numbered leaves with ruled margins, cont. binding in vellum sheet from
an early 13th century mss. of the Gospels
in ink with red capitals, slightly rubbed,
worming, ties missing.
(Christie's, King
    St.) $335   £150

NAVIRE D'ARGENT
Edited by Adrienne Monnier, No. 5 (2
copies), 11 (2 copies), 12, 6 issues, contributions by D. H. Lawrence, Jean Prevost,
Rilke and others, illustrations, original
wrappers, part of cover of vol. 1 missing,
repaired, uncut — Paris, 1925-26.
(Sotheby's,
    Chancery Lane) $22   £10

NEALE, J. P.
'Mansions of England' — 2 vols., 392
plates on 196 pages, india paper, half
morocco, gilt, 4to — 1847.
(Phillips) $270   £120

NECKER, JACQUES
'De l'Administration des Finances de la
France' — 3 vols., 1st Edn., slight brown-
ing, cont. mottled calf, rubbed — Paris,
1784.
(Sotheby's, New Bond
    Street) $180   £80

NEEDLEWORK, THE DICTIONARY OF
6 vols., plates, illus., some leaves detached,
original cloth, spine chipped, g.e., 4to —
n.d.
(Christie's S.
    Kensington) $90   £40

NELSON, HORATIO
'Letters from the Leeward Islands' — no.
196 of 300 copies, frontispiece, illustra-
tions and map by Geoffrey Wales, original
cloth, folio — Golden Cockerel Press, 1953.
(Christie's S.
    Kensington) $100   £45
A.L.s Nelson and Bronte, 2pp. 4to,
Madalena, Dec. 1803, to Hugh Elliot, H.M.
Minister at Naples 'A most severe winter
has almost knocked me up . . .'.
(Phillips) $1,035 $460

NELSON, THOMAS (Publisher)
'A New General Atlas' — engraved title,
29 hand coloured maps, some spotting and
soiling, cont. half calf, rebacked in cloth,
soiled — Edinburgh, 1840.
(Christie's S.
    Kensington) $65   £28

NERCIAT, ANDREA DE
'Les Aphrodites ou Fragments Thali-
Priapiques' — 4 vols., engraved frontis-
piece and a few plates, morocco backed
boards, gilt spines, t.e.g. — Paris, 1864.
(Sotheby Parke Bernet
    Monaco) $1,575   £700

'Felicia ou Mes Fredaines' – 20 illustrations, coloured by hand by artist, unsewn in original wrappers – Paris, 1928.
(Sotheby's,
Chancery Lane) $45 £20

NERUDA, PABLO (Chilean Poet and Nobel Prize Winner)
Fine collection of autograph poems and papers accompanied by Neruda's drawings, notes and signatures, also three letters dated 1956, 30 leaves quarto all on notes Neruda's personal headed paper, written one side in green ink, one photograph.
(Sotheby's New Bond
Street) $3,375 £1,500

NESBIT, EDITH
'A Pomander of Verse' – 1st Edn., limited to 750 copies, presentation copy inscribed by author, title and cover design by Laurence Housman, original cloth gilt, rubbed – 1895.
(Sotheby's,
Chancery Lane) $68 £30

NETTLEFORD, F. J. AND FORRER, R.
'The Collection of Bronzes and Castings in Brass and Ormolu' – plates, original cloth, large 4to – Privately printed, 1934.
(Christie's S.
Kensington) $55 £25

NEVILL, RALPH
'British Military Prints' – plates, some coloured, original pictorial cloth, spine faded – 1909.
(Christie's S.
Kensington) $33 £15

NEVILLE, ALEXANDER
'De Furoribus Norfolciensium Ketto Duce. Liber Unus, Eiusdem Norvicus' – 1st Edn., first issue, two titles within woodcut borders, one with woodcut device, 6 printed tables at end, cont. panelled calf, bookplate of John, Earl of Hyndford – 1575.
(Christie's, King
St.) $225 £100

'NEW CYCLOPAEDIA OF BOTANY and Complete Book of Herbs'
2 vols. in one, hand coloured frontis and 99 plates, upper margins repaired, cont. half morocco, inner hinges broken – London, W. M. Clark and Huddersfield, R. Brook, n.d.
(Christie's S.
Kensington) $65 £30

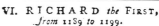

VI. RICHARD the FIRST, from 1189 to 1199.

RICHARD, for boist'rous courage chiefly known
Wasted his years in countries not his own;
A pris'ner long, at last untimely slain;
England had small advantage from his reign.

G   RICHARD

'NEW HISTORY OF ENGLAND FROM THE INVASION OF JULIUS CAESAR TO THE END OF GEORGE THE SECOND'
32 wood engraved illustrations, calf gilt, upper cover loose, original pictorial wrappers bound in, soiled and slightly worn, g.e. – Printed for T. Carnan, 1781.
(Sotheby's,
Chancery Lane) $125 £55

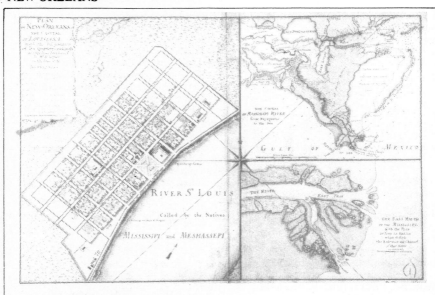

Plan of New Orleans, and maps of the Mississippi, c. 1722. (Sotheby's)

NEW ORLEANS
'Plan of New Orleans, Capital of Louisiana;
The Course of the Mississippi River from
Bayagoulas to the sea; the East Mouth of
the Mississippi' — mss. on paper, three
drawings by unidentfied hand in blank ink,
each drawing finely executed, 2 sheets
joined, stained, some slight tears, dust
soiled — no place or date, circa 1722.
(Sotheby's, New Bond
    Street)   **$900**   **£400**

NEW TESTAMENT, COPTIC
'Novum Testamentum Aegyptium Vulgo
Copticum et in Latinum sermonem con-
vertit David Wilkins' — 1st Edn., engraved
title, light browning and staining, later
18th century mottled calf, gilt, worn spine
— Oxford, 1716.
(Sotheby's, New Bond
    Street)   **$360**   **£160**

NEW TESTAMENT, HEBREW
'Evangelium Matthaei ex Hebraeo Fideliter
Redditum' — Hebrew and Latin versions
of St. Matthew, staining, modern dark
blue suede — Martin Iuvenum, Paris, 1555.
(Sotheby's, New Bond
    Street)   **$200**   **£90**

NEWBATTLE COLLIERY
An album of photographs — 1924.
(Tessa Bennett,
    Edinburgh)   **$65**   **£28**

NEWCASTLE, WILLIAM CAVENDISH, DUKE OF
'A General System of Horsemanship in All
its Branches' — 2 vols., double page engraved title to the 1658 Antwerp edition,
62 plates some in vol. II in colour, some
tears, discolouration, cont. mottled calf,
gilt, a little worn, bookplate of Richard
Hill of Thornton, Yorkshire, folio — J.
Brindley, 1743.
(Sotheby's, New Bond
    Street)   **$4,275**   **£1,900**

NEWTE, THOMAS
'Prospects and Observations on a Tour of
England and Scotland' – 1st Edition, 23
engraved plates, lacks map, some spotting,
cont. calf, gilt, joints worn, 4to – 1791.
(Sotheby's, New Bond
   Street) $125   £55

NEWTON, C. T.
'History of Discoveries, at Halicarnasus,
Cnidus, and Branchidae' – with folio
volume of plates, 3 vols., cloth – 1863.
(Bonham's) $425   £190

NEWTON, SIR ISAAC
'Observations upon the Prophesies of
Daniel, and the Apocalypse of St. John' –
1st Edn., a few marginal dampstains, cont.
calf, gilt, front cover detached, worn,
signature of Tho. Nordman, 1750 on title
– J. Darby and T. Browne, 1733.
(Sotheby's
   London) $80   £35
'Opticks' – 1st Edn., title in red and black,
19 engraved folding plates, ink smears on
title, foxing, edges browned, cont. calf
panelled and rebacked – 1704.
(Christie's, King
   St.) $4,050   £1,800

**NEWTON, SIR ISAAC – WHISTON,
WILLIAM**
'Sir Isaac Newton's Mathematick Philo-
sophy More Easily Demonstrated' – 1st
Edn., half title, 9 folding engraved plates,
2 damaged, tables, dampstained, cont.
panelled calf, rubbed – 1716.
(Sotheby's, New Bond
   Street) $540   £240

NICHOLSON, W. – KIPLING, R.
'An Almanac of Twelve Sports' – coloured
plates by Nicholson, slight offsetting,
original cloth backed pictorial boards,
extremeties slightly rubbed – New York,
1898.
(Christie's S.
   Kensington) $110   £50

NICOLAI, JOHANNIS
'Libri IV De Sepulchris Hebraeorum' – 8
engraved plates, 5 folding, 1 torn, 3 with
overslips, cont. vellum – Leiden, apud
Henricum Teering, 1706.
(Christie's S.
   Kensington) $190 $85

NICOLAY, REV. C. G.
'The Oregon Territory' – frontispiece,
folding map, original wrappers, slightly
soiled, cloth box – 1846.
(Sotheby's,
   Chancery Lane) $110   £50

NICOLSON, HAROLD
'The English Sense of Humour' – 1st Edn.,
buckram gilt, uncut, no. 550 of 550 copies
– Dropmore Press, 1946.
(Lawrence of
   Crewkerne) $22   £10

NIGER, FRANCISCUS
'Grammatica' – 1st Edn., 242 leaves of 247,
24 lines, roman letter, a little musical
printing, wormed, some browning and staining, 19th century boards, worn, covers
detached – Venice, 1480.
(Sotheby's, New Bond
   Street) $1,125   £500

NIGHTINGALE, FLORENCE
'Notes on Nursing' – 1st Edn., original
cloth, rubbed, stitching worn – 1859.
(Christie's S.
   Kensington) $100   £45

NIGHTINGALE, FLORENCE AND VERNEY, LADY FRANCES
'Sketches from Nature with Pen and Pencil' – 1st Edn., inscribed by Florence Nightingale, wood engraved illustrations, original cloth gilt, g.e. – 1877.
(Sotheby's,
Chancery Lane) $80   £35

NIMMO, W.
'History of Stirlingshire' – 2 volumes, 2 folding maps, half calf – 1880.
(Tessa Bennett,
Edinburgh) $36   £16

NOBLE, JOHN
'Descriptive Handbook of the Cape Colony' – 2 lithoed plates, 1 folding, folding map, slightly torn, original cloth, slightly rubbed – 1875.
(Sotheby's,
Chancery Lane) $80   £35

NOE, COMTE A. DE
'Memoires Relatifs a l'Expedition Anglaise' – some dampstains, 2 maps, 19 coloured plates, calf – 1826.
(Phillips) $80   £35

NOLLET, ABBE JEAN ANTOINE
'Lecons de Physique Experimentale' – vols. II-V of six, 4 vols., ninth, eight, 1st and 7th Edns., 77 engraved folding plates, some loose, a few frayed, cont. calf, worn, 2 spines missing, 1 spine partly missing – Paris, 1748-83.
(Sotheby's
London) $100   £45

NORDEN, F. L.
'Voyage d'Egypte et de Nubie' – 3 vols. including volume of plates, the 2 vols. of text bound in one, 1st Edn., large paper copy, 162 engraved plates, maps and plans, rubbed, large folio – Copenhagen, 1755.
(Sotheby's, New Bond
Street) $3,375   £1,500

NORDEN, JOHN
'Speculum Britanniae, Cornwall' – engraved title, ded., 2 maps and plates, illus. in text, calf rebacked – 1728.
(Phillips) $990   £440

NORDENSKIOLD, A. E.
'The Voyage of the Vega round Asia and Europe' – 2 vols., plates, folding maps, some slightly torn, illustrations, cont. half morocco, slightly rubbed, t.e.g. – 1881.
(Sotheby's,
Chancery Lane) $95   £42

NORTH, SIR DUDLEY AND OTHERS
A collection of 26 pamphlets from the 17th century, mainly relating to politics or trade, in one volume, a few margins slightly browned and frayed, some slightly wormed, but not affecting text, a few leaves loose, bookplate of Paul Panton, cont. panelled calf, slightly rubbed – 1684-92.
(Sotheby's
London) $1,575   £700

Voyage d'Egypte et de Nubie, by F.L. Norden. (Sotheby's)

NORTHUMBERLAND, THE DUCHESS OF
'Castles of Alnwick and Warkworth' –
dedication leaf signed by author, 31
plates, one coloured, illustrations, occasional slight spotting, some prints loosely
inserted, title laid down, cont. morocco
backed boards, rubbed, with a volume of
plates of the same area – 1824.
(Christie's S.
   Kensington) $225   £100

NORTON, THOMAS
'A Warning agaynst the dangerous practises
of Papistes' – 2nd Edn., slight browning,
some shaving, modern red morocco by
Riviere, gilt – John Daye, circa 1570.
(Sotheby's, New Bond
   Street) $360   £160

NORWAY
A small half morocco album of photographs
– 1897.
(Tessa Bennett,
   Edinburgh) $12   £5

NOTT, JOHN
'The Cook's and Confectioner's Dictionary'
– frontispiece detached and margins
frayed, some soiling and spotting, crudely
repaired with adhesive tape – 1723.
(Christie's S.
   Kensington) $55   £25

NOTT, STANLEY CHARLES
'Chinese Jade Throughout the Ages' –
plates, some coloured illustrations –
Batsford, 1936.
(Christie's S.
   Kensington) $65   £28

**NOUVELLE MORALITE D'UNE
PAUVRE FILLE VILLAGEOISE**
Ms. on vellum, a copy of a 16th century
printed book, 16 leaves, vignette on title
page, early 19th century French red
morocco gilt, g.e., silk doublures – circa
1800.
(Sotheby Parke Bernet
   Monaco) $10,125   £4,500

**NOVOTNY, FRITZ AND DOBAI,
JOHANNES**
'Gustav Klimt' – illustrations, some
coloured, most full page, original cloth,
dust jacket, slipcase – Salzburg, 1967.
(Christie's S.
   Kensington) $160   £70

DESCRIPTIVE CATALOGUE OF CONJURING TRICKS, FROM HENRY NOVRA'S MAGICAL REPOSITORY, 95, Regent Street, London. W. PART I. LONDON: PRINTED BY G. STUART, 47, GT. WINDMILL STREET, HAYMARKET. 1860.

NOVRA, HENRY
'Descriptive Catalogue of Conjuring Tricks
from Henry Novra's Magical Repository' –
Part I, original wrappers, soiled, a few tears,
one repaired – Printed by G. Stuart, 1860.
(Sotheby's,
   Chancery Lane) $495   £220

**NUGENT, G. MARQUIS OF WEST
MEATH**
Miniature in uniform on card, draft appli-
cation for the Turkish gold medal Egypt,
1801, printed order signed by Fitzroy
Somerset (Lord Raglan) – 1850 etc.
(Phillips) $100   £45

NUTTER, M. E.
'Carlisle in the Olden Time' – litho-
graphed plates on India paper, cont.
morocco backed cloth, slightly soiled –
Carlisle, 1835.
(Sotheby's,
   Chancery Lane) $270   £120

OATES, TITUS, D. D.
'The Witch of Endor or the Witchcrafts of the Roman Jesebel' — 1st Edn., cont. black morocco, gilt fillets and panel with corner sprays, rubbed, folio — 1679.
(Sotheby's, New Bond
Street) $405   £180

O'BRIEN, FITZJAMES
'A Gentleman from Ireland' — 1st Edn., text browned, original printed wrappers, in hard folder — New York, 1858.
(Sotheby's,
Chancery Lane) $22   £10

O'BRIEN, R. BARRY
'The Irish Nuns at Ypres, an Episode of the War' — original blue cloth, 3 photographic illustrations, free endpaper signed by 13 of the nuns at Ypres — 1915.
(Lawrence of
Crewkerne) $11   £5

OCKLEY, SIMON (Translator)
'The Improvement of Human Reason, Exhibited in the Life of Hai Ebn Yokdhan' — engraved frontis and plates, frontis cut down and mounted, spotted throughout, cont. panelled calf, rebacked and recornered — Printed for W. Bray, 1711.
(Christie's S.
Kensington) $160   £70

O'CONNOR, FRANK
'Lords and Commons' — 1st Edn., limited to 250 copies, original linen backed boards, uncut, unopened — Cuala Press, Dublin, 1938.
(Sotheby's,
Chancery Lane) $65   £28

'The Wild Bird's Nest, Poems from the Irish' — 1st Edn., limited to 250 copies, presentation copy inscribed by author, original linen backed boards, soiled — Cuala Press, Dublin, 1932.
(Sotheby's,
Chancery Lane) $101   £45

'Three Tales' — 1st Edn., no. 34 of 250 copies, original linen backed boards, slightly creased, uncut, unopened — Cuala Press, Dublin, 1941.
(Sotheby's,
Chancery Lane) $95   £42

O'DONOVAN, JOHN (Editor)
'The Tribes and Customs of Hy-Many' — map, one folding table, occasional spotting, cont. cloth — Dublin, 1843.
(Christie's. S.
Kensington) $22   £10

OFFICE DE LA SEMAINE SAINTE
Latin and French, engraved frontispiece, woodcut monogram on title, three engraved plates, cont. French red morocco, g.e., scuffed and rubbed — Paris, 1701.
(Christie's, King
St.) $380   £170

O'FLAHERTY, LIAM
'The Assassin' — 1st Edn., presentation copy, inscribed by author, original cloth, dust jacket — 1928.
(Sotheby's,
Chancery Lane) $90   £40

OGILBY, JOHN
'The Road from King's Lynn to Norwich' — hand coloured engraved map, 14 x 18in., framed and glazed — late 17th century.
(Christie's S.
Kensington) $90   £40

'The Roads from London to Bath and Wells' — engraved map, hand coloured in outline, 13½ x 18in., repaired at fold, framed and glazed — 1676.
(Christie's S.
Kensington) $80   £35

'Britannia or the Kingdom of England and the Dominion of Wales Actually Surveyed' — 98 of 100 engraved double page strip maps, many maps with faint dampstain, occasional spotting, old calf, very worn, upper cover detached — 1698.
(Christie's
St. James) $7,875   £3,500

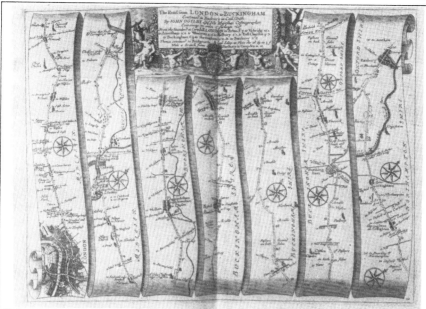

Strip map from John Ogilby's Britannia. (Christie's)

OGILVIE-GRANT, W. R.
'Game Birds' – 2 vols., 39 plates, 38 coloured, illus., original cloth, joints slightly torn, spines soiled, t.e.g. – n.d. (Christie's S.
   Kensington)   **$33**   **£15**

OGLESBY, CATHERINE
'French Provincial Decorative Art' – coloured plates, illustrations, original cloth, dust jacket – 1951. (Christie's S.
   Kensington)   **$33**   **£15**

OLD WORLD HOUSE, THE – Its Furniture and Decorations –
2 vols., original morocco – 1924.
(Bonham's)   **$70**   **£32**

OLDHAM, J. BASIL
'Shrewsbury School Library Bindings' – no. 99 of 200 copies, coloured frontispiece, plates, original cloth, 4to – Oxford, 1943. (Christie's S.
   Kensington)   **$250**   **£110**

OLEARIUS, ADAM
'The Voyages and Travels of the Ambassadors in Persia' – translated by J. Davies, 2 vols. in one, engraved title and printed title laid down, 3 maps and 2 portraits only, old calf, folio – 1662.
(Phillips)   **$80**   **£35**

OLIPHANT, LAURENCE
'Narrative of the Earl of Elgin's Mission to China and Japan' – 2 vols., 1st Edn., 20 coloured lithos, 5 folded maps, half title first blank and 16 page publisher's catalogue in vol. I, irregular collation, but complete, signature of Sarah Tyrconnel on titles, original cloth, gilt – 1859. (Sotheby's
   London)   **$200**   **£90**

OLIVER, LIEUT. SAMUEL PASFIELD
'Madagascar and Malagasey' – 24 coloured lithographed plates, slightly spotted, map and plan original cloth – 1866. (Christie's S.
   Kensington)   **$100**   **£45**

O'NEILL

O'NEILL, A.
'Annals of Brechin Cricket, 1849-1927' –
plates, cloth – Brechin, 1927.
(Tessa Bennett,
    Edinburgh) $18   £8

O'NEILL, EUGENE
'The Iceman Cometh' – 1st Edn., presentation copy, inscribed by author, original
cloth, dust jacket repaired – New York,
1946.
(Sotheby's,
    Chancery Lane) $1,685   £750

OPIE, JOHN
'Lectures on Painting' – portrait, plates,
occasional slight spotting, cont. half calf,
rubbed – 1809.
(Christie's S.
    Kensington) $100   £45

ORCHARD, THE
Text figures, lacks some pages, morocco,
small 4to – 1597.
(Phillips) $50   £22

ORDNANCE SURVEY
'An Entirely New and Accurate Survey of
the County of Kent with Part of the County
of Essex' – 3 of 4 linen backed folding
sheets, engraved by Thomas Foot, published by William Faden, each approx. 25 x
37in., cont. case with morocco label, worn
– January, 1801.
(Lawrence of
    Crewkerne) $160   £70

ORDNANCE SURVEY
Isle of Wight, Plymouth – two linen
backed folding maps, printed in electro-
type, each approx. 27½ x 39½in. – 1872-76.
(Lawrence of
    Crewkerne) $55   £25

ORIENTAL ANNUAL
4 vols., 88 plates, green morocco tooled in
gilt and blind with stamp of Howdah on
Elephant – 1835-8.
(Phillips) $110   £50

ORIOLI, G.
'Adventures of a Bookseller' – 1st Edn., no.
111 of 300 copies, signed by author, origi-
nal wrappers, unopened – G. Orioli,
Florence, 1937.
(Sotheby's,
    Chancery Lane) $155   £70

**ORLERS, JAN AND VAN HAESTENS,
HENRIK**
'Description and Representation de Toutes
Les Victoires Tant Par Eau que Par Terre
. . . Souz La Conduite et Gouvernement
de Maurice de Nassau' – 1st Edn., engraved
title, 42 double page engraved plates and
plans, 1 double page engraved map of the
Netherlands, cont. calf, worn, folio –
Leyden, 1612.
(Sotheby's, New Bond
    Street) $1,910   £850

ORME, EDWARD
'An Essay on Transparent Prints' – plates,
some coloured, some transparent, russia,
worn – 1807.
(Sotheby's, New Bond
    Street) $785   £350
'Orme's Collection of British Field Sports'
– oblong folio, wrappers missing, fac-
simile edition, illustrated title, list of
contents, 20 colour plates after Samuel
Howitt, some plates dampstained –
Charles Traylen, Guildford, n.d.
(Lawrence of
    Crewkerne) $90   £40

**ORMEROD, GEORGE AND HELSBY,
THOMAS**
'The History of the County Palatine and
City of Chester' – 3 vols. in 5, 2nd Edn.,
plates and maps, some folding, some hand
coloured, illustrations in the text, cont.
half morocco, rubbed – 1882.
(Sotheby's,
    Chancery Lane) $350   £155

ORR, WILLIAM AND CO.
'The Travelling Atlas of England and
Wales' – cont. red morocco gilt with flap
a.e.g., engraved title, contents, 45
coloured lithographic plates, folding map
of England and Wales, North Wales, South
Wales and 42 county maps, some loose –
circa 1852.
(Lawrence of
    Crewkerne) $200   £90

ORTELIUS, ABRAHAM
'Africae Tabula Nova' – hand coloured
engraved map, 14½ x 19½in., slightly torn
at fold, framed and glazed – Antwerp, 1570.
(Christie's S.
    Kensington) $245   £110

ORWELL, GEORGE
'Animal Farm' – 1st Edn., original cloth,
dust jacket – 1945.
(Sotheby's,
    Chancery Lane) $290   £130
'Down and Out in Paris and London' – 1st
American Edn., original cloth, uncut, dust
jacket – New York, 1933.
(Sotheby's,
    Chancery Lane) $335   £150
'Nineteen Eighty Four' – 1st Edn., original
cloth, discoloured, dust jacket repaired –
1949.
(Sotheby's,
    Chancery Lane) $110   £50

OSBALDISTON, W. A.
'The British Sportsman' – plates, 4to, half
calf, binding defective – 1792.
(Bonham's) $270   £120

OSBORN, LIEUT. S.
'Stray Leaves from an Arctic Journal' – 4
tinted plates, folding map, calf gilt – 1852.
(Phillips) $110   £50

OTTLEY, W. Y. AND TOMKINS, P. W.
'Engravings of the Most Noble the Marquis of Stafford's Collection of Pictures'
– 4 vols. in one, 291 engraved plates, 13
plans, some spotting, lacks half title,
cont. half morocco, one cover detached,
very worn, large folio – 1818.
(Sotheby's, New Bond
    Street) $720   £320

OUGHTON, THOMAS
'Ordo Judiciorum; sive, methodus proce-
dendi in negotiis et litibus in foro ecclesias-
tico-civili Britannico et Hibernico' – 2
vols., 2nd Edn., library stamps on title
pages, cont. mottled calf, very worn –
1738.
(Sotheby's
    London) $45   £20

OVED, S.
'The Book of Necklaces' – fine quarter
morocco, plates – 1953.
(Tessa Bennett,
    Edinburgh) $13   £6

OVID
'The Amores' translated by E. Powys
Mathers – no. 194 of 350 copies, plates
by J. E. Laboureur, original morocco
backed cloth, t.e.g. – Golden Cockerel
Press, 1932.
(Christie's S.
    Kensington) $135   £60

'Les Matamorphoses Gravees sur Les
Desseins des Meilleurs Peintres Francais.
Par les soins des Srs Le Mire et Basan
Graveurs' – 141 engraved plates, cont.
French mottled calf, gilt, worn, g.e. –
Paris, 1767-70.
(Sotheby's, New Bond
    Street) $270   £120
'Metamorphosis' – in German, 1 vol. only,
engraved additional title and plates after
Johann von Sandrart, some spotting, cont.
calf, rebacked, worn, folio – Nurnberg,
1698.
(Christie's S.
    Kensington) $245   £110
'Verwandlungen in Kupfern von Mehrern
Kunstlern Deutschlands Vorgestellt . . .
Zweite Auflage' – 3 parts in one vol.,
3 engraved title pages, 135 engraved
plates, slightly spotted and soiled, cont.
boards – Augsburg, 1822.
(Sotheby's, New Bond
    Street) $168   £75

OVINGTON, JOHN
'The Voyage to Suratt in the Year 1689' –
1st Edn., 2 folding engraved plates and
printed folding table, torn, 18th century
calf, joints rubbed, covers scuffed, 8vo –
1696.
(Christie's
    St. James) $540   £240

OWEN, JOHN AND BOWEN, EMANUEL
'Britannia Depicta or Ogilby Improved' –
4th Edn., engraved title and 273 road
maps, some stains, modern calf backed
boards, 4to – 1736.
(Christie's S.
    Kensington) $1,080   £480

**OXFORD ENGLISH DICTIONARY,
COMPACT EDITION**
2 vols., cloth complete text micrographi-
cally reproduced with magnifier in case –
Oxford 1972.
(Lawrence of
    Crewkerne) $65   £30

**'OXFORD PAMPHLETS ON WORLD
AFFAIRS ETC.'**
About 74 bound in 13 vols., red morocco
– 1939-42.
(Phillips) $34   £15

PAGE, PHILIP
'The Cumberland Hotel' – limited to
500 copies, unnumbered, original morocco,
slipcase – Golden Cockerel Press, 1933.
(Christie's S.
  Kensington) $18 £8

PAGE, T.
'The Art of Shooting Flying' – cont. calf
gilt with dentelles, a good copy – J.
Crouse, Norwich, 1766.
(Lawrence of
  Crewkerne) $110 £50

PAINE, THOMAS
'Common Sense' and 'Rights of Man' – two
works in one vol., cont. calf, rubbed and
cracked – 1791-1792.
(Christie's S.
  Kensington) $55 £25
'Life and Works' – 10 vols., buckram – New
New York, 1925.
(Tessa Bennett,
  Edinburgh) $75 £34

PALGRAVE, WILLIAM GIFFORD
'Narrative of a Year's Journey Through
Central and Eastern Arabia' – 2 vols., 3rd
Edn., engraved portrait, 1 folding map,
coloured in outline, 4 folding plans, half
title in vol. II, advert leaf at end of each
vol., original cloth, gilt – 1866.
(Sotheby's
  London) $170 £75

PALLADIO, ANDREA
'Les Quatres Livres de l'Architecture' –
title and fly titles within woodcut architectural border, woodcut illus. and plans,
mostly full page, cont. sprinkled calf, gilt
spine, folio – Paris, 1650.
(Sotheby's, New Bond
  Street) $945 £420

'Quattro Libri dell'architettura' – 4 parts
in one vol., titles in woodcut border,
numerous woodcut illustrations in text,
late 18th century or early 19th century
notes, 18th century mottled calf, worn,
folio – Appresso Bartolomeo Carampello,
Venice, 1581.
(Sotheby's, New Bond
  Street) $785 £350
'The Architecture . . . the Whole Revised
Designs and Published by Giacomo Leoni'
– books 3 and 4 in one vol. only, 12
engraved plates, 15 double page, text in
English, French and Italian – Printed by
John Watts, n.d.
(Christie's S.
  Kensington) $95 £42

PALLAS, P. S.
'Travels Through the Southern Provinces
of the Russian Empire 1793 and 1794
translated from German by F. W. Blagdon'
– 2 vols., 1st Edn. in English, 51 engraved
plates, 44 hand coloured, 4 folding engraved
maps, engraved vignettes in text, most
hand coloured – 1802-03.
(Sotheby's, New Bond
  Street) $1,235 £550

PALMER, SIR G.
'Les Reports' – portrait after Lely by
White, folio, old craft – R. and E.
Atkyns, 1678.
(Bonham's) $56 £25

PALMER, SAMUEL
'An English Version of the Eclogues of
Virgil' – 14 etched and photograved
plates after Palmer, original cloth, lower
joint torn, small folio – 1883.
(Christie's S.
  Kensington) $675 £300

A BOWL OF SILVER is examined, and found to contain nothing. In a moment it is mysteriously filled with bonbons, and afterwards with blazing punch, in quantity sufficient to fill a dozen bowls of the same size. The audience pronounce it to be delicious.

PALMER, WILLIAM H. 'Robert Heller'
'Robert Heller, His Doings' — spotted —
Melbourne, circa 1875.
Another Edition — Glasgow, 1875.
Illustrations, original wrappers, slightly
worn or stained.
(Sotheby's,
   Chancery Lane) $190   £85

PALOU, FRANCISCO
'Relacion Historica de la Vida y Apostoli-
cos Tareas del Venerable Padre Fray
Junipero Serra y de las Misiones que
Fundo en la California Septentrional' —
1st Edn., portrait, folding map of Cali-
fornia, a clean copy in con. vellum —
Mexico City, 1787.
(Sotheby's, New Bond
   Street) $2,250   £1,000

PAMPHLETS
'A Collection of 31 pamphlets dealing with
English Political Affairs, etc.' — slight
browning or soiling, wrappers or disbound
— 1710-4.
(Sotheby's
   London) $135   £60

RELACION HISTORICA
DE LA VIDA
Y APOSTOLICAS TAREAS
DEL VENERABLE PADRE
FRAY JUNIPERO SERRA,
Y de las Misiones que fundó en la California Sep-
tentrional, y nuevos establecimientos de Monterey.

ESCRITA
Por el R. P. L. Fr. FRANCISCO PALOU,
Guardian actual del Colegio Apostólico de S.
Fernando de México, y Discipulo del
Venerable Fundador:
DIRIGIDA
A SU SANTA PROVINCIA
DE LA REGULAR OBSERVANCIA
DE Nrô. S. P. S. FRANCISCO
DE LA ISLA DE MALLORCA.
A EXPENSAS
DE VARIOS BIENHECHORES.

Impressa en México, en la Imprenta de Don Felipe de Zúñiga
y Ontiveros, calle del Espíritu Santo, año de 1787.

*Relacion Historica .... del .... Padre Fray
Junipero Serra, by F. Palou. (Sotheby's)*

PAMPHLETS
A collection of 18 pamphlets, etc. in one
volume — some browning and soiling, half
calf, worn, one cover detached, Including
one by William Wilberforce — 1744-1819.
(Sotheby's
   London) $215   £95
PAMPHLETS
A collection of 76 political pamphlets —
some leaves soiled and frayed, a few torn or
spotted, many disbound, 19 bound
together in 4 vols., cont. half calf, defective,
a few in wrappers — 1785-1820.
(Sotheby's
   London) $245   £110
PANORAMA
'A Description of the Colosseum . . . and
eight coloured sections of the Panorama
of London, embossed by Messrs. Dobbs,
Bailey and Co.' — 22 plates, 8 coloured
and embossed, illus., cont. cloth, slightly
soiled, disbound — 1845.
(Christie's S.
   Kensington) $85   £38

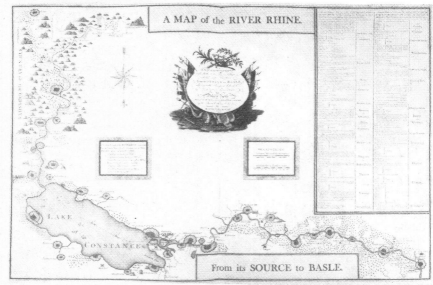

Map of the River Rhine by Matthias Koops. (Sotheby's)

PANORAMIC RIVER MAPS
KOOPS, MATTHIAS

'A Map of the River Rhine'; 'A Map of the River Maes'; 'River Scheldt' all 1797 – 9 double page remarkably detailed engraved maps, finely coloured in cont. hand, individual emblematic dedication cartouches, dated 1796, repaired, discoloured in places, atlas folio – M. Koops, June- Dec. 1797.

(Sotheby's, New Bond Street)	$3,600	£1,600

PANSERON, P.

'Grand et Nouveau Vignole' – engraved title, 80 plates, cloth backed boards, folio – circa 1870.

(Phillips)	$90	£40

PANTHEON, THE

. . . or History of the Heathen Gods and Heroes of Antiquity – wood engraved frontispiece and 27 full page illustrations by W. Green, lacking endpapers, cont. sheep, worn -- Printed for Osborne and Griffin, 1793.

(Sotheby's, Chancery Lane)	$80	£35

The Pantheon, illustrated by W. Green. (Sotheby's)

PAPA LOVECHILD SERIES
'The Aquatic Party' – 7 wood engraved
illustrations signed by J. R. B. coloured by
hand, one double page, original pictorial
wrappers – Dean and Son, 1865.
(Sotheby's,
    Chancery Lane) $45   £20

PAPWORTH, J. B.
'Hints on Ornamental Gardening' – 1st Edn.,
27 coloured aquatint plates, 1 tinted plan
with overslip, half title, some dampstains
and soiling, original boards, rebacked, uncut,
4to – 1823.
(Sotheby's, New Bond
    Street) $495   £220
'Select Views of London' – 76 coloured
aquatints, half calf, repaired – 1816.
(Sotheby's, New Bond
    Street) $2,475   £1,100

PAQUET, FRERES
'Modes et Costumes Historiques' – coloured
vignette, title, 96 hand coloured plates,
half morocco, worn – circa 1864.
(Phillips) $315   £140

PARDOE, JULIA
'The Beauties of the Bosphorus . . . illustrated by W. H. Bartlett' – steel engraved
additional title, 2 portraits, 84 plates and
one map, cont. calf, rubbed, lower cover
detached – n.d.
(Christie's S.
    Kensington) $135   £60

PARE, AMBROSE
'The Works of Ambrose Pare, translated
out of Latin and compared with the
French by Tho. Johnson' – engraved title
and numerous woodcuts throughout, 2nd
English Edn., folio, old calf rebacked,
some plates repaired – R. Coates and W.
Dugard, 1649.
(Bonham's) $1,080   £480
'Les Oeuvres . . . Avec Les Figures & Por-
traicts, Tant de l'Anatomie que Des
Instruments de Chirurgie & Des Plusieurs
Monstres' – 2nd Collected Edn., woodcut
portraits, illustrations in text, wormholes,
waterstaining, 19th century calf, worn,
folio – G. Buon, Paris, 1579.
(Sotheby's, New Bond
    Street) $3,375   £1,500

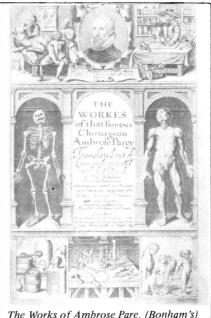

The Works of Ambrose Pare. (Bonham's)

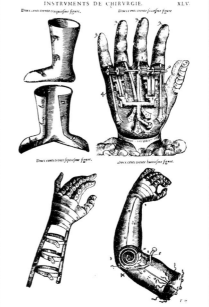

Les Oeuvres by Ambrose Pare. (Sotheby's)

273

'The Works' translated out of Latin and compared with the French by Th. Johnson — 1st English Edn., engraved title, 323 woodcuts, stained, torn, frayed, mended, worming, cont. calf, rebacked, folio — Th. Cotes and R. Young, 1635.
(Sotheby's, New Bond
　　Street)　　　　　$1,575　　　£700

PARIS, JOHN AYRTON
'Philosophy in Sport' — 3 vols., illustrations, cont. boards, extremeties rubbed — 1827.
(Christie's S.
　　Kensington)　　　$200　　　£90

PARIS, MATTHEW
'Historia Maior' — slightly stained, cont. calf, rubbed upper joint slightly split, crest stamped in gilt on covers, folio — Zurich, in officina Froschoviana — 1589.
(Christie's S.
　　Kensington)　　　$110　　　£50

PARISH WATSON AND CO.
'Chinese Pottery of the Han, T'ang and Sung dynasties' — 17 coloured plates, original cloth backed boards, slightly soiled, 4to — New York, 1917.
(Sotheby Humberts
　　Taunton)　　　　$45　　　£20

PARK, MUNGO
'Travels in the Interior Districts of Africa ... with an Appendix Containing Geographical Illustrations of Africa by Major Rennell' — 3rd Edn., engraved portrait, 3 engraved folding maps, 5 engraved plates, cont. calf, slightly worn — 1799.
(Sotheby's, New Bond
　　Street)　　　　$135　　　£60

PARKINSON, JOHN
'Paradise in Sole' — 2nd Edn., engraved additional title, illustrations, cont. calf, rubbed, spine chipped, folio — 1656.
(Christie's S.
　　Kensington)　　　$290　　　£130

PARLIAMENTARY BLUE BOOK
Papers relating to treatment of slaves in the colonies — 1818.
(Sotheby's, New Bond
　　Street)　　　　$22　　　£10
Price and Quality of Beer — original wrappers, uncut — 1819.
(Sotheby's, New Bond
　　Street)　　　　$22　　　£10

PARNELL, THOMAS
'Poems' — selected by Lennox Robinson, 1st Edn., limited to 200 copies, original linen backed boards, uncut, unopened — Cuala Press, Dublin, 1927.
(Sotheby's,
　　Chancery Lane)　　$50　　　£22

PARNELL, DR. THOMAS AND GOLDSMITH, OLIVER
'Poems on Several Occasions ... published by Mr. Pope ... to which is prefixed The Life of Dr. Parnell, written by Dr. Goldsmith' — 1st Edn., 2 copperplate engravings after S. Wale, contents leaf inserted at end, cont. half red morocco gilt — 1770.
(Sotheby's
　　London)　　　　$110　　　£50

PAROLES PEINTES
5 vols., 52 etched plates by Arp, Braque,
Chagall, Giacometti, Miro, Moore and
others, 34 coloured, to illustrate cont.
French poetry by Aragon, Jean Paulhan
and others, unsewn in original wrappers,
uncut, folders, slipcases – O. Lazar Vernet,
Paris, 1962-75.
(Sotheby's,
   Chancery Lane) $2,250   £1,000

PARRISH, MAXFIELD – WHARTON, E.
'Italian Villas and their Gardens' – plates,
one detached, the coloured ones by Parrish,
original cloth, stitching worn – 1904.
(Christie's S.
   Kensington) $110   £50

PARRY, CAPTAIN W. R.
'Journal of a Second (Third) Voyage for
the Discovery of the North West Passage'
– 1st Edn., 51 engraved plates including
11 aquatints and 10 folding maps and
charts. Uniformly bound, cont. purple
diced calf, rubbed, spines faded, gilt –
1824-26.
(Sotheby's, New Bond
   Street) $335   £150

PASCAL, BLAISE
'Les Provinciales' Lettre escritte a un
provincial par un de ses amis. Paris,
January 1656 to March 1657 – 18 issues,
minor waterstaining, uncut and unopened
– Elzevier, Leyden, 1656-57.
(Christie's, King
   St.) $1,575   £700

PASCIN, JULES – WARNOD, ANDRE
'Petites Filles dans la Rue' – frontispiece
and 34 illustrations by Pascin, 4 double
page, all coloured by hand, original
wrappers, spine torn, folder and slipcase
– Paris, 1925.
(Sotheby's,
   Chancery Lane) $650   £290

PASS, C. DE

'Hortus Floridus' – plates, limited edition
on hand made paper, vol. 2, small oblong
folio, boards, morocco back – Cresset
Press, 1929.
(Bonham's) $45   £20

PASSEBON, HENRY S. DE

'Plan de Plusieurs Batiments de Mer' –
engraved title and 17 plates, modern cloth
backed boards, oblong folio – Marseilles,
circa 1750.
(Sotheby's
    Belgravia) $4,950   £2,200

PATRIARCHS. (The testament of the
Twelve Patriarchs, translated by Robert
Grosseteste)
Black letter, 12 woodcut illustrations in
text, mss. inscriptions, browned and soiled,
lacking title and last leaf, calf, rebacked,
rubbed, in a calf backed cloth folding box
– late 17th century.
(Sotheby's
    London) $75   £35

PATRICK, SYMON

'Mensa Mystica; or A Discourse conerning
the Sacrament of the Lords Supper . . .
(with) Aqua Genitalis, a Discourse concerning Baptism' – 2 parts in one vol., 2nd
Edn., William Wordsworth's copy, general
title signed 'Wordsworth', slight browning
and soiling, the second part lacking all
after G5, panelled calf, slightly worn –
Strassburg, 1587.
(Sotheby's
    London) $45   £20

PAUL, HERMANN – RABELAIS, FRANCOIS

'La Vie Tres Horrifique du Grand Gargantua' – initials printed in red, 108 wood
engraved illustrations, decorations by
Paul, staining, original wrappers, slightly
discoloured – Pichon, Paris, 1921.
(Sotheby's,
    Chancery Lane) $15   £7

PAULUS, VENETUS

'Logica' – 48 leaves, double column, gothic
letter, one woodcut initial, diagram, worming, 16th century marginalia, wrappers –
Petrus de Quarengiis, Venice, 1500.
(Sotheby's, New Bond
    Street) $360   £160

PAVLOVA, ANNA

Charming signed photograph of Anna
Pavlova, signed in Russian to Vladimir
Ouranofsky, 15 x 20cm., red velvet
mount, framed and glazed – 28 September
1912.
(Sotheby's, New Bond
    Street) $495   £220

PAXTON, SIR J.

'Magazine of Botany and Register of
Flowering Plants' – vol. II only, 47 coloured
and one tinted plate, woodcut illus., cont.
half morocco, corners rubbed, front inner
hinge split – 1844.
(Christie's S.
    Kensington) $200   £90

PAYNE, A. H. – BICKNELL, W. I.

'Illustrated London' – 3 parts in two vols.,
printed title in vol. 2, engraved title in vol.
1, plates by Payne, occasional slight spotting, cont. half calf, rubbed – n.d.
(Christie's S.
    Kensington) $70   £32

PEACH, R. E.
'Historic Houses in Bath' – 3 vols., extra illustrated mainly with portraits, cont. half morocco, joints slightly rubbed – 1883.
(Christie's S.
Kensington) $810 $360

PEACHEY, CAROLINE (Translator)
'Later Tales of Hans Christian Andersen published between 1867 and 1868' – 1st English Edn., 8 engraved plates, plates by A. W. Cooper and others, original red cloth gilt, slightly stained, Herbert Bowes Lyon's copy with inscription – Bell and Duddy, 1869.
(Sotheby's,
Chancery Lane) $135   £60

PEACHEY, EMMA
'The Royal Guide to Wax Flower Modelling' – four hand coloured plates, a little browning, cont.hard grained morocco, rubbed – 1851.
(Christie's S.
Kensington) $110   £48

PEACOCK, FRANCIS
'Sketches Relative to the History and Theory but More Especially to the Practice of Dancing' – 1st Edn., rather browned throughout, modern cloth – Aberdeen, 1805.
(Sotheby's, New Bond
Street) $110   £50

PEARCH, G.
'A Collection of Poems . . . by Several Hands' – 2 vols., 1st Edn., half titles, engraved vignette on titles and at head of first text leaves, ads. on verso of final leaf of vol. I, a few leaves slightly spotted, cont. calf backed boards, slightly rubbed – 1768.
(Sotheby's
London) $135   £60

PEARSE, COL. HUGH WODEHOUSE
70th Regiment
Autograph mss. 'Rough Diary in India and Afghanistan 1875-80' – folio half morocco gilt, very neatly written on 362 pp., 3 plans one hand drawn, details of routes of marches, chiefly concerned with routine regimental duties.
(Lawrence of
Crewkerne) $270   £120

PEEBLESSHIRE AND ITS OUTLAND BORDERS
Map, cloth – Peebles, n.d.
(Tessa Bennett,
Edinburgh) $18   £8

'PEG'S COMPANION'
Nos. 1-532 in 23 volumes – 1921-32.
(Sotheby's,
Chancery Lane) $1,170   £520

PELBARTUS, OSWALD DE THEMESWAR
'Stellarium Corone Benedicte Marie Virginis in Laudem' – cont. calf over wooden boards, restitched, rebacked, remains of brass clasps preserved, folio – Hagenau, March 1501.
(Christie's, King
St.) $225   £100

PEMBROKE, HENRY, EARL OF
'A Method of Breaking Horses and Teaching Soldiers to Ride, designed for the use of the army' – 2nd Edn., two folding plates, cont. sprinkled calf, gilt, head and foot of spine chipped – 1762.
(Sotheby's, New Bond
Street) $315   £140

PENDRAGON; OR, THE CARPET KNIGHT HIS CALENDAR
1st Edn., advert leaf at end, browned, 18th century panelled calf, gilt, rubbed, upper joint split, 8vo – For John Newton, 1698.
(Sotheby's, New Bond
Street) $22   £10

PENE DU BOIS

PENE DU BOIS, RAOUL
26 pen and watercolour costume and
stage designs etc. for Joan of Arc, some
heightened in silver, one with material
samples attached, 3 with colour cards
and written suggestions for materials.
All numbered in red crayon, various sizes
— 1948.
(Sotheby's, New Bond
    Street)   **$945**   **£420**

PENNANT, THOMAS
'Some Account of London, Westminster
and Southwark' — 2 vols., 139 plates, extra
illustrated, some plates lacking, cont. calf,
worn, covers detached, folio — n.d.
(Christie's S.
    Kensington)   **$85**   **£38**

PENZER, N. M.
'The Book of the Wine-Label' — plates,
original cloth, dust jacket — 1947.
(Christie's S.
    Kensington)   **$27**   **£12**

PEPYS, SAMUEL
'Memoirs' Edited by Richard, Lord
Braybrooke — 2 vols., 1st Edn., 13 engraved

portraits and plates, one folding, half titles,
some spotting and staining, later half
morocco, slightly rubbed — 1825.
(Christie's S.
    Kensington)   **$110**   **£50**
'The Diary' — 10 vols., Edited by Henry B.
Wheatley, original cloth, t.e.g. — 1920.
(Christie's S.
    Kensington)   **$45**   **£20**

PERCIVAL, ROBERT
'An Account of the Island of Ceylon' —
1st Edn., 4 folding engraved maps, some
leaves slightly spotted, cont. calf, gilt spine,
slightly rubbed, 4to — 1803.
(Sotheby Humberts
    Taunton)   **$155**   **£70**

PERCY, THOMAS
'The Hermit of Warkworth' — 2nd Edn.,
wood engraved illustrations, some full
page, cont. half morocco spine chipped —
Alnwick, 1807.
(Christie's S.
    Kensington)   **$70**   **£32**

PEREGRINUS
'Sermones peregrini de Tempore et de
Sanctis' — 1st Edn., 173 leaves of 176, 40
lines, semi gothic letter, some worming,
staining and discolouring, modern boards,
rubbed, folio — Strasbourg, circa 1474-77.
(Sotheby's, New Bond
    Street)   **$900**   **£400**

PERRAULT, CHARLES
'A Treatise of the Five Orders of Columns
in Architecture' — translated by John
James, engraved frontis, title, 7 plates and
24 head pieces, initials and tail pieces by
John Sturt, cont. calf, rebacked, worn,
folio — 1708.
(Sotheby's, New Bond
    Street)   **$495**   **£220**

PERRIER, FRANCOIS
'Eigentyke Afbeeldinge van Hondert
Aldervermaerdste statuen op antique
beelden' — engraved title and 86 engraved
plates of 100 by Cornelis van Dalen, title
torn and partly repaired and other plates
torn, marginal numbering in ink, cont.
mottled calf, gilt spine, folio — N.
Visscher, Amsterdam, 1702.
(Christie's, King
    St.)   **$170**   **£75**

'Roman Statues' – 100 fine engravings of sculptures, engraved title and 100 plates, index, half calf, folio – Rome, 1638. ·
(Tessa Bennett,
   Edinburgh) $180   £80
'Segmenta Nobilium Signorum et Statuarii' – engraved title with dedication addressed to Roger Duplessis, engraved index at end and 100 engraved plates on 51 leaves, mounted on guards, old thick paper boards, very worn and rubbed, folio – J. J. de Rubies, Rome, 1638.
(Sotheby's, New Bond
   Street) $335   £150

PERRIN, M.
'Fables Amusantes' – 4th Edn., engraved frontispiece, one illustration and one decoration, cont. sheep, slightly worn – Law, Cadell and Elmsley, 1785.
(Sotheby's,
   Chancery Lane) $33   £15

PERRY, GEORGE
'Conchology or the Natural History of Shells' – 58 hand coloured engraved plates, occasional light offsetting, 19th century green half morocco worn and stained, folio – William Miller, 1811.
(Sotheby's, New Bond
   Street) $360   £160

'PERSIA'
Hand coloured map – Ortelius, circa 1630.
(Phillips) $135   £60

PERSIUS, FLACCUS, AULUS
'Satyrae' – 64 leaves of 72, 54 lines of commentary and headline, gothic letter, light staining, cont. French blindstamped calf, very worn, folio – Nicholaus Wolf, Lyon, 1499.
(Sotheby's, New Bond
   Street) $292   £130

PETER PARLEY'S ANNUAL . . 1860, 1865, 1869, 1883
4 volumes, coloured frontispiece and end-pieces, numerous wood engraved illustrations, third lacking frontispiece, slightly spotted, some leaves loose, original decorated gilt cloth, worn and faded, some joints torn, hinges weak, and a duplicate of the second, defective – 1860-83.
(Sotheby's,
   Chancery Lane) $45   £20

Le Magicien divertissant.

PETIT MAGICIEN, LE, OU RECUEIL D'EXPERIENCES, TIREES DE LA MAGIE BLANCHE ET DES AMUSEMENTS DE SCIENCES
Wood engraved frontispiece and 40 illustrations on 10 leaves, somewhat spotted, corner torn, cont. wrapping – Delarue, Paris, 1860.
(Sotheby's,
   Chancery Lane) $325   £145

PETRARCA, FRANCESCO
'De Remediis Utriusque Fortunae', Edited by Nicolas Lucarus, 160 leaves of 166, roman letter, woodcut device at end, wormed, light waterstaining, 18th century calf, gilt, rebacked, corners worn, folio – Cremona, 1492.
(Sotheby's, New Bond
   Street) $540   £240

PETRONIUS
Complete Works, limited edition signed by
Jack Lindsay, illustrated by Norman
Lindsay, half vellum gilt – n.d.
(Phillips) $180   £80

PETRUS COMESTOR
'Historia Scholastica' – 49 leaves of 254,
45 lines and headline, double column, gothic
letter, initials in red and blue, rubricated,
wormed, waterstained, frayed and dogeared,
disbound, folio – Strasbourg, 1483.
(Sotheby's, New Bond
    Street) $380   £170

PETRUS DE ROSENHEIM
'Rationarium Evangelistarum' 1502;
Marcellus – 'Passio Petri et Pauli Apostolo-
rum ac Disputatio Eorundem Contra
Simonem Quemdam Magnum' 1499;
Poenitias Cito, 2nd Edn., 1490;
Andreas De Escobar 'Modus de Confitendi'
1480; Basil, Saint and Archbishop of
Caesarea 'De Legendis Antiquorum Libris
Opusculum Divinum' 1502; Herbanus
Maurus 'De Institutione Clericorum' 1504 –
six works in one volume, cont. German
blindstamped pigskin over wooden boards.
(Sotheby's, New Bond
    Street) $5,850   £2,600

PETRUS, TOMMAI 'Ravennas'
'Aurea Opuscula' – gothic letter, some early
ms. notes, slight browning and soiling,
modern vellum boards, ties – Quentel,
Cologne, 1508.
(Sotheby's, New Bond
    Street) $495   £220

PETTIGREW, T. J.
'A History of Egyptian Mummies' – 13
plates after G. Cruikshank, four coloured,
some spotted, cont. speckled calf, rubbed
– 1834.
(Christie's S.
    Kensington) $135   £60

PFINTZING, MELCHIOR
'Die Geuerlicheiten und Einstils der
Geschichten des Loblichen Streyt Paren
und Hochberumbten Helds un Ritters
Herr Tewrdannckhs' – 118 woodcuts by
Hans Schauffelein and Hans Burghmair,
cont. Nuremberg binding of pigskin over
wooden boards, clasps intact, folio –
Nuremberg, 1517.
(Sotheby Parke Bernet
    Monaco) $157,500 £70,000

PHILBY, H. ST. JOHN B.
'A Pilgrim in Arabia' – no. 262 of 350
copies, portrait, original morocco backed
cloth, spine stained, t.e.g. – Golden
Cockerel Press, 1943.
(Christie's S.
  Kensington) $270   £120

PHILIP III, KING OF SPAIN 1598-1621
'Carta Executoria de Hidalguia' – illuminated mss. on vellum, 74 leaves, 34 lines
on gothic script in brown ink, ruled in
red, large illuminated initials, two historiated, one small miniature and 3 full
page miniatures with silk guard between,
cont. velvet covered boards, spine very
worn, folio – Granada, 6 September, 1603.
(Christie's, King
  St.) $1,685   £750

PHILIP, PRINCE, DUKE OF
EDINBURGH
Typed letter to Andre Deutsch, the
publisher, 27 lines folio from Sandringham
January 1978 about his preface to a book,
and another – 1978.
(Lawrence of
  Crewkerne) $135   £60

PHILIPPE, CHARLES LOUIS
'Bubu de Montparnasse' – no. 79 of
130 copies, numerous illustrations by
Dunoyer de Segonzac with a separate
suite of illustrations limited to 60 copies,
unbound, original wrappers and slipcase
– Paris, 1929.
(Sotheby Parke Bernet
  Monaco) $15,750   £7,000

PHILIPS, JOHN
'Cyder. A Poem' – 1st Edn., large paper
copy, engraved frontis (inlaid), a trifle
wormed in some lower inner margins, cont.
panelled calf, rebacked – 1708.
(Sotheby's
  London) $135   £60

PHILIPS, MIDSHIPMAN JOHN
'An Authentic Journal of the Late Expedi-
tion under the command of Commodore
Anson' – some cont. marginalia, a little
soiling, cont. calf, rubbed, joints and
spine cracked – 1744.
(Christie's S.
  Kensington) $405   £180

PHILLIP, ARTHUR
'The Voyage to Botany Bay' – engraved
portrait, title and 53 plates and charts,
cont. calf, worn – John Stockdale, 1789.
(Christie's S.
  Kensington) $945   £420

PHILLIPS, PHILIP
'The Forth Bridge in its Various Stages of
Construction' – 2nd Edn., plates, some
double page, original cloth, soiled –
Edinburgh, n.d.
(Christie's S.
  Kensington) $70   £32

PHILPOTTS, EDEN.
'The Girl and the Faun' – no. 304 of 350
copies, signed by author and artist,
coloured plates and illustrations by Frank
Brangwyn, presentation inscription from
author, original parchment backed boards,
slightly rubbed, t.e.g., 4to – 1916.
(Sotheby Humberts
  Taunton) $360   £160
Ten volumes of novels, all 1st Edns.,
including 'The Runaways'; 'The Enchanted
Wood'; 'A Dartmoor Village'; 'The Hidden
Hand'; 'The Changeling' – signed by
author – 1928-54.
(Sotheby Humberts
  Taunton) $470   £210

PHOTIUS

PHOTIUS, Patriarch of Constantinople
'Librorum quos legit Photius Patriarcha
excerpta et censurae' – 1st Edn., edited
by David Hoeschelius, Greek text, device
on title, blank fore corner torn from last
leaf, a few rust spots and marginal stains,
cont. vellum boards, soiled, Harvard
College bookplate and release stamp, folio
– Augsburg, Joannes Praetorius, 1601.
(Sotheby's
    London) $200   £90

PHOTOGRAPH ALBUM

Album of 44 cabinet photographs and 4
photographic postcards of American actors
and actresses and some European and
English composers and singers, original
morocco with clasp, rubbed, spine defective – New York, circa 1872-1911.
(Sotheby's, New Bond
    Street) $630   £280

PHOTOGRAPHS

Collection of about 350 photographs and
film stills of Martha Graham, Alicia
Markova, Anton Dolin, Tallulah Bankhead
and many others by Marcus Blechman,
Seymour and others, various sizes – circa
1935-50.
(Sotheby's, New Bond
    Street) $200   £90

PHYBUS, WILLIAM

'The Amusing Companion' – a few leaves
spotted, morocco backed boards – Hull,
1818.
(Sotheby's,
    Chancery Lane) $290   £130

PICART, B.

'Impostures Innocentes or a Collection
of Prints' – portrait plates, half leather,
worn, folio – J. Boydell, London, 1756.
(Sotheby Parke Bernet
    Monaco) $1,575   £700

PICASSO, PABLO – LEIRIS, MICHEL

'Balzac en Bas de Casse et Picasso Sans
Majuscules' – 8 full page lithographed
portraits of Balzac by Picasso, a reproduction of another, unsewn, uncut,
●riginal cloth portfolio – Louise Leiris,
Paris, 1957.
(Sotheby's,
    Chancery Lane) $720   £320

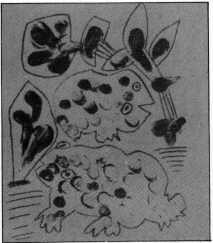

PICASSO, PABLO – TZARA, TRISTAN

'De Memoire d'Homme' – 9 full page
lithographs by Picasso including title,
original wrappers, uncut, red half morocco
folder, slipcase – Bordas, Paris, 1950.
(Sotheby's,
    Chancery Lane) $585   £260

PICASSO, PABLO – BUFFON, COMTE GEORGES LOUIS LECLERC DE

'Eaux Fortes Originales Pour Les Textes
de Buffon' – 31 etched plates by Picasso,
unsewn in original wrappers, folder,
slipcase damaged, folio – Martin Fabiani,
Paris, 1942.
(Sotheby's,
    Chancery Lane) $9,900   £4,400

PICASSO, PABLO — ARISTOPHANES
'Lysistrata' translated by Gilbert Seldes
— 6 etched plates by Picasso, 30 illustrations in text, original decorated boards,
uncut, folder, no. 901 of 1,500 copies,
signed by artist — Limited Editions Club,
New York, 1934.
(Sotheby's,
   Chancery Lane) $810   £360

PICASSO, PABLO — LEIRIS, MICHEL
'Balzac en Bas de Casse et Picasso Sans
Majuscule' — 8 full page lithographed
portraits of Balzac by Picasso, a reproduction of another about limitation
statement, unsewn, uncut, in original
cloth portfolio — Louise Leiris, Paris,
1957.
(Sotheby's,
   Chancery Lane) $630   £280

PICASSO, PABLO — CESAIRE, AIME
'Corps Perdu' — 32 etched plates by Picasso
including cover design, original wrappers,
uncut, folder, slipcase — Editions Fragrance,
Paris, 1950.
(Sotheby's,
   Chancery Lane) $2,475   £1,100

'PICTORIAL STATIONERY'
A collection of 149 sheets of notepaper
with engraved views of the British Isles,
a few slightly soiled, loose.
(Sotheby's,
   Chancery Lane) $515   £230

PICTURESQUE EUROPE
The British Isles — 2 vols., steel engraved
plates, cont. morocco, gilt — n.d.
(Christie's S.
   Kensington) $55   £25

PICTURESQUE EUROPE
6 vols., engraved additional titles, plates
and illustrations after various artists,
original pictorial cloth, slightly soiled, some
inner hinges broken — n.d.
(Christie's S.
   Kensington) $245   £110

PIGAGE, NICOLAS DE
'Le Galerie Electorale de Dusseldorff ou
Catalogue raisonne et Figure de ses Tableaux'
— 2 vols., one of plates, engraved title
vignettes, six other engraved illustrations,
30 full page engraved plates, 18th century
calf, rebacked, spine and joints rubbed,
oblong folio — Basle, 1778.
(Christie's, King
   St.) $270   £120

PIGNORIA, LORENZO
'De Servis et Eorum Apud Veteres Minis-
teriis Commentarius' — 1st Edn., numerous
woodcut illus., several full page, one folding,
late 17th century calf, gilt, interlacing
cypher of Gaston de France, Duc d'Orleans
in panels of spine, hinges cracked, 4to —
Augsburg, 1613.
(Sotheby's, New Bond
   Street) $405   £180

PIGOT, JAMES AND CO.
'British Atlas of the Counties of England'
— 40 hand coloured engraved maps only,
mounted on cloth, 2 folding, lacking
Pigot's New Map of the Environs of
London, slight soiling, cont. half calf, worn,
g.e., folio — 1831.
(Christie's S.
   Kensington) $785   £350
'New Commercial Directory for Scotland
for 1825-26' — calf, thick, one hand
coloured map — 1826.
(Tessa Bennett,
   Edinburgh) $55   £24

PILULAND, ELIAS
'Hocus Pocus, die Taschenspielerkunst
Leicht zu Lernen, Ingleichen Schone
Kunstgriffe vor Spieler' – engraved frontis-
piece and woodcut illustrations, boards,
slightly stained – Frankfurt und Leipzig,
circa 1730.
(Sotheby's,
Chancery Lane) $855   £380

PINARD, A.
'Traite du Palper Abdominal au Point de
Vue Obstetrical et de la Version par
Manoeuvres Externes' – 1st Edn., 27
illustrations, new half calf – Paris, 1878.
(Bonham's) $675   £300

PINELLI, BARTOLOMEO
'Istoria Romana' – 101 plates, title and a
few preliminary leaves creased, cont.
green roan backed boards, worn, oblong
folio – Rome, 1818-19.
(Sotheby's, New Bond
Street) $360   £160

PINKERTON, ALLAN
'Claude Melnotte as a detective and other
stories' – fifteen thousand, manuscript
dedication on front free-end paper by the
author to Sir John Duke, Baron Coleridge,
Lord Chief Justice, plates, original decorated cloth, soiled – 1880.
(Christie's S.
Kensington) $27   £12

PIRANESI, FRANCESCO
'Il Teatro d'Ercolano' – double page
engraved title, 8 of 9 double page plates,
half title, repaired and mounted, disbound,
folio – Rome, 1783.
(Sotheby's, New Bond
Street) $270   £120

PISARRO, LUCIEN
'Notes on the Eragny Press and a Letter to
J. B. Manson' – limited to 500 copies,
plates, original boards – Cambridge, 1957.
(Christie's S.
Kensington) $170   £75

PITCAIRN, ARCHIBALD
'The Philosophical and Mathematical
Elements of Physick . . . translated by John
Quincy' – 2nd Edn., cont. calf, 8vo. – W.
Innys, 1745.
(Sotheby's, New Bond
Street) $200   £90

PITOU, LOUIS ANGE
'Voyage a Cayenne' – 2 vols. in one, 2
engraved frontis., minor foxing, cont. half
calf, hinges cracked, 8vo – Paris, 1805.
(Christie's
St. James) $155   £70

PLAGUE
'A Historical Narrative of the Great Plague
of London 1665 and some other remarkable plagues ancient and modern' – old
calf, rebacked, 8vo – W. Nicoll, 1769.
(Sotheby's, New Bond
Street) $135   £60

PLANETE, LA PREMIERE REVUE DE BIBLIOTHEQUE
Edited by Louis Pauwels, nos. 1-32, num-
erous illustrations, some coloured, original
wrappers – Paris, 1961-67.
(Sotheby's,
Chancery Lane) $110   £50

PLANSON, ANDRE – BARONCELLI, JEAN DE
'Vingt Six Hommes' – lithographed vig-
nette, on title, 36 illustrations by Planson,
11 full page, unsewn in original wrappers,
uncut, slipcase, slightly worn – Archat,
Paris, 1842.
(Sotheby's,
Chancery Lane) $15   £7

PLATT, SIR HUGH
'A Closet for Ladies and Gentlewomen'
with 'Delights for Ladies to Adorne their
Persons, Tables, Closets and Distillatories'
– two works in one vol., pages enclosed
within woodcut border, cont. calf, recornered, worn – 1632.
(Christie's, King
    St.) $1,125   £500
'The Jewell House of Art and Nature' – 1st
Edn., 3 architectural woodcut titles, woodcut arms of Earl of Essex on verso, woodcut illustrations and initials, 19th century
calf a little rubbed – 1594.
(Christie's, King
    St.) $225   £100

PLAUTUS, CASPAR
'Nova Typis, Transacta Navigatio, Nova
Orbis Indiae Occidentalis' – engraved title,
19 engraved plates, including portrait of
Columbus, engraved illustration and
woodcut design, foxing, cont. limp vellum
– 1621.
(Christie's, King
    St.) $2,700   £1,200

PLAW, J.
'Sketches for Country Houses, Villas and
Rural Dwellings' – sepia aquatints, half
morocco – 1803.
(Sotheby's, New Bond
    Street) $495   £220

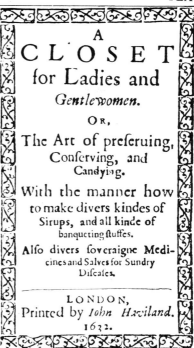

A Closet for Ladies and Gentlewomen,
by Sir Hugh Platt. (Christie's)

Nova Typis, Transacta Navigatio, Nova Orbis Indiae Occidentalis, by Caspar Plautus.
(Christie's)

PLAYFAIR, WILLIAM
'Thoughts on the Present State of French Politics' – folding maps, hand coloured, second in outline only, original boards, upper cover detached – 1793.
(Christie's S.
  Kensington) $55   £25

PLAYFORD, J.
'Musical Companion' – 2 parts in one vol., oblong, half calf, title and two leaves of table and last leaf in facsimile – 1667.
(Bonham's) $22   £10

PLAZZONUS, F.
'De Partibus Generationi Inservientibus, Lib II' – engraved frontispiece, vellum – 1664.
(Bonham's) $245   £110

PLESHCHEEV, ALEXANDRA
'Our Ballet' (1673-1896) – 1st Edn., numerous photographs and drawings, decorations on title page and in text, modern morocco backed boards, original upper wrapper bound in – St. Petersburg, 1896.
(Sotheby's, New Bond
  Street) $45   £20

PLINIUS SECUNDUS, GAUIS CAECILIUS
'Opera' – device on title and last page, 18th century vellum gilt spine, label – Venice, 1518.
(Sotheby's, New Bond
  Street) $225   £100

PLOT, ROBERT
'The Natural History of Oxfordshire' – folding map and 16 engraved plates, half morocco gilt, folio – Oxford, 1705.
(Phillips) $290   £130
'The Natural History of Staffordshire' – engraved title, folding map, plates, calf upper cover detached, folio – Oxford, 1686.
(Phillips) $1,080   £480

PLUTARCH
'La Prime Parte Delle Vite' – device on title and last leaf, Italian red morocco, gilt, joints repaired but a particularly nice example, bookplate of J. Bizzarro, in a cloth case – Golito, Venice, 1555.
(Sotheby Parke Bernet
  Monaco) $7,875   £3,500

'Les Vies Des Hommes Illustres . . . translatees par M. Jaques' – 2 vols., title page of vol. 2 repaired with the loss of a few letters, cont. parchment – 1654.
(Christie's S.
  Kensington) $65   £28
'The Lives of the Noble Grecians and Romans' – 5 vols., limited edn., translated by T. North, illustrated by T. L. Poulton, original buckram, t.e.g. – Nonesuch Press, 1929.
(Phillips) $80   £35

POE, EDGAR ALLAN
'The Bells' – illustrated by E. Dulac, cloth gilt – Hodder, n.d.
(Phillips) $100   £45

POELINITZ, CARL LUDWIG BARON VON
'Amusements des Eaux de Spa' – Nouvelle Edn., 2 of 4 parts in one volume, 2 engraved titles, 2 engraved frontispieces and 7 folding plates, cont. calf, rubbed – Amsterdam, 1652.
(Sotheby's, New Bond
  Street) $80   £35

POGANY, WILLY AND GOETHE, J. W. VON
'Faust' translated by Abraham Hayward – coloured plates by Pogany, original cloth, slightly soiled – 1908.
(Christie's S.
  Kensington) $40   £18

POGANY, WILLY – WAGNER, RICHARD
'Tannhauser' – mounted coloured plates by Pogany, original cloth, slightly soiled – n.d.
(Christie's S.
  Kensington) $70   £32

POISSON, J. B.
'Cris de Paris' – engraved title 72 fine engraved plates, cont. red morocco gilt, arms of J. Bignon, 1747-84, the royal librarian, gilt on sides, very slight wear – Paris, 1775.
(Sotheby Parke Bernet
  Monaco) $49,500   £22,000

POLE, THOMAS
'The Anatomical Instructor or an Illustration of the Modern Methods of Preparing and Preserving the different parts of the Human Body' – New Edn. with additional notes, 10 folding plates, advertisement leaf at end, original boards, uncut, 8vo – J. Callow, 1813.
(Sotheby's, New Bond
  Street) $80   £35

POLISH MILITARY UNIFORMS
'Rocznik Woyskony Krolestwa Polskiego,
Na Rok, 1824' — original blue cloth, 46
tissued coloured lithographs of soldiers in
uniform with captions, some with super-
scripts which appear to indicate changes
in the uniforms in November 1826 —
Warsaw, circa 1827.
(Lawrence of
    Crewkerne) $515   £230

POLITICAL CARTOONS
A collection of about 100 lithographs by H.
H. and H. B. — folio — circa 1830.
(Tessa Bennett,
    Edinburgh) $95   £42

'POLLOCK'S JUVENILE DRAMA —
DOUGLAS'
11 hand coloured plates loose as issued,
one incomplete and made up from
duplicate, text in original wrappers.
Together with a list of published titles —
n.d.
(Christie's S.
    Kensington) $70   £30

POLO, MARCO
'The most Noble and Famous Travels' —
no. 543 of 1,050 copies, plates and maps,
original vellum backed cloth, gilt — 1929.
(Sotheby's,
    Chancery Lane) $95   £42

PONTEY, WILLIAM
'The Forest Pruner; or, Timber Owner's
Assistant' — 3rd Edn., 8 plates, some fold-
ing, some hand coloured, occasional spott-
ing, original boards, joints split — 1810.
(Christie's S.
    Kensington) $70   £32

POOLE, BENJAMIN
'Coventry: its History and Antiquities' —
lithographed plates, some tinted, some
folding, original cloth, gilt, slightly soiled
— 1870.
(Sotheby's,
    Chancery Lane) $125   £55

POPE, ALEXANDER
'An Essay on Man, being the First book of
Ethic Epistles. To Henry St. John, L.
Bolingbroke' — 1st quarto edn., title in red
and black with engraved vignette, engraved
head and tail pieces, half title, cont. calf
backed marbled boards, worn — 1734.
(Sotheby's
    London) $135   £60

POPE, ALFRED
'The Old Stone Crosses of Dorset' — green
half morocco gilt, t.e.g., rest uncut, folding
map, 34 tissued and mounted black and
white plates, very good copy — Chiswick
Press, 1906.
(Lawrence of
    Crewkerne) $45   £20

POPE, A. U.
'A Survey of Persian Art' — 6 vols., original
edition, 1,482 plates many coloured and
numerous illustrations, cloth — Oxford,
1938-39.
(Sotheby Parke Bernet
    Monaco) $15,750   £7,000

POPE PAUL III — 1534-49.
Papal document on vellum with calligraphic
heading and lead portrait seal.
(Phillips) $1,170   £520

POPHAM, A. E.
'The Drawings of Leonardo da Vinci' —
plates, cloth — 1931.
(Phillips) $18   £8

'POPULAR COUNTY HISTORIES' — 15
volumes, original cloth — 1885-1900.
(Sotheby's,
    Chancery Lane) $225   £100

PORTAL

PORTAL, P.
'La Pratique des Accouchements Soutenue
d'un Grand Nombre d'Observations' –
portrait and 8 plates, 1st Edn., cont. calf,
rebacked – G. Martin, Paris, 1685.
(Bonham's) $855   £380

PORTEFEUILLE
18th century French red morocco, spine
gilt with fleur de lys in compartments and
in corners of covers, lined with cont. gilt
flowered paper, engraved lock in brass with
key.
(Sotheby Parke Bernet
    Monaco) $5,625   £2,500
Another 18th century French red morocco,
rather worn, with a miscellaneous collection of menus, photographs etc.
(Sotheby Parke Bernet
    Monaco) $3,375   £1,500

PORTER, ROBERT KER
'Travelling Sketches in Russia and Sweden'
– 2 vols. in one, 39 plates of 41, many
coloured, a few folding, one torn, vol. 2
lacks half title, some foxing and offsetting,
cont. dark blue half calf, rubbed, lower
joint split – 1809.
(Sotheby's
    London) $160   £70

PORTLAND, DUKE OF
'Fifty Years and More of Sport in Scotland'
– frontispiece and other plates, cloth, small
folio, first edition – 1933.
(Tessa Bennett,
    Edinburgh) $49   £22

**PORTRAITS AND CHARACTERS OF
THE KINGS OF ENGLAND**
2 parts, wood engraved vignette on title,
33 illustrations coloured by hand, original
pictorial wrappers, soiled and worn – John
Harris, n.d.
(Sotheby's,
    Chancery Lane) $40   £18

POTTER, BEATRIX
'The Tale of Mr. Tod' – original boards,
coloured plates, 1st Edn. – 1912.
(Tessa Bennett,
    Edinburgh) $15   £7
'The Roly Poly Pudding' – 1st Edn.,
illustrations, a little soiling, original cloth
– 1908.
(Christie's S.
    Kensington) $27   £12

Watercolour drawing of Greenhouses and
Cucumber Frames among Trees and
Shrubbery – inscriptions in various hands
in verso including H. B. Potter and 'sent
among packing paper to her cousin, Mary
Hutton' – framed and glazed.
(Sotheby's,
    Chancery Lane) $1,685   £750

Two watercolour drawings of clumps of
toadstools on one sheet – slightly spotted
and soiled, inscribed on the back by
the artist 'Dunkeld'.
(Sotheby's,
    Chancery Lane) $830   £370

POTTER, STEPHEN (Editor)
'Minnow Among Tritons, Mrs. S. T.
Coleridge's Letters to Thomas Poole' –
no. 470 of 675 copies, portrait,
original cloth – The Nonesuch Press, 1917.
(Christie's S.
   Kensington) $18   £8

POUND, EXRA
'Cavalcanti Poems' – 1st Edn., no. 165 of
200 copies, signed by author, original
vellum backed boards, slipcase – 1916.
(Sotheby's
   Chancery Lane) $450   £200
'Exultations' – 1st Edn., original boards,
slightly worn, uncut – 1909.
(Sotheby's,
   Chancery Lane) $65   £28
'Selected Poems' Introduction by T. S.
Eliot – 1st Edn., original cloth, spine
faded, rubbed – 1928.
(Sotheby's,
   Chancery Lane) $15   £7

POUQUEVILLE, F.
'Travels through the Morea, Albania' – 2
plates, some annotations in pencil, later
cloth – 1806.
(Christie's S.
   Kensington) $65   £28

POWELL, R. HUTCHINSON
'A Medical Topography of Tunbridge
Wells' – map and litho plates – Tunbridge
Wells, 1846.
(Bonham's) $45   £20

POWYS, JOHN COWPER
'Lucifer' – 1st Edn., no. 344 of 500 copies,
signed by author, wood engraved illustrations by Agnes Miller Parker, original
morocco backed cloth, gilt, unopened –
1956.
(Sotheby's,
   Chancery Lane) $100   £45

POWYS, LLEWELYN
'The Book of Days' – no. 238 of 300
copies, full page illustrations by Elizabeth
Corsellis, original morocco backed cloth,
t.e.g., folio – Golden Cockerel Press, 1937.
(Christie's S.
   Kensington) $200   £90

'Glory of Life' – no. 262 of 277 copies,
frontispiece and illustrations by Robert
Gibbings, original parchment backed cloth,
t.e.g., folio – Golden Cockerel Press, 1934.
(Christie's S.
   Kensington) $425   £190

POWYS, T. F.
'Fables' – 1st Edn., no. 492 of 750 copies
signed by author, 4 illustrations by Gilbert
Spencer, original cloth, slightly damp-
stained, t.e.g., dust jacket – 1929.
(Sotheby's,
   Chancery Lane) $45   £20
'Goat Green or the Better Gift' – no. 79
of 150 copies, signed by author, frontis-
piece and full page illustrations by Gwenda
Morgan, original morocco backed cloth,
dust jacket spotted, t.e.g. – Golden
Cockerel Press, 1937.
(Christie's S.
   Kensington) $110   £50

POZZO, ANDREA
'Rules and Examples of Perspective proper
for Painters and Architects, etc. In English
and Latin' – 2 engraved titles, frontis,
tear repairs and 102 plates, two stained,
some soiling, last leaf of text laid down,
cont. calf, rebacked, old covers laid down,
folio – John Sturt, 1707.
(Christie's S.
   Kensington) $470   £210

PRATT, ANNE
'Flowering Plants, Grasses, Sedges and Ferns
of Great Britain' – 6 vols., coloured plates,
occasional spotting, original cloth, extreme-
ties slightly rubbed, g.e. – n.d.
(Christie's S.
   Kensington) $145   £65
'Wild Flowers' – 2 vols., coloured plates,
modern morocco backed cloth – n.d.
(Christie's S.
   Kensington) $45   £20

'THE PREACHER'
Presentation copy by the artist Owen
Jones, illuminated text, some damp-
staining, carved wooden covers – 1849.
(Phillips) $135   £60

PRENNER

PRENNER, G. G.
'Illustri fatti Farnesiani . . . Palazzo di
Caprarola' – half calf, 41 plates, lacks
title, plate no. 19 defective folio, circa
1748.
(Phillips) $191   £85

PRESCOTT, W. H.
'Historical Writings' – 9 vols., cloth –
1857-60.
Also W. Robertson – Works – 8 vols.,
portraits, calf rubbed, 8vo – 1825.
(Phillips) $33   £15
'History of the Conquest of Mexico' – 3
vols., 2 maps, slight tear, original cloth –
1843.
(Phillips) $80   £36

PRETRUS MAGISTER
'Canonis Missae Interpretario, cum Addition-
ibus' – 211 leaves of 212, 34 lines, gothic
letter, woodcut initials, lightly waterstained,
18th century mottled sheep, spine worn –
Salamanca, 1499.
(Sotheby's, New Bond
    Street) $900   £400

PREVOST D'EXILES, A.
'Histoire du Chevalier des Grieux et de
Manon Lescaut' – 2 vols., 8 plates, cont.
calf, gilt spines, little worn – Amsterdam,
Paris, 1753.
(Sotheby Parke Bernet
    Monaco) $5,850   £2,600

PRICE, L.
'Tauromachia' – coloured litho, title, 25
coloured litho plates, quarter morocco,
original silk boards – 1852.
(Phillips) $1,125   £500

PRICE, RICHARD
'Observations on the Nature of Civil
Liberty - and the Justice and Policy of the
War with America' – 2nd Edn., modern
half calf – 1776.
(Christie's S.
    Kensington) $55   £25

PRICE, R. K.
'Astbury, Whieldon and Ralph Wood
Figures, and Toby Jugs' – limited to 500
copies, plates, some coloured and folding,
original buckram backed boards, corners
bumped, dust jacket – 1922.
(Christie's S.
    Kensington) $290   £130

PRICE, S.
'Illustrations of the Fungi of Our Fields
and Woods' – hand coloured illus., cloth
gilt, 4to – 1865.
(Phillips) $180   £80

PRICE, UVEDALE
'A Dialogue on the distinct characters of
the Picturesque and the Beautiful' – 1st
Edn., half title, last leaf blank, cont. calf,
upper hinge split – Hereford, 1801.
(Sotheby's
    London) $225   £100

PRIDEAUX, MATHIAS
'An Easy and Compendious Introduction
for Reading all sorts of Histories' – 3
parts in one vol., 2nd Edn., general title
in red and black – 17th century style
panelled calf – 1650.
(Sotheby's, New Bond
    Street) $65   £28

PRIDEAUX, S. T.
'Aquatint Engraving' – illus., cloth gilt,
t.e.g. – 1909.
(Phillips) $100   £45

PRIEST, CAPTAIN C. D.
'The Birds of Southern Rhodesia' – 4
vols., map, coloured plates, buckram,
worn – 1933-36.
(Phillips) $245   £110

PRIESTLEY, J. B.
'The Town Major of Miraucourt' – no.
28 of 5,252 copies, signed by author,
original vellum boards, slipcase, slightly
soiled, 8vo – 1930.
(Sotheby Humberts
    Taunton) $70   £32

PRIESTLEY, JOSEPH
'Miscellaneous Observations Relating to
Education, more Especially as it Respects
the Conduct of the Mind' – 1st Edn.,
lacking half title, some leaves spotted,
modern half calf – Bath, 1778.
(Sotheby's,
    Chancery Lane) $135   £60
'The History and Present State of
Discoveries Relating to Vision, Light
and Colours' – 1st Edn., folding engraved
table frontispiece, 15 folding engraved
plates only of 24, cont. half calf, worn
– 1772.
(Sotheby's, New Bond
    Street) $65   £30

PRINCE, C. LEESON
'Observations upon the Topography and Climate of Crowborough Hill, Sussex' – 2nd Edn., inscribed by the author, plates, illustrations, cont. half parchment, slightly soiled – Lewes, 1898.
(Christie's S.
Kensington) $25   £12

PRINGLE, W. J.
'Melrose Abbey, in twelve photographic Views' – 13 actual photographs mounted, additional photograph inserted, cont. half morocco, rubbed – 1870.
(Sotheby's,
Chancery Lane) $180   £80

JE SUIS LE TAUREAU DU BÉTAIL DE SACRIFICE

PRINNER, ANTON
'Le Livre Des Morts des Anciens Aegyptiens' – 67 etched plates by Prinner, 33 pp. illustrations and 34 pp. text, unsewn in original wrappers, uncut, folder and slipcase, folio – Robert Godet, Paris, 1948.
(Sotheby's,
Chancery Lane) $425   £190

PRIOR, THOMAS
'An Authentick Narrative of the Success of Tar Water in curing a great number and variety of distempers' – small stain and hole in title, name erased, cont. marbled boards, calf spine, worn, 8vo – Dublin, 1746.
(Sotheby's, New Bond
Street) $22   £10

PRICHARD, JAMES COWLES
The Natural History of Man – 2nd Edn., 40 of 49 engraved plates, all but 5 hand-coloured after George Catlin, numerous illustrations in text, 1 plate dog eared, a few small tears, some soiling, original cloth, slightly worn – 1845; the same, 2 vols., 4th Edn., edited by Edwin Norris, 62 engraved plates, 58 hand coloured, illustrations in text, original cloth gilt, stained, contents loose – 1855.
(Sotheby's, New Bond
Street) $158   £70

'The Natural History of Man' – 2nd Edn., plates, mostly hand coloured, some slightly shaved, illustrations, occasional slight spotting, cont. calf, extremeties rubbed – 1845.
(Christie's S.
Kensington) $100   £45

PROCHAZKA, BARONESS L. H.
'The Abduction or the Marvels of Mesmerism' – 3 vols., 1st Edn., lacking front endleaf in vol. 3, original cloth, tear in spine of vol. 2, uncut – 1850.
(Sotheby's,
Chancery Lane) $400   £180

PROCTER, W. R.
'Memorials of Manchester Streets' – plates, cloth gilt – 1874.
(Phillips) $40   £18

PROKOSCH, FREDERIC
'Death at Sea' – 1st Edn., original cloth – New York, 1940.
(Sotheby's,
Chancery Lane) $11   £5

PROKOFIEV

PROKOFIEV, SERGE
Typed letter signed, in French, 1 page,
quarto, Chateau de Vetraz, par Anne-
masse (Haute Savoie), 30 July 1928, to
Henri Prunieres, the eminent French musi-
cologist, requesting his assistance in obtain-
ing an entry visa for Boris Assafieff, who
wishes to visit France.
(Sotheby's, New Bond
    Street) $338   £150

THE
PROTESTATION
OF THE GENERALL
ASSEMBLIE OF THE
CHURCH OF SCOTLAND, AND OF
THE NOBLEMEN, BARONS,
GENTLEMEN, BORROWES, MI-
NISTERS AND COMMONS;

Subſcribers of the Covenant, lately
renewed, made in the high Kirk, and at the
Mercate Croſſe of Glaſgow, the 28, and 29.
of November 1638.

Printed at Glaſgow by George Anderſon,
in the Yeare of Grace, 1638.

**THE PROTESTATION OF THE
GENERALL ASSEMBLIE OF THE
CHURCH OF SCOTLAND**
8 leaves, woodcut on titles, woodcut
initial on next leaf, modern calf, 1st Edn.
of first book printed in Glasgow – G.
Anderson, Glasgow, 1638.
(Sotheby's
    Edinburgh) $585   £260

**PROUT, SAMUEL – ROSCOE,
THOMAS**
'The Tourist in Italy' – 2 vols., engraved
additional titles and plates after Prout,
spotting, cont. morocco, spines slightly
soiled and rubbed – 1830-1.
(Christie's S.
    Kensington) $180   £80

PROUT, SAMUEL
'Hints on Light and Shadow' – New Edn.,
20 tinted lithographic plates after Prout,
slight spotting, original cloth, affected by
damp, folio – 1876.
(Christie's S.
    Kensington) $40   £18

**PROUT, SAMUEL AND HARDING,
J. D.**
'One Hundred and Four Views of
Switzerland and Italy, adapted to illustrate
the works of Byron, Rogers, Eustace, and
other works on Italy' – 2 vols. in one,
104 engraved plates, a little light spotting,
cont. half morocco, rubbed, folio –
Jennings and Chaplin, 1833.
(Christie's S.
    Kensington) $315   £140

PSALTER
Use of Sarum with canticles, litany and
Office of the Dead in Latin, some headings
in French – illuminated mss. on vellum,
138 leaves of probable 171, 18th century
sheep covered boards, early 19th century
antique style calf, gilt in morocco backed
case – East Anglia, early 14th century.
(Christie's, King
    St.) $22,500   £10,000
PSALTER, THE or PSALMS OF DAVID
No. 385 of 500 copies, original cloth, t.e.g.
– Golden Cockerel Press, 1927.
(Christie's S.
    Kensington) $80   £35

PSALTER IN LATIN
Illuminated mss. on vellum, 75 psalms only, 54 leaves, 20 lines, bound in random sequence in 19th century antique style calf over wooden boards by Claessens, bevelled edges — Northern France, first quarter of 13th century.
(Christie's, King
St.) $5,625   £2,500

PSALTERIUM FERIALE
Illuminated ms. on vellum, 97 leaves including 4 blank, written in brown ink in gothic rounded hand, double column, late 18th century calf, arms of Duke of Roxburghe on both covers — Attavante, Florence, late 15th century.
(Christie's, King
St.) $20,250   £9,000

PSALTER
'Psalterium Dauticum Materna Lingua Expositum' — gothic letter, printed in red and black, French and Latin text, title with large woodcut, slight browning and soiling, 18th century French mottled calf, labels, spine gilt, rubbed — Paris, 1500.
(Sotheby's, New Bond
Street) $855   £380

PUCCINI, GIACOMO — FORZANO, GIOVACCHINO
Signed autograph libretto of 'Suor Angelica' 89 pages only of 94, 6 pages of rough draft on Puccini's writing paper and 4 pages of proofs, altogether 99 pages — February 1917.
(Sotheby's, New Bond
Street) $2,250   £1,000

PUGH, EDWARD
'Cambria Depicta' — 1st Edn., 71 hand coloured aquatint plates, 2 advertisement leaves at end, slight browning and soiling, cont. calf, rebacked, rubbed — 1816.
(Sotheby's, New Bond
Street) $585   £260

PUGH, P. D. GORDON
'Heraldic China Mementoes of the First
World War' — plates, original cloth, large
4to — Newport, 1972.
(Christie's S.
   Kensington) $22   £10

PUGIN, A. C. AND HEATH, C.
'Paris and its Environs' — 2 vols., engraved
vignette titles and 202 views on 101
plates, cont. cloth, rubbed — 1831.
(Sotheby's,
   Chancery Lane) $110   £50

PUGIN, A. AND LE KEUX, J.
'Specimens of the Architectural Antiquities of Normandy' — engraved title and 68
plates only, some double page, 2 hand
coloured, a few stained, cont. morocco
backed cloth, rubbed, t.e.g. — n.d.
(Christie's S.
   Kensington) $50   £22

PUGIN AND ROWLANDSON
'The Microcosm of London' — 96 coloured
plates, 3 vols., 4to, boards worn — 1904.
(Bonham's) $70   £32

*Purchas His Pilgrimage, by
Samuel Purchas. (Sotheby's)*

PUNCH
71 volumes, illus. half calf gilt, 1 vol.
unbound, 4to — 1893-1940.
(Phillips) $155   £70

PURCELL, E.
'Sketches in Lithography' — 26 of 40
uncoloured lithographed plates of rural
and domestic scenes, animals etc., stitched
as issued, oblong folio — 1822.
(Christie's
   St. James) $145   £65

PURCHAS, SAMUEL
'His Pilgrims' — 4 vols., 1st Edn.
'Purchas His Pilgrimage' — 4th Edn., issue
with dedication to King Charles, 5 vols. in
all, engraved title page to vol. 1 dated
1624, 88 engraved maps, engravings or
woodcuts in text, some leaves slightly
damaged, cont. calf, folio — 1625-26.
(Sotheby's, New Bond
   Street) $6,750 £3,000

PURMANN, MATTHAEUS GOTTFRIED
'Chirurgia Curiosa or Observations and
Operations in the Whole Art of Chirurgery'
— 5 engraved folding plates, foxing through-
out, cont. sprinkled calf, joints cracked,
folio — 1706.
(Christie's, King
   St.) $290   £130

PYNE, J. B.
'Lake Scenery of England' — tinted litho-
graphed title and 24 plates, illustrations,
original cloth, worn, loose.
(Sotheby's,
   Chancery Lane) $180   £80

PYNE, W. H.
'The Costume of Great Britain' — coloured
vignette on title, 60 coloured aquatint
plates, spotting, cont. red straight grained
morocco panelled in gilt and blind, rubbed,
g.e., folio — 1808.
(Sotheby's, New Bond
   Street) $1,800 £800
'The History of the Royal Residences' —
3 vols., 100 hand coloured plates,
a few leaves detached, some soiling and
browning, mainly marginal, cont. red
straight grained morocco, gilt, soiled and
rubbed, inner hinges worn — 1819 water-
marks earlier.
(Christie's S.
   Kensington) $1,350 £600

QUARLES, FRANCIS
'Emblemes' – 2 parts in one vol., engraved
titles and full page illustrations, cont.
panelled calf, worn – n.d.
(Christie's S.
   Kensington) $135   £60
'Hedessa or the History of Queene Ester' –
1st Edn., title with woodcut device, woodcut coat of arms on verso, browning and
soiling, modern mottled calf, rubbed, g.e. –
1621.
(Sotheby's, New Bond
   Street) $335   £150

QUARTERLY MEDICAL JOURNAL
vols. I – II, half calf – 1892-1903.
(Bonham's) $90   £40

QUARTO, THE
Vols. 1-4, plates and illustrations, original
boards, worn, vol. 1 lacks spine, 4to –
1896-8.
(Sotheby Humberts
   Taunton) $85   £38

QUENNELL, NANCY (Editor)
'The Epicure's Anthology' – no. 64 of
150 copies signed by artist, frontispiece
and illustrations by Osbert Lancaster,
original morocco, t.e.g., unopened –
Golden Cockerel Press, 1936.
(Christie's S.
   Kensington) $110   £50

QUERELLES, CHEVALIER DE
'Hero et Leander' – engraved plain frontis,
8 plates printed in colour by Debucourt,
one torn, half title, later morocco backed
boards, gilt spine, rubbed – Didot L'Aine,
Paris, 1801.
(Sotheby's, New Bond
   Street) $720   £320

QUEVEDO-VILLEGAS, F.
'Pablo de Segovia' – portrait, illustrated
by Daniel Vierge, vellum, 4to – 1892.
(Phillips) $45   £20

QUILLERMOZ, EMILE
'Visages de Musiciens' – no. 104 of 229
copies, presentation copy inscribed by
author to Frank Brangwyn, plates, illus.,
original wrappers, soiled, folio – Paris,
1920.
(Christie's S.
   Kensington) $90   £40

QUILLET, CLAUDE
'Callipaedia, or the art of getting pretty
children, translated from the Latin by
several hands' – 1st English Edn.,
engraved frontispiece, 3 pp. advertisements
at end, cont. panelled calf, rebacked –
Bernard Lintott, 1710.
(Sotheby's, New Bond
   Street) $170   £75

QUIN, MICHAEL J.
'A Steam Voyage down the Danube' – 2
vols., 2nd Edn., 9 lithographed plates,
some spotting, cont. calf, gilt – 1835.
(Sotheby's,
   Chancery Lane) $135   £60

QUINCY, J.
'Dispensatory of the Royal College of
Physicians' – frontispiece, old calf, rebacked
– 1721.
(Bonham's) $45   £20
'Lexicon Physico-Medicum or a New
Medicinal Dictionary' – 3rd Edn., a few
woodcut diagrams, cont. calf gilt, 8vo –
J. Osborn and T. Longman, 1726.
(Sotheby's, New Bond
   Street) $90   £40

QUINONES, JUAN DE
'Tratado de las Langostas muy util y
Necessario' – 1st Edn., engraved device on
title, old inscriptions and drawings of
locusts on title, late 19th century cloth
backed boards – Madrid, 1620.
(Sotheby's, New Bond
   Street) $335   £150

RABELAIS, F.
'Oeuvres' – 3 vols., large paper, rubricated, 3 frontispieces, portrait, 17 plates after Picart, cont. dark blue morocco, gilt, g.e., by Derome le jeune with his ticket – Amsterdam, 1741.
(Sotheby Parke Bernet
    Monaco) $146,250   £65,000

RACINE, J.
'Oeuvres' – 7 vols., portrait and 12 plates by Duclos and others after Gravelot, cont. French red morocco, the Reliure de Present designed by Gravelot with flat gilt spines to his design, g.e. – Paris, 1768.
(Sotheby Parke Bernet
    Monaco) $153,000   £68,000

'Oeuvres' – 7 vols., 12 engraved plates, slight browning, scored calf, slightly rubbed and faded – Paris, 1768.
(Sotheby's, New Bond
    Street) $405   £180
'Phedre and Hippolyte' – early 18th century French red morocco, gilt, gilt flowered endpapers, a trifle rubbed – J. Ribou, Paris, 1677.
(Sotheby Parke Bernet
    Monaco) $5,400   £2,400

RACKHAM, ARTHUR
Watercolour drawing of a snow coloured slope with conifer trees, signed twice, the first signature painted over, captioned on back 'Montana, 1913'. Framed and glazed with the title and artist's address on back.
(Sotheby's,
    Chancery Lane) $810   £360
'Book of Pictures, with an introduction by Sir Arthur Quiller-Couch' – no. 170 of 1,030 copies signed by the artist, mounted coloured plates by Rackham, stained, original cloth, soiled, t.e.g. – 1913.
(Christie's S.
    Kensington) $245   £110

'Aesop's Fables' – plates, 13 coloured and illustrations by Rackham, a few leaves creased, slight spotting, original cloth – 1912.
(Christie's S.
    Kensington) $78   £35

'Alice's Adventures in Wonderland' –
coloured plates, cloth gilt, thumbed –
1907.
(Tessa Bennett,
   Edinburgh) $25   £11
'The Allies Fairy Book' – no. 308 of 525
copies signed by the artist, mounted
coloured plates by Rackham, original
cloth, t.e.g. – 1916.
(Christie's S.
   Kensington) $290   £130
'Little Brother and Little Sister, and
other tales by the Brothers Grimm' – no.
441 of 525 copies signed by the artist,
mounted coloured plates by Rackham,
original cloth, slightly soiled, t.e.g. – 1917.
(Christie's S.
   Kensington) $315   £140
'Shakespeare (W) A Midsummer Night's
Dream' – mounted, coloured plates by
Rackham, original cloth, soiled – 1908.
(Christie's S.
   Kensington) $67   £30
'The Ring of the Nibelung – R. Wagner' –
coloured plates by Rackham, original cloth
– 1939.
(Christie's S.
   Kensington) $85   £38
'The Romance of King Arthur' – coloured
plates, cloth gilt – 1917.
(Tessa Bennett,
   Edinburgh) $50   £22
'The Tempest – W. Shakespeare' – mounted
coloured plates by Rackham, original cloth
– 1926.
(Christie's S.
   Kensington) $100   £45
'Undine' – coloured plates, cloth gilt –
1909.
(Tessa Bennett,
   Edinburgh) $65   £30

RACKHAM, ARTHUR – BARRIE, J. M.
'Peter Pan in Kensington Gardens' –
mounted coloured plates by Rackham,
frontispiece detached, original cloth,
soiled – 1906.
(Christie's S.
   Kensington) $108   £48
RACKHAM, ARTHUR – EVANS, C. S.
'The Sleeping Beauty' – mounted and
coloured frontispiece and illustrations by
Rackham, marginal tear to one leaf,
original cloth backed boards, soiled 4to. –
1920.
(Christie's S.
   Kensington) $34   £15

RACKHAM, ARTHUR – IRVING,
WASHINGTON
'Rip Van Winkle' – 50 mounted coloured
plates by Rackham, original cloth, slightly
affected by damp – 1924.
(Christie's S.
   Kensington) $78   £35

RACKHAM, ARTHUR – LEVER,
CHARLES
'Charles O'Malley, the Irish Dragoon' –
plates by Rackham, original cloth, spine
faded – 1899.
(Christie's S.
   Kensington) $40   £18

RACKHAM, ARTHUR – MALORY, SIR
THOMAS
'The Romance of King Arthur . . . abridged'
– 23 plates, 16 coloured by Rackham, one
detached, original cloth, slightly soiled –
1917.
(Christie's S.
   Kensington) $90   £40

RACKHAM, ARTHUR – WAGNER,
RICHARD
'Das Rheingold et Die Walkure' – mounted
coloured plates by Rackham, one detached
with a little loss, text spotted, original
parchment backed boards, soiled, inner
hinges cracked – Frankfurt, 1910.
(Christie's S.
   Kensington) $100   £45

RADEMAKER, ABRAHAM
'Kabinet van Nederlandsche Outheden en
Gezichten' – 6 vols., Robert Southey's
copy, titles, printed in red and black, 300
engraved views, caption in Dutch, French
and English, browning, cont. calf, worn –
Amsterdam, 1725-33.
(Sotheby's, New Bond
   Street) $3,375   £1,500

RAEMAEKERS, LOUIS
'The Great War. A Neutral's Indictment' –
limited to 1,050 copies, 100 mounted
plates by Raemaekers most coloured,
original half buckram, soiled, folio – 1916.
(Christie's S.
   Kensington) $45   £20

RAFFALD

RAFFALD, ELIZABETH
'The Experienced English Housekeeper' –
10th Edn., author's signature on 1st text
page as usual, engraved portrait, 3 engraved
folding plates, last two with very small
marginal tears, ad. leaf at end, a few leaves
slightly spotted, outer margins of preliminaries just frayed, cont. sheep, lacking
upper cover – 1786.
(Sotheby's
   London) $110   £50

RAFFLES, MRS. S.
'Memoir of the Life . . . Sir Thomas
Stamford Raffles' – portrait, 10 maps and
charts, calf gilt, 4to – 1830.
(Phillips) $190   £85

RAILWAY ACTS
'An Act for Making the Railway from
Aylesbury to join the London and
Birmingham Railway 1836'.
Another for making and maintaining a
Railway or Tram Road in the County of
Carnarvon, 1825.
(Tessa Bennett,
   Edinburgh) $65   £28

RAINOLDS, WILLIAM
'De iusta reipub. Christianae in rrges (sic)
impios et haereticos authoritatte' – ruled in
red throughout, device on title, printing
flaw on small 8vo, cont. limp vellum, arms
of James Beaton (1517-1603) Archbishop
of Glasgow, gilt on sides, signature of
Andrew Fletcher of Saltoun on final paste
down, spine defective – Paris, Guillaume
Bichon, 1590.
(Sotheby's
   London) $225   £100

RALEIGH, SIR WALTER
'The Discoverie of the large and beautiful
Empire of Guiana' – no. 561 of 975 copies,
plates and maps, original vellum backed
cloth, gilt – 1928.
(Sotheby's,
   Chancery Lane) $55   £24
'The History of the World' – title printed
in red and black, engraved portrait and 8
double page maps, some browning and
soiling, half calf, worn, folio – 1677.
(Sotheby's, New Bond
   Street) $125   £55

RAMBERT, EUGENE AND ROBERT, PAUL
'Les Oiseaux dans la nature' – 3 vols.,
engraved additional titles, plates including
60 mounted chromolithographs after
Robert, some slightly damaged, unbound
as issued in original portfolio, slightly
soiled, folio – n.d.
(Christie's S.
   Kensington) $125   £55

RAMSAY, ALLAN
'The Gentle Shepherd' – plates, spotting
some soiling, cont. calf, joints worn –
Edinburgh, 1808.
(Christie's S.
   Kensington) $65   £30

RAMUSIO, GIOVANNI BATTISTA (Editor)
'Delle Navigatione et Viaggi' – 3 vols.,
complete set, water staining with minor
defects, recent vellum backed boards,
folio – Della Stamperia di Giunti, Venice,
1554-1574-1556.
(Christie's, King
   St.) $2,700   £1,200

RANSONNET, BARON EUGENE DE
'Sketches of the Inhabitants, Animal Life
and Vegetation of Ceylon' – 26 lithographed plates, 3 coloured, slightly soiled,
loose as issued in original cloth, portfolio,
worn, lacks ties, folio – Vienna, 1867.
(Sotheby Humberts
   Taunton) $245   £110

RAPHAEL SANZIO
'Raccolta delle Opere di Raffaello disegn-
nate ed incise da Niccola Consoni' –
engraved title, 50 plates, all mounted, cont.
vellum boards, soiled – 19th century.
(Sotheby's
   London) $18   £8

RASMUSSEN, AXEL (Editor)
'Den Blaa Trylleserie Udsogte Tricks med
Kort, Monter, Cigaretter og Torklaeder' –
12 cols., illustrations, original pictorial
wrappers, a few detached, circa 1949-51.
'Smaa Korrtricks fra Magikeren' – 5 vols.,
spotted, original wrappers, circa 1955 –
Hegnsborg, 1949-55.
(Sotheby's,
   Chancery Lane) $11   £5

RATIONAL RECREATIONS, THE MOST
MARVELLOUS EXPERIMENTS, THE
MOST ASTOUNDING FEATS OF
LEGERDEMAIN, THE MOST PUZZLING
NUMERICAL EXERCISES
2nd Edn., wood engraved frontispiece,
border to title and illustrations, original
boards, slightly worn, uncut — Knight &
Lacey, 1825.
(Sotheby's,
   Chancery Lane) $380   £170

RAWLE, EDWIN JOHN
'Annals of the Ancient Royal Forest of
Exmoor' — cloth backed boards, stained,
partly uncut, partly unopened, title in red
and black, 2 photographic plates, folding
map — Taunton, 1893.
(Lawrence of
   Crewkerne) $27   £12

RAWSTHORNE, L.
'Gamonia or the Art of Preserving Game' —
15 coloured plates, nice copy in original
green morocco gilt, g.e., cloth slipcase, 8vo
— 1837.
(Sotheby's, New Bond
   Street) $1,575   £700

RAY, JOHN
'A Collection of English Proverbs˙ — 2nd
Edn., title in red and black, 18th century
calf, joints rubbed — Cambridge, 1678.
(Christie's, King
   St.) $170   £75

RAYE, C.
'A Picturesque Tour Through the Isle of
Wight' — 24 coloured aquatints, minor
soiling, original half leather — 1825.
(Sotheby's, New Bond
   Street) $450   £200

RAYMOND, J.
'An Itinerary Containing a Voyage Made
Through Italy' — engraved title, engravings
in text, old russia, broken, some leaves cut
— 1648.
(Bonham's) $90   £40

RAYNER, SIMEON
'The History and Antiquities of Haddon
Hall' — 2 vols., 38 lithographed plates —
Derby, Robert Moseley, 1836-7.
(Christie's S.
   Kensington) $55   £25

READ, ALEXANDER
'Chirurgorum Comes or the Whole Practice
of Chirurgery begun by the Learned Dr.
Read continued and completed by a member of the College of Physicians in London'
— 1st Edn., engraved plate of surgical instruments, printed in double columns, rust
hole, cont. panelled calf, 8vo — 1687.
(Sotheby's, New Bond
   Street) $945   £420

READE, CHARLES
'The Course of True Love Never Did Run
Smooth' — blue half morocco by Bickers
and Son, t.e.g. — 1857.
(Christie's S.
   Kensington) $80   £35

RECIPE BOOK
Mss. recipes for soups, cakes, puddings,
bread and wine etc., 100 in all, calf backed
boards — late 18th century.
(Tessa Bennett,
   Edinburgh) $40   £18

RECREATIONS IN SCIENCE OR A
COMPLETE SERIES OF RATIONAL
AMUSEMENTS
by the author of 'Rational Amusements' —
folding frontispiece with 35 wood engraved
illustrations, slightly spotted, original
boards, worn, lacking spine — Effingham
Wilson, 1830.
(Sotheby's,
   Chancery Lane) $290   £130

'RECUEIL DES PLANCHES DU
SYSTEME ANATOMIQUE FAISANT
PARTIE DE L'ENCYCLOPAEDIE
METHODIQUE'
Plates, occasional spotting, modern half
morocco, ex library copy — Paris, 1825.
(Christie's S.
   Kensington) $65   £30

REDON, ODILON – FLAUBERT, GUSTAVE

'Le Tentation de Saint Antoine' – 22 lithographed plates by Redon, 15 wood engraved illustrations after Redon and 5 key plates, maroon morocco, t.e.g., original wrappers, bound in, slipcase by Rene Kieffer, folio – Ambroise Vollard Paris, 1933.
(Sotheby's,
Chancery Lane) $5,175 $2,300

REDON, ODILON AND OTHERS – BAUDELAIRE, CHARLES

'Les Fleurs du Mal' – etched frontispiece by Pierre Leroy, olive green morocco, covers with geometric design tooled in silver, t.e.g., original wrappers bound in, slipcase by Rene Kieffer, no. 256 of 1,000 copies – Presses de la Cite, Paris, 1945.
(Sotheby's,
Chancery Lane) $1,685   £750

REDOUTE, P. J.

'Les Liliacees', – 8 vols. in 4, 464 plates of 486, all but one in colour and hand finished, lacking portrait and titles to vols. II and VIII, short tears, crudely repaired, some cropping, staining and foxing, cont. green half morocco, spines gilt, slightly worn, folio t.e.g., folio – Paris, 1802-16.
(Sotheby's, New Bond
Street) $30,375   £13,500

REGENSBURG

'Des Heyligen Reichs Freyen Statt Regenspurg Wachtgerichts und Baw-Ordnung' – woodcut arms on title, some leaves soiled, slightly dampstained, disbound, uncut – Regensburg, 1657.
(Sotheby's, New Bond
Street) $90   £40

REID, A.

'Kinghorn - A Short History' – frontispiece and photographic plates, cloth – Kirkcaldy, 1906.
(Tessa Bennett,
Edinburgh) $27   £12
'The Regality of Kirriemuir' – frontispiece map and plates, cloth – 1909.
(Tessa Bennett,
Edinburgh) $36   £16

REID, ROBERT

'Elevation of the New Exchange and Other Buildings erecting in the City of Edinburgh for the Accommodation of the Court of Justice' – large aquatint engraving.
(Tessa Bennett,
Edinburgh) $40   £18

REID, THOMAS

'An Enquiry into the Human Mind on the Principles of Common Sense' – 2nd Edn., cont. calf, 8vo – Edinburgh, 1765.
(Sotheby's, New Bond
Street) $80   £35
'Essay on the Active Powers of Man' – half title and advert leaf, cont. calf, 1st Edn., – Edinburgh, 1788.
(Tessa Bennett,
Edinburgh) $270   £120

REINAGLE, GEORGE PHILIP

'Illustrations of the Battle of Navarin' – mounted title and plan, 12 lithographed plates, slight staining and spotting, half calf – C. Hullmandel, 1828.
(Christie's S.
Kensington) $585   £260

REINECCIUS, CHRISTIAN
'Janua Hebraeae Linguae Veteris Testamenti' – Latin and Hebrew, 7th Edn., title printed in red and black, engraved frontispiece, cont. calf over thin wooden boards, worn – Leipzig, 1756.
(Sotheby's, New Bond
   Street) $40   £18

RELAND, ADRIAN
'De Nummis Veterum Hebraeorum' – 1st Edn., engraving on title, some folding, original vellum, soiled – W. Broedelet, Utrecht, 1709.
(Sotheby's, New Bond
   Street) $270   £120

RELPH, JOHN
'An Enquiry into the Medical Efficiacy of a New Species of Peruvian Bark' – original boards, new label, uncut, 8vo – James Phillips, 1794.
(Sotheby's, New Bond
   Street) $80   £35

REMMELIN, JOHAN AND SPAHER, MICHAEL OF TYROL
'A Survey of the Microcosme or the Anatomy of the Bodies of Man and Woman . . . corrected by Clopton Havers' – title and 4 engraved plates, a few stains or dustmarks but a very good copy, old half calf, very worn, folio – Dan Midwinter and Tho. Leigh, 1702.
(Sotheby's, New Bond
   Street) $3,825   £1,700

RENARD, LOUIS
'Atlas de la Navigation et du Commerce' – 2nd Edn., title printed in red and black, engraved vignette and planisphere, portrait of George I, 28 engraved maps and charts, with text, original boards, uncut, calf spine, worn, folio – Regner and Josua Ottens, Amsterdam, 1739.
(Sotheby's, New Bond
   Street) $9,000   £4,000

Atlas de la Navigation et du Commerce by Louis Renard. (Sotheby's)

RENAULT, MALO – ADAM, PAUL
'Le Serpent Noir' – coloured etched
frontispiece and 106 illustrations by
Renault, black morocco, inside border
gilt, silk doublures and end leaves, g.e.
original embossed pictorial wrappers
bound in, slipcase by Canape – Pour les
Cent Bibliophiles, Paris, 1913.
(Sotheby's,
  Chancery Lane) $225   £100

RENNIE, JOHN
The Civil Engineer's Drawings, Proposals and
Estimates for the building of a stone bridge
over the River Whiteadder, Berwickshire,
signed and dated by Rennie with 11 double
page coloured plans, half calf, folio –
1800-1801.
(Tessa Bennett,
  Edinburgh) $1,550   £690

**REPRESENTATION, THE, OF THE
LEASEHOLDERS AND CONTRACTORS
INTERESTED IN THE HOUSES AND
BUILDINGS IN PICKETT STREET,
NEAR TEMPLE BAR . . .'**
24 engraved plates and plans, 11 folding,
a few partially hand coloured, original
boards, worn and loose – circa 1810.
(Sotheby's, New Bond
  Street) $495   £220

REPTON, HUMPHRY
'Odd Whims and Miscellanies' – 2 vols. in
one, 9 hand coloured engraved plates, half
titles, a few leaves slightly soiled, cont.
calf, worn, 8vo – 1804.
(Sotheby Humberts
  Taunton) $95   £42

RESTORATION OF CHARLES II
Mss. in ink containing 'A Sermon Preacht
upon the Most Happy Restoration of His
Most Sacred Majesty'. Dedication illuminated in colours and gold with initials,
cont. black morocco, rubbed and cracked
– 1666.
(Christie's, King
  St.) $200   £90

REYNOLDS, J.
'The Triumph of the Gods Against Murther'
– plates, small folio, half calf, title
defective – 1656.
(Bonham's) $70   £32

RHEIN, DER
'Von Mainz bis Coln' – folding engraved
panorama, spotted, torn, text browned,
original boards, rebacked, rubbed –
Mayence, D. Kapp, n.d.
(Sotheby's,
  Chancery Lane) $170   £75

**RHEINTHAL, DAS VON BINGEN BIS
ZUM LURLEY**
8 lithographed sections and front coloured
by hand, one hinge repaired, front soiled
and rubbed, in box form, cloth case –
Germany, circa 1850.
(Sotheby's,
  Chancery Lane) $785   £350

RHYNE, W. TEN AND BREYNIUS, J.
'Herbarium Vivum' – 100 leaves of
pressed flowers captioned in Latin with a
few notes in Dutch, blindstamped calf,
worn and wormed, the Plesch copy, folio
– Holland and Danzig, 1658-70.
(Sotheby's, New Bond
  Street) $540   £240

RICCOBONI, MARIE JEANNE
'Oeuvres Completes' – 6 vols., engraved frontispieces, half titles, cont. red half roan, label, spines gilt, slightly rubbed – Paris, 1818.
(Sotheby's, New Bond
   Street) $200   £90

RICE, WILLIAM
'Indian Game' – 10 plates, original cloth, gilt, slightly rubbed – 1884.
(Sotheby Humberts
   Taunton) $40   £18

RICHARDS, WALTER
'Her Majesty's Army' – 3 vols., coloured plates, original cloth – Virtue, n.d.
(Phillips) $145   £65

RICHARDSON, JOHN
'A Grammar of the Arabick Language' – partly disbound, original boards, backstrip lacking – 1776.
(Christie's S.
   Kensington) $135   £60

RICHARDSON, M.
'Stirling Castle and Other Poems' – with an etching and 4 drawings, by D. Y. Cameron, buckram, author's presentation copy – 1934.
(Tessa Bennett,
   Edinburgh) $13   £6

RICHARDSON, MOSES A.
'A Collection of Armorial Bearings . . . in the Parochial Chapel of Saint Andrew' – engraved title, vignette and plates, occasional slight spotting, cont. cloth – Newcastle, 1818.
(Christie's S.
   Kensington) $33   £15

RICHARDSON, T. M.
'The Castles of the English and Scottish Border' – 2 original parts only, 6 mezzotint plates, slight soiling, original cloth backed wrappers, soiled, folio – Newcastle, 1834.
(Christie's S.
   Kensington) $80   £35
'Sketches in Italy, Switzerland, France, etc.' – lithographed title, 25 plates, spotting, original morocco backed cloth, rubbed, folio – 1841.
(Christie's S.
   Kensington) $1,575   £700

RICHTER, G. M.
'Engraved Gems of the Greeks, Etruscans and Romans' – 2 vols., plates, original cloth, dust jackets – 1968-71.
(Christie's S.
   Kensington) $55   £25

RICKETTS, CHARLES – GRAY, JOHN (Translator)
'Spiritual Poems' – frontispiece and decorative borders by Ricketts, cont. reversed calf by Bumpus, foot of spine chipped – 1896.
(Christie's S.
   Kensington) $45   £20

RIDDELL, J.
'Tracts Legal and Historical' – cloth – Edinburgh, 1835.
(Tessa Bennett,
   Edinburgh) $5   £2

RIDER, WILLIAM
'Views in Stratford upon Avon and its Vicinity' – 5 mounted India paper plates, slight spotting, original boards, folio – Warwick and Leamington, 1828.
(Christie's S.
   Kensington) $65   £30

RITCHIE, L.
'Heath's Picturesque Annual for 1832, North Italy, Tyrol and the Rhine' – 26 plates, including frontis, engraved title, morocco gilt, g.e. – 1832.
(Phillips) $105   £48

RITSON, JOSEPH (Editor)
'Robin Hood, A Collection of All the Ancient Poems, Songs, Ballads now extant, relative to that Celebrated English Outlaw' – 2 vols., 1st Edn., woodcut illustrations in text, cont. calf, gilt, rebacked, worn – 1795.
(Sotheby's, New Bond
   Street) $65   £30

RITTERSHAUS, EMIL
'Rheinlands Sang und Sage' – engraved title and 19 plates, original pictorial cloth, slightly soiled, g.e., folio – Bonn, 1899.
(Christie's S.
   Kensington) $180   £80

RIVERIUS

RIVERIUS, LAZARUS
'The Universal Body of Physick in Five
Books . . . translated into English by
William Carr' – 2 folding tables, 2
glossary at end, new calf, folio – Henry
Eversden, 1657.
(Sotheby's, New Bond
   Street) $425   £190
'Praxis Medica' – 2nd Edn., 2 vols. in one,
old vellum – Paris, 1644-45.
(Bonham's) $85   £38

ROBERT
'Carte de l'Isle de Saint-Domenique' –
double page – 1767. Four others including
one of Caribbean.
(Phillips) $70   £32

ROBERT-HOUDIN, JEAN EUGENE
'Memoirs of Robert-Houdin, Ambassador,
Author and Conjuror, written by himself'
– 2 vols., 1st English Edn., original cloth,
slightly worn and faded, uncut – 1859.
(Sotheby's,
   Chancery Lane) $305   £135

La Corne d'abondance.

'Confidences d'un Prestidigitateur' – 2
vols., 1st Edn., 16 illustrations, a few
leaves spotted and soiled, uncut – Paris,
1859.
(Sotheby's,
   Chancery Lane) $200   £90
'The Secrets of Stage Conjuring translated
and edited by Professor Hoffmann' – 1st
English Edn., illustrations, original pictorial
cloth – 1881.
(Sotheby's,
   Chancery Lane) $110   £50

The Secrets of Stage Conjuring, by Jean Eugene Robert-Houdin. (Sotheby's)

ROBERTON, JOHN
'The Generative System' – 5th Edn.,
enlarged, edited by Thomas Little, engraved
portrait, 17 plates with explanatory text,
some plates spotted, new half calf, uncut –
J. J. Stockdale, 1824.
(Sotheby's, New Bond
   Street) $55   £25

ROBERTS, DAVID
A collection of 47 tinted lithographed plates,
views of the Holy Land, Syria, Idumea,
Arabia, Egypt and Nubia by L. Haghe after
Roberts, 2 plates with text, some spotting
and staining, large folio – F. G. Moon,
1841-49.
(Christie's
   St. James) $1,235   £550

ROBERTS, EMMA
'Hindoostan' – 2 vols. in one, 2 vignette
titles, 99 engraved plates, half calf, 4to –
Fisher and Son, n.d.
(Phillips) $145   £65

ROBERTS, W.
'Memorials of Christie's – 2 vols., frontis-
piece, one coloured, plates, original cloth,
vol. 2, stitching shaken, t.e.g. – 1897.
(Christie's S.
   Kensington) $90   £40

ROBERTSON, G.
'General View of the Agriculture of
Kincardineshire' – portrait frontispiece,
map, plate and 9 tables, original boards,
uncut – 1813.
(Tessa Bennett,
   Edinburgh) $125   £55

ROBERTSON, J.
'Treatise of Such Mathematical Instruments'
– portable case, 9 plates, mottled calf gilt
– 1757.
(Phillips) $135   £60

ROBERTSON, W.
'Historical Disquisition concerning India' –
2 folding maps, 4to, old calf, broken –
1791.
(Bonham's) $31   £14

ROBERTSON, WILLIAM
'Works' – 9 volumes, engraved frontis-
piece, folding maps, cont. calf, gilt spines,
rather rubbed, 8vo – 1802-3.
(Sotheby Humberts
   Taunton) $40   £18

ROBIDA, A. – VILLON, FRANCOIS
'Oeuvres' – numerous illustrations by
Robida, prospectus inserted, brown half
morocco floral design on spine, t.e.g.,
original pictorial wrappers bround in –
Paris, 1897.
(Sotheby's,
   Chancery Lane) $65   £28

ROBINS, W. P.
'Etching Craft' – illustrated, cloth backed
boards – 1924.
(Phillips) $36   £16

ROBINSON, EMMA
'Cesar Borgia' – 3 vols., cont. morocco,
gilt, endpapers decorated with drawings
coloured from Nature by G. Crisp, St.
Peter's Coll. – 1846.
(Christie's S.
   Kensington) $100   £45

ROBINSON, NICHOLAS
'A New Theory of Physick and Diseases
founded on the Principles of the New-
tonian Philosophy' – 16pp. catalogue of
books published by Bettesworth at end,
cont. panelled calf, spine gilt, 8vo. – 1725.
(Sotheby's, New Bond
   Street) $290 £130

ROBINSON, P. F.
'Rural Architecture, or a Series of Designs
for Ornamental Cottages' – 1st Edn., 96
lithoed plates, Tyrconnel bookplate, later
half parchment, spine gilt – 1823.
(Sotheby's
   London) $125   £55

ROBINSON, ROBERT
'Thomas Bewick, His Life and Times' –
green cloth paper label, frontispiece portrait, 25 tissued plates, autograph letter,
black and white illustrations – Newcastle,
1887.
(Lawrence of
   Crewkerne) $90   £40

ROBINSON, WILLIAM (Editor)
'The Garden' – 6 vols., illustrations, cont.
morocco – 1872-74.
(Christie's S.
   Kensington) $45   £20

ROBINSON, W. HEATH (Illustrator)
'Danish Fairy Tales and Legends' – 16
plates by Heath Robinson, inscription on
title, original cloth gilt, slightly soiled,
t.e.g. – Bliss, Sands and Co., 1897.
(Sotheby's,
    Chancery Lane) $100   £45

**ROBINSON, WILLIAM E 'Chung Ling
Soo'**
'Spirit Slate Writing and Kindred
Phenomena' – 1st Edn., 66 illustrations,
original pictorial cloth, slightly damp-
stained – New York, 1898.
(Sotheby's,
    Chancery Lane) $190   £85

ROBSON, G. F.
'Scenery of the Grampian Mountains' –
coloured map, 41 coloured aquatints,
half morocco, worn – 1819.
(Sotheby's, New Bond
    Street) $1,460   £650

**ROCHEGROSSE, GEORGES – FRANCE,
ANATOLE**
'Thias' – etched vignette on title coloured
by hand, 14 illustrations by E. Decisy after
Rochegrosse, scarlet morocco gilt, inside
borders gilt, marbled endpapers, t.e.g. –
Librairie des Amateurs, Paris, 1909.
(Sotheby's,
    Chancery Lane) $115   £52

**ROCHEGROSSE, GEORGES –
BAUDELAIRE, CHARLES**
'Les Fleurs du Mal' – etched frontispiece,
2 plates, 6 coloured section titles, wood
engraved head and end pieces by Rochegrosse, brown half morocco, t.e.g.,
original wrappers bound in by P. Affolter
– Librairie des Amateurs, Paris, 1917.
(Sotheby's,
    Chancery Lane) $200   £125

Baudelaire's 'Les Fleurs du Mal' illustrated by Georges Rochegrosse. (Sotheby's)

ROCHESTER, JOHN WILMOT, EARL OF
'Poems, etc. On Several Occasions: with
Valentinian: A Tragedy' – marginal worm-
ing, affecting a few letters in some head-
lines, cont. calf, rebacked – Jacob Tonson,
1696.
(Christie's S.
   Kensington) $90   £40

ROCHEFOUCAULT, FRANCIS DUC DE LA
'Moral Maxims' – no. 271 of 350, original
parchment backed boards, rubbed,
unopened – Golden Cockerel Press, 1924.
(Christie's S.
   Kensington) $90   £40

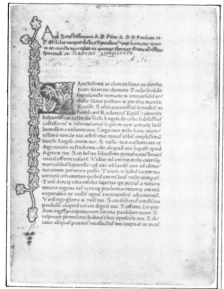

RODERICKUS ZAMORENSIS
'Speculum Vitae Humanae' – 1st Edn.,
142 leaves of 150, initial 'S' in burnished
gold, cont. calf backed wooden boards,
worn and wormed, rebacked with paper,
17th century ownership inscription of
convent at Albi, folio – Rome, 1468.
(Sotheby's, New Bond
   Street) $5,400   £2,400

ROEDERER, J. G.
'Icones Uteri Humani, Observationes
Illustratae' – 7 full page plates, folio, new
boards, calf back – Gottingen, 1759.
(Bonham's) $405   £180

ROESSLIN, EUCHARIUS
'Der Swangern Frauwen Und Hebammen
Rosengarten' – title in woodcut border
and full page woodcut of the author, 19
woodcuts in text, 18th century half calf
with text of the Ducal Library of Gotha
and the date 1776 impressed on cover –
1776.
(Bonham's) $56,250   £25,000

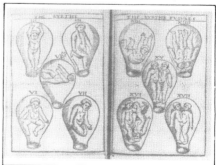

'The Byrth of Mankinde' translated by T.
Raynald – title in fine woodcut border,
woodcut initials, 1st English Edn., disbound in vellum case – London, 1540.
(Bonham's) $3,600   £1,600

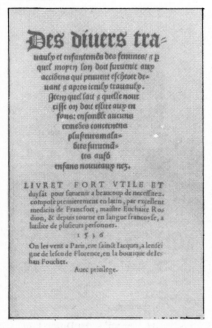

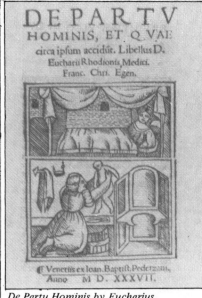

De Partu Hominis by Eucharius Roesslin. (Bonham's)

'Des Divers Travaux et Enfantemens de Femmes, et Par Quel Moyen Lon Doit Survenir Aux Accidens Qui Peuvent Eschoir Devant et Apres Iceulx Travaux' – fine woodcut initials, 20 woodcuts of foetus in uteri and delivery chair in text, 1st French Edn., cont. limp vellum in slipcase – J. Foucher, Paris, 1536.
(Bonham's) $9,900   £4,400
'De Partu Hominis' – large woodcut on title, woodcuts throughout, colophon leaf with printer's device, vellum – 1537.
(Bonham's) $720   £320
'Kreuterbuch von aller Kreuter Gethier Gesteine und Metal Naturnutz und Gebrauch' – fine woodcut title and numerous woodcuts throughout represent-ing herbs, animals, etc., cont. stamped calf over oak boards with clasps, folio – Frankenfurt am Meyn, 1536.
(Bonham's) $13,500   £6,000

ROGERS, SAMUEL
'Human Life, A Poem' – 1st Edn., margins soiled, original boards, backstrip torn, stitching shaken – 1819.
(Christie's S.
  Kensington) $27   £12

The 1536 edition of Roesslin's 'Kreuterbuch'. (Bonham's)

ROHAULT DE FLEURY, CH.

'La Messe Etudes Archeologiques sur ses Monuments' – 8 vols. in two text, 8 vols. in four of plates, soiled, 4to – Paris, 1883-87.

(Phillips) $65   £28

ROHDE, E. SINCLAIR

'The Old English Gardening Books' – plates and text illustrations, canvas backed – 1924.

(Tessa Bennett, Edinburgh) $75   £34

ROHMER, SAX

'She Who Sleeps' – 1st Edn., presentation copy, inscribed by author to Will Goldston, original cloth, spine gilt, slightly soiled, torn – 1928.

(Sotheby's, Chancery Lane) $80   £35

'White Velvet' – 1st American Edn., presentation copy, inscribed by author to Will Goldston, original cloth, slightly soiled, spine slightly faded – New York, 1936.

(Sotheby's, Chancery Lane) $50   £22

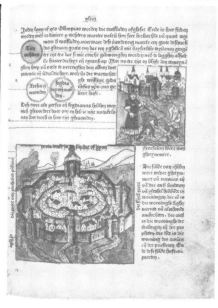

ROLEWINCK, WERNER

'Fasciculus Temporum' – 1st Dutch Edn., numerous illustrations and coats of arms all coloured, uncoloured device at end, rubricated throughout, stains and other minor imperfections, 17th century vellum, soiled, folio – Johann Veldener, Utrecht, 1480.

(Sotheby's, New Bond Street) $4,274   £1,900

'Fasciculus Temporum' – 72 leaves, 40 lines, gothic letter, initials in red or blue, woodcut illustrations, staining, 19th century half calf, worn, folio – Johann Veldener, Louvain, 1476.

(Sotheby's, New Bond Street) $2,700   £1,200

ROLFE, FREDERICK, 'Baron Corvo'

'The Songs of Meleager' – 1st Edn., limited to 750 copies, decorations by author, original cloth gilt, very slightly soiled, t.e.g. – First Edition Club, 1937.

(Sotheby's, Chancery Lane) $85   £38

'The Rubaiyat of Omar Khayyam' – coloured plates by Hamzeh Carr, slightly soiled, original cloth – 1924.

(Christie's S. Kensington) $72   £32

ROLT, RICHARD
'An Impartial Representation of the
Conduct of the Several Powers of Europe,
engaged in the Late General War . . . 1739
. . . 1748' – 4 vols., 2nd Edn., slight browning, cont. calf, rebacked, rubbed – 1754.
(Sotheby's, New Bond
    Street) $90   £40

ROMBAUDI, A. – CHAMPEVILLE, PAUL DE
'Les Rebelles' – engraved frontispiece,
vignette on title and 9 illustrations, 3 full
page, half morocco, original wrappers
bound in – A. Belinac, Paris, 1905.
(Sotheby's,
    Chancery Lane) $31   £14

ROME
Important collection of 400 16th and 17th
century engraved maps, plans, views and
other plates of Rome, public buildings,
amphitheatres, baths, tombs, etc., 13
plates by Antonio Lefreri dated 1547-60,
others by Duchetti, Beatrizel, Ligorio and
others, 17th century gilded Spanish calf,
large folio – Rome, n.d.
(Sotheby's, New Bond
    Street) $4,050   £1,800

ROME
'Nuova Raccolta di Principali Vedute di
Roma' – 100 engravings some mounted,
oblong, boards – Rome, 1786.
(Bonham's) $225   £100

RONALDS, ALFRED
'The Fly Fisher's Entomology' – 6th Edn.,
10 of 20 hand coloured plates only, cont.
cloth, spine torn – 1862.
(Christie's S.
    Kensington) $27   £12

RONGE, JOH. AND BERTHA
'A Practical Guide to the English Kinder
Garten, being an Exposition of Froebel's
System of Infant Training, accompanied
by a Great Variety of Instructive and
Amusing Games' – 1st Edn., lithographed
frontispiece and 70 plates, dampstained,
spotting, original cloth, faded – J. S.
Hodson, 1855.
(Sotheby's,
    Chancery Lane) $63   £28

ROPS, FELICIEN – GYP, OCTAVE, UZANNE AND OTHERS
'Feminies' – 8 coloured etched plates after
Rops, wood engraved borders after L.
Rudnicki, half morocco, uncut, original
coloured pictorial wrappers after Georges
de Feure, bound in, uncut – Pour les
Bibliophiles Contemporaines Paris, 1896.
(Sotheby's,
    Chancery Lane) $1,080   £480

'ROSAMUND, COUNTESS OF CLARENSTEIN'
3 vols., 1st Edn., half titles, 3 advert leaves in vol. I, some pencilled notes in text, 'Lady Tyrconnel with kind regards from the Miss Watsons, Sept. 1841' on front flyleaf in vol. I, cont. mottled calf, gilt, spines slightly worn — 1812.
(Sotheby's
London) $65   £30

ROSCOE, THOMAS
'The Tourist in Italy' — engraved addtional title and plates after S. Prout, original morocco, corners bumped, g.e. — 1831.
(Christie's
Kensington) $50   £22
'Continental Tourist . . . Italy, France and Switzerland' — 3 vols., 3 engraved titles and 129 plates, some spotting, text in French and English, cloth gilt, g.e., 4to — circa 1840.
(Phillips) $225   £100

ROSE, GILES
'A Perfect School of Instructions for the Officers of the Mouth' — 1st Edn., 42 woodcuts, tears, worming, cont. calf worn, spine defective, joints cracked, 12mo. — 1682.
(Christie's
St. James) $450   £200

ROSE, THOMAS
'Westmorland, Cumberland, Durham and Northumberland' — 3 vols., plates, titles, plates by T. Allom and others, quarter morocco — 1833.
(Phillips) $380   £170

ROSENDALE, H. G.
'Queen Elizabeth and the Levant Company' — plates, original parchment backed cloth, slightly soiled — 1904.
(Christie's S.
Kensington) $45   £20

ROSENTHAL, LEONARD
'Au Jardin des Gemmes' — no. 986 of 2,200 copies, coloured plates by Leon Carre, original wrappers, backstrip cracked and rubbed, 4to — Paris, 1924.
(Christie's S.
Kensington) $50   £22

ROSS, ALEXANDER
'Adventures of the First Settlers on the Oregon or Columbia River: Being a Narrative of the Expedition Fitted out by John Jacob Astor to Establish the Pacific Fur Company' — 1st Edn., folded engraved map, original cloth — 1849.
(Sotheby's, New Bond
Street) $720   £320

ROSS, FREDERICK
'The Ruined Abbeys of Britain' — 2 vols., coloured plates, illustrations, original cloth, slightly rubbed, folio, n.d.
(Christie's S.
Kensington) $65   £28

ROSS, J. AND FUNN, H.
'The Book of the Red Deer and Empire Big Game' — plates, buckram, limited edition 190/500 copies — 1925.
(Tessa Bennett,
Edinburgh) $45   £20

ROSS, SHEARER W.
'Rutherglen Lore' — cloth — Paisley, 1922.
(Tessa Bennett,
Edinburgh) $13   £6

ROSSETTI, CHRISTINA
'Goblin Market and Other Poems' — 1st Edn., wood engraved frontispiece and title after D. G. Rossetti, rather spotted, original cloth gilt, uncut — 1862.
(Sotheby's,
Chancery Lane) $155   £70
'The Prince's Progress and Other Poems' — 1st Edn., presentation copy, inscribed by the artist, wood engraved frontispiece and pictorial title after D. G. Rossetti, spotting, original cloth gilt, spine soiled, uncut — 1866.
(Sotheby's,
Chancery Lane) $360   £160

'Speaking Likenesses' – 1st Edn., wood
engraved frontispiece, original cloth, gilt,
g.e. – 1874.
(Sotheby's,
    Chancery Lane) $170   £75

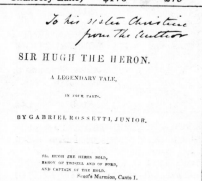

ROSSETTI, DANTE GABRIEL
'Sir Hugh the Heron' – 1st Edn., presentation copy, inscribed to his sister Christine
from the author, loose with original
wrappers, autograph note by W. M. Rossetti
in folder and calf slipcase, rubbed – G.
Polidori's Private Press, 1843.
(Sotheby's, New Bond
    Street) $4,725   £2,100

ROSSI
'Villa Pamphilia' – engraved title, portrait
and plates, some folding, folio, old calf
worn – 1650.
(Bonham's) $360   £160

ROSSI, MARIO M.
'Pilgrimage in the West' – translated by J.
M. Hone, limited to 300 copies, original
linen backed boards, uncut, unopened –
Cuala Press, Dublin, 1933.
(Sotheby's,
    Chancery Lane) $45   £20

ROSSINI, LUIGI
'Le Antichita Romane' – 101 engraved
plates, one torn cleanly, some marginal
fraying and soiling, title and covers worn
and detached, large folio – Rome, 1829.
(Christie's S.
    Kensington) $4,050   £1,800

ROTHERHITHE TUNNEL
Chevalier Benjamin Schlick Ms. in ink in
French, two fine full page illustrations
and two lengthwise sections of tunnel,
sepia wash, ink and watercolour, margins
ruled in gold, signed by Schlick and dated
1837, blue paper covered folder, disbound, g.e., folio – 1837.
(Christie's
    St. James) $630   £280

ROUND ABOUT OUR COAL FIRE OR
CHRISTMAS ENTERTAINMENTS
4th Edn., 7 woodcut illustrations, 8pp.
advertisements, torn, slightly spotted,
half roan, slightly rubbed – J. Roberts,
1734.
(Sotheby's,
    Chancery Lane) $1,170   £520

ROUSSEAU, J. J.
'Reflexions sur la Parure des Femmes' –
15pp. autograph with corrections, in
album, linen folder.
(Phillips) $1,215   £540

'Collection Complete des Oeuvres' —
portrait and 30 plates without text, each
plate is in two states, one and sometimes
both in Ricci's first state, straight grain red
morocco, gilt by Canape, folio — Brussels,
1774-83.
(Sotheby Parke Bernet
   Monaco) $4,050   £1,800
'Oeuvres' — 39 vols. in 37, large paper on
papier velin, 83 plates, some coloured after
Moreau, Boucher and others, some plates
avant la lettre, cont. French red morocco,
spines flat gilt a la grotesque, gilt edges —
Paris, 1788-93.
(Sotheby Parke Bernet
   Monaco) $81,000   £36,000

ROUSSET, F.
'Traite Nouveau de l'Hysterotomotokie,
ou Enfantement Caesarien' — 1st Edn., calf
— Paris, 1581.
(Bonham's) $2,925   £1,300

ROUTLEDGE'S EVERY BOY'S ANNUAL
1864, 1865, 1867, 1876, 1877 (2 copies),
1880, 1885, 1889
10 volumes, numerous wood engraved
plates and illustrations, one frontispiece
and title page detached, some leaves loose,
first in half calf, hinges and joints weak,
one in cloth, remainder in original cloth,
gilt, slightly worn, a few covers detached.
Selections from Routledge's Every Boy's
Annual, extra number, original cloth,
slightly worn.
(Sotheby's,
   Chancery Lane) $360   £160

ROUX, JEAN L. F. POLYDORE
'Ornithologie Provencale' — 117 litho-
graphed plates of birds by Beisson after
Roux bound without title or text, brown
half roan a little rubbed, 4to — Paris,
circa 1825.
(Christie's
   St. James) $360   £160

ROWE, GEORGE
'Forty Eight Views of Cottages and
Scenery at Sidmouth, Devon' — 48 litho-
graphed plates, india paper mounted,
light spotting, cont. olive green morocco,
rubbed — John Wallis, Sidmouth, 1826.
(Christie's S.
   Kensington) $810   £360

ROWLANDSON, THOMAS
'Caricature Etching Illustrating Boswell's
Tour of the Hebrides' — 20 plates,
slightly soiled, unbound in cloth portfolio
— n.d.
(Christie's S.
   Kensington) $80   £35

ROWLEY, W.
'Treatise on the New Discovered Dropsy of
the Membranes of the Brain' — 1st Edn.,
modern boards, original wrappers, bound
in — 1801.
(Bonham's) $110   £50

ROYAL COMMISSION OF ANCIENT
MONUMENTS AND CONSTRUCTIONS
OF SCOTLAND
9th Report, Outer Hebrides, Skye and the
Small Isles — cloth — Edinburgh, 1928.
(Tessa Bennett,
   Edinburgh) $100   £44

ROYAL ILLUSTRATED ATLAS, THE
Engraved title and coloured maps, mostly
double page, cont. calf – n.d.
(Christie's S.
   Kensington) $245   £110

ROYAL SOCIETY
'The Philosophical Transactions and
Collections to the end of the year 1700'
— First 3 vols., 2nd Edn., 12 vols. lacking
VI part 1, engraved plates and table, cont.
calf, hinges and spines worn, small 4to.
(Christie's
   St. James) $360   £160

RUDAUX

RUDAUX, ED. – ZOLA, EMILE
'Nouveaux Contes a Ninon' – 2 vols.,
etched frontispiece and 30 illustrations by
Rudaux, half morocco, original wrappers
bound in, t.e.g., by Champs Strodbants,
no. 429 of 500 – Conquet, Paris, 1886.
(Sotheby's,
    Chancery Lane) $90   £40

RUDDER, SAMUEL
'A New History of Gloucestershire' – 8
plates only, title detached, cont. calf, worn,
rebacked, folio – Cirencester, 1779.
(Christie's S.
    Kensington) $65   £30

RUEFF, JACOB
'Hebammen' – woodcuts throughout,
modern vellum, staining, worming –
Zurich, 1569.
(Bonham's) $720   £320

'De Conceptu et Generatione Hominis; De
Matrice et Eius Partibus' – title printed
in red and black and fine woodcut border,
numerous whole page and other woodcuts
by J. Ammann, modern vellum – Frankfurt,
1587.
(Bonham's) $1,125   £500

'De Conceptu et Generatione Hominis; De
Matrice et Eius Partibus, Nec Non De
Conditione Infants in Utero' – title in red
and black with woodcut, woodcuts throughout, 8 whole page by Jost Ammann, old
panelled calf, rebacked – Frankfurt, 1587.
(Bonham's) $2,925   £1,300

RULEAU, J.
'Traite de l'Operation Cesarienne' – 1st
Edn., old French calf – Paris, 1704.
(Bonham's) $315   £140

RULIMAN, LEO
'Conjuring Books' – catalogues no. 16-46,
31 issues, some with supplementary lists,
original wrappers, slightly worn, loose in
folder – New York, 1922-43.
(Sotheby's,
    Chancery Lane) $245   £110

RUMPF, GEORG, E.
'Thesauraus Imaginum Piscium Testaceorum' – engraved portrait frontispiece
and title, 60 plates, half calf, folio – P.
de Hondt, 1739.
And another edition in German but
affected by damp – 1773.
(Tessa Bennett,
    Edinburgh) $135   £60

EFFIGIES
GEORGII EVERHARDI RUMPHII, HANOVIENSIS ÆTAT LXVIII.

'Thesaurus Imaginum Piscium Testaceorum' — engraved additional title, slightly rubbed, portrait and 60 plates, light spotting, cont. speckled calf, rubbed, joints cracked, folio — The Hague, 1739.
(Christie's S.
   Kensington) $875   £390

RUMPH, GEORG EBERHARDUS
'D'Amboinische Rariteitenkamer Behelzende eene Beschryvinge . . .' — engraved title page, title printed in red and black, engraved vignette, engraved portrait, 60 engraved plates, dampstained, cont. calf, gilt spine, rubbed, folio — J. Roman, Amsterdam, 1741.
(Sotheby's, New Bond
   Street) $787   £350
'Thesaurus Imaginum Piscium Testaceorum Quales sunt Cancri, echinometra, stellae marinae etc.' — title in red and black with engraved vignette by Picart, engraved frontis, portrait and 60 engraved plates, later half calf, folio — The Hague, 1739.
(Christie's
   St. James) $573   £255

RUPP, I. DANIEL
'History of Lancaster County To Which is Prefixed a Brief Sketch of the Early History of Pennsylvania' — 4 lithographed plates only of 5, folding printed table, list of subscribers, some browning and soiling, cont. calf, rubbed — Lancaster, Penn. 1844.
(Sotheby's, New Bond
   Street) $22   £10

RUSHWORTH, JOHN
'The Tryal of Thomas (Wentworth) Earl of Stafford . . . upon an Impeachment of High Treason . . . Begun in Westminster-Hall the 22 of March 1640' — 2nd Edn., engraved portrait frontis, half calf, slightly rubbed — 1700.
(Sotheby's
   London) $65   £30

RUSKIN, JOHN
'Praeterita' — 24 original parts, printed wrappers — 1885-87.
(Phillips) $56   £25
'Modern Painters' — 6 vols., including index, cloth gilt — 1892-1898.
(Phillips) $80   £35
'Works' — 39 vols., limited to 2,062 copies, plates, some coloured, original cloth, spines faded — 1903-12.
(Christie's S.
   Kensington) $900   £400

RUSKIN, JOHN AND TURNER, J. M. W.
'The Harbours of England' — one of 250 copies, 14 plates, original cloth, slightly rubbed — 1895.
(Sotheby's,
   Chancery Lane) $45   £20

RUSSELL, ALEXANDER
'The Natural History of Aleppo, and parts adjacent' — 1st Edn., 17 plates, a few spots and stains, one plate detached, cloth spine, 4to — '1856' (1756).
(Sotheby's, New Bond
   Street) $101   £45

RUSSELL, GEORGE 'A.E.'
'Enchantment and Other Poems' — 1st Edn., no. 437 of 542 copies, original cloth backed boards, uncut — New York and London, 1930.
(Sotheby's,
   Chancery Lane) $50   £22

RUSSELL

RUSSELL, GEORGE W.
'A Plea for Justice' – 1st Edn., original
wrappers – Irish Homestead Limited,
Dublin, 1920.
(Sotheby's,
    Chancery Lane) $18   £8

RUSSELL, M.
'Polynesia or an Historical Account of . .'
– folding map and vignette, cloth, 2nd
Edn. – 1843.
(Tessa Bennett,
    Edinburgh) $36   £16

RUSSELL, P.
'An Account of Indian Serpents' – 2 vols.
in one complete set, portrait, 6 plain and
85 on 81 coloured plates, soiling, russia,
gilt, rebacked, folio – 1796-1801.
(Sotheby's, New Bond
    Street) $1,125   £500

RUSSELL, RICHARD
'A Dissertation on the use of sea water in
the diseases of the Glands' translated from
the Latin – 2nd Edn., engraved frontispiece, 1 plate, cont. calf – W. Owen and
R. Goadby, 1753.
(Sotheby's, New Bond
    Street) $55   £25

RUSSELL, THOMAS
'Sonnets and Miscellaneous Poems' – 1st
Edn., with preliminary and final blanks,
but prelim, blank slightly soiled and
frayed, disbound, loose in folder – 1789.
(Sotheby's
    London) $225   £100

RUSSELL, W. H.
'A Memorial to the Marriage of Edward,
Prince of Wales and Alexandra, Princess
of Denmark' – lithographed title and
plates, original morocco backed cloth,
worn – n.d.
(Christie's S.
    Kensington) $155   £70

RUTHERFORD, ERNEST
'Radioactive Substances and their
Radiations' – 1st Edn. inscribed by author,
original cloth, joints worn, 8vo – Cambridge
1913.
(Christie's
    St. James) $180   £80

RYCAUT, SIR PAUL
'The History of the Present State of the
Ottoman Empire' – 3 parts in one vol.,
12 engraved plates, title slightly soiled and
with ownership inscription deleted, upper
hinge weak, cont. calf, slightly rubbed –
For John Starkey, 1682.
(Sotheby's
    London) $225   £100

RYFF, W. H.
'Schwangerer Frawen Rosengarten' – title
printed in black and red with woodcut, 73
woodcuts of birth figures, instruments,
limp brown vellum – Frankfurt am Main,
1561.
(Bonham's) $1,800   £800

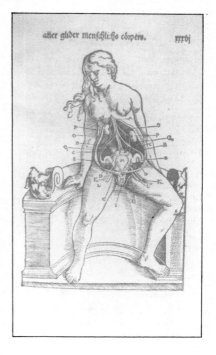

'Frawen Rosegarten von Vilfaltigen
Sorglichen Zulfallen und ge Brechen der
Mutter und Kinder' – large woodcut,
printed black and red on title and numerous
woodcuts throughout, modern vellum, folio,
in cloth cover and slipcase – Frankfurt,
1545.
(Bonham's) $12,375   £5,500

SACHS, EDWIN
'Sleight of Hand' – 1st Edn., original cloth gilt, spine and part of lower cover faded.
'The Bazaar' 1877.
And another three copies.
(Sotheby's,
   Chancery Lane) $146   £65

SACKVILLE-WEST, VICTORIA
'The Garden: – 1st Edn., no. 57 of 750 copies, signed by author, original buckram gilt, t.e.g. – 1946.
(Sotheby's,
   Chancery Lane) $70   £32

SADLEIR, MICHAEL
'Forlorn Sunset' – presentation copy signed by author, coloured frontispiece by John Piper, 1947.
(Christie's S.
   Kensington) $33   £15

'XIX Century Fiction' – a Bibliographical Record, 2 vols., limited edition, plates, buckram, dust jackets, 4to – 1951.
(Christie's
   St. James) $247   £110

SAHBI – SOULIE, FREDERIC
'Le Lion Amoureux' – engraved frontispiece and 18 illustrations, blue morocco gilt with floral bouquet, inside borders gilt, marbled endpapers, t.e.g., original wrappers bound in, no. 92 of 500 – Conquet, Paris, 1882.
(Sotheby's,
   Chancery Lane) $80   £35

ST. ANDREW'S UNIVERSITY
'Catalogue Librorum in Bibliotheca' – folio, uncut, presentation copy – 1826.
(Tessa Bennett,
   Edinburgh) $22   £10

ST. DENIS, RUTH
Album containing photographs, postcards, pictorial press cuttings, prints, Japanese prints, lithographic fashion plates etc, with a portfolio containing 2 scrapbooks and mounted press cuttings of about 350 of Erte's costume designs and pictorial designs collected by Ruth St. Denis and Pearl Wheeler. Some coloured, folio – 1915-36.
Posters (3) one a duplicate of Ruth St. Denis' performances – 1948.
(Sotheby's, New Bond
   Street) $90   £40

Important collection of approximately 500 photographs of Ruth St. Denis, Ted Shawn, the Denishawn Dancers including Martha Graham. Some coloured, some duplicates, some signed and inscribed. Various sizes – 1912-1970.
(Sotheby's, New Bond
   Street) $1,800   £800

ST. JOHN, JAMES AUGUSTUS
'Views in the Eastern Archipelago Borneo, Sarawak, Labuan . . . by Bethune, Heath and others' — lithographed title and 24 plates, 3 folding, one torn, some spotting, cont. half morocco, rubbed, spine chipped, small folio — 1847.
(Christie's S.
   Kensington) $200   £90

SAINT-LEON, ARTHUR M.
'Coppelia Ballet en 3 Actes de Mr. St. Leon et Musique de Mr. Leo Delibes' — manuscript of the libretto, choreographic instructions in different hand, ink, pencil and red and blue crayon, stained or spotted, cont. cloth back boards, corners s, worn — circa 1871.
(Sotheby's, New Bond
   Street) $110   £50

SALESBURY, WILLIAM
'A Dictionary in Englysche and Welshe' — 1st Edn., interleaved copy, black letter, title in woodcut border, numerous ms. notes, 17th century hands, dampstained, 17th century calf, worn, bookplate of Richard Mostyn of Penbedw, small 4to — 1547.
(Sotheby's, New Bond
   Street) $5,400   £2,400

SALIS, H. R. DE
'Bradshaw's Canals and Navigable Rivers of England and Wales' — 1st Edn., folding map in pocket at end, variety of modern newspaper clippings, photocopies, letters etc., original cloth, worn, 8vo — 1904.
(Sotheby's, New Bond
   Street) $75   £35

SALLUST, CAIUS CRISPIUS
'Belli Catalinarii et Jugurthini Historiae' — cont. red morocco gilt, joints rubbed, g.e., dull gold floral end-papers — William Ged, Edinburgh, 1739.
(Christie's, King
   St.) $515   £230
'Opera Omnia' — rubricated, device on title, early 18th century blue morocco, spine flat gilt with leafy tendrils, gilt panelled sides, g.e., worn — Plantin, Leiden, 1597.
(Sotheby's, New Bond
   Street) $123   £55

SALMON, N.
'The History of Hertfordshire' — folding map, calf rebacked, folio — 1728.
(Phillips) $135   £60

SALMON, THOMAS
'A New Geographical and Historical Grammar' — 9th Edn., 22 engraved folding maps, bookplates of Marbury Hall, cont. calf gilt, upper hinge weak, slightly worn — 1764.
(Sotheby's
   London) $135   £60

SALMON, WILLIAM
'Botanologia, the English Herbal' — 1st Edn., first issue, additional engraved title page, botanical woodcuts in text, damaged, defective, cont. calf, worn, spine repaired, folio — 1710.
(Sotheby's, New Bond
   Street) $1,125   £500
'The Family Dictionary or Household Companion' — 4th Edn., half title, some leaves wormed, browned, recipe in cont. hand on half title, cont. panelled calf, upper cover detached, lower hinge split — 1710.
(Sotheby's, New Bond
   Street) $33   £15

SALMONIA
'Or Days of Fly Fishing' — engraved plates, half calf, 2nd Edn. — 1829.
(Tessa Bennett,
   Edinburgh) $27   £12

SALON DE 1883-1905
22 volumes, lacking 1900, many photo-gravure plates, original cloth, some joints cracked and spines loose, folio — Paris, 1883-1905.
(Christie's
   St. James) $765   £340

SALZMANN, C. G.
'Unterhaltungen fur Kinder und Kinderfreunde' — 8 vols. in 4, wood engraved heads and tail pieces, cont. calf backed boards, slightly worn — Siegfried Lebrecht Crusius, Leipzig, 1778-87.
(Sotheby's,
   Chancery Lane) $180   £80

SAMAIN, ALBERT
'Hyalis' – limited to 100 copies, plates by
C. Picart le Doux, morocco, gilt, original
wrappers bound in, 4to – 1909.
(Phillips) $78   £35

SAMARITAN MANUSCRIPT
Bible, Hebrew leaf from a Samaritan
manuscript of the Pentateuch, part of the
Book of Numbers, on vellum, double
columns, written on both sides, imperfect –
14th or 15th century.
(Sotheby's, New Bond
    Street) $200   £90

SAMBUCUS, JOHANNES
'Emblemata' – lacks all before A3, woodcut
emblems, wormed with loss of a few letters,
later calf, worn – n.d.
(Christie's S.
    Kensington) $45   £20

SAMUELSON, JAMES
'The Honey-Bee; Its Natural History,
Habits, Anatomy and Microscopical
Beauties' – lithographed plates, original
cloth – 1860.
(Christie's S.
    Kensington) $65   £28

SANDERS, CHARLOTTE
'The Little Family written for the Amusement and Instruction of Young Persons'
– 2 vols. in one, 1st Edn., cont. sheep,
worn – R. Cruttwell, Bath, 1797.
(Sotheby's,
    Chancery Lane) $80   £35

SANDERUS, ANOTNIUS
'Chorographia Sacra Brabantiae' – 3 vols.,
titles with engraved vignettes, 65 engraved
plates including 59 double page plates, 6
folding, dampstains, cont. calf, worn,
folio – The Gaue, 1726-27.
(Christie's
    St. James) $1,575   £700

SANDFORD, CHRISTOPHER (Translator)
'The Garden of Caresses' – no. 7 of 275
copies, this with 6 extra illustrations
signed by artist in pencil, specially bound,
illustrations by Gertrude Hermes, original
vellum soiled, t.e.g. – Golden Cockerel
Press, 1934.
(Christie's S.
    Kensington) $335   £150

SANDRART, J. VON
'Illustrations to the Old Testament' – 142
engravings with text, some worming,
vellum, oblong 4to – Nurnberg, before
1700.
(Phillips) $225   £100

SANDYS, G.
'A Relation of a Journey - containing a
Description of the Turkish Empire of
Egypt, of the Holy Land etc.' – engraved
title, double page map and plates, 3rd Edn.,
cont. calf – R. Allot, 1632.
(Bonham's) $315   £140
'Relation of a Journey . . .' – engraved
title cut round and mounted, folding
plate damaged, no double page map,
James Bindley bookplate, calf gilt, w.a.f.
1615 – 1610.
(Phillips) $247   £110

SANGER, 'LORD' GEORGE
'Seventy Years a Showman' – 1st Edn.,
illustrations, original pictorial wrappers,
discoloured, upper cover damaged at
edges – 1908.
(Sotheby's,
    Chancery Lane) $80   £35

SANKEY, F. F.
'Familiar Instructions in Medicine and
Surgery with Observations, on the means
of maintaining the health of men on ship
board' – with 91 pp. appendix, 1 plate,
cloth, paper label – British Press, Malta,
1846.
(Sotheby's, New Bond
    Street) $155   £70

SANSON, LE SIEUR
'Carte de la Manche' – engraved chart
hand coloured in outline, 23 x 32 in.,
spotted, framed and glazed – Chez Hubert
Taillot, Paris, 1692.
(Christie's S.
    Kensington) $65   £30
'Le Royaume de l'Angleterre' – engraved
map, hand coloured in outline, 32 x 32½in.,
slightly spotted, framed and glazed –
Paris, 1693.
(Christie's S.
    Kensington) $90   £40

SANSON, NICOLAS
'Royaume de la Chine' – hand coloured engraved map, slightly stained, framed and glazed, 10¾ x 7¾in. – mid 17th century.
(Christie's S.
Kensington) $27   £12

SANSON AND ROSSI
'British Isles' – double page folio map – 1697.
(Tessa Bennett,
Edinburgh) $50   £22

SASSOON, SIEGFRIED
'Memoirs of a Fox Hunting Man' – no. 129 of 300 copies, signed by author and artist, seven plates by William Nicholson, original parchment, dust jacket, t.e.g. – 1929.
(Christie's S.
Kensington) $180   £80

SAUGRAIN, CLAUDE MARIN
'Nouveau Voyage de France, geographique, historique et curieux . . .' – engraved folding map and 11 folding plates, cont. calf, worn – Paris, 1750.
(Sotheby's, New Bond
Street) $50   £22

SAUNDERS, JOHN CUNNINGHAM
'A Treatise on some practical points relating to the diseases of the eye to which is added a short account of the author's life and his method of curing congenital cataracts by J. R. Farre' – 1st Edn., portrait, 8 plates, 7 coloured, new boards, uncut, 8vo – Longman, 1811.
(Sotheby's, New Bond
Street) $225   £100

SAUNDERS, WILLIAM
'A Treatise on the Structure, Economy and Diseases of the Liver' – 1st Edn., tree calf, rebacked, 8vo – G. G. and J. Robinson, 1793.
(Sotheby's, New Bond
Street) $225   £100

SAUVAN, J. B. B.
'Picturesque Tour of the Seine from Paris to the Sea' – 1st Edn., 24 hand coloured aquatint plates and map, some dampstains, red morocco, spine gilt, 4to – R. Ackermann, 1821.
(Sotheby's, New Bond
Street) $2,025   £900

SAVAGE, HENRY
'The Surgery, surgical pathology and surgical anatomy of the female pelvic organs' – 3rd Edn., revised and greatly augmented, 17 lithographed plates, woodcut illustrations in text, half title, new cloth, 4to – J. and A. Churchill, 1876.
(Sotheby's, New Bond
Street) $245   £110

SAVILE, GEORGE, MARQUESS OF HALIFAX
'Advice to a Daughter' – limited to 350 copies, this no. 19 of 75 on handmade paper and signed by artist, full page illustrations by Hester Sainsbury, original cloth, slightly soiled, t.e.g. – The Cayme Press, 1927.
(Christie's S.
Kensington) $22   £10

SAVORY, E.
'Sporting Pictures' – coloured plates, pictorial cloth, gilt, folio – n.d.
(Tessa Bennett,
Edinburgh) $45   £20

SAXTON, CHRISTOPHER AND HOLE, W.
'Oxoniensis' – hand coloured engraved map, 10½ x 15in., framed and glazed – early 17th century.
(Christie's S.
Kensington) $100   £45

SAXTON, CHIRSTOPHER AND KIP, WILLIAM
'Norfolciae' – hand coloured engraved map, 10½ x 15in., framed and glazed – early 17th century.
(Christie's S.
Kensington) $90   £40
'Durham' – hand coloured map – circa 1610.
(Tessa Bennett,
Edinburgh) $95   £42
'England and Wales' – hand coloured map – circa 1610.
(Tessa Bennett,
Edinburgh) $70   £32
'Notinghamiae' – hand coloured map, framed oak – circa 1610.
(Tessa Bennett,
Edinburgh) $67   £30

SCAMOZZI, VINCENT
'Oeuvres d'Architecture' – engraved additional title and 23 plates, some double page, woodcut and engraved illus. and diagrams many full page, stained, cont. calf, rubbed, detached, folio – Leiden, 1713.
(Christie's S.
Kensington) $315   £140

SCARPA, ANTONIO
'Practical Observations on the Principal Diseases of the Eyes. Translated by James Briggs' – 1st English Edn., 3 folding plates soiled, half calf – 1806.
(Bonham's) $245   £110

SCARRON, PAUL
'Le Virgile travesti en vers burlesques' – 2 vols., 8 engraved plates, a little browning, 19th century, slightly rubbed – Paris, 1726.
(Sotheby's
London) $100   £45

SCHAEBAELJE, JAN PHILIPSZ
'Emblemata Sacra – Bybelsche Figuren' – hand coloured woodcut ornament on title and hand coloured initials, additional engraved title, map and 213 engraved plates and illustrations, some plates badly stained, cont. vellum soiled, oblong folio – Amsterdam, 1653.
(Christie's, King
St.) $785   £350

SCHEDEL, HARTMANN
'Liber Chronicarum' – 1809 woodcuts, some double page and double page woodcut map by Wolgemuth and Pleydenwurff, 1st Edn., 325 leaves, folio, old vellum – Nuremburg, 1493.
(Bonham's) $15,300   £6,800
'Liber Cronicarum' – 298 leaves only of 366, lacking leaves in all sections with some leaves misbound, 51 lines and headline, gothic letter, numerous woodcut illus. in text, some dampstaining, 19th century half calf, rubbed, folio – Augsburg, Johann Schonsperger, I Feb. 1497.
(Sotheby's
London) $3,037   £1,350

SCHENK, PETER
'Icones Praetiorum et Villarum' – engraved title and 16 plates, last 2 repaired and defective, modern boards – Amsterdam, circa 1700.
(Sotheby's, New Bond
Street) $225   £100

SCHILLER, FRIEDRICH VON
'The Robbers', 2nd Edn. – 1795.
'Cabal and Love' – 1795.
'Fiesco' or 'the Genoese Conspiracy' – 1796. Three works in one volume, cont. calf, worn.
(Christie's S.
Kensington) $49   £22

SCHIMMELPENNINCK, MARY ANNE
'Theory on the Classification of Beauty and Deformity' – 2 folding charts of 4, 38 copper plates, mostly hand coloured, half calf, slightly rubbed, head of spine just faded – 1815.
(Sotheby's
London) $135   £60

SCHMID, HEINRICH ALFRED
'Arnold Bocklin' – 30 plates, illustrations, unbound as issued in original portfolio – Munich, 1901.
(Christie's S.
Kensington) $55   £25

SCHMID, HERMAN AND STIELER, KARL
'The Bavarian Highlands and the Salzkammergut' – numerous plates and illustrations, original blue embossed cloth, gilt, slightly rubbed, large 4to – 1874.
(Christie's
St. James) $270   £120

SCHMITZ, H.
'Encyclopaedia of Furniture' – illus., cloth gilt, 4to – 1926.
(Phillips) $33   £15

SCHOMBURGK, ROBERT H.
'Twelve Years in the Interior of Guiana' – tinted litho, title, list of subscribers, map, 12 litho plates, vignettes, original boards worn, folio – Ackermann, 1840.
(Phillips) $560   £250

SCHOTT, GASPAR
'Technica Curiosa' – 1st Edn., 58 engraved plates, some folding, full page engraved portrait, browning, modern half calf – Nuremberg, 1664.
(Sotheby's, New Bond
Street) $1,000   £450

SCHOTT

'Physica Curiosa' – half title, engraved
title, printed title in red and black, 60
plates, one folding, cont. vellum –
Wurzburg, 1667.
(Sotheby's, New Bond
    Street) $945   £420

SCHOTTMULLER, FRIDA
'Furniture and Interior Decoration of the
Italian Renaissance' – illustrations, origi-
nal cloth, 4to – Stuttgart, n.d.
(Christie's S.
    Kensington) $70   £32

SCHREINER, OLIVE
'Trooper Peter Halket of Mashonaland' –
1st Edn., frontispiece, original cloth,
slightly worn, t.e.g. – 1897.
(Sotheby's,
    Chancery Lane) $65   £30

SCHUBERT
Album – portrait, original Ausgabe, half
roan, defective – n.d.
(Bonham's) $22   £10

SCHWEGLER, JAKOB
'Gemalde der Kapellbrucke in Luzern' –
75 triangular lithographed plates by
Brothers Egli after Schwegler, one original
wrapper preserved, a little spotting, worn
– Lucerne, circa 1840.
(Sotheby's, New Bond
    Street) $495   £220

SCLATER, P. L. AND HUDSON, W. H.
'Argentine Ornithology' – 2 vols., some
foxing, 20 coloured plates, half morocco,
8vo – 1880-89.
(Sotheby's, New Bond
    Street) $1,235   £550

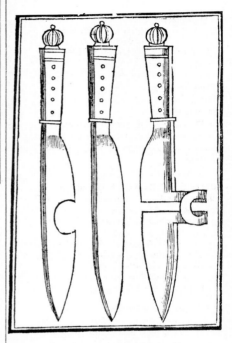

SCOT, REGINALD
'Discovery of Witchcraft proving the
Common Opinion of Witches contracting
with Devils, Spirits or Familiars to be but
Imaginery, Erronius Conceptions and
Novelties' – 2nd Edn., second or third
issue, woodcut illustrations, a few leaves
frayed, browning and staining, later calf,
rubbed, joints weak, corners pierced for
ties – R. C. for Giles Calvert, 1651.
(Sotheby's,
    Chancery Lane) $720   £320

SCOTLAND
'Scotland as it was in the Year 1745 and
Scotland in 1819' – original cloth backed
boards – London, 1825.
(Tessa Bennett,
    Edinburgh) $40   £18

SCOTT, JONATHAN
'Tales, Anecdotes and Letters from the
Arabic and Persian' – 1st Edn., 19th
century half calf, slightly rubbed –
Eddowes, Shrewsbury, 1800.
(Sotheby's,
   Chancery Lane) $65   £30

SCOTT, MICHAEL
'Physionomia Laqual Compilo Michael
Scotto, apreghi de Federico Romano' –
italic letter, title in woodcut border,
woodcut device on last leaf, modern
red morocco, spine gilt, gilt fillets and
corner sprays, g.e. by Ramage –
Francesco Bindoni and Malpheo Pasini,
Venice, 1533.
(Sotheby's, New Bond
   Street) $90   £40

SCOTT, PETER
'Morning Flight' – no. 323 of 750 copies
signed by Scott, portrait plates, some
coloured, original cloth, slightly soiled –
1935.
(Christie's S.
   Kensington) $145   £65

SCOTT, PETER – GALLICO, PAUL
'The Snow Goose' – no. 691 of 750
copies, signed by author and artist,
illustrations and 4 mounted coloured
plates by Scott, original cloth, t.e.g. –
1946.
(Christie's S.
   Kensington) $135   £60

SCOTT, SIR WALTER
Autograph letter signed to 'My Dear
Cunningham' regretting that he can no
longer be useful to him as a contributor
– 1 page, framed and glazed, dated 1828.
(Christie's S.
   Kensington) $65   £28
'Demonology and Witchcraft' – 6 engraved
plates after George Cruikshank, original
cloth, soiled, front inner hinge split –
1868.
(Christie's S.
   Kensington) $11   £5
'Marmion' – 9th Edn., cont. maroon
straight grained morocco, panelled in gilt,
extremeties gilt, with fore edge painting
of ships on stormy day with cliffs and
town in background – Edinburgh, 1815.
(Christie's S.
   Kensington) $110   £50

'The Life of Napoleon Bonaparte' – 9
vols., 2nd Edn., cont. calf, spines
slightly soiled – Edinburgh, 1827.
(Christie's S.
   Kensington) $72   £32
A.L.s Abbotsford 1830 in shaky hand
deploring the collecting of autographs,
slightly frayed and laid down with A.L.s.
3pp. Buller, Sir Redvers from Crediton,
1885 with cover.
(Phillips) $112   £50
'Provincial Antiquities and Picturesque
Scenery of Scotland' – 2 vols. in one, 2
engraved titles, 50 engraved plates, a few
slightly spotted, signature of Sarah
Tyrconnel on title, Tyrconnel bookplate,
cont. calf, rebacked, spine gilt, Tyrconnel
crest, coronet and initials, covers slightly
worn – 1826.
(Sotheby's
   London) $124   £55
'Waverley Novels' – 48 vols., engraved
frontispieces and titles spotted, cont. half
blue morocco, by M. Bell, Richmond, with
the Tyrconnel coronet and crest, gilt, on
spines, one upper cover slightly worn –
1829-33.
(Sotheby's
   London) $337   £150

SCOTTISH EXHIBITION, GLASGOW
Palace of History – 3 vols., original cloth,
gilt – 1911.
(Tessa Bennett,
   Edinburgh) $13   £6
Souvenir Album – plates, morocco,
oblong, printed for private circulation –
Glasgow, 1911.
(Tessa Bennett,
   Edinburgh) $18   £8
2 volumes, wrappers and official historical
catalogue, cloth – 1911.
(Tessa Bennett,
   Edinburgh) $7   £3

SCOTTISH HISTORY SOCIETY
16 volumes first series including nos. 1-57
and one vol. of third series.
(Tessa Bennett,
   Edinburgh) $335   £150

SCOTTISH NATIONAL GALLERY
Folio album containing photographs
and photogravures of paintings.
(Tessa Bennett,
   Edinburgh) $13   £6

Be Kind to Auld Grannie.

Be kind to auld Grannie, for noo she is frail,
As a time-shattered tree bending low to the gale,
When ye were wee bairnies, tot, tottling about,
She watched ye when in, and she watched ye when
out—
And aye when ye chanced in your daffin' and fun
To dunt yer wee heads on the cauld stany grun,
She lifted ye up, and she ki-sed you fu' fain,
Till a' your bit cares were forgotten again.
Then be kind to auld Grannie, for noo she is frail,
As a time-shattered tree bending low to the gale.

When first in your breast rose that feeling divine,
That's waked by the tales and the sangs o' langsyne,
Wi' auld warld cracks she would pleasure inspire,
In the lang winter nichts as she sat by the fire ;
Or melt your young heart wi' some Scottish lay,
Like the " Flowers o' the Forest," or " Auld Robin
Gray."
Though eerie the wind blew round our bit cot,
Grim winter and a' its wild blasts were forgot.
Then be kind to auld Grannie, for noo she is frail,
As a time-shattered tree bending low to the gale.

And mind, though the brief day of youth now is yours,
Time will wither its joys as wild winter the flowers,
And your step that's noo licht as the bound of the roe,
Wi' cheerless auld age may be feeble and slow ;
And the friends o' your youth to the grave may be
gane,
And ye on its brink may be tott'ring alane,
Oh, think how consoling some frien' would be then,
When the gloamin' o' life comes like mist o'er the glen.
Then be kind to auld Grannie, for noo she is frail,
As a time-shattered tree bending low to the gale,

SCOTTISH STREET LITERATURE
An extensive collection of broadside Penny
Ballads, 560 pieces, a number with small
wood or metal cuts, mounted two on a
page, in a half roan album — mostly late
19th century.
(Sotheby's
    Edinburgh) $1,170   £520

SCRATCHLEY, J.
'The London Dissector or System of
Dissection Practised in the Hospitals and
Lecture Rooms of the Metropolis' — 3rd
Edn., original boards, rebacked, uncut and
unopened, 8vo — John Murray, 1811.
(Sotheby's, New Bond
    Street) $55   £25

SCULTETUS, J.
'Armamentarium Chirurgiae' — engraved
title and 86 plates, 3 folding, 4 parts in
one vol., old vellum — 1692-93.
(Bonham's) $900   £400

SEARLE, RONALD
10 autograph letters signed, one typed, and
2 postcards incorporating an ink cartoon,
all to Nicolas Bentley, over 200 lines — n.d.
(Lawrence of
    Crewkerne) $45   £20

SECCOMBE, T. S.
'Army and Navy Birthday Book' — 12 wood
engraved plates, printed in colour by
Edmund Evans, illustrations, original cloth,
slightly soiled — 1881.
(Sotheby's,
    Chancery Lane) $55   £25

SEDER ARBA TRANIOT
Order of the Four Minor Fasts for
Sephardi Rite — engraved and printed
titles, 'Joodse' binding of brown calf,
elaborately gilt, roll tooled borders, centre
ornament, g.e., worn — Joseph Athias,
Amsterdam, 1689.
(Sotheby's, New Bond
    Street) $540   £240

SEEBOHM, HENRY
'The Geographical Distribution of the
Family Charadriidae of the Plovers,
Sandpipers, Snipes and their Allies' — 1st
Edn., numerous engravings in text, 21
hand coloured lithographs, original cloth,
worn, upper hinge weak, lower hinge split
— 1887-1888.
(Sotheby's, New Bond
Street) $585   £260

SEGUIN, L. G.
'Rural England' — limited edition, illus.,
vellum, gilt worn, t.e.g., folio — 1881.
(Phillips) $65   £30

SELBY, PRIDEAUX JOHN
'A History of British Forest-Trees' — illustra-
tions, cont. calf — 1842.
(Christie's S.
    Kensington) $27   £12

SELLER, JOHN
'Anglia Contracta' — frontispiece mounted,
hand coloured title, 7 general maps, 2
plates, table, 59 hand coloured maps, 2
views, calf.
(Phillips) $1,755   £780

SELWAY, N.
'The Golden Age of Coaching and Sport'
– coloured frontispiece and plates, limited
edition 500 copies, wrapper – 1972.
(Tessa Bennett,
    Edinburgh) $22   £10

SENECA, L. ANNAEUS
'Opera' – engraved portrait and title page,
woodcut initials, some browning, cont.
vellum, gilt, slightly soiled, folio –
Antwerp, Ex Officina Plantiniana Balthasaris Moretti – 1652.
(Christie's S.
    Kensington) $90   £40

ꟼrologo.

Aqui comieça el libro de lucio anneo feneca. que fe lla
ma de prouidencia de dios a lucillo.traſladado de la ꞁ
tin en lenguaie caſtellano: por mandado del muy alto
principe z muy poderoſo rey z ſeñor nueſtro ſeñor el
rey don Juan de Caſtilla z de leon.el ſegundo. ꟼoren
de el prologo dela traſlacion habla conel.

ꟼrologo enla traſlacion.

Ꞇlano dulçe es la ciencia. O muy ca ꞁ
tholico principe avn aquel lo ſiente
que nunca aprendio . Ca delepta el
ver.delecta el oyr. delepta alas de ꞁ
zes los otros ſentidos . Ꝺas la otra
deleytacion dela ciencia atodos ſo ꞁ
brepuja los otros plazeres . E no es
ſin razo. Ca pues el onbre es vna criatura mediana en
tre las ſuſtancias apartadas que llamamos los ange ꞁ
les z los animales yrracionales z brutos:deleytar ſe de
ue mas en aquello que le es comun conla natura an ꞁ
gelical. que en aquello que mejor o tan bien como el
ſienten las beſtias. ꟼero la errada coſtunbre z obſcuri
dad del ingenio baze en muchos poner ante lo ſenti ꞁ
ble. z derar que ſe tome de orin la parte intellectual ꝗ
es enel onbre mas alta. ꟼorende avn que la ciencia ſea
muy delectable. no ſe deleytan egual mente todos en
ella.Ca aſi como en muchas coſas de ꝗ los onbres to ꞁ
man plazer.no ſe alegran las beſtias. Aſi el gozo del ſa
ber.la dulçura del eſtilo eloquente. con que ſe buelgã
los eleuados ingenios. no ſolo no ꝉ gozan táto como
deuian. mas alas vezes avn ſe enojan algunos . Ꞓi es
de penſar que todos los que ſiguen las ciencias. ſienté
perfecta mente eſte plazer . Ca algunos aprenden por
ganar. Otros por fama o por otros fines diuerſos . E
                                            b ꞁ

'Cinco Libros' translated by Alonso de
Cartagena – 1st Edn. in Spanish, 127 leaves
of 132, 52 lines of commentary round 24
lines of text, gothic letter, fine woodcut
initial 'S', woodcut device at end, wormed,
water stained, cont. Spanish blindstamped
calf over wooden boards, very worn, folio –
Seville, 1491.
(Sotheby's, New Bond
    Street) $1,000   £450

SENEFELDER, ALOIS
'A Complete Course of Lithography' – 14
lithographed plates, one folding, the frontispiece coloured, some spotting, cont. half
calf, rubbed – R. Ackermann, 1819.
(Christie's S.
    Kensington) $810 $360

SENEX, J.
'An New Map of Rome' – engraved map,
19¼ x 21in., slightly rubbed at foot of fold,
framed and glazed – 1721.
(Christie's S.
    Kensington) $55   £25

SETON, ERNEST E. THOMPSON
'Life Histories of Northern Animals and
Account of the Mammals of Manitoba,
Grass eaters and Flesh eaters' – 2 vols.,
numerous maps and plates and illustrations
in text, original buckram, faded, 4to –
1910.
(Christie's
    St. James) $145   £65

SETON, G.
'St Kilda Past and Present' – cloth gilt,
small – 1878.
(Tessa Bennett,
    Edinburgh) $110   £50

SEVERAL DECLARATIONS
'The Several Declarations together with
Several Depositions concerning the Birth
of the Prince of Wales, at the Council
Chamber at Whitehall, Monday, the 22nd
of October, 1688' – half calf – Printed
by Charles Hill, Henry Hills and Thomas
Newcomb, 1688.
(Bonham's) $90   £40

SEVERN, WALTER
'The Golden Calendar' – chromolithographed title and dedication, 12 coloured
plates after Severn, original cloth, g.e.,
folio – Day and Son, n.d.
(Christie's S.
    Kensington) $45   £20

SEVIGNE, M. DE
'Receuil de Lettres' – 6 vols., portrait,
cont. red morocco, gilt, arms of Madame
Adelaide, daughter of Louis XV, gilt on
sides – Paris, 1738.
(Sotheby Parke Bernet
    Monaco) $112,500   £50,000

SHADWELL, THOMAS
'Bury Fair, a Comedy' – title soiled, some foxing.
'The Volunteers or the Stock Jobbers, a Comedy' – foxing, worming at end, 1st Edns., paper wrappers – 1689/1693.
(Christie's, King
St.) $146   £65

SHAKESPEARE, WILLIAM
'Comedies, Histories and Tragedies' – second impression, several tears, slight waterstaining, 19th century olive morocco gilt, arms of Sion College on upper cover, folio – 1632.
(Christie's, King
St.) $1,800   £800
'The Plays . . . with the corrections and illustrations of various commentators; to which are added notes by Sam. Johnson' – 8 vols., 1st Edn. of Johnson's Shakespeare, engraved portrait, half titles in vols. II-VIII, cont. sprinkled calf, gilt, labels, rubbed, bookplate of Lord Kinnaird – 1765.
(Sotheby's
London) $585   £260
'Poems and Sonnets' – limited to 470 copies, this no. 3 of 100 specially bound by Hiscox, decorations by John Buckland Wright, initials by Eric Gill, original morocco, t.e.g., slipcase, folio – Golden Cockerel Press, 1960.
(Christie's S.
Kensington) $315   £140

SHARP, CECIL AND OPPE, A. P.
'The Dance, an Historical Survey of Dancing in Europe' – 1st Edn., illustrations in text, frontispiece and 75 plates, 4 coloured, original decorated cloth, t.e.g. – 1924.
(Sotheby's, New Bond
Street) $33   £15

SHARP, MRS. JANE
'The Compleat Midwife's Companion or the Art of Midwifery Improv'd' – woodcut frontispiece and head pieces, 3rd Edn., old calf, rebacked – J. Marshall, 1724.
(Bonham's) $585   £260

SHARP, SAMUEL
'A Critical Enquiry into the Present State of Surgery' – 2nd Edn., cont. calf gilt, 8vo – Tonson and Draper, 1750.
(Sotheby's, New Bond
Street) $90   £40

SHAW, HENRY
'Alphabets, Numerals and Devices of the Middle Ages' – folio, half morocco, 48 plates, many coloured and heightened with gold, a very clean copy – 1845.
(Lawrence of
Crewkerne) $200   £90
'The History and Antiquities of the Chapel at Luton Park' – engraved title and 20 plates, spotted, cont. roan backed cloth, rubbed – 1829-30.
(Sotheby's,
Chancery Lane) $45   £20

SHAW, PETER
'Philosophical principles of Universal Chemistry' – cont. panelled calf, rebacked, 8vo – 1730.
(Sotheby's, New Bond
Street) $270   £120

SHAW, WILLIAM A.
'Manchester Old and New' – 3 vols., plates, illustrations, original cloth, gilt, slightly rubbed – 1894.
(Sotheby's,
Chancery Lane) $65   £28

SHEBBEARE, JOHN
'The Practice of Physic' – 2 vols., folding plate in vol. 1, rebacked, calf, 8vo – J. Hodges, 1755.
(Sotheby's, New Bond
Street) $90   £40

SHEDLOCK, EMMA L.
'A Trip to Music Land' – presentation copy, inscribed by the artist, 20 lithographed plates by J. King James, title slightly spotted, original cloth gilt – Blackie and Son, 1876.
(Sotheby's,
Chancery Lane) $55   £25

SHELLEY, PERCY BYSSHE
'Harriet and Mary, being the relations between them as shown by letters . . . edited by Walter Sidney Scott' – limited to 500 copies, this no. 16 of 100 signed by editor with collotype facsimiles and specially bound, portrait, original morocco, t.e.g., slipcase – Golden Cockerel Press, 1944.
(Christie's S.
Kensington) $110   £50

'Poetical Pieces . . . containing Prometheus Unmasked . . . The Cenci . . . Rosalind and Helen' – with original half titles, ads. and fly titles, some leaves slightly spotted, one margin with small perforation, original boards, spine barely rubbed, uncut – 1823.
(Sotheby's
London) $495   £220
'The Sensitive Plant' – coloured plates and other illustrations by Charles Robinson, parchment gilt, 4to – n.d. (circa 1920).
(Tessa Bennett,
Edinburgh) $45   £20
'Zastrozzi' – no. 85 of 200 copies, frontis and illus. by Cecil Keeling, original morocco backed boards, t.e.g., slipcase – The Golden Cockerel Press, 1955.
(Christie's S.
Kensington) $35   £15

SHENSTONE, WILLIAM
'Men and Manners, selected by Havelock Ellis' – no. 494 of 500 copies, original morocco backed boards, unopened, t.e.g., dust jacket – Golden Cockerel Press, 1927.
(Christie's S.
Kensington) $50   £22

SHEPHERD, J. C. AND JELLICOE, G. A.
'Italian Gardens of the Renaissance' – signed, plates, original cloth, soiled, corners worn, spine chipped, folio – 1925.
(Christie's S.
Kensington) $70   £32

SHEPHERD, T. H.
'Metropolitan Improvements of London in the Nineteenth Century' – additional engraved title, plan of Regent's Park and 158 engraved views of 79 plates, cont. half calf, slightly worn – 1827.
(Sotheby's, New Bond
Street) $270   £120

SHERER, JOHN
'Europe Illustrated' – First series, 2 vols., engraved titles and 117 plates only of 118, a few leaves slightly spotted, cont. half morocco, slightly rubbed – n.d.
(Sotheby's,
Chancery Lane) $335   £155

SHERINGHAM, HUGH AND MOORE, JOHN C. (Editors)
'The Book of the Fly Rod' – 13 plates including 4 coloured, by George Sheringham, original cloth, slightly rubbed, 4to – 1936.
(Sotheby Humberts
Taunton) $65   £28

SHERINGHAM, ROBERT
'De Anglorum Gentis Origine Disceptatio' – 1st Edn., Arbury Library book label, 18th century mottled calf, hinges cracked and rubbed – Cambridge, 1670.
(Sotheby's, New Bond
Street) $22   £10

SHEVCHENKO, ALEKSANDR
'Printsipy Kubisma', The Principles of Cubism and other Trends in Painting – 9 plates of Marionov, Goncharova, Shevchenko and others, 1 loose, printed on recto only, original lithographed wrappers, slightly soiled – Moscow, 1913.
(Sotheby's, New Bond
Street) $1,035   £460

SHIPP, HORACE
'The New Art'; a study of the principles of non representational art and their application in the work of Lawrence Atkinson – plates, original cloth – Cecil Palmer, 1922.
(Christie's S.
Kensington) $27   £12

SHIRLEY, THOMAS
'The Angler's Museum or the Whole Art of Float and Fly Fishing' – 1st Edn., engraved portrait, woodcut vignette on title, trade label of John Higginbotham, cont. sheep, worn, 12mo – 1784.
(Sotheby's, New Bond
Street) $380   £170

SHOBERL, F.
'The World in Miniature' — containing 516
hand coloured plates, 31 vols. morocco
gilt, worn, some covers detached — 1824.
(Phillips) $1,350   £600

SHOOTER, JOSEPH
'The Kaffirs of Natal' — frontis, plates, map,
original cloth gilt, slightly worn — 1857.
(Phillips) $110   £50

SHORT, THOMAS
'New Observations, Natural, Moral, Civil,
Political and Medical on City, Town and
Country Bills of Mortality — with an appen-
dix on Weather and Meteors' — advertise-
ment leaf before title, cont. calf, 8vo — T.
Longman and A. Millar, 1750.
(Sotheby's, New Bond
    Street) $200   £90

SHUCKARD, W. E.
'British Bees' — 15 hand coloured plates,
occasional light spotting, original cloth,
rubbed — 1866.
(Christie's S.
    Kensington) $33   £15

SIBLY, EBENEZER
'The Medical Mirror or Treatise on the
Impregnation of the Human Female Shewing the Origin of Diseases' — 1st Edn., engraved portrait, frontispiece, 4 plates,
original boards, uncut, 8vo — For the
author, n.d.
(Sotheby's, New Bond
    Street) $155   £70

SIDDONS, G.
'The Cabinet Maker's Guide — Dying,
Lacquering etc' — 4 plates, half morocco,
5th Edn. — Madras, 1840.
(Tessa Bennett,
    Edinburgh) $18   £8

SIDDONS, MRS. SARAH
'An Abridgement of Paradise Lost' — 1st
Edn., signature of Mrs. Siddons, slightly
spotted, from the library of Edw. Willes,
original boards, spine slightly torn,
unopened — 1822.
(Sotheby's
    London) $90   £40

SIDMOUTH, THE BEAUTIES DISPLAYED
One folding aquatint plate, cut down,
boards, joints cracked — J. Wallis, Sidmouth,
n.d.
(Christie's S.
    Kensington) $78   £35

SIDMOUTH, THE BEAUTIES DISPLAYED
2nd Edn., seven hand coloured aquatint plate
plates, map, cont. green half calf, upper
joint split — J. Wallis, Sidmouth, n.d.
(Christie's S.
    Kensington) $292   £130

SIGNATURE
A Quadrimestrial of Typography and
Graphic Arts. Edited by Oliver Simon —
nos. 1-15 and New Series 1-6, original cloth
backed folders with decorative paper
boards, ties, colour and black and white
illustrations, contributions from Paul
Nash, James Laver, Graham Sutherland
etc. — 1935-40 and 1946-48.
(Lawrence of
    Crewkerne) $380   £170

SILESIO, MARIANO
'The Arcadian Princesse' — 1st Edn.,
additional engraved emblematic title,
edges browned, old calf, worn, rebacked,
spine defective and wormed — 1635.
(Christie's, King
    St.) $425   £190

SILICUS, ITALICUS, G.
'Bellorum, quae Romani adversus Poenos
gesserent' — title laid down, portion of
last leaf of text excised, cont. vellum,
worn — Basle, per Henricum Petrum, 1543.
(Christie's S.
    Kensington) $56   £25

SILLAR, DAVID
'Poems' — preface by R. Burns, uncut,
original boards — Kilmarnock, 1789.
(Phillips) $290   £130

SILTZER, CAPTAIN FRANK
'The Story of British Sporting Prints' —
plates, 4 coloured, original cloth, slightly
rubbed — n.d.
(Christie's S.
    Kensington) $155   £70

SILVESTRE, ISRAEL AND OTHERS
'A collection of engravings of Chateaux,
Palaces, Gardens and Prospects, mostly
French' — 154 plates, 56 plates mounted,
stained, browned cont. vellum, gilt,
soiled and worn, bookplate of Marquis of
Grantham, oblong 4to — Paris, circa 1649-
61.
(Sotheby's, New Bond
    Street) $1,800   £800

SIMMONS, W.
'Detection of the Fallacy of Dr. Hull's
Defence of the Caesarian Operation' –
new half calf – Manchester, 1800.
(Bonham's) $155   £70

SIMMS, RUPERT
'Bibliotheca Staffordiensis' – no. 119 of
200 copies, cont. cloth, rubbed, t.e.g., 4to
– Lichfield, 1894.
(Sotheby Humberts
    Taunton) $30   £14

SIMON, F.
'Bits of Old Edinburgh' – 10 etched plates
and text in portfolio, limited edition 250
copies, large paper copy on india paper –
Edinburgh, 1855.
(Tessa Bennett,
    Edinburgh) $27   £12

SIMON, RICHARD
'The History of the Origin and Progress
of Ecclesiastical Revenues' – 1st Edn. in
English, some leaves browned, rust holes
in 17, cont. mottled calf, repair to head
of spine – 1685.
(Sotheby's
    London) $65   £30

SIMOND, LOUIS
'Journal of a Tour and Residence in Great
Britain' – 2 vols., 21 tinted aquatint
plates, illustrations, cont. half calf,
rubbed, 2 covers detached – Edinburgh,
1815.
(Sotheby's,
    Chancery Lane) $100   £45

SIMPSON, SIR J. Y.
'The Obstetric Memoirs and Contributions'
edited by W. O. Priestly and H. R. Storer –
2 vols., cloth worn – Edinburgh, 1855-56.
(Bonham's) $180   £80

SIMPSON, W.
'Glasgow in the Forties' – frontispiece and
plates, buckram gilt, limited edition 242/
500 copies – Glasgow, 1899.
(Tessa Bennett,
    Edinburgh) $20   £9

SIMPSON, WILLIAM
'The Seat of War in the East, First and
Second Series' in one volume, 76 plates of
79, some spotted, dampstains, cont. red
half morocco, rubbed, gilt, t.e.g., folio –
1855-56.
(Sotheby's, New Bond
    Street) $405   £180

SIMSON, FRANK B.
'Letters on Sport in Eastern Bengal' – 7
plates only of 10, A.L.s from author
inserted, later half morocco, slightly
rubbed and faded, t.e.g. – 1886.
(Sotheby Humberts
    Taunton) $1,575   £700

SINCLAIR, GEORGE
'Hortus Gramineus Woburnensis' – cont.
calf gilt, folio, brass clasps, 1st Edn., folding plan and specimens of seeds, some
heightened with hand colouring, portraits –
1816.
(Lawrence of
    Crewkerne) $675   £300

SINGER, C. J.
'The Earliest Chemical Industry' – limited
edition, colophon engraved by S. Gooden,
illus., cloth, folio – 1948.
(Phillips) $180   £80

SINTON, T.
'Family and Genealogical Sketches' –
cloth, small folio – Inverness, 1911.
(Tessa Bennett,
    Edinburgh) $50   £22

SIREN

SIREN, O.
'Chinese Paintings in American Collections'
– 2 vols., plates, cloth, folio – 1928.
(Phillips) $135   £60

SIRKIS, JOEL
'She'Eilot U'Teshuvot (Responsa)' – 1st
Edn., title in large woodcut wreath orna-
ment surrounded by winged cherubs,
worming, browning, modern cloth, folio –
Johann Wust, Frankfurt am Main, 1697.
(Sotheby's, New Bond
  Street) $100   £45

SITWELL, DAME EDITH
'Alexander Pope' – 1st Edn., limited to
200 copies, signed by author, this no. 209,
frontispiece, original cloth, soiled – 1930.
(Sotheby's,
  Chancery Lane) $11   £5

'Bucolic Comedies' – 1st Edn., presentation copy, inscribed by author, original
boards, small portion missing from spine
– 1923.
(Sotheby's,
  Chancery Lane) $55   £25

SITWELL, SIR OSBERT
'Dickens' – 1st Edn., presentation copy,
inscribed by author, original boards, dust
jacket – 1932.
(Sotheby's,
  Chancery Lane) $75   £35

'Dumb Animal and Other Stories' – 1st
Edn., presentation copy signed by author
to Gerald Gould, original cloth, spine
faded – 1930.
(Sotheby's,
  Chancery Lane) $90   £40

SITWELL, SACHEVERELL
'Doctor Donne and Gargantua; Canto the
Second' – 1st Edn., limited to 35 copies, 2
illustrations by Gino Severini, original
boards, backstrip worn, rubbed – Favil
Press, 1923.
(Sotheby's,
  Chancery Lane) $380   £170

**SITWELL, SACHEVERELL AND BLUNT,
WILFRED**
'Great Flower Books' – limited to 2,045
copies, coloured plates, original half cloth,
inner hinges cracked, dust jacket torn, ex
library copy, folio – 1956.
(Christie's S.
  Kensington) $315   £140

SKELTON, JOSEPH
'Oxonia Antiqua Restaurata' – 2 vols.,
132 engraved plates on india paper only,
folding map mounted on linen, some
leaves slightly spotted or soiled, modern
half morocco – Oxford, 1823.
(Sotheby's,
  Chancery Lane) $675   £300

SKELTON, V. AND OTHERS
'The Vinland Map and the Tartar Relation'
– plates – Yale University Press, 1965.
(Tessa Bennett,
   Edinburgh) $15   £7

SKENE, W.
'The Highlanders of Scotland' – cloth,
Stirling, 1902.
(Tessa Bennett,
   Edinburgh) $20   £9

**SKETCHES AND MEMORANDA OF
THE WORKS OF THE TUNNEL UNDER
THE THAMES**
10 plates, one folding map, one double
paged plan slight spotting and soiling,
original wrappers, worn, oblong 12mo –
Harvey and Darton – 1827.
(Christie's S.
   Kensington) $108   £48

SKIRA, ALBERT
'Les Tresors de l'Asie' – 5 vols., mounted
coloured illustrations, original cloth, 4to –
Geneva, 1960-63.
(Christie's S.
   Kensington) $110   £50

SKUES, G. E. M.
'The Way of a Trout with a Fly' – 2nd
Edn., three plates, some spotting, original
cloth, spine torn – 1928.
(Christie's S.
   Kensington) $22   £10

SLADE, A.
'Records of Travels in Turkey, Greece' –
some annotations in pencil, later cloth –
1806.
(Christie's S.
   Kensington) $65   £28

**SLAVE TRADE
BLUE BOOKS**
Correspondence relating to the Slave Trade,
a collection of 17 Blue Books, original
blue printed wrappers, 7 with torn spines,
folio – 1857-70.
(Sotheby's, New Bond
   Street) $225   £100

SLAVERY
'Two letters on Slavery, by an Eminent
and Learned Jurist' – 4 leaves, slight
browning, sewn as issued – Philadelphia,
1841.
(Sotheby's, New Bond
   Street) $50   £22

SLEZER, JOHN
'Theatrum Scotiae' – 57 of 60 fine double
engravings of Scottish views, some repairs,
lacking title, some plates missing, view of
Edinburgh defective, half calf, worn, folio
– 1718.
(Sotheby's, New Bond
   Street) $785   £350

SLOANE, SIR HANS
'An Account of the Most Efficacious
Medicine for the Soreness, Weakness and
several other distempers of the Eyes' –
17pp., half title, short tear in last leaf
mended, new cloth, uncut – Dan. Browne,
1745.
(Sotheby's, New Bond
   Street) $125   £55

SLOANE, W. M.
'Life of Napoleon Bonaparte' – 4 vols.,
illus., quarter vellum, 4to – 1906.
(Phillips) $90   £40

S. M.
'Manners and Customs of the French' –
no. 250 of 250 copies, 10 engraved plates
coloured by hand, original half buckram,
slightly stained, uncut – Leadenhall
Press, 1893.
(Sotheby's,
   Chancery Lane) $90   £40

SMART, CHARLES
'Practical Observations on Angling, in
the River Trent' – edges just soiled,
original boards, slightly defective, uncut –
Newark, S. & I. Ridge, etc., 1801.
(Sotheby's
   London) $425   £190

SMART, CHRISTOPHER
'A Collection of Seven Works' – 4 vols.,
all but one 1st Edn., browning and soiling,
cont. half calf, worn, covers detached –
1746-65.
(Sotheby's, New Bond
   Street) $2,700   £1,200

SMELLIE, WILLIAM
'A Treatise on the Theory and Practice of
Midwifery' – 2 vols., vol. 1 fourth and
vol. 2, fifth editions, cont. calf, spine gilt
with morocco labels, uniform set, bookplate of Lord Minto, 8vo – D. Wilson,
1766-68.
(Sotheby's, New Bond
   Street) $225   £100

SMILES, S.
'Lives of Boulton and Watt' – portrait frontispiece and illustrations, cloth – 1865.
(Tessa Bennett,
    Edinburgh) $55   £24

SMITH, ADAM
'An Inquiry into the Nature and Causes of the Wealth of Nations' – 2 vols., 1st Edn., cont. tree calf, gilt – W. Strahan and T. Cadell, 1776.
(Sotheby's, New Bond
    Street) $5,850   £2,600
'An Inquiry into the Wealth of Nations' – 2 vols., edited by J. Rogers, cloth – Oxford, 1880.
(Tessa Bennett,
    Edinburgh) $45   £20

SMITH, C.
22 English county maps, including Kent, Lancaster and Middlesex, a few damp-stained, coloured in outline – 1808.
(Phillips) $300   £135

SMITH, CHARLES HAMILTON
'The Ancient Costume of Great Britain and Ireland, from the seventh to the sixteenth century' – 'improved edition', hand coloured aquatint, additional title and 60 plates, light marginal browning, cont. half morocco, worn, folio, republished by the new proprietor, J. Dowding, n.d.
(Christie's S.
    Kensington) $335   £150

SMITH, CHARLOTTE
'The Banished Man' – 4 vols., 1st Edn., half titles in 3, cont. tree calf, joints and spines cracked, 12mo – 1794.
(Christie's S.
    Kensington) $470   £210

SMITH, G.
'New Pocket Plan of London' – folding engraved map, coloured in outline, 16½ x 29½in., mounted on cloth, dampstained, original wallet – 1819.
(Christie's S.
    Kensington) $33   £15

SMITH, GEORGE
'A Collection of designs for Household and Interior Decoration' – 157 of 158 hand coloured engraved plates only, 4to – 1808.
(Christie's S.
    Kensington) $155   £70

SMITH, GEORGE, OF KENDAL
'Institutiones Chirurgicae or Principles of Surgery' – cont. calf – Henry Lintot, 1732.
(Sotheby's, New Bond
    Street) $100   £45

SMITH, J. J.
'Die Orchideen von Java' – 1 vol. of plates for vols. 1-6, and vol. 6 text only, cloth backed boards – 1905.
(Phillips) $70   £30

SMITH, JOHN
'England's Improvement Reviv'd' – cont. sheep, rubbed, head of spine chipped – Tho. Newcombe for Benjamin Southwood and Israel Harrison, 1673.
(Christie's S.
    Kensington) $290   £130

SMITH, JOHN
'The Portrait of Old Age wherein is contained a sacred anatomy both of soul and body' – 3rd Edn. corrected, cont. calf, rebacked – E. Withers, 1752.
(Sotheby's, New Bond
    Street) $90   £40

SMITH, JOHN
'Select Views in Italy' – 72 engraved views, morocco gilt, g.e. 4to – 1796.
(Phillips) $450   £200

SMITH, JOHN THOMAS
'Antiquities of London and its Environs' – engraved title, 96 engraved plates, 3 in red and black, including one or two aquatints, title slightly spotted, Tyrconnel bookplate, cont. half roan, worn – 1791-1800.
(Sotheby's
    London) $155   £70
'Etchings of Remarkable Beggars, Itinerants and Traders in London' – etched title and 43 plates, a few margins lightly stained, modern half morocco, large – 1815.
(Christie's S.
    Kensington) $200   £90

SMITH, ROBERT (Rat Catcher to the Princess Amelia)
'The Universal Directory for Taking Alive and Destroying Rats' – with 6 plates inserted, 4 folding, additional water colour inserted of a stoat – For the author, 1768.
(Lawrence of
    Crewkerne) $135   £60

SMITH, SOUTHWOOD
'The Philosophy of Health or an Exposition of the Physical and Mental Constitution of Man' – 3rd Edn., 2 vols., woodcut illustrations, half calf, spine gilt, 12 mo. – 1847.
(Sotheby's, New Bond
    Street) $80   £35

SMITH, THOMAS
'The Young Artist's Assistant in the Art of Drawing in Water Colours' – 22 engraved and aquatint plates, 14 hand coloured, cont. half green roan, hinges rubbed – watermark, 1829.
(Sotheby's
    London) $270   £120

SMITH, T. J.
'Nollekens and His Times' – 2 vols. in four, extra illustrated by the insertion of 350 portraits, views etc., a few in colour, half morocco, gilt – 1829.
(Sotheby's, New Bond
    Street) $360   £160
'Ancient Topography of London' – engraved additional title, hand coloured 32 plates, occasional slight spotting, cont. half morocco, rubbed – 1815.
(Christie's S.
    Kensington) $168   £75

SMITH, WILLIAM
'A New & Compendious History of the County of Warwick' – engraved title, map and 60 plates, rather spotted and soiled throughout, cont. cloth, rebacked, rubbed – Birmingham, 1830.
(Sotheby's,
    Chancery Lane) $245   £110

SMITH, WILLIAM STEVENSON
'A History of Egyptian Sculpture and Painting in the Old Kingdom' – plates, original cloth, dust jacket – 1949.
(Christie's S.
    Kensington) $70   £30

SMITHSONIAN CONTRIBUTIONS TO KNOWLEDGE
4 vols., various plates some coloured, a few leaves detached, various cont. bindings, worn, large 4to, ex library copy – New York and Washington, 1848-53.
(Christie's S.
    Kensington) $33   £15

SMOLLETT, TOBIAS
'Peregrine Pickle' – 4 vols., 4 plates, calf gilt, upper cover, vol. 1 detached, 1784.
(Phillips) $33   £15
'The History of England' – 11 vols., 1763-60.
'Continuation of the History – 5 vols., 1763-63 – 16 vols. altogether in various editions, cont. calf.
(Christie's S.
    Kensington) $85   £38

SMYTH, LIEUTENANT W. AND LOWE, F.
'Narrative of a Journey from Lima to Peru' – 1st Edn., 13 engraved or lithoed plates, including 3 maps, 2 folding, frontis. spotted, cont. half calf, hinges split – 1836.
(Sotheby's
    London) $225   £100

SOANE, SIR JOHN
'Sketches in Architecture' – 1st Edn., 54 engraved plates including several aquatints, light spotting mostly marginal, cont. half calf, worn, folio – 1793.
(Sotheby's, New Bond
    Street) $1,080   £480

SOBIESKI, J. AND STUART, C. E.
'Lays of the Deer Forest' – 2 vols., 2 frontispieces and plates, fine straight grained morocco, 1st Edn. – 1848.
(Tessa Bennett,
    Edinburgh) $110   £48

SOBREVIELA, MANUEL AND BARCELO, NARCISSO Y
'Voyages a Peru 1790-1794. Collection de Planches' – 12 hand coloured plates, 1 folding map, cont. calf backed boards, rubbed and soiled – Paris, 1809.
(Sotheby's, New Bond
    Street) $65   £30

SOIXANTE VUES DES PLUS BEAUX PALAIS, MONUMENTS ET EGLISES DE PARIS, CATHEDRALES ET CHATEAUX DE FRANCE
Engraved title page, plan and 60 plates, spotting and soiling, original cloth backed boards, worn – Paris, n.d. but most plates 1818.
(Christie's S.
    Kensington) $80   £35

SOLOMKO

SOLOMKO, SERGE DE — GAUTIER, THEOPHILE
'Mademoiselle de Maupin' — 2 vols., 19 etched plates and one illustration by Pennequin after Solomko, g.e., original wrappers bound in, by Canape, no. 3 of 1,020 copies and an original water colour by Solomko — Librairie des Amateurs, Paris, 1914.
(Sotheby's,
  Chancery Lane) $720   £320

SOLON, L.
'Inventions Decoratives' — engraved plates, cont. half morocco, spine torn with loss, folio — Paris, 1866.
(Christie's S.
  Kensington) $125   £55

SOLVYNS, BALTHAZAR
'A Collection of 250 coloured etchings, descriptive of the Manners, Customs and Dresses of the Hindoos' — 12 sections in 2 vols., 1st Edn., 250 hand coloured etched plates including 11 double page views, slight browning and soiling, 19th century red morocco backed cloth, spine gilt, rubbed and soiled, large folio — Calcutta, 1799.
(Sotheby's, New Bond
  Street) $2,700 $2,700 £1,200

SOMERFIELD, SIGNOR T.
'Descriptive Catalogue of Entirely New and Superior Wonders in the Art of High-Grade Prestidigitation, Magical Apparatus, Necromantic Mysteries etc.' — cloth, original wrappers bound in, soiled and faded, a few tears repaired — Paulton Bros, Wolverhampton, circa 1870.
(Sotheby's,
  Chancery Lane) $380   £170

SOMERSET
Sale particulars. The Somerset estates of the Rt. Hon. Lord Ashburton, folio paper wrappers, 2nd Edn., key plan and 9 folding plans partly coloured with two photographic illus., repaired — 30 May 1894.
(Lawrence of
  Crewkerne) $13   £6

SOMERSET
A collection of approx. 50 assignments with abstracts of titles, sale particulars etc. mainly 19th century relating mainly to Hinton St. George but also to South Pemberton and Crewkerne. With mss. Surveyor's Journal of G. C. Hale, 1836-40.
(Lawrence of
  Crewkerne) $55   £25

'SOMERSETSHIRE; WILTSHIRE'
Engraved map, extracted from Drayton's
Poly-Olbion, 10 x 13in., framed and glazed
— 1612 or later.
(Christie's S.
 Kensington) $85 £38

SOMERVILLE, W.
'The Chace' — 1st Edn., frontis., boards,
new calf spine, cloth slipcase, 4to — 1735.
(Sotheby's, New Bond
 Street) $225 £100

SOMM, HENRY
'La Berline de l'Emigre' — frontispiece and
5 etched plates by author, frontispiece
coloured by hand and heightened by gold,
maroon straight grained morocco, original
wrappers bound in. No. 4 of an unspeci-
fied limitation on japon, signed by author
— Paris, 1885.
(Sotheby's,
 Chancery Lane) $135 £60

SOMMER, H. OSKAR (Translator)
'Stories and Fairy Tales' of Hans Christian
Andersen — 2 volumes limited to 300
large paper copies, hand made paper,
frontispieces, illustrations, ornamental
borders, initials by Arthur Gaskin, original
buckram gilt, uncut, dust jackets, slightly
soiled — Allen, 1893.
(Sotheby's,
 Chancery Lane) $315 £140

THE SONG OF SONGS
No. 69 of 750 copies, illustrations by Eric
Gill, original cloth, unopened, t.e.g., dust
jacket — Golden Cockerel Press, 1925.
(Christie's S.
 Kensington) $315 £140

**SONGS AND POEMS OF THE REBELS
WHO FOUGHT AND DIED FOR
IRELAND IN EASTER WEEK, 1916**
1st Edn., original wrappers, cloth folder,
morocco backed cloth, slipcase, slightly
rubbed — Dublin, 1916.
(Sotheby's,
 Chancery Lane) $70 £32

335

SONNINI

SONNINI, C. S.
'Travels in Upper and Lower Egypt Translated from the French' – portrait, 27 plates, folding map, torn, foxed, cont. half calf, worn, joints defective – 1800.
(Sotheby's, New Bond
   Street)   **$125**   **£55**

SOUTHEY, ROBERT
'The Minor Poems' – 3 vols., 1st Edn., presentation copy to William Wordsworth, original boards, spines worn, uncut – 1815.
(Sotheby's, New Bond
   Street)   **$1,915**   **£850**

SOUTHGATE, A.
'Narrative of a Tour through Armenia, Kurdistan, Persia and Mesopotamia' – 2 vols., original cloth, soiled, inner hinges cracked – 1840.
(Christie's S.
   Kensington)   **$90**   **£40**

SOUVENIR DE BOULOGNE SUR MER
Continuous folding strip containing 25 hand finished coloured lithographed costume plates of peasants, fishermen etc., 256 x 15cm. in original red folder lettered in gilt, worn, unsigned and undated – circa 1860.
(Christie's
   St. James)   **$190**   **£85**

'SOUVENIR OF SCOTLAND'
120 chromo. views, cloth gilt – T. Nelson, 1891.
(Phillips)   **$55**   **£25**

SOUVENIR PROGRAMMES
Collection of over 200 souvenir programmes for the Ballet Theatre, Royal Ballet, Ballet Russe, Martha Graham, Mordkin and his Russian Ballet, Serge Diaghileff's Ballet, Ruth St. Denis, etc., illustrations, many coloured, original wrappings, 1916-73. Together with 33 dance, ballet, opera and cinema programmes many with illustrations and original wrappers, some defective, various sizes.
(Sotheby's, New Bond
   Street)   **$495**   **£220**

SOUVENIRS DE MARINE CONSERVES
31 plates, half calf worn, folio – Fernique, n.d.
(Phillips)   **$335**   **£150**

SOWERBY, JAMES AND OTHERS
'English Botany' – 3rd Edn., edited by John T. Boswell Syme, 13 vols., hand coloured plates, original half morocco, spines rubbed, some partly disbound, t.e.g. – 1902.
(Christie's S.
   Kensington)   **$630**   **£280**

SOYER, A.
'The Pantropheon' – engraved portrait and 41 plates, 2 double page and mounted on guards, some spotting, original cloth, gilt, worn, t.e.g. – 1853.
(Christie's S.
   Kensington)   **$65**   **£28**

SPAIN
'Retrotos de Los Espanoles Illustres con un Epitome de sus Vidas' – engraved portraits, limp leather, some leaves stained – Madrid, 1791.
(Bonham's)   **$200**   **£90**

SPARRMAN, ANDERS
'A Voyage Round the World with Captain Cook in H.M.S. Resolution' – no. 255 of 350 copies, frontispiece and illustrations by Peter Barker-Mill, folding map, original cloth, t.e.g., folio – Golden Cockerel Press, 1944.
(Christie's S.
   Kensington)   **$380**   **£170**

SPECTATOR, THE
8 vols., engraved frontispieces and titles, cont. marbled calf, repaired – n.d.
(Christie's S.
   Kensington)   **$70**   **£32**

SPEED, JOHN
'Cumberland' – hand coloured map, inset plan – R. Rea, 1663.
(Phillips)   **$155**   **£70**
'Italia' – hand coloured engraved map, 15 x 23 in. framed and glazed as a tray – George Humble, 1626.
(Christie's S.
   Kensington)   **$245**   **£110**
'Norfolk' – hand coloured map, 15 x 19½in., small marginal tears, framed and glazed – mid 18th century.
(Christie's S.
   Kensington)   **$200**   **£90**
'Oxfordshire' – hand coloured map, inset town plan, arms – 1611.
(Phillips)   **$495**   **£220**

'Buckinghamshire' – hand coloured,
mounted and framed map – 17th century.
(Tessa Bennett,
    Edinburgh)   **$112**   **£50**
'Rutlandshire' – hand coloured map –
H. Overton, circa 1720.
(Phillips)   **$94**   **£42**
'The Countie and Citie of Lyncolne' –
hand coloured engraved map, 15 x 20in.,
repaired at fold, framed and glazed –
1610.
(Christie's S.
    Kensington)   **$247**   **£110**
'The Countie Pallatine of Lancaster' –
engraved map, 15 x 19¾in., repaired at top
centre, framed and glazed – G. Humbell,
1610.
(Christie's S.
    Kensington)   **$247**   **£110**
'The County of Warwick' – hand coloured
map, 15½ x 20½in., torn and repaired,
framed and glazed – 1612 or later.
(Christie's S.
    Kensington)   **$135**   **£60**
'The Isle of Man' – hand coloured engraved
map, 15 x 21in., repaired at fold, no
imprint, framed and glazed – 1646.
(Christie's S.
    Kensington)   **$180**   **£80**
'Yorkshire' – engraved map, hand coloured
in outline, 15 x 20¼in., slightly rubbed at
foot of fold, framed and glazed – Sudbury
and Humbe, 1612.
(Christie's S.
    Kensington)   **$146**   **£65**

SPEKE, JOHN HANNING

'Journal of the Discovery of the Source
of the Nile' – 1st Edn., 2 engraved portraits, plates including 1 coloured map
and text engravings, folding map in pocket
at end, 34 page catalogue at end, frontis,
and one section partly detached, cont.
signature of Sarah Tyrconnel on title page,
original cloth, uncut, gilt, inner hinges
weak – 1863.
(Sotheby's
    London)   **$125**   **£55**

SPELMAN, HENRY

'The History and Fate of Sacrilege' and
'Valor Beneficorum' or 'A Valuation of
All Ecclesiastical Preferments in England
and Wales' – 1695/8.
(Sotheby's, New Bond
    Street)   **$40**   **£18**

SPENCE, JOSEPH

'Observations, Anecdotes and Characters
of Books and Men' – cont. polished calf
– 1820.
(Christie's S.
    Kensington)   **$40**   **£18**
'Polymetis' – 1st Edn., engraved portrait,
41 plates, a few double page or folding,
engravings in text, short tear in plate 24,
tears in some upper margins, lower inner
corners wormed at beginning, some foxing,
cont. calf, joints split, worn, folio – 1747.
(Sotheby's
    London)   **$40**   **£18**

SPENCER, EDMUND

'Travels in Circassia, Krim, Tartary, etc.' –
2 vols., 1st Edn., 4 lithoed plates, 2
coloured, 2 engraved folding maps, original
cloth, splits in hinges – 1837.
(Sotheby's
    London)   **$145**   **£65**

SPENSER, EDMUND

'The Shepheardes Calender' – edited by
F. S. Ellis, limited to 231 copies, printed in
red and black, 12 full page illustrations by
A. J. Gaskin, ornamental woodcut initials,
original holland backed boards, spine
slightly soiled, uncut, 4to – 1896.
(Sotheby's,
    Chancery Lane)   **$470**   **£210**

STAEL-HOLSTEIN

STAEL-HOLSTEIN, Mme. A. L. G. DE
'Corinne, ou l'Italie' – 1st Edn., 2 vols.,
slight spotting, rubbed, 8vo – Paris, 1807.
(Sotheby's, New Bond
    Street)   **$315**   **£140**

SPITZER, FREDERIC
Collection – 6 volumes, plates, some
coloured, half morocco gilt – 1890-92.
(Phillips)   **$425**   **£190**

'SPORTING MAGAZINE, THE'
9 volumes only, engraved titles, plates,
occasional spoiling, cont. russia backed
marbled boards, some covers detached,
some spines torn with loss – 1793-1828.
(Christie's S.
    Kensington)   **$380**   **£170**

SPRATT, GEORGE
'Obstetric Tables' – 2nd Edn., 2 vols., 19
plates, 2 tinted and 13 coloured, brown
stain, original green cloth, paper labels,
4to – John Churchill, 1835.
(Sotheby's, New Bond
    Street)   **$335**   **£150**

SPRY, WILLIAM
'Life on the Bosphorus' – portrait, plates,
a few leaves detached, original cloth, gilt,
spine torn, t.e.g. – 1895.
(Christie's S.
    Kensington)   **$55**   **£25**

SQUIRE, J. C.
'The Rugger Match' – no. 12 of 50 copies
on large paper, signed by author, original
wrappers – Privately published, 1922.
(Sotheby's,
    Chancery Lane)   **$27**   **£12**

STACKHOUSE, THOMAS
'A New History of the Holy Bible' – 2
vols., plates, cont. calf, worn, repaired,
folio – 1752-53.
(Christie's S.
    Kensington)   **$70**   **£32**

STAFFORD, W. C. AND BALL, CHARLES
'Italy Illustrated' – 2 vols., engraved plates,
half calf, gilt – n.d.
(Phillips)   **$270**   **£120**

'STAFFORDSHIRE'
6 hand coloured maps including Greenwood
(1), Morden (3) – C. Smith, J. Cary, 1801-30.
(Phillips)   **$78**   **£35**

STAFFORDSHIRE
Hand coloured showing the Hundreds with
key, compass rose and vignette of Lich-
field Cathedral, approx. 25½ x 31½in. –
Greenwood and Co. Feb. 1830.
(Lawrence of
    Crewkerne)   **$45**   **£20**

STANFIELD, CLARKSON
'Coast Scenery' – engraved title and 39
plates, some leaves spotted, cont. half
calf, rubbed – 1836.
(Sotheby's,
    Chancery Lane)   **$145**   **£65**

STANFORD, JOHN
'Stanford's London Atlas of Universal
Geography' – half morocco, some rubbing,
a.e.g., 44 colour maps, fly leaf inscribed by
author – 1882.
(Lawrence of
    Crewkerne)   **$9**   **£4**

STANFORD, SIR WILLIAM
'Les Plees del Coron' – bound with 'An
Exposition of the Kinges Prerogative' –
old calf worn, (S.T.C. 23221 and 23213)
– R. Tottel, 1567-68.
(Phillips)   **$315**   **£140**

**STANHOPE, PHILIP, EARL OF
CHESTERFIELD**
'His Correspondence with Various Ladies'
– no. 64 of 480 copies, decorations by
Jeanne Bellon, original cloth – Franfrolico
Press, n.d.
(Christie's S.
    Kensington)   **$45**   **£20**

STANLEY, A. PENRHYN
'Sinai and Palestine' – frontis maps and
plans, original cloth, 3rd Edn. – 1856.
(Tessa Bennett,
    Edinburgh)   **$22**   **£10**

STANLEY, H. M.
'In Darkest Africa' – 2 vols., 1st Edn., folding coloured maps, plates, spotting and
original cloth – 1890.
(Christie's S.
    Kensington)   **$65**   **£30**

STARK, FREYA.
'Space, Time and Movement in Landscape'
– no. 487 of 500 copies signed by author,
original morocco backed boards, slip case,
oblong 4to – The Compton Press, n.d.
(Christie's S.
    Kensington)   **$65**   **£28**

STAUNTON, SIR GEORGE LEONARD
'An Authentic Account of an Embassy from the King of Great Britain to the Emperor of China . . . taken chiefly from the Papers of the Earl of Macartney' — 2 vols. only of 3 lacking volume of plates, 1st Edn., engraved portrait frontispieces, cont. half calf, covers detached gilt — 1797.
(Sotheby's, New Bond
Street) $27   £12

STEAD, W. J.
'Jersey' — engraved map, 15 x 26in., slightly soiled, torn at fold, framed and glazed — 1799.
(Christie's S.
Kensington) $90   £40

STEELE, SIR RICHARD AND ADDISON, JOSEPH
'The Tatler by Isaac Bickerstaff' — nos. 1-271, original issue in periodical form, no index, cont. calf, gilt, cracked, rubbed, folio — 1709-10.
(Sotheby's, New Bond
Street) $495   £220

HOW TO WRITE

STEIN, GERTRUDE
'How to Write' — 1st Edn., limited to 1,000 copies, presentation copy, inscribed by author, original boards — Plain Edition, Paris, 1931.
(Sotheby's,
Chancery Lane) $360   £160
'Operas and Plays' — 1st Edn., limited to 500 copies, original wrappers, slipcase — Plain Edition, Paris, 1932.
(Sotheby's,
Chancery Lane) $170   £75

'Matisse, Picasso and Gertrude Stein with Two Shorter Stories' — 1st Edn., limited to 500 copies, original wrappers, slipcase — Plain Edition, Paris, 1932.
(Sotheby's,
Chancery Lane) $225   £100

'The Autobiography of Alice B. Toklas' — 1st Edn., plates, slightly spotted, original cloth, soiled, with signature of Arthur Bliss — New York, 1933.
(Sotheby's,
Chancery Lane) $80   £35

STEINEL, KURT
'Abracadabra, Magier, Gaukler, Taschenspieler' — no. 37 of 85 copies, one of 39 with an extra illustration, 6 coloured lithographs signed and numbered by Steinel, unbound, folio — Offenbach am Main, 1970.
(Sotheby's,
Chancery Lane) $45   £20

STEINLEN, ALEXANDRE THEOPHILE
'Dans la Vie' — portrait, 99 coloured illustrations and cover design by Steinlen, cloth backed boards, original wrappers bound in — Sevin et Ret, Paris, 1901.
(Sotheby's,
Chancery Lane) $110   £48

STEINMETZ, ANDREW
'The Gaming Table, Its Votaries and Victims' — 2 vols., 1st Edn., spotted, lower hinges of vol. I split, original cloth, faded and worn, uncut — Tinsley Brothers, 1870.
(Sotheby's,
Chancery Lane) $45   £20

STENDHAL, M. DE
'Le Rouge et Le Noir' — 2 vols., 1st Edn., cont. half calf, blind stamped a la cathedral, slightly worn — Paris, 1831.
(Sotheby Parke Bernet
Monaco) $40,500   £18,000

STEP, EDWARD
'Favourite Flowers of Garden and Greenhouse' — 4 vols., coloured plates, cont. half morocco, extremities rubbed, t.e.g. — 1896-7.
(Christie's S.
Kensington) $245   £110

STEPHENS

STEPHENS, WILLIAM
'Dolaeus on the cure of the Gout by Milk
Diet to which is prefixed an essay on Diet'
— cont. panelled calf — London and Dublin,
1732.
(Sotheby's, New Bond
    Street)   **$125**   **£55**

**STEPHENSON, J. AND CHURCHILL,
J. M.**
'Medical Botany' — numerous coloured
plates, 3 vols., half calf, worn — 1834-
36.
(Bonham's)   **$990**   **£440**

STEPHENSON, P. R.
'Policemen of the Lord, a political
satire' — no. 5 of 500 copies, full page
illustrations by Beresford Egan, later
limp morocco, soiled — The Sophistocles
Press, n.d.
(Christie's S.
    Kensington)   **$22**   **£10**

STERN, F. C.
'A Study of the Genus Paeonia' — coloured
plates, illus., original cloth — 1946.
(Christie's S.
    Kensington)   **$270**   **£120**

STERNE, LAURENCE
'Sentimental Journey Through France
and Italy' — no. 138 of 500 copies, plates
by J. E. Laboureur, original cloth, t.e.g.,
dust jacket — Golden Cockerel Press,
1928.
(Christie's S.
    Kensington)   **$200**   **£90**
'The Life and Opinions of Tristram
Shandy' — 3 vols., no. 3 of 500 copies,
plates by J. E. Laboureur, original cloth,
t.e.g., dust jacket — Golden Cockerel Press,
1928.
(Christie's S.
    Kensington)   **$191**   **£85**
'The Life and Opinions of Tristram Shandy,
Gentleman' — 9 vols. in five, 1st Edn., cont.
calf, gilt spines, worn, five in cloth cases,
leather labels — York and London, 1760-
67.
(Sotheby's, New Bond
    Street)   **$1,687**   **£750**

STEUART, H.
'The Planters' Guide' — frontispiece and
plates, cloth gilt — 1848.
(Tessa Bennett,
    Edinburgh)   **$22**   **£10**

Among the many heads that have played
upon the passions of the public, this is one
[*takes the head*] that did cut a capital figure
in that way. This is the head of JONAS, or
the card-playing conjuring Jew. He could
make matadores with a snap of his fingers,
command the four aces with a whistle, and
get odd tricks. But there is a great many
people in London, besides this man, famous
for playing odd tricks, and yet no conjurors
neither. This man would have made a great
figure in the law, as he is so dexterous a con-
veyancer. But the law is a profession that
does not want any jugglers. Nor do we need
any longer to load our heads with the weight

STEVENS, GEORGE ALEX.
'A Lecture on Heads' — wood engraved
frontispiece and illustrations by Charlton
Nesbit, cont. calf gilt, slightly rubbed,
original wrappers bound in — Vernon and
Hood, 1802.
(Sotheby's,
    Chancery Lane)   **$110**   **£50**

STEVENS, WALLACE
'The Man with the Blue Guitar' — 1st Edn.,
original cloth, spine faded — New York,
1937.
(Sotheby's,
    Chancery Lane)   **$85**   **£38**

STEVENSON, R. L.
'A Child's Garden of Verses' — 1st Edn.,
original cloth, soiled, t.e.g. — 1885.
(Sotheby's,
    Chancery Lane)   **$33**   **£15**
'Kidnapped' — original red cloth, folding
map, adverts., 1st Edn. — 1886.
(Tessa Bennett,
    Edinburgh)   **$27**   **£12**

'The Master of Ballantrae' – original red cloth, adverts., 1st Edn. – 1889.
(Tessa Bennett,
Edinburgh) $7   £3
'The Works' – 26 vols., Vailima edition, no. 977 of 1,060 copies, frontispieces, 2 coloured, facsimiles, original cloth gilt, t.e.g., spines slightly faded, all but one unopened – 1922-23.
(Sotheby's,
Chancery Lane) $225   £100

STEWART, CECIL
'Topiary' – no. 125 of 500 copies, illustrations by Peter Barker-Mill, original half cloth – Golden Cockerel Press, 1954.
(Christie's S.
Kensington) $27   £12

STEWART, MAJOR GENERAL D.
'Sketches of the Character, manners . . . of the Highland Regiments' – 2 vols., folding hand coloured map, calf gilt, rubbed, 8vo – 1825.
(Phillips) $100   £45

STIELER, KARL AND OTHERS
'TheRhine from its Source to the Sea' – 2 vols., new edition, plates, cont. half morocco, rebacked, old spines laid down, t.e.g. – Philadelphia, 1893.
(Christie's S.
Kensington) $270   £120

STILLINGFLEET, EDWARD BISHOP
'Origines Britannicae or the Antiquities of the British Churches' – 1st Edn., title printed in red and black, cont. calf, splits in joints, rubbed, folio – 1685.
(Sotheby's, New Bond
Street) $65   £30

STITT, J. C.
'List of English Ladies' Armorial Book Plates' – inscribed by author, about 160 original and facsimile bookplates, ms. additions by G.H. Viner, cloth, 4to – n.d.
(Phillips) $65   £28

STOCKWOOD, JOHN
'The Treatise of Figures at the end of the Rules of Construction in the Latine Grammar Construed' – bound with several other imperfect grammatical works, cont. calf, rubbed and thumbed – n.d.
(Christie's, King
St.) $540   £240

STODDART, JOHN
'Remarks on the Local Scenery and Manners in Scotland 1799-1800' – 2 vols., 32 tinted plates, cont. tree calf, gilt, gilt spines, morocco labels, rubbed – W. Miller, 1801.
(Sotheby's, New Bond
Street) $155   £70

STOKER, BRAM.
'Dracula' – 1st Edn., some soiling, original cloth, soiled – 1897.
(Christie's S.
Kensington) $225   £100

STOLL, MAXIMILIAN
'Rationis Medendi' – 1st Edn., 3 vols., spotting and water staining, cont. calf, slight worming, 8vo – Vienna, 1777-1780.
(Christie's
St. James) $135   £60

STONE, FRANCIS
'Picturesque Views of all the Bridges . . . of Norfolk' – lithographed title and 84 plates, a few spotted, one repaired, cont. half morocco, slightly rubbed.
(Sotheby's,
Chancery Lane) $315   £140

STONE, REYNOLDS (Editor)
'Wood Engravings of Thomas Bewick' – no. 571 of 1,000 copies signed by editor, collotype plates, original cloth, dust jacket – 1953.
(Christie's S.
Kensington) $55   £25

STONE, SARAH (of Piccadilly)
'A Complete Practice of Midwifery consisting of 40 cases or observations of that valuable art' – half title, some dampstains, new half calf – T. Cooper, 1737.
(Sotheby's, New Bond
Street) $380   £170

STONER, FRANK
'Chelsea, Bow and Derby Porcelain Figures' – original red cloth gilt, t.e.g., 5 colour plates and 112 black and white plates – Newport, 1955.
(Lawrence of
Crewkerne) $80   £35

STORER, J. S.
'The Antiquarian Itinerary' – 7 vols.,
engraved plates, occasional spotting, cont.
half morocco, slightly rubbed – 1815-18.
(Christie's S.
   Kensington) $135   £60

STOSCH, PHILLIP
'Pierres Antiques Gravees' – 70 engraved
plates, titles and text in Latin and French,
occasional spotting, cont. calf, worn, folio
– Bernard Picart, Amsterdam, 1724.
(Christie's S.
   Kensington) $135   £70

**STOTHARD, THOMAS – DEFOE,
DANIEL**
'La Vie et Les Aventures de Robinson
Crusoe' – 3 vols., 19 engraved plates by
Delvaux after Stothard and others, folding
map, somewhat spotted, half morocco,
t.e.g. – Verdiere, Paris, 1799.
(Sotheby's,
   Chancery Lane) $54   £24

STOW, JOHN
'The Survey of London continued to this
present yeere 1618' – woodcut device on
title, slight staining and foxing, cont. calf
worn, joints cracked – 1618.
(Christie's, King
   St.) $110   £50

STOWE, HARRIET BEECHER
'Uncle Tom's Cabin' – wood engraved
portrait, vignette on title, 27 plates after
Cruikshank, original cloth, slightly soiled,
g.e. – 1852.
(Sotheby's,
   Chancery Lane) $55   £25

STOWE, JOHN
'Annales' – B. L. woodcut border to
title, cont. calf gilt, rebacked, folio, 1631.
(Phillips) $96   £40

STRABO
'Geographia' – 318 leaves only of 320,
some ms. notes, some dampstaining,
vellum boards, defective, folio – Treviso,
1480.
(Sotheby's, New Bond
   Street) $945   £420

STRAUSS, JOHAN JANSZ.
'Sehr Schwere Wiederwertige und Denck-
wurdige Reysen durch Italien, Griechen-
land, Lifland, Moscau und Unterschiedliche
andere Lander . . . aus dem Hollandischen
Ubersetzt von Andreas Muller' – 1st
German Edn., 20 engraved double page
plates by J. Kip and C. Decker including
one map, cont. calf, crowned cypher on
covers, spine gilt, slightly worn, folio –
Amsterdam, 1678.
(Sotheby's, New Bond
   Street) $720   £320

STRAUSS, RICHARD
Autograph sketch leaf of 'Munchen, ein
Gedachtiniswalzer' – 1st version, short
score, 40 filled staves, in pencil with
alterations in ink, with his signature and
date 1939 added later, oblong folio, 1939.
(Sotheby's, New Bond
   Street) $3,825   £1,700

STRAVINSKY, IGOR
'Apollon Musagete, Ballet en deux
Tableaux' – 1st Edn., piano score with
errata leaf and duplicate, original printed
wrappers, folio – Edition Russe de
Musique, Berlin, 1928.
(Sotheby's, New Bond
   Street) $55   £25

STREATFIELD, THOMAS
'Lympsfield and it's Environs, being . . .
original drawings, with manuscript
descriptions of that village . . . 1832' –
11 pen, ink and grey wash drawings, 12pp.
of mss. text, a.l.s., by the author bound in,
morocco backed wrappers.
(Christie's S.
   Kensington) $515   £230

Dearest, then I'll
LOVE THEE MORE.
—·o:o·—

London:—H. SUCH, Printer & Publisher.
123, Union Street, Boro'—S.E.
and at 83, White Cross-street, **City.**

The Insult by America on the
BRITISH FLAG

AIR,—" RED, WHITE & BLUE."

OLD England the pride of the nation,
Whose flag proudly floats in the breeze,

Two broadsides from the William Harvey collection of Street Literature.
(Sotheby's Edinburgh)

STREET LITERATURE
Collected by William Harvey, F.S.A. SCOT.
c. 150 pieces mostly broadside ballads but
including souvenirs of 'Visit of the British
Tank'; a poem 'The Mitherless Bairn'
printed on silk etc. Some of Scottish
interest particularly Dundee but many of
the ballads of English origin, in a half
leather album with ms. title as quoted —
late 19th/early 20th century.
(Sotheby's,
    Edinburgh) $495   £220

STREET LITERATURE
A collection of Ballads, Songs and
Snatches with other ephemeral literature,
c. 215 pieces, mounted in a half leather
album, mostly 19th century.
(Sotheby's
    Edinburgh) $765   £340

**STRICKLAND, HUGH EDWIN AND
MELVILLE, A. G.**
'The Dodo and Its Kindred' — 18 plates,
mostly lithographic, containing 2 coloured
and one folding map, illustrations in text,
cont. blue cloth, gilt, 4to — 1848.
(Christie's
    St. James) $225   £100

KING
PIPPIN.

A NEW SONG.

*Sung with unbounded applause by S. T. D. L.—r,
Bart. at a late Whig Dinner.*

Tune—" Derry down."

1.
I sing of KING PIPPIN, the chief of his race,
The joy of the garden, the pride of the place—
The pride of the place—not forgetting the tree—
And of all our Whig Apples, King Pippin for me.'
      Sing down down, down derry down.

*A song from an album of 19th century
Street Literature. (Sotheby's Edinburgh)*

STRONG

STRONG, L. A. G.
'The Hansom Cab and the Pigeons' —
limited to 1,212 copies, frontispiece and
illustrations by Eric Ravillious, original
cloth, unopened, dust jacket slightly torn
— Golden Cockerel Press, 1935.
(Christie's S.
   Kensington) $40   £18

STRUTT, JOSEPH
'A Complete View of the Manners, Customs,
Arms, Habits, etc., of the Inhabitants of
England' — 3 vols., 158 engraved plates,
some slightly spotted, Tyrconnel book-
plate, cont. calf., rebacked in vellum,
Tyrconnel crest and coronet, gilt, fore
corners slightly worn — 1775-6.
(Sotheby's
   London) $90   £40
'Sports and Pastimes of the People of
England' — 2nd Edn., 40 engraved plates,
3 hand coloured, Tyrconnel bookplate,
cont. calf, gilt borders, Tyrconnel crest on
upper cover, rebacked, fore corners slightly
worn — 1810.
(Sotheby's
   London) $110   £50
'A Complete View of the Dress and Habits
of the People of England' — 2 vols., 142 of
143 sepia engraved plates, a few leaves
spotted, lacks first leaves, Tyrconnel bookplate, cont. half vellum, Tyrconnel crest
and coronet, gilt, on spines — 1796-9, but
plates in vol. II watermarked 1802.
(Sotheby's
   London) $67   £30

**STUART, JAMES AND REVETT,
NICHOLAS**
'The Antiquities of Athens' — 4 vols., new
edition, 2 engraved portraits, frontis in
vol. 4 and 190 plates only, spotting, cont.
half morocco, rubbed, inner hinges cracked
or broken, folio — Priestley and Weale,
1825-30.
(Christie's S.
   Kensington) $245   £110

STUART, JOHN
'Sculptured Stones of Scotland' — 2 vols.,
plates, half morocco, worn, folio — 1856-
67.
(Phillips) $125   £55

STUART, ROBERT
'Views and Notices of Glasgow in Former
Times' — tinted lithographed title and
plates, one loose, original cloth, rebacked
preserving original backstrip — Glasgow,
1848.
(Sotheby's,
   Chancery Lane) $45   £20

STUBBE, HENRY
'A Justification of the Present War against
the Netherlands' — 2 folding plates.
'A Further Justification of the Present War
. . .' — 1st Edn., engraved frontispiece and
4 plates, two folding, 2 works in one vol.,
cont. calf, spine defective — 1673.
(Christie's, King
   St.) $225   £100

STUBBS, GEORGE
'An Illustrated Lecture of Sketching' — 17
lithographed plates, some mounted and
coloured, some spotting, soiling, original
cloth, soiled, binding, folio — n.d.
(Christie's S.
   Kensington) $65   £28

STUDDY, G. E.
Pen and ink drawing heightened with white
of Bonzo and Ooloo laughing together
with a golliwog and bowl in the foreground,
signed and dated '29, somewhat creased and
soiled, one slight tear, on fine tracing paper,
mounted on card.
(Sotheby's,
   Chancery Lane) $125   £55

STUDIO, THE
32 volumes, various bindings – 1897-1917.
(Christie's S.
   Kensington) $292   £130
STUDIO, THE
An Illustrated Magazine of Applied and Fine
Art . . . vols. 1-142, original cloth, some
spines faded, some soiled, 4to – 1893-1951,
plus 2 special issues.
(Christie's S.
   Kensington) $3,375   £1,500
STUDIO, THE
'Year Book of Decorative Art 1910' –
illustrations, some coloured, original cloth,
inner hinges cracked – n.d.
(Christie's S.
   Kensington) $55   £25

SUE, EUGENE
'Mysteres de Paris' – 10 vols. in five, green
morocco gilt – 1843.
'Juif Errant' – 10 vols., green morocco gilt –
1844.
(Phillips) $112   £50

SUETONIUS, TRANQUILLUS CAIUS
'The Lives of the Twelve Caesars . . . done
into English by Several Hands' – 1st Edn.,
12 engraved portraits, bookplate of Hugh
Cecil Earl of Lonsdale, cont. panelled
calf, spine gilt, slightly worn – 1688.
(Sotheby's
   London) $55   £25

SULLIVAN, E.
'The Book of Kells' – coloured plates –
Studio, 1933.
(Tessa Bennett,
   Edinburgh) $70   £32

SULLIVAN, EDMUND J.
'Maud' by Alfred, Lord Tennyson – limited
to 520 copies signed by the artist, illustrations by Sullivan, some coloured, original
cloth backed boards, slightly soiled, dust
jacket, 4to – 1922.
(Christie's S.
   Kensington) $63   £28

SUMME
'The Summe of The Conference between
John Rainolds and John Hart' – cont.
calf, upper cover detached – Geor. Bishop,
1584.
(Christie's S.
   Kensington) $45   £20

SURTEES, ROBERT SMITH
'Ask Mamma, Plain or Ringlets, Facey
Romford's Hounds, Sponge's Sporting Tour,
Handley Cross, Hawbuck Grange' – 6 uni-
form red half calf gilt, spines worn, t.e.g.,
rest uncut, vignette titles, coloured plates
by Leech, Browne etc., black and white
illustrations in text – n.d.
(Lawrence of
   Crewkerne) $157   £70
'Handley Cross' – 1st Edn. in book form,
17 coloured plates, calf gilt – 1854.
(Phillips) $170   £75
'Sporting Novels' – 6 vols., coloured plates,
half morocco gilt – 1890.
(Phillips) $225   £100

SUTHERLAND, WILLIAM
'The Shipbuilder's Assistant' – 10 folding
plates only, soiled and torn, mss. annota-
tions, cont. calf, rubbed – 1711.
(Christie's S.
   Kensington) $45   £20

SWAN, ABRAHAM
'The British Architect' – 2nd Edn., 60
engraved plates, modern mottled calf, label,
gilt, folio – 1750.
(Sotheby's, New Bond
   Street) $157   £70
'A Collection of Designs in Architecture' –
vol. 2 only, 65 engraved plates, modern
morocco, slightly rubbed, folio – 1757.
(Christie's S.
   Kensington) $110   £50

SWAN, JOSEPH AND LEIGHTON,
JOHN M.
'Views of the Lakes of Scotland' – 2 vols.,
engraved titles and plates, original cloth,
slightly rubbed – Glasgow, 1836.
(Sotheby's,
   Chancery Lane) $200   £90

SWARBRECK, S. D.
'Sketches in Scotland' – tinted lithographed
title and 25 views on 24 plates, mostly
rather soiled or spotted, one slightly torn,
edges frayed, cont. morocco backed cloth,
slightly worn – 1845.
(Sotheby's,
   Chancery Lane) $495   £220

SWIFT, JONATHAN
'Miscellanies in Prose and Verse' – title
soiled, imprint slightly rubbed, mid 18th
century ownership inscription along fore
margin, upper corners of last few leaves
wormed, cont. calf, rubbed, joints and
spines cracked – 1711.
(Christie's S.
 Kensington) $123 £55
'Travels by Lemuel Gulliver' – 2 vols., no.
88 of 480 copies, illustrations and map by
David Jones, mostly hand coloured, origi-
nal half cloth, slightly soiled – Golden
Cockerel Press, 1925.
(Christie's S.
 Kensington) $405 £180
'Directions to Servants' – limited to 380
copies, illustrations by John Nash, original
parchment backed boards, slightly rubbed –
Golden Cockerel Press, 1925.
(Christie's S.
 Kensington) $110 £50
'Miscellaneous Poems' – no. 89 of 375
copies, illustrations by Robert Gibbings,
original parchment backed boards, dust
jacket, slightly torn – Golden Cockerel
Press, 1928.
(Christie's S.
 Kensington) $45 £20
'Selected Essays' – vol. I, limited to 450
copies, illustrations by Jon Farleigh,
original parchment backed boards, slightly
rubbed, unopened – Golden Cockerel
Press, 1925.
(Christie's S.
 Kensington) $94 £42
'Travels into Several Remote Nations of
the World, by Lemuel Gulliver' – 2 vols.,
no. 171 of 480 copies, 40 wood engraved
illustrations by David Jones, some
coloured by hand, original half cloth, uncut,
4to – 1925.
(Sotheby's,
 Chancery Lane) $560 £230

SWINBURNE, ALGERNON C.
'The Springtide of Life' – limited edition
signed by artist A. Rackham, coloured
plates, original vellum gilt – 1918.
(Phillips) $380 £170
'Laus Veneris' – no. 350 of 750 copies,
frontispiece and illustrations, some full
page by John Buckland-Wright, original
cloth backed boards, t.e.g. – Golden
Cockerel Press, 1948.
(Christie's S.
 Kensington) $80 £35
'Locrine' – 1st Edn., ownership inscription
of Manley Hopkins, 32pp. of publisher's
adverts. dated October 1887 at end, origi-
nal cloth – 1887.
(Christie's S.
 Kensington) $33 £15
'Lucretia Borgia' – no. 286 of 350 copies,
frontispiece and illustrations by Reynolds
Stone, original cloth, t.e.g., folio – Golden
Cockerel Press, 1948.
(Christie's S.
 Kensington) $101 £45
'Pasiphae' – limited to 500 copies, this no.
72 of 100 with an extra plate and specially
bound by Sangorski and Sutcliffe, frontis-
piece and illustrations some full page by
John Buckland-Wright, original boards,
t.e.g. – Golden Cockerel Press, 1950.
(Christie's S.
 Kensington) $213 £95
'Lucretia Borgia' – Introduction by
Randolph Hughes, no. 19 of 300 copies,
one of 30 specially bound with collotype
facsimile of a portion of Swinburne's mss.,
wood engraved vignette on title and 6
illustrations by Reynolds Stone, original
white morocco, gilt, t.e.g., slipcase, small
folio – 1942.
(Sotheby's,
 Chancery Lane) $425 £190

Gulliver's Travels, illustrated by David Jones. (Sotheby's, Chancery Lane)

Lucretia Borgia by A. C. Swinburne, illustrated by Reynolds Stone. (Sotheby's, Chancery Lane)

SWISS EMBROIDERED BINDING
'Prieres Ecclesiastiques avec l'Exercise du Pere de Famille' — oval black fabric covered boards with single lobed indentations in each side, embroidered with silver thread with floral motif, fabric, slightly worn, repaired, 680 x 320mm. approx. — Perrin, Geneva, 1566.
(Sotheby's, New Bond
    Street) $5,400   £2,400

'SWITZERLAND:
Its Scenery and People . . . with historical . . . text based on the German of Dr. Gsell-Fels' — 22 plates only, illustrations, some leaves of text lacking, original cloth, spine torn, partly disbound, small folio — 1881.
(Christie's S.
    Kensington) $100   £45

SWITZERLAND
'Nouvelle Carte de la Suisse' — map coloured in outline — W. Faden, 1799.
(Phillips) $157   £70

SYDENHAM, THOMAS
'The Entire Works Newly Made English - the third edition by John Swan' — advertisement leaf bound at beginning, cont. calf gilt — E. Cave, 1753.
(Sotheby's, New Bond
    Street) $157   £70
'The Whole Works' — 1st Edn. in English, translated by John Peachey, spotted, damp-stained, cont. calf, rebacked — 1696.
(Sotheby's, New Bond
    Street) $110   £50

SYLVIUS, FRANCISCUS DE LA BOE
'A New Idea of the Practice of Physic . . . translated by Richard Bower' — only edn. in English, cont. calf, repaired — Printed for Brabazon Aylmer, 1675.
(Sotheby's, New Bond
    Street) $765   £340

SYMINGTON, A.
'Pen and Pencil Sketches of Faroe and Iceland' — cloth — 1892.
(Tessa Bennett,
    Edinburgh) $45   £20

SYMPSON, SAMUEL
'A New Book of Cyphers' — engraved title page, 19th century half morocco, joints and corners slightly rubbed — 1726.
(Sotheby's, New Bond
    Street) $80   £35

SYNGE, JOHN M.
'Poems and Translations' — 1st Edn., limited to 50 copies, original buckram backed boards, t.e.g., uncut — Printed for John Quinn, New York, 1909.
(Sotheby's,
    Chancery Lane) $235   £105
'Some Letters to Lady Gregory and W. B. Yates, selected by Anne Saddlemyer' — 1st Edn., no. 257 of 500 copies, original linen backed boards, uncut, unopened — Cuala Press, Dublin, 1971.
(Sotheby's,
    Chancery Lane) $18   £8

TABLE OF PRICES
'Clock and Watch Making, Aberdeen' –
1797.
(Tessa Bennett,
Edinburgh) $135   £60

TACITUS, PUBLIUS CORNELIUS
'Opera' – woodcut ornaments, cont.
vellum, gilt slightly soiled, folio –
Antwerp, Ex Officina Plantiniana
Balthasaris Moreti – 1658.
(Christie's S.
Kensington) $90   £40

TAGORE, SUBINDRO MOHUN
'Taravati, a Tale Translated into English'
– author's presentation copy to the
Marchioness of Ripon, Vicereine of
India, blue decorated velvet, 8vo., with
ten others – Calcutta, 1881.
(Christie's
St. James) $80   £35

TALLENTS, FRANCIS
'A View of Universal History' – 9 folding
engraved tables, slightly spotted, half
calf, worn, folio – 1758.
(Sotheby Humberts
Taunton) $155   £70

TALLIS, JOHN
'History and Description of the Crystal
Palace' – 3 vols. in two, engraved plates,
cont. morocco, gilt, slightly rubbed – 1851.
(Sotheby's,
Chancery Lane) $215   £95
'World Atlas' – 22 double page engraved
maps, hand coloured in outline, title
lacking, some spotting, slight tears to
some folds, cont. cloth, rebacked, n.d.
(Christie's S.
Kensington) $225   £100

TALLIS MAPS
28 coloured in outline, vignettes, various
parts of the world – London Printing Co.,
circa 1840.
(Phillips) $200   £90

TANNER, JOHN
'The Hidden Treasures of the Art of
Physick, Fully Discovered' – 1st Edn.,
errata leaf at end, title dust soiled, cont.
calf, spines renewed – Printed for George
Sawbridge, 1659.
(Sotheby's, New Bond
Street) $900   £400

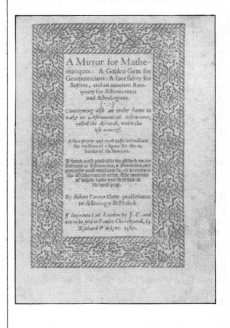

TANNER, ROBERT
'A Mirror for Mathematiques; a Golden
Gem for Geometricians; a Sure Safety
for Saylers . . . containing an order howe
to make an astronomical instrument
called the Astrolab, with the use thereof' –
1st Edn., woodcut initials and 16 woodcuts
in text, title in woodcut border, ownership
inscription and date, sprinkled calf
gilt by W. Pratt – 1666.
(Bonham's) $3,825   £1,700

TAPLIN, WILLIAM
'The Sportsman's Cabinet or a Correct
Delineation of the Various Dogs Used in
the Sports of the Field' – 2 vols., 1st Edn.,
engraved frontis, 2 additional engraved
titles, 24 plates, woodcut vignettes by
Bewick, spotting and soiling, cont. red
straight grained morocco, gilt, rubbed, 4to
– 1803-04.
(Sotheby's, New Bond
    Street) $855   £380

TASSO, T.
'Jerusalem Delivree' – 2 vols., 2 frontispieces, 2 engraved titles, 20 plates and 43
vignettes by Le Roy and others after
Gravelot, cont. French green morocco, gilt,
arms of Merard de St. Just, gilt on sides,
pink silk liners, gilt edges, with the Rahir
bookplate – Paris, 1774.
(Sotheby Parke Bernet
    Monaco) $126,000   £56,000
'La Gerusalemme Liberata' – 2 vols., upper
margin repaired of vol. I, later calf backed
boards, rubbed, ex library copy, 4to – 1807.
(Christie's S.
    Kensington) $33   £15

TASTU, MADAME AMABLE
'Education Maternelle. Simples Lecons
d'un Mere a ses Enfants' – coloured frontispiece, numerous illustrations, including
hand coloured maps, original half leather,
bit worn – Paris, 1861.
(Sotheby Parke Bernet
    Monaco) $450   £200

TATE, GEORGE '
'The History of·Alnwick' – 2 vols., 21
lithographed plates, 2 coloured, extra
illustrated with 21 engraved plates, cont.
morocco, spines faded – Alnwick, 1866-
69.
(Christie's S.
    Kensington) $135   £60

TATHAM, C. H.
'Etchings . . . of Ancient Ornamental
Architecture . . . in Rome' – 3rd Edn.,
101 plates only, some soiling, later cloth,
covers detached, partly disbound, folio –
1810.
(Christie's S.
    Kensington) $50   £22

TATLER, THE
106 volumes – 1925-65.
(Sotheby's,
    Chancery Lane) $1,215   £540

TAUCHNITZ EDITIONS
About 190 volumes various, original
wrappers, some torn or lacking, a few
disbound, 12 mo. – Leipzig, 1852-1930.
(Christie's S.
    Kensington) $560   £250

TAUNT, HENRY W.
'Oxford' – presentation copy from the
Oxfordshire Licensed Victuallers' Central
Protestation Association to Major C. H.
St. Hill' – gilt, joints rubbed, g.e., small
4to – Oxford, n.d.
(Christie's S.
    Kensington) $65   £30
'New Map of the River Thames from
Oxford to London' – maps and original
photos inserted, cloth – 1873.
(Phillips) $270   £120

TAUVRY, DANIEL
'A New Rational Anatomy Containing an
Explication of the Uses of the Structure of
the Body of Man and Some Other Animals'
– made English from the 3rd Edn.,
engraved frontispiece, 21 engraved plates,
library stamps, panelled calf, rebacked –
D. Midwinter and Tho. Leigh, 1701.
(Sotheby's, New Bond
    Street) $225   £100

TAVERNIER, JEAN BAPTISTE

'A Collection of Several Relations and
Treatises, Singular and Curious . . . Not
Printed Among His First Six Voyages . . .
published by Edmund Everard' — 2 parts
in one volume, folding engraved map and 8
folding plates, 4 with their own descriptive
leaves of text, cont. sprinkled sheep,
slightly rubbed, spine chipped, folio —
1680.
(Sotheby's, New Bond
    Street)   **$720**   **£320**

TAYLOR, GEORGE AND SKINNER, ANDREW

'Maps of the Roads of Ireland' — engraved
vignette title, dedication, key, folding
general map, torn, and 288 maps, Subscribers' List, cont. diced calf, joints rubbed
— 1778.
(Sotheby's,
    Chancery Lane)   **$450**   **£200**

TAYLOR, ISAAC

'Scenes in America' — 2nd Edn., engraved
plates and folding map, spotted, original
morocco backed boards, worn — 1822.
(Christie's S.
    Kensington)   **$45**   **£20**

TAYLOR, J.

'Voyage Pittoresque en Espagne, en Portugal
et sur la Cote d'Afrique, de Tanger a
Tetouan' — 3 vols., including 2 vols. of
plates, 164 engraved plates only of 165, half
titles, rather spotted, cont. morocco backed
cloth, rubbed, g.e. — Paris, 1826-32.
(Sotheby's,
    Chancery Lane)   **$515**   **£230**

TAYLOR, JEAN AND ANN

'City Scenes or a Peep into London' —
etched title and 28 plates each with 3
illustrations, neatly coloured by a former
owner, slightly spotted, original cloth, g.e.
— Harvey and Darton, 1828.
(Sotheby's,
    Chancery Lane)   **$315**   **£140**

TAYLOR, JEREMY

'A Selection from his Works made by
Martin Armstrong' — limited to 320 copies,
original cloth backed boards — Golden
Cockerel Press, 1923.
(Christie's S.
    Kensington)   **$110**   **£50**

'City Scenes' by J. & A. Taylor.
(Sotheby's, Chancery Lane)

'The Great Exemplar' — 3rd Edn., addditio-
nal engraved title and plates, one detached,
first few leaves detached, cont. calf, rubbed,
joints split, folio — 1657.
(Christie's S.
    Kensington)   **$40**   **£18**

TAYLOR, CAPTAIN PHILLIP MEADOWS

'Tippoo Sultaun; a Tale of the Mysore
War' — 3 vols., 1st Edn., lacks half titles,
cont. half green calf, gilt, lacks label —
1840.
(Sotheby's
    London)   **$90**   **£40**

TEALBY, NORMAN

'Voltaire, Candide and Other Romances' —
blue cloth gilt, black and white illustrations
— 1928.
(Lawrence of
    Crewkerne)   **$11**   **£5**

TELFORD, THOMAS AND McADAM, JOHN LOUDON

First Report of the Select Committee on the road from London to Holyhead 1819; papers relating to building a bridge over the Menai Strait; 2 folding maps, 2 engraved diagrams, 1819; Report of the Select Committee on Mr. McAdam's Petition 1823; 9th Report of the Commission for Roads and Bridges in the Highlands of Scotland, large folding map, diagrams 1821; 6 works in one vol., cont. half calf, rubbed, with McAdam's 'Remarks on the Present System of Road Making' – 3rd Edn., original boards, worn, upper cover partly detached, 1820.
(Christie's
   St. James) $146   £65

TELL TALE, THE OR UNIVERSAL MUSEUM

A collection of 82 tales, 4 vols., each with engraved title and 12 plates, some leaves spotted, cont. half calf, rubbed and slightly worn – I. Roe, 1803-05.
(Sotheby's,
   Chancery Lane) $225   £100

TELLIER, JULES

'Abd-el-Rhaman in Paradise' – no. 142 of 400 copies, frontispiece and full page illustrations by Paul Nash, original cloth backed boards, dust jacket, t.e.g. – Golden Cockerel Press, 1928.
(Christie's S.
   Kensington) $110   £50

'Abd-el-Rhaman in Paradise' – translated by Brian Rhys, no. 323 of 400 copies, wood engraved frontis, vignette on title and 2 illustrations by Paul Nash, original buckram backed boards, t.e.g., slightly affected by damp, 8vo – 1928.
(Sotheby's,
   Chancery Lane) $85   £38

TEMPLE, SIR EDMUND

'Life of Pill Garlick' – hand coloured folding frontis, half calf, gilt – 1813.
(Phillips) $50   £22

TEMPLE, SIR RICHARD CARNAC

'The Itinerary of Ludovico di Verthema of Bologna' – limited edition on Japan vellum, original vellum backed cloth, uncut – 1928.
(Sotheby's,
   Chancery Lane) $55   £24

TEN COMMANDMENTS
'Jhesus. the Floure of the Commandments of God' — woodcut on title and full page woodcut of Crucifixion on verso of title, woodcut device of Caxton and de Worde, niger morocco by Zaehnsdorf, original binding preserved as doublures, folio — Wynkyn de Worde, 14 September, 1510.
(Christie's, King
 St.) $20,250 £9,000

TENNENT, SIR J. EMERSON
'The Wild Elephant and the method of capturing and taming it in Ceylon' — 1st Edn.,.3 plates and 19 illustrations, inscribed by the author on half title, original cloth, rubbed and slightly soiled — 1867.
(Sotheby's
 London) $100 £45

TENNYSON, ALFRED LORD
'The Poetical Works' — 12 vols., original cloth in a hinged box — 1891.
(Christie's S.
 Kensington) $40 £18
'The Idylls of the King' — decorated parchment gilt, 21 tissued and mounted plates by Eleanor Fortescue Brickdale, signed by artist, out of series of 350 — 1911.
(Lawrence of
 Crewkerne) $55 £24

TERELIUS, DOMENICO
'De Generatione et Partu Hominis, Libri Due' — woodcut initials, 1st Edn., vellum in cloth case, a fine large copy — Alexandrum Marsilium, 1578.
(Bonham's) $810 £360

TERENCE
'Comoediae' — a nice copy in cont. French violet morocco gilt with wide dentelle border on sides, gilt spines, g.e., joints worn — Baskerville, Birmingham, 1772.
(Sotheby's, New Bond
 Street) $675 £300

TESTAMENT, THE, OF THE TWELVE PATRIARCHS, THE SONS OF JACOB
Translated by Robert Grosthead — 14 woodcuts, including one on title, soiling and staining, cont. sheep, soiled — M. Clark for the Company of the Stationers, 1684.
(Sotheby's,
 Chancery Lane) $225 £100

TEXIER, EDMUND
'Voyage Pittoresque en Hollande et en Belgique' — illustrations by M. M. Rouargue Freres, title with engraved vignette, 22 engraved plates, including 2 coloured by hand, cartonnage polychrome, g.e., 8vo — Paris, 1857.
(Sotheby's, New Bond
 Street) $405 £180

THAYER, EMMA HOMAN
'Wild Flowers of the Pacific Coast' – 24 coloured plates, title signed by author, presentation inscription torn, original cloth soiled, inner hinges cracked, g.e., 4to – New York, 1887.
(Christie's S.
Kensington) $50   £22

No. 271. The Substitution Trunk

THAYER, F. G.
67 catalogues and supplements in 54, 1914 – 1944. Numerous illustrations, one in original leatheroid, the remainder original wrappers or as issued, some inserted or bound in cloth folders, various sizes – Los Angeles, 1914-1944.
(Sotheby's,
Chancery Lane) $380   £170

THEATRE, THE
Illustrated Monthly magazine devoted to the Drama and Music – 46 volumes altogether, illustrations, some leaves detached or loose, decorated cloth, original wrappers bound in, some hinges weak, spines faded – New York, 1901-27.
(Sotheby's, New Bond
Street) $1,000   £450

THEMISTIUS
'Opera' – 1st Edn., woodcut device of Aldus on title and last page, woodcut initials and headpieces, Archbishop Cranmer's copy with inscription, also signature of John, Lord Lumley and 'Bound for Henry, Prince of Wales' calf gilt with his arms and Tudor rose, red edges, folio – Heirs of Aldus and Andreas Asulanus, Venice, May 1534.
(Christie's, King
St.) $7,875   £3,500

THEOBALD, JOHN
'The Young Wife's Guide in the Management of Her Children' – 3rd Edn., 2 works in one volume, half title to first work, rough calf, covers loose – W. Griffin, 1764.
(Sotheby's, New Bond
Street) $80   £35

THEOBALD, J. AND CO.
'Special Catalogue of Conjuring Tricks' – 4th Edn., leaves discoloured, n.d. Another copy, 6th Edn., n.d. Bound together in cloth folders, soiled. With 'Catalogue of Conjuring Apparatus, Electrical Goods' – 633rd thousand, stained, repaired, original wrappers, illustrations – 1899.
(Sotheby's,
Chancery Lane) $155   £70

THEOCRITOS, BION AND MOSCHUS
'The Complete Poems translated by
Jack Lindsay' – no. 480 of 500 copies,
plates by Edward Hutton, original
parchment, t.e.g., folio – The Franfrolico
Press, 1929.
(Christie's S.
Kensington) $90 £40

**'THESAURUS ARABICO SYRO
LATINUS'**
Later half vellum, rubbed, soiled – Rome,
1636.
(Christie's S.
Kensington) $245 £110

**THEVENIN, CHARLES – LACHIZE,
HENRI**
'Une Amazone sous le Premier Empire' –
etched frontispiece, vignette on title, 5
plates and 20 illustrations, parchment
backed boards, t.e.g., original wrappers
bound in, no. 577 of 675 – Garrington,
Paris, 1902.
(Sotheby's,
Chancery Lane) $20 £9

THEVENOT, JEAN DE
'Travels into the Levant' – in three parts,
1st Edn. in English, 3 engraved plates and
engraved illustration of 'Malabar Cyphers'
cont. mottled calf rubbed, joints split,
spine chipped, folio – 1687.
(Christie's, King
St.) $225 £100

THIELICHE, H.
'Ethics of Sex', 1964.
'Nymphomania' and other similar, d.w.s.
(Phillips) $7 £3

THIRTY YEARS' WAR
44 pamphlets in German in one volume, 6
folding engraved plates, woodcut or woodcut
arms on 12 titles, 17th century ms., vellum
boards, spine damaged – Regensburg,
Stralsund, Frankfurt and other places, 1626
-33.
(Sotheby's, New Bond
Street) $945 £420

THOMAS, A. H. AND THORNLEY, I. D.
(Editors)
'The Great Chronicle of London' – no. 58
of 500 copies, plates, original morocco by
Saehnsdorf, t.e.g. – 1938.
(Sotheby's,
Chancery Lane) $215 £95

THOMAS AQUINAS
'Summa, Prima Secundae' – 1st Edn., woodcut device at end printed in red, initials at
beginning in blue and red and first few
leaves rubricated, waterstained, some
worming and marginalia, cont. South
German blindstamped calf over wooden
boards, rebacked, rubbed, folio – Peter
Schoeffer, Mainz, 8 November, 1471.
(Sotheby's, New Bond
Street) $8,550 £3,800

THOMAS, DYLAN
'Deaths and Entrances' – 1st Edn., presen-
tation copy, inscribed by author, original
cloth, dust jacket – 1946.
(Sotheby's,
Chancery Lane) $155 £70
'Under Milk Wood' – 1st Edn., original
cloth, slightly soiled – 1954.
(Sotheby's,
Chancery Lane) $70 £32
'18 Poems' – 1st Edn., first issue, half
title and title slightly spotted, original cloth,
uncut – Sunday Referee and Parton Book-
shop, 1934.
(Sotheby's,
Chancery Lane) $157 £70
'Portrait of the Artist as a Young Dog' –
1st Edn., original cloth – 1940.
(Sotheby's,
Chancery Lane) $157 £70

'The Map of Love' – 1st Edn., first issue, one of 100 copies, original cloth, owner's signature – 1939.
(Sotheby's,
Chancery Lane) $78   £35

THOMAS, ISSAIAH
'The History of Printing in America . . . edited by Marcus A. McCorrison from the second edition' – portrait, original cloth, slipcase – Barre, Mass, 1970.
(Christie's S.
Kensington) $15   £7

THOMAS, R. S.
'Laboratories of the Spirit' – no. 109 of 215 copies, cont. morocco backed cloth by Sangorski and Sutcliffe, publisher's box – Gregynog, 1976.
(Christie's S.
Kensington) $145   £65

THOMAS, WILLIAM THOMAS 'W. T. Moncrieff'
'The Adventures of a Ventriloquist or the Rogueries of Nicholas, containing the following entertainment, so successfully performed by Mons. Alexandre at the Adelphi Theatre' – 2nd Edn., etched frontispiece coloured by hand, morocco backed boards – Duncombe, 1823.
(Sotheby's, New Bond
Street) $350   £155

THOMPSON, C.
'Travels in France, Italy, Turkey, etc.' – 3 vols., 8 folding maps with cont. hand colouring, 13 engraved plates, mainly folding, full cont. calf, spines gilt, 1st Edn. – Reading, 1744.
(Tessa Bennett,
Edinburgh) $190   £85

'The Adventures of a Ventriloquist, or the Rogueries of Nicholas', by W. T. Thomas. (Sotheby's, New Bond Street)

THOMPSON, EDWARD
'Sailor's Letters Written to his select
friends in England, during his Voyages and
Travels in Europe, Asia, Africa and America'
– 2 vols., 1st Edn., advert. leaf at beginning
of vol. 2, cont. calf, one cover defective –
1766.
(Sotheby's
London) $200   £90

THOMPSON, SIR HENRY
'Clinical Lectures in Diseases of the
Urinary Organs' – 1st Edn., illustrations,
2 leaves advertisements at end, original
cloth – John Churchill, 1868.
(Sotheby's, New Bond
Street) $135   £60

THOMPSON, W.
'The English Flower Garden' – 2 vols. in
one, 23 hand coloured plates, original
cloth, rubbed – 1854.
(Christie's S.
Kensington) $155   £70

THOMSON, HUGH – AUSTEN, JANE
'Pride and Prejudice' – one of 275 large
paper copies, mounted India paper frontis
and illustrations by Thomson, original
buckram, faded, corners bumped – 1894.
(Christie's S.
Kensington) $18   £8

THOMSON, HUGH – BARRIE, J. M.
'Quality Street' – mounted coloured
plates by Thomson, original cloth, foot
of spine slightly torn, dust jacket, torn –
n.d.
(Christie's S.
Kensington) $34   £15

THOMSON, HUGH AND SHAKESPEARE, WILLIAM
'The Merry Wives of Windsor' – no. 243 of
350 copies signed by the artist, mounted
coloured plates by Thomson, original
vellum, soiled, ties lacking, t.e.g. – 1910.
(Christie's S.
Kensington) $95   £42

THOMSON, JAMES
Fore-edge Painting – Poems, painting of
Congreve Street, Birmingham, under the
gilt, morocco gilt – circa 1870.
(Phillips) $125   £25
'Seasons' – wood engravings by T. Bewick,
modern boards, calf back – J. Wallis, 1805.
(Bonham's) $65   £28

THOMSON, J.
'Illustrations of China and Its People' –
4 volumes, a series of 200 photographs
with letterpress, original cloth gilt, folio
– Chiswick Press, 1873.
(Tessa Bennett,
Edinburgh) $2,925   £1,300
'History of Dundee' – edited by J.
McLaren, folding map, list of subscribers,
cloth gilt – Dundee, 1874.
(Tessa Bennett,
Edinburgh) $27   £12
'New General Atlas' – 34 hand coloured
double page folio maps, half leather,
maps badly folded and some dusty – 1814
- 1816.
(Tessa Bennett,
Edinburgh) $315   £140

'The Atlas of Scotland' – key map,
double maps of rivers and mountains, 58
fine double engraved maps, all coloured
by hand, cont. half russia, worn, folio –
Edinburgh, 1832.
(Sotheby's
Edinburgh) $785   £350

THORBURN, ARCHIBALD
'Game Birds and Wild Fowl of Great
Britain and Ireland' – 30 coloured plates
by author, original cloth, faded and rubbed,
spine slightly torn, t.e.g., folio – 1923.
(Christie's S.
Kensington) $675   £300

'British Birds' – 4 vols., 80 coloured plates by author, one torn, original cloth, faded and rubbed, t.e.g., 4to – 1915-16.
(Christie's S.
　Kensington)　　$560　　£250

THORNBURY, WALTER
'Old and New London' – 6 vols., frontispieces, illustrations, some leaves detached, cont. half morocco, rubbed – n.d.
(Christie's S.
　Kensington)　　$33　　£15

THORNHILL, R. B.
'The Shooting Directory' – 1st Edn., 6 hand coloured aquatints, 2 engraved plates, 3 folding tables, half calf, gilt, rubbed – 1804.
(Sotheby's, New Bond
　Street)　　$425　　£190

THORNTON, J.
'A New Family Herbal or Popular Account of the Natures and Properties of Various Plants' – woodcuts by T. Bewick, 1st Edn., with half title, half blue morocco gilt, m.e. – 1810.
(Bonham's)　　$145　　£65

'The Temple of Flora' by R. J. Thornton. (Bonham's)

THORNTON, ROBERT JOHN
'The Temple of Flora' or 'Garden of Nature Being Picturesque Botanical Plates of the New Illustration of the Sexual System of Linnaeus' – 5 engraved calligraphic titles, coloured frontispieces including mezzo tint of Linnaeus in Lapland dress and 28 superb plates of flowers, printed in colour and finished by hand, cont. full red morocco, worn, g.e., folios – 1799 – 1808.
(Bonham's)　　$29,250　　£13,000

THOROTON, ROBERT
'The Antiquities of Nottinghamshire' – 3 vols., 2nd Edn., engraved titles and 96 plates only, illustrations, some leaves slightly spotted, cont. half morocco, gilt spine, slightly rubbed – 1790-96.
(Sotheby's,
　Chancery Lane)　　$180　　£80

THROSBY, JOHN
'The History and Antiquities of the town and county of the town of Nottingham' – engraved portrait and plates, one folding, 2 folding tables, cont. russia, rebacked, worn – Nottingham, 1795.
(Sotheby's, New Bond
　Street)　　$180　　£80

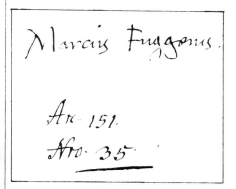

THUCYDIDES
'Thucydides cum Scholiis et Antiquis et Utilibus' – title in Greek and Latin, text in Greek, woodcut device on last page, bound in 16th century calf for Marcus Fugger, Marcus Fugger's signature inside front cover, folio – Hervagius, Basle, 1540.
(Sotheby Parke Bernet
　Monaco)　　$16,875　　£7,500

THULDEN, THEODOR VAN
'Les Travaux d'Ulisse' – 1st Edn., engraved
armorial title and 58 engraved plates, 1
folding, bookplate of William Gilpin, with
his signature 1752, old vellum boards,
rebacked, 19th century cloth pasted on
covers, folio – Paris, 1633.
(Sotheby's, New Bond
   Street)   **$360**   **£160**

THURLOE, JOHN
'A Collection of the State Papers . . . edited
by Thomas Birch' – 7 vols., 1st Edn., some
browning and soiling, lacking portrait, half
roan, worn, a few covers loose or detached,
shelf marks on spines, folio – 1742.
(Sotheby's
   London)   **$225**   **£100**

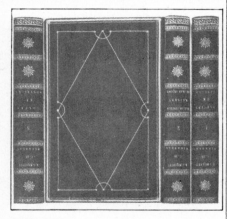

TIBULLUS, A.
'Elegies . . . avec les Notes et Recherches de
Mythologie . . . suivies des Baisers de Jean
Second' – 3 vols., Grand Papier Velin, por-
trait, 13 plates after Borel and Marillier,
avant la lettre, cont. green morocco, gilt,
g.e., silk liners by Bozerain, signed at foot
of spine – Tours & Paris, 1795.
(Sotheby Parke Bernet
   Monaco)   **$40,500** **£18,000**

TIELCKE, I. G.
'Beitrage zur Kriegs Kunst und
Geschichte des Krieges von 1756 bis 1763'
– 6 vols., folding plates, cont. half calf,
rebacked, worn – Freyburg, 1776-86.
(Christie's S.
   Kensington)   **$290**   **£130**

TILLOTSON, JOHN
'The New Waverley Album' – plates,
original cloth, gilt, inner hinges slightly
cracked, g.e. – n.d.
(Christie's S.
   Kensington)   **$45**   **£20**

TIMAR – GOETHE, JOHAN WOLFGANG VON
'Faust' – initials printed in red, etched
frontispiece and 41 illustrations by Timar,
11 full page, slightly worn, uncut –
Moulin de Pen Mur, Paris, 1943.
(Sotheby's,
   Chancery Lane)   **$31**   **£14**

TIMAR – MILLER, HENRY
'Tropique de Cancer' – 24 full page
coloured lithographs and illustrations in
text by Timar, unsewn in original wrappers,
uncut, folder, slipcase – Deux Rives, Paris,
1947.
(Sotheby's,
   Chancery Lane)   **$112**   **£50**

TIMBS, JOHN
'Curiosities of London' – engraved
additional title and plates, cont. half calf,
rubbed, spine faded – n.d.
(Christie's S.
   Kensington)   **$45**   **£20**

TIMMS AND WEBB
'Select Furniture in all Styles' – cloth,
folio – n.d.
(Tessa Bennett,
   Edinburgh)   **$11**   **£5**

TIMPERLEY, C. H.
'A Dictionary of Printers and Printing' –
plates, a few folding, slight browning, later
cloth, soiled, 4to, ex library copy – 1839.
(Christie's S.
   Kensington)   **$90**   **£40**

TIPPING, H. A.
'English Homes' – 9 vols., complefe set,
numerous illustrations, cloth, folio –
1920-37.
(Sotheby Parke Bernet
   Monaco)   **$11,250** **£5,000**

TISSOT, SAMUEL AUGUSTE ANDRE
'An Essay on Disease Incidental to
Literary and Sedentary Persons' – 1st Edn.
in English, cont. calf, spine gilt – Edward
and Charles Dilly, 1768.
(Sotheby's, New Bond
   Street)   **$200**   **£90**

TITMARSH, M. A.
'Our Street' — 1st Edn., 16 coloured plates, cont. half calf, rubbed, 8vo.
(Sotheby Humberts
Taunton) $45 £20
'Mrs. Perkins' Ball' — 22 hand coloured plates, one folding, some slightly spotted, cont. half calf, rather rubbed, 8vo — n.d.
(Sotheby Humberts
Taunton) $108 £48

TOLKIEN, J. R. R.
Autograph statement signed ('In all my works I take the part of the trees as against all their enemies'), on an oblong slip of paper.
(Sotheby's, New Bond
Street) $350 £155
'The Hobbit' — 1st Edn., 10 full page illustrations, map endpapers, cont. inscription on fly leaf, original cloth, somewhat soiled, 8vo — 1937.
(Sotheby's,
Chancery Lane) $395 £175
'The Lord of the Rings' — 3 vols., 1st Edn., folding maps, cuttings attached to lower endpapers of two vol., original cloth, spines slightly faded, 8vo — 1954-55.
(Sotheby's,
Chancery Lane) $560 £250

TOMASO DE GIESU, FR.
'Travagli di Giesu . . . Tradotti . . da Christoforo Ferrera e Samoayo et Hora di Nuouo dalla Castigliani dal P. Lodovico Flori' — woodcut device on title page, cont. limp vellum — Venice and Genoa, circa 1678.
(Sotheby's, New Bond
Street) $11 £5

TOMBLESON, W.
'Panoramic View of the Thames' — folding coloured panorama, original cloth — J. Reynolds — n.d.
(Phillips) $110 £50
TOMBLESON AND FEARNSIDE
'Views of the Rhine' — engraved title, folding panorama and 68 plates, half cont. morocco — London, 1832.
(Tessa Bennett,
Edinburgh) $650 £290
'Thames' — engraved vignette title and dedication, 79 plates, foxing, torn, original blindstamped leather, worn, inside hinge broken — n.d.
(Sotheby's, New Bond
Street) $540 £240
'Eighty Picturesque Views on the Thames and Medway' — engraved title and 80 plates, slightly soiled and spotted, cont. blindstamped calf, worn, spine loose.
(Sotheby's,
Chancery Lane) $405 £180

TOMLINSON, H. M.
'All Our Yesterdays' — no. 570 of 1,025 copies, portrait, original cloth — 1930.
(Sotheby Humberts
Taunton) $29 £13
'Thomas Hardy' — 1st Edn., no. 666 of 761 copies, signed by author, portrait, original cloth, uncut — New York, 1929.
(Sotheby's,
Chancery Lane) $40 £18

TOOKE, J. H.
'Diversions of Purley' — 2 vols., 2 plates with extra colour plate inserted, diced calf gilt, 4to — 1708-1805.
(Phillips) $55 £25

TORENT, EVELIO — MIRABEAU, OCTAVE
'Le Jardin des Supplices' — coloured frontispiece by Rodin, marbled brown morocco, slightly rubbed, inside borders gilt, uncut, original wrappers bound in, no. 107 of 150 copies — Charpentier et Fasquelle, Paris, 1899.
(Sotheby's,
Chancery Lane) $200 £90
'Le Journal d'Une Femme de Chambre' — brown marbled calf, inside borders gilt, uncut, hand titled wrappers bound in — Charpentier et Fasquelle, Paris, 1900.
(Sotheby's,
Chancery Lane) $112 £50

TORENT, EVELIO – LE SAGE, ALAIN RENE
'Le Diable Boiteux' – 9 coloured plates by Torent, black morocco, inside borders gilt, marbled endpapers, t.e.g., original wrappers bound in, slipcase, by Rene Kieffer, no. 12 of 500 copies – Glomeau, Paris, 1913.
(Sotheby's,
Chancery Lane) $100 £45

TORQUEMADA, JUAN DE
(Franciscan)
'Primera (Tercera) parte de los Veinte i un libros Rituales i Monarchia Indiana' – 3 vols., enlarged title by Irala in each vol., a hand coloured folding map of the Americas and the East Indies in vol. I, later 18th century Spanish tree sheep, rubbed, folio – Madrid, 1723.
(Sotheby's, New Bond
Street) $2,475 £1,100

TOSCANELLO, ORATIO
'Modo di Studiare le Pistole Famigliari di M. Tullio Cicerone' – woodcut device on title and at end, woodcut initials and ornaments, title slightly soiled, old limp vellum, lacking ties – Gabriel Giolito de Ferrari, Venice, 1568.
(Sotheby's, New Bond
Street) $75 £35

TOSI, P. A.
'Monumento Sepolcrale di Roma' – plates only, cloth backed boards worn – 1836.
(Phillips) $35 £15

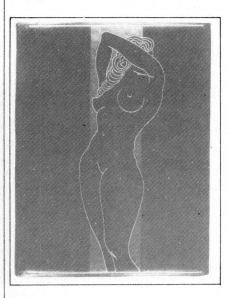

TOUCHAGUES – VERLAINE, PAUL
'Chansons pour Elle' – 36 coloured lithographed illustrations by Touchagues, 5 full page, slightly spotted, black morocco, t.e.g. original pictorial wrappers bound in, by T. Braillon – Editions du Belier, Paris, 1944.
(Sotheby's,
Chancery Lane) $810 £360

TOULOUSE LAUTREC – JOYANT, MAURICE
'Henri de Toulouse Lautrec 1864-1901' – 2 vols., colour frontis. to vol. 2, numerous plates, original pictorial cover, stitching broken, 4to – Paris, 1926-27.
(Christie's
St. James) $495 £220

TOURNEFORT, J. P. DE
'A Voyage into the Levant' – 3 vols., engraved, folding map, 152 plates of 153, one detached another torn, cont. calf, joints cracked – 1741.
(Christie's S.
Kensington) $200 £90

TOURTEL, MAY
'Rupert Little Bear Library' – no. 1-46,
illustrations, some crudely hand coloured,
original boards, soiled, one upper cover
detached, backstrips detached – n.d.
(Christie's S.
Kensington) $65   £28

TOUSBERG, C.
'Norske Folkelivsbilleder' – worn and
disbound, oblong folio – Christiania,
1854.
(Christie's S.
Kensington) $180   £80

TOWNSEND, JOSEPH
'The Physician's Vade Mecum being a
Compendium of Nosology and Thera-
peutics for the Use of Students' – 3rd
Edn., bound with blank leaves in matching
vellum slipcase – T. Cox and Dilly, 1795.
(Sotheby's, New Bond
Street) $45   £20

TOWNSON, ROBERT
'Travels in Hungary, with a short account
of Vienna in the Year 1793' – folding
engraved map, coloured in outline and
engraved plates, some folding, cont. calf,
rebacked – 1797.
(Sotheby Parke Bernet
Monaco) $3,150   £1,400

TOZER, H. F.
'Greece Pictorial, Descriptive and
Historical' – illustrations, cloth gilt – 1882.
(Phillips) $70   £32

TRACTS
A collection of 12 tracts, many relating to
Scotland, some to the 1745 rebellion,
together 12 works in one volume, some
with advert. leaves, holed, minor defects,
8vo, various places – 1695-1791.
(Sotheby's, New Bond
Street) $55   £25

TRACTS
A collection of 27 early 18th century
sermons relating to various subjects including charity schools, overseas missions,
thanksgivings for Marlborough's victories
etc., 27 works in one volume, some margins browned, cont. panelled calf, worn,
loose, 8vo – 1707-10.
(Sotheby's, New Bond
Street) $65   £30

'TRADES, BOOK OF, OR LIBRARY OF THE USEFUL ARTS'
3 volumes, parts 1 and 2, 3rd Edn., 66 of
67 engraved plates, one loose, spotted and
discoloured, original roan backed boards,
worn – Tabard and Co., 1806-7.
(Sotheby's, Hodgson's
Rooms) $245   £110

TRAITE ABREGE DES PIERRES FINES
Cont. calf, worn – N. F. Valleyre, 1769.
(Sotheby Parke Bernet
Monaco) $2,025   £900

TRAITE DES BATIMENTS PROPRES A LOGER LES ANIMAUX
50 engraved plates, 2 stains at beginning,
light foxing, cont. half calf, rubbed, folio
– Leipzig, 1802.
(Sotheby's, New Bond
Street) $495   £220

TRANSITION
Edited by Eugene Jolas and Elliot Paul,
9 issues, contributions by James Joyce,
Samuel Beckett, Gertrude Stein and
others, plates and illustrations, original
wrappers, worn – Paris and The Hague,
1927-35.
(Sotheby's,
Chancery Lane) $270   £120

TRASK, JOHN E. AND LAURVIK, J. NILSEN
Catalogue de Luxe of the Department of
Fine Arts Panama-Pacific International
Exposition – 2 vols., plates, original
vellum backed boards, slightly rubbed, 4to,
t.e.g. – San Francisco, 1915.
(Sotheby's,
Chancery Lane) $225   £100

TREDGOLD, THOMAS
'The Steam Engine . . . a New Edition . . .
Extended to the Science of Steam Naval
Architecture' – edited by W. S. B.
Woolhouse, 2 vols., 2 portraits, detached,
42 double page plates, 34 folding plates
and 47 plates, cont. half calf, worn.
Together with appendices A, B, C and D
contained in one volume – 1838 and
1840-2.
(Christie's S.
Kensington) $135   £60

TREMOIS — JOUNANDEAU, MARCEL
'Endymion' — 11 etched plates by
Tremois including cover design, unsewn in
original wrappers, uncut, cloth backed
folder, slipcase, folio, no. 18 of 65 copies,
with extra suite of etchings on japon nacre
— Bibliophiles de l'Union Francaise, Paris,
1953.
(Sotheby's,
    Chancery Lane)   **$1,395**   **£620**

TRENCH, F. W.
'A Collection of Papers relating to the
Thames Quay with Hints for Improvements
in the Metropolis' — 17 plates and plans,
some folding and some hand coloured in
outline — 1827.
(Christie's S.
    Kensington)   **$315**   **£140**

**TRENCHARD, JOHN AND GORDON,
THOMAS**
'Cato' Serious and Cleanly Meditations
upon a House of Office . . . to which is
added the Bog House, a poem in Imitation
of Milton' — title and last leaf slightly
soiled — 1723.
(Christie's S.
    Kensington)   **$78**   **£35**

TRICKS OF THE TOWN LAID OPEN
. . . or A Companion for Country
Gentlemen
Title cropped, one page of advertisements,
slight staining, modern half calf using
old boards — 1746.
(Christie's, King
    Street)   **$190**   **£85**

TRIGG, DR.
'Secrets Arcana's and Panacea's with his
most experienced Secrets' — pagination
jumps from p. 112 to 127 but apparently
complete, cont. sheep — R. D. for Dixy
Pafe, 1665.
(Sotheby's, New Bond
    Street)   **$945**   **£420**

TRIGGS, H. INIGO — TANNER, HENRY
'Some Architectural Works of Inigo Jones'
— plates, original cloth, rubbed — Batsford,
n.d.
(Christie's S.
    Kensington)   **$72**   **£32**

TRINDER, MARTIN
'The English Olive Tree or a Treatise on
the Use of Oil and the Air Bath' — 2nd
Edn., original grey wrappers, uncut — For
the author, 1802.
(Sotheby's, New Bond
    Street)   **$65**   **£30**

TRISTRAM, H. B.
'The Land of Israel; a Journal of Travels in
Palestine' — 1st Edn., 4 coloured lithos,
8 engraved views, 2 folded maps, one
coloured, one coloured in outline, half
title, signature of Sarah Tyrconnel on title,
original cloth, gilt — 1865.
(Sotheby's
    London)   **$200**   **£90**
'The Great Sahara' — 1st Edn., 11 engraved
plates, 2 folded maps, coloured in outline, 32 page publisher's catalogue at end,
signature of Sarah Tyrconnel on title,
original cloth, gilt — 1865.
(Sotheby's
    London)   **$94**   **£42**

TROLLOPE, ANTHONY
'Australia and New Zealand' — 2 vols., 2nd
Edn., 8 colour printed maps, 7 folded, oval
Guisachen bookplate, cont. polished calf
by Tout, triple gilt fillet, spine gilt, red and
green morocco labels — 1873.
(Sotheby's, New Bond
    Street)   **$245**   **£110**

TROTTER, WILLIAM EDWARD
'Views of the Environs of London' –
engraved title and 24 plates, slightly
spotted, original cloth, gilt, rubbed,
joints split.
(Sotheby's,
    Chancery Lane) $115   £52

TROY, THE SIEGE OF
Engraved frontispiece and one illustration,
browning, corners frayed, original wrappers, soiled and frayed – n.d.
(Christie's S.
    Kensington) $7   £3

TRUSLER, JOHN
'The Progress of Man and Society' – 1st
Edn., issue with vignette at foot of page
241, illustrations, slight staining, cont.
sheep, joints cracked – 1791.
(Christie's S.
    Kensington) $110   £48

TRYON, THOMAS
'The Way to Health, Long Life and Happiness' – 3rd Edn. to which is added a
discourse on the philosopher's stone,
pagination of pp. 305-312, cont. calf,
upper cover loose – Sold by Most Book-
sellers, 1697.
(Sotheby's, New Bond
    Street) $585   £260
'Some Memoirs of the Life of Thomas
Tryon late of London, merchant, written
by himself' – 1st Edn., folding portrait
of author by R. White with his horoscope
on verso, cont. panelled calf, spine rubbed
– T. Sowle, 1705.
(Sotheby's, New Bond
    Street) $250   £110

TUER, ANDREW W.
'Old London Street Cries' – coloured
frontispiece, illustrations, original boards,
rubbed – 1885.
(Christie's S.
    Kensington) $33   £15
'History of the Horn Book' – illustrations,
three facsimile horn books in wallet at
back, original cloth, soiled – 1897.
(Christie's S.
    Kensington) $215   £95

TUKE, SAMUEL
'Description of the Retreat, an Institution
near York for Insane Persons, of the
Society of Friends' – 1st Edn., engraved
frontispiece and two diagrams, title and
plates waterstained, original boards, upper
cover detached, spine chipped, 4to – York,
1813.
(Christie's
    St. James) $360   £160

TULL, JETHRO
'The Horse-Hoeing Husbandry: or, an
Essay on the Principles of Tillage and
Vegetation' – with the supplement,
very slightly spotted, later panelled calf,
folio – 1733-40.
(Sotheby's
    London) $585   £260

TULLY, RICHARD
'Narrative of a Ten Years' Residence at
Tripoli in Africa' – 2nd Edn., 7 coloured
aquatint plates, folding map, foxed, some
offsetting, calf, very worn, lacks one
cover, 4to – 1817.
(Sotheby's, New Bond
    Street) $90   £40

TURBERVILLE, A. (Editor)
'Johnson's England' – 2 vols., plates –
Oxford, 1933.
(Tessa Bennett,
    Edinburgh) $13   £6

TURNER, CAPTAIN SAMUEL
'Account of an Embassy to Teshoo Lama
in Tibet' – folding map, 13 plates, half
calf gilt, 4to – 1806.
(Phillips) $405   £180

TURNER, DANIEL
'The Art of Surgery' – 5th Edn. corrected,
2 vols., engraved portrait frontispiece, one
folding plate, cont. calf – C. Rivington and
J. Clarke, 1736.
(Sotheby's, New Bond
    Street) $155   £70
'De Morbis Cutaneis a treatise of disease
incident to the Skin' – 1st Edn., engraved
portrait by Vertue after I. Richardson,
advertisement leaf at end, spotted or
browned throughout, cont. calf gilt – R.
Bonwicke, 1714.
(Sotheby's, New Bond
    Street) $500   £220

SINGLE ADMISSION

Exhibition of the Royal Academy, 1839.

Admit to the Private View on Friday, May 3rd.

Miss Jones

No Ticket can be used unless the Name of the Bearer be inserted, and that of the Member from whom it has been received.

The Doors to be opened at Twelve o'Clock.

JMW Turner RA

TURNER, J. M. W.
Printed ticket, signed 'J. M. W. Turner RA', admitting Miss Jones to the private view of the exhibition of the Royal Academy, to be held on 3 May 1839, printed in blue ink on card, with ms. insertions, oblong octavo.
(Sotheby's, New Bond
   Street)   **$180**   **£80**

'The Seine and the Loire' – Introduction by M. Huish, 61 steel engraved plates, quarter morocco, new edition, small folio – 1895.
(Tessa Bennett,
   Edinburgh)   **$58**   **£26**
'The Rivers of France' – engraved title and 60 plates, some spotting, original cloth, spine soiled and torn – n.d.
(Christie's S.
   Kensington)   **$90**   **£40**
'Picturesque Views of the Southern Coasts of England' – half calf, spines gilt, marbled boards, with 80 tinted plates and vignettes as called for, 2 vols. – 1826.
(Lawrence of
   Crewkerne)   **$630**   **£280**
TURNER, J. M. W. AND WATTS, ALARIC A.
'Liber Fluviorum' – engraved title and 60 plates, some slightly spotted, cont. morocco gilt, slightly rubbed, g.e. – 1853.
(Sotheby's,
   Chancery Lane)   **$140**   **£62**

TURNER, LAURENCE
'Decorative Plaster in Great Britain' – frontispiece, illustrations, original cloth, slightly soiled – 1927.
(Christie's S.
   Kensington)   **$85**   **£38**

TURNER, SHARON
'History of England from the Norman Conquest to the Reigns of Edward Sixth, Mary and Elizabeth' – 5 vols., 1st Edn., spotting, cont. calf, rubbed – 1814-29.
(Sotheby's, New Bond
   Street)   **$65**   **£30**

TWO CITIES, LA REVUE BILINGUELLE DE PARIS
Edited by Jean Fanchette, nos. 1-9 in 8 parts, text in English and French, contributions by Lawrence Durrell, Henry Miller, Rilke and others, illustrations, coloured wrappers – Paris, 1959-64.
(Sotheby's,
   Chancery Lane)   **$80**   **£35**

TYRRELL, JAMES
'The General History of England' – 3 vols. in five, 1st Edn., engraved frontispiece, some browning and soiling, cont. calf, worn – 1697-1704.
(Sotheby's, New Bond
   Street)   **$65**   **£30**

UDALL, WILLIAM
'The Historie of the Life and Death of
Mary Stuart' — some leaves slightly soiled,
cont. calf, rebacked, rubbed — Printed by
John Haviland, sold by William Sheares,
1636.
(Christie's S.
   Kensington)   **$50**   **£22**

ULLOA, ANTONIO DE
'A Voyage to South America . . . translated from the Original Spanish' — 2 vols.,
3rd Edn., 7 folding plates, including map,
cont. mottled calf, some wear — 1772.
(Sotheby's, New Bond
   Street)   **$245**   **£110**

UNAMUNO, MIGUEL DE
Autograph letter signed, 3 pages, octavo,
on headed letter paper to Rector of
University of Salamanca, March 1906, to
F. A. Gelmormini.
(Sotheby's, New Bond
   Street)   **$200**   **£90**

'THE UNIVERSAL FAMILY BIBLE'
Engraved title, hand coloured plates, cont.
morocco, upper joint split, extremeties
rubbed — n.d.
(Christie's S.
   Kensington)   **$65**   **£30**

UNIVERSAL HISTORY, AN
'from the earliest account of time' — 21
vols., 2nd Edn., 69 plates, 39 maps,
slight worming, cont. calf, gilt spines,
slightly rubbed, 8vo — 1747-54.
(Sotheby's, New Bond
   Street)   **$157**   **£70**

**UNIVERSAL MAGAZINE OF KNOW-
LEDGE AND PLEASURE . . . ARTS
AND SCIENCES, THE**
vols. 1, 2, 4, 7-15, 17-19, 15 vols. altogether, engraved titles, frontis, plates
and maps, cont. calf backed marbled
boards, joints split, spines worn, 8vo —
1747-56.
(Sotheby's, New Bond
   Street)   **$900**   **£400**

UPCOTT, WILLIAM
Unusually affectionate autograph letter
signed, 1 page, octavo, London Institution,
17 May 1832, to Miss Sophie Smith,
discussing collecting, autograph address
leaf, seal.
(Sotheby's, New Bond
   Street)   **$90**   **£40**
Autograph letter signed, 3 pages, octavo,
London Institution, 15 October 1819, to
George Russell, expressing his approbation
of Mr. Raffles and discussing collecting.
(Sotheby's, New Bond
   Street)   **$90**   **£40**

URE, D.
'History of Rutherglen and East Kilbride'
— 20 engraved plates including folding
map, subscribers' list — Glasgow, 1793.
(Tessa Bennett,
   Edinburgh)   **$135**   **£60**

URSINUS, ZACHARIAS
'Summe of Christian Religion' — translated by H. Parre, calf worn, 8vo — Oxford,
1587.
(Phillips)   **$80**   **£35**

USSHER, JOHN
'A Journey from London to Persepolis'
— coloured plates, cloth gilt — 1865.
(Phillips)   **$80**   **£35**

UVAROV, S. S. COUNT
'Essay on the Mysteries of Eleusis' —
folding frontispiece, original boards,
uncut, slightly worn, with 3 others, 8vo —
1817.
(Sotheby's, New Bond
   Street)   **$56**   **£25**

UZANNE, O.
'Son Altesse la Femme' — no. 100 of 100
copies on Papier du Japon, plates by
Rops and others, red morocco gilt, inner
gilt borders inlaid in cream and blue, silk
liners, by David, joints rather worn —
Paris, 1885.
(Sotheby Parke Bernet
   Monaco)   **$1,685**   **£750**

VAENIUS, OTTO
'Historia Septem Infantium de Lara' —
40 engraved plates, titles and captions
to plates in Spanish and Latin, cont.
vellum boards, soiled — Antwerp, 1612.
(Sotheby's, New Bond
    Street) $450   £200

VALENTIA, GEORGE VISCOUNT
'Voyages and Travels in India, Ceylon,
the Red Sea, Abyssinia and Egypt' — 3
volumes, 69 engraved plates, maps, 3
vignettes, some leaves slightly soiled,
original boards, worn, 4to — 1809.
(Sotheby Humberts
    Taunton) $270   £120

VALENTINE, J. (Photographer)
'Photographic Groups of Eminent
Personages' — cloth gilt — circa 1875.
(Tessa Bennett,
    Edinburgh) $18   £8

VALENTINO, RUDOLPH
T. L's. carbon copy, one page, New York,
n.d. to Editor of the Chicago Tribune,
angrily replying to a personal attack on
Valentino. In Valentino's hand, top edge
roughly trimmed affecting text.
(Sotheby's, New Bond
    Street) $270   £120

VALENTINUS, MICHAEL BERNHARD
'Polychresta Exotica in Curandis Affecti-
bus Contumacissimis Probatissima . . . et
nova Herniarum Cura' — engraved plates,
2 folding, light browning, modern parchment boards — Frankfurt, 1700.
(Sotheby Parke Bernet
    Monaco) $4,050   £1,800

**VALERIANO BOLZANI, GIOVANNI
PIERIO**
'Les Hieroglyphiques' — engraved archi-
tectural and historiated title, numerous
woodcut illustrations, foxing, gilt
episcopal arms, gilt spine, folio — P.
Frellon, Lyon, 1615.
(Christie's, King
    St.) $335   £150

VALERY, PAUL
'Odes' — limited to 150 copies, wood
engravings by Paul Vera, original wrappers,
half morocco case, folio — Paris, 1920.
(Sotheby Parke Bernet
    Monaco) $3,600   £1,600

**'VALUABLE SECRETS IN ARTS,
TRADES'**
Staining, original calf, slightly rubbed —
New York, Evert Dycknick, 1809.
(Christie's S.
    Kensington) $65   £28

VANCOUVER, GEORGE
'Voyages de Decouvertes a l'Ocean
Pacifique du Nord autour du Monde' —
1st French Edn., 3 vols., engraved chart
and 17 engraved folding plates, foxing,
with atlas containing 10 double page
maps and 6 plates of coastal profiles,
occasional spotting and dampstaining,
three 4to volumes in original paper
wrappers, uncut as issued, boxed individ-
ually, folio atlas bound in modern boards
— Imprimerie de la Republique, Paris,
1800.
(Sotheby Humberts
    Taunton) $2,025   £900
'A Voyage of Discovery to the North Pacific
Ocean and Round the World' — 3 vols., 1st
Edn., lacks atlas, 18 engraved plates,
charts, cont. mottled calf, gilt fillets
and borders, gilt crest on covers, vol. 3
rebacked — 1798.
(Sotheby's, New Bond
    Street) $1,575   £700
'Voyage of Discovery to the North Pacific
Ocean and Round the World' — 3 vols.,
text and atlas vol., 1st Edn., spotted and
offset, marginal tears, original boards,
original paper labels, rebacked, atlas spine
missing, all uncut, 4to and folio — 1798.
(Sotheby's, New Bond
    Street) $3,600   £1,600

George Vancouver's 'Voyage of Discovery to the North Pacific'. (Sotheby's, New Bond Street)

VAN DONGEN, KEES – MONTHERLANT, HENRI DE
'Les Lepreuses' – 25 coloured lithographed illustrations by Van Dongen, including cover design, unsewn in original wrappers, uncut, folder and slipcase – Paris, 1947. (Sotheby's,
Chancery Lane) $180   £80

VAN DYCK, SIR ANTHONY
'Le Cabinet des Plus Beaux Portraits' – title in red and black, engraved device, 100 portraits by Pontius, Hollar and others, 19th century calf, gilt, g.e., worn, upper cover detached, folio – Antwerp, circa 1655.
(Sotheby's, New Bond
Street) $1,690   £750

VAN EVRIE, JOHN H.
'Negroes and Negro 'Slavery': The first an Inferior Race: The latter its Normal Condition' – frontis, title stained, some spotting, original cloth, spine torn with some loss – New York, 1861.
(Christie's S.
Kensington) $70   £32

Montherlant's 'Les Lepreuses', illustrated by Kees Van Dongen. (Sotheby's, Chancery Lane)

VAN GOGH, VINCENT

Early autograph contribution to an album of about 5,000 words on 6 pages written but not dated during residence in England in 1876 when he was 23 – excerpts from Bible and some hymns.
(Sotheby's, New Bond
Street) $1,235   £550

Printed invitation to the funeral of Van Gogh on 30 July, 1890, the day after his death, sent by his mother and brother Theodore, one page, quarto, blank edged paper, mss. alterations, repaired.
(Sotheby's, New Bond
Street) $1,000   £450

VAN OEST, G. (Publisher)

'Le Temple d'Angkor Vat' – 3 parts in 7 volumes, numerous photographic plates on thick paper, some folding plates, folio – Les Editions G. Van Oest, Paris, 1929.
(Sotheby's, New Bond
Street) $1,170   £520

VAN REUSSELAER, MRS. JOHN KING

'The Devil's Picture Books' – inscribed by author, related A.L.s pasted down at back plates, some coloured, original cloth, spine torn, inner hinges weak, t.e.g. – New York, 1890.
(Christie's S.
Kensington) $65   £30

VANITY FAIR

Spy cartoons, collection of approximately 130 coloured prints – circa 1889 to 1890.
(Tessa Bennett,
Edinburgh) $255   £114

VANITY FAIR ALBUM, THE

Vols. 1-7, vol. one, 3rd Edn., coloured portraits, original cloth – n.d.
(Christie's S.
Kensington) $630   £280

VARCHI, BENEDETTO L'HERCOLANO

Venice, F. Giunta e fratelli, 1580 – 'Apologia de gli Academici di Bianchi di Roma contra M. Lodovico Castelvetro da Modena in forma d'uno spaccio di Maestro Pas1uino . . .', with the final errata/device leaf, light waterstaining in lower margins – Parma, Seth Viotto, 1558.
(Sotheby's, New Bond
Street) $180   £80

VARGAS PONCE, JOSEF

'Descripciones de las Islas Pithiusas y Baleares' – 3 folding tables, lacks portrait, a few marginal worm holes, bookplate, 19th century red morocco, gilt floral border and large Spanish Royal arms (Ferdinand VII) on sides, 8vo – Madrid, 1787.
(Sotheby's, New Bond
Street) $337   £150

VARRO, MARCUS TERENTIUS

'Pars Librorum Quattuor et Viginti de Lingua Latina' with 'Libri de re Rustica' – 2 works in one volume, cont. Lyonnaise calf, rebacked, in morocco bound folding cloth box – Paris, 1543 and 1563.
(Sotheby's, New Bond
Street) $450   £200

VARTHEMA OF BOLOGNA, LUDOVICO DI

'The Itinerary' – no. 416 of 975 copies, maps, Prospectus loosely inserted, original vellum backed cloth, gilt – 1928.
(Sotheby's,
Chancery Lane) $50   £22

VAUGHAN, ROBERT

Fine 17th century autograph ms. containing biographical and heraldic notices of Owen Gwynedd and other Welsh worthies, 52pp. , bound with 18th century ms. notes and a 17th century A.L., half roan, 4to.
(Sotheby's, New Bond
Street) $1,912   £850

Autograph letter by the Welsh antiquary Robert Vaughan. (Sotheby's, New Bond Street)

Autograph drafts of 5 letters, 4 signed, to Mr. Vaughan of Trosgood and others, concerning The Book of Llandaff and other mss., 5 pages, small 4to – 1654-58. (Sotheby's, New Bond
Street) $1,125   £500

VAUGHAN WILLIAMS, RALPH
Autograph letter signed, 3 pages, oblong octavo, White Gates, Dorking, 12 November, to Mr. Pearl discussing the possibility of assisting a foreign musician named Keller, and suggesting that if his committee were unable to help, the Parliamentary committee for refugees might be able to do so.
(Sotheby's,
Chancery Lane) $67   £30

VAUX, BARON C. M. DE
'Les Grands Fusils de France' – no. 171 of 500 copies, 1st Edn., 50 coloured lithograph plates of birds, cont. blue morocco gilt, rubbed, original wrappers bound in, large 4to – Paris, 1898.
(Sotheby's, New Bond
Street) $855   £380

VECELLIO, CESARE
'Habiti Antichi et Moderni di Tutto il Mondo' – ornamental woodcut title, 506 full page woodcuts of costumes, woodcut device on verso of last leaf, foxing, cont. vellum – Venice, 1598.
(Christie's, King
St.) $945   £420

VEGA, CARPIO, LOPE DE
'Arcadia' – woodcut architectural title border, shaved, woodcut portrait, ornament and initial, waterstaining, 17th century calf, rubbed, joints worn – Madrid, 1611.
(Christie's, King
St.) $585   £260

VEGETIUS RENATUS, FLAVIUS
'De Re Militaris' Liber II, III and IV
only of V, illuminated mss. on vellum,
70 leaves, 19th century brown morocco
gilt by Pagnant — School of Tours,
last quarter of 14th century.
(Christie's, King
    St.) $51,750   £23,000

VELA, B. A. DE ORSUA Y
'Historia de la Villa Imperial de Potosi'
— 3 vols., Hanke (1) 'Bartolome Arzans
de Orsua y Vela's History of Potosi,'
facsimiles, buckram gilt, large 4to. —
Rhode Island, 1865.
(Phillips) $65   £30

VELLEIUS PATERCULUS, GAIUS
'Historiae Romanae, Libri due,
accurante S. A. Phillippe' — large
paper copy, engraved frontispiece by
Fessard, cont. French citron morocco,
g.e. — J. Barbou, Paris, 1754.
(Sotheby's, New Bond
    Street) $145   £65

**VELLY, L'ABBE, VILLARET, M. AND
GARNIER, M.**
'Histoire de France' — 30 vols., vols. 1-8
new edition, cont. mottled calf, spines
chipped — Paris, 1761-60-86.
(Christie's S.
    Kensington) $170   £75

VELSER, MARCUS
'Chronica Der Weitberuempten . . . statt
Augsburg: 3 parts; Antiqua Monumenta;
Das Ist Alte Bilder, Gemahlde unnd
Schrifften . . . zu Augspurg' — together 4
parts in one volume. 1st German Edn.,
translated by Englebert Werlich, woodcut
device on both titles, over 200 woodcuts
in text, 23 large. Slightly brown and
dampstained, bookplate and stamp of
Harvard College Library, cont. half calf,
worn, folio — Frankfurt, 1595.
(Sotheby's, New Bond
    Street) $540   £240
'Rerum Biocarum Libri Quinque' — 1st
Edn., title with large engraving, slightly
damaged, woodcut device at end, cont.
limp vellum, slightly worn and soiled —
Augsburg, 1602.
(Sotheby's, New Bond
    Street) $75   £35

VENICE
20 engraved views after Vincenze Chilone,
cont. half calf, inner hinge cracked —
Venice, 1800.
(Christie's S.
    Kensington) $200   £90

VENICE
Engraved views on three sheets, hand
coloured, 15½ x 41in., laid down, slightly
torn — n.d.
(Christie's S.
    Kensington) $200   £90

VENICE, COLLEGIUM AROMATARII
Certificate of proficiency in the art of
blending aromata and permission to practice pharmaceutical arts to Franciscus Faber,
aged 20, signed by the syndics of the guild.
Illuminated ms. on vellum, cont. Venetian
red morocco, richly gilt tooled in four
panels, floral paste down endpapers, 2
paper flyleaves — Venice, 16 June, 1694.
(Christie's, King
    St.) $1,800   £800

VENIERO, FRANCESCO
'I Discorsi . . . sopra i tre libri dell'anima
d'Aristotele' — device on title, woodcut
initials, a little marginal worming, some
foxing and slight soiling, old limp vellum
— Venice, A. Arrivabene, 1555.
(Sotheby's
    London) $225   £100

Letter by Giuseppe Verdi on his publisher's notepaper. (Sotheby's, New Bond Street)

VENN, THOMAS, TACQUET, ANDREW AND OTHERS
'Military and Maritine (sic) Discipline in Three Books' — Book 1, Military Observations; Book 2, An Exact Method of Military Architecture; Book 3, The Compleat Gunner. Separate title to each part, 2 engraved frontispieces and 11 folding plates, woodcut and engraved diagrams, cont. calf, gilt spine — 1672.
(Christie's, King
   St.) $630   £280

VERDI, GIUSEPPE
Autograph letter signed, 1 page, small quarto, no date or place, to unnamed correspondent, announcing his departure to Enghien.
(Sotheby's, New Bond
   Street) $560   £250
Autograph letter signed, 2 pages, octavo, St. Agata, November 1891 to Salvatore Marchese de Castrone in Vienna, with envelope.
(Sotheby's, New Bond
   Street) $900   £400
Autograph letter signed, 2 pages, octavo, St. Agata, October 1891, announcing he is writing 'Falstaff'.
(Sotheby's, New Bond
   Street) $1,125   £500

Copy of letter to Milan music publisher Francesco Lucca, 1 page, quarto, Milan on Lucca's headed notepaper, 14 October, 1845, suggesting Lucca arrange a contract with Benjamin Lumley for him to write an opera in London instead of Italy in 1846, subscribed with note in French, light marginal foxing — 1845.
(Sotheby's, New Bond
   Street) $315   £140

VERGA, GIOVANNI
2 autograph letters signed, 4 pages, quarto and octavo, Catania, November 1882 and May 1916 to unnamed correspondents, one praising a book sent to him.
(Sotheby's, New Bond
   Street) $90   £40

VERLAINE, PAUL
'Fetes Galantes' — numerous illustrations in colour by A. Ribaudi, original stained vellum in slipcase — Paris, 1903.
(Sotheby Parke Bernet
   Monaco) $7,875   £3,500
'Hombres' — 1st Edn., original wrappers, backstrip split, uncut — Paris, 1904.
(Sotheby's,
   Chancery Lane) $24   £11

VERLAINE

'Oeuvres Libres' — 12 coloured plates and decorations in text, unsewn in original wrappers, uncut, unopened, slipcase — Brussels, 1948.
(Sotheby's,
    Chancery Lane) $135   £60
'Parallelement' — illustrations by E. Chimot, one of 25 copies on Japon ancien with the plates in four states and an original drawing by the artist inserted, wrappers, in a broken half leather slipcase — Paris, 1931.
(Sotheby Parke Bernet
    Monaco) $6,300   £2,800
'Romances Sans Paroles' — 1st Edn., 300 copies printed, a number of ms. corrections, dark blue morocco by Gruel, original wrappers preserved, presentation copy inscribed to M. Leon Vanier by author — Sens, 1874.
(Sotheby Parke Bernet
    Monaco) $14,625   £6,500

VERNE, JULES

Autograph letter signed, 1 page, octavo, headed notepaper of the Societe Industrielle d'Amiens, Amiens, Sept. 1897 to unnamed correspondent, slightly browned.
(Sotheby's, New Bond
    Street) $450   £200

Autograph letter signed, 1 page, Amiens, April 1899, to Robert, integral blank.
(Sotheby's, New Bond
    Street) $360   £160

'Cinq Semaines en Ballon et Voyage au Centre de la Terre' — wood engraved illustrations after Riou and Montaut, , original cloth, slightly stained, g.e., large 8vo — Paris, Hetzel, 1876.
(Sotheby's,
    Chancery Lane) $90   £40
'De La Terre a la Lune, suivi de Autour de la Lune' — wood engraved illustrations after Montaut, Bayard and de Neuville, misbound, without the first six leaves of the second work, original cloth, slightly worn, g.e., large 8vo — Paris, Hetzel, 1877.
(Sotheby's,
    Chancery Lane) $56   £25
'Vingt Mille Lieues sous les Mers' — wood engraved illustrations after de Neuville and Riou, original cloth, g.e., large 8vo — Paris, Hetzel, 1880.
(Sotheby's,
    Chancery Lane) $90   £40

'Voyage au Centre de la Terre' by Jules Verne. (Sotheby's, Chancery Lane)

*'De la Terre a la Lune' by Jules Verne.
(Sotheby's, Chancery Lane)*

*'Vingt Mille Lieues sous les Mers' by Jules
Verne. (Sotheby's, Chancery Lane)*

VERNET, HORACE
Autograph letter signed, 1 page, octavo,
Paris, August 1857, to Madame Champein,
with autograph envelope, stamped and
postmarked and a carte de visite photograph.
(Sotheby's, New Bond
    Street) $65   £30

VERNET, HORACE – LAURENT, P. M.
'Histoire de Napoleon 1er' – wood engraved
illustrations after Vernet and Hippolyte
Bellange, brown calf gilt, slightly rubbed,
inside borders gilt, marbled endpapers, t.e.g.,
by Asper – Plon, Paris, 1870.
(Sotheby's,
    Chancery Lane) $27   £12

VERNON, JOHN
'The Compleat Compting-House: or, the
Young Lad taken from the Writing-School,
and fully instructed, by way of Dialogue, in
all the Mysteries of a Merchant' – 5th Edn.,
browned, cont. panelled calf, rubbed, upper
cover detached – 1722.
(Sotheby's
    London) $125   £55

VERSE PAMPHLETS
19 works in one volume, includes works by
Pope, Thomas Rogers, George Bubb
Doddington, Sir Charles Hanbury Williams
and others, edges of some early pamphlets
uncut, cont. sprinkled calf, folio – 1733-
46.
(Christie's, King
    St.) $4,950   £2,200

**VERTES, MARCEL – COLETTE,
SIDONIE GABRIELLE**
'La Vagabonde' – 15 coloured lithographed
plates by Vertes, loose, original wrappers,
uncut, folder and slipcase, presentation
copy – Paris, 1927.
(Sotheby's,
    Chancery Lane) $290   £130

VERTOT, ABBOT RENE AUBERT DE
'The History of the Revolutions in Spain
. . . Made English . . . By Mr. Morgan' –
2 vols. in 4, cont. mottled calf, slightly
rubbed – 1724.
(Christie's S.
    Kensington) $33   £15

VERTOT

'The History of the Knights of Malta' –
2 vols., 1st Edn., engraved portraits, folding
maps, slight browning and marginal soiling,
holed, cont. calf, worn, rebacked and
repaired, folio – 1728.
(Sotheby's, New Bond
    Street) $495   £220
'Histoire des revolutions de Portugal' –
folding map and 2 plates, 1,712 bound
with

LACOMBE, J.

'Histoire des revolutions de l'empire de
Russie' – 1760, wormed top right hand
margin, not affecting text, half calf.
(Phillips) $100   £45

VERVE

Vol. VIII 29 and 30 (Suite de 180 Dessins
de Picasso) Paris, 1954.
Vol. VI, 21 and 22 (Matisse) 1948; vol. IV,
13 (Matisse) 1945. Plates, boards, worn,
folio.
(Sotheby Parke Bernet
    Monaco) $2,475   £1,100

VERWER, PIETER ADRIAEN

'Historie van het Verlatene en Gelukkige
Weesiut, Charlotte Summers' – 2 vols.,
2nd Edn., engraved plates, soiled, a few
pages torn with loss, soiling, cont. calf,
extremities rubbed, inner hinges split –
Amsterdam, 1751.
(Christie's S.
    Kensington) $45   £20

VEVER, HENRI

'La Bijouterie Francaise' – 3 vols., plates,
illustrations, unopened, original wrappers,
soiled – Paris, 1906-08.
(Christie's S.
    Kensington) $270   £120

VIAL, CHARLES DE SAINBEL

'Elements of the Veterinary Art, containing an essay on the Celebrated Eclipse' –
2 parts in one vol., bookplate of Arthur
Hugh Smith Berry at Marbury Hall, cont.
half calf, slightly rubbed – 1797.
(Sotheby's
    London) $155   £70

VIALART, CHARLES, BISHOP OF AVRANCHES

'Geographia Sacra' – half title, 10 double
plage engraved folding maps with cartouches, mounted on guards, half vellum
paper, cracking, folio – Amsterdam, 1703.
(Sotheby's, New Bond
    Street) $765   £340

VIARDOT, PAULINE

Autograph letter signed, 1 page, octavo,
no place 'jeudi 20', to unidentified
correspondent.
(Sotheby's, New Bond
    Street) $180   £80

VICARY, THOMAS

'The English Man's Treasury with the
True Anatomie of Man's Body' – black
letter, full page woodcut of a skeleton,
original limp vellum – Bar. Alsop and
Tho. Fawcet, 1633.
(Sotheby's, New Bond
    Street) $765   £340

VICO, AENEAS

'Augustarum Imagines' – engraved title,
plates – Venice, 1558.
(Phillips) $180   £80

'VICTORIAN COUNTY HISTORIES, HAMPSHIRE AND THE ISLE OF WIGHT'

6 vols. including index, plates and maps,
some folding, some coloured, original
cloth, slightly rubbed – 1900-14.
(Sotheby's,
    Chancery Lane) $155   £70

VICTORIA, QUEEN

'Leaves from the Journal of Our Life in
the Highlands' – 2 coloured plates,
illustrations, original pictorial cloth, corners rubbed, g.e., with dedication to Lady
Waterfarle from Victoria R., Christmas
Eve, 1869 – 1868.
(Christie's S.
    Kensington) $90   £40

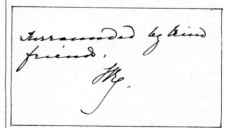

Autograph letter signed, 3 pages, octavo,
on black-edged letter paper head 'Osborne',
1 August 1869, to an unnamed person,
offering warm condolences on the death of
his or her son.
(Sotheby's, New Bond
    Street) $180   £80

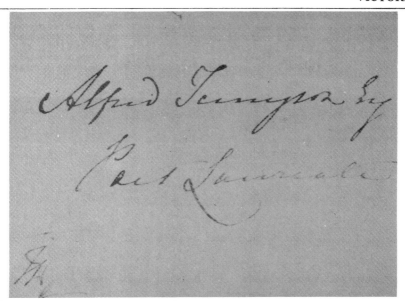

Autograph letter from Queen Victoria to Tennyson. (Sotheby's, New Bond Street)

Remarkable long A.L., signed 'V.R.I.' to Alfred Tennyson, lamenting the death of her 'truest and most devoted' John Brown, 9pp., 8vo, Osborne, 14th August 1883, on black-edged paper, with autograph envelope. (Sotheby's, New Bond Street) $3,600   £1,600

Her first A.L. to Alfred Tennyson thanking him for the dedicatory epilogue to 'Idylls of the King' – 4pp., 8vo, Windsor Castle, 26th February, 1873, on black-edged paper, signed, with autograph envelope. (Sotheby's, New Bond Street) $1,170   £520

Fine photograph of the Queen in old age, signed and inscribed in Italian 'Victoria RI Firenze – Aprile 1893', depicting her dressed in black with a white veil and seated, reading, at a desk which bears a portrait of Prince Albert (by W. & D. Downey), note on reverse by D. E. Colnaghi, to whom it was sent from the Queen by Sir H. Ponsonby, unevenly trimmed for framing, 11 x 7in. (Sotheby's, New Bond Street) $630   £280

Queen Victoria at Firenze, 1893. (Sotheby's, New Bond Street)

VICTORIUS, PETRUS
'Vararium Lectionum Libri XXV' – 1st
Edn., large woodcut of the Medici arms
on title, woodcut initials, many historiated,
some damp and water staining, title
soiled, old limp vellum, folio – Florence,
1553.
(Sotheby's, New Bond
    Street) $110   £50

VIDA, MARCUS HIERONYMUS
'Dialogi de rei publicae dignitate' – italic
letter, title within woodcut border, errata
leaf, cont. sheep, worn, signature of
Andrew Fletcher of Saltoun on title
– Cremona, Vicenzo Conti, 1556.
(Sotheby's
    London) $135   £60

VIDAL, E. E.
'Picturesque Illustrations of Buenos Ayres
and Monte Video' – 1st Edn., 24 coloured
aquatint plates, 4 folding, text watermarked 1818, original red cloth, spine gilt,
foot chipped, g.e. – R. Ackermann, 1820.
(Sotheby's, New Bond
    Street) $6,300   £2,800

VIDAL, PIERRE – LOUYS, PIERRE
'Les Aventures du Roi Pausole' – new
edition, 82 illustrations by Vidal, t.e.g.,
original wrappers bound in, slipcase by
Rene Kieffer – Blaizot, Paris, 1906.
(Sotheby's,
    Chancery Lane) $945   £420

'Picturesque Illustrations of Buenos Ayres' by E. E. Vidal. (Sotheby's, New Bond Street)

VIERGE, DANIEL – BERGERAT,
EMILE
'L'Espagnole' – wood engraved half title,
frontispiece and 19 illustrations by
Bellenger after Vierge, red morocco, g.e.,
original pictorial wrappers bound in –
Paris, 1891.
(Sotheby's,
    Chancery Lane) $75   £35

VIERGE, DANIEL – QUEVENDO,
FRANCISCO DE
'Pablo de Segovia el Gran Tacano, traduit
par J. H. Rosny' – definitive edition,
portrait frontispiece after Velasquez,
3 plates and numerous editions by Vierge,
black half morocco, slightly rubbed,
original wrappers, bound in, no. 133 of 455
copies – Paris, 1902.
(Sotheby's,
    Chancery Lane) $35   £15

VIEUSSENS, RAYMOND DE
'Novum Vasorum Corporis Humani
Systema' – title in black and red, additional
engraved title showing anatomy lesson,
original blue-grey boards, slightly faded
and stained, uncut – Amsterdam, 1705.
(Sotheby's, New Bond
    Street) $945   £420

VIEUX PARIS, LE
'Album Pittoresque' – lithographed title,
list of plates and 24 coloured plates, some
slightly soiled, loose as issued in original
cloth backed board portfolio, worn, lacks
some ties – Paris, n.d.
(Sotheby's,
    Chancery Lane) $225   £100

'VIEWS IN LONDON'
45 mounted india paper plates engraved by
Charles Heath after Dewint, Westall and
MacKenzie, occasional spotting, cont.
half morocco, slightly rubbed – n.d.
(Christie's S.
    Kensington) $125   £55

VIEXMONTIUS, CLAUDIUS
'Christliche Vermahnung zu Wahrer,
Ernster Buss und Besserung des Lebens' –
1st Edn. in German, edited and translated
by Caspar Franck, old boards – D.
Sartorius, Ingolstadt, 1583.
(Sotheby's, New Bond
    Street) $75   £35

VIGNAU, LE SIEUR DE
'L'Etat Present de La Puissance Ottomane'
– cont. calf, rebacked – 1687.
(Christie's S.
    Kensington) $75   £55

VIGNOLA, GIACOMO BAROZZIO DA
'Regola delli cinque ordini d'architettura
. . . con la nuova aggionta di Michel-
Angelo Buonaroti' – engraved portrait
frontis and 42 engraved plates in text,
woodcut vignette on title, text in Italian,
Dutch, French and German, partly in
black letter, a few small spots and stains
slightly affecting text and plates, two
tiny burns in text, two or three pages very
slightly soiled, cont. limp vellum, slightly
stained, folio – Amsterdam, Johan and
.Cornelius Blaeu, 1640.
(Sotheby's
    London) $360   £160

VIGNY, ALFRED DE
'Eloa ou la Soeur des Anges' – 1st Edn.,
red morocco, gilt, g.e., original wrappers
preserved, by G. Mercier, 1912 – Paris,
1824.
(Sotheby Parke Bernet
    Monaco) $8,100   £3,600

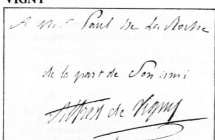

'Les Consultations du Docteur-Noir.
Stello' – 1st Edn., cont. red morocco gilt,
binding by Duplanil, signed on front cover,
presentation inscription from author to
M. Paul de la Roche – Paris, 1832.
(Sotheby Parke Bernet
Monaco) $54,000   £24,000

VILAIN XIIII – PHILIPPE, JEAN
JACQUES, VICOMTE
'Memoire sur les Moyens de Corriger les
Malfaiteurs et Faineans' – 1st Edn., 4
folding engraved plates, waterstained,
modern calf backed boards, entirely uncut
– Ghent, 1775.
(Christie's, King
St.) $360   £160

VILLARS, M. DE
'The Count of Gabalis' – calf, worn –
1680.
(Sotheby's, New Bond
Street) $155   £70

VILLEFOSSE, H. DE
'Eloge des Pierreries' – no. 25 of an
edition of 30 on 'pur chiffon du marais'
with original lithograph by Andre Derain
as frontispiece, wrappers unopened,
board slipcase – Cartier, Paris, 1947.
(Sotheby Parke Bernet
Monaco) $1,575   £700

VINCENT, NATHANIEL
'The Morning-Exercise against Popery' –
7 copies, various calf bindings.
(Sotheby's, New Bond
Street) $110   £50

VINCENT, WILLIAM
'The Voyage of the Neachus' – frontispiece,
maps, charts, cont. half calf, part of spine
lacking, worn – 1797.
(Christie's S.
Kensington) $33   £15

VINCENZO, MARIA DI S. CATERINA
DA SIENA
'Il Viaggio all Indie Orientali' – 1st Edn.,
engraved frontis, cont. vellum rubbed, in
buckram box, folio – F. Mancini, Rome,
1672.
(Sotheby's, New Bond
Street) $270   £120

VIOLET-LE-DUC, E. E.
'Dictionnaire Raisonne de l'Architecture
Francais' – illus., 10 vols., half morocco,
worn – Paris, 1868-73.
(Bonham's) $110   £50

VIRGILIUS MARO, PUBLIUS
'The Bucolicks ... with an English Trans-
lation ... by John Martyn' – engraved
portrait, hand coloured plate and two
maps, cont. calf, rubbed, joints and spine
cracked – 1749.
(Chrsitie's S.
Kensington) $110   £50
'Opera' – some staining, cont. vellum,
soiled, last leaf holed, inner hinges
cracked, folio – Basle, ex officiana
Sebastiani Henric Peni, 1613.
(Christie's S.
Kensington) $45   £20

'Opera' – 5 vols. in two, engraved throughout, titles with engraved vignettes,
numerous engraved illustrations in text,
some full page, 19th century red morocco,
gilt, g.e. – The Hague, 1757-65.
(Sotheby's, New Bond
Street) $1,125   £500

VIRTUE'S
... 'Picturesque Views of Great Britain –
Kent' – frontispiece, map and 130
engravings, 2 vols., old calf, worn – 1749.
(Bonham's) $90   £40

VISSCHER, NICOLAUS
Theatrum Biblicum
5 parts in one volume, 462 plates, half
calf, worn, covers detached – Amsterdam,
1674.
(Christie's S.
Kensington) $785   £350

VISSCHER, N. J.
'Historiae Sacrae Veteris Quam Novi
Testamenti' – 2 parts in one, 144 plates,
half calf, oblong – circa 1700.
(Phillips) $180   £80

VITAL, CHAIM ETZ CHAIM
A classic work of Kabbalah − 5th Edn.,
modern blue cloth, folio − Shabtae Ben
Zion and Menachem Segal, Shklov, 1800.
(Sotheby's, New Bond
   Street) $360   £160

VITRUVIUS, P.
'Architecture ou Art de Bien Bastir . . .
mis de Latin en Francoys par Jan Martin' −
2nd French Edn., 152 fine woodcuts, late
16th century, olive morocco, arms of
Charles de Valois 1573-1650, gilt on sides
and his cypher in corners and compartments
of spine, folio − Paris, 1572.
(Sotheby Parke Bernet
   Monaco) $72,000   £32,000
'L'Architetettura di Marco Vitruvio
Pollione Tradotta e Comentata dal
Marchesa Berardo Galiani' − 2nd Edn.,
engraved frontispiece and 25 engraved
plates after Galiani, 11 woodcuts in text
by Lucchesini, slightly browned, 19th
century half red morocco, folio − Fratelli
Terres, Naples, 1790.
(Sotheby's, New Bond
   Street) $135   £60

Tranfferatur mens ad Architætarentini & Eratofthenis cyrenei cogitata,
Hi enim multa & grata a mathematicis rebus hominibus inuenerunt, Itaqi
cum in cæteris inuentionibus fuerint grati, in eius rei concertationibus ma
xime funt fufpecti. Alius enim alia ratione explicare curauit, quod delo im
perauerat refponfis apollo, uti aræ eius quantum haberet pedum quadra/
torum, id duplicaretur, & ita fore, ut hi qui effent in ea infula tunc religio/
ne liberarentur, Itaqi architas cylindrorum defcriptionibus, eratofthenes
organica melolabi ratione idem explicauerunt.

'De Architectura' − 2nd, first dated Edn.,
80 leaves of 86, 43 lines and headline,
roman letter, a few woodcut diagrams,
light stains − Christophorus de Pensis,
Venice, 1495-96.
(Sotheby's, New Bond
   Street) $5,400   £2,400

VLAMINCK, MAURICE DE
Autograph letter signed, 1 page, quarto
March 1932 to M. Delamain, integral
blank.
(Sotheby's, New Bond
   Street) $180   £80

VLIET, J. VAN
'Les Arts et Les Metiers' − 18 etched plates,
printed on tinted paper, cut close, mounted,
tree calf album, worn, folio.
(Sotheby Parke Bernet
   Monaco) $11,250   £5,000

VOGEL, JOHANN
'Die Moderne Bau Kunst' − 2nd Edn., title
in red and black, engraved frontis, 59 plates
on 50 sheets, cont. half calf, folio −
Hamburg, 1726.
(Sotheby's, New Bond
   Street) $785   £350

**VOGT, CARL AND SPECHT
FRIEDRICH**
'The Natural History of Animals, (Class
Mammalia. . .)' − 2 vols., subscriber's
edn., plates, illustrations, original cloth,
head and foot of spines slightly torn − n.d.
(Christie's S.
   Kensington) $27   £12

VOIGHT, HANS HENNING 'ALASTAIR'
'Fifty Drawings' − limited to 1,025 copies,
plates, original cloth backed boards, t.e.g.
− New York, 1925.
(Christie's S.
   Kensington) $180   £80
'Prevost d'Exiles (A.F.) Manon Lescaut'
− no. 23 of 1,850 copies, plates by
'Alastair', a little spotting, original cloth,
dust jacket − 1928.
(Christie's S.
   Kensington) $125   £55
'Wilde (Oscar) The Sphinx' − limited to
1,000 copies, plates by 'Alastair', original
buckram, gilt, slightly soiled, t.e.g. − 1920.
(Christie's S.
   Kensington) $315   £140

VOLTURE, V. DE
'Letters of Affaires, Love and Courtship' −
translated by J. Davies, portrait, some
spotting, calf rebacked − 1657.
(Phillips) $215   £95

VOLNEY

VOLNEY, C. F.
'Travels Through Syria and Egypt . . .
1783-85' – 2 vols., 2nd Edn. in English, 3
folding engraved plates, 2 folding engraved
maps, slight browning, cont. tree calf,
worn, upper covers detached – 1788.
(Sotheby's, New Bond
Street) $65 £30
'L'Alfabet Europeen Applique Aux
Langues Asiatiques' – folding tables, half
title, cont. calf backed boards, worn –
Paris, 1819.
(Sotheby's, New Bond
Street) $100 £45

VOLT, ALESSANDRO
Document signed being a prospectus for
the University of Pavia for academic year
1817-18, printed on both sides with mss.
insertions, oblong folio.
(Sotheby's, New Bond
Street) $450 £200

VOLTA, GIOVANNI SERAFINO
'Ittiolitologia Veronese del Museo
Bozziano' – 1st Edn., 76 engraved plates
of fish fossils, 20 folding including map,
lacks title and text, plates complete,
damp stained, cont. wrappers, uncut,
folio – Verona, 1796.
(Sotheby's, New Bond
Street) $900 £400

VOLTAIRE, F. M. A. DE
'Candide ou L'Optimisme' – 1st Paris Edn.,
a few leaves spotted, cont. calf backed
boards, label, spine slightly torn, upper
hinge weak – Lambert, Paris, 1759.
(Sotheby's, New Bond
Street) $180 £80
'Oeuvres Completes' – 70 vols., a fine set
of Kehl Voltaire, 108 engraved plates by
Baquoy and others after Moreau, avant la
lettre, cont. red morocco, gilt, g.e., silk
liners by Bradel, with his ticket, with the
Franchetti book label – Kehl, 1785-89.
(Sotheby Parke Bernet
Monaco) $393,750 £175,000
'Romans et Contes' – 3 vols., 57 plates
by Baquoy and others after Marillier,
Moreau and others, a fine set in cont.
French red morocco, gilt, g.e., the Duc de
la Valliere, Beckford, Laurence Currie copy
– Bouillon, 1778.
(Sotheby Parke Bernet
Monaco) $99,000 £44,000

Voltaire's 'Romans et Contes'. (Sotheby
Parke Bernet, Monaco)

Autograph letter signed 'V', 2 pages,
quarto, no place, 20 September 1762, to
his friend Francois de Chennevieres.
(Sotheby's, New Bond
Street) $900 £400

'Elemens de la Philosophie de Neuton' —
1st Edn., frontispiece, portrait, 7 engraved
plates, calf, spine very worn, Bengesco
1570; Babson 120, 8vo — Amsterdam,
1738.
(Sotheby's, New Bond
    Street) $168   £75
'Candide, ou l'Optimisme, traduit de
l'Allemand'. De Mr. le Docteur Ralph, 299
pages, ornament on title, short tear in D4
(Wade 1; Moritz 59; Besterman F), 1759;
'Candide . . . Seconde Partie', 132 pages,
ornament on title, 1761, 2 vols. in one,
slight spotting and staining, cont. calf
backed boards, very worn, 12mo — 1759-
61.
(Sotheby's, New Bond
    Street) $270   £120

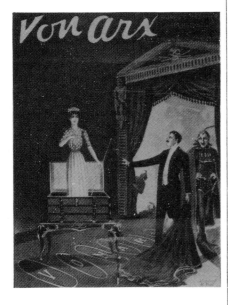

VON ARX
'World's Premier Illusionist and All
American Company, conjuror with two red
devils, female assistant in patriotic dress
standing in trunk on table' — coloured
lithograph, a few splits, tears and holes —
28 x 21in. — St. Paul, Standard (Show
Printers, circa 1910).
(Sotheby's,
    Chancery Lane) $135   £60

VOSMAR, A.
'Description d'un Nouvelle . . . Porc a
large groin, ou Sanglier Afrique' — 18
hand coloured plates, morocco gilt —
Amsterdam, 1767.
(Phillips) $405   £180

VOSSIUS, ISAAC DE LUCIS
'Natura et proprietate' — 1st Edn., woodcut device on title, woodcut diagrams in
the text, cont. calf, rubbed, Willems 1296,
small 4to — Amsterdam, L. & D. Elzevir,
1662.
(Sotheby's, New Bond
    Street) $270   £120

VUILLARD, EDOUARD
Autograph letter signed, 1 page octavo on
letter card, postmarked Paris, May 1912,
to Madame Godebska, address on verso,
stamped and postmarked.
(Sotheby's, New Bond
    Street) $245   £110

VUILLEMIN, A.
'La France et Ses Colonies. Atlas Illustre' —
111 hand coloured engraved maps, cont.
morocco backed boards, gilt, folio —
Paris, 1883.
(Sotheby's, New Bond
    Street) $585   £260

**VUILLIER, GASTON — MERIMEE,
PROSPER**
'Colomba' — 13 plates and 16 illustrations
by Bouchery after Vuillier, blue half
morocco, original wrappers bound in,
t.e.g., no 270 of 1,200 copies — Librairie
des Amateurs, Paris, 1913.
(Sotheby's,
    Chancery Lane) $22   £10

VULLIANY, LEWIS
'Examples of Ornamental Architecture' —
2nd Edn., engraved title and 40 plates,
spotting, cont. half morocco, rubbed,
folio — n.d.
(Christie's S.
    Kensington) $95   £42

WAAGEN, GUSTAV FRIEDRICH
'Treasures of Art in Great Britain' — 4
vols., cont. calf, gilt spines, 8vo — 1854-57.
(Christie's
   St. James) $315   £140

WAAL, R. B. DE
'World Bibliography of Sherlock Holmes
and Dr. Watson' — illustrations, 4to — 1974.
(Phillips) $50   £22

WADD, WILLIAM
'Mems, maxims and memoirs' — 1st Edn., a
few plates, advertisement leaf at end,
original boards, spine repaired, new label,
uncut — Callow and Wilson, 1827.
(Sotheby's, New Bond
   Street) $50   £22

WADDESDON MANOR
The James de Rothschild Collection. Ellis
Waterhouse Paintings 1967/Svend Eriksen;
Sevres Porcelain, 1968, 2 vols. together,
numerous plates, cloth, in dust jackets, 4to.
(Christie's
   St. James) $495   £220

WADE, ALLAN
'A Bibliography of the Writings of W. B.
Yeats' — 2nd Edn., revised, illustrations,
original cloth, dust jacket — 1958.
(Sotheby's,
   Chancery Lane) $125   £55

WADE-GERY, H. T.
'Terpsichore and Other Poems' — 2nd Edn.,
limited to 370 copies, original cloth backed
boards, rubbed, lower hinges cracked —
Golden Cockerel Press, 1922.
(Christie's S.
   Kensington) $22   £10

WADSWORTH, JAMES
The copies of certaine letters which have
passed betweene Spaine and England in
matter of Religion' — 1st Edn., errata leaf
at end, cont. sheep, spine defective at
foot — 1624.
(Sotheby's
   London) $11   £5

WAGNER, RICHARD
'Wieland der Schmeidt' — printed in
brown and black, calf gilt, large pictorial
design on upper cover, t.e.g. — Ernst
Ludwig Presoe, Leipzig, 1911.
(Sotheby's,
   Chancery Lane) $33   £15
Autograph letter signed, 1 page, octavo,
Munich, February 1865 to Gottfried
Semper, architect, integral blank.
(Sotehby's, New Bond
   Street) $720   £320
Good autograph letter signed, 3 pages,
octavo, Paris, October 1860 railing against
truncated version of Tannhauser in
Germany.
(Sotheby's, New Bond
   Street) $1,350   £600
Good autograph letter signed, 1 page,
octavo, no place, April 1871, to his
publisher E. W. Fritsch.
(Sotheby's, New Bond
   Street) $675   £300
'The Rheingold and the Valkyrie' — large
pictorial parchment gilt, t.e.g., 34 tissued
and mounted plates by Arthur Rackham,
no. 627 of 1,150 copies, signed by artist —
1910.
(Lawrence of
   Crewkerne) $55   £24

WAIN, LOUIS
'Annual for 1913' — parchment backed
boards, coloured plate and many illustra-
tions — 1913.
(Tessa Bennett,
   Edinburgh) $22   £10
'Cat's Cradle' — illus., cloth backed boards
— Blackie, n.d.
'Daddy Cat' — illus., cloth backed boards
— Blackie, n.d.
(Phillips) $85   £38

WALFORD, EDWARD
'Old and New London' — 6 vols. in 3,
plates, illustrations, cont. half calf, one
cover detached, rubbed.
(Sotheby's,
   Chancery Lane) $50   £22

Legal manuscript concerning a lawsuit in Wales in 1599. (Sotheby's, New Bond Street)

WALES
Ms. concerning an action for the Manor
of Sully in Glamorgan, heard before
Justices John Croke and Thomas
Estcourt at Cardiff on 9th July 1599,
vellum, 15 x 22in., trace of seal.
(Sotheby's, New Bond
    Street) $450   £200

WALES
Fine autograph account by Richard
Robert Jones ('Dick of Aberdaron'), 4
pages, 4to, with a portrait, detailing his
fruitless attempts between 1835 and 1837
to secure publication of his dictionary
of Welsh, Greek and Hebrew. Self-educated,
he was proficient in Greek, Latin, Hebrew,
French, Italian and Spanish and had some
knowledge of Syriac and Chaldaic. His
English, however, was never good.
(Sotheby's, New Bond
    Street) $495   £220

WALEY, ARTHUR
A.L. signed, 2 pages, 8vo, British Museum,
24th December, no year, to Clive Bell,
praising his verse.
(Sotheby's, New Bond
    Street) $168   £75

WALKER, A.
'Gatherings from Graveyards particularly
those of London with a Concise History
of the modes of interments among
Different nations' — engraved and printed
titles, errata slip, original cloth, uncut —
Longman, etc., 1839.
(Sotheby's, New Bond
    Street) $90   £40

Autobiographical manuscript by Sir Edward Walker, 1676. (Sotheby's, New Bond Street)

WALKER, SIR EDWARD
Long autobiographical ms. in defence of
his character and his execution of the
office of Garter King of Arms, 88pp.
sewn in marble wrappers, folio — 15th
November, 1676.
(Sotheby's, New Bond
    Street) $1,080   £480

WALKER, GEORGE
'The Costume of Yorkshire Illustrated by
a Series of 40 Engravings' — folio, morocco
backed boards, spine gilt, coloured frontispiece and 40 coloured plates after Walker
by Ernst Kaufmann, title and text in
English and French, dampstained, no. 220
of 600 copies — Leeds, 1885.
(Lawrence of
    Crewkerne) $380   £170

WALKER, J.
'Universal Atlas' — 26 double page part
coloured, half calf, 8vo — 1814.
(Phillips) $50   £22

WALKER, JOHN
'Elements of Elocution, Being the Sub-
stance of a Course of Lectures on the
Art of Reading, delivered at several
Colleges in the University of Oxford' —
2 vols., 1st Edn., half titles, cont. tree
calf, gilt — 1781.
(Sotheby's, New Bond
    Street) $200   £90

'WALLACE'
The Magician, The World's Greatest
Illusionist — stock poster with birds, bats
and female spirits flying between a cracked
globe held by a red devil and conjuror's
hands, coloured lithograph, torn at upper
corners, with a slight loss of printed surface,
30 x 20in. — Birmingham, Moody Bros.,
circa 1920.
(Sotheby's,
    Chancery Lane) $90   £40

WALLHAUSEN, JOHANN JACONI VON
'Romanische Kriegskunst' – 2 vols. in one, engraved historiated title and 21 double page plates, cont. vellum, ties missing, folio – Frankfurt, 1616.
(Christie's, King
St.) $405   £180

WALL MAP
AMERICA
BLAEU, W. J.
'Nova Americae sive Novi Orbis Tabula' – large engraved map, inset maps of Arctic and Antarctic regions, borders surrounded by printed descriptive text in Latin, French and Dutch, some repairs, stained, mounted on linen in light wooden frame, approx. 47 x 66in. – N. Visscher, Amsterdam, after 1657.
(Sotheby's, New Bond
Street) $16,875   £7,500

WALPOLE, HORACE
'Correspondence' – Edited by W. S. Lewis, 'Yale Edition', original cloth, dust jacket, 33 vols. – 1937-65.
(Sotheby's, New Bond
Street) $495   £220

'The Castle of Otranto' – Jeffrey's Edn., 7 printed coloured plates with gold borders, slight browning, cont. red straight grained morocco, label, spine gilt, slightly rubbed – 1796.
(Sotheby's, New Bond
Street) $380   £170

WALPOLE, HUGH
'The Apple Trees' – no. 93 of 500 copies signed by author, illustrations by Lynton Lamb, original morocco backed boards – Golden Cockerel Press, 1932.
(Christie's S.
Kensington) $85   £38
'Works' – 7 vols., all limited editions, signed by the author, 3 vols., unopened, original cloth backed boards, extremities rubbed – 1921-35.
(Christie's S.
Kensington) $33   £15

WALPOLE, ROBERT
'Memoirs Relating to European and Asiatic Turkey; Travels in Various Countries of the East, being a Continuation of the Memoirs' – 2 vols., 1st Edns., 27 engraved plates, plans and maps, some browning, cont. calf, spines gilt, covers detached – 1845.
(Sotheby's, New Bond
Street) $360   £160

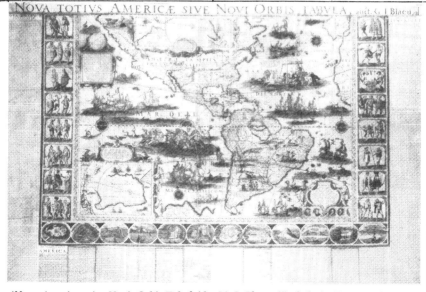

'Nova Americae sive Novis Orbis Tabula' by W. J. Blaeu. (Sotheby's, New Bond Street)

WALSH, J. H.
'The Economical Housekeeper' – lacks
frontis, quarter morocco, worn – 1857.
(Phillips) $100   £45

WALSH, ROBERT
'Constantinople' – 2 vols. in one, engraved
plates, morocco gilt, 4to – n.d.
(Phillips) $125   £55

WALSH, T.
'Journal of the Late Campaign in Egypt'
– numerous folding and other maps and
plates, some coloured, half calf, 1st Edn.
– 1803.
(Bonham's) $200   £90

WALSINGHAM, FRANCIS, S. J.
'A Search Made Into Matters of Religion' –
1st Edn., title soiled, stains, worm holes,
18th century calf, some wear, small 4to –
English College Press, St. Omer, 1609.
(Sotheby's, New Bond
    Street) $180   £80

WALTERS, H.
'Incunabula Typographica Catalogue of
Books, Printed in the Fifteenth Century' –
illustrated, calf gilt – 1906.
(Phillips) $65   £28

WALTON, IZAAK
'The Life of Mr. Rich Hooker' – 1st Edn.,
imprimatur and errata leaves, a little
worming in lower margins, slight soiling,
repair to I7, cont. sheep, spine worn –
1665.
(Sotheby's
    London) $90   £40
'Love and Truth' – 1st Edn., modern calf,
outer and lower edges uncut – 1680.
(Christie's, King
    St.) $495   £220
WALTON, IZAAK AND COTTON, C.
'The Compleat Angler' – copper and wood
engravings, half morocco – 1823.
(Tessa Bennett,
    Edinburgh) $15   £7

WALWYN, WILLIAM
'Physick for Families . . . in all distempers'
– 1st Edn., cont. sheep, fine copy – J.
Winter for Robert Horn in Gresham
College Court, 1669.
(Sotheby's, New Bond
    Street) $810   £360

**WANDA'S, THE 'MYSTERIOUS
HAND'**
Heads of performers on large coins,
coloured lithograph, short tears and
creasing at centre fold – 47 x 31½in.
– Paris, Affiches Louis Galice, circa 1912.
(Sotheby's,
    Chancery Lane) $135   £60

WANLEY, NATHANIEL
'The Wonders of the Little World or a
General History of Man in Six Books' –
1st Edn., cont. calf gilt, spine gilt, hinges
repaired, folio – T. Basset and others, 1678.
(Sotheby's, New Bond
    Street) $200   £90

WARBURTON, ELIOT
'The Crescent and the Cross; or Romance
and Realities of Eastern Travel' – 2 vols.,
3rd Edn., cont. polished calf, labels, spines
gilt, rubbed – 1845.
(Sotheby's, New Bond
    Street) $100   £45

WARD, EDWARD 'NED'
'The London Spy' Nov. 1698–April 1700 –
complete set of 18 issues, some staining
and foxing throughout, some offensive
words heavily crossed out in ink, later
boards, small folio – Printed and sold by
J. How, 1699-1700.
(Christie's, King
    St.) $1,080   £480

WARD, REV. JOHN
'Diary extending from 1648 to 1679' –
half calf, with an account of Shakespeare's
last illness and death – H. Colburn, 1839.
(Sotheby's, New Bond
Street) $40   £18

WARE, SIR JAMES
'De Scriptoribus Hiberniae' – 1st Edn.,
minor flaws, calf, worn – Dublin, 1639.
(Sotheby's, New Bond
Street) $135   £60

WARNER, P. F.
'The Cricketer' – 13 cols. various, illustra-
tions, cont. cloth, some worn, 4to – 1923-
37.
(Christie's S.
Kensington) $145   £65

WARNER, RICHARD
'Antiquitates Culinariae, or Curious tracts
Relating to the Culinary Affairs of the Old
English' – engraved title and 2 coloured
plates, including double page Peacock
Feast, half morocco, slightly rubbed and
worn, 4to – 1791.
(Sotheby Humberts
Taunton) $430   £190
'A Walk through some of the Western
Counties of England' – 1st Edn., title with
woodcut vignette, sepia aquatint frontis,
woodcut road maps in text, half title,
advertisement leaf at end, slight browning,
half calf, joints split, rubbed – Bath, 1800.
(Sotheby's
London) $100   £45

WARNER, REV. RICHARD
'The History of Bath' – engraved plates,
one mounted, slightly spotted and soiled,
cont. half calf, rebacked, slightly rubbed
– 1801.
(Sotheby's,
Chancery Lane) $110   £48

WARNERY, C. E. VON
'Remarks on Cavalry . . . translated from
the original by G. F. Koehler' – 1st English
Edn., 31 engraved plates, modern brown
half morocco, spine gilt, from library of
the Royal Institution, 4to – 1798.
(Sotheby's, New Bond
Street) $110   £50

WARREN, J. G. H.
'A Century of Locomotive Building by
Robert Stephenson and Co.' – illustrated,
cloth, morocco backed – 1923.
(Bonham's) $55   £25

WARWICK, EDEN
'Nasology or Hints Towards the Classifi-
cation of Noses' – woodcuts, half
morocco, t.e.g. – Richard Bentley, 1848.
(Sotheby's, New Bond
Street) $55   £25

WARWICKSHIRE
Hand coloured showing the Hundreds with
key, compass rose and vignette of Warwick
Castle, approx. 25½ x 31½in. – Greenwood
and Co., Feb. 1830.
(Lawrence of
Crewkerne) $40   £18

**WASHINGTON, WILSON G. AND
VALENTINE, J.**
A series of photographs of Scottish
scenery and a few others, continental
views, oblong, binding very poor – circa
1890.
(Tessa Bennett,
Edinburgh) $11   £5

WATERING PLACES OF GREAT BRITAIN
Vignette title, 33 engraved views on india
paper, some foxing, cloth – 1831.
(Phillips) $200   £90

WATERLOO
6 tinted lithographed plates by Vanderheet,
original boards, disbound, spine lacking,
folio – Brussels, n.d.
(Christie's S.
Kensington) $55   £25

WATERTON, CHARLES
'Wanderings in South America' – portrait,
frontis., half morocco gilt, t.e.g. – 1825.
(Phillips) $225   £100

WATSON, P. W.
'Dendrologia Britannica' – vol. 2 only,
hand coloured plates, boards – 1825.
(Phillips) $245   £110

WAUGH, EVELYN
'Black Mischief' — one of 250 copies signed by author, plates, original cloth, spine and edge of upper cover faded, t.e.g., others uncut, 8vo — 1932.
(Christie's
St. James) $135   £60
'Vile Bodies' — 1st Edn., pictorial title, original cloth, soiled, worn — 1930.
(Sotheby's,
Chancery Lane) $170   £75

A.L. signed, 1 page, 8vo, Piers Court, Stinchcombe, Glos., 23rd October 1954, to Mrs. F. J. Stopp, thanking her for the gift of her translation of Albertus Magnus' 'De Adhaerendo Deo', woodcut heading, autograph envelope.
(Sotheby's, New Bond
Street) $168   £75

Succinct autograph letter signed, 1 page, octavo, Royal Crescent Hotel, Brighton, 25 June no year, to Nicholas Bentley, the illustrator — 'Alas, impossible . . .'
(Sotheby's, New Bond
Street) $56   £25

WEAVER, JOHN
'An Essay Towards the History of Dancing' — 1st Edn., title within double line border, woodcut headpiece, small stains, cont. panelled calf, rebacked — For Jacon Tonson, 1712.
(Sotheby's, New Bond
Street) $630   £280

WEAVER, LAURENCE
'Houses and Gardens by Lutyens' — plates, cloth backed boards, t.e.g., folio, two copies — 1914.
(Christie's
St. James) $215   £95

WEBER, CARL MARIA
Letter signed in English, 1 page, octavo, Great Portland St., London, March, 1826, to F. Kennith, saying he cannot sit for his portrait.
(Sotheby's, New Bond
Street) $495   £220
Letter signed in English, 1 page, octavo, Great Portland St., London, May, 1826, to Mr. Moralt, integral address leaf.
(Sotheby's, New Bond
Street) $830   £370
Autograph letter signed, 1 page, octavo, no place or date, to Friedrich Kind, librettist, integral address leaf, trace of seal, with note of authentication.
(Sotheby's, New Bond
Street) $1,350   £600

WEBSTER, D.
'Original Scottish Rhymes with Humourous and Satirical Songs' — Paisley, 1835.
(Tessa Bennett,
Edinburgh) $18   £8

WEBSTER, JOHN
'The Displaying of Supposed Witchcraft' — Imprimatur leaf before title, title ruled in red, title slightly discoloured, cont. calf, rebacked, folio — J. M. 1677.
(Sotheby's, New Bond
Street) $540   £240

WEHNERT, ALFRED
'Tales for Children' by Hans Christian
Andersen – 47 plates by E. H. Wehnert,
57 illustrations in text by W. Thomas and
others, staining, splitting, original cloth
gilt, slightly worn, g.e. – Bell and Duddy,
1861.
(Sotheby's,
    Chancery Lane) $95   £42

WEIGEL, CHRISTOPHE
'Historiae Celebriores Veteris Novi Testamenti Iconibus Representatae' – 2 parts
in one volume, engraved titles, 239
copper plates, slightly soiled, cont. calf,
worn, folio – Endter, Nuremberg, 1712.
(Sotheby's, New Bond
    Street) $425   £190

WEISSENBACH, JOHANN CASPAR
'Damons desz Unseelingen Hirten Einfal-
tige Cither, mit Teutschen Seiten Gespan-
net; Dasz ist Wunderlichen Weltgedanckken
Erster' – 1st Edn., incomplete, 2 works in
one volume, slightly spotted and dampstained, cont. vellum slightly soiled –
Johann Hubschlein, Feldkirch, 1678.
(Sotheby's, New Bond
    Street) $45   £20

WEISSER, PROF. LUDWIG
'Bilder Atlas sur Weltgeschichte' – illus.,
half calf, gilt, folio – Stuttgart, 1885.
(Phillips) $100   £45

WELFORD, RICHARD (Editor)
'History of Newcastle and Gateshead' –
3 volumes, original cloth, gilt – 1884-87.
(Sotheby's,
    Chancery Lane) $75   £35

WELLESLEY, DOROTHY
'Selected Poems' – 1st Edn., presentation
copy inscribed by author to Elizabeth
Kyle, original cloth, dust jacket – 1949.
(Sotheby's,
    Chancery Lane) $13   £6

WELLINGTON, A., 1st DUKE OF
A.Ls. to Earl (Later Marquis) of West
Meath, Spanish govt. does not allow British
officers to serve with their troops . . . 1811;
unable to help Col. Roberts, I have comm-
anded armies now for 14 years 1814;
Commission on vellum signed Arthur
Wellesley appointing West Meath Col. of
Militia (1808); and other pieces include
letter from West Meath asking the Duke
not to call.
(Phillips) $245   £110
Important group of A.Ls. (one unsigned)
to West Meath, 16pp., 1838-46, on state of
crime in Ireland, House of Lords procedure,
Poor Law amendment, lack of accurate
information about Ireland.
(Phillips) $400   £180
Series of 7 A.Ls. to the Earl of West Meath
'My dear Lord', March-May 1819 advising
caution, one torn in fold without loss.
(Phillips) $245   £110
A.Ls., 2 pp. 4 to Calais, 1817 to General
Count Woronzouw, Commander of
Russian Army, about capacity of Boulogne,
Calais and Dunkirk harbours, marginal
tear without loss.
(Phillips) $180   £80

WELLS, H. G.
'Christina Alberta's Father'; 'The Open
Conspiracy'; 'The Man who could Work
Miracles?' – 1st Edns., presentation copies
inscribed by author to Gerald Gould,
original cloth, worn – 1928/1936.
(Sotheby's,
    Chancery Lane) $200   £90
'The Country of the Blind' – no. 145 of
280 copies, frontispiece and illustrations
some full page by Clifford Webb,
original parchment backed cloth, t.e.g. –
Golden Cockerel Press, 1939.
(Christie's S.
    Kensington) $170   £75

WELLS

Autograph postcard signed, full page, 8vo, Italy, n.d., to Miss Atkinson, about the Fabian Society.
(Sotheby's, New Bond
   Street)   **$90**   **£40**
'The First Men on the Moon' – 1st Edn., plates, original cloth, spine soiled, slightly soiled – 1901.
(Sotheby's,
   Chancery Lane)   **$65**   **£30**
'The Invisible Man' – 1st Edn., original cloth, slightly faded – 1897.
(Sotheby's,
   Chancery Lane)   **$65**   **£30**
'The Outline of History' – 2 vols., coloured plates, illus., original cloth – 1925.
(Christie's S.
   Kensington)   **$22**   **£10**
'The Time Machine' – 1st Edn., a few leaves spotted, original cloth, soiled and buckled, uncut – 1895.
(Sotheby's,
   Chancery Lane)   **$110**   **£48**
'The War of the Worlds' – 1st Edn., soiled, original cloth, inner hinges cracked – 1898.
(Christie's S.
   Kensington)   **$20**   **£9**
'Select Conversations with an Uncle' – 1st Edn., slightly discoloured and spotted, original cloth, spine soiled, rubbed, t.e.g. – 1895.
(Sotheby's,
   Chancery Lane)   **$110**   **£48**
'The Country of the Blind' – no. 78 of 280 copies, wood engraved frontis and 4 illustrations by Clifford Webb, 2 full page, original vellum backed cloth, t.e.g., 4to – 1939.
(Sotheby's,
   Chancery Lane)   **$290**   **£130**

Good series of 23 A.Ls. and P.Cs. signed, 45 pages, 4to and 16mo, 15th January 1912 to 10th January 1927, to Newman Flower at Cassell's, chronicling his turbulent relationship with that publisher.
(Sotheby's, New Bond
   Street)   **$1,620**   **£720**

WELSH, COL. JAMES

'Military Reminiscences' – 2 vols., 2nd Edn., 21 aquatint plates, 17 maps and plans, 20 wood engraved plates and illustrations, cont. half calf, worn – 1830.
(Christie's S.
   Kensington)   **$95**   **£42**

WENTWORD, J. A. (Editor)

'Janie Ellise's Recipes 1846-1859 . . . foreword by Elizabeth Craig' – no. 51 of 265 copies signed by Craig, illus., original morocco – 1974.
(Christie's S.
   Kensington)   **$55**   **£25**

WERFEL, FRANZ

'Der Weg Der Verheissung' – 1st Edn., presentation copy, inscribed by author, original pictorial wrappers, slightly worn – Paul Zsolnay, Vienna, 1935.
(Sotheby's,
   Chancery Lane)   **$4**   **£2**

H. G. Wells' 'The Country of the Blind', illustrated by Clifford Webb. (Sotheby's, Chancery Lane)

THE

DESIDERATUM:

O R,

ELECTRICITY

Made PLAIN and USEFUL.

By a Lover of Mankind, and of Common Senſe.

LONDON:

Printed And Sold by W. Flexney, under Gray's-Inn Gate, Holborn; E. Cabe, Ave-mary Lane; George Keith, in Little Carter Lane; George Keith, Grace-Church Street; T. Smith, under the Change; and at the Foundery, in Moorfields.
MDCCLX.

WESLEY, JOHN
'Primitive Physick or an Easy and
Natural Method of Curing Most
Diseases' – 31st Edn., green morocco, gilt
title on upper cover, 1825.
Another edition of the same, 1843.
(Sotheby's, New Bond
   Street)   **$65**   **£28**
'The Desideratum of Electricity made Plain
and Useful by a Lover of Mankind and of
Common Sense' – 1st Edn., marbled
boards, new calf spine – 1760.
(Sotheby's, New Bond
   Street)   **$585**   **£260**

WESSELY, NAFTALI HERZ
'Chochmat Shlomo' (On the Wisdom of
Solomon) – 1st Edn., cont. half calf, worn
– Berlin, 1780.
(Sotheby's, New Bond
   Street)   **$65**   **£30**

WEST INDIES
Series of mss. notes in form of a letter
criticising the management of the colonies
and the running of plantations. Mention
of the emancipation of the negro – circa
1850.
(Tessa Bennett,
   Edinburgh)   **$95**   **£42**

WEST, REBECCA
6 Autograph letters signed and typed to
Nicolas Bentley and his wife, in all 300
lines with many interesting references to
literary matters and other writers etc. –
1955-68.
(Lawrence of
   Crewkerne)   **$180**   **£80**

WESTALL, RICHARD
'Victories of the Duke of Wellington' –
1st Edn., 12 hand coloured aquatint
plates, 1 watermarked, torn, spotted,
cont. half black morocco, spine gilt,
damp marked – 1819.
(Sotheby's, New Bond
   Street)   **$200**   **£90**

WESTALL, W.
'Great Britain Illustrated' – vignette title,
116 plates, some spotting, half morocco,
gilt, 4to – 1830.
(Phillips)   **$245**   **£110**

WESTWOOD, J. O.
'The Cabinet of Oriental Entomology' –
42 hand coloured lithographed plates,
cont. half morocco, extremities rubbed –
1848.
(Christie's S.
   Kensington)   **$1,800**   **£800**
'Palaeographia Sacra Pictoria' – col. title
and plates, morocco gilt – 1843-45.
(Phillips)   **$170**   **£75**

WHATELEY, THOMAS
'Observations on Modern Gardening and
Laying out Pleasure Grounds, Parks,
Farms, Ridings etc.' – a new edition with
notes by Horace Walpole, Earl of Orford,
6 hand coloured engraved plates, modern
green half morocco, 4to – 1801.
(Christie's
   St. James)   **$380**   **£170**

WHEATLEY, H. B.
'Reliques – Later Reliques' – 2 vols.,
limited editions, signed by artist, lithos
by T. R. Way, original boards, rubbed,
4to – 1896-97.
(Phillips) $65   £28

WHEELER, PEARL
Interesting collection of 43 A.Ls. approx.
230 pages. New York, Rangoon, Manila
among other places, May 1922 –
September 1926, describing her journeys
to Europe and East with Denishawn
Dancers. All in portfolio with 'Letters
to My Mother' written on upper cover,
worn.
(Sotheby's, New Bond
    Street) $125   £55

WHEELWRIGHT, HORACE WILLIAM
'Sporting Sketches at Home and Abroad' –
later cloth, 8vo – 1866.
(Sotheby Humberts
    Taunton) $75   £35
'A Spring and Summer in Lapland . . . by
an Old Bushman' – cont. polished calf, a
little rubbed – 1864.
(Christie's S.
    Kensington) $55   £25

WHISTLER, JAMES MCNEILL
'Eden Versus Whistler, The Baronet and
the Butterfly' – 1st Edn., spotted, original
cloth backed boards, uncut – Paris, 1899.
(Sotheby's,
    Chancery Lane) $22   £10

Autograph invitation, signed with his
stylized butterfly, to breakfast at 12 o'clock,
on Sunday 22 July at Tite Street, on a stiff
card.
(Sotheby's, New Bond
    Street) $180   £80

WHISTLER, LAURENCE AND FULLER, R.
'The Work of Rex Whistler' – plates,
original cloth, dust jacket – 1960.
(Christie's S.
    Kensington) $180   £80

WHITAKER, C. W.
'Illustrated History of Enfield' – 2 folding
plans, plates, cloth, gilt – 1911.
(Phillips) $70   £32

WHITAKER, T. D.
'The History and Antiquities of the
Deanery of Craven in the County of York'
– 1st Edn., portrait, 36 engraved and
aquatint plates, cont. half russia, rubbed,
4to – 1805.
(Christie's S.
    Kensington) $100   £45

WHITE, CHARLES
'A Treatise on the Management of Preg-
nant and Lying-In Women' – 1st Edn., 2
plates, cont. calf, inscribed on fly leaf –
Edward and Charles Dilly, 1773.
(Sotheby's, New Bond
    Street) $585   £260

WHITE, GEORGE
'A Practical Treatise on Weaving' – 20
engraved plates, dampstained, one folding,
one double page and mounted on guards,
original cloth, joints cracked – 1846.
(Christie's S.
    Kensington) $22   £10

WHITE, GILBERT
'The Works in Natural History – Com-
prising the Natural History of Selborne,
the Naturalist's Calendar, Miscellaneous
Observations', with a Calendar and
Observations by W. Marwick – 2 vols.,
original boards, paper labels, uncut, 4
plates, one folding and 2 hand coloured –
For J. White, 1802.
(Lawrence of
    Crewkerne) $110   £50
'The Natural History and Antiquities of
Selborne' – new edition and engraved
additional title, plates, illus., original
cloth, g.e. – 1834.
(Christie's S.
    Kensington) $22   £10

'A Rich Cabinet, with a Variety of Inventions . . .' by John White.(Sotheby's, Chancery Lane)

WHITE, GLEESON AND OTHERS
'Modern Book Plates and Their
Designers' – illustrations, some coloured,
original wrappers, torn, rebacked – The
Studio, 1898.
(Christie's S.
   Kensington) $36   £16

WHITE, JOHN
'A Rich Cabinet with a Variety of Inven-
tions, Unlock'd and Open'd for the
Recreation of Ingenious Spirits in their
Vacant Hours' – 3rd Edn., engraved title,
woodcut illustrations, some spotting, half
morocco – William Gilbertson, 1658.
(Sotheby's,
   Chancery Lane) $1,035   £460

WHITEHEAD, W.
'Poems on Several Occasions, with the
Roman Father, a Tragedy' – 1st collected
edition, cont. calf gilt, slightly defective
– 1754.
(Sotheby's
   London) $11   £5

WHITFIELD, CHRISTOPHER
'Together and Alone' – no. 249 of 500
copies, illustrations by John O'Connor,
original cloth, t.e.g. – Golden Cockerel
Press, 1945.
(Christie's S.
   Kensington) $27   £12

WHITMAN, WALT.
'Two Rivulets' – 6 parts bound in one
volume, 1st Edn., original half calf,
slightly rubbed and soiled – Camden, New
Jersey, 1876.
(Sotheby's,
   Chancery Lane) $135   £60

A.L. signed, to Alfred Tennyson, 2 pages,
8vo, Washington 2nd September 1872,
thanking him for a photograph sent, and
discussing the weather, etc.
(Sotheby's, New Bond
   Street) $2,025   £900

WHITWORTH, RICHARD
'The Advantages of Inland Navigation' –
1st Edn., cont. red morocco gilt, label
and spine tooled with flower and acorn
ornaments, rubbed, g.e. – 1766.
(Sotheby's, New Bond
   Street) $720   £320

WHYMPER, EDWARD
'Travels among the Andes' – lacks supple-
ment, plates, cloth – 1892.
(Phillips) $50   £22

WHYTE, JAMES CHRISTIE
'History of the British Turf' — 2 vols.,
illustrations, some leaves detached, rebacked,
worn — 1840.
(Christie's S.
Kensington) $40   £18

WHYTE, ROBERT
'Observations on the Nature, Causes and
Cure of those Disorders which have been
commonly called Nervous Hypochondriac
or Hysteric' — 1st Edn., advertisement
leaf, cont. calf — Edinburgh, 1765.
(Sotheby's, New Bond
Street) $425   £190

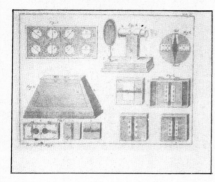

WIEGLEB, JOHANN CHRISTIAN
'Die Naturliche Magie' — 2nd enlarged
edn., 12 folding engraved plates, 3 diagrams in text, cont. half calf, slightly
rubbed — Berlin and Stettin, 1782.
(Sotheby's,
Chancery Lane) $280   £125

WIELAND, CHRISTOPH MARTIN
'Beytrage zur Geheimen Geschichte des
Menschlichen Verstandes und des Herzens.
Aus den Archiven der Natur Gezogen' —
2 parts in one volume, slightly spotted and
soiled, cont. half calf, slightly rubbed —
Reuttlingen, 1776.
(Sotheby's, New Bond
Street) $65   £28
'Socrates out of his Senses' — 2 vols. in
one, 1st English Edn., translated by Mr.
Wintersted, cont. calf, gilt, label — For T.
Davies, 1771.
(Sotheby's, New Bond
Street) $245   £110

WILD, ROGER — BAUDELAIRE, CHARLES
'Les Fleurs du Mal' — etched frontispiece
and 11 plates by Wild, slightly spotted,
cont. buckram, spine slightly discoloured —
Emile-Paul Freres, Paris, 1942.
(Sotheby's,
Chancery Lane) $30   £14

'WILD SPORTS OF THE WEST WITH LEGENDARY TALES AND LOCAL SKETCHES'
— 2 vols., aquatint plates,
1st Edn. — 1832.
(Tessa Bennett,
Edinburgh) $65   £30

WILDE, OSCAR
'The Ballad of Reading Gaol' — 1st End.,
limited to 830 copies, original cloth,
soiled, uncut — 1898.
(Sotheby's,
Chancery Lane) $190   £85
'Works' — 14 vols., limited edition, cloth,
gilt, slightly soiled — London and Paris,
1908.
(Sotheby Parke Bernet
Monaco) $945   £420
'Sir Arthur Savile's Crime and Other
Stories' — 1st Edn., original boards, cover
design by Charles Ricketts, slightly soiled
— 1891.
(Sotheby's,
Chancery Lane) $125   £55

WILHELM, G. T.
'Unterhaltungen aus der Naturgeschichte
des Planzenreichs' — 10 vols., the botanical
section complete, very numerous coloured
plates, cont. half calf — Augsburg, 1810-20.
(Sotheby Parke Bernet
Monaco) $8,550   £3,800

WILKES, JOHN
'The North Briton' No. XVII — woodcut
caricature of William Hogarth in upper part
of first page, folio — 21 May, 1763.
(Christie's, King
St.) $100   £45
'Encyclopaedia Londonensis' — 15 vols.
only, engraved dedication, plates and maps,
cont. calf — 1810-28.
(Christie's S.
Kensington) $720   £320

WILKINS, BISHOP JOHN
'The Discovery of a World in the Moone' –
1st Edn., woodcut diagram on title, 5 other
woodcuts, one full page, cont. calf, worn,
repaired – 1638.
(Christie's, King
St.) $630   £280

WILKINS, JOHN
'An Essay Towards a Real Character and a
Philosophical Language' – 1st Edn., cont.
calf, rubbed, folio – 1668.
(Sotheby's, New Bond
Street) $360   £160

WILKINS, W.
'Atheniensia or Remarks . . . of Athens' –
double page plan, half calf gilt – 1816.
(Phillips) $125   £55
'The Antiquities of Magna Graecia' – 73
plates and plans, recent blue half calf,
gilt spine, uncut, folio – Cambridge, 1807.
(Sotheby's, New Bond
Street) $315   £140

WILKINSON, R.
'General Atlas of the World' – 3rd Edn.,
engraved title and 49 hand coloured maps,
cont. half calf, worn – 1822.
(Christie's S.
Kensington) $85   £38

WILKS, COLONEL MARK
'Historical Sketches of the South of India'
– 3 vols., 1st Edn., 2 folding engraved
maps, partly hand coloured, Tyrconnel
bookplate, cont. calf, Tyrconnel crest,
gilt, on covers, hinges split, one cover
detached – 1810-17.
(Sotheby's
London) $75   £35

WILLIAM I, KING OF PRUSSIA
4 Autograph letters signed, 11 pages, Berlin
and elsewhere, January 1868-November
1868 to Empress Augusta and Princess
Louise of Prussia on political and family
matters, with autograph telegram and
photograph.
(Sotheby's, New Bond
Street) $405   £180

WILLIAM III
Document signed 'William R' at head,
ordering the Earl of Jersey, Ranger of
Hyde Park, to take measures to increase
the park's stock of deer, 1 page, folio –
Kensington, 1st June 1699.
(Sotheby's, New Bond
Street) $270   £120

WILLIAM IV
Series of eleven A.Ls. signed 'William',
17 pages, 4to, St. James's, Bushy House,
and the Admiralty, 28th April 1817 to
1828, to Sir Richard Puleston, announcing
his marriage, discussing his health and his
tours abroad, etc.
(Sotheby's, New Bond
Street) $560   £250

WILLIAM IV
3 A.Ls. scored through and torn across,
Hanover 1818-19, Lords Brougham (7, three
with initials), Derby (6, three private)
1858-67, W. Lamb, Lord Melbourne (3, two
brief) 1828-38, Sir Robert Peel (5, 3 private,
2 signed only), Lord Whitworth (8)
addressed to West Meath, etc., loosely
inserted in green letter file.
(Phillips) $145   £65

WILLIAMS, A. M.
'Engravings of Celebrated Shorthorns' –
15 etched plates, calf gilt, oblong 4to –
1881.
(Phillips) $190   £85

WILLIAMS, GEORGE
'The Holy City' – 2 vols., 2nd Edn., 16
tinted lithographic plates – 1849.
(Lawrence of
Crewkerne) $75   £35

WILLIAMS

WILLIAMS, HAROLD
'Book Clubs and Printing Societies of
Great Britain and Ireland' — limited to 750
copies, original cloth, slightly soiled, printed
at the Curwen Press for the First Edition
Club — 1929.
(Christie's S.
  Kensington) $27   £12

WILLIAMS, HELEN MARIA
'A Tour of Switzerland' — 2 vols., half title
in vol. I, some leaves slightly browned,
cont. calf, rubbed, hinges split — 1798.
(Sotheby's,
  Chancery Lane) $115   £52

WILLIAMS, LIEUT. COLONEL
'England's Battles' — 6 vols., engraved
additional title and portrait in vol. I,
plates, cont. half calf, rubbed — n.d.
(Christie's S.
  Kensington) $90   £40

WILLIAMS, WILLIAM
'Occult Physick or the Three Principles in
Nature' — 1st and only edn., some orna-
mental woodcut headings, short marginal
tear, new mottled calf — Tho. Leach, H.
Marsh, 1660.
(Sotheby's, New Bond
  Street) $720   £320

**WILLIAMSON, GEORGE C. AND
ENGLEHEART, HENRY**
'George Engleheart, miniature painter to
George III' — no. 15 of 53 copies, linen
covered boards, slightly soiled, t.e.g.,
others uncut, privately printed, folio —
1902.
(Christie's
  St. James) $155   £70

WILLIAMSON, HENRY
'Dandelion Days' — yellow cloth gilt, t.e.g.,
uncut, no. 111 of 200 copies on hand made
paper, signed by author — 1930.
(Lawrence of
  Crewkerne) $155   £70

WILLIAMSON, JAMES A.
'The Voyage of the Cabots' — no. 441 of
1,050 copies, plates and maps, original
vellum backed cloth, gilt — 1929.
(Sotheby's,
  Chancery Lane) $85   £38

WILLIAMSON, THOMAS
'Oriental Field Sports' — 41 hand coloured
and aquatint plates, cont. straight grained
maroon morocco, gilt spine tooled with
hunting scenes in compartments, slightly
rubbed — Edward Orme, n.d.
(Sotheby's, New Bond
  Street) $495   £220

WILLICH, A. F. M.
'Lectures on Diet and Regimen' — 3rd Edn.,
cont. calf, rubbed — 1800.
(Christie's S.
  Kensington) $22   £10

WILLINK, DANIEL
'Amsterdamsche Buitensingel' — 2nd Edn.,
additional engraved title, 16 engraved
plates, most folding, slight browning,
cont. half vellum boards, worn —
Amsterdam, 1738.
(Sotheby's, New Bond
  Street) $400   £180

WILLIS, NATHANIEL PARKER
'Canadian Scenery' — 2 vols., 2 additional
engraved titles, map, frontispiece, 117
engraved plates after Bartlett, purple
half morocco boards, g.e. — n.d., circa
1842.
(Christie's
  St. James) $900   £400
'American Scenery' — 2 vols., steel
engraved portrait, additional titles and 117
plates after W. H. Bartlett, one map, a
little marginal browning, small library
stamps on verso of titles, cont. half
morocco, rubbed — 1840.
(Christie's S.
  Kensington) $585   £260

**WILLIS, N. P. AND COYNE, J.
STIRLING**
'The Scenery and Antiquities of Ireland
illustrated by W. H. Bartlett' — 2 vols.,
steel engraved additional titles, 118
plates and one map, portrait lacking,
staining and spotting, cont. half calf,
rubbed, joints worn, ex library copy, 4to
— George Virtue, n.d.
(Christie's S.
  Kensington) $290   £130

Carl Willmann, Hamburg.

1279. Der indische Fakir.
The floating Ind an Fakir. Suspension aérienne ou scène du Fakir.

Ich bin infolge weitverzweigter Verbindungen stets vom Neuesten unterrichtet.

WILLMANN, CARL
4 catalogues including the 24th, 26th and
28th editions, one with portrait torn and
6 supplements, 10 vols. in 5 – Hamburg,
circa 1883-1915.
(Sotheby's,
   Chancery Lane) $585 £260

WILLOUGHY, F.
'Ornithology' – 1st English Edn., translated by J. Ray, 80 plates, one mounted,
title in facsimile, some repairs, calf, folio
– 1678.
(Phillips) $630 £280
'Ornithologiae Libri Tres' – cont. calf,
folio, worn, 1st Edn., title in red and black
with arms of the Royal Society, 77 engraved
plates, diagrams in text, 2 folding tables,
some leaves and plates with dampstains –
1676.
(Lawrence of
   Crewkerne) $400 £180

WILSON, SIR C. W.
'Picturesque Palestine' – plates with
supplement, 5 vols., 4to, original gilt –
Virtue – n.d.
(Bonham's) $180 £80

WILSON, D.
'Memorials of Edinburgh in Olden Times'
– folding plan, steel engraved plates,
wood engravings, half morocco –
Edinburgh, 1873.
(Tessa Bennett,
   Edinburgh) $40 £18

**WILSON, JAMES AND CHAMBERS,
ROBERT**
'The Land of Burns' – vol. 1 only,
engraved additional title and plates after
David Hill, cont. morocco, spine rubbed
– 1840.
(Christie's S.
   Kensington) $40 £18

WILSON, JOHN
'General View of the Agriculture of
Renfrewshire . . . drawn up for the con-
sideration of the Board of Agriculture' –
engraved plate and folding frontis, cont.
half calf, rubbed, joints cracked –
Paisley, 1812.
(Christie's S.
   Kensington) $85 £38

WILSON, PROFESSOR JOHN
'Scotland Illustrated in a Series of 80
Views' – additional engraved title and 76
plates only, some spotting, cont. half calf,
worn, upper cover detached, g.e. – 1845.
(Christie's S.
   Kensington) $65 £30

WILSON, SIR JOHN
'The Royal Philatelic Collection' – portraits, some coloured plates, original
morocco, rubbed – The Dropmore Press,
1952.
(Christie's S.
   Kensington) $100 £45

WILSON, M.
'Life of William Blake' – limited edition,
illus., quarter vellum gilt – Nonesuch
Press, 1927.
(Phillips) $50 £22

WILSON, MATTHEW
'Mercy and Truth or Charity Maintayned by Catholiques' — 1st Edn., cont. limp vellum, soiled, small 4to — English College Press, St. Omer, 1634.
(Sotheby's, New Bond
Street) $135   £60

WILSON, ROBERT THOMAS
'History of the British Expedition to Egypt' — portrait, three folding maps, cont. half calf, rebacked, covers detached. Together with the 4th Edn. of the same work — 2 vols. — 1802 and 1803.
(Christie's S.
Kensington) $80   £35

WILSON, THOMAS (Dancing Master)
'A Description of the Correct Method of Waltzing . . . Part 1 only' — 1st Edn., one of 250 copies, one engraved folding frontispiece and 2 engraved plates, 4 plates of engraved music, encased in modern boards with original endpapers, label on spine, uncut — For the author, 1816.
(Sotheby's, New Bond
Street) $100   £45

WIMPHELING, JACOB
'De Conceptu et Triplici Mariae Virginis Gloriosissimae Candore Carmen' — 40 leaves, 28 lines, roman letter, woodcut on title page of Virgin and Child, water stained, dust soiled, modern boards — Johann Bergmann, Basle, 1494.
(Christie's S.
Kensington) $1,125   £500

WINKLES, H. AND B.
'Architectural and Picturesque Illustrations of the Cathedral Churches of England and Wales' — 3 vols., additional engraved titles, engraved plates and plans, some spotting, cont. half roan, rubbed, vol. I rebacked — 1836-42.
(Sotheby's
London) $90   £40
'Cathedral Churches of Great Britain' — 2 vols., plates, cloth gilt, 4to — 1836-38.
(Phillips) $100   £45

WINSLOW, JACOBUS BENIGNUS
'The Uncertainty of the Signs of Death and the Danger of Precipitate Interments and Dissections' — 1st English Edn., 6 plates, cont. calf, rebacked, bookplate — Stansby Alchorne, Tower of London, M. Cooper, 1746.
(Sotheby's, New Bond
Street) $335   £150

WINTER, CARL
'The Fitzwilliam Museum' — limited to 1,526 copies, this 'K' of 26 copies letter A to Z, plates, a few coloured, original cloth, publisher's box — Trianon Press, 1958.
(Christie's S.
Kensington) $70   £32

WINTER, G. S.
'Tractatio Nova et Auctior de Re Equaria' — text in Latin, German, French and Italian, engraved title, 37 engraved plates, recent leather, gilt, folio — Nuremberg, 1687.
(Sotheby Parke Bernet
Monaco) $27,000   £12,000

WINTERBOTTOM, THOMAS
'An Account of the Native Africans in the Neighbourhood of Sierra Leone' — 2 vols. in one, 2 engraved maps, modern half morocco — 1803.
(Sotheby's, New Bond
Street) $405   £180

WIRELESS
93 assorted volumes of Modern Wireless, Popular Wireless, Wireless Construction, Wireless Weekly and Wireless and Television Review — 1922-37.
(Sotheby's,
Chancery Lane) $1,170   £520

A
TREATISE
OF
Wounds.

BY
RICHARD WISEMAN,
ONE OF
His Majeſtie's Serjeant-Chirurgeons.

L O N D O N,
Printed by *R. Norton,* for *Richard Royſton,*
Bookſeller to His moſt Sacred MA-
JESTY, MDCLXXII.

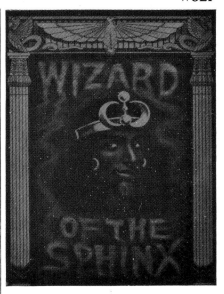

WIZARD OF THE SPHINX
Head within Egyptian arch, coloured
lithograph, short tears at edges, 27 x 19in.
— circa 1905.
(Sotheby's,
    Chancery Lane) $225   £100

WISEMAN, RICHARD
'A Treatise of Wounds' — 1st Edn., short
marginal tear, cont. sheep, worn, torn at
top of spine — R. Norton for Richard
Royston, 1672.
(Sotheby's, New Bond
    Street) $1,350   £600

WITHER, GEORGE
'Speculum Speculativum or, a considering-
glasse' — some staining and soiling, polished
calf, gilt — 1660.
(Sotheby's
    London) $33   £15

WITHERING, WILLIAM
'An Account of the Scarlatina and Sore
Throat . . . as it appeared in Birmingham in
1778' — 1st Edn., half title and last page
rather dust soiled, new red cloth — T.
Cadell and others, 1779.
(Sotheby's, New Bond
    Street) $720   £320

WITT, JOHAN DE 1625-72
Letter signed, 1 page, folio, The Hague,
April, 1666, to his cousin condoling him
on death of his wife.
(Sotheby's, New Bond
    Street) $315   £140

WOLF, HUGO
Autograph letter signed, 2 pages, octavo,
June 1884, discussing his accommodation
problems, autograph envelope, stamped and
postmarked.
(Sotheby's, New Bond
    Street) $675   £300
Autograph letter, 3 pages, octavo, Vienna,
December 1896, to a friend urging him
to end feud with Paul Muller.
(Sotheby's, New Bond
    Street) $1,170   £520

WOLF, J.
'Sammlung Mehrerer Abbildungen
Verschiederer Vogel' — ms. title, 24
leaves, most with 2 attractive watercolours of birds, soiling, some drawings
unfinished, half sheep, worn, some scraps
still pasted to versos, oblong small 8vo —
circa 1840.
(Sotheby's, New Bond
    Street) $675   £300

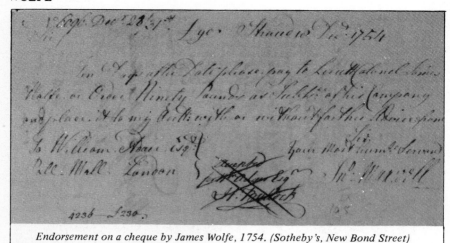

Endorsement on a cheque by James Wolfe, 1754. (Sotheby's, New Bond Street)

WOLFE, JAMES
Endorsement signed 'Jam. Wolfe' on a
cheque made out to him 'Lieutt-Colonel
James Wolfe' for £90 by John Maxwell on
his banker, William Adair of Pall Mall,
Wolfe's endorsement transferring the sum
to John Tozer, narrow oblong octavo, a
small tear in one edge — 18-31 December
1754.
(Sotheby's, New Bond
    Street)   **$560**   **£250**

WOLFF, JOSEPH
'Travels and Adventures' — 2 vols., green
half morocco, spines gilt, t.e.g., frontispiece portrait, appendix — 1860.
(Lawrence of
    Crewkerne)   **$65**   **£28**

WOLLASTON, WILLIAM
'The Religion of Nature Delineated' —
dampstaining, cont. calf, worn — 1726.
(Sotheby's, New Bond
    Street)   **$70**   **£30**

WOLSEY, THOMAS
Privy Council warrant signed ('Thomas
Wulcy'), directing the buying of wine in
Flanders, also signed by Thomas Howard,
2nd Duke of Norfolk, Richard Fox, Bishop
of Worcester and others, 1 page, 4to, dated
from Richmond 25 November (1513), the
receipt 6 December, cont. docket.
(Sotheby's, New Bond
    Street)   **$2,925**   **£1,300**

WOLVERIDGE, J.
'Speculum Matricis, or the Expert Midwives Handmaid Catechistically Composed'
— engraved frontispiece, 8 plates, antique
calf — 1671.
  (Bonham's)   **$335**   **£150**

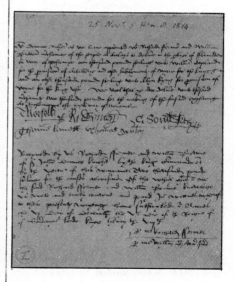

*Privy Council warrant signed by Thomas
Wolsey, 1513. (Sotheby's, New Bond Street)*

WOMACK, BISHOP LAURENCE
'The Examination of Tilenus before the
Triers' – 1st Edn., damp stains, cont.
mottled calf, neatly rebacked – For R.
Royston, 1658.
(Sotheby's, New Bond
   Street) $55   £25

WOMAN'S RELIQUARY, A.
Edited by Edward Dowden, 1st Edn.,
limited to 300 copies, signed by author on
title, original linen backed boards, spine
soiled and faded, uncut – Cuala Press,
Dundrum, 1914.
(Sotheby's,
   Chancery Lane) $55   £25

WONG TOY SUN, THE WORLD FAMED
Chinese dragon carrying lantern above
caricature of the conjurer at side of text,
ink and watercolour drawing, signed Wiggin,
soiled and frayed, mounted on brown paper,
30 x 15in. – circa 1920.
(Sotheby's,
   Chancery Lane) $90   £40

WOOD, ESTHER AND OTHERS
'Modern Bookbindings and Their
Designers' – illustrations, some coloured,
some leaves soiled, modern morocco
backed cloth – The Studio, 1899.
(Christie's S.
   Kensington) $40   £18

WOOD, JOHN
'The Origin of Building or the Plagiarism
of the Heathens' – plates, boards, uncut,
canvas spine added, folio – Bath, 1741.
(Sotheby's, New Bond
   Street) $380   £170

WOOD, N.
'Practical Treatise on Railroads' – 6
folding plates, no adverts., boards, 8vo –
1825.
(Phillips) $135   £60

WOOD, W.
'The East Neuk of Fife' – cloth –
Edinburgh, 1887.
(Tessa Bennett,
   Edinburgh) $55   £24

WOOD, W.
'A Catalogue of Shells, British and
Foreign' – illustrated with 480 figures,
8 fine hand coloured plates, half calf –
1828.
(Tessa Bennett,
   Edinburgh) $13   £6

'WOODCUTS'
82 16th century mounted woodcut illustrations, mainly of biblical scenes, 18th
century half calf, worn – 1821.
(Christie's S.
   Kensington) $135   £60

WOODMAN, PHILIP
'Medicus Novissimus or the Modern
Physician' – new half calf – J. N. for
Chr. Coningsby, 1712.
(Sotheby's, New Bond
   Street) $55   £25

WOODS, GEORGE
'An Account of the Past and Present State
of the Isle of Man; including . . . a Sketch
of its Mineralogy' – 1st Edn., cont. tree
calf, neatly rebacked – 1811.
(Sotheby's
   London) $11   £5

WOODS, J.
'Letters of an Architect from France,
Italy and Greece' – 2 vols., 21 plates,
cloth gilt, worn, 4to – 1828.
(Phillips) $70   £32

WOODTHORPE, R. G.
'The Lushae Expedition 1871-72' –
frontis., map, half calf – 1873.
(Phillips) $45   £20

WOODVILLE, WILLIAM
'Medical Botany' – 4 vols. in two, 2nd Edn.,
254 engraved plates only, later cloth
backed boards – 1810.
(Christie's S.
   Kensington)   **$450**   **£200**

WOODWARD, GEORGE MURGATROYD
'Elements of Bacchus' – 1st Edn., 40 hand
coloured aquatint caricature portraits of
the most celebrated bon vivants in Great
Britain, cont. calf, very worn, scarce –
William Holland, 1792.
(Sotheby's, New Bond
   Street)   **$200**   **£90**

WOODWARD, JOHN
'The State of Physick and of Diseases . . .
more particularly of the Small Pox' – cont.
panelled calf, bookplate of St. John's
College, Oxford – T. Horne and R. Wilkin,
1718.
(Sotheby's, New Bond
   Street)   **$125**   **£55**

WOODWARD, JOSIAH
'An Account of the Societies for Refor-
mation of Manners, in London and
Westminster' – 1st Edn., engraved portrait,
hinges torn, cont. panelled calf, very
slightly worn – For B. Aylmer, 1699.
(Sotheby's
   London)   **$135**   **£60**

WOOLF, LEONARD
Eighteen autograph and typed letters
signed, 26 pages 4to and 8vo, one P.C.,
Clifford's Inn, Tavistock Square, the
Nation and Monk's House, 1906-1937, to
Clive Bell and Julian Bell, discussing
aesthetics and politics.
(Sotheby's, New Bond
   Street)   **$1,395**   **£620**

WOOLF, VIRGINIA
'Between the Acts' – 1st Edn., original
cloth, spine faded – Hogarth Press, 1941.
(Sotheby's,
   Chancery Lane)   **$11**   **£5**
'Kew Gardens' – no. 282 of 500 copies,
decorations by Vanessa Bell, slightly
spotted, original decorated boards, rubbed,
lacking spine, uncut – Hogarth Press, 1930.
(Sotheby's,
   Chancery Lane)   **$70**   **£32**
'On Being Ill' – 1st Edn., no. 86 of 250
copies, original vellum backed boards,
uncut – Hogarth Press, 1930.
(Sotheby's,
   Chancery Lane)   **$405**   **£180**

The autograph ms. of the first draft of
Quentin Bell's biography of his aunt,
Virginia Woolf, with autograph revisions
and corrections throughout, 5 vols., 8
pages, insertions, paste-overs and sketches
by Bell, extra large 4to and folio.
(Sotheby's, New Bond
   Street)   **$4,275**   **£1,900**

Fine series of 25 autograph or typed letters signed and 16 P.Cs., 50 pages, 4to and 8vo, 52 Tavistock Square and Monks House, 1927-36, to Julian Bell, containing Bloomsbury gossip and literary and artistic commentaries as well as detailing the progress of her writing and giving him various small commissions.
(Sotheby's, New Bond
Street) $7,875   £3,500

Important autograph journal and notebook kept during travels to Italy, Greece and Turkey, 1906, 1908, 1909, 145 pages, green cloth, quarto.
(Sotheby's, New Bond
Street) $19,125   £8,500

Fine series of 45 letters, 14 of them autograph and 31 typed, and 8 P.Cs., upwards of 100 pages, folio, 4to and 8vo, Tavistock Square, Monk's House and elsewhere, 13th March 1927 to 18th October 1938, to her nephew Quentin Bell, urging him to develop his talents and exchanging Bloomsbury gossip.
(Sotheby's, New Bond
Street) $10,800   £4,800

A. L. signed, 1 page, 4to, Richmond, no date, to Brett, traces of mount, arranging a meeting, discussing how busy she is, etc.
(Sotheby's, New Bond
Street) $393   £175

THE 🜔 DIAL

Autograph inscription written at the head of Clive Bell's article on her, 'Virginia Woolf', printed in The Dial, December 1924: 'Please return to Mrs. Woolf, 52 Tavistock Sq., W.C.1/London', the pages of the article torn out, folded, soiled.
(Sotheby's, New Bond
    Street) $225   £100

Fine early series of 21 A.Ls. signed and one typed letter, mostly 8vo, 61 pages, 22 Hyde Park Gate and Corby Castle, 1896-1903, to her brother Thoby, containing personal and family news.
(Sotheby's, New Bond
    Street) $10,125   £4,500

Notebook containing autograph accounts of her earnings from books and articles and from work with the B.B.C., July, 1928 to December 1937, c. 30 pages, boards, 12mo.
(Sotheby's, New Bond
    Street) $1,687   £750

WOOLLEY, HANNAH
'The Compleat Servant Maid or the Young Maidens' Tutor' — 4th Edn., engraved frontis., later calf rubbed, joints cracked, 12mo — 1685.
(Christie's
    St. James) $180   £80

WORCESTER, MARQUIS OF
'Century of Names and Scantlings of Inventions' — half calf, 12mo — Glasgow, 1767.
(Phillips) $75   £35

WORDSWORTH, WILLIAM
'Peter Bell' — 2nd Edn., inscribed by the author to John Sproat on title, engraved frontispiece, a little foxing on title, hole on half title and tear in margin of frontispiece skilfully repaired, morocco by Riviere, g.e., 8vo — 1819.
(Christie's, King
    St.) $123   £55

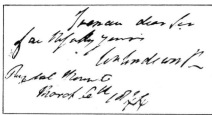

Literary autograph letter signed, 2 pages, octavo, Rydal Mount, 6 March 1844, to an unnamed correspondent, allowing him to make use of the poems which he proposes, but asking him, if he wishes to select 'The Labourer's Noon-day Rest', to alter the first line of the fifth stanza to 'Each field is then a hallowed spot' or, if he chooses, to omit it altogether.
(Sotheby's, New Bond
   Street) $540   £240

'The Excursion' – 2nd Edn., slightly spotted, later half calf – 1820.
(Sotheby's, New Bond
   Street) $90   £40
'The River Duddon' – 1st Edn., later half calf – 1820.
(Sotheby's, New Bond
   Street) $100   £45
'Poems in Two Volumes' – 2 vols. in one, 1st Edn., half titles, cont. half calf, lower hinge cracked – 1807.
(Sotheby's, New Bond
   Street) $1,000   £450

WORDSWORTH, WILLIAM AND COLERIDGE, S. T.
'Lyrical Ballads' – 2 vols., 1st Edn., vol. I second issue, levant morocco, spines faded, slipcase, g.e. – London, 1798-1800.
(Christie's S.
   Kensington) $630   £280

WORLIDGE, THOMAS
A select collection of Drawings from Curious Antique Gems – a proof set of 183 engraved plates, unaccompanied by the text, on large paper, including the two additional plates of Medusa and Hercules, cont. black blind panelled morocco, rubbed, uncut, 4to – 1768.
(Christie's, King
   St.) $135   £60

WORLD MAP
ARNOLDI, ARNOLDO DI
'Descrittione Universale dei Terra Con l'Uso del Navigare, Anno 1669' – very large and remarkably detailed engraved map of the world, lettered in Italian throughout, 10 sheets joined, mounted on canvas, framed, 41 x 73in. – Pietro Petrucci, Siena, 1669.
(Sotheby's, New Bond
   Street) $15,750   £7,000

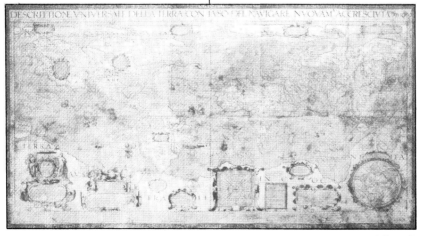

'Descrittione Universale dei Terra' by Arnoldo di Arnoldi. (Sotheby's, New Bond Street)

405

WORLIDGE, JOHN
'Dictionarium Rusticum & Urbanicum, or,
a Dictionary of all Sorts of Country Affairs'
— 1st Edn., woodcut illustrations, cont.
panelled calf, defective — 1704.
(Sotheby's
London) $155   £70

WORLIDGE, THOMAS
'A Select Collection of Drawings from
Curious Antique Gems' — portrait, 182
plates, 26 additional proof plates, morocco
gilt, g.e., 4to — 1768.
(Phillips) $135   £60

WORSLEY, SIR RICHARD
'Museum Worsleyanum' — 2 vols., illus.,
includes many fine views in Greece and
Turkey, half morocco, folio — 1824.
(Phillips) $335   £150

WOTTON, WILLIAM
'Reflections Upon Ancient and Modern
Learning' — 1st Edn., cont. panelled calf,
armorial bookplate of Thomas Isted of
Middle Temple — J. Leake for Peter Buck,
1694.
(Sotheby's, New Bond
Street) $380   £170

WOUVERMAN, P.
'Oeuvres . . . gravees d'apres ses meilleurs
Tableaux . . dedies a Comte de Clermont,
Prince du Sang' — engraved title, portrait
and 92 engravings mostly by Moyreau,
marbled boards worn, large folio — Paris,
1737-62.
(Phillips) $11,250   £5,000

WRIGHT, EDWARD
'Sketches in Bedlam or Characteristic traits
of Insanity' — 2nd Edn., half title, original
cloth backed boards, label worn, uncut —
Sherwood, Jones and Co., 1824.
(Sotheby's, New Bond
Street) $270   £120
'Some Observations made in Travelling
through France, Italy, &c. in the Years
1720, 1721 and 1722' — 2 vols. in one,
1st Edn., 41 plates, three folding, 1
full page woodcut, tear in vol. I, cont.
calf, gilt spine, worn — 1730.
(Sotheby's
London) $135   £60

WRIGHT, G. N.
'China in a Series of Views' — 2 vols.
illustrated by T. Allom, 125 plates,
morocco gilt, covers detached — 1843.
(Phillips) $200   £90
'The Rhine, Italy and Greece' — In a
series of drawings by Col. Cockburn, Major
Irton, Messrs. Bartlett, Leitch and
Wolfensberger, 2 vols. in one, steel engraved
titles and 71 plates, spotting, cont. half
morocco by Hatchard and Co., rubbed, g.e.,
4to — Fisher Son and Co., n.d.
(Christie's S.
Kensington) $400   £180
'The Shores and Islands of the Mediterranean' — drawn by Sir Grenvil Temple,
W. L. Leitch, Major Irton and Lieut. Allen,
steel engraved additional title, 59 plates
only and 1 folding map, spotting, cont.
half morocco by Hatchard and Co.,
rubbed, g.e., 4to — Fisher Son and Co.,
n.d.
(Christie's S.
Kensington) $180   £80
'France Illustrated' — 4 vols. in two,
engraved plates, morocco gilt, 4to —
Faber, n.d.
(Phillips) $290   £130
'The Rhine, Italy and Greece' — 2 vols. in
one, engraved titles and 63 plates only of
71, one loose, a few slightly spotted,
cont. morocco, gilt spine, slightly rubbed,
g.e. — 1841-42.
(Sotheby's,
Chancery Lane) $315   £140
'China' — 4 vols. in two, cont. mottled
calf gilt, inner and outer dentelles by
Saunders, 4 vignette titles, 124 engraved
plates, plates in good state — circa 1843.
(Lawrence of
Crewkerne) $315   £140

WRIGHT, G. N. AND BUCKINGHAM,
L. F. A.
'Belgium, The Rhine, Italy, Greece' —
2 vols., 2 vignette titles, engraved plates,
morocco gilt, 4to — Fisher, n.d.
(Phillips) $450   £200

WRIGHT, JOHN
'The Fruit Grower's Guide' — 2 vols. only,
title vignettes and 25 plates, occasional
slight spotting, original cloth — n.d.
(Christie's S.
Kensington) $155   £70

WRIGHT, THOMAS
'A Treatise, shewing the possibilitie, and conveniencie of the reall presence of our Saviour in the blessed Sacrament' — 1st Edn., device on title, somewhat stained and soiled, 19th century blind stamped calf — Antwerp, Ioachim Trognesius (London V. Sims) 1596.
(Sotheby's
London)　　$135　　£60

WRIGHT, THOMAS AND BARTLETT, W.
'The History and Topography of the County of Essex' — 2 vols., engraved vignette titles and 100 plates on India paper, folding map, coloured in outline, some spotting throughout, cont. half morocco, gilt, slightly rubbed — 1831-35.
(Sotheby's,
Chancery Lane)　　$315　　£140

WURTTEMBERG
Collection of over 100 letter signed by rulers of Wurttemberg in the 18th and 19th centuries — 1701-1860.
(Sotheby's, New Bond
Street)　　$585　　£260

WYLDE, JAMES (Editor)
'The Circle of the Sciences' — 3 vols., plates, illustrations, list of plates neatly repaired, cont. half calf, rubbed — n.d.
(Christie's S.
Kensington)　　$40　　£18

WYNKYN DE WORDE
Facsimile published by Cambridge University Press — 'The Frere and the Boy' — parchment backed boards, limited edition, 250 copies — 1907.
(Tessa Bennett,
Edinburgh)　　$18　　£8

' X '
A quarterly review, edited by David Wright and Patrick Swift — vols. 1 and 2, two sets, contributions by Samuel Beckett, Robert Graves and Ezra Pound, illustrations, original wrappers, some worn.
Another copy of vol. 1, limited to 800 copies, original boards — 1956-61.
(Sotheby's,
Chancery Lane)　　$50　　£22

XENOPHON
'The Institution and Life of Cyrus the Great from the Original Greek made English by Francis Digby and John Norris' — 2 vols. in one, 1st Edn., of this translation, engraved title, some minor defects, bookplate of Earl of Lonsdale, cont. calf, worn, upper hinge weak — For Matthew Gilliflower and James Norris, 1685.
(Sotheby's, New Bond
Street)　　$67　　£30

'De Cyri Institutione libri octo' — Greek text, 1st English Edn., 19th century calf gilt, 4to — Melchisidec Bradwood, Eton College, 1613.
(Sotheby's, New Bond
Street)　　$155　　£70

'Cyropaedia De Cyri Institutione libri octo' — Greek text, 1st Edn. in England, ms. marginal notes, 19th century calf gilt, 4to — Melchisidec Bradwood, Eton College, 1613.
(Sotheby's, New Bond
Street)　　$200　　£90

'Cyropaedia or the Institution and Life of Cyrus the First of that name, King of the Persians' — additional engraved title, old calf, folio — 1632.
(Christie's
St. James)　　$190　　£85

Y

YARRELL, W.
'A History of British Fishes' — 2 vols., 3rd Edn., portrait, numerous woodcut illustrations in text, cloth, slightly rubbed — 1859. (Sotheby's
London) $65   £28

YATES, WILLIAM
'A Map of the County of Stafford' — hand coloured engraved map, 58 x 42in., mounted on cloth in a calf slipcase, worn — 1775. (Christie's S.
Kensington) $110   £50

YEATS, JACK
'Sailing Sailing Swiftly' — 1st Edn., inscribed by author, illustrations by author, original cloth, soiled — 1933. (Sotheby's,
Chancery Lane) $72   £32

YEATS, JACK B.
'A Lament for O'Leary' — translated by Frank O'Connor, 1st Edn., no. 52 of 130 copies, vignette on title and 6 illustrations by Yeats, original linen backed boards, uncut, unopened — Cuala Press, Dublin, 1940. (Sotheby's,
Chancery Lane) $855   £380

'La La Noo' — 1st Edn., no. 172 of 450 copies, original linen backed boards, uncut, unopened — Cuala Press, Dublin, 1943. (Sotheby's,
Chancery Lane) $450   £200

YEATS, W. B.
'A Packet for Ezra Pound' — 1st Edn., limited to 425 copies, presentation copy, inscribed by author to Edith Sitwell, original cloth backed boards, label on spine, slightly damaged — Cuala Press, Dublin, 1929. (Sotheby's,
Chancery Lane) $810   £360

'A Wind Among the Reeds' — 1st Edn., original decorated vellum gilt designed by Althea Gyles, t.e.g., bookplate loosely inserted — Caradoc Press, 1902. (Sotheby's,
Chancery Lane) $405   £180

'Four Plays for Dancers' — 1st Edn., illustrations by Edmund Dulac, original cloth backed decorated boards, faded — 1921. (Sotheby's,
Chancery Lane) $33   £15

'Modern Poetry' — 1st Edn., limited to 1,000 copies, original wrappers, spine slightly faded — British Broadcasting Corporation, 1936. (Sotheby's,
Chancery Lane) $45   £20

'The Tower' — 1st Edn., original cloth gilt, cover design by T. Sturge Moore, unopened, dust jacket — 1928. (Sotheby's,
Chancery Lane) $245   £110

'A Full Moon in March' — 1st Edn., green cloth gilt, 1935; 'Wheels and Butterflies' — 1st Edn., green cloth gilt, 1934; 'Secret Rose' — 1st Edn., blue cloth, gilt, 1897. (Phillips) $90   £40

'A Speech and Two Poems' — 1st Edn., no. 41 of 70 copies, presentation copy inscribed by author, original wrappers — Dublin, 1937. (Sotheby's,
Chancery Lane) $517   £230

A.L. signed, 1 page 8vo, Nassau Hotel, Dublin, 27th February, no year, to an unnamed correspondent, expressing sympathy for his work but declining to take part.
(Sotheby's, New Bond
   Street) $168   £75

A.L. signed, 1 page 8vo, 18 Woburn Buildings, no date, to Clive Bell, quoting three lines of verse about hermits:
   '. . . and the third
     giddy with his hundred years
     sang unnoticed like a bird'
(Sotheby's, New Bond
   Street) $337   £150

'A Vision' — illustrations, original cloth backed boards, dust jacket — 1937.
(Sotheby's,
   Chancery Lane) $63   £28
'Cathleen ni Hoolihan' — 1st Edn., no. 5 of 8 copies, printed on vellum, in red and black, original vellum gilt, uncut, silk ties — Caradoc Press, 1902.
(Sotheby's,
   Chancery Lane) $1,575   £700
'Dramatis Personae' — 1st Edn., original cloth gilt — 1934.
(Sotheby's,
   Chancery Lane) $72   £32
'Herne's Egg' — 1st Edn., maroon cloth, gilt — 1938.
(Phillips) $27   £12
'Last Poems and Two Plays' — 1st Edn., limited to 500 copies, original linen backed boards, uncut — Cuala Press, Dublin, 1939.
(Sotheby's,
   Chancery Lane) $54   £24
'Per Amica Silentia Lunae' — 1st Edn., 1,500 copies printed, original cloth gilt, cover design by Sturge Moore, slightly worn, spine faded — 1918.
(Sotheby's,
   Chancery Lane) $33   £15

'Responsibilities: Poems and a Play' — 1st Edn., no. 160 of 400 copies, original linen backed boards, unopened — Cuala Press, Dundrum, 1918.
(Sotheby's,
   Chancery Lane) $67   £30
'Stories from Carleton' — cloth, Camelot Series, 1889; five others, uniform green cloth gilt — 1923-25.
(Phillips) $45   £20

'Stories of Red Hanrahan and the Secret Rose' – 1st illustrated Edn., 2 coloured plates, 12 full page illustrations, decorations and cover design by Norah McGuiness, original cloth gilt – 1927.
(Sotheby's,
Chancery Lane) $108 £48

'The Death of Synge and Other Passages from an Old Diary' – 1st Edn., limited to 400 copies, original cloth backed boards, unopened – Cuala Press, Dublin, 1928.
(Sotheby's,
Chancery Lane) $85 £38

'The Trembling of the Veil' – 1st Edn., no. 986 of 1,000, signed by author, portrait, original boards, faded – 1921.
(Sotheby's,
Chancery Lane) $22 £10

'Wheels and Butterflies' – 1st Edn., original cloth gilt – 1934.
(Sotheby's,
Chancery Lane) $18 £8

'THE YELLOW BOOK' – 13 vols., plates, original pictorial cloth, soiled, a few spines frayed at head, joints of one vol. torn – 1894-97.
(Christie's S.
Kensington) $170 £75

YITZHAK BEN SHESHET, RIBASH
'Teshuvot' Responsa – 1st Edn., title in border of foliate sprays, masks, etc., repaired, wormed, waterstained, modern dark brown calf, folio – Elieser Soncino, Constantinople, 1546-47.
(Sotheby's, New Bond
Street) $1,800 £800

YORKE, PHILIP
'The Royal Tribes of Wales' – plates, some marginal soiling, cont. morocco, rubbed, front free endpaper lacking – Wrexham, 1799.
(Christie's S.
Kensington) $75 £35

YOUNG, ARTHUR
'A Six Weeks Tour Through the Counties of England and Wales' – 2nd Edn., folding engraved frontis, cont. calf, rubbed, joints and spine cracked – 1769.
(Christie's S.
Kensington) $110 £50

'A Tour in Ireland' – 2 vols., 2nd Edn., 5 engraved plates, cont. calf, slightly rubbed – 1780.
(Sotheby's,
Chancery Lane) $360 £160

'The Farmer's Kalendar' – 1st Edn., half title, cont. calf, lower cover defective – 1771.
(Sotheby's
London) $155 £70

'A Six Months Tour Through the North of England' – 4 vols., 1st Edn., 27 engraved plates only of 28, 6 folding printed tables, cont. sprinkled calf, joints split, rubbed – 1770.
(Sotheby's
London) $157 £70

'The Farmer's Letters to the People of England' – 2nd Edn., slight browning, inscription on title, cont. sprinkled calf, worn – 1768.
(Sotheby's
London) $67 £30

'Travels with a View to Ascertaining the Cultivation, Wealth, Resources and National Prosperity of the Kingdom of France' – 1st Edn., 3 folding maps, 1 coloured, half calf, very worn, covers loose, 4to – Bury St. Edmunds, 1792.
(Sotheby's, New Bond
Street) $202 £90

YOUNG, DAVID (Perth)
'National Improvements Upon Agriculture in 27 Essays' – 3 plates, 2 folding, cont. sprinkled calf, label slightly worn – Edinburgh, 1785.
(Sotheby's, New Bond
Street) $85 £38

YOUNG, GEORGE
'A History of Whitby and Streoneshalh Abbey' – 2 vols., 3 folding engraved maps and plants, aquatint frontis and 12 plates, spotting and foxing, later half calf, rubbed, 8vo – Whitby, 1817.
(Sotheby's, New Bond
Street) $145 £65

'A Treatise on Opium Founded upon Practical Observations' – advertisement leaf at end, cont. calf gilt – A. Millar, 1753.
(Sotheby's, New Bond
Street) $135 £60

YOUNG, JOHN
'A Catalogue of the . . . Collection . . . of
. . . John Jules Angerstein' — engraved
plates, occasional slight staining, text in
English and French, original morocco
backed boards, upper cover detached —
1823.
(Christie's S.
   Kensington) $63   £28

YOUNG, T.
'Course of Lectures on Natural Philosophy'
— 2 vols., cloth gilt — 1845.
(Phillips) $190   £85

THE YOUTHFUL JESTER.

fhall have your name written in letters of
gold, madam, and upon the front of the
building, madam : fixteen, feventeen,
eighteen, nineteen, twenty."—" I will
not pay a farthing more," faid the
duchefs. " Charity hides a multitude of
fins, (replied Nafh) twenty-one, twenty-
two, twenty-three, twenty-four, twen-
ty-five."—" Nafh ! (faid the lady) you
frighten

**YOUTHFUL JESTER, THE, OR
REPOSITORY OF WIT AND INNOCENT
AMUSEMENT,** containing Moral and
Humorous Tales, Merry Jests, Laughable
Anecdotes and Smart Repartees
Compiled by Richard Johnson, 1st Edn.,
wood engraved frontispiece and 12 illus-
trations, one or more leaves inserted from
another copy, original Dutch floral boards,
restitched, rebacked, 32mo — E. Newbery,
circa 1790.
(Sotheby's,
   Chancery Lane) $225   £100

**YOUTH'S RECREATION OR MERRY
PASTIMES**
In 2 parts, Part I containing delightful and
profitable Stories, Novels, Merry Jests,
Witty Sayings and Pleasant Tales, Bulls,
Blunders, and Puns, with many other
Merry Conceits, Part II Strange and Won-
derful Histories or Stories of Giants,
Pigmies, Fairies, Witches and Sorcerers
with the strange things they have done,
this part not being in the former impression,
2nd Edn., engraved frontispiece with three
illustrations, stained, slightly wormed, cont.
calf, rebacked, 12 mo — G. Conyers and T.
Ballard, 1704.
(Sotheby's,
   Chancery Lane) $225   £100

YRIARTE, CHARLES
'Venice' — plates, illustrations, original cloth
cloth, inner hinges split — 1880.
(Christie's S.
   Kensington) $40   £18

YULE, CAPTAIN HENRY
'A Narrative of the Mission to the Court
of Ava in 1855' — large linen backed
folding map and 29 lithographed and
engraved plates, some coloured, some
tinted, some foxing, half calf, rebacked —
1858.
(Christie's
   St. James) $90   £40

YUNKERS, ADJA
Nude Dancers — woodcut printed in
colours, 1941, on laid paper, signed and
dated in pencil, trimmed to the subject,
laid at the upper corners, framed, 345 x
259mm.
(Christie's, King
   St.) $337   £150

Y—WORTH, WILLIAM
'Introitus Apertus ad Artem Distillationis
or the Whole Art of Distillation' — 2 plates
only, adverts at end, corners wormed, old
calf, upper cover detached — Joh. Taylor,
1692.
(Christie's S.
   Kensington) $90   £40

ZAHN, JOHANNES

'Specula Physico-Mathematica-Historica Notabilium ac miraculium scientorum in qua mundi oeconomia' – 3 parts in 2 vols., 1st Edn., 3 engraved title pages, 3 engraved portraits, 57 engraved maps and plates, 29 folded or double paged, 16 double page tables, half title only in vol. I, a few wormholes, very slightly affecting a few plates and margins, a few leaves slightly torn in margin, 1 folding plate torn, cont. German blindstamped pigskin over boards, slightly rubbed, lacks ties, folio – Nuremberg, Lochner, 1696. (Sotheby's
London) $1,530   £680
'Oculus Artificales Teledioptricus Sive Telescopium' – 2 vols., 1st Edn., slightly spotted, some leaves brown, cont. vellum boards, soiled, corner of vol. I worn, folio – Wurzburg, 1685-6.
(Sotheby's
London) $1,300   £580

ZANONI, J.

'Rariorum Stirpium Historia' – portrait, frontis, 185 fine plates, half morocco, folio – Bologna, 1742.
(Sotheby's, New Bond
Street) $675 $300

ZANOTTI, G.

'Le Pitture di P. Tibaldi e di N. Abbati, esistenti nell' Instituto di Bologna' – plates, large folio, boards, vellum back – From the Signet Library – 1756.
(Bonham's) $495   £220

ZATTA, ANTONIO

'Atlante Novissimo' – 4 vols., 217 double page engraved maps, 5 cosmographical charts, maps mounted on guards, cont. mottled calf, spines gilt, worn, worming – Antonio Zatta, Venice, 1775-85.
(Christie's
St. James) $9,450   £4,200

ZAUBERSCHAU DIREKTOR KASSNER

'Meoma – Was ist Meoma, Mensch oder Maschine', illustration of mechanical apparatus with woman's head, coloured lithograph, fold mark, 18½ x 13½in. – Hamburg, Adolph Friedlander, circa 1925.
(Sotheby's,
Chancery Lane) $135   £60
Der geheimnissvolle Madler Koffer, head and shoulders portraits of Kassner and female assistant, coloured lithograph, 18½ x 13½in. – Hamburg, Adolphe Friedlander, circa 1925.
(Sotheby's,
Chancery Lane) $168   £75

ZEILLER, MARTIN

'Itinerarum Hispaniae Oder Raiss Beschreibung Durch . . . Hispanien und Portugal' – 1st Edn., engraved title with medallion portrait, and view, stains, cont. vellum boards, small 8vo – Nuremberg, 1637.
(Sotheby's, New Bond
Street) $200   £90

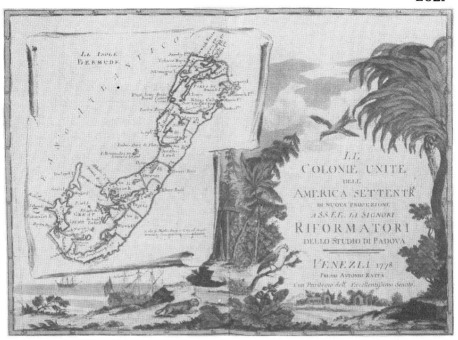

'Atlante Novissimo' by Antonio Zatta. (Christie's, St. James)

ZENTNER, L.
'A Select Collection of Landscapes from the Best Old Masters' – English and French text, 56 engraved plates, slight spotting, original boards, linen spine, oblong 4to.
(Sotheby's, New Bond
   Street)   **$360**   **£160**

ZIMMERMANN, JOHAN GEORG
'Solitude Considered with Respect to its Influence upon the Mind and the Heart' – 1st Edn. in English, cont. calf – C. Dilly, 1791.
(Sotheby's, New Bond
   Street)   **$200**   **£90**

ZINANNI, G.
'Delle Uova e Dei Nidi Degli Uccelli' – frontis, 3 engraved titles, 30 plates, vellum, stained, 4to – Venice, 1737.
(Sotheby's, New Bond
   Street)   **$450**   **£200**

ZOLA, EMILE
'La Terre' – presentation copy inscribed by author, margins browned, cont. half morocco, rubbed, original wrappers bound in – Paris, 1887.
(Christie's S.
   Kensington)   **$70**   **£32**
Autograph letter signed, 1 page octavo, Paris, January 1900 integral blank, damp-stained, three autograph visiting cards, signed.
(Sotheby's, New Bond
   Street)   **$315**   **£140**
Autograph letter signed, 3 pages, May 1886 to art critic Gustave Geffroy, dated 1885 in error.
(Sotheby's, New Bond
   Street)   **$247**   **£110**

ZOLI, FEDERICO.
'Pas de Cinq' – 16 ink and wash drawings of groups of dancers coloured in pink, wrappers torn and defective – Germany, 1845.
(Sotheby's, New Bond
   Street)   **$105**   **£48**

ZOOLOGICAL

ZOOLOGICAL SOCIETY
'Proceedings of the Committee of Science and Correspondence of the Zoological Society of London' – 13 vols. 1832-1910, together with 14 vols., original cloth, 8vo. (Christie's
St. James) $65   £30

ZORGDRAGER, C. G.
'Bloeyende Opkomst Der Aloude en Heden-daagsche Groenlandsche Visschery' – engraved title and 13 plates and maps, some folding, half title – Amsterdam, 1720. (Sotheby's
Belgravia) $1,350   £600

'Tableaux . . . de la Suisse' by Zurlauben and Laborde. (Sotheby's, New Bond Street)

ZSCHOKKE, J. H. D.
'The Bravo of Venice' – a romance translated from German by M. G. Lewis, 1st English Edn., cont. tree calf, split, 8vo – 1805. (Sotheby's, New Bond
Street) $105   £48

ZUALLART, JEAN
'Il Devotissimo Viaggio di Gerusalemme' – 1st Edn., engraved title, full page portrait and 51 maps, views and plans in text, 2 or 3 full page, browning, 19th century boards, covers detached – Rome 1587. (Sotheby's, New Bond
Street) $2,250   £1,000

ZURLAUBEN, B. F. A., BARON DE AND LABORDE, J. B. DE
'Tableaux Topographiques, Pittoresques, Physiques, Historiques, Moraux, Politiques, Litteraires, de la Suisse' – 2 vols. in 4, 224 plates of views, 6 plates of medals, 11 plates of portraits, 7 folding maps, cont. calf, gilt, slightly worn, folio – Paris, 1780-86. (Sotheby's, New Bond
Street) $24,750   £11,000

ZWEIG, STEFAN
Autograph letter to Sir Thomas Beecham in English, 1 p., Hallam St., London, 1938. (Sotheby's, New Bond
Street) $630   £280

ZWEITES TOILETTEN-GESCHENK
'Ein Jahrbuch fur Damen 1806' – 1st Edn., engraved frontispiece by F. Bartel and 19 engraved plates by Schenk, Philipson and Netto, one folding engraved plate of dance notation, 24 pages of printed music, cont. limp wrappers, spine defective – George Voss, Leipzig, 1806. (Sotheby's, New Bond
Street) $155   £70

ZWINGER, THEODOR
'Theatrum Botanicum das ist neu volkommens Krauter-Buch' – engraved frontis, folding portrait and numerous woodcuts in the text, lightly foxed throughout, cont. calf, worn, folio – Basie, 1696. (Sotheby's
London) $2,135   £950